FOR REFERENCE

Do Not Take From This Room

Faiths across Time

5,000 Years of Religious History

VOLUME 3: 1400–1849

J. Gordon Melton

◯ ABC-CLIO

Santa Barbara, California • Denver, Colorado • Oxford, England

Library of Congress Cataloging-in-Publication Data
Melton, J. Gordon.
    Faiths across time : 5,000 years of religious history / J. Gordon Melton.
        pages cm
    Volume 1. 3500 BCE-499 CE — Volume 2. 500-1399 — Volume 3. 1400-1849 — Volume 4. 1850-2009.
    Includes bibliographical references and index.
    ISBN 978-1-61069-025-6 (hardcover : alk. paper) — ISBN 978-1-61069-026-3 (ebook) 1. Religion—History.
    2. Religions—History. I. Title.
    BL80.3.M45 2014
    200.9—dc23   2013024419

ISBN: 978-1-61069-025-6
EISBN: 978-1-61069-026-3

18 17 16 15 14   1 2 3 4 5

This book is also available on the World Wide Web as an eBook.
Visit www.abc-clio.com for details.

ABC-CLIO, LLC
130 Cremona Drive, P.O. Box 1911
Santa Barbara, California 93116-1911

This book is printed on acid-free paper ∞
Manufactured in the United States of America

About the Author

J. Gordon Melton is the Distinguished Professor of American Religious History at the Institute for Studies of Religion at Baylor University in Waco, Texas. In addition, for the last 45 years, he has headed the Institute for the Study of American Religion, which he founded in Evanston, Illinois, in 1968, and has overseen the publication of its hundreds of scholarly texts and reference works on religion, a number of which he authored. Among his recent texts are the *Encyclopedia of American Religions* (8th edition, 2009), *Religious Celebrations: An Encyclopedia of Holidays, Festivals, Solemn Observances, and Spiritual Commemorations* (2011), and *Religions of the World: A Comprehensive Encyclopedia of Belief and Practice* (2010).

Contents

Volume 3
1400–1849 CE

1400–1499 CE

Introduction: 1400s

The 15th century would become the transition point between the medieval and modern world, with the European discovery (or rediscovery) of the existence of the Americas during its last decade. Before that transition happened, however, other changes were occurring and preparing the way for the reorientation of Europe around the Atlantic Ocean.

The century opens with the Roman Catholic Church in trouble. While Boniface IX reigned in Rome, a somewhat powerful rival, Benedict XIII (r. 1394–1423), is acknowledged by Sicily, Scotland, and, most notably, Castile and Aragon. Mutual negotiations fail to heal the schism, and in 1409 a third pope is elected. The major step to healing the schism would not occur until 1414 when at the Council of Constance, one pope resigns and the two others are deposed. Benedict would continue to hold court until his death in 1423, and a successor would be elected, but after the action of the council, his authority was severely limited.

The Council of Constance would also attempt to deal with another emerging problem, a potential schism in Moravia and Bohemia. The calls for reform by Czech reformer John Hus were seen as a symptom of needed reform throughout the church, though any attempt to carry out the needed reforms appeared to be lost in power struggles between popes and councils, and the elusive hope of reuniting the Roman Catholic Church and the Eastern Orthodox churches centered on Constantinople.

The Council at Constance would answer the call for reform that had started in the previous century by John Wycliffe in England and was carried on by Hus by inviting him to Constance with a pledge of safe-conduct, only to condemn him and burn him at the stake. His supporters would rally around his martyrdom and later create the first Protestant church, while continuing the cry for reform through the century.

The cause of reform would be greatly served by an event little heralded at the time, the development of movable type and the printing of the Bible (in Latin) as the first product of the new technology. The printing made the Bible more accessible in the West, at least to those few who read Latin, but the new technology would spread and become available to the next wave of reformers who would appear in the next century.

After lengthy negotiations between Rome and Constantinople, a formal agreement for reunion would be worked out at the Council of Florence in 1439, but the efforts of the Eastern church's representatives would be all for naught when they returned to Constantinople where church leaders rejected their concessions and refused to accept their reunion agreement.

The prospects of the Eastern church were growing ever more grim as the Turkish Muslims steadily reduced the territory of the former Byzantine Empire, whose real authority was largely limited to the city and immediate environs of Constantinople. The city itself was periodically the target of Turkish forces and in what would be a trauma for the Christian world, finally fell in 1453. The fall of the Byzantine capital would end whatever hope remained of Christians eventually reconquering the Holy Land and set up the Ottoman Empire for the invasion of central Europe, as its armies would now head west across the Balkans toward the Adriatic and north along the Danube into Romania and Hungary to finally arrive at the gates of Vienna.

Once established in Constantinople, Ottoman emperor Mehmed II quickly moves north along the Danube with Belgrade as a first major target. His quest to enlarge his realm leads him into conflict with an obscure Wallachian prince, Vlad III. Though greatly outnumbered, Vlad is able to score some victories using a combination of guerrilla and terrorist tactics. Vlad has also inherited the program of the anti-Muslim Christian coalition known as the Order of the Dragon, which his father had joined. In the 20th century, Vlad will become known by his name as the son of the Vlad Dragon (or Dracul) and become infamous as Dracula. After dealing with Vlad, Mehmed will redirect his energies. No longer pushing north, he will concentrate on the southern Balkans and consolidate his attention on conquering Bosnia and Albania, which will become and remain majority Muslim communities to the present. The push north would not be resumed until the 1520s.

The fall of Constantinople and the upward trajectory of the Turkish Muslims is again partially compensated for by the fall of Granada, the last Muslim stronghold in Spain, and the completion after several centuries of the reconquest of the Iberian Peninsula by Christian forces. Though the Spanish will attempt the invasion of Morocco, the island of Gibraltar will, for all practical purposes, become the boundary between the Christian and Muslim worlds in the western Mediterranean.

The fall of Granada will occasion a great disaster for the large Spanish Jewish community. They are already drawing the attention of the Spanish Inquisition founded in 1479, but now receive the additional blow of being exiled first from Spain (1492) and a year later from Portugal. The new anti-Jewish measures will work for their long-term good, as they are welcomed into the Ottoman lands and will find their way to the Americas.

The fall of Constantinople provides an opportunity for the Russians to declare their independence from the city's patriarch, and to go even further and proclaim themselves the new Rome. The church has developed powerful centers in Kiev and Moscow and is aligned with the monarch. The powerful Golden Horde, Muslim Mongols, which had long held hegemony over Russia, also faces a crisis in the years immediately after the fall of Constantinople, and by the end of the 1450s split into several factions, a prelude to their losing control of their Russian lands.

Even as the Turks are on the rise in Asia Minor, the Ming Dynasty, which pushed aside the Mongol Yuans

at the end of the last century, are settling into their new leadership role. A family coup just as the century begins brings Yhu Di, better known as the Yongle emperor (1402–1424), to the throne. Having come to the throne as he did, he is motivated to legitimize his reign, which he does in spectacular fashion. He makes massive changes that will include moving the capital from Nanjing to Beijing, where he will construct the palace complex that comes to be known as the Forbidden City.

Though largely favoring Confucianism, he will initially dispose of some leading Confucian scholars, part of the effort to head off any attack upon his rule on technical grounds. He will then, however, favor the development of both Buddhist and Taoist centers in the capital.

Shortly after becoming emperor, he had a vision of Avalokitesvara (aka Guan Yin) and invited Deshin Shekpa, the fifth Gyalwa karmapa, the head of the Karma Kagyu school of Tibetan Buddhism, to Nanjing, and begins to build a relationship with the Tibetans that bypasses the head of the Sakyapa school, courted and favored by the Yuan rulers. He also moves to build the Porcelain Pagoda in Nanjing, which at 250 feet is designed to be one of the tallest buildings in his realm.

Possibly the most notable accomplishment of the Yongle emperor, at least relative to religion, is the initiation of the Temple of Heaven and Earth, the largest temple complex in China, where he and his successors will thrice annually lead the ceremonies that renew the connections between the country and the spiritual world. It is built on the southeastern edge of the city even as the Forbidden City is erected as the new city central. Continuing the policy of responding to all the religions in his realm, the emperor will promote Confucianism and build several notable mosques, including one in Nanjing and one in Beijing. Among his several contributions to Taoism is the Purple Cloud Temple in Hubei Province.

Just as the Yongle emperor was creating the Forbidden City and Temple of Heaven and Earth, in Tibet the Buddhist monk Tsongkhapa, one of Tibet's most learned leaders, was completing his creation of a new approach to Buddhism, which he explained in his two works: *Great Exposition of the Stages of the Path* and *Great Exposition of the Secret Mantra*. Following his death in 1419, his followers created a new school of Tibetan Buddhism, the Gelugpa, and founded monasteries as places to train and initiate monks. The abbot of Gendun Monastery, known as the Ganden Tripa, emerged as the official head of the new Gelugpa school.

Buddhism continues to flourish in Japan with the support of the shogun and his administration. So established has Zen, the meditative form of Japanese Buddhism, become that Japan experiences a reform movement among those who feel the tradition has been destroyed by its success.

Through the century, the Delhi Sultanate continues to dominate northern India and from its lands it continues to make raids into the south, where a set of Hindu kingdoms maintains control. The tensions between Hindus and Muslims will, as the century is drawing to a close, lead the 30-year-old mystic Nanak to make his famous declaration, "There is neither Hindu nor Mussulman [Muslim], so whose path shall I follow? I shall follow God's path. God is neither Hindu nor Mussulman and the path which I follow is God's." His attempt to reconcile the two religions will become the foundation upon which in the next several centuries the new religion of Sikhism will build.

ca. 1400

East and Southeast Asia: China
Islam

Muslims, the majority of the residents of Ningxin Province, initiate construction on the Great Mosque of Tongxin. It will outwardly resemble a Buddhist temple, constructed as the Hui Muslim community is going through a period of sinicization. It survives as one of the largest mosques in the Ningxia Hui Autonomous Region.

ca. 1400

East and Southeast Asia: Malaysia
Islam

Iskandar Shah, a renegade from Singapore, founds the Malacca Sultanate, a Muslim center in what is now Malacca, Malaysia.

ca. 1400

Europe: Italy
Judaism

Reacting to rising anti-Semitism, Italian Jews begin to centralize authority and meet in synods to make decisions on proper responses to their changing condition. These synods would be called periodically over the next few centuries as conditions dictated.

1400

Europe: England
Christianity

The new Exeter Cathedral, which replaced the 12th-century Norman original and upon which work had been pursued for over a century, is finally completed. Among its significant features is an astronomical clock that along with the time shows the positions of the major heavenly bodies.

1400

Europe: Germany
Christianity

Wenceslaus, the king of the Germans, who was also the king of Bohemia, is accused of neglecting his duties in the greater part of his empire. The electors meet and depose him. He had never been able to make the trek to Rome and receive formal coronation from the pope. After his deposition, he remains on the throne in Bohemia. The electors chose Rupert II (r. 1400–1410), the Palatine Elector, as the new king of the Germans.

1400

Europe: Greece
Christianity

The expansion of the Roman Catholic Church among the Greek islands through the 14th century, which has led to the erecting of several dioceses, continues with the erection of the Diocese of Mykonos.

1400

Europe: Italy
Christianity

Only 10 years after the last jubilee celebration, Boniface IX leads a new Jubilee Year. Having missed the 1390 jubilee, due to royal support of the Avignon pope, numerous French pilgrims now flock to Rome. During part of the year an epidemic spreads through Rome, but Pope Boniface remains in the city.

1401

Europe: England
Christianity

The British parliament under King Henry IV passes *De heretico comburendo,* making heresy a capital offense with death to be inflicted by burning at the stake. The statute is largely prompted by the activity of the Lollards, the followers of John Wycliffe.

Among the early victims of the law is William Sawtrey, a Roman Catholic priest and follower of John Wycliffe who headed a parish in Norwich and rejected a number of Catholic practices from the veneration of saints to the efficacy of pilgrimages. Crucial to the charges of heresy is his rejection of transubstantiation.

1401

Europe: Italy
Christianity

The design of Italian artist Lorenzo Ghiberti wins first prize in the competition to create the bronze doors for the Baptistery of the cathedral in Florence. Though originally presenting a design with scenes from the Christian Old Testament, he was subsequently asked to change his proposal and do scenes from the New Testament. After completing these, he did an additional set of Old Testament scenes for another door. These second doors came to be considered one of the great art works of the century, and Michelangelo would term them the "Gates of Paradise."

1402

East and Southeast Asia: China
Chinese Religions

The Jianwen emperor is overthrown by his uncle Zhu Di (a son of the former Hongwu emperor) and dies during the brief rebellion. Zhu Di then assumes the Chinese throne as the Yongle emperor (r. 1402–1424). In his drive to legitimize his actions, he initiates an effort to falsify records concerning the rebellion that leads him to conduct a massive purge of Confucian scholars in the capital. The most renowned of the scholars became known as the Four Martyrs, among whom was Fang Xiaoru, the former emperor's tutor. Zhu Di also decides to relocate the capital from Nanjing to Beijing, where he launches construction of a

The Yongle emperor, who from 1402 to 1424 was the third emperor of China's Ming Dynasty, gained the throne by usurping it from his nephew, the Jianwen emperor. (Private Collection/The Bridgeman Art Library)

vast new palace complex that becomes known as the Forbidden City.

The Yongle emperor broadly promotes what he understands to be Chinese culture and liberally supports Daoism, Confucianism, and Buddhism (though showing some favor to Confucianism). At the same time he develops a dislike of all things Mongolian and moves to suppress remnants of Mongolian culture. His attachment to Buddhism is manifest in the erection of the Porcelain Pagoda in Nanjing, Bao'ensi (or "Temple of Gratitude"). More than 250 feet tall, when originally built it was one of the largest buildings in the country.

In Beijing, the Yongle emperor will initiate the building of the Zhenjue Temple along the Changye River.

1402

East and Southeast Asia: Japan
Buddhism

A Chinese diplomatic mission arrives in Japan and is entertained by the shogun Yoshimitsu, who in 1494 had entered the religious life as a Buddhist monk. The Chinese, however, present him with a crown and the robes of state and a new title as the "King of Japan." He is also cited as a "subject" of the Ming Empire. Diplomatic relations between the two countries, which have been bad for more than a century, improve and evolve from this point.

1402

Europe: Spain
Christianity
Construction begins on the new cathedral in Seville, Spain. It will be constructed on the site of the city's former mosque, which had remained in disrepair since a earthquake damaged it 50 years previously.

1402

Southwest Asia and North Africa: Asia Minor
Islam
The Battle of Ankara. The Central Asian ruler Timur attacks the Ottoman Empire led by the sultan Bayezid. During the battle, the sultan is captured, and his army defeated. The sultan's sons escape and would for the next decade fight among themselves over the succession to the throne. Meanwhile Bayezid dies in captivity in 1403.

1403

East and Southeast Asia: China
Buddhism
The Yongle emperor, a devout Buddhist, has a vision of Avalokitesvara (aka Guan Yin) and invites Deshin Shekpa, the fifth Gyalwa karmapa, head of the Karma Kagyu school of Tibetan Buddhism, to visit China. This invitation initiates a diplomatic effort to court a relationship with the Tibetans through the leader of one of its primary schools that continues the relationship the previous Yuan Dynasty had established through the Sakyapa school.

1403

East and Southeast Asia: China
Chinese Religions

The Jinshan God Temple, dedicated to the spirit of Jinshan or "Gold Mountain," an island off the coast of Shanghai (and now a district of Shanghai), is converted into the City God Temple for Shanghai.

1403

East and Southeast Asia: Thailand
Buddhism
The Golden Buddha, officially known as Phra Phuttha Maha Suwan Patimakon, the world's largest solid gold statue, possibly created in the 13th century, is moved from Sukhothai to the Kingdom of Ayutthaya, after the latter kingdom had come to the fore in what is now Thailand.

1403

Europe: Albania
Christianity
Gjergj Kastrioti is born. He will later become a leader of the Albanian people under the name Skanderbeg.

1403

Europe: Spain
Judaism
Christians in Toledo riot against the very prosperous Jewish community. A large synagogue built in the 13th century, which had been the center of the Jewish community, was seized and transformed into a church dedicated to Santa Maria La Blanca.

1404

Europe: Bohemia
Christianity
King Sigismund of Hungary issues the *Placetum Regium,* which decrees that papal bulls could not be disseminated in Hungary without the consent of the king.

1404

Europe: England
Christianity
Thomas Langley (r. 1405), a British priest, is selected as the new bishop of London. Largely because of his role in the deposition and execution of King Richard II (1399),

Pope Innocent VII blocked his installation. Henry IV appointed Langley as England's chancellor.

1404

Europe: England
Christianity
British king Henry IV has Richard le Scrope, the archbishop of York, executed for his role in a failed coup aimed at driving King Henry IV from the throne.

1404

Europe: Italy
Christianity
Pope Boniface IX dies after a brief illness and is succeeded by Pope Innocent VII (r. 1404–1406). Innocent's papacy is contested by the presence of the rival Pope Benedict XIII (now considered an antipope) at Avignon. Benedict will become known for his anti-Semitic attitudes.

1405

East and Southeast Asia: China
Buddhism
Nyamed Sherib Gyaltshan, a teacher of the Bon religion of Tibet, founds the Menri monastery, which will serve as the major center of learning for the movement until the 1950s. The abbot of Menri is recognized as the spiritual leader of the Bon religion.

1405

Europe: England
Christianity
Thomas Langley, England's chancellor, is selected as the new archbishop of York. Again, Pope Innocent VII, who had blocked Langley's appointment as bishop of London, blocked his installation in his new office. He subsequently excommunicated both Langley and King Henry IV. The election was quashed.

ca. 1406

Europe: France
Christianity
The second of two bell towers added to the front of the Cathedral of Our Lady of Amiens is finished. The cathedral now stands as the tallest complete cathedral in France, with a stone-vaulted nave reaching a height of 138.8 feet. The Cathedral of Saint Peter of Beauvais is slightly taller, but will never be completed.

1406

East and Southeast Asia: China
Chinese Religions
Simultaneously with the building of the Forbidden City, the Yongle emperor begins work on the Temple of Heaven and Earth, the largest temple complex in China, where the elaborate ceremonies that renew the connections between the country and the spiritual world would be conducted. Once completed, toward the end of his reign, he (or his representative) would conduct three ceremonies annually on the 15th day after the New Year, the summer solstice, and the winter solstice.

1406

Europe: Austria
Judaism
After several centuries of relative peace in Austria, the burning of the Vienna synagogue, followed by riots and lootings, signals the beginning of a time of trouble for the Jewish community.

1406

Europe: England
Christianity
Pope Innocent VII selects Robert Hallam, the chancellor of the University of Oxford, as the new archbishop of York; however, his nomination is vetoed by King Henry IV.

1406

Europe: England
Christianity
The excommunication imposed on England's chancellor is lifted and he is appointed and installed as the bishop of Durham, though he continues to hold a high post in the government of King Henry IV.

1406

Europe: Italy
Christianity

Pope Innocent VII dies unexpectedly and is succeeded by Pope Gregory XII (r. 1406–1415). Gregory is chosen by a conclave consisting of a mere 15 cardinals. He agrees that if, upon his elevation to his new office, Benedict XIII, the rival papal claimant residing at Avignon (and now considered an antipope), renounces his office, he will also resign and allow a new election of a consensus pope to occur. Such an action would have brought to an end the ongoing schism (1378–1417) that was dividing the loyalties of all Europe. Benedict refuses to resign, however, and the schism continues.

1406

Europe: Netherlands
Christianity
Thomas à Kempis enters the Monastery of Mount St. Agnes in Zwolle, the Netherlands, a community founded by the Brethren of the Common Life, disciples of Gerard Groote's new form of devotion. Thomas will lead a quiet life, spending his time in devotional exercises and copying manuscripts. He is known to have copied the Bible at least four times. He will also author the devotional classic, *The Imitation of Christ,* which will go through numerous printings through the century.

1407

East and Southeast Asia: China
Buddhism
Deshin Shekpa, the fifth Gyalwa karmapa, head of the Kagyu school of Tibetan Buddhism, arrives in Nanjing where he is received by thousands of monks. He subsequently meets with the Yongle emperor. He performs several ceremonies for the imperial family and receives a variety of gifts, including a new title, "Precious Religious King, Great Loving One of the West, Mighty Buddha of Peace." A number of miraculous occurrences were attributed to his visit.

1407

East and Southeast Asia: China
Buddhism
The Yongle emperor (China), a devotee of Tibetan Buddhism, gives the title Tai Situpa to the monk Chokyi Gyaltsen, a close disciple of the fifth karmapa (who heads the Karma Kagyu school of Tibetan

Buddhism). The karmapa subsequently appoints Chokyi Gyaltsen as the abbot of Karma Goen, then the Karma Kagyu's principal monastery. He becomes the first in a lineage of tulkus (or reincarnated lamas) that continues to the present day. The Tai Situpa is considered to be an emanation of bodhisattva Maitreya.

1407

Europe: England
Christianity
The vacancy in the chair of the archbishop's office at York is finally resolved when Henry Bowet, the bishop of Bath and Wells, is transferred and elevated to become the archbishop of York.

1407

Europe: Serbia
Christianity
Serbian ruler Stephan Lazarevic begins construction of the monastery of Manasija, located near Despotovac, originally intended as his burial place. It would feature a church with five domes and resemble a castle with a high surrounding protective wall connecting 11 watchtowers.

1407

Russia, Central Asia, and the Caucasus: Russia
Christianity
Cyprian, the metropolitan of Kiev, Moscow, and All Russia, dies. Ecumenical Patriarch Matthew of Constantinople initially appoints Photius with the title of metropolitan of Kiev and Vladimir and he takes up his post in Kiev. However, wishing to remove himself from the influence of the Roman Catholic rulers of Poland, he moves to Moscow and emerges as the metropolitan of Moscow and All Russia (r. 1408–1431). He takes over at a point at which the church suffered greatly from the effects of recent natural disasters across the Russian countryside and is essentially broke. He speaks no Russian and can expect no support from Constantinople, which is suffering under the loss of revenue due to the rise of the Ottoman Empire.

1408

East and Southeast Asia: China
Buddhism

Deshin Shekpa, head of the Karma Kagyu school of Tibetan Buddhism, completes his visit to Nanjing and begins his return to Tibet.

1408

East and Southeast Asia: China
Islam

Maharaja Karna, the ruler of Poni (Brunei), visits Nanjing, China, and is welcomed by the Yongle emperor. Unfortunately, the maharaja becomes ill and dies while in the city, and the emperor sees to his royal burial, bestowing posthumously the title King Gong Shun.

1408

East and Southeast Asia: China
Islam

Abdul Majid Hasan, the sultan of Brunei, travels to China and while in Nanjing dies. He was only 28 years old. He is buried in Nanjing, and his tomb remains a tourist attraction.

1408

East and Southeast Asia: Japan
Buddhism

Ashikaga Yoshimochi (r. 1394–1428) had officially been the shogun since 1394, but in fact, power continued in the hands of his father Ashikaga Yoshimitsu. Yoshimitsu dies in 1408 and finally Yoshimochi assumes power as shogun. Envoys from China arrive to perform special rites for the deceased Yoshimitsu and then to acknowledge his son as the new king of Japan.

Yoshimitsu's villa near Kyoto is converted into a Zen temple called Kinkaku-ji (or Temple of the Golden Pavilion), in accord with his final wishes. The three-story temple is named for the gold leaf that covers the exterior of the second and third floors.

1408

Europe: England
Christianity

The "Constitutions of Oxford" support the attacks on reformer John Wycliffe by banning his books and forbidding the translation of scripture into English by unlicensed laity, branding such activity as heretical.

1408

Europe: Hungary
Christianity

Sigismund, the king of Hungary (and later king of the Germans and Holy Roman emperor), founds the Order of the Dragon, a knightly military order modeled on those that had been prominent during the Crusades. Sigismund designates St. George as the order's patron saint, thus making reference to the saint's legendary defeat of a dragon. The order, whose members would be drawn from the elites of European society, would come to include among its members Vlad II, the prince of Wallachia (Romania). Vlad became known as Vlad Dracul (*dracul* being the Romanian word for dragon). His son and later successor to the throne would be known as Vlad Dracula (*dracula* being a diminutive form of *dracul).* The order's members swore to defend Christianity and wage war against its enemies, most notably the Ottoman Turks.

1408

Russia, Central Asia, and the Caucasus: Russia
Christianity

Tatars conducting raids in Russia burn the Trinity Lavra of St. Sergius, the Russian Orthodox Church's most important monastery. It had been constructed in wood and will be rebuilt with stone. A team of Serbian monks, who had found refuge in the monastery after the Battle of Kosovo (1389), will construct Russia's first stone cathedral as part of the monastery complex.

1409

East and Southeast Asia: China
Chinese Religions

The Yongle emperor gives a boost to the emerging cult built around the goddess Tianhou (or Tin Hau), aka Matsu, whose worship has been spreading in Fujien Province. He names her the Celestial Concubine Who Protects the Nation and Defends the People. Tianhou has become a popular deity for seafarers and fishermen.

1409

East and Southeast Asia: China
Buddhism

Tibetan lama Tsongkhapa, popularly known as Je Rinpoche, the learned teacher of the Kadam tradition of Tibetan Buddhism, who had mastered all of the Tantric Buddhist texts, inaugurates the Monlam Great Prayer Festival at the Lhasa Jokang and with his disciples founds Ganden Monastery, located on Wangbur Mountain, some 30 miles from Lhasa. Ganden would become the lead monastery of the reformed Gelugpa (or those from Ganden) school of Tibetan Buddhism, which saw itself reviving the Kadam tradition originally established by Atisha in the 11th century.

1409

Europe: England
Christianity
England strengthens its antiheresy laws by passing the Suppression of Heresy Act. Heresy is now also considered an offense against the common law.

1409

Europe: France
Christianity
Responding to the direction of Pope Benedict XIII, work begins on the Cathedral of Saint Siffredus at Carpentras in Provence, France. It would take 150 years to complete, but served the diocese until 1801 when it was absorbed into the Diocese of Avignon.

1409

Europe: Italy
Christianity
With the backing of King Charles V of France, a number of cardinals of the church call a council to meet at Pisa (Italy) to act to end the schism created by the presence of two rival popes, each with significant support across Europe. The cardinals' plan to depose both of the current popes, Benedict XIII and Gregory XII, is accepted by those in attendance, and a new pope, who takes the name Alexander V (r. 1409–1410), is elected. The two popes deposed by the council did not respond to its action and continue in office, and the church now faces further scandal with three rivals to the papal throne. The fallout from the Council of Pisa will lead to the Council of Constance.

ca. 1410

East and Southeast Asia: China
Islam
The Yongle emperor sees to the construction of the Hanximen Mosque in Nanjing and the Dapiyuan Mosque in Xi'an, and orders the reconstruction and repair of mosques throughout his realm, including the Great Mosque of Xi'an, originally constructed in the eighth century.

ca. 1410

Russia, Central Asia, and the Caucasus: Russia
Christianity
Andrei Rublev, often cited as Russia's greatest medieval painter of Orthodox icons, creates an icon of the Holy Trinity, which depicts the Trinity as three angels who visit the patriarch Abraham.

1410

East and Southeast Asia: China
Buddhism
Deshin Shekpa, head of the Kagyu school of Tibetan Buddhism, upon his return to Tibet turns his attention to the monastery at Tsurphu, which had suffered severe damage by an earthquake during his absence in China.

1410

Europe: France
The French Franciscan nun Colette, empowered with several bulls issued by Pope Benedict XIII (now considered an antipope), based in Avignon, founds a monastery from which she initiates a reform of the Poor Clares (the female branch of the Franciscans). She had started her effort following a vision of St. Francis of Assisi. She will go on to found a new reform branch of the movement popularly referred to as the Colettine Poor Clares.

1410

Europe: Germany
Christianity
Rupert II, the king of the Germans, dies and is laid to rest in the recently completed Church of the Holy

Spirit in Heidelberg, Germany. He is succeeded by Sigismund of Luxemburg (r. 1411–1437), the king of Hungary.

1410

Europe: Italy
Christianity
After less than a year in office, Pope Alexander V (now considered an antipope by the Roman Catholic Church) dies. Cardinal Baldassare Cossa oversees his burial and then succeeds him as Pope John XXIII (r. 1410–1415). He is currently also considered an antipope by the Roman Catholic Church.

1410

Europe: Poland
Christianity
The Battle of Grunwald. The Teutonic Knights (officially the Order of Brothers of the German House of Saint Mary in Jerusalem), having lost any rationale for their existence with the Christianization of the Baltic countries, continue as a power in northern Europe from their base at Marienburg (near Danzig), Poland. That power is, however, broken by a Polish-Lithuanian army, which decisively defeats the order, which has to retreat to its castle headquarters.

1410

Europe: Spain
Christianity
Martin, the king of Aragon, dies without a male heir. Aragon is thrown into some confusion relative to a successor and the crown remains vacant for two years.

Ferdinand, the regent of the Kingdom of Castile, leads the army in conquering the town of Antequera (Spain), which is taken from the Muslim kingdom of Granada.

1410

Southwest Asia and North Africa: Asia Minor
Christianity
Euthymios II (r. 1410–1416) succeeds Matthew I as the new ecumenical patriarch.

1411

East and Southeast Asia: China
Chinese Religions
As part of preparing Beijing for its future role, the Yongle emperor has the Confucian Temple renovated, including extensive repairs to the main building, the Dacheng Hall.

1411

Europe: England
Christianity
Pope John XXIII (later to be designated as an antipope) appointed Thomas Langley, the bishop of Durham in England, as a cardinal, but Langley refused to accept the title.

1412

Europe: Spain
Christianity
Two years after King Martin of Aragon died without a male heir, Ferdinand I (r. 1412–1416), the son of King John of Castile, is chosen as the new king of Aragon and begins a new dynasty of Aragonese rulers. Ferdinand had previously turned down the crown of Castile, instead becoming the regent for John II, the new king of Castile, who took office as a minor.

1412

Europe: Ukraine
Christianity
Pope Gregory XII officially erects the Diocese of Lviv (Ukraine).

1413

East and Southeast Asia: China
Chinese Religions
The Yongle emperor supports the development of Taoism at Wudang Mountain in the northwest of Hubei Province by building the Purple Cloud Temple. The temple enshrines the Taoist deities Zhen Wu, the Shouzi Mother, and the ubiquitous Guan Yin. It will be a popular site for prospective mothers who come to pray for a male child. The emperor

also supports the construction of the Taihe temple and the Jin (or Gold) Palace (taking its name from the gold and copper used to build it) at Wudang Mountain, which had been a center for Taoism since the eighth century.

1413

Europe: England
Christianity

British king Henry IV dies and is buried at Canterbury Cathedral rather than Westminster Abbey, where kings were normally interred. He is succeeded by Henry V (r. 1413–1422).

1413

Europe: Scotland
Christianity

With Europe divided over two claimants to the papal throne, Scotland sided with Pope Benedict XIII (who would later be considered an antipope). Thus, when the founders of a new St. Andrews University for the nation need incorporation and patronage, they turn initially to the bishop of St. Andrews, Henry Wardlaw, and he then seeks the approbation of Benedict, who grants full university status in a set of six papal bulls.

1413

Europe: Serbia
Christianity

Bogdan, a court official under Stephan Lazarevic, the ruler of Serbia, initiates the building of Kalenic Monastery near the town of Kragujevac. The interior will be decorated with a number of frescoes attributed to Master Radoslav, who will later create the famous illuminated Radoslav Gospel.

1413

Southwest Asia and North Africa: Asia Minor
Islam

Following a decade of fighting for control of the Ottoman Empire, one of the former sultan's sons, Mehmed I Çelebi (r. 1413–1421), emerges victorious and is named sultan. He would reestablish the empire and move his capital to Edirne (earlier known as Adrianople) near the Turkish-Bulgarian border.

1414

Europe: Wales
Christianity

Henry Chichele (r. 1414–1443), the bishop of the diocese of St. David's in Wales, becomes the new archbishop of Canterbury.

1414

Russia, Central Asia, and the Caucasus: Russia
Christianity

Vasily I, the grand prince of Vladimir and prince of Moscow, arranges the marriage of his daughter Anna to Byzantine emperor John VIII Palaiologos.

1414–1417

Europe: Germany
Christianity

In the midst of the scandal caused by the existence of three rival popes, the German king Sigismund (who later became the Holy Roman emperor) calls for a council of the church's leaders to gather at Constance (Konstanz) in Germany near the Swiss border. There is a simple plan to either depose or accept the resignation of all three reigning popes and elect a single new pope. As the council begins, Sigismund travels to France, England, and Burgundy in an unsuccessful attempt to convince the three rival popes to resign.

Soon after the council begins, Pope Gregory XII offers his resignation (1415). It is accepted and for the next two years the council works on effecting the deposition of the two remaining popes, condemning the actions of the 1409 council at Pisa, and finally electing the successor to Gregory, Martin V (r. 1417–1431).

In ending the schism in the papacy, it is agreed that the lineage of popes that passes through Urban VI, Boniface IX, Innocent VII, and Gregory XII would be considered the legitimate popes. Those lineages that pass through Alexander V and John XXIII and through Clement VII and Boniface XIII are set aside, and these popes are henceforth considered antipopes.

The council also treats matters of needed church reforms. It initially reviews and condemns the teachings of British reformer John Wycliffe. It then gives an audience to Jan Hus, the reformer from Prague, whose opinions it also condemns. Then, in spite of promising safe passage, it orders the execution by

Woodcut showing Jan Hus (ca. 1369–1415) at the stake. Hus was a Bohemian theologian and priest who established a religious reform movement that was strongly influenced by the teachings of the English theologian John Wycliffe. Hus was burned as a heretic in 1415. (iStockphoto.com)

burning of his colleague Jerome of Prague (May 30, 1416), and then of Hus himself (July 6, 1415).

Though praised for ending the Great Schism, in light of the 16th-century Protestant Reformation, the Council of Constance is equally condemned for the execution of John Hus, whom Protestants will come to see as a forerunner of their movement. The Council of Constance is now considered the 16th Ecumenical Council by the Roman Catholic Church. It is not recognized as authoritative by the Eastern Orthodox Church.

1415

Europe: Czech Republic
Christianity

The knights and nobles of Bohemia and Moravia, who favored the church reforms advocated by John Hus, send the *protestatio Bohemorum,* a letter of protest, to the Council of Constance. It condemns the execution of Hus, who had been granted safe passage by the council. The Holy Roman emperor Sigismund answers the Bohemians by announcing that he will personally take steps to crush all the Hussites and the Wycliffites in the land. Hussites in Bohemia rally around John Hus's demand that both elements of the Eucharist (the bread and wine) be given to communicants, while general church practice of the time offered only the bread.

1415

Europe: France
Judaism

Antipope Benedict XIII, now in control in Avignon, issues a bull denying employment to Jews in the manufacture of various Christian ceremonial items such as crucifixes.

1415

Europe: France
Christianity

The Battle of Agincourt. King Henry V of England invades France and scores a major victory.

1415

Southwest Asia and North Africa: Morocco
Christianity

Portuguese forces under King John I capture Ceuta, a Moroccan city east of the Straits of Gibraltar. Two years later, a diocese centered on the city will be established under the authority of the archbishop of Lisbon, and the city will remain a Christian conclave in North Africa.

1415

Southwest Asia and North Africa: Morocco
Christianity

The Portuguese occupy Ceuta, which today is a city of Spain located on the north coast of Morocco. They have as their goal the domination of the African coast and the expansion of Roman Catholic Christianity.

JAN HUS (CA. 1370–1415)

Jan Hus was a Bohemian theologian and priest who established a religious reform movement that was strongly influenced by the teachings of the English theologian John Wycliffe. Tried and convicted as a heretic by the Catholic Church at the Council of Constance, Hus was burned at the stake in 1415. Following his death, the Hussite movement was seen as a precursor to the Protestant Reformation.

Jan Hus was born ca. 1370 in Husenic, southern Bohemia. At the University of Prague, he studied theology, earning bachelor of arts, bachelor of theology, and master of arts degrees. In ca. 1400, Hus was ordained as a Catholic priest, and soon after accepted a position with the Bethlehem Chapel, which promoted the practice of preaching in the Czech language. During that time, Hus studied the writings of the English theologian and reformer John Wycliffe. Hus came to admire Wycliffe's philosophy, particularly for its realism. In 1403, Hus objected to the condemnation of Wycliffe's work by the University of Prague. He subsequently translated Wycliffe's *Trilogus* into the Czech language.

As a priest, Hus soon engendered animosity among the other priests by denouncing rampant abusive practices by the clergy in his sermons. He also advocated the distribution of the elements in the Eucharist in both kinds (i.e., bread and wine), rather than just the bread, as had become common in Catholic services. In his writings, Hus declared that the scriptures held ultimate authority over the church. He held that clergy members should be spiritual leaders only and should not become involved in government or politics. He asserted that only God has the power to establish doctrine or forgive sinners, and he argued that no Christian should obey an order given by a clergy member that was clearly wrong.

In 1414, Hus was summoned to the Council of Constance to justify his philosophy and writings. In defending himself, Hus agreed to renounce certain views that were attributed to him if they could be proven false by the scriptures, but he refused to acknowledge that some of those views were truly his own. In the end, his belief that the office of pope did not exist by divine order, but by order of the church to govern in a practical manner, proved to be quite unpopular to a church that was attempting to unite itself under one pope after a 40-year-long crisis. Hus was subsequently pronounced a heretic and was burned at the stake in Konstanz, Germany on July 6, 1415.

KATHARINE HABER

1416

East and Southeast Asia: China
Buddhism
Tongwa Donden, the child recognized as the sixth karmapa, the head of the Karma Kagyu school of Tibetan Buddhism, is born in east Tibet into poor circumstances. He initially identifies himself to a disciple of the former karmapa during a chance encounter with his mother. The student subsequently took the child to one of the Karma Kagyu monasteries where he demonstrated some precocious abilities that confirmed his identity as the reincarnated karmapa.

Jamyang Choje Tashi Palden, a disciple of Tsongkhapa, founder of the Gelugpa school of Tibetan Buddhism, founds Drepung Monastery, located immediately west of Lhasa.

Gedun Drupa, a century later to be designated the first Dalai Lama, becomes the disciple of Tsongkhapa, the founder of the Gelugpa school of Tibetan Buddhism.

1416

Europe: Spain
Christianity
In one of the last acts of his brief regime, King Ferdinand of Aragon agrees to the deposition of papal claimant Benedict XIII, now considered an antipope, a decision that helped to end the lengthy schism in leadership in the Roman Catholic Church, divided over the previous generation among three claimants to the papal office.

1416

Europe: Spain
Christianity
Ferdinand I of Aragon dies and is succeeded by his son Alfonso the Magnanimous (r. 1416–1458). Alfonso will inherit additional territory through his regime and emerge as king of most of Spain, Sicily, Corsica, Sardinia, and Naples (southern Italy). While his predecessor had supported the effort to depose Pope Benedict XIII, Alfonso will come to support the claims of Benedict, who will be excommunicated in 1417.

Work begins on a complete rebuilding of the Romanesque cathedral at Girona, Spain, along Gothic lines. The new design includes an enlarged nave that will (at some 70 feet) become the widest Gothic nave in the world and the second widest nave of all, surpassed only by St. Peter's Basilica in Rome.

1416

Southwest Asia and North Africa: Asia Minor
Christianity
Joseph, the long-term metropolitan of Ephesus (r. 1393–1416), is named the new ecumenical patriarch, succeeding Matthew I.

1417

Sub-Saharan Africa: Ethiopia
Christianity, Judaism
Christian subordination of the Ethiopian Muslims leads to new laws being passed in Egypt aimed at regulating both the Jewish and Christian minorities.

1417

Europe: England
Christianity
King Henry V designates English as the language of record within the British government.

1417

Europe: England
Christianity
John Oldcastle, a follower of John Wycliffe in Herefordshire, who had been convicted of heresy and subsequently attempted to stir up a rebellion against the king, is captured and executed.

1417

Europe: Italy
Christianity
Pope Martin V has the Church of the Twelve Apostles, damaged in the earthquake that hit Rome in 1348 and left abandoned, restored and returned to use.

1417

Europe: Spain
Christianity
Pope Benedict XIII, one of three claimants to the papal throne, refuses to resign as demanded by the Council of Constance. When he is declared a schismatic and excommunicated, he leaves Perpignan in southern France for Valencia (Spain). He still is considered the reigning pope only in the Spanish kingdom of Aragon, where he will remain until his death in 1423.

1417

Europe: Switzerland
Christianity

As part of the agreement that ended the Great Schism in the Roman Catholic Church (1378–1417), the three current popes are abandoned and Pope Martin V (r. 1417–1431) is elected to continue the papal line. Pope Martin will respond positively to the petitions of the Jewish community to the pressure being applied by the Franciscans. Martin, in contrast to the anti-Semitism of his rival Benedict XIII in Avignon, issues several bulls supportive of Italian Jews.

1418

East and Southeast Asia: China
Buddhism
Khedrup Gelek Pelzang (popularly called Khedrub Je), a disciple of Tsongkhapa, the founder of the Gelugpa school of Tibetan Buddhism, founds Baiju Monastery in Gyantse District (Tibet).

1418

Europe: Austria
Christianity
Nicolaus Seyringer (r. 1418–1425) begins his tenure as abbot of Melk Monastery, a Benedictine center overlooking the Danube River. While in office, he will lead a new reform movement, which calls for the adoption of a stricter discipline for the monks, and is credited with reinvigorating monastic life throughout Austria and southern Germany.

1418

Europe: Italy
Judaism, Christianity
Italian Jews meeting at Forli petition Pope Martin V to withdraw a set of laws promulgated by Pope Benedict XIII (now considered an antipope), which they have found most oppressive. Martin yields to their request.

1418

Southwest Asia and North Africa: Persia
Islam
Queen Goharshad, the wife of Shah Rukh of the Timurid Dynasty, orders the construction of the Goharshad Mosque in Mashhad, Persia, known for its beauty and intricate design.

1419

East and Southeast Asia: China
Buddhism
Jamchen Choje Shakya Yeshe, a close disciple of teacher/monk Tsongkhapa, the founder of the Gelugpa school of Tibetan Buddhism, founds Sera Monastery in Lhasa, the capital of Tibet.

Following Tsongkhapa's last major teaching sessions on Tantric Buddhism, he entrusts the perpetuation of his Tantric learning to one of his disciples, Gyu Sherab-senggey. Sherub-senggey would later found two monastic schools in central Tibet that focused on these teachings.

Shortly before passing away, Tibetan teacher/monk Tsongkhapa gives his hat and robe, the symbols of his office, to his successor Gyeltsabjey, who becomes the abbot of Ganden Monastery and the head of the Gelugpa school of Tibetan Buddhism.

1419

Europe: Czech Republic
Christianity
Divisions in Bohemia and Moravia, which had become more pronounced since the burning of John Hus as a heretic in 1414, come to a head with a procession by Hus's supporters through the streets of Prague. The burgomaster and several Catholic town consuls are tossed from their windows onto the street. None were killed as they landed in a pile of manure. Several weeks later, the king of Bohemia Wenceslaus IV dies, reputedly from the shock he suffered over the Prague events. Weneeslaus's widow, Queen Sophia, sent an army to Prague to quell the Hussites, but it only succeeded in destroying a large portion of the city.

1419

Europe: Italy
Christianity
Giovanni di Bicci de' Medici, one of Florence's leading citizens, offers to pay for a new church building to replace the Basilica di San Lorenzo (where the Medici family worshiped), and he commissioned a leading architect of the era, Filippo Brunelleschi, to design it. The basilica has a history dating to the original church on the site constructed in the fourth century. The new building would be officially completed at the

time Pope Pius II visited the city, though construction would continue through the rest of the century.

1419

Europe: Lithuania

The cathedral at Vilnius burns. In the 1420s, as Lithuania is elevated from the status of grand duchy to that of kingdom and Grand Duke Vytautas is preparing to be crowned as the first king of Lithuania, he will build a significantly larger Gothic cathedral to replace the one that has been lost. He will be buried in the new cathedral (1430).

1420

East and Southeast Asia: China
Chinese Religions

The Xiannong Altar and the Temple of Agriculture, a complex of sacred buildings and storehouses that supply the water that the Chinese emperors draw for the purpose of making sacrifices to the sacred forces of agriculture, are constructed in Beijing adjacent to the Temple of Heaven. Here, each spring, the emperor will perform rituals aimed at ensuring a bountiful harvest. In the main Jufu Hall, the emperor dons farming clothes and leads a ritual plowing of land to demonstrate respect to the god of agriculture. The temple remained in use into the 20th century.

1420

East and Southeast Asia: China
Islam

Muslims in China, in the process of turning Cangzhou, Hebei Province, into one of the country's largest Muslim centers, build the Cangzhou Grand Mosque. The Qur'an will initially be translated into Chinese in Cangzhou.

1420

Europe: England
Christianity

Archbishop of Canterbury Henry Chichele comes into conflict with Pope Martin V after threatening to declare a jubilee designed to bring pilgrims to Canterbury (and thus divert them from Rome). Pope Martin protests. The issue is a key incident in a long-running conflict over power in the British church. Chichele has been trying to prevent his rival, Henry Beaufort, bishop of Winchester, from being appointed papal legate.

1420

Europe: England
Christianity

The Treaty of Troyes. King Charles recognizes Henry of England as his successor and, while claiming that his son Charles was illegitimate, disinherits him. He also betroths his daughter Catherine of Valois to King Henry.

1420

Europe: Italy
Christianity

Pope Martin V continues the trend demonstrated by his immediate predecessors in attempting to suppress efforts to reform the church in directions he considers to be heretical. He issues a papal bull calling upon the secular authorities to eradicate all of the heretics in their individual realms, especially the followers of John Hus and John Wycliffe. The bull initiates the Hussite Wars, a series of military actions against the followers of John Hus in Bohemia over the next 15 years.

1420

Europe: Portugal
Christianity

Prince Henry the Navigator is appointed governor of the well-endowed Order of Christ, the Portuguese successor to the Knights Templar.

1420

Europe: Portugal
Christianity

Portuguese under the leadership of Prince Henry rediscover the Madeira Islands in the Atlantic Ocean west of Morocco and begin to colonize them.

1420

Southwest Asia and North Africa: Morocco
Islam

Marinid ruler Abu Said Othman is assassinated. He is succeeded by his infant son Abdul Haq (r. 1420–1465), who will enjoy a lengthy rule.

1420-1421

Europe: Austria
Judaism

Culminating more than a decade of action against the Jewish community, Albert, the duke of Austria, with the backing of the Roman Catholic Church, orders the imprisonment and forcible conversion of all the Austrian Jews. In the immediate aftermath of the order, some converted and others left the country. Many of the wealthy Jews were arrested and stripped of their property. Children taken into custody were forced to become Christians, though Pope Martin V soon intervened to stop that practice. The pogrom climaxed on March 12, 1421, when Austrian authorities burned 92 men and 120 women at the stake just outside the wall of Vienna. The Vienna synagogue, which had been burned in 1406 and subsequently rebuilt, was again destroyed.

March 25, 1420

Europe: Czech Republic
Christianity

The Battle of Sudomer. Jan Žižka, the leader of the Hussite army in southern Bohemia, defeats a Catholic army in what is the first major battle of the Hussite wars. Following the battle he settles with his army at a highly defensible location and founds a new settlement called Tabor. It will become the center of a new utopian community.

As it evolves, the Taborite community develops egalitarian views, choosing its leaders in a democratic election; adopts a millenarian perspective focused on a belief in the imminent return of Christ; and imposes a very disciplined code of conduct, given the warlike conditions under which they have emerged.

Holy Roman Emperor Sigismund responds to Pope Martin V's bull against the Hussites and marches an army to Prague. They are unable to overcome the defenders of the city and begin negotiations with the Hussites. They demand church reform, including the serving of the Eucharist in both kinds (bread and wine) and the divestment of the church of its temporal powers and wealth. Sigismund rejects their

demands, which had been compiled into a brief statement known as the "Four Articles of Prague." When hostilities resume, the Hussites decisively defeat Sigismund's army and Bohemia largely falls under Hussite control.

1421

East and Southeast Asia: China
Chinese Religions

The Forbidden City is finished to the point of being inhabitable, and the capital of the Ming Dynasty moves from Nanjing to Beijing.

1421

Europe: Austria
Judaism

A wave of anti-Judaism hits Austria and authorities arrest and expel Jews. In Vienna, members of a synagogue die when it is burned with the members within it. Jews are banned from the city, and the financially strapped Duke Albert V confiscates their property. The expulsion from the capital heralds similar action by cities throughout the country over the next generation.

1421

Southwest Asia and North Africa: Asia Minor
Islam

Ottoman sultan Mehmed I Çelebi dies and is buried in a mausoleum located near the Great Mosque in Bursa. He is succeeded by his son Murad II Kodja (r. 1421–1451).

1421–1422

Europe: Czech Republic
Christianity

A Catholic army from Germany again attempts to crush the Hussites in Bohemia, but experiences a series of defeats first at the town of Žatec (August) and then more decisively at the Battle of Deutschbrod (January 6, 1422). With Bohemia now relatively safe from outside intervention, divisions among the Hussites come to the fore.

Jan Želivský, a former Roman Catholic priest who had emerged in the 1420 demonstrations of the

Hussites in Prague, emerges as a popular leader in Prague with his greatest support coming from the poorer sections of the city. The town council eventually orders his arrest, which occurs on March 9. He is subsequently executed by decapitation.

1422

Europe: England
Christianity

Following a string of victories that almost brought him to the French throne, British king Henry V dies suddenly leading his army near Paris. He is succeeded by his infant son, not yet a year old, later crowned as King Henry VI (r. 1422–1461, 1470–1471). The country would be controlled by regents during much of his reign.

1422

Europe: France
Christianity

King Charles VI of France dies. He has left his kingdom to the recently deceased Henry V of England, whose army controls northern France, including the city of Paris. Some consider passing the crown to the infant Henry VI of England, but in the end, the French throw their support to the previously disinherited son, Charles VII (r. 1422–1461), who is proclaimed king of France. His territory includes the southern two-thirds of France apart from Aquitaine.

1422

Russia, Central Asia, and the Caucasus: Russia
Christianity

The Russian Orthodox Church declares Sergius of Radonezh the patron saint of the Russian state.

1423

East and Southeast Asia: Japan
Buddhism

Shogun Ashikaga Yoshimochi, following the example of his father, cedes authority to his 18-year-old son, Ashikaga Yoshikazu. Yoshikazu is an alcoholic and dies two years later, and Yoshimochi must reassume the shogun's office.

1423

Europe: Italy
Christianity

The schismatic pope Benedict XIII dies and the three cardinals who had remained loyal to him elect a successor who takes the name Clement VIII. He has a following only in parts of Spain.

1423

Russia, Central Asia, and the Caucasus: Russia
Christianity

Amid his work of rebuilding the Russian Church, Metropolitan Photius of Moscow authors a number of items of ecclesiology, among them his study of the episcopacy, the *Order of Selection and Installation of Bishops* (1423).

1423–1424

Europe: Italy
Christianity

The Council of Constance (1414–1418) had suggested the calling of periodic councils to discuss church matters, thus in 1423 Pope Martin V called for a council to meet at Pavia (Italy). When plague was spotted in the city soon after it convened, the council was hastily moved to Siena. The first set of decrees follows up on the Council of Constance by condemning John Wycliffe and Jan Hus, denouncing the still schismatic Pope (antipope) Benedict XIII, and calling for vigilance against heresy. Following the selection of Basel (Switzerland) as the site for the next council, the work at Siena ended abruptly.

1423–1424

Europe: Scotland
Christianity

The 1423 Treaty of London leads to the release of the Scottish king James I from captivity. He had been in custody for 18 years, but soon after his return to Scotland, he marries and is crowned King James I at the traditional site for Scottish rulers, the abbey at Scone.

April 27, 1423

Europe: Czech Republic
Christianity

Ming Dynasty Emperors of China

Reign	Emperor
1368–1398	Hongwu
1398–1402	Jianwen
1402–1424	Yongle
1424–1425	Hongxi
1425–1435	Xuande
1435–1449	Zhengtong
1450–1457	Jingtai
1457–1464	Tianshun
1465–1487	Chenghua
1488–1505	Hongzhi
1505–1521	Zhengde
1521–1567	Jiajing
1567–1572	Longqing
1572–1620	Wanli
1620	Taichang
1620–1627	Tianqi
1627–1644	Chongzhen

The Battle of Hořice. The major division among the Hussites who now control Bohemia reaches a decisive point when the more extreme element, the Taborites, led by Jan Žižka, defeat the more moderate Hussites, called Utraquists (for their emphasis on offering the Eucharist in both kinds). After the battle, representatives of the two sides concluded an armistice.

1424

Europe: Italy
Christianity
Pope Martin, who had previously moved his residence from St. Peter's Basilica to the Church of Santa Maria Maggiore, again relocates to the Basilica of Santi Apostoli.

1424

Southwest Asia and North Africa: Asia Minor
Christianity
Manuel II Palaiologos (r. 1391–1425) dies and is succeeded by his son John VIII Palaiologos (r. 1425–1448),

who inherits a greatly diminished Byzantine Empire, now reduced to Constantinople and its immediate environs.

1424–1425

East and Southeast Asia: China
Chinese Religions
The Yongle emperor dies and is succeeded by his son, the Hongxi emperor (1424–1425), who lasts only a year before dying. He is succeeded by his son, the Xuande emperor (r. 1425–1435). Prior to his death, the Hongxi emperor had decided to move the capital back to Nanjing, but he dies before the relocation could be implemented.

1425

East and Southeast Asia: Japan
Shinto
The main hall at Kibitsu Jinja, a Shinto shrine in Okayama Prefecture, is reconstructed. The new building is the second largest *honden* (the building where the *kami* are enshrined) in Japan.

1425

Europe: Italy
Christianity
Frances, a young woman of an aristocratic family in Rome and a visionary, founds the Olivetan Oblates of Mary, an order of nuns attached to the Church of Santa Maria Nova. The members do not adopt a cloistered life, as did most monastic communities of women, nor do they take formal vows, and they are thus able to combine a life of intense prayer and contemplation with duties in the community in service to people in need. Frances would eventually be canonized, and the order become popularly known as the Oblates of Saint Frances of Rome.

1425

Russia, Central Asia, and the Caucasus: Russia
Christianity
Vasily I, the grand prince of Vladimir and prince of Moscow, dies and is succeeded by his 10-year-old son Vasily II Vasiliyevich (r. 1425–1462).

1426

Europe: England
Christianity

After being blocked for a number of years by the archbishop of Canterbury, but following British king Henry V's death, Henry Beaufort, the bishop of Winchester, is named a cardinal and papal legate. One of his strong supporters, John Kemp, is named archbishop of York.

1426–1427

Europe:
Christianity

The Germans again attempt to regain control of Bohemia from the Hussites, but are defeated in two major battles at Ústí nad Labem (1426) and Tachov (1427). Following the victory at Tachov, the Hussites took to the offensive and conducted a variety of raids into those neighboring states that had supported the German attempts to invade Bohemia. During this time, the Hussites also received support from Poland (a thoroughly Catholic country at this time), which wanted to prevent any German incursions eastward.

1427

Europe: Italy
Christianity

Bernardino of Siena, a Franciscan friar known for his spirited preaching against witches, homosexuals, and Jews, is summoned to Rome to stand trial on charges of heresy for his promotion of the devotion to the Holy Name of Jesus, then considered somewhat suspect as an innovation in devotion. Following his acquittal, Pope Martin V offers him the bishopric of Siena, but he turns it down.

1427

Europe: Portugal
Christianity

The Portuguese discover the Azores, which are subsequently targeted for colonization.

1427

Russia, Central Asia, and the Caucasus: Russia
Christianity

Cyprian, the metropolitan of Moscow and All Russia, moves against the Strigolniki, a Christian movement that developed in the previous century under the leadership of some low-ranking priests and spread among the poorer elements of the Russian population. The Strigolniki opposed the church's hierarchy and its identification with the aristocracy and renounced those sacraments whose administration is accompanied by the payment of fees to the clergy. The church considers it a heresy, and it appears to have run its course by the end of the 15th century.

1428

East and Southeast Asia: China
Buddhism

The Qingquan Temple near Beijing is rebuilt and adopts its present name, Dajue Temple. At the time it receives large statues of the Trikala Buddhas—the past (Dipamkara), present (Sakyamuni), and future (Maitreya) Buddhas. Destroyed and rebuilt in the 20th century, Dajue will reemerge as the Lingquan Monastery complex. Among its claims to fame is a large thousand-year-old ginkgo tree.

1428

East and Southeast Asia: Japan
Buddhism

Before Shogun Ashikaga Yoshimochi dies, he directs that his successor be chosen by lots between his sons. The choice falls to Ashikaga Yoshinori (r. 1429–1441), his sixth son, who was, at the time, serving as the chief abbot of Tendai Buddhism.

1428

Europe: England
Christianity

Following up on decrees from the Council of Constance, Pope Martin V has the remains of British reformer John Wycliffe exhumed, burned, and the ashes cast into the River Swift.

1428

Europe: Italy
Christianity

King Alfonso V, who rules over Sicily, orders the Jews of his realm to convert to Roman Catholicism.

Emperors of Japan, 1318–1557 CE

Namboku Period: The Southern Court	
1318–1339	Go-Daigo
1339–1368	Go-Murakami
1368–1383	Chokei
1383–1392	Go-Kameyama
Namboku Period: The Northern Court	
ca. 1331–1333	Kogon
ca. 1336–1348	Komyo
ca. 1348–1351	Suko
1353–1371	Go-Kogon
1374–1382	Go-Enyu
Muromachi Period	
1392–1412	Go-Komatsu
1412–1428	Shoko
ca. 1428–1464	Go-Hanazono
ca. 1464–1500	Go-Tsuchimikado
1500–1526	Go-Kashiwabara
1526–1557	Go-Nara

1428

Europe: Spain
Christianity
Yeshaq I, the ruler of Ethiopia, dispatches two dignitaries to the court of Alfonso of Castile. They carry a letter proposing a mutual alliance against the Muslims. Alfonso responded positively, and then sent a group of artisans to Ethiopia, but they never made it to their goal. The alliance was never consummated due to the problems of communication between the two rulers.

1428–1429

Europe: France
Christianity
British forces, already in control of northern France, push south and lay siege to Orléans. The fall of the city would place the French crown in jeopardy. The siege set the stage for the emergence of Joan of Arc (or Jeanne d'Arc). As the siege continues, the teenage girl, having been in communication with supernatural beings she believed to be angels, presented herself to King Charles, whom she immediately recognized even though he had disguised himself as one of his courtiers. In a private conversation, she revealed knowledge of personal secrets about him that he had voiced only in his private prayers.

After receiving the blessing of Charles VII, Joan of Arc is freed to lead French forces in breaking the siege at Orléans. The event turned the momentum of the hostilities in France's favor and led to the decisive Battle of Patay, at which French forces proved victorious. Subsequently the French move north and occupy Rheims, after which Charles would finally be formally crowned as king of France in Rheims Cathedral.

1429

East and Southeast Asia: China
Buddhism
Ngor Evam Choden monastery is founded in Tsang, central Tibet. It will become the lead monastery of the Ngor Sakya sub-school of the Sakya School of Tibetan Buddhism. The Ngor tradition was established by Ngorchen Kunga Zangpo (1382–1457) and has become the largest group of Sakya Buddhists.

1429

Europe: Italy
Judaism, Christianity
Pope Martin V issues a bull calling upon the Franciscans to refrain from their targeting of the Jewish community with their preaching activity. The Franciscans are also ordered to stop interfering with the Jews' relationships with their immediate neighbors and stop infringing upon their rights in general. The Franciscans largely ignore the bull.

Among the Franciscans, John of Capistrano and Bernardine of Siena lead a movement to instill a stronger discipline among the Franciscan communities. The pair emphasize devotion to the Holy Name of Jesus, which leads to their being summoned to Rome to answer accusation of heresy. John speaks to the inquisitors and is acquitted by a Commission of Cardinals that had been appointed to judge them. John would himself emerge as an active inquisitor and a major voice in Italy and then in Bohemia and Germany against both the Jews and various heretics.

Medieval illustration depicting the arrival of Joan of Arc (1412–1431) at Chinon Castle. Joan of Arc, the French peasant who believed herself destined by God to help the French defeat the British, became a saint and remains a powerful symbol of French nationalism. (Bettmann/Corbis)

1429

Europe: Serbia
Christianity

Radoslav, a Serbian scribe from Dalša, creates the Radoslav Gospel, an illustrated hand-written codex of the New Testament Gospels, noteworthy for its several miniatures picturing the four evangelists (Matthew, Mark, Luke, and John). The original is now located in the Russian National Library, St. Petersburg.

1429

Russia, Central Asia, and the Caucasus: Russia
Christianity

The monks Sawaty, Gherman, and Zosima relocate to the Solovetsky Islands in the White Sea (northwest Russia) and found the New Wilderness hermitage.

Within a few years it evolves to become Solovetsky Monastery, one of the country's most important and renowned monastic establishments.

1430

East and Southeast Asia: China
Islam

Fire destroys the Jingjue Mosque in Nanjing. The famous Moslem navigator Zheng He calls the emperor's attention to the problem and the government orders the rebuilding of the mosque.

1430

Europe: Belgium
Christianity

In Bruges, Philip III, Duke of Burgundy founds the Order of the Golden Fleece, a Christian chivalric order, as part of the celebration of his marriage to Infanta Isabella, the daughter of King John I of Portugal. Limited originally to 24 members, it evolves into one of the most elite and prestigious orders in Europe.

1430

Europe: France
Christianity

Joan of Arc's brief career as a soldier ends when she is captured by Burgundian forces as she attempted to lift the siege of Compiègne. Her captors turn her over to the English.

1430

Europe: Greece
Christianity, Islam

The Ottoman forces under Murad II conquer Thessaloniki. Shortly thereafter the monks of Mount Athos pledge allegiance to him. Murad subsequently recognizes the monasteries' sacred status and rights to their properties. This act will later be reiterated by Sultan Mehmed II after the fall of Constantinople and will allow the monastic communities to survive in a semi-autonomous state during the centuries of Ottoman rule of the Greek peninsula.

1430

Europe: Italy
Christianity

Cosimo de' Medici of Florence commissions Italian artist Donatello, already noted for his many religious sculptures, to produce a bronze statue of a youthful David, representing the future king of Israel. Donatello's most famous work, it is the first known free-standing nude statue to appear in Europe since ancient times.

1430

Europe: Poland
Christianity

As part of the ongoing struggles between the Poles and Germans, Hussites storm the Pauline monastery at Częstochowa (Poland) and plunder the sanctuary.

The monastery chapel houses the icon known as Our Lady of Częstochowa. In the chaos surrounding the attempt to leave with the icon, a soldier struck the image with his sword and left two deep scars. They have remained visible in spite of attempts to cover them.

1430

Europe: Switzerland
Christianity

An organ is constructed in the Valère Basilica in Sion, the capital of the canton of Valais. It survives to the present as the world's oldest still functioning organ.

1431

Europe: Czech Republic
Christianity

In spite of a decade of failure in trying to crush the Hussites, Frederick I, the elector of Brandenburg, leads another army into Bohemia and initially lays siege to the city of Domažlice. When reinforcements arrive on August 14, the invading force is completely defeated and flees in rapid retreat.

1431

Europe: France
Christianity

The British occupation government in France, based at Rouen, places Joan of Arc on trial for heresy, though no evidence of her holding or voicing any heretical opinions had been produced. In what history has judged as an extremely irregular proceeding, Joan is found guilty and is burned at the stake (May 30). Charles VII, who owes his throne to Joan, does nothing to attempt to save her.

1431

Europe: Italy
Christianity

Pope Eugene IV (r. 1431–1447) succeeds Martin V on the papal throne.

1431

Europe: Switzerland
Christianity

Pope Martin V calls for a church council to convene at Basel, but he dies before it can convene. Joan of Arc appeals the case against her to the coming church council at Basel, but her appeal is ignored by her British captors.

1431

Europe: Switzerland
Christianity
The council called by Pope Martin V meets at Basel, but is dismissed by Pope Eugene IV who rejects the expressed desires of some to greatly limit papal power. The group continues to meet at Basel through the decade and issues a statement claiming the supremacy of church councils over the pope.

1431

Russia, Central Asia, and the Caucasus: Russia
Christianity
Photius, the metropolitan of Moscow and All Russia, dies. The office remains vacant for six years.

1432

Europe: Belgium
Christianity
Flemish artist Jan van Eyck paints the altarpiece for the church at Ghent, now considered the epitome of Dutch medieval art.

1432–1433

East and Southeast Asia: China
Buddhism
Gyu Sherab-senggey, to whom Tsongkhapa had entrusted the spreading of his teachings on Tantric Buddhism, founds Saygyu Monastery at Yagshilung in Tsang Province of central Tibet. This monastery would also be known as Tsang Togyu, or the Tantric College of Tsang, Upper (Central) Tibet. After entrusting the school to Dulngapa Pelden-zangpo, he travels to Lower Central Tibet (U Province) and founds Maygyu Monastery, the Tantric College of Lower Central Tibet, near Lhasa, at Nordzin-gyeltsen.

1433

East and Southeast Asia: Japan
Buddhism

The shogun Ashikaga Yoshinori, himself a Tendai Buddhist priest, is called upon to suppress a rebellion of the increasingly militant monks from Enryaku-ji, the Tendai monastery on Mt. Hiei. While the rebellion is unsuccessful, it heralds more serious trouble to come in the next century.

1433

Europe: Italy
Christianity
Pope Eugene IV is forced to issue a second papal bull that declares his earlier bull dismissing the Council of Basel to be null and void. In guarded terms he recognizes the legitimacy of the gathering.

1433

Europe: Holy Roman Empire
Christianity
Sigismund of Luxemburg (r. 1433–1437) becomes the emperor of the Holy Roman Empire. He is the last emperor of the House of Luxemburg.

1433

Europe: Netherlands
Christianity
Dutch mystic Lidwina of Schiedam, who became famous during her life for her fasting, healing people, and as a holy woman, dies. Though some thought she was under the influence of an evil spirit, after her death, her grave became a place of pilgrimage and devotees constructed a chapel over it.

1433–1434

Europe: Switzerland, Czech Republic
Christianity
Hussite envoys arrive in Basel, Switzerland, to open negotiations on ending the periodic incursions by Catholic forces into Bohemia. It will take more than a year of negotiations to reach an agreement. In the meantime, the moderate Utraquists and more extreme Taborite Hussite factions again find themselves battling each other. This time the Utraquists defeat and all but annihilate the Taborites. The Hussite Wars (1419–1434) finally come to an end.

Statue of Cosimo de' Medici in the Plaza degli Uffizi in Florence, Italy. A wealthy Florentine banker and statesman, Cosimo de' Medici (1389–1464) was the first member of a line of de facto rulers of Florence during the Italian Renaissance. (William Perry)

1437

Europe: Italy

The Dominicans petition Cosimo de' Medici the Elder to fund their renovation of the large monastic complex near his home in Florence, which they had inherited two years earlier. He does so, and they create several structures, including a private cell and a library, largely for him. The renovated complex will come to be the home of a number of famous works of art.

Cosimo de' Medici commissions Fra Angelico, now a resident of San Marco, to accept the task of decorating the monastery as part of its renovation. His contributions turn it into a major work of art in itself. Masterpieces include the *Last Judgment* altarpiece and the *Maesta* (Madonna enthroned) *with Saints.*

1437

Europe: Scotland
Christianity

King James I of Scotland is assassinated, though his queen and six-year-old son survive. His son is quickly crowned as James II in ceremonies at Holyrood Abbey, an Augustinian abbey in Edinburgh.

1437

Europe: Spain
Christianity

King Alfonso V takes a cup, which some claimed to have been the cup used by Jesus of Nazareth at the Last Supper, from its resting place in Saragossa to the cathedral in Valencia where it remains until the present.

1437

Europe: Switzerland
Christianity

Pope Eugene IV dissolves the Council of Basel and summons the bishops to Ferrara, Italy, where they will be joined by representatives of the Eastern Greek churches.

1437

Russia, Central Asia, and the Caucasus: Russia
Christianity

Patriarch Joseph II of Constantinople names Isidore, a Russian monk residing in Constantinople, where he headed a monastery, as the metropolitan of Kiev, Moscow, and All Russia. He is deeply involved in the plans of Byzantine Emperor John and Patriarch Joseph for a union of the Orthodox churches with the Roman Catholic Church.

1437

Southwest Asia and North Africa: Morocco
Islam, Christianity

A Portuguese expedition to Tangier proves disastrous. The Moroccans take as a prisoner Henry the Navigator's brother Fernando, who never returns to his homeland.

1438

East and Southeast Asia: China
Buddhism

Khedrup Gelek Pelzang (better known as Khedrup Je), one of the main disciples of Lama Tsongkhapa (the founder of the Gelugpa school of Tibetan Buddhism), begins his seven-year tenure as the third Ganden Tripa, the administrative head of the Gelugpa school, and the abbot of Ganden Monastery. He will later be designated the first Panchen Lama.

1438

Europe: England
Christianity

British king Henry VI and Henry Chichele, the archbishop of Canterbury, found All Souls' College, at Oxford University. The original structures at the college include a large chapel (constructed 1438–1442).

1438

Europe: Italy
Christianity

Mark of Ephesus, archbishop of Ephesus (Asia Minor), attends the Council of Florence (1438–1445 CE) and rejects the addition of the *filioque* clause to the Nicene Creed, which he considers an act of heresy. He further rejects the idea of the universal jurisdiction of the pope relative to the church. Of the several Eastern Orthodox bishops present at the council, he is the only one to refuse to sign its decrees. While in the minority at the time, he will later be considered a saint by the Eastern Orthodox churches.

1438

Europe: Italy
Christianity

The church council, which has been meeting at Basel, reconvenes in Ferrara (Italy) and then moves on to Florence in 1439. It makes significant progress in the negotiation of reunification with several Eastern churches and reaches a key agreement on the use in the Western church of the *filioque* clause in the Niceno-Constantinopolitan Creed. It also defines the number of the sacraments (seven) and approves a statement on the doctrine of purgatory.

1438

Europe: Italy
Western Esotericism, Traditional Religions

Greek scholar Georgius Gemistus, aka Plethon, accompanies Byzantine emperor John VIII Palaiologos to the Council of Florence, along with his students Bessarion, Mark Eugenikos and Scholarios. Though present to assist the proposed reunion of the Eastern Orthodox and Roman Catholic churches, his major accomplishment is the reintroduction of the philosopher Plato to the Western world, which has the effect of challenging the domination that Aristotle had come to possess in Western European thought. While in Florence, he establishes a temporary school at which he delivers lectures on the differences in the thought of Plato and Aristotle. Plethon is himself a Neoplatonist.

As a result of his contact with Plethon, Cosimo de' Medici founds a Platonic Academy in Florence and places humanist scholar Marsilio Ficino in charge. Ficino would proceed to translate all Plato's works, the *Enneads* of Plotinus, and various additional Neoplatonist works into Latin. Ficino would also proceed to translate the collection of Greek texts discovered by Leonardo da Pistoia, which came to be known as the Hermetic Corpus, most notably the *Corpus Hermeticum* of Hermes Trismegistos, a major Esoteric work.

1438

Southwest Asia and North Africa: Morocco
Judaism

A special Jewish section of the city, the Mellah, is established at Fez, Morocco. It has a high wall around it and a single entrance. Its original purpose is to supply a protective home, but it later serves to keep the community isolated and ostracized. It will also become the model of other such Jewish communities in Morocco.

1438–1439

Russia, Central Asia, and the Caucasus: Russia
Christianity

The Russian metropolitan Isidore attends the Council of Florence (Italy, 1438–1439). Following the council, the pope names him a papal legate to Russia and Lithuania.

ca. 1439

Europe: Italy
Christianity

Florentine artist Donatello completes his bronze statue of the biblical David that had been commissioned by Cosimo de' Medici.

1439

East and Southeast Asia: Japan
Buddhism

A division among the leaders of the shogun's family places Ashikaga Mochiuji, the shogun's representative in Kamakura, against the country's leadership in Kyoto. Shogun Ashikaga Yoshinori attacks Kamakura. Mochiuji and his eldest son Yoshihisa kill themselves to escape capture. Unfortunately, a fire breaks out and destroys Fian-ji, the temple in which they had taken refuge, and it spreads to surrounding temples, burning many to the ground.

1439

Europe: France

With the completion of its north tower, the building of the Cathedral of Our Lady of Strasbourg reaches completion. The second tower is never initiated. This tower would, in 1647, following the destruction by fire of the spire of St. Mary's church, Stralsund, transform the cathedral into the world's tallest building, a status it enjoyed into the 19th century.

1439

Europe: Germany, Austria
Christianity

Albert II (1437–1439), the king of Germany, dies. He is succeeded by Frederick III (r. 1437–1493), who will rule for over a half-century. He also inherits the title of duke of Austria.

1439

Europe: Switzerland
Christianity

Those church leaders who remained and attempted to continue the Council of Basel suspend and then formally depose Pope Eugene IV, whom they label a heretic. They subsequently elect a new rival pope who takes the name Felix V (r. 1439–1449); he will attempt to exercise authority for the next decade. Now considered an antipope by the Roman Catholic Church, he received his strongest support from France and Germany.

1439

Southwest Asia and North Africa: Asia Minor
Christianity

The aging ecumenical patriarch Joseph, who strongly supported the emperor's proposal to reunite the Eastern Orthodox and Roman Catholic churches, dies while attending the Council of Florence and is buried in Italy. He is succeeded as patriarch by Metrophanes II (r. 1440–1443), who shares his pro-unionist position. Metrophanes is the former bishop of Cyzicus in Asia Minor and had also attended the Council of Florence.

Upon his return from the Council of Florence, Byzantine emperor John VIII forces Patriarch Metrophanes and all the bishops in his jurisdiction to submit to papal authority. One bishop, Markos Eugenikos, the metropolitan of Ephesus, refused to submit and to sign the document of union. As the union required unanimous agreement, his refusal prevented the union. Unpopular even in his own diocese, he encounters a popular uprising and is forced to flee. He leaves Ephesus and settles in Rome, outside the emperor's reach.

1439–1443

East and Southeast Asia: China
Buddhism

A eunuch named Li Tomng collects the funds for the construction of the Fahai Temple on the southern edge of Beijing. The main hall is decorated with a set of murals, reputedly the best preserved in China, that depict Buddhist worship. They are created by painters from the Ming Dynasty court, with one mural depicting the emperor and his wife worshipping the many Buddhas and bodhisattvas.

ca. 1440

Europe: England
Christianity

Shortly before her death, Margery Kempe, a Christian laywoman, completes the dictation of *The Book of Margery Kempe,* the first autobiography in the English language. The book describes her

MARGERY KEMPE (CA. 1373–CA. 1440)

Margery Kempe was a pious laywoman and pilgrim who became the subject of the first autobiography written in English. Born ca. 1373, Kempe was the daughter of John Brunham, a rich merchant of King's Lynn in Norfolk, England. She married John Kempe, another merchant of King's Lynn. She ran her own successful brewery, which indicated that Kempe was a member of the local elite. Misfortunes, however, came into her life. When her first child was born, Kempe suffered a spiritual crisis. Her perception of her own sinfulness increased when her business failed. Kempe's response to the loss was a determination to dedicate her life to piety and chastity, which led to her severing sexual relations with her husband. John did not feel the same way, and he insisted on his conjugal rights; the couple produced 14 children during the first 20 years of their marriage. They battled constantly over Kempe's growing commitment to chastity. Adding to Kempe's husband's and neighbors' woes, Kempe became increasingly prone to hysterical outbursts of sobbing and weeping.

In 1413, Kempe joined a party of pilgrims with the goal of visiting Rome, Santiago de Compostela (in Spain), and Jerusalem. Although initially welcomed, Kempe soon alienated her fellow pilgrims because of her incessant weeping. Kempe's first sight of Jerusalem was an intensely emotional experience. Two German pilgrims had to come to her assistance to prevent her from falling off her mount; as she viewed the sites of Jesus of Nazareth's suffering and death, Kempe became even more distraught. She could not keep herself from crying and roaring. That kind of crying lasted for many years after that time, despite anything that anyone might do, and she suffered much contempt for it. Most people found Kempe's outbursts to be extremely irritating, although some saw them as genuine expressions of devotion.

ABC-CLIO

interesting life as a devout Christian, her relatively extensive pilgrimages to various holy sites in both Europe and Asia, and her intimate conversations with God.

ca. 1440

Europe: Greece
Traditional Religions
Following his return to Greece from the Council of Florence, Greek Neoplatonist philosopher Georgius Gemistus, aka Plethon, founds a school at which he advocates a return to polytheism. He erects statues to the ancient Greek deities and some of his students begin to adopt his Pagan perspective and offer worship to the statues.

1440

East and Southeast Asia: Japan
Buddhism
Nisshin (1407–1488), a Nichiren priest, is arrested by the shogun for authoring *Establishing Righteousness to Protect the Nation*, published as part of an effort to have Japan adopt Nichiren Buddhism as the national religion. Tortured in order to obtain a recantation, he was finally released after the shogun is murdered (1441) and a new shogun assumes office. He resumes

his preaching activity, though hampered with a split tongue acquired in the torture sessions.

1440

Europe: Italy
Christianity

Humanist scholar Lorenzo Valla completes his essay *De falso credita et ementita Constantini Donatione declamatio,* in which he demonstrates that the document known as the *Donation of Constantine,* widely cited as evidence the emperor Constantine I gave the Western Roman Empire to the Roman Catholic Church out of gratitude for having been cured of leprosy by Pope Sylvester I, was not a product of the fourth century. He dated the document to the eighth century. While largely ignored during Valla's lifetime, the essay will make a significant impact over the next few centuries. Initially published in 1517, it would be cited by Protestants as part of their case against papal control of the church. Valla would later reveal that other reputedly ancient texts were forgeries, most notably the letter that Jesus of Nazareth was supposed to have sent to King Abgarus of Edessa.

1440

Europe: Serbia
Islam

The Muslim Ottoman army unsuccessfully besieges Belgrade, the Christian citadel on the Danube River.

1440

Russia, Central Asia, and the Caucasus: Russia
Christianity

On his way to take up his post, Isidore, the recently appointed metropolitan of Moscow, stops in Budapest, where he issues an encyclical asking all the Russian bishops to line up behind the proposed union of the Orthodox and Catholic churches.

1440–1449

East and Southeast Asia: Japan
Buddhism

Zen master Ikkyu (1394–1481), a student of Kanzan Eden and of Kaso Sodom, both of the lineage of Soho Myocho (the founder of Daitoku-ji), emerges as critic of the degeneration of Zen in Japan in the shadow of its success and patronage by the wealthy and powerful elements of society. In this regard, he writes a number of poems, many assembled in his *Crazy Cloud Collection* (ca. 1480).

1441

Europe: England
Christianity

British king Henry VI founds Eton College, an independent school for teenage boys, and commissions the building of the college chapel. Due to the War of the Roses in England, the chapel would never be completed. King Henry VI also founds King's College of Our Lady and Saint Nicholas in Cambridge, and commissions the erection of its large campus church. Begun in 1446, the church, complete with the world's largest fan-vault, would take 70 years to finish (1515).

Henry Chichele, the archbishop of Canterbury, dies, and Pope Eugene IV appoints John Stafford (1443–1452) as his successor.

1441

Europe: Italy
Christianity

Construction begins on the Pazzi Chapel, commissioned by Andrea Pazzi, head of the Pazzi family, one of Florence's wealthiest families. When finished in the 1460s, it will be considered one of the masterpieces of Renaissance architecture.

1441

Europe: Netherlands
Christianity

Thomas à Kempis completes the Christian devotional classic, *The Imitation of Christ.* The book is the epitome of what was termed the modern devotion, originally developed by Dutch mystic Gerard Groote based on techniques in which individuals learn to meditate upon and project themselves into the imagery of Biblical scenes.

1441

Europe: Portugal
Christianity

Portuguese explorers operating along the African coast bring the first consignment of African slaves to Lisbon, Portugal.

1441

Russia, Central Asia, and the Caucasus: Armenia
Christianity

The leadership of the Armenian Apostolic Church, which had moved from Armenia to Sis in Armenian Cilicia in 1292, is transferred back to Echmiadzin in Armenia. At this time, Armenians in Cilicia organized as a separate ecclesiastical domain, though remaining a branch of the Armenian Apostolic Church. The former catholicos Gregory IX Mousabegian (1439–1446) did not return to Armenia, but remained at Sis, the former capital of Cilicia, and became the head of the Cilician lineage of Armenian Catholicos. In Armenia, Kirakos I Virapetsi was named the new catholicos.

1441

Russia, Central Asia, and the Caucasus: Russia
Christianity

Isidore, the new metropolitan of Kiev and Moscow, assumes his post in Russia and begins to advocate for the plan of union between the Eastern Orthodox churches and the Roman Catholic Church, which the council has developed. When he presides in services at the Cathedral of the Dormition in Moscow, he processes with a Catholic cross leading the way and names Pope Eugene IV during the liturgy. For his proclamation of the proposed union from the pulpit in the cathedral, he encounters widespread opposition. Prince Basil II of Moscow has him arrested and a synod of Russian bishops depose him. He is subsequently locked up in the Chudov Monastery.

1441–1442

East and Southeast Asia: Japan
Buddhism

Shogun Ashikaga Yoshinori is murdered and his eight-year-old son Ashikaga Yoshikatsu (r. 1442–1444) succeeds him.

1442

East and Southeast Asia: China
Islam

Sassiz Mirza and Muslims in Kashgar, Xinjiang (China), build the Id Kah Mosque on a site used for worship since the 10th century. Initially a relatively small structure, it will grow to become the largest mosque in China.

1442

East and Southeast Asia: China
Buddhism

The Minzhong Temple in Beijing undergoes a large-scale renovation and is renamed as the Confu Temple (and is now known as the Fayuan Temple).

1442

East and Southeast Asia: Japan
Buddhism

Ouchi Morimi builds a five-story pagoda adjacent to Koshaku-ji, a the temple built by his older brother, samurai Ouchi Yoshihiro, at Yamaguchi City. The 90-foot pagoda is recognized as an architectural work of art; however, the adjacent temple would be moved to another location. In 1690, a temple named Ruriko-ji, which had been built at a different location, would be moved to the site next to the five-story pagoda. The pagoda survives as one of the oldest in Japan.

1442

Europe: England
Christianity

King Henry VI founds both Bordeaux University and King's College, Cambridge, the latter to receive the graduates of Eton College, founded just a year earlier.

1442

Europe: Italy
Christianity

Pope Eugene issues the papal bull *Illius qui,* which grants full remission of sins to any who take part in any military expeditions against the (Muslim) Saracens. In this case, the Saracens to whom the pope referred are Africans residing along the western Atlantic coast who have been taken as slaves by the Portuguese.

Pope Eugene reverses the favorable attitude of his predecessor and turns on the Jewish community. He forbids Italian Jews from building any new synagogues, lending money with interest, holding public office, or testifying against any Christian in court.

1442

Europe: Spain

The Borja family of Valencia, Spain, emerge as important church leaders when Alfonso de Borja, serving as a diplomat with King Alfonso V of Aragon, worked an agreement between the king and Pope Eugene IV, whose unpopularity had forced him to leave Rome. The pope had refused to recognize Alfonso's right to rule over Naples. Once the agreement to recognize Alfonso is in place, Pope Eugene returns to Rome. For his work, Alfonso de Borja is named a cardinal. He will later become pope.

1443

Europe: Italy
Christianity

The dedication of the church of San Marco becomes a high point in the renovation of the large Dominican monastic complex in Florence.

1443

Russia, Central Asia, and the Caucasus: Russia
Christianity

The deposed metropolitan of Kiev and Moscow, Isidore, a prisoner at Chudov Monastery, escapes and flees to Rome, where he is warmly received. The Russians use the occasion to declare their independence from Constantinople, and without the approval of the ecumenical patriarch name Jonah (r. 1448–1461), the bishop of Ryazan and Murom, as the new metropolitan of Moscow.

1443

Southwest Asia and North Africa: Asia Minor
Christianity

Metrophanes II dies, and Gregory III Mammas (r. 1443–1450) succeeds him as the new ecumenical patriarch.

1443–1444

Europe: Albania
Christianity, Islam

Skanderbeg and a group of Albanian warriors defect from the Ottoman army and head for Kruje, a fortress town in Albania. Skanderbeg subsequently gains control over the fortress by deceiving the local magistrate with a forged letter signed by the sultan. He then organizes Albanian resistance to Ottoman rule, which takes the form of the League of Lezhë, an alliance of Christian Albanian princes.

The Christian league is able to keep the Ottomans from controlling Albania for the next 20 years.

November 10, 1443

Europe: Bulgaria
Christianity

The Battle of Varna. Pope Eugene IV pledges a substantial amount of the papal income to support a crusade against the Muslim advance in Bulgaria. Władysław III of Poland and the Hungarian John Hunyadi take up the cause and lead an army that encounters the forces of the Ottoman Empire under Sultan Murad II along the Black Sea. The Christian forces are defeated and the crusade ends.

With the situation in the Papal States resolved, Pope Eugene IV returns to Rome after an absence of almost 10 years.

1444

Sub-Saharan Africa: Senegal
Christianity

In their drive ever southward, the Portuguese sailing along the African coast pass the desert and reach Senegal.

1444

East and Southeast Asia: Japan
Buddhism

The 10-year-old Japanese shogun Ashikaga Yoshikatsu dies after a fall from a horse. He is succeeded by his 8-year-old brother, Ashikaga Yoshinari (aka Yoshimasa, r. 1449–1490), though there is a five-year hiatus before he is formally appointed to the office.

1444–1446

Southwest Asia and North Africa: Asia Minor
Islam

Following his victory over the Hungarian forces of Janod Hunyadi, the Ottoman Sultan Murad II Kodja retires and turns the throne over to his teenage son, who begins to reign as Mehmed II. Murad begins a life of quiet contemplation. Mehmed calls his father to return to the throne he had abandoned and after some persuasion he finally comes out of retirement and rules for another five years.

1445

Europe: Italy
Christianity
Pope Eugene IV summons Dominican monk Fra Angelico, who had become known for his paintings, to Rome, where he completes frescoes for several chapels.

1445

Europe: Spain
Judaism
A rabbi Nathan in Arles compiles a concordance to the Hebrew Bible to assist those Jews forced into debates (disputations) with Christians. To accomplish his task, he adopts the Christian ordering of the biblical books and introduces the Christian numbering of chapters and verses, which Christians had introduced in the previous century. His concordance will be the model for future such work by both Christians and Jews in the next centuries.

1445

Russia, Central Asia, and the Caucasus: Russia
Christianity, Islam
Vasily II, the prince of Moscow and grand prince of Vladimir, battles the forces of the Kazan Khanate led by Olug Moxammat, resulting in his being taken prisoner. The citizens of his realm have to raise a ransom for his release. Upon his return, Dmitry Shemyaka, who had ruled in his absence, has Vasily blinded. Thought officially still the prince, it will take him several years to gather his support and regain his power.

1446

Europe: Scotland
Christianity

Sir William St. Clair, a grand master of the Knights Templar, had Rosslyn Chapel (officially the Collegiate Chapel of St. Matthew) constructed near Rosslyn Castle, then the family home outside of Edinburgh. Among its major uses is the celebration of Catholic masses for the faithful departed, most notably the deceased members of the Sinclair family.

1446

South Asia: Afghanistan
Islam
Muslims in Herat, Afghanistan, build the Friday Mosque of Herat, the city's first mosque. It is located on a site formerly occupied by two Zoroastrian fire temples that had been destroyed by an earthquake and fire.

1447

East and Southeast Asia: China
Buddhism
Gyelwa Gedun Drup, a monk of the Gelugpa school of Tibetan Buddhism, later posthumously named the first Dalai Lama, founds Tashilhunpo Monastery located at the foot of Drolmari (or Tara's Mountain), Shigatse, Tibet's second largest city, located south and west of Lhasa. The successive abbots of Tashilhunpo would come to be designated the "Panchen Lama" (meaning "great scholar") and by the 17th century emerge as the second most important leader in the Gelugpa school.

1447

South Asia: China
Islam
Muslims in Beijing build the Dongsi Mosque. It houses a stone tablet inscribed with a poem in praise of the Prophet Muhammad written by Zhu Yuanhang, the first Ming Dynasty emperor.

1447

Europe: Italy
Christianity
Pope Eugene IV dies and Nicholas V (r. 1447–1455) begins his reign in Rome. His plans for refurbishing

Courtyard of the Jama Masjid (Friday Mosque) in Herat, western Afghanistan. Construction was begun in the 13th century and completed in the 15th century. (Sven Dirks)

the city as the capital of Christendom focus on St. Peter's Basilica, which he wishes to rebuild. To that end, he begins pulling down part of the basilica and gathering marble from the ruins of the Coliseum.

Humanist scholar Lorenzo Valla visits Rome and meets the new Pope Nicholas, who hires him as an apostolic secretary in the Curia and commissions him to make a set of translations of Greek texts (including those written by Pagans) into Latin.

1447–1448

Europe: Romania
Christianity

Boyars (feudal lords) in Wallachia, with the support of Hungarian regent John Hunyadi, rise against Wallachian prince Vlad II Dracul. They kill him and blind his eldest son Mircea, who is then buried alive. Their action prompts the involvement of the Ottoman sultan who places Vlad III (called Dracula, or son of Dracul) on the throne. Vlad III's emergence then leads to

Hunyadi's invading Wallachia, driving Vlad into exile, and placing his own ally Vladislav II in place.

1447–1448

Russia, Central Asia, and the Caucasus: Russia
Christianity

The three founders of Solovetsky Monastery in northern Russia—Sawaty, Gherman, and Zosima—are canonized and the monastery becomes a place of pilgrimage. Philip Kolychev (r. 1448–1456), its new superior, begins an energetic building program that includes two cathedrals, the Uspemnsky (built 1452–1457) and the Preobazhenski (built 1556–1564).

1448

Europe: Germany
Christianity

Pope Nicholas V appoints Nicolas of Cusa, already the papal legate to Germany, as a cardinal. A mystic, with theological leanings suspected of being pantheistic, he nevertheless escaped any charges of heresy. His wide-ranging works were reprinted and circulated throughout Europe through the next century.

1448

Europe: Italy
Christianity

Pope Nicholas V establishes the Vatican library by combining a set of codices accumulated by previous popes with his own personal collection. He will add a number of manuscripts from the imperial library of Constantinople.

1448

Europe: Kosovo
Christianity, Islam

Second Battle of Kosovo. Leading a coalition of forces from the Kingdom of Hungary and Wallachia, John Hunyadi battled a coalition of forces of the (Muslim) Ottoman Empire under Sultan Murad II. Two days of heavy fighting left the Ottomans in command of the field. This was the last battle at which the Christian Balkan states were able to provide significant resistance to the Ottomans' advance into Europe.

1448

Southwest Asia and North Africa: Egypt
Islam, Judaism

Sultan Jaqmaj issues a decree banning Jewish and Christian physicians from treating Muslim patients.

1448–1449

Southwest Asia and North Africa: Asia Minor
Christianity

Byzantine emperor John VIII Palaiologos dies (1448) and is succeeded by his son Constantine XI Palaiologos (r. 1449–1453), the last of the Byzantine emperors, who will die during the siege and fall of Constantinople.

1449

East and Southeast Asia: China
Buddhism

Eunuch Wang Zhen is arrested and executed. Six years previously, he had constructed a family shrine in the eastern part of Beijing, which is now appropriated by the authorities. The shrine had followed the common building pattern of a Buddhist temple, and it was transformed into what is now known as the Zhihua Temple. It would later house the wood blocks used for printing the famous edition of the Buddhist scriptures by the Qianlong emperor in the 1730s.

1449

East and Southeast Asia: China
Buddhism

The Battle of Tumu Fortress. Mongol forces defeat the Chinese Ming army led by the Zhengtong emperor, who is captured and imprisoned. His younger brother, Zhu Qiyu, is installed as the Jingtai emperor (1449–1457).

1449

East and Southeast Asia: China
Buddhism

The eunuch Wang Zhen, a court official in charge of protocol for the Ming emperor, becomes a victim of court intrigue and is executed. The Zhihua Temple, a family temple he had constructed six years previously, is confiscated and becomes a public temple. Its seven halls would come to house a copy of the Qianlong edition of the Buddhist scripture printed in the 1730s.

1449

Europe: Albania
Christianity, Islam

The Albanians under Skenderbeg rout the Ottoman forces attempting to invade Albania under Sultan Murat II.

1449

Europe: Denmark

Construction finally begins on a new cathedral in Aarhus where the previous cathedral had been destroyed in 1330. The Cathedral of St. Clement will be built in the Gothic style.

1449

Europe: Greece
Christianity
Thomas Palaiologos, the youngest surviving son of Eastern Roman Emperor Manuel II Palaiologos, is named the Despot of Morea (as the Peloponnesian peninsula was then known).

1449

Europe: Italy
Christianity
Felix V, the pope elected by the group of bishops opposed to Eugene IV, resigns and the dissenting bishops recognize Nicholas V as the rightful pope. After resigning as pope, Felix is given a cardinal's hat.

ca. 1450

East and Southeast Asia: China
Buddhism
Nyingma master Ratna Lingpa assembles a number of the Tantric texts, which had been preserved at Ukpalung Monastery in central Tibet since the 10th century by Zurpoche Shakya Jungney and his successors, and creates a collection known as the Nyingma Gyudbum, now an essential text of the Nyingmapa school of Tibetan Buddhism. This work becomes a major step in the defining of the Nyingmapa tradition.

1450

East and Southeast Asia: China
Buddhism
The former Ming ruler, the Zhengtong emperor, is released by the Mongols and returns to Beijing where his brother now rules. His brother places him under house arrest within the Forbidden City and his outside contacts are severely limited.

1450

Europe: Germany
Christianity
In Mainz, Johannes Gutenberg, who has perfected a form of interchangeable type that could be produced in large quantities and also invented a new type of printing press, begins printing a copy of the Bible (in Latin).

1450

Europe: Italy
Christianity
Nicholas V proclaims 1450 a Jubilee Year in Rome, and numerous pilgrims flock to the city. Nicholas uses the income generated by the event to underwrite further architectural and cultural improvements in the city. He declares that future jubilees will be celebrated every 50 years.

1450

Southwest Asia and North Africa: Asia Minor
Christianity
Athanasius II (r. 1450–1453) succeeds Gregory III Mammas to become the new ecumenical patriarch.

1451

South Asia: India
Hinduism
The Somnath Temple, a prominent Shiva temple located on the western coast of Gujarat, one of the 12 Jyotirlinga shrines and a favorite target of Muslims who have become a significant power in the region, is destroyed by Mahmud Begda, the sultan of Gujarat. It is later rebuilt.

1451

South Asia: India
Islam
Bahlul Khan Lodi ascended the throne of the Delhi Sultanate and initiates the Lodi Dynasty, which will rule northern India into the 1520s. Lodi Dynasty rulers are ethnic Afghans and religiously Sunni Muslims.

1451

Europe: Germany, Netherlands
Christianity
Cardinal Nicholas of Cusa, the bishop of Brixen (South Tyril), orders the Jews of Holland to wear a badge to identify themselves amid their Christian neighbors.

1451

Southwest Asia and North Africa: Asia Minor
Islam

Ottoman sultan Murad II Kodja dies, and for the second time his son Mehmed II (r. 1451–1481) assumes the throne.

1452

Europe: England
Christianity

After a long career in the church and in government, John Kemp (r. 1452–1454) was named archbishop of Canterbury. Pope Nicholas V added to the honor by also naming him cardinal-bishop of Santa Rufina.

1452

Europe: France
Christianity

A religious play in honor of Joan of Arc is staged at Orléans. Those who make a pilgrimage to the city to see the play are granted an indulgence (for the remission of temporal punishment for sin).

1452

Europe: Holy Roman Empire
Christianity

Frederick the Peaceful (r. 1452–1493) becomes the emperor of the Holy Roman Empire.

1452

Europe: Italy
Christianity

Pope Nicholas V crowns Frederick III as Holy Roman emperor in St. Peter's Basilica. It is the last instance of an emperor being crowned at Rome.

1452

Europe: Portugal
Christianity

Directed largely to Portuguese king Alphonso V, Pope Nicholas issued the bull *Dum Diversas* in which he gives his broad blessing on the subjugation of Saracens, Pagans, and other "enemies of Christ" and permits the Portuguese to abduct the inhabitants and consign them to perpetual slavery. This text will later be used to sanction the African slave trade.

1452–1456

Europe: France
Christianity

A retrial of Joan of Arc is authorized by Pope Calixtus III to examine the irregularities accompanying her conviction in 1431. Inquisitor-General Jean Brehal takes the lead in the proceeding, which includes testimony by more than a hundred witnesses. Brehal's final summary claimed Joan was a martyr and pointed the finger at Bishop Pierre Cauchon, a prominent prosecutor in the case, who is himself charged with heresy. In the end, the court reversed Joan's conviction and declared her innocent.

There is minimal immediate reaction to the court's decision. Only in the 19th century is she rediscovered and a campaign launched for her beatification. She would finally be canonized in 1920.

1453

East and Southeast Asia: China
Buddhism

The sixth karmapa, the head of the Karma Kagyu school of Tibetan Buddhism, dies, and the school is left in the charge of two of the karmapa's leading students, Bengar Jampal Zangpo and the first gyaltsap (regent), Goshir Paljor Dondrup. Once the seventh karmapa was identified, they would become his main instructors.

1453

Europe: Germany
Judaism

The ritual blood libel accusation spread through Breslau with the encouragement of Franciscan friar and inquisitor John of Capistrano (later canonized). It leads to the expulsion of the Jews from the city.

1453

Europe: Italy
Christianity

French knight Geoffrey de Charny II bequeaths a piece of cloth believed to be the burial shroud of Jesus of Nazareth to the royal House of Savoy in northern Italy. The shroud will later come to be housed in Turin, Italy, and will be known as the Shroud of Turin.

Mehmed II was a 15th-century Turkish sultan who made the Ottoman Empire a major power in the early modern world. Mehmed conquered the city of Constantinople and brought the Byzantine Empire to an end. This watercolor portrait was created around 1453. (The Gallery Collection/ Corbis)

About the same time, Pope Nicholas V acquires a piece of cloth believed to picture the face of Jesus of Nazareth and dating from the week of his death from some relatives of the emperor of the Byzantine Empire. This relic would later make its way to the Monastery of the Holy Face in Alicante, Spain.

1453

Southwest Asia and North Africa: Asia Minor
Islam
Upon assuming the throne in 1451, the youthful Sultan Mehmed II focuses his attention on capturing Constantinople, beginning with taking control of the

Bosporus Strait. The city fell after a 57-day siege. Following his successful entry into the city, he took the title of Caesar of Rome, indicating his understanding that he had conquered what had once been the Roman Empire. He would soon turn his attention to extending his empire into Europe proper.

1453

Southwest Asia and North Africa: Asia Minor
Islam, Christianity
Constantinople falls, and its transformation into Istanbul begins. Both Byzantine emperor Constantine XI Palaiologos (r. 1449–1453) and Ecumenical Patriarch Athanasius II die in the fighting.

Among those caught in Constantinople when it falls is Isidore, the metropolitan of Kiev and Moscow. He escapes, makes his way to Rome, and is eventually consecrated as bishop of Sabina. Eventually, Pope Pius II names him Latin patriarch of Constantinople and archbishop of Cyprus, but in neither case is he able to exercise any real jurisdiction.

1453

Southwest Asia and North Africa: Asia Minor
Judaism
Ottoman sultan Mehmed II confirms Rabbi Moshe Kapsali as the chief rabbi of Constantinople. He also establishes a special tax to support the appointment of a rabbinic authority over the Jewish communities throughout the Ottoman Empire.

1454

East and Southeast Asia: China
Chinese Religions
Emperor Daizon constructs the Long'an Temple in Beijing.

1454

East and Southeast Asia: China
Buddhism
The future seventh karmapa, the reincarnated head of the Karma Kagyu school of Tibetan Buddhism, is born as Chodrag Gyamtso in the town of Kyilha in northern Tibet. At the time of the child's birth, Cho Paljor, a student of the sixth karmapa who had passed

away the year before, has a dream that the karmapa would be reborn at Kyilha. He searched out the child and identified him. Several weeks later he is given to the school, who raise him as their future leader.

1454

Europe: England
Christianity

John Kemp, the archbishop of Canterbury, dies and is succeeded by Thomas Bourchier (r. 1454–1486), formerly the bishop of Ely.

1454

Europe: Greece
Christianity

Following the Ottoman conquest of Greece, they return the 11th-century Daphni Monastery outside of Athens, which had been taken over by French Roman Catholic crusaders in 1206, to Greek Orthodox monks. The monastery houses a number of famed mosaics.

1454

Europe: Italy
Christianity

Pope Nicolas V preaches a crusade whose goal is the retaking of Constantinople, which had fallen to the Ottoman (Muslim) Turks the previous year. He receives little support from the European states, however, and his words fall on deaf ears. Like other European rulers, the pope seems heavily focused on more local issues, not the least being the rebuilding of Rome's ecclesiastical architecture (most notably St. Peter's Basilica) and the creation of new art as a step in the elevation of the papacy, now reestablished in Rome with both the Avignon era and the Great Schism with its rival popes behind it.

1454

Southwest Asia and North Africa: Asia Minor
Christianity, Islam

Ottoman sultan Mehmed II selects Gennadius II Scholarius (r. 1454–1456), a scholar monk, as the successor to the office of ecumenical patriarch. He is considered the ethnarch (governor) of the

Christian *millet* (a semiautonomous religious community), and as such assigned responsibility over all Orthodox Christians (both Greeks and non-Greeks) within the Ottoman realm. The anti-Western Gennadius is chosen after some consideration by Mehmed, as he wanted someone who would not attempt a new appeal to the West for help in overthrowing his empire.

Since Mehmed has converted the patriarchal basilica, the Hagia Sophia, into a mosque, Gennadius established his headquarters at the Church of the Holy Apostles.

1454

Southwest Asia and North Africa: Egypt
Christianity

Bedouins attack, plunder, and severely damage St. Anthony's Monastery, the fourth-century monastic establishment in southern Egypt.

1455

Europe: Italy
Christianity

Pope Calixtus III (r. 1455–1458) succeeds Nicholas V on the papal throne. He is the first representative of the Borgia family to become pope. He would appoint his youthful nephew Rodrigo (later Pope Alexander VI) as a cardinal.

1455

Europe: Poland
Christianity

The combined forces of Poland and Lithuania finally capture the Teutonic castle headquarters at Marianburg, the world's largest brick castle, in the midst of the Thirteen Years' War. In the final Second Peace of Thorn (1466), the Teutonic order loses control of its former lands to Poland.

1455

Europe: Portugal
Christianity

The Papal bull *Romanus Pontifex* grants the Portuguese a trade monopoly for newly discovered countries in Africa and Asia.

1456

Europe: Italy
Christianity

After a comet appears in the sky over Europe, Pope Calixtus III issues an edict for the faithful to pray for deliverance from "The Devil, the Turk, and the Comet."

Pope Calixtus also issues the bull *Inter Caetera,* which reaffirms the practice of the Portuguese in placing non-Christians they encounter in their exploration of the African coast into a state of servitude (slavery). The bull appears to directly conflict with the 1435 bull of Pope Eugene IV that declared all persons, including Muslims and other non-Christians, to have been created in the image of God and to have a soul. Eugene denied Christians the right to take away the liberty of others, especially non-Christians.

Pope Calixtus formally pronounces Joan of Arc innocent of the charges of witchcraft (working malevolent magic) and of heresy, the charges that led to her condemnation and execution in 1431.

1456

Europe: Serbia, Romania
Christianity, Islam

The Siege of Belgrade (aka the Siege of Nándorfehérvár). The Muslim forces of the Ottoman sultan Mehmed II attack the town of Belgrade (along the Danube River in what today is Serbia). The town is defended by Christian Hungarian John Hunyadi. His success in preventing the capture of Belgrade blocks the expansion of the Ottoman Empire along the Danube for some 70 years. The pope, who had called upon Catholic believers to pray for victory, happily celebrates Hunyadi's accomplishment by including the Feast of the Transfiguration in the calendar of the Western church each year on August 6.

With Hunyadi focused on Belgrade, Vlad II Dracula (1456–1462), who had briefly ruled Wallachia in 1448, leads his supporters into his native land and deposes and kills Vladislav II, whom Hunyadi had placed on the throne. Vlad shows his support of the Romanian Orthodox church by building a new church at Târgşor (near where his father and older brother had been killed), and he contributed substantively to the Snagov Monastery and the Comana Monastery.

Believing the boyars (feudal lords) to be a major problem in Wallachia (modern Romania) due to their constant infighting, he turns on them, removes them from office, and replaces them with people loyal to his centralized government.

1456

Southwest Asia and North Africa: Asia Minor
Christianity

The Church of the Holy Apostles having fallen into a state of disrepair, the ecumenical patriarch Gennadius moves his office to the Church of the Pammakaristos in Istanbul. Shortly after making the move, Gennadius resigns his office and is succeeded by Isidore II (r. 1456–1462), another known opponent of the union of the Eastern church with the Roman Catholic Church.

1457

East and Southeast Asia: China
Buddhism

The Jingtai emperor, who had assumed the throne of China when his brother was captured by the Mongols, falls ill and provides the opening for the former emperor (a prisoner in the forbidden city) to reclaim his throne. He comes to power as the Tianshun emperor (r. 1457–1464).

1457

East and Southeast Asia: China
Chinese Religions

The massive Dashengshou Wan'an Temple (the Temple of Great Holy Longevity and Eternal Peace), a Vajrayana temple in Beijing located to the west of the Forbidden City, which had burned to the ground in 1368, is redesigned, rebuilt, and renamed as the Miaoying (Divine Retribution) Temple. It is dominated by a large white pagoda in a style reminiscent of Tibetan architecture.

1457

East and Southeast Asia: Japan
Buddhism

Rennyo (1415–1499) becomes the head of Honganji, at the time a poor and somewhat dilapidated Jodo

RENNYO (1415–1499)

Rennyo was a Japanese Buddhist monk and reformer. Rennyo was born as Hoteimaru in 1415. Although it was on the basis of the works of his forebear, Shinran, that Japanese True Pure Land Buddhism (Jodo Shinshu) was founded, it was not until Rennyo appeared that True Pure Land Buddhism was interpreted in such a manner that the ordinary people of Japan could participate in its practice. This is not to say that during Shinran's time there were no lay practitioners of Jodo Shinshu, but rather that it was Rennyo who made Shinran's teachings available in colloquial Japanese so that they could be understood by the ordinary people.

It is in this sense that Rennyo has been lauded in the Jodo Shinshu tradition as the restorer of the Jodo Shinshu piety. He is known as Chuku Shonin (the master who restored [the tradition] in midcourse) or Gosaiko no Shonin (the master who was the restorer [of the tradition]). As a restorer of Shinran's teaching, Rennyo explained how a follower could practice the single-minded faith of Jodo Shinshu by giving up all other practices.

In a sense, Rennyo was also a reformer of the True Pure Land Buddhist tradition. Scattered throughout his letters one can find encouragement to continue the practice of reciting the six-letter name of Amida Buddha (*Rokuji no Myogo*), procedures for giving up practices that are not conducive to generating a single-minded faith in Amida Buddha (also known as Amitabha or *Shinjin Ketsujo*), and caution against slandering other religious traditions.

Much of what is known about Rennyo has been derived from memoirs written by his disciples and followers, the letters that he wrote, and writings by others concerning the doctrine and history of Shinran's teachings. Among the memoirs, the best-known of the collections is the *Goichidaiki Kikigaki* (*Record of Words and Deeds*). The most important source for the reinterpretation of the full expression of Shinran's life of *nembutsu* (gratitude) lies in Rennyo's letters, many of which were compiled by Rennyo's grandson, Ennyo, into a collection known as *Ofumi* (*Letters*), which has become better known within the Nishi-Honganji system as the *Gobunsho* (another word for "Letters"). Rennyo died in 1499.

LESLIE S. KAWAMURA

Shinshu temple in the Otani district of Kyoto. The temple was important as the site of the mausoleum of Shinran, the founder of the Jodo Ahinshu sect, but at the time was but one of a number of loosely associated temples.

1457

Europe: England
Christianity
Reginald Pecock, Bishop of Chichester, stands trial for heresy. In the process of writing against the contemporary supporters of John Wycliffe (the Lollards),

he questions the infallibility of the Roman Catholic Church. He is found guilty himself of heresy, a capital offense. Pecock publicly recanted his heretical views, resigned his office (1459), and retired to obscurity at Thorney Abbey.

1457

Europe: Moldavia
Christianity
Stephen III (r. 1457–1504) begins his almost half a century of rule over the nation of Moldavia. He makes a pledge that he will build and endow a church for

every victory he has over the surrounding nations of Poland, Hungary, and Turkey. By the end of his life, he has built 40 such churches. These unique churches are noted for the fresco paintings on the exterior walls that depict biblical scenes.

1457–1458

Russia, Central Asia, and the Caucasus: Russia
Christianity

Isidore, the Orthodox metropolitan of Kiev and Moscow, having escaped Constantinople after its fall to the Ottomans, submits to Rome. Meanwhile a new metropolitan of Moscow has been appointed in Russia, independent of the ecumenical patriarch, Gregory of Constantinople. Thus Patriarch Gregory appoints a new metropolitan of Kiev (Ukraine now being under the control of Poland) and upon his arrival at his new residence, the new bishop, also named Gregory, begins a reorganization of his diocese. The patriarch revises his title to become Metropolitan of Kiev, Galychyna and All Russia.

1457–1464

East and Southeast Asia: China
Buddhism

Two Buddhist monks, Pu Hi and Yuan Hong, collect funds to rebuild a village temple in Beijing that had originally been constructed in the 12th century. The temple had collapsed in the distant past and was all but forgotten. Once reconstructed, with some funds coming from the emperor, it is named Hongci Guangji and continues as an important Buddhist center. The temple complex will come to include a scripture library that now holds over 100,000 books, including a copy of the Ming edition of the Tripitaka (the Buddhist scriptures) printed in the 1730s.

Daxiong Hall of the reconstructed temple has a unique roof ridge, the only Buddhist temple in Beijing with such a structure. It is decorated with a gold lotus and a word in Sanskrit meaning "everlasting world." The hall houses statues of the three Trikala Buddhas—Dipamkara, Sakyamuni, and Maitreya—and the 18 arhats (enlightened ones).

1458

Europe: Greece
Islam

Sultans of the Ottoman Empire, 1280–1512

Reign	Osmanli Dynasty
1280–1324	Osman I
1324–1360	Orhan
1360–1389	Murat I
1389–1402	Bayezid I, the Thunderbolt (deposed)
1402–1403	Isa (claimed Asia Minor)
1402–1411	Suleiman (claimed Rumelia)
1409–1413	Mesa (claimed Rumelia)
1413–1421	Mehmed I (claimed Asia Minor, 1402–1413)
1421–1451	Murat II (abdicated in favor of Mehmet II, 1444–1446)
1451–1481	Mehmed II, the Conqueror
1481–1512	Bayezid II (deposed)

The forces of the Ottoman Empire overrun Athens. Sultan Mehmed II orders that no looting or destruction of the city occur, under pain of death. He does, however, convert the Parthenon into the city's main mosque.

1458

Europe: Italy
Christianity

Pope Calixtus III dies and is succeeded by Pope Pius II (r. 1458–1464).

1458

Europe: Spain
Christianity

Alphonso V, the king of Aragon, dies and is succeeded by his brother John II (called the Faithless) (r. 1458–1479).

1458

Southwest Asia and North Africa: Asia Minor
Islam, Christianity

Ottoman Sultan Mehmed II initiates construction of the Eyüp Sultan Mosque on the European side of Istanbul near the Golden Horn and outside the walls of the old city. It is the first mosque that the Ottomans build (as opposed to adapting older buildings) following their conquest of the city. The mosque is built adjacent to the tomb of Abu Ayyub al-Ansari, who led the original Arab Muslim attempt to take Constantinople in 670. Al-Ansari's tomb had become a pilgrimage site, and it is believed to contain several items formerly owned by the Prophet Muhammad.

1459

East and Southeast Asia: Japan
Buddhism

Shogun Yoshimasa completely rebuilds the eighth-century temple to the goddess Kannon at Kamakura. It houses a large golden statue of the goddess, as well as 18 figures donated by Yoshimasa representing the various incarnations or forms she is believed to have assumed. Previously, the shogun had given the temple a dried camphor tree, which had been hollowed out to make a container of holy water.

1459

Europe: Romania
Islam, Christianity

Ottoman Sultan Mehmed II demands that Vlad III Dracula, the ruler of Wallachia, pay the *jizya* tax (a standard amount demanded of non-Muslims in the Ottoman Empire). Vlad refuses to admit that Wallachia was part of the empire and thus will not pay the tax. He kills the Ottoman envoys by having their turbans nailed to their heads, claiming that they had refused to properly acknowledge his status by removing their "hats."

The sultan moves against Vlad by sending an army under the Bey of Nicopolis, Hamza Pasha, to Wallachia. Vlad responds with a surprise attack. Following his victory, he has the survivors, including Hamza Pasha, impaled. Impalement had become his favorite form of execution, a fact that would later have him nicknamed Vlad the Impaler (aka Vlad Tepes).

1459

Russia, Central Asia, and the Caucasus: Russia
Islam

Qulpa, the brother of the khan of the Golden Horde, poisons his brother Berdi Beg (aka Berdibek). The Horde, already rent with turmoil, begins to break up into a number of factions.

1460

Europe: Italy
Christianity

Pope Pius II proclaims a crusade against the Ottoman Turks who now reign in Constantinople. The crusade will last for three years and end with no visible success.

1460

Europe: Scotland
Christianity

Scottish king James II dies from an accident caused by an exploding cannon during at the siege of Roxburgh Castle as he attempted to reclaim land in southern Scotland near the famous abbey at Kelso. Following his death, his infant son James III is hastily crowned at Kelso Abbey, rather than being taken to the traditional site, Scone Abbey. Kelso Abbey, one of the largest and wealthiest in Scotland, was under the control of monks of the Tironensian order, a 12th-century French monastic order.

1460–1461

Europe: Greece
Islam, Christianity

The Ottoman sultan Mehmed conquers the despotate of Morea in Greece (1460) and the empire of Trebizond (1461) in northeastern Asia Minor, thus completing his dismantling of the Byzantine Empire.

1461

Europe: England
Christianity

The lengthy struggle between the House of York and the House of Lancaster (known as the War of the Roses) for control of England ends with Henry VI (Lancaster) being deposed and imprisoned. His cousin, Edward of York, who reigns as Edward IV (r. 1461–1470), succeeds him as king,

1461

Europe: France
Christianity

King Charles VII dies and is succeeded by his son Louis XI (r. 1461–1483). Louis gains a reputation for being superstitious in part derived from his including a number of astrologers among his personal advisors.

1461

Europe: Greece, Italy
Christianity

Thomas Palaiologos, the former despot of Morea, who had fled to Italy when Greece was added to the Ottoman Empire the year previously, makes a gift of what is believed to be the head of the biblical apostle Andrew, long the property of the church in Petras, Greece, to Pope Pius II. The relic is taken to Rome and placed in St. Peter's Basilica. As the surviving male of his family, the pope and most European rulers recognize him as the Byzantine emperor, though he will never be able to regain the throne in Constantinople.

1461

Europe: Italy
Christianity

Pope Pius II, born in the province of Siena, canonizes Saint Catherine of Siena. He also authorized the building of a cathedral in his hometown, now called Pienza.

1461

Russia, Central Asia, and the Caucasus: Russia
Christianity

Jonas, the metropolitan of Moscow and All Russia, dies. He is succeeded by Theodosius, the archbishop of Rostov. Theodosius is the first metropolitan to be appointed by the grand prince of Moscow since the fall of Constantinople to the Ottomans. He becomes the new head of the Russian Orthodox Church, which now exists independently of the patriarch residing in Constantinople. Theodosius attempted, unsuccessfully, to purge the clergy ranks of uneducated and unfit priests, but found himself unable to recruit enough capable clergy. He also had to contend with the loss of juridiction of those areas of his diocese that had fallen under the control of Poland (whose rulers were Roman Catholic) and which he feared might be lost to Roman Catholicism.

1461

Southwest Asia and North Africa: Asia Minor
Christianity

The abandoned Church of the Holy Apostles in Istanbul is pulled down by the Ottoman rulers who construct the Fatih Mosque on the site.

Sultan Mehmed II designates Bishop Hovakim of Bursa as the patriarch for all Armenian subjects of the Ottoman Empire.

1462

Europe: Greece
Christianity

The monks of St. Michael's Monastery at Mantamados create an icon of the archangel Michael, which will later become famous as a wonderworking icon as reports of miracles cluster around it.

1462

Europe: Italy
Christianity

In an address on the issue of slavery directed primarily to the Portuguese, Pope Pius II condemns as a great crime the enslavement of newly baptized Christians. He thus sanctions the enslavement of non-Christians who had been captured in the Portuguese takeover of lands along the African coast (Morocco).

1462

Europe: Romania
Islam, Christianity

Mehmed II comes into conflict with Vlad III Dracula, the prince of Wallachia, with whom he had spent many childhood years. Vlad had ambushed and captured several Ottoman forces, only to subsequently announce his plans to impale some 23,000 of the captive Turks. Upon hearing the news, Mehmed II abandons his siege of Corinth and launches an attack on Wallachia. His attack begins poorly, as he suffers many casualties as the result of a surprise attack in the middle of the night. Vlad appears to have planned to personally kill the sultan.

In the end, reacting to Vlad's scorched earth policies and unexpected brutality, Mehmed II withdrew from the campaign and turned the task of its completion to Vlad's brother Radu. Heading a relatively small force that included some local boyars (feudal lords) who had turned against Vlad, Radu eventually moves on Targoviste, Vlad's capital, and drives him into exile. Radu assumes administrative control of Wallachia.

Vlad, a Romanian Orthodox Christian, is arrested after he arrives in Hungary, a Roman Catholic country.

1462

Europe: Romania
Christianity, Islam

Sultan Mehmed II enters Wallachia (modern Romania) with a large army. Vlad III Dracula, the prince of Wallachia, unable to directly challenge the force, fights a guerrilla war that includes a famous raid on the sultan's camp in the middle of the night aimed at assassinating the sultan. As a result, the sultan personally withdraws and leaves the final attack on Vlad to his brother Radu, who drives Vlad from the capital at Targoviste and replaces him as prince or voivode. Vlad moves into exile in Hungary and Radu rules as a puppet of the Ottomans.

After the encounter with Vlad Dracula, the Ottomans would not renew their move north along the Danube for a generation. Mehmed turns his attention to other targets around the Mediterranean Basin.

1462

Europe: Russia
Christianity

Vasily II (r. 1425–1462), the grand prince of Moscow, dies and is succeeded by his co-regent, his son Ivan III Vasilyevich (1462–1505). Ivan begins immediately to see himself as the successor to the emperors of the overrun city of Constantinople and uses the term Czar (or Caesar) to describe himself. He consolidates his rule over the neighboring states.

1462

Russia, Central Asia, and the Caucasus: Russia
Christianity

Vasily II, the prince of Moscow and grand prince of Vladimir, dies and is succeeded by his son Ivan III Vasilyevich (aka Ivan the Great, r. 1462–1505). During his lengthy reign, he will triple the territory of the Muscovite state, end its subservience to the Mongols, and renovate the Kremlin, the religious and political heart of Moscow.

1462

Southwest Asia and North Africa: Asia Minor
Christianity

Ecumenical Patriarch Isidore II dies. His death initiates a period of instability in the patriarch's office and several patriarchs (Joseph I and Sophronios I) come and go. Former patriarch Gennadius returns twice to the office prior to the emergence of Mark II in 1466. The dating of the reigns of the patriarchs between Isidore and Mark is in dispute.

1463

Europe: Bosnia
Islam

Sultan Mehmed leads the Ottoman forces in the conquest of Bosnia. Almost immediately, the new Muslim rulers launch construction of the Emperor's Mosque, a wooden structure dedicated to the sultan, Muhammad al-Fatih, the conqueror of Constantinople.

Mehmed issues a *firman* (decree) to the Franciscans of Bosnia, who had submitted to Ottoman rule. It grants members of the order freedom to move freely within the empire and lead Roman Catholic worship in the churches and monasteries located in what is now Ottoman territory, and promises freedom from persecution, insult, and disturbance. Mehmed recognizes them as citizens of the empire who are under his protection and offers his desire for peace throughout the empire as the rationale for the *firman*.

1463

Europe: Italy

Both Venice and Padua claim to possess the relics of Luke, the first-generation Christian who is credited with writing two books of the New Testament, the Gospel of Luke and the Acts of the Apostles. The bones in each location were exhumed and examined, those in Padua being declared authentic. They were subsequently enshrined in the Basilica of Santa Giustina.

1463

Europe: Serbia
Christianity

Patriarch Arsenios II, the head of the Serbian Orthodox Church, dies and no successor is elected. The vacancy of the patriarch's chair has the effect of abolishing the Serbian patriarchate, and the Serbian church comes under the direct jurisdiction of the ecumenical patriarch in Constantinople.

1463

Southwest Asia and North Africa: Asia Minor
Islam
In Istanbul, Mehmed II initiates construction of what will become Topkapi Palace.

1464

Sub-Saharan Africa: Mali
Islam
As the Mali Empire fades, the Songhai Empire, a Muslim state, emerges in western Africa, and the first emperor, Sonni Ali (r. 1464–1493), begins his regime.

1464

East and Southeast Asia: China
Buddhism
The Tianshun emperor, ruler of the Ming Dynasty of China, dies and is succeeded by his son, the Chenghua emperor (r. 1464–1487).

1464

Europe: Italy
Christianity
Pope Paul II (r. 1464–1471) succeeds Pius II on the papal throne. Prior to his election, the cardinals reached a number of agreements with the future pope, including a limitation on the number of cardinals at 24, the appointment of bishops to the more prominent posts to be made only with the consent of the cardinals, and the calling of an ecumenical council within three years. Paul backed off his consent to the agreements once in office.

1464

Russia, Central Asia, and the Caucasus: Russia
Christianity
Metropolitan Theodosius resigns and picks Philip I (r. 1464–1473), the archbishop of Suzdal, to succeed him as the head of the Russian Orthodox Church, the metropolitan of Moscow and All Russia.

1465

East and Southeast Asia: Japan
Buddhism
Alarmed at the revival of Hongan-ji, the Jodo Shinshu temple in the Otani district of Kyoto, and after accusations of heresy against the temple, an armed force from Mt. Hiei, the Tendai Buddhist center, attacks Otani and causes significant destruction. They are finally persuaded to retreat by the payment of a sum of money. Rennyo, the priest in charge of Hongan-ji, is forced to leave Kyoto.

1465

Southwest Asia and North Africa: Morocco
Islam, Judaism
Abdul Haq, the sultan of the Marinid Dynasty, appoints a Jew, Aaron ben Batash, as his vizier. The negative reaction to his decision includes his assassination. Sharif Muhammad al Jati (r. 1465–1471) seizes power, and the Marinid Dynasty comes to an end in Morocco. Anti-Jewish riots in Fez and other Moroccan cities lead to many deaths.

1465–1466

Southwest Asia and North Africa: Asia Minor
Christianity
Mark II, the bishop of Adrianople, becomes the ecumenical patriarch. He is a controversial choice and opposed by a segment of the church's leadership. The Ottoman sultan favors him as an opponent of any union with the Roman Catholics. He is in office only a year before Mehmed II appoints him the new archbishop of Ohrid, the primary religious post in Bulgaria, which now existed as an Ottoman state. Mark was succeeded by Symeon I, who hailed from Trebizond, a kingdom of Asia Minor recently incorporated into the Ottoman Empire. He was the patriarch for only a brief time before being forced off the throne under accusations of simony (having purchased his office) and was succeeded by Dionysios I (r. 1467–1471).

1466

East and Southeast Asia: China
Buddhism
The large monastic complex now known as Baogue Monastery was largely destroyed during the early years of the Ming Dynasty. Emperor Xianzong orders its rebuilding, at which time it is renamed Ciren Monastery.

1467–1477

East and Southeast Asia: Japan
Buddhism

After 20 years on the throne, Shogun Ashikaga Yoshimasa had produced no heir. To avoid any succession problems, in 1464 he adopted his younger brother, Ashikaga Yoshimi, then serving as the abbot of a Jōdo Shu Buddhist monastery. However, the next year, his wife produced an heir who was named Yoshihisa. The attempt to avoid a succession conflict had created one, as forces began to line up behind each claimant to the throne.

By 1467, open hostilities, termed the Odin War, had erupted and hostilities would spread to various parts of Japan and continue for the next decade. The war would become an important watershed for religion in Japan as armies regularly ransacked and destroyed Buddhist temples and Shinto shrines wherever they roamed. In and around Kyoto especially, most temples were destroyed and had to be rebuilt after the war. Among the more prominent temples destroyed were Tenryu-ji, Myoshin-ji, and Daitoku-ji in Kyoto.

April 28, 1467

Europe: Italy
Christianity

In the village of Genazzano, attendees at a public festival see a large cloud descend on the local church and upon the cloud's dissipation, a painting of the Blessed Virgin Mary holding the infant Jesus appears where none had been before. The church is, at the time, undergoing substantial repairs, slowed by the lack of resources. The town immediately becomes the target of pilgrimages, and miracles are recorded by those who prayed before the picture. It was later discovered that the picture had disappeared at about the same time from a church in Scutari, Albania, recently overrun by Turkish Muslims. The painting is now known as Our Lady of Good Counsel.

ca. 1468

South Asia: India
Hinduism

The 19-year-old Srimanta Sankaradeva composes his initial work, Uddhava Samvāda, a verse-rendering of a small portion of the Hindu Vaishnava holy book, the Srimad Bhāgavata in the language of Assam, and begins to initiate people in his new faith, a monotheistic version of Hindu Vaishnava religion built around the belief that Lord Krishna is the One, Eternal, and Absolute and stressing unqualified devotion to him. He prohibits the worship of deities other than Krishna. He subsequently spreads the belief/practice of bhakti throughout Assam (eastern India).

Srimanta Sankaradeva's lengthy career, while largely limited to Assam, parallels the development of bhakti yoga elsewhere, most notably in Bengal around Chaitanya Mahaprabhu.

1468

Europe: Albania
Christianity, Islam

Following the death of the Albanian military hero Skanderbeg, the Turkish Ottomans are finally able to reabsorb Albania into the Ottoman Empire. Gradually, most Albanians convert to Islam. Skanderberg's resistance has thwarted plans by the Ottomans to carry their conquests into old Byzantine territory in northern Italy.

1468

Europe: Bosnia
Islam

Following up on the conquest of Asia Minor and Greece, Muslim forces overrun Bosnia. Here, where a larger percentage of the upper classes have remained aloof from the Christian Church, a majority will convert to Islam.

1468

Europe: Scotland
Christianity

King James III annexes the Orkney Islands to Scotland from Norway. St. Magnus Cathedral, the seat of the bishop of Orkney, is now placed under the oversight of the archbishop of St. Andrews, who appoints Scots to the seat of the bishop of Orkney, the first being Bishop Robert Reid (r. 1541–1558).

1468

Southwest Asia and North Africa: Morocco
Christianity

Anticipating the future conquest of the city, the Portuguese form a diocese of Tangier, though the first bishop is unable to take up residence there.

1469

South Asia: India

Nanak, the founder of the Sikh religion, is born in what is now Pakistan.

1469

Europe: Austria
Christianity

Frederick III, the Holy Roman emperor, who is also the duke of Austria, finally persuades Pope Paul II to establish bishoprics in Vienna and Wiener Neustadt, an achievement his predecessors had been unable to accomplish. The large cathedral-like St. Stephen's Church is designated Vienna's new cathedral.

1469

Europe: Spain
Christianity

Ferdinand, the heir to the throne of Aragon, marries Isabella, the heiress to the crown of Castile. Their nuptial agreement carries a provision that once on the throne, they will exercise power as co-rulers.

1469

Russia, Central Asia, and the Caucasus: Russia
Christianity

Ivan III of Russia married the daughter of Thomas Palaiologos, the former despot of Morea (that is, the Peloponnese peninsula) and claimant to the throne of Constantinople as he was the brother of the deposed Constantine XI, the last reigning Byzantine emperor.

1470

Europe: England
Christianity

A successful coup deposes King Edward IV and returns King Henry VI (r. 1470–1471) to his throne in England. Edward takes refuge in Burgundy (France).

1470

Europe: Italy
Christianity

Pope Paul II issues a bull providing for a Jubilee (or Holy) Year to be celebrated every 25 years.

1471

Europe: England
Christianity

After a mere six months on the throne, Henry VI of the House of Lancaster is again deposed by his cousin Edward IV (r. 1471–1483) of the House of York, who resumes his rule of England. Shortly after Edward again becomes king, Henry dies, and his heir is killed in battle.

St. Stephen's Cathedral in Vienna, Austria. It was originally constructed as a Romanesque church in the 12th century, with Gothic architectural features added in the 14th century. The church was elevated to the rank of cathedral in 1469. (Maria Zoroyan/Dreamstime.com)

1471

Europe: England
Christianity

Former British king Henry VI dies while imprisoned by King Edward. Rumors circulate that he was murdered as he knelt praying. Subsequently, miracles are attributed to his agency, and some begin to think of him as both a saint and a martyr. A personal cult began to emerge around him and was encouraged by Henry VII Tudor. A catalog of miracles associated with him would be compiled at St George's Chapel, Windsor, where he was interred. The devotion to Henry VI would be manifest for a generation (until the Protestant Reformation swept through England).

Following Henry's death, King Edward IV (r. 1471–1483) officially begins his second tenure on the throne.

1471

Europe: Italy
Christianity

Pope Sixtus IV (r. 1471–1484) is elected. He is credited with establishing the Sistine Chapel and building the Vatican Archives adjacent to the Vatican Library.

The Malermi Bible, the first translation of the Bible into Italian, is printed. It was translated using the Latin Vulgate version.

1471

Europe: Spain
Christianity

Construction begins on the new Cathedral of Astorga (Spain), which will replace the older Romanesque building. Begun as a Gothic church, by the time it is finished it will incorporate a variety of architectural styles.

1471

Southwest Asia and North Africa: Asia Minor
Christianity

Ecumenical Patriarch Dionysius I is deposed after being accused of having at one time converted to Islam. Even after defending himself by showing his uncircumcised penis, he was forced from his office, and former patriarch Symeon I (r. 1471–1475) was appointed in his stead.

1471

Southwest Asia and North Africa: Morocco
Christianity

After failing a generation earlier, the Portuguese finally take control of Tangier on Morocco's Atlantic coast south of Gibraltar. The Roman Catholic bishop of Tangier is finally able to move to the city and take up his assigned post.

1472

Europe: England
Christianity

Construction on the western towers of York Minster, formally the Cathedral and Metropolitical Church of St. Peter in York, is completed, which occasions the rebuilt church's consecration. York Minster is the second largest Gothic cathedral of northern Europe. The great east window, added in 1408, is the largest expanse of medieval stained glass in the world.

1472

Europe: Italy
Christianity

The first printed edition of Dante's *Divine Comedy* appears. The epic poem, which includes his tour of heaven, purgatory, and hell, was not published during Dante's lifetime. It included the placement of various contemporaries in hell, including popes Nicholas III and Boniface VIII, and negative reflections on a spectrum of corrupt church leaders (both lay and clerical) through the ages. It also assigns a place in hell to alchemists, diviners, astrologers, and magicians.

1472

Europe: Scotland
Christianity

Pope Sixtus IV elevated the see of St. Andrews (Edinburgh) to an archbishopric.

1472

Russia, Central Asia, and the Caucasus: Russia
Christianity

Zoe Palaiologina, a niece of the last Byzantine emperor Constantine XI, who had died when the city fell to the Ottomans, marries Prince Ivan III of Russia. The marriage arrangements had been initiated in 1469 by Pope Paul II as a step toward uniting the Eastern Orthodox and Roman Catholic churches. The marriage ceremony was held at the Dormition Cathedral in Moscow, but given the opposition of Theodosius, the Russian metropolitan of Moscow, to any union, the pope's effort went for naught. Zoe converts to Russian Orthodoxy.

1472

Southwest Asia and North Africa: Morocco
Islam, Judaism

In Morocco, Sharif Muhammad al Jati is overthrown by the Wattisid chief Muhammad al Shaikh (r. 1472–1505) who establishes the rule of the Wattisid dynasty, which will rule Morocco until 1554. The Wattasids are a Zenata Berber family. The new ruler invites those Jews who had fled in 1465 to return to Fez and pick up their life there.

1473

East and Southeast Asia: China
Buddhism

An addition is made to the Zhenjue Temple originally built earlier in the century in Beijing along the banks of the Changhe River—the unique Diamond Throne Pagoda structure consisting of a large square base that supports five pagodas. The temple is one of a number of Buddhist temples constructed along the riverfront, but over the years only 10 such five-tower pagodas will be erected in China. Four of the 10 are in Beijing, with Zhenjue being the oldest.

1473

East and Southeast Asia: Japan
Buddhism

In the midst of the Odin War over the succession to the shogun's throne between Shogun Ashikaga Yoshimasa's younger brother and adopted son, Ashikaga Yoshimi, and his infant son Ashikaga Yoshihisa (r. 1473–1489), Yoshimasa retires in favor of his son. His son is, however, still a child and Yoshimasa retains the power of the office.

1473

East and Southeast Asia: Japan
Buddhism

Jodo Shinshu priest Rennyo, driven out of Kyoto and having created a new power base in Yoshizaki, issues the first set of guidelines for Jodo Shinshu followers.

1473

Europe: Germany
Christianity

Work on the massive cathedral at Cologne, Germany, which had proceeded for two centuries, ceases with the cathedral largely incomplete, though being used for worship and display of relics to pilgrims.

1473

Europe: Italy
Christianity

Catherine, a young woman from a prominent family of Genoa, experiences a life-changing mystical experience, which she later describes as a sense of the overpowering love of God for her. She will dedicate her life to service to the poor and ill. Operating from a hospital in Genoa, she combined her daily worship, frequent mystical confrontations, and service to the community for the next four decades. She is later canonized and named the patroness of the hospitals of Italy.

1473

Russia, Central Asia, and the Caucasus: Russia
Christianity

Metropolitan Philip dies and is succeeded as the Orthodox metropolitan of Moscow by Gerontius (r. 1473–1489), the bishop of Kolomna.

1473

Southwest Asia and North Africa: Palestine
Judaism

Muslims riot in Jerusalem and target the Jewish synagogue, which is destroyed. Reacting to the anti-Jewish sentiments, the Muslim authorities charge a heavy fee in exchange for the reconstruction of the synagogue.

1474

East and Southeast Asia: China
Buddhism

Gyuchen Kunga-dondrub, a disciple of the prominent Gelugpa Tibetan Buddhist teacher, establishes Uto Jampel-ling Monastery in the Upper U Province of central Tibet. This monastery/school is commonly referred to as the Upper Tantric College.

1474

East and Southeast Asia: Japan
Buddhism

Zen master Ikkyu Sojun becomes the chief priest of Dai Toku-ji, the famous Zen temple in Kyoto that now lies in ashes as a result of the Onin War. He will spend the last years of his life trying to revive the temple and its work.

1474

Europe: Spain
Christianity

King Henry IV of Castille dies, and his sister is crowned as Queen Isabella I of Castile. Isabella is married to Ferdinand II, the heir to the throne of Aragon.

1474

Russia, Central Asia, and the Caucasus: Russia
Christianity

An earthquake hits Moscow. It destroys the new cathedral of the Dormition, then in the midst of a massive reconstruction, a project initiated two years previously with the support of Grand Prince Ivan III by Philip I, the Orthodox metropolitan of Moscow. Ivan III subsequently initiated the building of a new cathedral modeled on the Cathedral of the Dormition in Vladimir, Russia. The building is completed in 1479.

1475

East and Southeast Asia: Japan
Buddhism

Ouchi Masahiro, a general in the Onin War, retires to his family's ancestral domains at Yamaguchi, where he works to reproduce Kyoto culture. Among his artistic accomplishments is Joei-ji, a Zen temple. He invites the monk Sesshu, a painter and garden designer who had recently returned to Japan from a stay in China, to design the temple's garden, which he created in the image of a painting he had previously done.

1475

Europe: Germany
Judaism

Encouraged by the Franciscan friar Bernandino de Feltre, the blood libel accusation spreads through the city of Trent following the disappearance of a Christian child named Simon. Several Jews are tortured and the entire Jewish community is expelled from the city. Later, the missing child is canonized as a Christian saint.

1475

Europe: Italy
Christianity

Johannes Müller von Königsberg (aka Regiomontanus), a German mathematician, astronomer, and astrologer, travels to Rome, where Pope Sixtus IV commissions him to begin work on reforming the Julian calendar. He died in 1476 before he could make much progress.

1475

Europe: Italy
Christianity

Pope Sixtus IV celebrates a Holy Year. He commissions the construction of the Sistine Chapel and a bridge over the Tiber River, which will be named for him.

1475

Europe: Moldavia
Islam, Christianity

The Battle of Vaslui. The army of Stephen the Great of Moldavia hands the Ottoman forces a major defeat. Sultan Mehmed follows the next year with a siege of Suceava, the Moldavian capital, but is unable to conquer it or the key Moldavian stronghold, the Castle of Târgu Neamţ. He retreats back to Constantinople.

1475

Southwest Asia and North Africa: Asia Minor
Christianity

The reign of Ecumenical Patriarch Symeon I was marked by the church falling steadily behind on the annual payments it was due to make to the sultan. Unable to raise the funds, Symeon was forced out of office and replaced with Raphael I (r. 1475–1476), who promised to make the annual payments of the church to the sultan.

1475–1479

Russia, Central Asia, and the Caucasus: Russia
Christianity

Ivan III commissions the building of the Cathedral of the Dormition, a Russian Orthodox Church commemorating the Dormition (death) of the Theotokos (i.e., the Blessed Virgin Mary). It is located on Cathedral Square within the Moscow Kremlin. Regarded as the mother church of Orthodox Russia, it would become the site for the coronation of the Russian monarchs for the next three centuries. It is also the site for the internment of most of the metropolitans and patriarchs of the Russian Orthodox Church.

ca. 1476

Europe: England
Christianity

The first edition of Chaucer's *Canterbury Tales* (1387–1400) is printed by William Caxton. It offers a spectrum of stories of pilgrims making their way to the shrine of martyr, saint, and former archbishop Thomas à Becket at Canterbury Cathedral.

1476

Russia, Central Asia, and the Caucasus: Russia
Christianity

Ivan ends Russia's subserviency to its former Mongol ruler when he refuses to pay the annual tribute to the khanate known as the Golden Horde. Before the Mongols could reassert their hegemony, the Mongol state fell apart.

1476

Russia, Central Asia, and the Caucasus: Russia
Christianity

Prince Ivan III initiates the construction of the Church of the Holy Spirit at the Trinity Lavra of St. Sergius, the Russian Orthodox Church's key monastery. It is unique as one of the few Russian churches topped with a bell tower. The earliest glazed tiles used for decorating the interior of a church in Russia are found in its sanctuary.

1476

Southwest Asia and North Africa: Asia Minor
Christianity

The ecumenical patriarch Symeon I, an alcoholic and immensely unpopular in the Greek community of Constantinople, was unable to raise the funds he had promised to deliver to the sultan. He was deposed and imprisoned. He was succeeded by a layman, Manuel Christonymos, who had a lengthy track record for his financial skills. The day before his consecration to the high office, he made his vows as a monk and would reign as Maximos III (r. 1476–1482). He would introduce a time of stability and relative prosperity into the life of the church.

1477

Europe: Austria
Christianity

Charles, the duke of Burgundy, was killed in the Battle of Nancy and King Louis XI of France took control of Burgundy and incorporated it into France proper. Mary, the daughter of Charles, inherited the crown of the duchy, and shortly afterward married Maximilian, the archduke of Austria, which had the effect of giving the Habsburg rulers of Austria and Germany control of the remainder of the Burgundian territory (the Low Countries), which fell under Habsburg control.

Following his marriage, Maximilian was admitted into the Order of the Fleece, the elite prestigious Christian knightly order that had been founded by the Duke of Burgundy in 1430. The order thus comes under Habsburg control and later develops both an Austrian-German branch and a Spanish branch. (In 1493, Maximilian would become the Holy Roman emperor, and his successors on the throne would regularly be admitted into the order.)

1477

Europe: Portugal
Christianity

Alfonso V, the king of Portugal, retires to a monastery and his son Joao II (John II) begins to rule as king. Joao will become king in his own right four years later.

1477

Sweden
Sten Sture the Elder, the regent of Sweden (r. 1470–1497), and Jacob Ulvsson, the archbishop of Uppsala, found Uppsala University, the oldest in Scandinavia.

1478

East and Southeast Asia: Japan
Buddhism
Jodo Shinshu Rennyo selects a new site in Kyoto for Hongan-ji (destroyed in 1465) and begins rebuilding. The first service in the new memorial hall for Shinran was held the next year.

1478

Europe: Italy
Christianity
Pope Sixtus IV sets the Feast of the Conception of the Virgin Mary to be celebrated on December 8. Sixtus officially tolerates both those who refer to the conception of the Virgin as "Immaculate" and those who reject the designation.

1478

Europe: Italy
Christianity
Pope Sixtus IV formally annuls the decrees of the Council of Constance.

1478

Spain
Christianity
Boniface Ferrer, a Carthusian monk, completes his translation of Bible into Valencian, the Catalan language, spoken in the Valencian community in Spain.

1478

Europe: Spain
Christianity

Pope Sixtus IV issues the bull *Exigit Sinceras Devotionis Affectus,* which sanctions the establishment of the Inquisition in the Kingdom of Castile (Spain). Its primary function is rooting out Jews who have formally converted to Christianity, but continue to practice Judaism in the privacy of their home. Such individuals are variously referred to as Marranos, New Christians, and *conversos.*

1478–1479

Europe: Albania
Christianity, Islam
The citadel at Kruje, which had become the center of remaining resistance to Ottoman rule in Albania, finally falls to Ottoman forces. Sultan Mehmed II follows by laying siege to Shkodra, which falls in 1479. The Albanian victories will be the last battles in which Mehmed personally leads the Ottoman army.

ca. 1479

East and Southeast Asia: Indonesia
Islam
Sunan Kalijaga, one of the Wali Songo (the group of nine Muslim saints who helped initially establish Islam in Indonesia), leads in the construction of Masjid Agung Demak (or Demak Great Mosque), one of the oldest of the Indonesian mosques. It is located at Demak in central Java, Indonesia.

1479

Europe: Spain
Christianity
John II of Aragon dies and is succeeded by his son Ferdinand II (r. 1479–1516), who emerges as the King of Aragon and the husband of Queen Isabella of Castile. Almost all of Spain is now united.

1479

Europe: Spain
Christianity
Don Alonso de Cárdenas, the master of the Order of Santiago, a Spanish religious/military order, initiates the expansion of the chapel dedicated to the Virgin Mary at Merida, Spain. It will become the main church of the city and a major center of the order.

1479

Russia, Central Asia, and the Caucasus: Russia
Christianity

According to tradition, a young girl named Matrona has an apparition of the Blessed Virgin Mary in which the location of an icon of the Virgin as the Mother of God (Theotokos) is revealed. The icon is discovered and eventually placed in the new Theotokos Monastery of Kazan, which is constructed over the spot where the icon had been uncovered.

1479

Russia, Central Asia, and the Caucasus: Russia
Christianity

Metropolitan Gerontius of Moscow dedicates the recently reconstructed Cathedral of the Dormition in Moscow, though work on the interior will continue for the next generation.

1479

Russia, Central Asia, and the Caucasus: Russia
Christianity

Joseph Volotsky, a prominent Russian Orthodox monk who was the most prominent advocate of the merging of the power of the secular government with the religious authority structure (a concept known as caesaropapism) within the Russian Orthodox Church and the leader of a faction who advocated monastic landownership of property, founds Joseph Volokolamsk Monastery. At Joseph's request, the monastery will be removed from the jurisdiction of the archbishop of Novgorod and placed under the direct authority of Russian Prince Vasilii III and the metropolitan of Moscow. It will later serve as a prison for church leaders who dissented from royal authority. Over the next centuries, the monastery will become one of the wealthiest in Russia and a major landowner.

1480

Europe: Spain
Judaism, Christianity

King Ferdinand and Queen Isabella introduce the Inquisition to Spain, its original task being the handling of the cases of Jews who had formally converted to Christianity but were accused of secreting keeping their original faith. Isabella also orders her court painter not to allow any Jews to participate in the painting of images of Jesus or Mary.

1480

Europe: Switzerland
Christianity

Franciscan brother Bartolomeo d'Ivrea experiences a vision of the Blessed Virgin Mary, which leads to the founding of the sanctuary of the Madonna del Sasso, part of a large monastic complex on a hill above the city of Locarno.

1480

Russia, Central Asia, and the Caucasus: Russia
Christianity

The refusal of Grand Prince Ivan III of Russia to pay tribute to the Mongols who had ruled Russia for several centuries culminated in a confrontation between the Russians and the forces of Akhmat, khan of the Great Horde, which became known as the Great Standoff on the Ugra River. Gerontius, the Orthodox metropolitan of Moscow, adds his voice to those calling for resisting the Mongols at all costs. In the end, the Mongol army chose to retreat, and Mongol-Tatar domination of Russia came to an end.

1480

Southwest Asia and North Africa: Palestine
Christianity

Responding to a project initiated by the Burgundians, European rulers combine efforts for an extensive reconstruction and renovation of the roof of the Church of the Nativity in Bethlehem. England supplies the lead, the Kingdom of Burgundy the wood, and Venice the labor.

1480–1481

Europe: Italy
Islam, Christianity

The Ottomans invade Italy and target Rome. Otranto falls, but even as the Ottoman Empire changes rulers, the effort is stalled, Otranto is recaptured by a Christian army, and the Ottomans are pushed out of Italy.

An auto-da-fe in Madrid's Plaza Mayor during the Spanish Inquisition, 17th century. The auto-da-fe was the sentencing phase of an Inquisition trial conducted by the Catholic Church against suspected heretics. (Jupiterimages)

1481

Europe: Italy
Christianity

Leonardo da Vinci initiates work on *The Adoration of the Magi,* an altarpiece for the Monastery of San Donato at Scopeto. It is the first of many major works of sacred art he will complete over the next two decades.

1481

Europe: Portugal
Christianity

Pope Sixtus IV issues a papal bull, *Aeterni regi,* in which the right of Portugal to capture and enslave the native residents of West Africa is reaffirmed.

1481

Europe: Spain
Christianity, Judaism

The Spanish Inquisition stages its first auto-da-fe (act of faith), in which those accused of heresy are marched through the streets and church authorities pronounce their sentence. The condemned are then turned over to secular authorities who carry out the executions by burning the victims at the stake. This formality of shifting the custody of the condemned to the state formally disassociates the church from the shedding of blood.

1481

Southwest Asia and North Africa: Asia Minor
Islam, Christianity

Ottoman sultan Mehmed dies, most likely from poison given him over time by his son and successor Bayezid II (r. 1481–1512).

1481–1482

Sub-Saharan Africa: Ghana
Christianity

The Portuguese establish El Mina, a trading settlement, on the West African "Gold Coast" (now Ghana), which became Portugal's major West African center for its enterprises in the region. Here they build Sao Jorge da Mina Castle at what is the first European settlement in West Africa.

1482

Sub-Saharan Africa: Democratic Republic of the
Congo, Republic of the Congo
Christianity

Portuguese explorer Diogo Cão reaches the mouth of the Congo River.

1482

Europe: Italy
Christianity

Construction begins on the Cathedral of the Annunciation of the Virgin Mary in Vicenza, Veneto, in northern Italy.

1482

Europe: Spain
Christianity

Spanish Christian forces invade the emirate of Granada, the main part of the Iberian Peninsula still under Muslim control, and score an early victory, capturing Alhama de Granada. It initiates, however, a decade of warfare.

1482

Southwest Asia and North Africa: Asia Minor
Christianity

Ecumenical Patriarch Maximos III dies and for the third time former patriarch Symeon I (r. 1482–1486) ascends the throne.

1483

East and Southeast Asia: Japan
Buddhism

The large complex of structures that became the new Hongan-ji is completed by its head priest Rennyo. The Jodo Shinshu temples from around Japan acknowledge it as their head temple, and almost all of the Jodo Shinshu community recognize it as their point of unity.

Once Hongan-ji was rebuilt, Rennyo turned to oppose a heresy that had appeared at Bukko-ji, a Jodo Shinshu temple in Kyoto, whose priests suggested that faith in the temple leader would ensure rebirth in the Western Paradise. Belivers were asked to have faith in the leader, make donations to the temple, and have their name added to a list of registered believers. The struggle with the Bukko-ji heresy would engage Rennyo for the rest of his life.

1483

Europe: England
Christianity

Edward IV, king of England, dies and is succeeded by his 12-year-old son, Edward V (r. 1483). Never formally crowned, he survives as king only a couple of months before being pushed aside in a coup by his uncle Richard, Duke of Gloucester, who took the throne as Richard III (r. 1483–1485). Richard sent the young Edward to the Tower of London where he dies under still debatable circumstances.

1483

Europe: France
Christianity

King Louis XI dies and is succeeded by his 13-year-old son Charles VIII (r. 1483–1498).

1483

Europe: Germany
Christianity

Martin Luther is born at Erfurt, Saxony.

1483

Europe: Italy
Christianity

Pope Sixtus IV celebrates the first mass in the Sistine Chapel, a building named for him, whose construction he had initiated in 1475. The chapel is located in the Apostolic Palace, the official residence of the pope.

1483

Europe: Spain
Christianity

The Spanish rulers name Dominican priest Tomas de Torquemada as inquisitor-general of Spain. The stakes in the increasing tensions between the Christian and Jewish communities are further raised by the expulsion of all Jews from the province of Andalusia. Additional attention is focused upon those Jews who have formally converted to Christianity, who are distrusted by both the non-Jewish Christian community and the continuing Jewish community. The Inquisition increasingly focuses its attention on Jewish Christians believed to be continuing to practice Jewish rituals in the privacy of their homes.

1484

Europe: Italy
Christianity
Pope Innocent VIII (r. 1484–1492) succeeds Sixtus IV as pope.

1484

Europe: Italy, Germany
Christianity, Traditional Religions

Pope Innocent VIII initiates what will become the great witch hunt of the next centuries with his papal bull *Summis desiderantes* authorizing severe measures against magicians and witches (those who practice malevolent magic) in Germany. The bull is occasioned by a related set of social problems caused by weather changes that contribute to failed crops, widespread starvation, and a rising crime rate.

1484

Southwest Asia and North Africa: Asia Minor
Christianity
Ecumenical Patriarch Symeon I hosted an international gathering of Eastern Church leaders, including representatives of the patriarchates of Antioch, Jerusalem, and Alexandria, for a synod that was held at Istanbul. At issue was the preparation of a liturgy to recognize converts from the Roman Catholic Church, as numerous people were being received into Orthodoxy as the Ottoman Empire expanded into lands formerly under the control of Catholic rulers. The synod also condemned the acts of the Council of Florence, which

POPE INNOCENT VIII (1432–1492)

Innocent VIII was the pope from 1484 to 1492. His original name was Giovanni Battista Cibo. As pope, Innocent VIII at first showed little interest in sponsoring a crusade against the Ottoman Turks, in spite of the threat that they now posed to Italy. In 1489, however, Cem (Djem), brother of Sultan Bayezid II and pretender to the Ottoman throne, arrived in Rome. Innocent now had a useful political pawn in his hands, since releasing Cem could spark civil war in the Ottoman Empire, and the mere threat to do so could put a brake on Ottoman expansion in the Balkans.

Innocent summoned a crusade congress to Rome to consider how to make the most of this advantage and overcome the practical problems of mounting an expedition against the Turks. The congress met in March 1490, but its deliberations ultimately came to nothing. Of the two powers on which such an expedition would depend, Venice was reluctant to renew the war against the Turks, and Hungary was in a weak position following the death of its king, Matthias I (Corvinus). Nevertheless, the possession of Cem was a useful lever against Bayezid, who was careful to cultivate Innocent by sending him a gift in 1492—the iron head of the Holy Lance, which was supposed to have pierced Christ's side during the crucifixion.

JONATHAN HARRIS

had worked out a plan for the reunion of the Roman Catholic and Eastern Orthodox churches.

1484

Southwest Asia and North Africa: Egypt
Christianity

Bedouins attack and plunder the eighth-century monastery of St. Paul in the desert of southern Egypt. As a result, the site is abandoned for over a century, though it is eventually reoccupied.

November 25, 1484

Europe: Germany
Western Esotericism

On the same day that witnessed a solar eclipse, Europeans see a "grand conjunction" of the planets Jupiter and Saturn, all the more notable as four additional planets also gathered close by (there being only seven known planets at the time). Astrologers view the Saturn-Jupiter conjunction as an indication of significant changes in both religious and secular power relationships. This particular grand conjunction occurs in the astrological sign of Scorpio, a sign that influences radical, revolutionary events, epidemics, and widespread death. As they considered the implication of this heavenly event, astrologers initially suggested that dramatic changes in all social spheres were soon to occur and that a "rebel" who would upset both the religious and secular order was about to emerge. Later they would tie it to the birth of Martin Luther (b. 1483, in the sign of Scorpio).

By this time, the learned are familiar with the work of Muslim scholar Abu Ma'shars, *De magnis coniunctionibus,* which initially presented a theory of "grand conjunctions." He also predicted the arrival of a "little prophet" whom he described in some detail. He noted that many people would be attracted to his new doctrine.

1485

Europe: England
Christianity

King Richard III (r. 1483–1485) of England is killed during the Battle of Bosworth Field, considered the last battle of the Wars of the Roses that pitted the House of York against the House of Lancaster. He is succeeded by Henry VII (r. 1485–1509), the first monarch of the House of Tudor.

1485

Europe: Germany
Christianity

Empowered by a papal bull, Dominican priests and inquisitors Heinrich Kramer and Jacobus Sprenger issue a treatise on witchcraft, the *Malleus Maleficarum* (i.e., *The Hammer of Witches*), which becomes a manual for the persecution of people accused of working malevolent magic. Though later widely used, the book is quite controversial when initially released. It is condemned by the theological faculty of Cologne for its proposal of utilizing unethical and illegal procedures and its innovative and un-Catholic doctrine of demonology.

1485

Asia Minor
Islam

Authorities in the Ottoman Empire forbid all movable-type printing using Arabic characters. This law has particular reference to the printing of the Qur'an, which has heretofore always been reproduced by being copied by hand.

August 22, 1485

Europe: England
Christianity

British king Richard III is killed in battle with the forces of Henry Tudor, who succeeds him on the throne as Henry VII (r. 1485–1509).

September 14, 1485

Europe: Spain
Christianity

Pedro de Arbués, the head inquisitor of Aragon, is assassinated as he prays in the cathedral at Zaragoza (Spain). His death is a sign of the unpopularity of the Inquisition in Aragon, where it was interpreted as an attack on local political rights. In the aftermath of the assassination, however, some Jewish families (all formal converts to Christianity) are implicated in the death, and with local support are targeted by the

Inquisition. Several dozen were executed, 13 by being burned at the stake.

1486

Sub-Saharan Africa: Namibia
Christianity
Portuguese explorer Diogo Cão reaches what he called Cape Cross, named for the large stone cross he erected (present-day Namibia).

1486

Sub-Saharan Africa: Senegal
Christianity
Initial Roman Catholic missionary efforts in what is now Senegal lead to the baptism of Behemoi, a Senegalese chief who had visited Lisbon, and the subsequent founding of the first Catholic parishes.

1486

South Asia: India
Hinduism
Vyasatirtha, a leading Vaishnava scholar and teacher, becomes head of the prominent Tirumala Venkateswara Temple near Tirupati, Andhra Pradesh. The new wealth allows both the Vimana (inner shrine) and the roofing to be plated with gold.

1486

East and Southeast Asia: China
Buddhism
The 11-year-old child later to become the second Dalai Lama is recognized as the reincarnation of Gendun Drupa, the founder and first abbot of Tashilhunpo monastery, a primary institution of the Gelugpa school of Tibetan Buddhism. He is given his vows as a novice monk and the ordination name of Gedun Gyatso.

1486

East and Southeast Asia: Japan
Buddhism
Tendai priest Shinzei (1443–1495), who had a lengthy career at Mount Hiei, comes out of retirement to take charge of Saikyo-ji, a temple in Omi Province.

During his retirement years, he has experimented with the practice of reciting the Nembutsu (the name of Amida Buddha) and begun to lecture on the results. After refurbishing the temple and making it his headquarters, he promotes the idea of blending Nembustu recitation and the observance of the traditional Buddhist precepts. The idea finds a popular reception, and over a hundred temples are founded in neighboring provinces. His work leads to the emergence of a new Shinzei Tendai subsect.

1486

East and Southeast Asia: Japan
Shinto
A fire does significant damage at the Ise Shrine, the major Shinto shrine in Japan. It will allow an opening for the emergence of the Yoshida Jinja, a competing shrine, which innovative theologian Yoshida Kanetomo has been promoting as the original Japanese shrine.

1486

Europe: England
Christianity
John Morton (r. 1486–1500), the former bishop of Ely, succeeds Thomas Bourchier as archbishop of Canterbury. A financial genius, he is able to set the finances of both the country and the archdiocese in order and pay for the building of the central tower of Canterbury Cathedral and the Gateway Tower at Lambeth Palace (the residence of the archbishop of Canterbury when in London).

1486

Europe: Germany
Christianity
Maximilian I (r. 1486–1519) becomes the emperor of the Holy Roman Empire, ruling jointly with his father Frederick III (d. 1493).

1486

Europe: Italy
Christianity
The youthful and naïve Italian philosopher Giovanni Pico della Mirandola brashly challenges European scholars by asserting his willingness to defend each

of some 900 theses he had assembled from his reading of various Greek, Latin, Hebrew, and Arabic texts. When this list is examined by theologians at the Vatican, it is found to contain 13 heretical statements. Though he immediately recants, Pico is arrested and briefly imprisoned.

1486

Europe: Spain
Judaism

In Toledo, some 750 Jews who had formally converted to Christianity but been found guilty of lapsing back into their Jewish faith are marched from the Church of San Pedro Martir to the city's cathedral where they will formally be reconciled to the Christian faith. They are forced to recant, fined 20 percent of their property, and forbidden to wear decent clothes or hold public office.

1486

Southwest Asia and North Africa: Asia Minor
Christianity

Ecumenical Patriarch Symeon I is again driven off the throne and is succeeded by Niphon II (r. 1486–1488), formerly the metropolitan of Thessaloniki.

1486

Southwest Asia and North Africa: Morocco
Islam

Muhammad al Shaikh, the ruler of Morocco, captures the Songhai's salt mines in Taghaza (northern Mali) and plans to move against the Songhai source of gold.

1487

Sub-Saharan Africa: South Africa
Christianity

Portuguese explorer Bartolomeu Dias lands at Mossel Bay near the Cape of Good Hope.

1487

East and Southeast Asia: China
Buddhism

The Chenghua emperor in China dies and is succeeded by his son, the Hongzhi emperor (1487–1505).

1487

Europe: Germany
Christianity

Frederick the Wise (r. 1487–1525) becomes the elector of Saxony. As the ruler of Saxony, one of the more powerful states within the Holy Roman Empire, he is one of a select few who will meet to select the new Holy Roman emperor when the throne becomes vacant.

1487

Europe: Spain
Christianity

Pope Innocent VIII confirms Tomas de Torquemada as the grand inquisitor of Spain.

1488

Sub-Saharan Africa: South Africa
Christianity

Portuguese explorer Bartolomeu Dias sails around the Cape of Good Hope, an important milestone in the attempt by the Portuguese to set up a direct trade route to India, China, and Southeast Asia. The Portuguese effort will lead to the significant spread of Christianity, primarily in the form of Roman Catholicism, through the 16th century.

1488

Sub-Saharan Africa: South Africa
Christianity

Portuguese explorer Bartolomeu Dias rounds the Cape of Good Hope and returns to his homeland with news that Europeans could now bypass the land routes in the Islam-controlled Middle East and trade directly with East Africa, India, and points east.

1488

East and Southeast Asia: China, Macau
Chinese Religions

Residents of what will become Macau build a temple to Matsu (or Tianhou), the empress of heaven in traditional Chinese mythology and a goddess of seafarers. The A-Ma Temple is one of the oldest temples in Macau.

1488

East and Southeast Asia: Japan
Buddhism

An Ikkō Buddhist group (a variant of Jodo Shu Pure Land Buddhism) initiates an uprising in Kaga Province, Japan, and drives the shogun out of the province and the surrounding region. They will remain in control for more than 30 years.

1488

East and Southeast Asia: Japan
Buddhism

Hosokawa Matsumoto, a Japanese warlord serving under the shogun, rebuilds Ryoan-ji, a prominent Rinzai Zen temple in Kyoto, which had been destroyed during the Ōnin War (1467–1477). The temple had originally been built in the 11th century. He adds a rock garden as a prominent feature of what will become the burial site for the leaders of the Hosokawa clan. The "garden," whose function is to incite meditation, is cared for daily by the monks.

1488

Europe: Bohemia
Christianity

Followers of the late reformer John Hus in Prague publish the first complete Bible in the Czech language.

1488

Europe: Germany
Western Esotericism

Johann Lichtenberger, a German priest who served as an astrologer in the court of Holy Roman emperor Frederick III, issues a work on the grand conjunction of Jupiter and Saturn in the astrological sign of Scorpio that had taken place in 1484. The book will go through some 32 editions over the next generation. He sees the

Rock garden at Ryoan-ji, a Rinzai Zen Buddhist temple founded in 1488 in Kyoto, Japan. Zen claims to differ from other Buddhist schools in its emphasis on seated meditation as a means of achieving enlightenment. (Chuongy/Dreamstime.com)

conjunction as one of the signs of the end time. He believes that shortly the church will experience great storms, that rulers will go to war with one another, and that life will become hell for the common people (due to a variety of negative events beyond their control: disease, war, natural catastrophes). In the midst of these tragedies, the "little prophet," a well-known prophetic figure among the astrologically minded, will appear and usher in the last days. As Martin Luther emerges on the scene and the Protestant Reformation begins, many will view Luther as a fulfillment of Lichtenberger's predictions.

1488

Europe: Italy
Judaism
Abraham ben Hayyim, an Italian Jewish printer in Soncino, publishes the first complete printed edition of the Hebrew Bible. Earlier in the century, the first Jewish presses had been established in Italy. The text includes marks that assist in the cantillation (ritual chanting) of the scripture during the Sabbath liturgy.

1488

Europe: Netherlands
Christianity
Dutch painter Hieronymus Bosch joins the very conservative Roman Catholic Brotherhood of Our Lady. He is known for his religious paintings, which depict scenes in rich and complex detail, possibly the most famous being a triptych known as *The Garden of Earthly Delights,* one panel of which shows hell and the variety of fantastic punishments awaiting sinners.

1488

Southwest Asia and North Africa: Asia Minor
Christianity
Two years after being selected as the ecumenical patriarch, Nephon is involved in a major scandal when it is revealed that he had been part of a conspiracy to obtain the vast wealth that former patriarch Symeon had accumulated. He is forced out of office and exiled, and the former patriarch Dionysius I, who had been living at a monastery in northern Greece, is again elected to the patriarch's office. He reigns from his monastic home and does not return to Istanbul.

1488

Southwest Asia and North Africa: Maghreb
Islam
Hafsid ruler Abu Umar Othman dies after a rule of 52 years. He is succeeded by Abu Zikriya Yahya (r. 1488–1489).

1489

East and Southeast Asia: Japan
Shinto
Yoshida Kanetomo, who has developed an innovative form of Shinto, moves to dislodge the centrality of the Ise Shrine in Japanese thought by claiming that the *goshintai* (the sacred body of the kami [gods]) had left Ise and flown to Yoshida. In this claim, he had the backing of the Urabe clan that controlled the *jingikan* (Bureau of Kami Affairs).

The Yoshida Shinto developed by Kanetomo had emphasized the central role of the kami, offered Shinto as the origin of both Buddhism and Confucianism, and offered a way of unifying the various major religious impulses in the country. In building the new important role to be played by Yoshida, he suggested that all the kami descended on Mount Yoshida every day, and he labeled the main kami enshrined there, Taigenshin, as the "kami of great origin." After challenging the role of Ise, he obtained the backing of the imperial court in Kyoto and was briefly able to promote Yoshida as the new central focus of Shinto.

1489

East and Southeast Asia: Japan
Buddhism
Rennyo retires as head of Hongan-ji and the Jodo Shinshu Buddhist community, and is succeeded by his son Jitsunyo.

1489

Europe: France
Christianity
French Roman Catholic authorities post 32 propositions attributed to the Waldensians on the door of the Cathedral of Our Lady at Embrun in southern France. This act heralded a campaign to suppress the movement, which was accused of heresy. These largely ineffective efforts against the Waldensians lead to a

SHINTOISM UNDER KANETOMO

Shintoism experienced a revival in the 15th century after many shrines were destroyed in the Onin War. Out of the ashes emerged Yoshida Kanetomo, who dedicated his life to their reconstruction (especially those most associated with his prominent family), the return of Shinto supremacy in the land, and the reestablishment of imperial authority. He recast Shintoism as the original faith and the source of Daoism, Confucianism, and Buddhism. He expounded a new theology built around an Esoteric teaching as found in the *Kojiki* and *Nihon Shoki* and Esoteric teachings that he claimed had been revealed by deities to his family (resulting in additional scriptural texts). Kanetomo became the leading figure in Shintoism, and his school would dominate the religion during the next centuries.

During the Edo period, the work of Kanetomo and his successors would lead to a shift in Shinto away from a primary dialogue with Buddhism to one with Confucianism. Especially in the writings of Yoshikawa Koretari, the deity Kuninotokotachi no Mikoto, identified with primal chaos, emerged as the central figure in the Shinto pantheon. The continued development of Shintoism in the 18th century set the stage for major developments in the 19th century. The variety of Shinto groups, later to constitute Sect Shintoism, began to emerge. The Fuji and Ontake sects emphasized the longstanding worship at sacred mountains. Spiritual healing, utilizing Shinto rituals, became the center of the Tenrikyo and Konkokyo religions.

J. GORDON MELTON

reaction a century later when French Protestants under their local military leader Lesdiguières would pillage the Embrun cathedral (1585).

1489

Europe: Germany
Christianity
A three-year-old local boy drowned in the river that flows through Altotting, Bavaria. His mother took the body into the local church and offered prayers before the wooden statue of the Virgin Mary at the high altar. The boy revived, and the miracle becomes news across Germany and throughout Europe. To accommodate the pilgrims at what became one of the most-visited shrines in Germany, the church was greatly expanded.

1489

Europe: Italy
Christianity

Pope Innocent VIII excommunicates King Ferdinand I of Naples and invites French king Charles VIII to join him in taking possession of the Kingdom of Naples. Hostilities between Naples and the Papal States will continue through the remainder of Innocent's papacy.

1489

Europe: Italy
Western Esotericism
Marsilio Ficino, who had spent the last half century translating Greek texts into Latin, had developed a strong interest in astrology that led to his drawing attention from the leadership of the Roman Catholic Church. Now a priest, he is accused of believing in and working magic and made to appear before Pope Innocent VIII. A capable scholar, he is able to mount a strong defense of his activity and escapes condemnation as a heretic. Several years later, he is able to proclaim that "this century appears to have perfected astrology."

Ficino would have a major influence in both reviving Neoplatonism as a philosophical option among Renaissance thinkers and sparking a new interest in astrology in the West.

1489

Europe: Spain
Christianity

As part of the reconquest of Spain, Christian forces capture Gaudix, and the old Visigoth church, which had been transformed into a mosque during the years of Muslim rule, is re-named the Church of Saint Mary of the Incarnation. Pope Innocent VIII subsequently designates it the seat of the reestablished bishopric.

1489

Europe: Spain
Christianity

A Roman Catholic priest, Mosen Pedro Mena, carries a piece of cloth believed to picture the face of Jesus of Nazareth dating to the week of his crucifixion, formerly the property of Pope Nicholas V, to Spain. Soon after the cloth's arrival, another priest, Father Villafranca, carries it in a procession through the countryside of Alicante, then in the midst of a drought. Reportedly, during the procession, the veil shed a tear and rain began to fall. The cloth is later enshrined in the Monastery of the Holy Face near Alicante.

1489–1490

East and Southeast Asia: Japan
Buddhism

The shogun Ashikaga Yoshihisa (r. 1473–1489), who has gradually assumed power as he grows to maturity, dies at an early age. His father, the former shogun Yoshimasa, who is still alive, resumes the office, but dies a year later. He is then succeeded by the son of his adopted son Ashikaga Yoshimi, who reigned as Ashikaga Yoshitane (r. 1490–1493, 1508–1521).

1489–1490

Russia, Central Asia, and the Caucasus: Russia
Christianity

Gerontius, the metropolitan of Moscow, dies and is succeeded by Zosimus the Bearded (r. 1490–1494). He is immediately confronted with the presence of what some considered widespread heresy in the church, the heretical group being termed Judaizers, or *Zhidovstvuyushchiye* (or "those who follow Jewish traditions"), a group whose origins were traced to Zacharia ben Ahron ha-Cohen, a scholar from Kiev who had moved to Novgorod and worked on translating Hebrew texts on astronomy, logic, and philosophy into Russian. The Russian priests who led the movement were accused of denying the Holy Trinity, the divine status of Jesus, and the immortality of the soul, and eschewing monasticism, the church hierarchy, and some ceremonies. A few were accused of abandoning the veneration of icons (i.e., iconoclasm). Gerontius advocates harsh repression, but Prince Ivan II, among whose advisors were followers, adopts a more lenient approach.

1490

Sub-Saharan Africa: Angola
Christianity

The Portuguese king Joao II sends teachers and Christian missionaries to Mani-Kongo, who ruled over territory in what today is Angola in southwest Africa. The missionaries succeed in converting him to Christianity. His son will later rule as Afonso I.

1490

Sub-Saharan Africa: South Africa
Christianity

Portuguese captain Bartolomeu Dias reaches the southern tip of Africa, the point now known as the Cape of Good Hope.

1490

South Asia: India
Islam

Ahmad ibn Mājid, Arab Muslim navigator and cartographer from what is now the United Arab Emirates, completes his most important work, the *Book of Useful Information on the Principles and Rules of Navigation,* an encyclopedic manual on sailing with particular reference to sailing the Indian Ocean. It would later be claimed that he accompanied Vasco de Gama on his pioneering voyage from the east coast of Africa to India, but evidence for his being with the Portuguese is disputed.

1490

East and Southeast Asia: Japan
Buddhism

Shogun Ashikaga Yoshimasa dies. He had been creating for himself a retirement villa with elaborate gardens that included an unfinished Rinzai Zen temple building. At the time of his death, he arranges for the gardens to continue as a Zen temple. The main structure, called Kannon Hall, was modeled on Kinkaku-ji, or "Golden Pavilion," a temple his grandfather Ashikaga Yoshimitsu had established. The hall is also called *Ginkaku* (the "Silver Pavilion"), as Yoshimasa had planned to cover the exterior in silver foil (as his grandfather's temple had been covered in gold leaf). The silver cover will never be added.

1490

Europe: Italy
Christianity

Dominican friar Savonarola moves to Florence where he launches a preaching mission emphasizing the judgments of the Last Days, which include claims of visions and direct communications from God and various saints. He quickly builds a large following. He strongly attacked what he saw as a secularized and worldly church, and called for reform.

1490

Europe: Italy
Judaism, Western Esotericism

Rabbi Elijah Delmedigo, a professor at the University of Padua, comments on the *Zohar*, a text that had appeared a century earlier and become a major text of Jewish mysticism built around the kabbalah. The *Zohar*'s publisher Moses de Leon ascribed the work to second-century rabbi Shimon bar Yochai, but Delmedigo refutes its ancient origin by noting it contains quotes from rabbis who had lived more recently.

1490

Russia, Central Asia, and the Caucasus: Russia
Christianity

The cathedral of the Nativity of the Virgin is built at Ferapontov Monastery in Vologda. It will become known for the extensive frescoes added by the noted artist Master Dionysius. They will cover some 6,500 square feet of the interior.

1490

Southwest Asia and North Africa: Asia Minor
Christianity

Ecumenical Patriarch Dionysus is for a second time deposed from office, seemingly under pressure applied by the monks on Mount Athos who had come to resent his policies. He is succeeded by Maximos IV (r. 1491–1497), a former monk from Athos who had become metropolitan bishop of Serres (northern Greece).

1490

Southwest Asia and North Africa: Asia Minor
Christianity

Two Christians from Malabar (India) arrive in Gazarta (southeast Asia Minor) to petition the patriarch Shemon IV, patriarch of the Nestorian Church of the East, to consecrate a bishop and send him to India. He responds by calling two monks from the monastery of Mar Awgin whom he consecrates as bishops (Mar Thomas and Mar John) and sends to Malabar.

1490–1491

East and Southeast Asia: China
Chinese Religions

Astronomers in China, Japan, and Korea record sightings of a bright comet during the winter of 1490–1491. More recently, astronomers have concluded that the 15th-century observers had seen a deep-space explosion that would later become the source of the annual Quadrantid meteor shower.

1490–1492

Europe: Italy
Christianity

Three closely placed churches that had served Turin, Italy, for the last millennium were demolished in favor of a new cathedral dedicated to St. John the Baptist. A bell tower erected in 1469 was maintained through the new construction.

1491

Sub-Saharan Africa: Congo, Angola
Portuguese missionaries—Franciscans, Dominicans, Canons of St. John the Evangelist—conduct their first explorations of the Congo River, which will lead to the development of a flourishing Roman Catholic mission through the next century.

The first church is soon erected in what is now Angola.

1491

Europe: Italy
Judaism
Franciscan friar Bernardino de Faltre, who had preached on the blood libel accusation in Trent, leading to the Jews being expelled from the city, preaches in Ravenna with similar results. Following the expulsion, Bernardino causes the synagogue to be destroyed.

1491

Europe: Spain
Judaism, Christianity
In LaGuardia, six Jews and five *conversos* (Jews who had formally converted to Roman Catholicism, but were charged with continuing to practice their Jewish faith) are accused of killing Christians.

1491

Russia, Central Asia, and the Caucasus: Russia
Christianity, Judaism
Skhariya the Jew (i.e., Zacharia ben Ahron ha-Cohen), the scholar considered to be the founder of the *Zhidovstvuyushchiye* (or "those who follow Jewish traditions"), which the Russian church leaders considered a heretical movement, is executed in Novgorod by the order of Prince Ivan III.

1491

Russia, Central Asia, and the Caucasus: Russia
Christianity
The Church of the Savior, called the New Church to distinguish it from the older Church of the Savior in Moscow, is established on the left bank of the Moskva River. Soon afterwards a monastery will be established adjacent to it. Novospassky Monastery will rise as one of a set of fortified monasteries surrounding Moscow.

November 25, 1491

Europe: Spain
Christianity
The Treaty of Granada, a temporary truce in the war between Spanish Christian forces and the city of Granada, is signed.

1492

Sub-Saharan Africa: Mali
Islam
As Askia Muhammad, Mamadou Toure ascends the throne at Timbuktu and over the next 37 years transforms the Songhai Kingdom into the largest empire in the history of West Africa. He restores the tradition of Islamic learning to the University of Sankore, thus giving Timbuktu its reputation as a major center of Islamic education. The focus he gave to Islam in the region would be a major obstacle preventing Christian forces gaining a foothold.

1492

Europe: Italy
Christianity
Pope Alexander VI (r. 1492–1503), the second member of the famous Borgia family to become pope, ascends the papal throne. He will be remembered as an able administrator and diplomat, but denounced for numerous violations of his priestly vows of celibacy, having had relations with a series of mistresses. Most serious, the morally offensive life of the papal court attracted significant criticism and would lead to the rise and fall of Florentine friar Girolamo Savonarola who preached against papal corruption and called church members to rise up and confront the church leaders, including the pope.

1492

Europe: Italy
Christianity
The sultan Bayazid II sends an object believed to be the Holy Lance (aka the Spear of Longinus or Spear of

Christ), reputedly the lance used to pierce Jesus's side as he hung on the cross (John 19:34), to Pope Innocent VIII. The sultan hopes by his action to influence the pope's continued internment of the sultan's brother who also happens to be a claimant to the Ottoman throne.

1492

Europe: Scotland
Christianity
Pope Innocent VII elevates the Diocese of Glasgow to an archdiocese.

1492

Europe: Spain
Judaism
The joint Roman Catholic rulers of Spain, Isabella I of Castile and Ferdinand II of Aragon, issue the Alhambra Decree (aka the Edict of Expulsion), which orders expulsion of all Jews from the kingdoms of Castile and Aragon (though not from the Kingdom of Navarre) and their territories and possessions. Released on March 31, the Jews have three months (until July 31) to comply. Rather than move, many Jews convert, accept baptism, and greatly enlarge the community of *conversos* or New Christians.

Though the order officially covers Castile and Aragon, in fact, all the Jews, some 100,000, will leave Spain and its territories of Sicily and Sardinia. Those who migrate head for Morocco or Asia Minor. The Ottoman Empire is the only country that openly welcomes the fleeing Jews. Sultan Bayezid II ridiculed the Spanish rulers for expelling a group that had been so useful to them.

1492

Europe: Spain
Christianity
Pope Alexander VI elevates the Diocese of Granada (Spain) to an archdiocese.

1492

Europe: Spain
Christianity
A representative of Spain's King Ferdinand and Queen Isabella signs a contract with Christopher Columbus commissioning him to seek a westward ocean passage to Asia. The rulers subsequently granted Columbus a set of guarantees relative to any discoveries. Upon completing his preparations, Columbus sails from the port of Palos with the goal of reaching Japan. Several months after he sets sail (October 11) he first sees land, which turns out to be the Bahamas. He subsequently lands on Cuba and Hispaniola.

1492

Europe: Spain
Christianity
Muhammad XII (r. 1487–1492), the last ruler of the Muslim Nasrid Dynasty, surrenders to the Christian Spanish kingdoms of Aragon and Castile, and thus brings the last Moorish dynasty in Spain to an end. The Nasrid Dynasty had risen to power following the defeat of the Almohad caliphate (1212) at the Battle of Las Navas de Tolosa.

1492

Southwest Asia and North Africa: Asia Minor
Islam, Judaism
In response to the Spanish expulsion of Jews and Muslims, Ottoman sultan Bayezid II sends the Ottoman navy to Spain to facilitate their evacuation and provide transport to Ottoman territory. Simultaneously, he issues a set of proclamations calling upon his subjects and especially government officials to welcome the refugees while granting the refugees permission to establish their residence and become Ottoman citizens.

January 2, 1492

Europe: Spain
Christianity, Islam
Muhammad XII, the last Muslim leader of Granada, surrenders Granada to the forces of Spanish rulers Ferdinand and Isabella. Some 200,000 Muslims leave Spain and immigrate to North Africa in spite of Spain's guarantee of property, laws, customs, and religion to the residents of the former Emirate of Granada.

October 12, 1492

Central America and the Caribbean:
   Dominican Republic
Christianity

Christopher Columbus and his crew arrive in the Bahamas. Over the next few weeks he visits Cuba and Hispaniola. In Hispanola, he encounters the Taino people, founds La Navidad (on Christmas Day), and introduces Roman Catholicism to the Americas.

November 1492

Europe: France
Christianity

A 280-pound meteorite falls in a wheat field near the village of Ensisheim, France. A young boy witnessed it and led the townspeople to a three-foot-deep crater where it lay. The people thought the object to be of supernatural origin. After seeing it King Maximilian of Germany declared that it must be a sign of the wrath of God against the French who were in a war with the Holy Roman Empire at that time. Maximilian ordered the rock to be moved to the church of Ensisheim where it could sit as a reminder of God's intervention. It stayed there until the French Revolution when the secular government seized it and moved it to a national museum at Colmar. Ten years later it was returned to the church and eventually moved to the town hall in Ensisheim where it rests today. The meteorite is now less than half of its original weight, the victim of souvenir hunters and scientists who removed samples from it for study while it lay in Colmar.

December 31, 1492

Europe: Sicily
Judaism

The year ends with the 100,000 Jews of Sicily being expelled from the country. They are given until January 12 to depart.

1493

Central America and the Caribbean: Dominican
    Republic
Christianity

On his second voyage to the Caribbean, Columbus finds the settlement of La Navidad destroyed and abandoned and he founds a new settlement, Port Isabella, soon renamed Santo Domingo, which emerges as the center of early Spanish activity in the region.

1493

Europe: Austria
Christianity

Holy Roman Emperor Frederick III (r. 1437–1493) bleeds to death following an attempt to amputate his leg. He is succeeded by his son Maximilian (r. 1483–1519), who had co-ruled with him for the previous decade. Unlike his father, Maximilian is never able to travel to Italy to be formally crowned emperor by the pope.

1493

Europe: Holy Roman Empire
Christianity

Those German rulers designated as electors meet and choose Maximilian (r. 1493–1519) as the new Holy Roman emperor.

1493

Europe: Italy
Christianity

Pope Alexander VI names his 18-year-old son Cesare Borgia, who had just completed his studies in theology at the University of Pisa, as archbishop of Valencia and a cardinal. Cesare would soon resign the post, but continue as an active force in the church from his position as a wealthy layman. Cesare Borgia is the brother of Lucrezia Borgia.

Pope Alexander VI names John Morton, the archbishop of Canterbury, the titular cardinal of the Church of St. Anastasia in Rome.

1493

Europe: Spain
Christianity

Christopher Columbus returns from his first voyage to the New World, meets with King Ferdinand and Queen Isabella, and departs for his second voyage. He leaves Cadiz with a flotilla of 17 ships and includes in his entourage 13 Roman Catholic priests. The voyage of exploration will last two years.

On this second voyage, Columbus will visit a number of islands not previously known to exist by Europeans—Dominica, Guadeloupe, Antigua, the North Leeward Islands (later the Netherland Antilles), Redonda, Puerto Rico, Montserrat, St. Croix, Jamaica, and the Virgin Islands. While finding a number of islands, he fails to locate a new continent. The priests will conduct the first formal Roman Catholic religious services in the New World.

Following Columbus's return from his initial discovery of the Caribbean Islands, the Spanish ask Pope Alexander to confirm their ownership of these newly found lands. He responds with three bulls, *Eximiae devotionis, Inter Caetera,* and *Dudum Siquidem,* that together grant rights to Spain like those granted earlier to Portugal relative to its African discoveries. Included in these bulls is the implicit sanction to enslave the native peoples (who are non-Christians).

1493

Europe: Spain, Portugal
Christianity
Pope Alexander V (1492–1503) issues a papal bull, the *Inter Caetara,* granting Spain the rights to all the new worlds discovered in the Americas west of a line 100 leagues west and south of the Azores and/or the Cape Verde Islands, which leads to a protest by Portugal.

1493

Southwest Asia and North Africa: Asia Minor
Judaism
Jews who have recently migrated from Spain establish the first printing press in Istanbul.

1494

Europe: England
Christianity
Lady Margaret Beaufort, Countess of Richmond and Derby, the mother of King Henry VII, sees to the publication of *The Scale of Perfection,* a book written by British mystic Walter Hilton, an Augustianian monk who had died a century earlier. The book becomes popular, goes through several printings in the next few decades, and becomes the first work written in English to gain a popular audience and circulate on the European continent.

1494

Europe: Italy
Judaism, Western Esotericism

The Medici family loses hegemony over Tuscany and its main city of Florence. The new authorities expel the Jews from the region. The Jews will only return when the Medicis regain control in 1513.

The controversial Italian intellectual Pico della Mirandola, a friend of Savanorola, dies, possibly from poisoning by his own secretary. Several of his works are published posthumously. His *Apologia* builds a case for Christianity from the Jewish mystical teachings based on the Kabbalah and leads to the development of a Christian approach to Esoteric teachings through the Kabbalah. His *Dissertation against Astrological Divination* argues against the practice of astrology, which he sees as contradicting Christian teachings on human free will.

1494

Europe: Scotland
Christianity
The first mention of Scotch whiskey in tax rolls makes note of a measure of malt going to Friar John Cor, which he will use to make the whiskey.

1494

Europe: Spain
Christianity
At the request of Christopher Columbus, Father Ramon Pane, one of the priests on the voyage to the Caribbean Islands, begins to write an account of the religion of the Taino people whom the expedition encounters on Hispaniola.

1494

Europe: Spain, Portugal
Christianity
In the Treaty of Tordesillas, papal opinions on the settlement of the newly discovered lands find formal agreement. Pope Alexander VI revises his earlier bull and grants Portugal new lands east of a line drawn 370 leagues west of the Azores and Cape Verde (i.e., Brazil and Africa), while Spain is given hegemony over the lands to the west of that line (including most of the Americas). France, Holland, and England will later challenge the exclusive rights assigned in the treaty. Pope Julius II confirmed the treaty in 1506.

Christopher Columbus receives ritual gifts from the cacique (chief) Guacanagarí on the island of Hispaniola. Engraving by Theodor de Bry (1528–1598). (Library of Congress)

1494

Russia, Central Asia, and the Caucasus: Russia
Christianity

Zosimus, the metropolitan of Moscow, who had spent his years in office fighting heresy, is himself accused of being a secret heretic, as well as being a homosexual. As a result, he is deposed from office. He is succeeded by Simon (r. 1499–1511), the hegumen (abbot) of the Troitse-Sergiyeva Lavra (monastery).

1494

Southwest Asia and North Africa: Maghreb
Islam

After several Hafsid rulers here were able to hold the throne only for a year or two, Muhammad IV (r. 1494–1526) begins his relatively lengthy rule.

1494–1495

Europe: Italy
Christianity

Having accepted the 1489 offer of Pope Innocent VIII to take over Naples, King Charles VIII of France brings his army into Italy, passes through, and subdues Florence, where the reforming friar Savonarola proclaims Charles as God's instrument for cleaning up and purifying the city's corruption. Upon entering Naples, Charles expels Alfonso II, who had just ascended the throne, and is crowned as the new king of Naples. Threatened by Charles's speedy success, an Italian coalition forms and soon forces Charles out of Naples and back to France.

1495

East and Southeast Asia: Japan
Buddhism

A tidal wave rushes inland at Kamakura and destroys the temple that houses the giant statue of Amida Buddha, the Daibutsu, the third destruction of the temple in less than a century. It is never rebuilt, and the statue has remained in an unsheltered condition ever since.

1495

Europe: France
Christianity

Construction begins on the Pro-cathédral of Sainte-Marie de Bastia on the island of Corsica. When finished, it would come to house the statue of Christ of the Miracles that two fishermen found floating in the Mediterranean in 1428.

1495

Europe: Italy
Christianity

Our Mother of Perpetual Help, an image of the Blessed Virgin Mary long associated with miracles, is taken from Crete and brought to Rome, and four years later installed at the Church of St. Matthew.

1495

Europe: Italy
Christianity

Leonardo da Vinci begins work on his painting *The Last Supper* for the refectory of the Convent of Santa Maria della Grazie in Milan. It will take him three years to complete. The work had been commissioned by his patron, Ludovico Sforza, the Duke of Milan, and depicts a scene from the Gospel of John, 13:21, in which Jesus announces that one of his apostles would betray him.

1495

Europe: Italy
Western Esotericism

The first major European outbreak of syphilis (aka *morbus gallicus* or the French disease) occurs among French troops besieging Naples, Italy. Astrologers will explain its origins relative to a prominent conjunction of the planets Jupiter and Saturn in 1484. On November 25, 1484, some six planets clustered in the astrological sign of Scorpio, during a solar eclipse, and the astrologically minded saw the occurrence as an indication of significant alteration of the social system.

1495

Europe: Italy, Croatia
Christianity

In Venice, Bernardin of Split prints the first Croatian lectionary, the first publication of selections of the Bible into the Croatian language.

1495

Europe: Lithuania
Judaism

Grand Duke Alexander expels the Jews from his realm and confiscates their property. He soon regrets his decision and reverses himself in 1503, when he invites the Jews to return and restores their property.

1495

Europe: Scotland
Christianity

Friar John Cor is cited as the distiller in the first written record of the existence of Scotch whiskey that appears in the Exchequer Rolls in Scotland.

1496

Europe: Austria
Judaism

Citing the blood libel, Austrian emperor Maximilian I expels the Jews from Carinthia and then from Styria, Austria.

1496

Europe: Italy
Christianity

The continued popularity of pilgrimages to Loreto to visit what many believe to be the residence of the Blessed Virgin Mary, reputedly transported by angels to Loreto, Italy, is signaled by the construction of a large basilica over the Holy House at Loreto. Once completed, a marble enclosure is added around the house itself (1507). Three years later, official approval for pilgrimages was given.

1496

Europe: Spain, France
Christianity

Joanna, the heir to the crown of both the neighboring kingdoms of Aragon and Castile, marries the Habsburg ruler of Burgundy, Philip the Handsome.

1496–1497

Europe: Portugal
Judaism

King Emanuel I of Portugal, who has married the daughter of King Ferdinand II of Aragon and Queen Isabella I of Castile, and thus stood ready to possibly inherit the Spanish throne and rule a united Iberian Peninsula, orders the expulsion of any Jews from Portugal who refuse to convert. Most Jews are forcibly converted prior to their eiminent expulsion. Because he values the Jews' economic contribution to his kingdom, he is slow to order the final expulsions.

1497

Sub-Saharan Africa: Mozambique
Christianity

During his stop at Mossel Bay (Mozambique), Portuguese explorer Vasco da Gama erects a cross, but the local residents destroy it after he leaves.

1497

Europe: Italy
Christianity

Savonarola, now head of a successful campaign to reform life in Florence, sends young boys around the city to collect any items associated with moral laxity, such as mirrors, cosmetics, immoral sculptures, musical instruments, fancy clothing, and many pieces of art. He then holds a giant Bonfire of the Vanities in which these are burned. The fire becomes the pinnacle of his success, which begins to wane.

May 4. Savonarola's Ascension Day occasions a riot that concludes with widespread public rejection of his reforms. Closed taverns reopen and public participation in condemned activities—dancing, singing, drinking, and gambling—appear throughout the city.

May 13. Pope Alexander VI excommunicates Savonarola.

1497

Europe: Italy
Christianity

Cardinal Oliviero Carafa has the relics of Saint Januarius, one of the patron saints of Naples, Italy, transferred to the cathedral of the city where he has a new crypt prepared to receive it. Since its completion in 1505, Naples has become the scene of the annual festival of Saint Januarius whose high point is the liquification of a vial of blood believed by the faithful to be that of the deceased saint.

1497

Europe: Portugal
Christianity

Vasco da Gama sails from Lisbon at the head of a fleet of four ships on a voyage that will take him around the Cape of Good Hope into the Indian Ocean. This voyage will introduce Christianity to East Africa and southern India.

1497–1498

North America: Canada
Christianity

John and Sebastian Cabot explore areas around Newfoundland and make first contact with the native population. Other Europeans will follow, open trade, and inadvertently spread diseases.

1497–1498

Southwest Asia and North Africa: Asia Minor
Christianity

Ecumenical Patriarch Maximos IV is forced to resign and is succeeded by former patriarch Nephon II (r. 1497–1498), called out of exile. He is in office only a year before being replaced by Joachim I (r. 1498–1502). This time, Nephon is exiled to Adrianople. From his place of exile, he will find support from the rulers of Wallachia and gradually accept their patronage.

1498

Sub-Saharan Africa: Kenya
Christianity, Islam

On a voyage from Portugal to India, Vasco da Gama arrives at Mombasa (Kenya), but the Arab rulers repel him. He subsequently lands at Malindi where he meets with the local sultan, who assigns him a pilot who can steer him to Calicut (or Kozhikode) in Kerala, India. A month later, he lands in India and initiates the Portuguese and Roman Catholic presence there.

1498

Central America and the Caribbean: Trinidad
Christianity

Columbus departs from Spain with six ships on what will be his third trip to the Caribbean Islands. He will first discover the island of Trinidad and reach South America along what is now the coast of Venezuela.

1498

Europe: France
Christianity

King Charles VIII of France dies without a living male heir. The throne goes to a cousin who will reign as King Louis XII (r. 1498–1515).

1498

Europe: Italy
Christianity

For centuries Venice maintained close ties to the Byzantine Empire and a large number of Greek-speaking people resided in the city. However, Roman Catholic authorities were hostile to the development of any competing Byzantine-style worship. Finally, in 1498, the church granted permission for the Greek community to found a confraternity to assist members of the local Greek-speaking community, which soon began to push for a Byzantine church. Construction on that church, dedicated to Saint George, would commence in 1539 and continue through the rest of the century. (In 1991, it would be designated the cathedral of a Greek Orthodox diocese.)

1498–1499

South Asia: India
Christianity

The Portuguese fleet led by Vasco da Gama lands at Kappadu near Calicut, India. Da Gama stays several months and then departs for home. Upon his return in 1499, da Gama is hailed as a hero for opening a direct sea route for trade with India. His voyage also has the secondary effect of opening India to the introduction of Portuguese Roman Catholicism.

April 8, 1498

Europe: Italy
Christianity

Following Pope Alexander VI's demand that Savonarola be arrested and executed, a crowd attacks the Convent of San Marco, and several people are killed. Savonarola surrenders himself to authorities. He is subsequently charged with heresy and various "religious errors" by the pope.

May 23. Following torture and his signing a confession, Savonarola is executed. Along with two companions, he is ritually stripped of his clerical office, labeled a heretic, and transferred to secular authorities. The three are then burned alive at the site of the Bonfire of the Vanities the previous year.

ca. 1499

South Asia: India
Sikhism

Nanak, a Hindu who met daily at the riverside for a time of meditation with a Muslim companion, waded into and disappeared beneath the surface of the water. Most believed that he had drowned, but three days later he came out of the river declaring "There is no Hindu, there is no Muslim." Mardana, his companion, and Nanaki, his sister, accept Nanak as their guru. The Sikh religion is thus founded as a resolution of the differences between Hinduism and Islam, beginning with the affirmation of one god. Soon afterward, Nanak and

Mardana begin a lengthy missionary journey around India and to the adjacent countries of Sri Lanka, Tibet, China, and Persia to spread the new faith.

1499

East and Southeast Asia: China
Chinese Religions

The large Confucian temple complex at Qufu, Shandong Province, the oldest of the Asian Confucian temples, is devastated by a fire. The Hongzhi emperor, himself a dedicated Confucian, sees to the complete reconstruction and expansion of the temple, completed in 1504.

1499

Europe: Italy
Christianity

Michelangelo, who sees himself as more of a sculptor than a painter, completes his *Pietà* (a statue of the deceased Jesus of Nazareth on the lap of his mother Mary after his crucifixion), originally commissioned by French cardinal Jean de Billheres for his funeral monument. Several centuries afterward it will be placed in St. Peter's Basilica, where it continues to reside.

1499

Europe: Spain
Christianity

Spanish archbishop Francisco Jiménez de Cisneros (aka Ximénes de Cisneros), frustrated over the slow rate of conversions of Muslims and Jews in Granada to Christianity, launches a program of forced Christian baptisms. His actions violate the treaty signed in 1491/1492, and also create a new class of citizens, the *conversos,* those Muslims and Jews who do formally convert. The forced conversions will lead to a local armed revolt (1501), which is quickly suppressed.

1499

Europe: Switzerland
Christianity

The Battle of Dornach. The Swiss defeat the forces of the Holy Roman Empire and force the emperor Maximilian to sign a peace treaty that recognizes the Swiss Confederacy as an autonomous entity independent from the Holy Roman Empire.

1499

Russia, Central Asia, and the Caucasus: Russia
Christianity

Gennadius, the Russian Orthodox archbishop of Novgorod the Great and Pskov (r. 1484–1504), completes the first complete codex of the Bible in the Slavic language. It has since become popularly known as the Gennady Bible.

1500–1599 CE

Introduction: 1500s

With the Great Schism (which saw three rival popes vying for power) behind them and the acceptance of the fall of Constantinople, which had the unintended consequence of leaving Rome as the major center of Christianity not under Islamic control, Roman Catholics began the 16th century with some optimism. The pope reflected this optimism by commissioning Michelangelo to complete the interior of the Sistine Chapel and a short time later laid the foundation of a new basilica to cover the spot where the apostle Peter is buried. It will arise as the greatest church building in all of Christendom. There is a seemingly small problem. Numerous voices are calling for reform in the church, so in 1512, Pope Julius opens a church council to address the church's needs. The bishops gather, unaware of the storm that is about to break loose.

The storm cloud appears in 1517 as a continent-wide campaign is being carried out to raise money to complete St. Peter's Basilica. A German priest/theologian, Martin Luther, complains about the doctrine underlying the practice of selling indulgences and in the process not only significantly undercuts sales but challenges papal authority. The mere act of calling for a debate on his 95 propositions or theses occasions a massive reaction to Rome and leads Luther into a more radical position in which he asserts the authority of the Bible over that of the pope as the interpreter of the Bible and the most authoritative voice in the church.

Luther's challenge occurs at a crucial moment in European history. A new sultan has emerged in Constantinople. Suleiman I, soon to be known as Suleiman the Magnificent, has just taken the throne of the Ottoman Empire (1520) and begins immediately to expand the empire northward. Belgrade fell in August 1521 and he quickly moved up the Danube

River where he defeated King Louis of Hungary, captured Buda, and occupied Transylvania. After a brief pause, in which he drove the Knights Hospitaller from their base on the Isle of Rhodes, he resumed his campaign in Hungary and on August 29, 1526, he defeated Louis II of Hungary at the Battle of Mohács. He now approached Vienna, and if Vienna fell, all of Europe was open to him.

The Holy Roman emperor, whose power had been a crucial factor in solving the Great Schism and now stood as the champion of the papacy and Catholicism, would continually be faced with a war on two fronts, one to his east with the intrusion of the Muslims and one in his own backyard with the troublesome followers of Martin Luther, the Protestants. In 1529, Suleiman stood before the gates of Vienna, but was turned back and was again defeated in 1532, stopping his advance for the moment. In spite of the defeat, Muslims now controlled much of central Europe from Hungary south to Greece.

Meanwhile, Europe was being rent asunder by the rise of the Protestants. From their initial centers in Wittenberg and Zurich, their influence spread across Scandinavia, and then to England and Scotland. From Geneva, Protestantism would spread through French-speaking Europe. The rise of the new movement emphasizing the power of faith and the peculiar authority of the Bible in the hands of believers would be punctuated by the issuance of the Augsburg Confession of Faith (1530), the first notable statement of the Protestant position; John Calvin's *Institutes of the Christian Religion* (1536), the first comprehensive theological text; and the Peace of Augsburg (1555), which brought a temporary end to hostilities between Catholic and Protestant forces battling for control of Germany, but more importantly provided for the existence of two religions in the lands of the Holy Roman Empire. The settlement at Augsburg was a small but no less monumental step toward creating the possibility of peaceful coexistence between believers of different religions.

Even as the Germans are working on Lutheran-Catholic issues, Queen Elizabeth in England, who takes the throne in 1558, articulates her Via Media, the path between the Reformed Protestantism of Geneva, which had come to dominate Scotland, and the Roman Catholicism still favored by many in her land. The new path becomes the diverse realm known as Anglicanism, an episcopally led Protestant church, which gains traction during the queen's long reign and is spread globally as England builds its worldwide empire.

By the end of the century, Europe is divided into two realms with Scotland, England, and Scandinavia firmly in the Protestant camp. Germany and Switzerland are divided into Protestant states and cantons and Catholic states and cantons. France remains Catholic, but grants Protestants toleration in the 1598 Edict of Nantes. Italy has remained Catholic and Spain has launched a new Counter-Reformation, which not only revives Christianity on the Iberian Peninsula but will lead to the much needed reform within the Catholic Church.

Leading the Catholic reform movement is a new religious order—the Jesuits—formed by a young Spanish soldier, Ignatius Loyola, who shapes his movement as a private spiritual army in the hands of the pope. With the Society of Jesus in hand, the Catholic Church makes two key thrusts. First, a cadre of young Jesuits will head east and carry Catholic Christianity to Asia—India, Malaysia, China, and Japan. Even as it loses northern Europe, the Catholic Church expands its territory, though it will take generations to grow its membership significantly. Second, the Jesuits would take the lead in recapturing lands from the Protestants. Poland is a notable battlefield, where Protestants gain a beachhead only to have it taken from them.

The early efforts at reforming the Catholic Church in the face of Protestant advances culminate in the Council of Trent, which meets for some 25 sessions in Trento and Bologna, Italy, spread out over the years from 1545 to 1563 under three different popes. As might be expected, the council condemned what it saw as the major Protestant heresies, but then set about redefining the church's faith and producing a set of teaching materials that helped standardize the church's life for the next four centuries.

The Reformation, by dividing Europe, also opens space for a spectrum of new religious movements to emerge. In Switzerland, a new Bible-based movement challenging the idea of an inclusive state church emerges. The movement, known as the Swiss Brethren, is rejected by both Catholics and Protestants and becomes a hunted and persecuted minority that mutates and survives as the Mennonite Church. Simultaneously, a theological challenge to Christian orthodoxy is initially offered by a Spanish physician,

Michael Servetus, who dies a martyr to the cause of what becomes Unitarianism, a form of Christianity that rejects the doctrine of the Triune God. Unitarianism will find an initial home in Poland and then achieve a more permanent minority status in Transylvania. It heralds the more intense challenges to major Christian beliefs that will remake Christendom in the 18th century.

The defeats at Vienna in 1529 and 1532 stopped Ottoman expansion in Europe, but did nothing to challenge Muslim control of central Europe. Though stymied in territorial expansion (primarily by geographical boundaries such as the Sahara Desert and the Caucasian Mountains), the Ottomans were able to establish their rule over their far-flung empire, which reached around the eastern Mediterranean and across North Africa (largely acquired by Suleiman II) and eastward to the Arabian Peninsula. The inhabited parts of Arabia were officially under the sharif of Mecca, who formally acknowledged Ottoman authority but operated largely as an autonomous local ruler. Later Muslim attempts to expand their European presence were blocked by the naval loss at Lepanto (1571).

Like the Ottomans in their realm, the Ming Dynasty had taken control of China and would through the century lead a vast and prosperous empire. Buddhists, Taoists, and Confucianists thrived, and Muslims and Christian minorities found space to grow. In neighboring Korea, Buddhism survived, but Confucianism enjoyed royal patronage and reigned supreme, while in Japan exactly the opposite is true.

Possibly the most important change in Asian religion occurs in the 1570s when Sonam Gyatso, the most prominent lama of the reformist Gelugpa school of Tibetan Buddhism, visits the Mongolian leader Altan Khan, who is attempting to revive and reunite the now splintered Mongolians. The cordial relations that quickly emerge between the two leaders will lead to Mongolia becoming a Buddhist country, with the Gelugpa school dominating, and the designation of Sonam Gyatso (and his immediate predecessors) as the Dalai Lama, a title roughly translated as "Ocean of Wisdom." From this point, the Gelugpa school, whose teachings have some resonance with all the other Tibetan Buddhist schools, would begin its emergence to political leadership of the country.

Even as Suleiman approached Vienna for the first time, a central Asian Muslim ruler would challenge the Delhi Sultanate, which had ruled northern India for the previous three centuries. Following his victory at the First Battle of Panipat in 1526. Babur quickly took possession of Delhi and the almost equally important city of Agra (officially the sultanate's capital) and initiates the Mughal Empire that will rule most of India until the British arrive in the 19th century. The Mughal rulers, beginning with Babur, will assume a much more aggressive stance toward Hinduism and will periodically unleash their power against Hindu shrines and temples. Many of the key issues between contemporary Muslims and Hindus originate as the Mughals exercise their control over their Hindu subjects.

Even as great empires—Ottoman, Ming, and Mughal—settle in for their lengthy run, the Christian lands are expanding into the new worlds that were initially discovered to exist by Europeans at the end of the previous century. By the Treaty of Tordesillas (1494), the Portuguese and Spanish have drawn a line down the middle of the Atlantic by which the Portuguese receive lands to the east (which includes Brazil and Africa), and Spain the rest of the Americas. Portugal will push its exploration of the African coast to its southern tip, round the Cape of Good Hope, and follow the Indian Ocean around the coast of East Africa to India and then beyond to Malaysia, Indonesia (the fabled Spice Island, and even China. By the end of the century, not only have the Portuguese introduced Christianity along the coast of Asia all the way to the Pacific, but the Catholic church has erected dioceses at Goa, India (1533, and elevated to an archdiocese in 1558), Malacca, Malaysia (1558), Macau (1576), and Funay, Japan (1588).

The Portuguese head start and hegemony in Asia would be challenged by the Spanish who commissioned the Portuguese sailor Ferdinand Magellan to sail to the Spice Islands by heading west. He would make it all the way to the Philippines, where he is killed in 1521. His sailors make it back to Europe, and from the Philippines the Spanish would begin to make their presence felt in the area, while the Philippines, by way of Mexico, would become the disseminating point for Spanish Catholicism to Asia.

Spain had already begun to colonize and plunder the Americas when the Treaty of Tordesillas was signed, and it moved immediately to take charge of its assigned territory, beginning with the Caribbean Islands and then moving westward to Mexico and finally north into the American southwest and south into the northern lands of South America. The Roman

Catholic Church went everywhere the Spanish went, and as the church grew to become the dominant faith in Spanish territory, the traditional religions of the Mayans and Incas and the other lesser known American Native peoples declined and eventually vanished. Major clashes would occur as the Spanish defeated the Mayans and the Incas, and the major religious news in the region became the swiftness of the Roman Catholic takeover of the religious life in their colonial territory.

Pope Julius erects the first Roman Catholic dioceses in the Americas in 1511, one in Puerto Rico and two on the island of Hispaniola (site of the current nations of Haiti and the Dominican Republic). Two years later a diocese is erected in Panama and the first is erected in Mexico in 1525. The first archdioceses (Mexico and Santo Domingo) appear in 1546, a testimony of the spread of the church among the Native population. The first South American diocese (in Venezuela) had appeared in 1531. While growth in the Caribbean is spectacular, European settlement of what is now the United States, and Canada, which begins in Florida (San Augustine) in the 1560s, will wait until the next century.

ca. 1500

South Asia: India
Islam, Hinduism
Sekandar Lodi (1488–1516), who heads the Delhi Sultanate, attacks and plunders Mathura in the heart of the land where the Hindu Lord Krishna was believed to have been born and lived most of his earthly life, along with his brother Balarama and consort Radha. Sekandar destroys many of the Hindu temples.

ca. 1500

South Asia: India
Hinduism
Shrimad Vallabhacharya founds the Pushtimarg, a Vaishnava Hindu devotional movement that emphasizes the idea that the love of God (Shri Krishna) is to be seen as an end in itself, not as a means to any other end.

Early in his career, Vallabhacharya participates in a great debate aranged by Krishnadevaraya, the ruler of the Vijayanagara Empire and himself a Vaishnava devotee, at which representatives of Vaishnavaites and disciples of the nondualistic teacher Shankaracharya discussed the philosophical question of dualism versus monism. The Vaishnava dualists were declared the winners.

ca. 1500

Europe: Estonia
Christianity

The steeple of the 13th-century St. Olaf's church in Tallinn, Estonia, is raised to a height of 522 feet. It thus becomes a sight visible far out in the Baltic Sea and useful to mariners sailing in and out of the city, and makes it the second tallest building in the world, second only to Lincoln Cathedral in England.

1500

South Asia: India
Christianity

Steeple of St. Olaf's Church in Tallinn, Estonia. From the time of the Protestant Reformation the church has been part of the Lutheran tradition. (Nickolay Khoroshkov/ Dreamstime.com)

Portuguese admiral Pedro Álvares Cabral arrives at Cochin and negotiates a treaty with the local ruler. He builds a trading post and upon his departure leaves 30 Portuguese and four Franciscan friars.

1500

South Asia: India
Christianity, Hinduism

Portuguese navigator Pedro Álvares Cabral founds the first European settlement in India at Kochi, a port city on the west coast of India in what is now the state of Kerala. It is a center of the Indian trade in spices.

1500

Europe: Belgium
Christianity

The new Cathedral of Our Lady at Antwerp, some 148 years in construction, is completed.

1500

Europe: Italy
Christianity

Pope Alexander VI proclaims a Year of Jubilee, inviting the faithful to make a pilgrimage to Rome, and includes in his proclamation a call for a crusade against the Ottoman Turks.

1500

Europe: Italy
Judaism

Rabbi Asher Lamlein launches a movement in northern Italy focused upon repentance and the imminent appearance of the messiah. His movement will spread into Germany before it runs its course and disappears.

1500

Europe: Spain
Christianity

Spanish cartographer Juan de la Cosa, the owner and captain of the *Santa María,* one of the ships used by Christopher Columbus on his first and second voyage to the Americas, designs the earliest European world map that incorporates information on the Americas in its presentation.

1500–1501

Europe: England
Christianity
John Morton, the archbishop of Canterbury, dies, and Thomas Langston, the bishop of Winchester, is named to succeed him, but dies from the plague a few weeks later before he can be consecrated to his office. Henry Deane (r. 1501–1503), the bishop of Salisbury, is then chosen to fill the vacant archbishopric.

1500–1599

South America: Brazil
Judaism
Sephardic Jews, expelled from Spain and Portugal, begin to arrive in Brazil. Most outwardly live as converts to Christianity.

1500–1700

Europe: Spain
Judaism
Many Jewish converts to Christianity and their descendants flee the threat of the Inquisition. Some move to the Netherlands, and a few set off for Recife, Brazil.

April 22, 1500

South America: Brazil
Christianity
Blown off course on his way to India, Portuguese explorer Pedro Alvares Cabral (ca. 1460–ca. 1526) lands on the coast of Brazil and claims it for Portugal.

1501

Sub-Saharan Africa: South Africa
Christianity
The Portuguese land at Mossel Bay, South Africa, and while there erect the first Christian church located south of the equator.

1501

East and Southeast Asia: China
Buddhism
The Xiaozong emperor transforms a mansion originally built by the Zhangzong emperor in the 13th century on the western outskirts of Beijing into the Ruiyan Nunnery. The site of the nunnery becomes famous for a large rock outcropping upon which a pagoda has been constructed.

1501

Europe: Bohemia
Christianity
The Hussites, proto-Protestant followers of John Hus, produce a hymnal for use by congregations during worship.

1501

Europe: Italy
Christianity
Pope Alexander VI scandalizes church leaders by attending, along with his children Cesare and Lucrezia, who were accused of having an incestuous relationship, the Banquet of Chestnuts, a Roman ball with all the elements of a public orgy.

1501

Europe: Portugal
Christianity
Having successfully petitioned the pope for permission to construct a monastery along the margins of the Tagus River at Lisbon, King Manuel I begins construction of the Monastery of St. Jerome (or Hieronymites Monastery). It will take some 70 years to complete but becomes the model of a new architectural style known as Manueline, a transition between the Gothic and the Renaissance. The monastery also becomes the symbol of Portugal's growing wealth derived from its colonial expansion and global trade. Once constructed, it would be a stopping point for sailors to have a moment of prayer before venturing out into the world. The monastery is placed in the hands of the relatively new Order of St. Jerome.

1501

Europe: Portugal
Christianity
On the day of the annual Christian Feast of the Ascension (of Jesus into heaven), Portuguese explorer Joao da Nova Castelia discovers an isolated volcanic island in the South Atlantic. He names it Ascension Island.

1501

Europe: Spain
Christianity

Responding to a rebellion in Granada in 1501, the Spanish rulers rescind the Alhambra Decree, which expelled the Jews from Spain, but protected the rights of the Muslim citizens. Authorities now mandate the conversion or emigration of the Muslims.

1501

Southwest Asia and North Africa: Persia
Islam

Shah Isma'il I establishes himself as the shah of Azerbaijan and initiates the Safavid Dynasty. He inherited a lineage of hereditary grand masters of the Safaviyeh order, a Shi'a Sufi order. He designates Shi'a Islam as the religion of his new Persian state. He immediately embarks on a campaign to bring all of Persia, at the time divided into a number of small kingdoms, under his rule, which occurs over the next decade. The rise of the Safavids would lead to a century-long struggle between it and the Ottoman Empire to the east.

Once in control of Persia, Ismail I enforced conversion of the heretofore Sunni population. Sunni imams were killed and/or exiled, and replaced with Shi'a imams whom he supported with salaries and land grants. In spite of his own Sufi origins, Ismail did not privilege the various Sufi orders other than the Ni-matullahi order, which prospered. The leaders of the Safavid dynasty ruled as head of both the government and the religious community.

1502

Central America and the Caribbean: Panama, Honduras
Christianity

Christopher Columbus makes his fourth and final trip to the New World. During this trip he has his first encounter with the island of St. Lucia and explores the shore of Panama, Honduras, and Costa Rica.

1502

Europe: Germany
Christianity

Frederick the Wise, Elector of Saxony, founds the University of Wittenberg.

1502

Europe: Spain
Christianity

Queen Isabella issues an order demanding that any remaining Moors choose between baptism into Christianity and expulsion from her realm.

1502

Southwest Asia and North Africa: Asia Minor
Christianity

When Ottoman sultan Bayezid I discovers that Joachim I had initiated construction of a stone church building without proper permission, he has the ecumenical patriarch deposed. Church leaders in Istanbul elect the former patriarch Nephon II to succeed again to the office, but he refuses, being happy in his new position with the church in Wallachia. Attention then turns to Pachomios I (r. 1503–1504), the metropolitan of Zichna (northern Greece). However, the former patriarch Joachim I (r. 1504) was able to reclaim his position by paying a large sum to the sultan. Unfortunately, he was not able to enjoy his new position as he died before the year was out and Pachomios I (r. 1504–1513) resumed the patriarch's throne.

1502

Southwest Asia and North Africa: Morocco
Christianity

The Portuguese seize Mazagan (which is renamed El Jadida) on the Atlantic coast of Morocco. They build a large fort and erect the Catholic Church of the Assumption.

1503

South Asia: India
Christianity

On his first voyage to India, Afonso de Albuquerque does battle with the Hindu ruler of the Kingdom of Calicut on Malabar Coast and is able to establish Calicut's rival on the throne at Kochi (or Cochin). Thankful for the help, the king of Cochin grants permission for Albuquerque to establish a Portuguese fort at Cochin, which will become a profitable trading post.

Vasco da Gama founds the Portuguese colony at Cochin, and the Portuguese erect St. Francis Church, the oldest European Christian church in India. In introducing Roman Catholicism to India, the work is placed directly under the jurisdiction of the Archdiocese of Lisbon.

1503

South Asia: India
Hinduism

The teenage future saint Chaitanya travels to Gaya with a group of peers and receives spiritual initiation from Iswar Puri, a Vaishnava *sannyasi* (one who has accepted the renounced life). The experience appears to have marked a change in the young man, as he now begins to manifest the unusual spiritual trance states that will be so prominent in later life and to manifest his appropriation of the Vaishnava tradition. In his native village, Nadia, he opens a school to teach and practice *kirtan*, the public dancing and chanting of the names of God.

1503

Europe: England
Christianity

Henry Deane, the archbishop of Canterbury, dies and is succeeded by William Warham (r. 1503–1532), formerly the bishop of London.

1503

Europe: England, Italy
Christianity

Pope Julius II issues a dispensation that sanctions the marriage of the future king Henry VIII of England to Catherine of Aragon. Catherine, the widow of Henry's brother, claimed to have remained a virgin during the brief period between the marriage and her husband's death. That technicality allows her marriage to Henry to proceed.

1503

Europe: Italy
Christianity

Pope Alexander VI dies. He is so unpopular that the priests of St. Peter's Basilica initially refuse to accept his body for interment. His immediate successor, Pope Pius III (r. 1503), goes so far as forbidding anyone from saying a requiem mass for him.

Pope Alexander is interred in St. Peter's Basilica. In the 19th century, his body would be transferred to the Church of Santa Maria in Montserrato degli Spagnoli (aka the Church of Holy Mary in Montserrat of the Spaniards), the National Church of Spain in Rome. The church is dedicated to the miraculous Virgin of Montserrat.

Pope Pius III (r. 1503) reigns for less than a month before dying. He is succeeded by Pope Julius II (r. 1503–1513).

1503

Europe: Poland
Judaism

Polish ruler Alexander Jagiellon (r. 1501–1506) appoints Rabbi Jacob Polak as the first chief rabbi of Poland. With a chief rabbi in place, the Jewish community finds itself able to develop a limited form of self-governance.

1503

Southwest Asia and North Africa: Asia Minor
Christianity

Eliya V, Patriarch of the Nestorian Church of the East, consecrates three additional bishops for India. Mar Yarbella is named as the metropolitan (archbishop) of the Indian church. He will be assisted by Mar Yakoob and Mar Denaha.

1503

Russia, Central Asia, and the Caucasus: Russia
Christianity

Nil Sorsky, a monk at the Kirillo-Belozersky Monastery, the largest monastery of northern Russia, emerges as the leader in the fight then engaging the Russian Orthodox Church against monastic ownership of land at the church's Synod of 1503 in Moscow.

May 28, 1503

Europe: Scotland, England
Christianity

Pope Alexander VI signs the papal bull confirming the marriage of King James IV of Scotland to Margaret Tudor of England, part of the negotiation of what was to be a treaty of everlasting peace between the two countries. Their marriage will be celebrated as the Union of the Thistle and the Rose.

1504

Central America and the Caribbean: Jamaica
Christianity

Using the *Ephemeris* produced by the 15th-century astrologer/astronomer Regiomontanus, Christopher Columbus successfully predicted a lunar eclipse in the skies of Jamaica that occurred on February 29. The event also successfully intimidated the local native residents of Jamaica upon whom Columbus depended for supplies.

1504

South Asia: India
Islam

Sultan Sikandar Lodī, the Muslim ruler of the Delhi Sultanate, founds Agra, Uttar Pradesh, India, and makes it his capital. It later became the capital of the Mughal Empire and was transformed into a major religious and cultural center.

1504

Europe: England
Christianity

John Fisher, a former tutor of the future king Henry VIII, is appointed bishop of Rochester.

1504

Europe: England
Christianity

After several centuries, construction is finally completed on the Bell Harry Tower, the main tower of Canterbury Cathedral.

1504

Europe: Moldavia

Prince Stephen of Moldavia dies after almost a half century on the throne. He is buried in Putna Monastery, which he had built in the 1460s. He endowed the church with a variety of holy objects, including the icon that he always carried into battle.

1504

Europe: Spain, England
Christianity

Catherine of Aragon, the daughter of King Ferdinand II of Aragon and Queen Isabella I of Castile, marries King Henry VIII of England.

1504

Russia, Central Asia, and the Caucasus: Russia
Christianity

A *sobor* (church council) in Moscow outlaws books of the Judaizing heretics and permits their being burned. As the church moves against the *Zhidovstvuy-ushchiye* (or "those who follow Jewish traditions"), who have lost the connections to the czar's family that had previously protected them to some extent, they are sentenced to death or exile.

1505

East and Southeast Asia: China
Chinese Religions

The Hongzhi emperor dies and is succeeded by the Zhengde emperor (r. 1505–1521) as the emperor of China. He would become known primarily for his indulgent and pleasure-driven behavior with an accompanying neglect of the country's affairs.

1505

Europe: Italy
Christianity

With the completion of the altarpiece at the Church of San Zaccaria in Venice, Giovanni Bellini is at the height of his lengthy career producing sacred art. The altarpiece depicts the Blessed Virgin Mary in conversation with the apostle Peter, Jerome (who translated the Bible into Latin), and two more recent Italian saints—Catherine and Lucy.

1505

Europe: Portugal
Christianity

The queen dowager Leonor of Viseu commissions a new translation of the Acts of the Apostles and of the General Epistles (i.e., the New Testament epistles of James, Peter, John, and Jude).

1505

Russia, Central Asia, and the Caucasus: Russia
Christianity

Grand Prince Ivan of Moscow dies and is succeeded by his son Vasili III (r. 1505–1533). With the Mongols to the East in disarray, his major concern will be the further consolidation of Russian lands under his regime and the continued rivalry for territory to his west with Poland and Lithuania, both Roman Catholic countries.

1506

Sub-Saharan Africa: Mozambique
Christianity

The first Portuguese Catholic missionaries arrive and begin work in southern Mozambique along the Zambezi River.

1506

East and Southeast Asia: Korea
Traditional Religions

King Chungjong (r. 1506–1544) begins his lengthy rule of Korea. With the support of those officials who had deposed the former king Yongsan-gun, he initiated the restoration of Confucianism to a central position in Korean life.

1506

Europe: Germany
Christianity

Astronomer Nicholas Copernicus becomes the canon of church properties in the Diocese of Ermland (Prussia).

1506

Europe: Germany
Judaism

Johannes Reuchlin begins his career of introducing the Christian church in Europe to the wisdom of Judaism by publishing his *De Rudimentis Hebraicis,* a grammar and lexicon.

1506

Europe: Italy
Christianity

Neglected during the years in which the popes resided in Avignon, plans for a new St. Peter's emerged during the 1400s. Finally, after much discussion, Pope Julius II lays the foundation stone of the new Basilica of St. Peter in Rome.

1506

Europe: Italy
Christianity

According to one report, Veronica's Veil, a piece of cloth believed by many to picture the face of Jesus and dating to the week of his crucifixion, is stolen while St. Peter's Basilica is being rebuilt. That cloth will change hands several times and will eventually be given to the Capuchin monastery in the village of Manoppello, Italy, where it remains to the present. According to other reports, the cloth that had been in Rome for many centuries was not stolen and remains in the new St. Peter's Cathedral to the present.

1506

Europe: Italy
Christianity

Pope Julius II officially founds the Swiss Guard, the elite unit who provide protection to the pope.

1506

Europe: Italy
Christianity

The new pope Leo X beatifies the wonderworking Francis of Paola, the founder of the Franciscan Order of Minims, who had died at the age of 91 only six years earlier. Six years later Leo would lead the ceremonies for Francis's canonization.

1506

Europe: Portugal
Christianity

Following months of suffering from the plague, residents of Lisbon place the blame on the Jewish community (consisting primarily of Jews who had been forcefully converted to Christianity). As Easter approaches, Dominicans rouse the public and call upon the public to destroy the *converso* community. A mob assembles and attacks the *conversos,* some 5,000 of whom are killed. In the aftermath, King Manuel turns on those who instigated the riot, executes them, and punishes many of the rioters. The rioting, however,

Christ Disputing with the Doctors, Albrecht Dürer, 1506. Oil on panel. Museo Thyssen-Bornemisza,Madrid, Spain. The painting depicts the New Testament scene of the young Jesus Christ debating with the elders in the Temple in Jerusalem. (Corbis)

spreads to other cities and becomes the occasion of the introduction of the Inquisition into Portugal.

1506

Europe: Spain
Christianity

Work is completed on the Cathedral of Saint Mary of the See in Seville, Spain. It replaces the Hagia Sophia in Constantinople as the largest cathedral in the world and remains the largest Gothic cathedral and the third-largest church in the world.

1506–1507

Europe: Italy
Christianity

German painter Albrecht Dürer visits Venice and produces a number of pieces of sacred art including an altarpiece, *The Adoration of the Virgin,* for the Church of Saint Bartholomew and a painting, *Christ Disputing with the Doctors.* Upon his return to Nurnberg in 1507, he will enter a highly productive period during which time he will produce a series of famous paintings.

1507

Sub-Saharan Africa: Mozambique
Christianity

The Portuguese establish a port and naval base on the island of Mozambique off the coast of northern Mozambique.

1507

East and Southeast Asia: China
Buddhism

Shortly after his preliminary identification as the future karmapa, the head of the Karma Kagyu school of Tibetan Buddhism, the status of the future eighth karmapa, Mikyo Dorje, is challenged by the parents of a second child who offer their son as a candidate to be the karmapa. Eventually, the school's regent arranged a meeting of the two children during which they were tested by being asked to choose items formerly owned by the previous karmapa. Mikyo Dorje passes the test and is proclaimed the karmapa. He in turn announces that the other child is also a reincarnated tulku of another recently deceased prominent lama.

1507

Europe: Italy
Christianity

Pope Julius II proclaims a new indulgence, the revenues from which will go toward the new Basilica of St. Peter.

1507

Europe: Spain
Christianity

Cardinal Ximenes assumes leadership of the Inquisition in Spain. During his decade of leadership, 40,000 people were arrested and some 2,000 executed. He is also named a cardinal by Pope Julius II.

1507

Southwest Asia and North Africa: Persia
Christianity, Islam

The Portuguese capture Hormuz (or Ormuz), an island and city off the coast of Persia that holds a commanding position at the entrance to the Persian Gulf. The action sets up a hostile relationship with the Persian Ismail I, who formerly had hegemony. Portuguese commander Afonso de Albuquerque began building the Fort of Our Lady of Victory, but his men refuse to work in the heat and abandon him. He is forced to withdraw from Hormuz while the schism in the Portuguese ranks is resolved.

1507

Southwest Asia and North Africa: Yemen
Christianity, Islam

A Portuguese fleet lands at Suq, the capital of Socotra, an archipelago in the Indian Ocean. They build a fortress and lay plans to disrupt/stop Muslim Arab commerce in the Indian Ocean, and secondarily to liberate the "Christians" (such as the Ethiopians) from Islamic rule. Their plans for Socotra do not prove successful and they abandon the fort several years later.

1508

Central America and the Caribbean: Puerto Rico
Christianity

Juan Ponce de Leon begins the Spanish settlement of the island of San Juan Baptista (now known as Puerto Rico).

1508

South Asia: India
Hinduism

Kalapahad, a former Hindu who converted to Islam and now the general serving the Bengal sultan Sulaiman Khan Karrani, makes a destructive raid through Orissa. His army destroys a number of Hindu temples, including the Sun Temple at Konark, where he breaks many of the deity statues (including many of the erotic statues that graced the temple's second level) and pulls down the towers.

1508

Europe: Germany
Christianity

Maximilian, the king of the Germans who had never made the trip to Italy to be formally crowned Holy Roman emperor by the pope, gains the assent of Pope Julius II to assume the title *Erwählter Römischer Kaiser* (or Elected Roman Emperor). The new title formally alters the custom dating to the time of Charlemagne that dictates that the Holy Roman emperor must be crowned by the pope.

1508

Europe: Italy
Christianity

Pope Julius II commissions Michelangelo to repaint the ceiling of the Sistine Chapel, currently covered with golden stars on a blue sky. At about the same time, he also commissions the artist Raphael to fresco his private library at the Vatican Palace. This becomes the first of a number of rooms in the palace that he paints, which are collectively regarded as his greatest work. Possibly the most famous is a work entitled *The School of Athens*. Both artists would work on their projects for many years.

1508

Europe: Portugal
Christianity
Funchal, a Portuguese town on the island of Madeira in the Atlantic Ocean, is formally elevated to the status of a city. By this time, work has proceeded on the Cathedral of Our Lady of the Assumption for a decade, and though it will not be completed for another decade, it is already available for regular worship. King Manuel I of Portugal, who had sent the architect to oversee the construction of the new cathedral, presented it with a large silver processional cross.

1508

Europe: Spain
Christianity
The papal bull *Universalis Ecclesiæ regimini* announces that no churches, monasteries, or religious foundations would be erected in the New World without the consent of the Spanish monarch. In addition he was granted a number of additional prerogatives including the setting of boundaries of any dioceses and the power to nominate candidates for the bishopric.

1508

Russia, Central Asia, and the Caucasus: Russia
Christianity
Russian ruler Ivan III completes the Cathedral of the Archangel in the Kremlin, Moscow. The cathedral honors the Muscovite rulers' patron saint, St. Michael, reflects the emerging power of the country, and provides a worthy place where the royal family can be buried.

1509

Central America and the Caribbean: Jamaica
Christianity
The Spanish begin settlement of Jamaica, and the Roman Catholic Church is established on the island.

1509

South Asia: India
Hinduism
Krishna Deva Raya (r. 1509–1529) begins his reign as the emperor of the Hindu-based Vijayanagara Empire, over which he will rule as it reaches the zenith of its power. A Vaishnava Hindu, he would pay particular attention to the Tirumala Venkateswara Temple to which he donates a number of valuables. He commissions statues of himself and his two wives to grace the temple grounds, which still stand at the temple exit.

Krishna Deva Raya had been formally initiated into Vaishnavism by Vyasatirtha, the outstanding scholar/teacher who headed the Tirumala Venkateswara Temple, and was like many of the Vijayanagara rulers a devotee of Venkateswara, one of the incarnations of the Hindu deity Vishnu.

1509

South Asia: India
Christianity
King Manuel I of Portugal sends a fleet of ships to India. He resolves the split in the Portuguese leadership by appointing Afonso de Albuquerque as the governor of Portuguese India, a position he would retain for the rest of his life.

Albuquerque determines that he will dominate the Muslim world and control the Asian spice trade. To this end, he commissions Diogo Lopes de Sequeira as head of a fleet to negotiate an initial agreement with Sultan Mahmud Shah of Malacca. The first effort proved a failure.

1509

Europe: England
Christianity
King Henry VII of England dies. His son Henry marries Catherine of Aragon, the widow of his late brother Arthur, and is crowned King Henry VIII (r. 1509–1547).

1509

Europe: Italy
Christianity
Pope Julius II, who had joined King Ferdinand of Aragon, Holy Roman Emperor Maximilian, and King

Louis XII of France to form the League of Cambrai against Venice, places the city-state under an edict of excommunication.

1509

Russia, Central Asia, and the Caucasus: Russia
Christianity

Work on the new Cathedral of the Archangel, dedicated to St. Michael, begun in 1505, having been completed (1508), Vasili III leads the dedication ceremonies. It will provide the primary burial site for Russian royalty for the next century.

1509

Southwest Asia and North Africa: Asia Minor
Christianity

The ecumenical patriarch Pachomius excommunicates Arsenius Apostolius, who had been appointed as bishop of Monemvasia over the Eastern rite Catholics of the island of Crete, at the time controlled by the Venetian Republic. Eastern rite Catholics follow a liturgy very like that of the Greek Orthodox, but acknowledge the authority of the pope. Once at his post, Arsenius had declared himself to be in communion with both the Orthodox patriarch of Constantinople and with the Roman Catholic Church. Finding his position unacceptable, Pachomius initially asked Arsenius to abdicate. Unable to otherwise resolve the issue, Pachomius acts, leading Arsenius to retire to Venice.

1509

Southwest Asia and North Africa: Maghreb
Islam, Christianity

Spanish armies invaded North Africa in a crusade against the Muslim rulers of Tripoli, Oran, and Bougie.

1509–1510

Europe: Germany
Christianity, Judaism

Johann Pfefferkorn, a converted Jew in the service of Holy Roman Emperor Maximilian I, launches a persecution of the Jews that leads to the deaths and/or expulsion of Jews from several German cities. He also obtains the authority to confiscate all Jewish books assumed to be directed against the Christian faith.

Pfefferkorn is opposed by Johannes Reuchlin whom Emperor Maximilian appoints to a commission to review Pfefferkorn's activities. In a survey of Jewish literature, he concludes that the number of books insulting to Christianity are very few and that Jews as a whole do not refer to them. In a counter-proposal, he asks the emperor to establish two Hebrew chairs at each German university and have the Jewish community supply the books necessary to support the new professors.

September 14, 1509

Southwest Asia and North Africa: Asia Minor
Islam

A massive earthquake strikes Istanbul and causes extensive damage. Over a hundred mosques are reportedly destroyed across northwest Asia Minor. In Istanbul, the dome of the recently completed Bayezid II Mosque is destroyed and one of its minarets collapses. The dome of Fatih Mosque splits open and the four great columns supporting it suffer damage. The Hagia Sophia, former church turned mosque, largely survives the quake, though one of its minarets is toppled. Most damage occurs inside where the plaster that had covered the Christian artwork falls off the walls.

ca. 1510

South Asia: India
Hinduism

Future Vaishnava saint and reformer Chaitanya Mahaprabhu assumes the renounced life as a sannyasin and leaves his hometown on Nadia. He moves to Puri, Orissa, where one of the most prominent of the Indian temples dedicated to Vishnu and Krishna is located, the Jagannath Temple. He will spend his remaining life in Puri and its environs, where King Maharaja Prataparudra will come to view him as a new incarnation of Krishna.

Chaitanya will develop a new form of Vaishnava religion with an exclusive focus on Krishna and the recitation of the Hare Krishna mantra as a primary form of bhakti (devotional) yoga. In the practice of his new religion, he often entered deep trance states.

Not a theologian, he will appoint six disciples, later known as the Six Goswamis of Vrindavan, to develop a systematic presentation of his approach, which comes to be known as Gaudiya Vaishnava

SHRI KRISHNA CHAITANYA (1486–1533)

Shri Chaitanya is one of the most influential teachers of Vaishnava Hinduism, and many of his devotees claim him to be an incarnation of Krishna, that most famous of Hindu deities. A contemporary of Martin Luther, he brought about a reformation in Hinduism in eastern India in the 16th century.

Chaitanya was born as Visvambhara Misra in Mayapur (now in West Bengal) in 1486. Though the early biographies contain hagiographic elements, including miraculous events that took place when he was a child, the general shape of his life is clear. Chaitanya became a scholar of Sanskrit at a youthful age. He married, but his marriage ended abruptly soon afterward when his wife died of a snake bite. Plans to remarry were subsequently aborted when he experienced spiritual transformation through an encounter with the noted ascetic Ishvara Puri of Gaya. Chaitanya had traveled to Gaya and was in a trance at a Vishnu shrine when Ishvara kept him from falling.

Chaitanya abandoned his role as teacher and became obsessed with a mystic passion for Krishna. Soon people began to acknowledge him as the incarnation of Krishna for this age and simultaneously as an embodiment of Radha, Krishna's lover. In about 1510, he became a *sannyasin,* traveled throughout India for a short while, and then settled in Orissa until his death in 1533.

Chaitanya adopted a personalist view of God and rejected the advaitist position that all is the impersonal One. For Chaitanya, Krishna is the Supreme Personality of God. Chaitanya left no extant writings though eight verses directly from him are recorded by others. These verses are known as the Siksastaka and mainly comprise devotional language about Krishna. The last verse reads: "I know no one but Krishna as my Lord, and he shall remain so even if he handles me roughly in his embrace or makes me brokenhearted by not being present before me. He is completely free to do anything and everything, for he is always my worshipful Lord unconditionally."

The *Chaitanya Charitamrita* is widely known through the publishing efforts of Sri Bhaktivedanta Swami Prabhupada, the founder of the modern International Society for Krishna Consciousness (ISKCON). Prabhupada published the *Charitamrita* in a deluxe 17-volume English edition in the 1970s. ISKCON has done more than any Hindu group to foster knowledge of Chaitanya and adoration of him as an incarnation of Krishna globally.

JAMES A. BEVERLEY

theology. The six theologians are Rupa Gosvamin, Sanatana Gosvamin, Gopala Bhatta Gosvamin, Raghunatha Bhatta Gosvamin, Raghunatha Dasa Gosvamin, and Jiva Gosvamin, all now honored by followers of Gaudiya Vaishnavism for their work.

1510

Central America and the Caribbean: Panama
Christianity
The Spanish found Santa María la Antigua del Darién, the first permanent European settlement on the American mainland, located on the Caribbean coast of what is now Panama.

1510

South Asia: India
Christianity, Judaism
Portuguese forces defeat the forces of the Muslim ruler of Bijapur, Ismail Adil Shah, who had just come to the throne, and establish a permanent settlement in Goa, on the coast of India. In defeating the Muslims, they win the initial support of the Hindu population. The Portuguese control of the Malabar coast also now includes the important port city of Cranganore (aka Kodungallur or Angamala).

In the wake of their conquest, Jews from both Spain and Portugal move to India.

1510

East and Southeast Asia: Myanmar
Buddhism
King Mingyinyo, a Theravada Buddhist, founds the First Taungoo Dynasty and unites Myanmar into a Buddhist state.

1510

Europe: England
Christianity
Anglican churchman John Colet founds St. Paul's School in London.

1510

Europe: England
Christianity

Humanist scholar Erasmus assumes duties as the professor of Greek at Cambridge University.

1510

Europe: France
Christianity
Benedictines in Normandy develop a new herbal-based liqueur, which will later be marketed as Benedictine Liqueur.

1510

Europe: Germany
Christianity
Martin Luther begins his tenure as professor of theology at the new University of Wittenberg.

1510–1511

Europe: Italy
Christianity
Martin Luther, a young Augustinian monk from Germany, makes a pilgrimage to Rome where he is appalled by the popular appropriation of Roman Catholicism relative to the acts of penance performed at the many shrines he visits and the selling of indulgences.

1510–1519

Europe: Italy
Christianity
A reform movement, later termed the Spirituali, emerges within the Roman Catholic Church in Italy. It emphasizes some ideas identified with Protestantism, especially the work of grace by the Holy Spirit, but as Protestantism developed abhorred the idea of schism. It would come to include a number of influential persons such as the artist Michelangelo and Cardinal Reginald Pole.

1511

Central America and the Caribbean: Puerto Rico, Dominican Republic
Christianity
Pope Julius II erected three dioceses in the New World, one on Puerto Rico and two on the island of Hispaniola (Santo Domingo Concepción de la Vega),

the first dioceses erected in the New World. The latter diocese was suppressed in 1527, while the Diocese of Santo Domingo soon covered a large portion of Latin America. As new countries are formed, dioceses are carved from it. It is elevated to an archdiocese in 1546. Meanwhile, the Diocese of Puerto Rico was renamed the Diocese of San Juan de Puerto Rico in 1924 and elevated as an archdiocese in 1960.

Initially, the developing dioceses of the Americas are placed under the Archdiocese of Seville. There is often a delay, sometimes for several years, between papal action erecting a new diocese (or archdiocese) and its formal organization and the consecration of its bishop.

1511

East and Southeast Asia: Malaysia
Christianity, Islam
The Portuguese led by Alfonso de Albuquerque capture Malacca (Malaysia), which holds a commanding position along the Strait of Malacca opposite Sumatra. The city is in a weakened state due to the widespread unpopularity of Sultan Mahmud Shah, a Muslim ruler who has privileged Muslim merchants to the detriment of those of other faiths. Upon taking the city, Albuquerque immediately builds a stone fortress, using stones from the city's mosque and the local cemetery.

Once securely in control, Albuquerque set about reordering trade relations with the diverse national groups who used Malacca as a trading center, winning the support of the Burmese, Thai, Indonesians, and Chinese. He also sought the location of the mysterious "Spice Islands" to the east, the ultimate source of the wealth passing through Malacca.

With the Portuguese in Malacca, Mahmud Shah settles in the rural outback of his former empire, where his descendants will eventually establish two new ruling sultanates, Johor and Perak, which will become a source of the spread of Islam to the Philippines.

1511

Europe: Italy
Christianity
Pope Julius, who had only a few years earlier joined an alliance with France against Venice, joins the Holy League with Venice and Aragon (Spain) against the French. Papal forces subsequently take the Italian cities of Modena and Mirandola from the French.

1511

Europe: Spain
Christianity
A mere five years after its completion, the dome of the Cathedral of Saint Mary of the See in Seville, Spain collapses. Work to replace it begins almost immediately.

1511

Russia, Central Asia, and the Caucasus: Russia
Christianity
Varlaam (r. 1511–1521), archimandrite (prior) of the Simonov Monastery in Moscow, succeeds Simon as metropolitan of Moscow and All Russia.

July 18, 1511

Europe: Italy
Christianity
Pope Julius II calls for the gathering of the Fifth Council of the Lateran to meet in Rome.

1512

Central America and the Caribbean: Caribbean
Christianity
Spain issues the Laws of Burgos, which propose the encomienda system, which outlaws slavery of Native Americans and forbids mistreatment and harsh punishments. At the same time, it requires Natives to engage in hard labor for their new Spanish overlords.

1512

Central America and the Caribbean: Cuba
Christianity
Dominican missionaries introduce the Roman Catholic Church to Cuba.

1512

Europe: Germany
Christianity
The monk Martin Luther completes his doctor of theology degree and becomes a professor at the recently formed University of Wittenberg.

During a meeting of the German parliament (Reichstag), the church at Trier displays its most holy relic, a coat believed to have been worn by Jesus of Nazareth. It had come to Trier in the fifth century as a gift from Helena, the mother of the emperor Constantine. It was transferred to the cathedral in the 12th century. After its viewing in 1215, it would not again be displayed until the 19th century (1844).

1512

Southwest Asia and North Africa: Asia Minor
Islam

A struggle between the sons of Ottoman sultan Bayezid II leads to the sultan's being deposed by his son Selim, who seizes the throne and initiates his own rule as Sultan Selim I (r. 1512–1520). Beyazid is forced into retirement, leaves Istanbul, and dies a month later.

May 3, 1512

Europe: Italy
Christianity

The first session of the Fifth Lateran Council convenes at Rome to consider questions of church unity and reform. It will meet off and on over the next five years.

1513

Central America and the Caribbean: Caribbean
Christianity

Spain issues the *Requerimento,* which calls upon the Native population of the new Spanish territories to accept the universal hegemony of the Roman Catholic Church and the rule of Spain in the Americas. If they refuse either clause, they may become targets of Spanish armies, forced conversion, and even slavery.

1513

Central America and the Caribbean: Panama
Christianity

The Roman Catholic Diocese of Santa María de La Antigua del Darién is erected. Its name was changed in 1520 to the Diocese of Panama. It becomes an archdiocese in 1925. Fray Juan de Quevedo is named as the first Catholic bishop in the continental Americas.

1513

Central America and the Caribbean: Trinidad
Christianity

Dominican priests begin a mission on Trinidad.

1513

South America: Venezuela
Christianity

The *Coronation of Sultan Selim I* from the "Hunername" manuscript by Lokman, Ottoman School, 16th century. Selim I ruled the Ottoman Empire from 1512 to 1520 and was an exceptional military commander who enlarged the empire's territory. (Topkapi Palace Museum, Istanbul, Turkey/The Bridgeman Art Library)

Dominican and Franciscan priests begin work on the coast of Venezuela.

1513

East and Southeast Asia: China
Buddhism
The Dahui Temple, originally referred to as the Giant Buddha temple, is constructed in Beijing. It houses a 50-foot copper statue of the Buddha (destroyed by the Japanese in the 1940s). Surviving are the 28 intricate clay statues, each some nine feet tall, of the Divine Guardians of the Law. Murals on the wall depict a man as he progresses through life, and with the help of the Buddha and the performance of good deeds he attains nirvana (the Buddhist heavenly state). The artwork at the temple is now considered a treasure of Chinese Buddhist art.

1513

East and Southeast Asia: China
Christianity, Chinese Religions
Alfonso de Albuquerque commissions Jorge Álvares to open relations with China. He lands at Lintin Island (Macau) on the Pearl River Delta in southern China. He is followed by Rafael Perestrello, who makes his way to Canton (Guangzhou). These lead to direct diplomatic and commercial relationships between China and a European nation. Simultaneously, Manuel I, the king of Portugal, commissions Fernão Pires de Andrade and Tomé Pires to open relations between the main Chinese court at Beijing and his court in Lisbon.

Subsequently, the Portuguese obtain rights to anchor ships in Macau's harbours and to engage in various trading activities. They do not obtain the privilege of staying ashore beyond the time needed to conduct their business.

1513

Europe: Spain
Christianity
Without disturbing the old cathedral in Salamanca, Spanish king Ferdinand V of Castile commissions the building of a new cathedral for the city. Following its consecration ater two centuries, both cathedrals have continued as active worship centers.

1513

Southwest Asia and North Africa: Asia Minor
Christianity
Returning to Constantinople from a visit to Wallachia, Theodolus, a monk accompanying the ecumenical patriarch Pachomius, murders him with poison. Theoliptos (r. 1513–1522) then sought and received the favor of Ottoman sultan Selim I, who appoints him as the next patriarch of Constantinople.

1513

Southwest Asia and North Africa: Asia Minor
Islam
Ottoman captain Piri Reis (aka Haci Ahmed Muhiddin Piri) prepares a map of the world as he knows it. The map is the oldest known Turkish atlas showing the Americas, and second only to the map prepared by Juan de la Cosa (1500).

1513–1514

Sub-Saharan Africa: Congo
Christianity
Nineteen-year-old Henrique, the son of Mani Kongo Mvemba Nzinga, the Christian king of Congo, leads a delegation whose aim is to vow fealty to Pope Julius II. By the time they arrive in Rome, early in 1514, Julius has been succeeded in office by Pope Leo X. The delegates present him with gifts and he grants a special dispensation for the consecration of the underage Henrique as a bishop.

March 9, 1513

Europe: Italy
Christianity
Giovanni di Lorenzo de' Medici, the son of the ruler of Florence, Lorenzo de' Medici, is elected to the papal office. Not yet a priest, he will subsequently be ordained, and on March 19 he takes office as Pope Leo X (r. 1513–1521). He will develop an open policy toward the Jewish community and sanctions their setting up a Hebrew printing press at Rome. The late pope Julius II will be buried in an elaborate tomb designed by Michelangelo, who will then begin work on his statue of Moses, meant to be the central figure amid the statues surrounding Julius's tomb.

November 1, 1513

Europe: Italy
Christianity
Following Michelangelo's completion of his work on the ceiling of the Sistine Chapel, Pope Leo X invites the first public viewing.

Raphael completes his commission of the altarpiece for the monks of the Benedictine Monastery of San Sisto in Piacenza. Known as the Sistine Madonna, it would be his last major work. It takes its name from its inclusion of an image of the second-century Saint Sixtus.

1514

Central America and the Caribbean: Costa Rica
Christianity
The first Catholic missionaries begin work in Costa Rica.

1514

Central America and the Caribbean: Cuba
Christianity
Franciscan missionaries initiate work in Cuba.

1514

Central America and the Caribbean: Dominican
  Republic
Christianity
Construction begins on the Basilica Catedral Santa Maria de la Encarnacion (aka Santa Maria la Menor), the first cathedral in the Americas. Roman Catholic leaders intended it to be the center for the church's expansion throughout the new Spanish territories in the New World. It would take several decades to complete and would finally be dedicated in the early 1540s.

1514

South Asia: India
Hinduism
Rupa and Sanatana, two brothers who had been forced into government service by the sultan of Bengal, Alauddin Hussein Shah, and hence are shunned by their fellow brahmins, meet Chaitanya Mahaprabhu for the first time. The meeting changes their lives.

They leave the service of the sultan and assume the renounced life of a sannyasin among Chaitanya's followers in Puri. Both brothers go on to become outstanding representatives of Gaudiya Vaishnava devotional thought as members of the influential Six Goswamis of Vrindavan, who had gathered around Chaitanya.

1514

South Asia: India
Christianity
Roman Catholic work in the Portuguese settlements of Cochin and Goa became two prominent mission stations within the Diocese of Funchal, based on the Madeira archipelago in the North Atlantic Ocean.

1514

Europe: Portugal
Christianity
Pope Leo X creates the Diocese of Funchal, based in the capital of the Madeira archipelago. It was placed under the authority of the Archdiocese of Lisbon, but given hegemony over all of the church's work in Portugal's foreign territory.

1514

Europe: Spain
Christianity
With the financial backing of Cardinal Francisco Jiménez de Cisneros, the Greek text of the New Testament was printed (but not published) as part of his Complutensian Polyglot Bible project. The completed Bible would be published in 1520.

1514

Southwest Asia and North Africa: Persia
Islam
The Battle of Chaldiran. To prevent the spread of Shi'a Islam into the Sunni Islamic Ottoman Empire, Sultan Selim I sends his army against that of Shah Ismail. Prior to the attack, the two had exchanged a set of increasingly hostile letters. The better-equipped Ottomans prevail after which they enter and briefly occupy the Persian capital, Tabriz. As quickly as he had attacked, Selim withdrew and retained control of almost none of the Persian territory.

1515

Sub-Saharan Africa: Ghana
Christianity
The Portuguese build Fort Santo Antonio at Axim on Ghana's southern coast.

1515

South Asia: India
Hinduism
Religious reformer and founder Lord Chaitanya Mahaprabhu visits the area near Mathura in Uttar Pradesh associated with the traditional life of Krishna, the incarnation of Lord Vishnu, who was believed to have grown up in Vrindavan. Through his spiritual awareness, he located the lost sites, one result being his founding of the modern town of Vrindavan. Subsequently, followers of Krishna, especially those who adhered to the form of Krishna devotion advocated by Chaitanya, are attracted to Vrindavan (and nearby sites also believed to be associatcd with Krishna), and temples began to be created. Soon after the town's establishment, Kapur Ram Das of Multan (Punjab) constructed the first temple in Vrindavan, the Madan Mohan Temple, located near the Kali Ghat.

1515

Europe: England
Christianity
Pope Leo X names Thomas Wolsey, Archbishop of York (England), to be a cardinal. Shortly thereafter, Henry VIII names him the lord high chancellor.

1515

Europe: France
Christianity
King Louis XII dies without a male, and his cousin Francis I (r. 1515–1547) inherits the throne and begins his long rule of France.

1515

Europe: Spain
Christianity
Spanish Catholics build the Church of Our Lady of the Remedies in Tenerife, Canary Islands.

1515

Europe: Spain
Christianity
Construction begins on the Cathedral of Juan de Albacete located in Albacete, Spain. It replaces a mosque that had stood on the site for many centuries.

1515

Southwest Asia and North Africa: Persia
Islam, Christianity
With little effort, Portuguese Indian governor Alfonso de Albuquerque recaptures Hormuz (Ormuz) at the mouth of the Persian Gulf. He keeps the local ruler on his throne, and Hormuz remains a Portuguese vassal state for the rest of the century.

1515–1516

Europe: France, Italy
Christianity
King Francis I of France and Pope Leo X negotiate a treaty, the Concordat of Bologna, that guaranteed the pope the right to collect the income from the Catholic Church in France, and the king of France the right to tithe the clerics, restrict their right of appeal over him to Rome, and nominate appointments to the top church positions, including archdiocese, diocese, and monastic establishments.

1516

South Asia: India
Hinduism
Krishna Deva Raya, the emperor of the Vijayanagara Empire, builds the Hundred-Pillared Mantapam (hall) at the Srikalahasti Temple, one of the important ancient Shiva temples of southern India.

1516

Europe: Denmark
Christianity

Pope Leo X sends the untactful papal nuncio Arcimboldi to Denmark with the goal of raising funds to rebuild St. Peter's Basilica in Rome.

1516

Europe: Germany
Christianity

German artist Matthias Grünewald completes work on his most famous piece, the altarpiece painted for the Monastery of St. Anthony in Isenheim, whose residents became most noted for their care of victims of the plague and those who had skin diseases. The monks were dedicated to Saint Anthony, the protector and healer of Saint Anthony's fire, a condition acquired from poisoning by ergot.

1516

Europe: Italy
Christianity

Pope Leo X names the bishop of Tortosa (Spain) and the future pope Adrian as the cardinal priest of the Basilica of Saints John and Paul in Rome.

1516

Europe: Italy
Judaism

The ruling doges of Venice discuss the possible expulsion of Jews and decide to allow them to remain in the city, but confine their residence to Ghetto Nuova, a small, somewhat inhospitable island. Though Jews had for centuries created Jewish communities within urban environs throughout Europe, often on the edge or outside the fortified walls of cities, the Venetians create the first Jewish ghetto, an area designated to maintain a Jewish presence with its associated economic advantages while keeping interaction between the Jews and Christians to a minimum. The establishment of formal ghettos will spread in Italy and then throughout Europe.

1516

Europe: Spain
Christianity

Joanna, the queen of Castile (r. 1504–1555), becomes the queen of Aragon (r. 1516–1555). Her eldest son,

Charles I (r. 1516–1556), already the king of Burgundy, joins her as co-ruler.

1516

Europe: Switzerland
Christianity

From Basel, Christian humanist scholar Erasmus (1466–1536) issues the Greek New Testament, the first publication of the text in the West in its original Greek. Heretofore, the Latin translation made by Jerome in the fourth century had been in common use. In fact, another edition of the Greek New Testament assembled by Cardinal Francisco Jiménez de Cisneros was set in print in Spain, but as Cisneros was working on a vast project to publish a number of texts in different languages of the complete Bible, he had delayed publication of his Greek text.

In the meantime, Erasmus had worked with a variety of surviving Greek manuscripts. It will be acknowledged by his scholarly colleagues as the most accurate version of the Greek text available. Added to the new edition is a fresh translation of the New Testament in Latin, which becomes controversial as it differs in places from the Vulgate translation of Jerome, then in common use.

Erasmus receives the exclusive privilege of publishing the Greek New Testament, which has the effect of blocking Cardinal Cisneros from publishing his Bible, which was ready in 1517. It will finally appear in 1520.

1516

Southwest Asia and North Africa: Yemen
Islam

The Mamluk rulers of Egypt annex Yemen. Their victory is short-lived as during the following year, the Mamluk governor surrenders to the Ottomans, and Ottoman forces take official control of Egyptian territory on the Arabian Peninsula. Over the next generation, the Ottomans will introduce strong Sunni Islamic influences into predominantly Shi'a Islamic Yemen.

1516–1517

Southwest Asia and North Africa: Asia Minor
Islam

DESIDERIUS ERASMUS (CA. 1466/1469–1536)

Desiderius Erasmus was one of the great humanist thinkers of the turn of the 16th century. He wrote on many different subjects, including theology and education, and his book *Moriae encomium (The Praise of Folly)* was one of the best-selling works of his age.

Erasmus was born on October 27, 1469 (or possibly 1466 or 1467) in Rotterdam, Holland (now the Netherlands). He went to Paris, France, in 1495 to begin studying theology, but he was impressed by the humanists in Paris and started to establish himself as a scholar. He came to widespread public attention when he wrote a preface to Robert Gaguin's history of France, published in 1495. He went in 1499 to England, where he met his lifelong friend Thomas More and the future Henry VIII. The next few years saw Erasmus moving around Europe, studying Greek, working on amending the corrupt text of Saint Jerome, and, as he saw it, restoring true theology. He published one of his most famous works, *Enchiridion militis Christiani (Handbook of a Christian Knight)*, in 1503. The work is a guide to Christian attitudes and behavior with an emphasis on constant warfare against sin. He was heavily influenced by the Franciscan friar Jehan Vitrier. The next year, he found a manuscript of Lorenzo Valla's *Annotationes* on the New Testament, which inspired him to revise the New Testament itself.

Erasmus wrote his famed work *The Praise of Folly* during 1509–1511 while he was staying in England at More's house. Primarily a satire targeting theologians and rhetoricians, the book became an instant best-seller when it was published.

In 1516, Erasmus published a huge edition of the works of Saint Jerome and an annotated Greek and Latin New Testament. Both of those were landmark books and widely acclaimed and reprinted, though many were shocked at Erasmus's giving priority to the Greek text over the Latin Vulgate version of the Bible. Martin Luther was one of his detractors, and Erasmus found himself debating the young reformer over Luther's idea that humans are totally corrupt and unable to do anything to aid their own salvation. He published those ideas in 1524 in *De libero arbitrio (Concerning Free Will)*.

During his last years, Erasmus suffered from ill health, the loss of friends, and the tumult that the early Reformation engendered. His last major work was *Ecclesiastes* (date unknown), a comprehensive treatise on the art of preaching. Erasmus died on July 12, 1536, in Basel, Switzerland.

ABC-CLIO

Having had success in a war with the Persians, Ottoman sultan Selim I regrouped his army and attacked the Mamluk Sultanate of Egypt who ruled much of southwest Asia. They relatively quickly defeated the Mamluks and took control of much of the territory of the older Muslim caliphate including Syria, Palestine, Arabia, and Egypt. The victory led to a major shift in power throughout the Mediterranean world.

The Ottoman victory also reshaped Eastern orthodoxy. The patriarchates of Alexandria, Antioch, and Jerusalem now came under the control of the Ottoman Empire. The sultan allowed the three patriarchates to remain autonomous jurisdictions, but on a less formal level, the three jurisdictions came under the influence of the ecumenical patriarch in Constantinople, simply because of the patriarch's closeness to the sultan and his appointment as the ethnarch of the Orthodox Christians. From this point, the role and influence of the ecumenical patriarch increased century by century. The first sign of this new situation occurred soon after Selim captured Jerusalem when the sultan granted Patriarch Theoleptus the right to maintain (and therefore control) the Church of the Holy Sepulchre, one of the most holy sites of Christendom.

After capturing Cairo, Sultan Selim I executes Tuman Bey, the last Mamluk ruler of Egypt, but leaves the Mamluks in power as an Egyptian ruling class.

Also, following the victory, Selim claims the title of caliph, while retaining Istanbul as his capital. The Ottomans thus took possession of the history of the previous Umayyad, Abbasid, and Fatimid/Mamluk caliphates. Now in control of the Muslim holy cities—Mecca and Medina—Selim also assumed a lesser version of the traditional title, Ruler of the Two Holy Shrines, terming himself the "Servant of the Two Holy Shrines." Selim took the emblems of his office, the sword and the mantle of Muhammad, both of which would find their way into the Topkapi Palace Museum, where they remain to the present.

1517

South Asia: India
Hinduism
Krishnadevaraya, the ruler of the Vijayanagara, visits the Tirumala Venkateswara Temple in Andhra Pradesh and makes lavish donations of gold and jewels.

1517

South Asia: Sri Lanka
Christianity
The Portuguese establish a fort at Colombo on the western coast of Sri Lanka. They begin to take control of the coastal area of the island and to introduce, often in a brutal manner, Roman Catholic Christianity.

1517

East and Southeast Asia: China
Buddhism
Gedun Gyatso, later to be designated the second Dalai Lama, becomes the abbot of Drepung Monastery, a monastery of the Gelupga school of Tibetan Buddhism.

1517

Europe: Germany
Judaism
Johannes Reuchlin initiates the Christian appropriation of Jewish mysticism as embodied in the Kabbalah with the publication of his *De Arte Cabbalistica.*

1517

Europe: Italy
Christianity
Some leading bishops and priests in Rome form the Oratory of Divine Love to reform the church through a new emphasis on piety and devotion.

March 15. The last session of the Fifth Lateran Council meets in Rome. Most of the decisions of the council would never be implemented.

July 3. Pope Leo X makes significant changes in the College of Cardinals by naming 31 new cardinals all at one time. This action culminates a purge of the college following the uncovering of a plot by several cardinals to poison the pope. He has one cardinal executed and dismisses a number of others, not otherwise involved in the plot, for living a decadent life incompatible with their office.

1517

Europe: Italy
Judaism
Italian Christian merchant Daniel Bomberg establishes a Hebrew press and publishes the Hebrew Bible.

His edition will include the commentaries. He will later publish both the Babylonian and Palestinian Talmuds (1521–1522).

1517

Europe: Italy
Christianity

The nuns at the Church of Saint Silvestro in Rome are forbidden to exhibit a piece of cloth they possess believed to picture the face of Jesus of Nazareth. Their image competes for attention with Veronica's Veil, another piece of cloth also believed to have Jesus's image, which is kept at St. Peter's Basilica. The image of Saint Silvestro is now housed in the Vatican.

1517

Russia, Central Asia, and the Caucasus: Belarus
Christianity

Operating in Prague, Roman Catholic monk Francysk Skaryna prints the first book (and the first selection from the Bible) in the Old Belarusian recension of Church Slavonic, *The Psalter.* Over the next two years he will additionally print 23 additional books of the Bible. His work is the first translation and publication of the Bible into an Eastern Slavic language.

1517

Southwest Asia and North Africa: Arabia
Islam

Barakat bin Muhammed, the sharif, that is, the local authority in Mecca, formally acknowledges the supremacy of the Ottoman caliph as leader of the Sunni Muslim world. He retains, however, considerable local autonomy in managing the affairs of the city and the mosque that is the object of the annual pilgrimage.

October 31, 1517

Europe: Germany
Christianity

German monk Martin Luther posts his Ninety-Five Theses (points for debate) concerning indulgences and other questionable issues relative to popular religious practices on the door of the Castle Church in Wittenberg.

1518

Central America and the Caribbean: Cuba
Christianity

Pope Leo X establishes the Diocese of All Cuba (including Louisiana and Florida). In 1522, the seat of the diocese was designated as the city of Santiago de Cuba.

1518

East and Southeast Asia: Japan
Shinto

The local lord Ouchi Yoshioki, who had recently traveled to the Ise Shrines, builds Yamaguchi Daijingu, a small version of Ise, at Yamaguchi. Like Ise, it possesses an outer and inner shrine, and is on a schedule to be rebuilt every 20 years.

1518

Europe: Germany
Christianity

February. In response to the circulation of Luther's 95 theses, Pope Leo orders the vicar-general of the Augustinian Order, to which Luther and several of his associates belong, to impose silence on them.

Biblical scholar Philipp Melanchthon joins the faculty at the University of Wittenberg.

May. Johann Tetzel (1465–1519), a Dominican monk and theologian who sold indulgences throughout Germany, counters Luther's 95 theses with 50 theses of his own.

1518

Europe: Italy
Christianity

The Italian artist Titian completes his large oil painting of the *Assumption of the Virgin,* which is installed on the high altar in the Basilica of Santa Maria Gloriosa dei Frari in Venice.

1518

Europe: Spain
Christianity

A small crowd gathers to watch as Martin Luther directs the posting of his Ninety-Five Theses, protesting the practice of the sale of indulgences, to the door of the castle church in Wittenberg, Germany. The Ninety-Five Theses would spark the birth of the Protestant religion and the subsequent Reformation. (Library of Congress)

The foundation is laid for the new cathedral of Granada on the site formerly occupied by the city's main mosque. For centuries under Muslim control, the emirate of Granada had surrendered to a coalition army of Spanish Christians in 1492.

1518

Russia, Central Asia, and the Caucasus: Russia
Christianity

Ecumenical Patriarch Theoleptos, who had been cultivating good relations with Grand Prince of Moscow Vasili III, who ruled what had become the largest independent predominantly Orthodox kingdom, dispatches the scholar Maximus the Greek as a consultant to the Russian church. His first accomplishment would be the production, in league with some Russian translators, of a Russian psalter. He would subsequently emerge as a leading voice opposing those who advocate the ownership of land and property by the monastic communities.

October 12–14, 1518

Europe: Germany
Christianity

Martin Luther is originally summoned to appear in Rome, but the summons is replaced with a meeting at Augsburg, in which Luther confronts Thomas Cardinal Cajetan (1469–1534). The pair discuss Luther's ideas that have begun to negatively affect the church's program in Germany, but Luther fails to back away from his theses.

1519

Europe: Germany
Judaism

MARTIN LUTHER (1483–1546)

Martin Luther, an Augustinian monk and professor of theology at the new University of Wittenberg, Saxony, began a relatively mild critique of the Roman Catholic Church at the beginning of the 16th century that quickly turned into a complete call for the reformation of the church. The Reformation movement he initiated would find support especially in northern Europe and result in the formation of the Evangelical (Lutheran) Church based in Germany and Scandinavia that would in subsequent centuries become a worldwide phenomenon.

Luther's studies and lectures led to a belief that Christian salvation focused on a new relationship with God that was based in faith in Christ rather than deeds of merit (such as pilgrimages, acts of piety, or the purchase of indulgences) done by the individual. He concluded that a Christian was also a sinner and hence undeserving of God's love. God nevertheless redeemed individuals and out of that new relationship started by God, the individual believer tried to conform his or her life to God's will. With this new insight, Luther turned his attention to Paul's letter to the Romans, out of which came his own personal experience of salvation. He came to feel that God had forgiven his sin and that he had received that salvation by faith and faith alone. Luther then moved from his intense personal experiences into the middle of a very public controversy. Johann Tetzel, a Dominican monk, traveled through Germany to sell indulgences. Any funds he raised were forwarded to Rome to cover the cost of building St. Peter's Cathedral.

Luther saw indulgences, especially the commercialization of them by Tetzel, as a practice built on bad theology and a complete misunderstanding of grace, faith, and biblical salvation. He decided to challenge the practice and did so by proposing 95 points for debate. These points were written down and the list, reputedly, nailed to the door of the parish church at Wittenberg on October 31, 1517. The sale of indulgences dropped dramatically. Tetzel attempted to recover by proposing a set of counterpoints. Luther and Tetzel's interaction led to a debate, though Tetzel would be replaced by theologian Johann Eck. The debate was held in 1519 in Leipzig. Luther built his defense by direct reference to the Bible, its text being cited to refute the rulings of popes and church councils. He claimed that both popes and councils had made mistakes, and was subsequently declared a heretic and excommunicated.

In response to the debate and subsequent excommunication, Luther made his case to a larger audience in three lengthy essays published in 1520. The *Appeal to the German Nobility* centered on the idea of the priesthood of all believers. The effect of asserting that every person was a priest had in effect removed some authority from parish priests and recast it in terms of the personal relationship between God and the believer. The whole concept would unfortunately soon be taken in some quite radical (and even violent) ways, much to Luther's consternation. He took up the subject of the church's elaborate sacramental system in *Baby-lonian Captivity of the Church* and concluded that only two of the church's sacraments, baptism and the Lord's Supper, met the criteria for continuation. On a lesser but not unimportant point, Luther argued that the cup of wine representing the blood of Christ should be given to the believers when the Lord's Supper was celebrated. Finally, Luther laid out a more systematic and complete understanding of faith in God, salvation, and the Christian life in *The Freedom of the Christian Man*.

Access to one of the new printing presses invented in the previous century by Johann Gutenberg, however, allowed the relatively quick circulation of Luther's writings, and their broad circulation led the emperor of the Holy Roman Empire to summon Luther to the meeting of its governing body, the Diet, which met at Worms. In defending his writings, Luther appealed to the Bible and to reason. The Diet condemned him, but the secular ruler of the region, Frederick, the elector of Saxony, was very protective of his university, its faculty, and Luther in particular. During the remaining 16 years of his life, Luther devoted much of his time to writing, and he completed a German translation of the Bible.

The Lutheran Reformation destroyed the religious unity of Europe, previously based in Roman Catholicism. The movement not only came to dominate much of northern Europe, but it created a situation in which further dissent led to the creation of modern Anglicanism in England, and the adherents of John Calvin's variant Reformation perspective came to control much of Switzerland, Holland, and Scotland. The whole Reformation would raise considerations of religious toleration and the status of minority dissenting religious groups, most notably the Mennonites and the Unitarians.

J. GORDON MELTON

The city of Regensburg, which has experienced a generation of decline, blames its problems upon the Jewish residents and expels them. The only remaining Jewish communities of importance in Germany are to be found at Worms and Frankfurt.

1519

Europe: Germany, Spain
Christianity
The Holy Roman emperor Maximilian dies. His son Philip having died in 1506, he is succeeded as emperor by his teenage grandson Charles V (r. 1519–1558). Charles had by marriage become the ruler of Aragon, Castile, and the Spanish colonies in Asia and the Americas. As the first person to rule both Castile-León and Aragon simultaneously in his own right, he is acknowledged as the first king of Spain. He also rules Burgundy. As he becomes aware of the extent of his domains and the wealth it was providing him, he also perceives his role as that of assuming leadership of Christendom and holding off any significant threat from the Islamic world as embodied in the Ottoman Empire.

1519

Europe: Spain
Christianity
Charles I, the king of Aragon and Castile (Spain), becomes Charles V (r. 1519–1555), the emperor of the

expansive Holy Roman Empire. A Roman Catholic, he will have to contend with both the Muslim Turkish threat entering his realm from the east and the religious reformation threatening to divide the territory under his authority from within. Like the king of Spain, he ruled much of Europe and had control of lands around the world.

1519

Europe: Switzerland
Christianity
Ulrich Zwingli moves from Einsiedeln to Zurich where he becomes head priest of the Grossminster, the main Roman Catholic church in the area.

1519–1521

Central America and the Caribbean: Mexico
Traditional Religions, Christianity
The Aztec leader Moctezuma welcomes Spanish conquistador Hernán Cortés and the 650 men accompanying him to the capital at Tenochtitlán. Moctezuma believes that Cortés could be the white-skinned deity Quetzalcoatl, whose return had been foretold in Aztec mythology. Meanwhile, Cortés and his men react to the riches the Aztecs have accumulated and are somewhat stunned by their practice of human sacrifice, which has a central role in their religion and public life. They systematically plunder Tenochtitlán and destroy the temples at which the sacrifices are conducted. Hostilities continue for several years, but the small force, armed with superior weaponry, prevails. The Spanish force defeats the Aztec empire, numbering some 25 million in 1521.

When the main Aztec temple is destroyed, the Spanish use its stones to erect a Catholic church.

1519–1522

Portuguese explorer Fernando Magellan leads an expedition that circles the globe, though he is killed when his ship stops in the Philippine islands.

July 4–14, 1519

Europe: Germany
Christianity

Emperors of the Aztec Empire, 1376–1521

Reign[1]	Name
1376–1396	Acamapichtli (chieftain at Tenochtitlán; traditional founder of Aztec royal house)
1396–1416	Huitzilihuitl (son)
1416–1427	Chimalpopoca (son)
1427–1440	Izcoatl (son of Acamapichtli)
1440–1469	Moctezuma I
1469–1481	Axayacatl (grandson of Izcoatl)
1481–1486	Tizoc
1486–1502	Ahuitzotl
1502–1520	Moctezuma II, Xocoyotzin (son of Axayacatl)
1520	Cuitláhuac
1520–1521	Cuauhtémoc (son of Ahuitzotl)

[1]Dates before 1468 are approximate.

Martin Luther debates Catholic theologian Johann Eck (1486–1543) at Leipzig. Eck compares Luther's thoughts to the ideas of John Hus who had been condemned as a heretic and executed by burning at the stake a century earlier. Luther asserts scripture as a greater authority than the pope or church councils.

ca. 1520

East and Southeast Asia: Philippines
Islam
Sharif Mohammed Kabungsuwan, a prince of Johor, flees Malaysia and establishes himself on Mindanao, southern Philippines, marries locally, and founds the Sultanate of Maguindanao, which rules parts of the island of Mindanao and becomes a point of dissemination of Islam through the islands.

ca. 1520

Southwest Asia and North Africa: Asia Minor
Islam, Christianity
Ottoman sultan Selim I orders a takeover of all Christian churches in his realms. He uses as his basis the fact that there was no written document (called a *firman*) that protected their right to exist and his own desire to convert everyone to Islam. At this point, the

AZTEC RELIGION

The religion of the Mexica evolved as they incorporated other divinities and other ethnic groups into the empire. The Mexica ruled from a theocratic position; every political and military decision depended upon consultation with the divine. The leader, the tlatoani, was "he who speaks," indicating that he communicated with both human and divine beings. Many pre-Hispanic images and some poetic texts recovered from the colonial era present the tlatoani preparing for communication with the divine. The first step in preparation for this event was to perform an auto-sacrificial bloodletting. Another method for assuring favor with the divine was the offering of human sacrifices.

The practice of human sacrifice was one of the most important tenets of Mesoamerican religion. In Mesoamerica, there were several types of human sacrifice: auto-sacrifice, sacrifice to emulate a divinity, and prisoner sacrifice. In each case, the idea that blood is the most precious fluid and that it must be offered to please specific divinities serves to justify the practice. In auto-sacrifice, a person, usually a tlatoani or a priest, lets blood from the earlobe, the hand, the tongue, or the genitals in imitation of the divinity Tlaloc, who offers his precious fluid—water—as the rain. The written records throughout Mesoamerica illustrate auto-sacrificial rituals practiced by warriors preparing for battle and by rulers requesting or receiving counsel from their ancestors.

Many of the rituals based upon the calendar included the practice of human sacrifice to emulate a divinity. The victims, often chosen from the local population, would be dressed as a specific divinity and sacrificed in imitation of that divinity. These sacrifices were often performed by decapitation, and the victim's skin would be used as the costume of a priest. In the ritual for celebrating the corn harvest dedicated to the divinity Xipe Totec, "The Flayed God," the victim's skin served as a metaphor for the dried cornhusks around the ripe ear of corn. Other divinities who received human sacrifices in imitation included Tlazoteotl, "She Who Eats Our Filth" (also known as Inn Tonan, "Our Mother"), and Tlaloc, the patron of rain who received the sacrifice of crying children to assure the proper amounts of rain. These sacrifices lean more to the agrarian focus of the empire than to the militaristic endeavors.

A third form of sacrifice combined both militaristic and fertility images. The practice of prisoner sacrifice became the motivating force behind the Mexica military machine. The Mexica believed that the blood of a sacrificed warrior taken captive in battle would nourish the sun and assure its daily path across the sky. This was performed in emulation of the Aztec sun god Nanahuatl, who sacrificed himself into a bonfire in the ancient city of Teotihuacan to become the sun. After this auto-sacrifice, the new sun then demanded that the other divinities who witnessed the event sacrifice themselves to feed him with enough energy to move across the sky. The Mexica wanted to assure the rising of the sun each day, so daily prisoner sacrifices were instituted. These were usually heart sacrifices.

(continued)

Prisoner sacrifice also resulted as the product of an alliance between Tenochtitlán and two neighboring states: Texcoco and Tlaxcala. During a severe drought, the rulers of the three states decided to implement the xochiyaoyotl, "Flowery War," in which warriors would be captured for sacrifice to the divinity Tezcatlipoca, the patron of the military class. The blood of these warriors was supposed to coax the divinity to return a magical obsidian mirror that predicted floods and droughts. Agrarian concerns once again became part of the mechanics of military warfare and conquest. The forces would meet in ritualized battle on a monthly basis for the purpose of taking captives to sacrifice.

ABC-CLIO

ecumenical patriarch Theoleptus uses his close relationship with the sultan to call the order into question and then present a counter case. He argued that when Constantinople had been conquered, all the churches of the city (with a few exceptions) were generally spared harm and have since been used for Christian worship. Theoleptus is eventually able to convince the sultan to rescind his original order.

1520

East and Southeast Asia: China
The Zhengde emperor offers the Portuguese embassy his blessing during a visit to Nanjing. The Portuguese, however, suffer under negative rumors circulated by their competitors, and following the Zhengde emperor's death the next year, are pushed out of the country by Chinese authorities.

1520

East and Southeast Asia: Indonesia
The Portuguese established a trading post in the village of Lamakera on the eastern side of Solor Island, one of the Lesser Sunda Islands of Indonesia. The work of converting the local population to Roman Catholicism begins.

1520

Europe: Denmark
Christianity
King Christian II, sensing the general dissatisfaction of his citizens with Rome and the particular problem created by papal nuncio Arcimboldi, who has been raising money for the building of St. Peter's Basilica, expels Arcimboldi from his realm and invites Lutheran theologians to Copenhagen, thus initiating the Protestant Reformation in the land. Christian subsequently initiates a series of changes that will lead to the establishment of a national church in Denmark. He forbids appeals to Rome and assigns final jurisdiction in ecclesiastical matters to the ruler and Diet.

1520

Europe: Germany
Christianity
August. Martin Luther issues the first of three important essays concerning the foundational issues upon which the Protestant Reformation will be built, *Appeal to the German Nobility,* in which he develops his understanding of the priesthood of all believers.

October. In his essay *The Babylobian Captivity,* Martin Luther tackles issues concerning the Christian sacraments, claiming that there are but two—baptism and the Lord's Supper.

November. In his essay on *Christian Liberty,* Martin Luther discusses the nature of faith and the love that flows from it.

December 10. Martin Luther responds to the papal bull threatening him with excommunication by publicly burning a copy of it.

1520

Europe: Holy Roman Empire
Christianity

As the relationship between Charles, the Holy Roman emperor, and Francis I of France deteriorated, Francis went to war with contested lands in Italy as the subject of hostilities. The Papal States will be deeply involved in the wars and suffer when its ally France loses. More importantly for the long run, the hostilities will focus the pope's attention away from the Reformation in Germany.

1520

Europe: Italy
Judaism

Solomon ibn Varga, a Sephardic Jew, writes an essay on the problems of Jewish persecution. He sees divine punishment behind contemporary Jewish suffering, but also blames current secular sources. Though written in Italy, *The Rod of Judah* will be published in the Ottoman Empire.

1520

Europe: Italy
Christianity

Spanish Muslim scholar al-Hasan ibn Muhammad al-Wazzan al-Fasi receives baptism from Pope Leo X and launches a new career in Italy that will include sharing information on Islam and North Africa with the European world. He will author an important book describing all he saw in his travels in Africa (1555), which would become a best-seller in its day.

1520

Europe: Spain
Christianity

Following the expiration of Erasmus's exclusive right to publish the Greek New Testament, Pope Leo X sanctions Cardinal Francisco Jiménez de Cisneros in the publishing of his monumental Complutensian Polyglot Bible, the first polyglot edition of the entire Christian scripture. Appearing in six volumes, the first four volumes contained Latin, Greek, Aramaic, and Hebrew texts of the Old Testament, and the fifth volume the Greek and Latin texts of the New Testament. Volume six includes a dictionary and various study aids.

Cardinal Cisneros, better known as Cardinal Ximenes, had been a leading cleric in Spain who also served as the confessor to the queen of Spain. By the time his Bible was actually published, he had died.

1520

Europe: Sweden
Christianity

Christian II, the ruler of Denmark, conquers Sweden. Several days after his being anointed by Swedish archbishop Gustav Trolle as the new ruler in Stockholm Cathedral, he had more than 80 of his political enemies, beginning with the bishops of Skara and Strängnäs, arrested and executed. All were charged with heresy.

1520

Southwest Asia and North Africa: Asia Minor
Islam

Sultan Selim I becomes unexpectedly ill and dies. He is succeeded by his son Suleiman I (r. 1520–1566), better known in the west as Suleiman the Magnificent. He would become the longest-reigning ruler of the Ottoman Dynasty.

1520–1521

Sub-Saharan Africa: Congo
Christianity

Henrique, the son of Mvemba Nzinga, the Christian king of Congo, who has been studying in Lisbon, is ordained a priest and shortly thereafter consecrated as a bishop. He returns home as the titular bishop of Utica (in Tunisia), as the Portuguese church leaders oppose the erection of a diocese in Congo. He will serve only two years and not be replaced following his death (ca. 1526).

June 15, 1520

Europe: Italy, Germany
Christianity

Pope Leo X (r. 1513–1521) issues *Exsurge Domine,* a papal bull that condemns 41 propositions taken from Luther's teachings and gives him 60 days to recant or be declared a heretic. Apostolic Nuncio Johann Eck carries the document with him to Germany.

August 28, 1520

Europe: Serbia
Islam, Christianity

The new sultan of the Ottoman Empire, Suleiman the Magnificent, captures the citadel of Belgrade (Serbia).

1521

Central America and the Caribbean: Guadeloupe
Christianity
Spanish Catholic priests attempting to set up a mission on the island of Guadeloupe are killed.

1521

Central America and the Caribbean: Mexico
Judaism
A number of Jews who had converted to Christianity have migrated to Mexico. To limit their growing influence, Spain issues a new regulation demanding that anyone planning to migrate to Spanish foreign territory must document at least four generations of Christian (i.e., Roman Catholic) ancestry. While slowing the flow of New Christians to Mexico, some are able to acquire the needed credentials by fraud and bribery.

1521

East and Southeast Asia: China
Chinese Religions
The emperor Zhengde dies and is succeeded by his cousin, the 14-year-old Zhu Houcong, who reigns as the Jiajing emperor (r. 1521–1567). The new emperor would come to live a life largely in isolation apart from the many young concubines he kept and Taoist priests. It is rumored he indulged in a search for immortality and to that end drank the menstrual blood of the concubines.

1521

East and Southeast Asia: China
Chinese Religions
The emperor Jiajing has a new temple constructed near the Miaoying Temple west of the Forbidden City that becomes the center over the next centuries for the maintainance of worship directed toward the emperors and the more notable of the country's leading court officials. Spirit tablets representing the former emperors are placed in the temple and each new emperor's name will be placed on a tablet in the main hall, while the names of honored government ministers are placed in a side hall.

1521

East and Southeast Asia: China
Confucianism
Chinese philosopher Wang Yangming criticizes the current dominant school of thought in China, the neo-Confucianism of Zhu Xi.

1521

East and Southeast Asia: Japan
Buddhism
The Japanese shogun Ashikaga Yoshitane loses in a power struggle for control of the country with the military commander Hosokawa Takakuni. Yoshitane withdraws to Awaji Island, and Takakuni sees to the installation of Ashikaga Yoshiharu (r. 1521–1546) as shogun. He would remain on the throne for almost a quarter of a century, but have little power as the shogunate was under the control of the Hosokawa clan.

1521

East and Southeast Asia: Malaysia
Christianity
Duarte Coelho, a Portuguese captain, constructs the first Roman Catholic church in Melacca on a hill overlooking the city. Jesuit missionary Francis Xavier will originally be buried in this church in 1553.

1521

East and Southeast Asia: Philippines
Christianity
Spanish explorer Ferdinand Magellan, after reaching the Marianas and Guam, arrives in the Philippines. On Cebu Island, he witnesses the baptism of the local ruler Rajah Humabon and his queen Hara Amihan as Christian. He then turns to do battle with Humabon's enemy, Datu Lapu-Lapu, on Mactan Island. Some of his men who survive him complete his voyage around the globe.

1521

Europe: Denmark
Christianity
After attempting sweeping reforms through his realm, King Christian II of Denmark is deposed and his uncle

WANG YANGMING (1472–1529)

Wang Yangming was one of the most influential Chinese philosophers in history. His ideas centered around the concept that knowledge and action were complementary. Wang's teachings were counter to the dominant school of Chinese thought because he believed that knowledge was innate within a person, not learned from books. His teachings greatly influenced Japanese intellectuals, particularly those responsible for Japan's modernization in the 19th century.

Wang was born Wang Shoujen in 1472 in a district southeast of Hangzhow, Chekiang. His family was one of scholars and officials, and the boy received a traditional education. Wang passed the examination for *chin-shih,* the highest academic degree, in 1499. As was normal in the well-organized Chinese society of the time, Wang entered the bureaucracy. Although Wang was a successful general and statesman, his greatest legacy was his philosophy. When he was born, the dominant school of thought was the neo-Confucianism of Zhu Xi. Zhu Xi lived during the 12th century. He was a Confucian scholar and studied the classical writings. He standardized the Four Books of Confucianism, which became the basis of the Chinese educational system, as well as the basis for examinations for candidates to enter the bureaucracy. Over the years, Zhu Xi's system became petrified and unchanging. Mastery of the past masterpieces, especially demonstrations of reading and memorization, quotations, and allusions were considered the most important criteria. Independent thinking and questioning was downplayed.

Wang criticized Zhu Xi's system openly by 1521. Wang believed that a person was born with the knowledge of right and wrong and the ability to do what was correct. Selfish impulses and thoughts kept a person from doing the right thing. Although Wang considered education and reading the Confucian classics to be important, he believed the path to truth was through developing a person's intuitive knowledge. Meditation to open one's mind to the truth was important. He presented four basic concepts.

Wang's teaching gave priority to willingness to work and taking one's social and political responsibilities seriously. Although his philosophy included both Daoist and Buddhist elements, Wang criticized both those philosophies for their renunciation of human relations and social responsibilities. His teaching spread quickly, despite the opposition of the followers of Zhu Xi. Wang's effect was also long-lasting in Japan, where the Oyo-mei school adopted his philosophy. Many of the 20th-century Japanese leaders who restored the emperor and opened Japan to Western ideas and technology were influenced by Wang.

TIM WATTS

Friedrich installed on the throne. Christian moves to Germany, where he is influenced by the Reformation and begins to side with the new Protestant movement.

1521

Europe: England
Christianity

In response to King Henry VIII's authoring *Assertio Septem Sacramentorum* (Defense of the Seven Sacraments) to refute Martin Luther's teachings, Pope Leo X conferred the title "Defender of the Faith" upon the British monarch.

1521

Europe: Germany
Christianity

On January 3, Pope Leo issues the bull *Decet Romanum Pontificem,* which formally excommunicates Martin Luther. Simultaneously, he asks Holy Roman Emperor Charles V to move more decisively against heretics in his realm. In April, Martin Luther appears before the Diet of the Holy Roman Empire convened at Worms to defend his ideas. It is here he is reputed to have made his famous statement concluding his defense, "Here I stand, I can do no other." Following the Diet of Worms, at which Luther is declared an outlaw, friends kidnap him and take him to Wartburg Castle for his protection. He will remain there almost a year.

Philipp Melanchthon completes the first Protestant systematic theological text, *Loci Communes.*

1521

Europe: Italy
Christianity

Leo responds to complaints by the Greek Catholics, Catholics who follow an Eastern Greek liturgy while acknowledging papal authority, by forbidding the clergy of the Latin rite to celebrate mass in Greek Catholic churches and stops future ordinations of Greek clergy by Latin bishops. This action presages the emergence of Eastern rite Catholics as an important semiautonomous segment of the Roman Catholic Church.

1521

Europe: Serbia, Hungary
Islam, Christianity

Ottoman sultan Suleiman the Magnificent disregards the truce signed by his predecessor and moves against Belgrade, which he takes from Hungary. Pope Leo responds by sending the Hungarians a large sum of money for their continued efforts against the Ottomans. The victory makes possible the further expansion of Islamic control of Eastern Europe.

1521

Russia, Central Asia, and the Caucasus: Russia
Christianity

Varlaam, the metropolitan of Moscow and All Russia, comes into conflict with Prince Vasily III as Varlaam refuses to sanction Vasily's divorce from his current (and childless) wife in order to marry another woman. Vasily removes the metropolitan from office and has him imprisoned in shackles in the Kyrilo-Beloozersky Monastery, located north of Moscow. Vasily subsequently appoints Daniel (r. 1522–1539), the hegumen (abbot) of Joseph-Volokolamsk Monastery, to succeed Varlaam, and Daniel eventually approves of the divorce.

1521

Southwest Asia and North Africa: Bahrain
Islam, Christianity

Determined to assume control of the local pearl industry, the Portuguese in the Persian Gulf under Antonio Correia invade Bahrain.

1521

Southwest Asia and North Africa: Palestine
Judaism

While residing in Sefed (now Zefat, in northern Israel), Joseph Caro completes his massive *House of Joseph,* his commentary on Jacob ben Asher's *The Four Columns,* a code of Jewish law compiled in the 14th century. Caro tracks each law to its Talmud origin, discusses its development, and offers his opinion on how best to observe it.

May 1521

Europe: Holy Roman Empire
Christianity

Pope Leo X signs a new treaty with the Holy Roman emperor Charles V. It represents a realignment against

France and provides for Milan and Genoa to move from French control to that of the empire, and Parma and Piacenza to be returned to the Papal States as soon as the French could be expelled.

December 1, 1521

Europe: Italy
Christianity
Pope Leo X dies and is succeeded by Pope Adrian VI (r. 1522–1523), a bishop from what is now Holland. He will be the last non-Italian elected as pope until the late 20th century.

1522

Sub-Saharan Africa: Mozambique
Christianity
The Portuguese construct the Chapel of Nossa Senhora de Baluarte, the oldest surviving European building in the southern hemisphere. It is located on the most eastern point of the island adjacent to Fort Sao Sebastiao (constructed beginning in 1558).

1522

Central America and the Caribbean: Mexico
Christianity
Franciscan friars arrive in Mexico.

1522

East and Southeast Asia: Indonesia
Islam
The Dutch, who have opened relations with the Javanese kingdom of Sunda, receive permission to build a port at what is now the city of Jakarta. They are seen as an ally who will help protect Sunda from the rising power of the Sultanate of Demak that has emerged in central Java.

1522

Europe: Germany
Christianity
Luther publishes the New Testament, which he has translated into German using the new Greek text prepared and recently published by Erasmus.

1522

Europe: Greece
Islam, Christianity
Forces of the Ottoman Empire lay siege to the Greek island of Rhodes and successfully drive the Knights of Saint John from their island stronghold. The victory gives the Ottomans control of the Eastern Mediterranean.

1522

Europe: Switzerland
Christianity
The second edition of *Novum Instrumentum omne,* the Greek New Testament prepared by Erasmus, appears. It will be this edition that will later be used by William Tyndale when he translates the first *English New Testament* (1526) and still later by translators of the Geneva Bible and the King James Version.

1522

Southwest Asia and North Africa: Asia Minor
Christianity
Ecumenical Patriarch Theoleptus, who had a cordial relationship with Selim, finds himself increasingly isolated under the successor regime. His status was undercut by charges of his leading an immoral private life. As trial looms before him, he dies. He is succeeded by Jeremias I (r. 1522–1545), the archbishop of Sofia (Bulgaria). Jeremias will have the longest reign of any ecumenical patriarch.

Summer 1522

Europe: Greece
Islam, Christianity
Forces of Suleiman the Magnificent lay siege to the stronghold of the Knights Hospitaller on the island of Rhodes in the Aegean. After holding out for five months, the knights surrender and leave the island for a new base on Malta.

Following the fall of Rhodes, the Roman Catholic Church reorganizes its work in the Greek Islands and elevates the Diocese of Naxos (founded in the 14th century) to an archdiocese, with jurisdiction over the other Greek island dioceses.

July 2, 1522

Europe: Switzerland
Christianity

Ulrich Zwingli and other priests petition the Roman Catholic bishop of Constance (Switzerland) for permission to marry.

1523

Europe: Belgium
Christianity

Two Flemish priests, Hendrik Voes and John of Esschen (Jan van Essen), are executed in Brussels after they refuse to recant their Lutheran beliefs.

1523

Europe: France
Christianity

Lutheran reformers Martin Bucer and Wolfgang Capito settle in Strasbourg. The city becomes a haven for a variety of Reform perspectives.

1523

Europe: Germany
Christianity

Martin Luther issues the *Order of Worship* with recommendations for reforming church worship in accordance with the Reformation ideas he had earlier expounded.

Luther defends himself before the Imperial Diet meeting at Worms. Afterward, Emperor Charles V declares him an outlaw.

1523

Europe: Italy
Christianity

Pope Adrian VI dies after less than two years in the papal chair. His papacy represents a hiatus in the papal administration. He tried to make reforms but was blocked by his own inexperience in papal politics and a variety of financial commitments made by his predecessor. He is succeeded by Clement VII (r. 1523–1534), born Giulio di Giuliano de' Medici. A member of the powerful Medici family, he comes to the office as a sophisticated leader with a broad apprehension of papal affairs.

1523

Europe: Switzerland
Christianity

Ulrich Zwingli starts the reformation in German-speaking Switzerland by issuing the "Sixty-seven Articles," which challenge papal authority, deny sacramental authority to the Eucharist, and call for eliminating a variety of non-biblical elements that have found their way into the church's life.

October. Church leaders in Zurich conduct the Second Zurich disputation that considers issues of images in the church and the worship of the mass. Zwingli denounces statues and images, arguing that they should be destroyed rather than become the object of veneration.

In his volume *A Brief Introduction to Christianity,* Zwingli issues the first official statement of Reformation doctrine.

Swiss religious leader Ulrich Zwingli, whose 16th-century Reformation movement played a key part in the Protestant break with the Catholic Church. (Library of Congress)

ULRICH ZWINGLI (1484–1531)

Ulrich Zwingli was a leader of the Protestant Reformation in Zurich, Switzerland, during the 16th century, where his reforms played a key part in the early Protestant break with the Catholic Church.

Zwingli was born on January 1, 1484, in the Toggenburg Valley in Switzerland. After several years of teaching Latin as a tutor, Zwingli was ordained as a Catholic priest. Zwingli later transferred to the Benedictine Abbey at Gensiedeln as the "people's priest," responsible for pastoral care. That position left him ample time for personal study. During that time, Zwingli accumulated a substantial library of 300–350 volumes. Correspondence with Desiderius Erasmus, the early church fathers, and texts critical of scholasticism led Zwingli to contemplate reform of the Catholic Church, especially after he learned Greek in order to make his own translations of biblical texts. In 1519, he transferred to the Great Minster, the main church at Zurich, and served through an outbreak of plague the first year. While there, he began to study the works of Martin Luther and came to agree on a theology based on *sola scriptura* in which the Bible replaced the pope and the church's hierarchy as ultimate authorities. He started to downplay the role of saints in his sermons by advising his parishioners to emulate the saints, not venerate them.

Like other reformers, Zwingli profoundly changed the style and content of the mass. Services were held while the congregation sat at wooden tables, with no elaborate trappings and no organ music, and involved only the chanting of psalms from the congregation itself. Communion was no longer a celebration of the real presence of Jesus Christ but a commemoration of the Last Supper and an act of thanksgiving; it was served on wooden platters and limited to four times a year. Zwingli's early reforms were an integral part of the Protestant break with the Catholic Church, and would have become even more important had he not died an untimely death in 1531.

MARGARET SANKEY

1523–1524

Europe
Western Esotericism
The conjunction of the planets Jupiter and Saturn, which occurs every 20 years, takes place in the constellation Pisces. It is all the more heralded, as all five of the other known planets are also gathered in Pisces as the event begins toward the end of 1523. This Grand Conjunction of the planets was not seen as heralding any positive potentials, and many among the astrologically oriented believe that it foretells the coming of a great deluge, such as that which occurred in the days of Noah.

1524

Central America and the Caribbean: Mexico
Christianity
A group of Franciscan friars formally establish a mission in and around Mexico City. One of their number, Fray Martín de Valencia, was also designated the commissioner general of the Inquisition

in New Spain. He held that office until 1528 when he was succeeded by a Dominican, Fray Vicente de Santa María.

1524

South Asia: India
Judaism

Moorish Arabs attack the Jewish community in Malabar (India), protesting their monopoly on various wanted commodities. The Jews, with no army to defend them, sought a haven from the ruler of Cochin. The king welcomed them and their new home became known as "Jew Town."

1524

Europe: Denmark
Christianity

Hans Mikkelsen and Christiern Pedersen complete and publish their translation of the New Testament in Danish.

1524

Europe: Denmark
Christianity

From Germany, Christian II, the deposed ruler of Denmark, publishes a Danish translation of the New Testament under the name *This is the New Testament in Danish directly from the Latin version*. It has been produced from Erasmus of Rotterdam's Latin Bible translation of 1516 and Luther's German New Testament. The preface included an attack on King Frederick I, the last Roman Catholic monarch to reign over Denmark, along with a petition against the Catholic Church in Denmark. As Friedrich still held power, he had the translation banned in his realm.

1524

Europe: Germany
Christianity

Johann Walther, a colleague of Martin Luther, issues a new hymnal that includes some hymns written by Luther. Its use in German churches reflects the attempt to increase lay participation in worship. This first Protestant hymnal has only eight hymns.

1524

Europe: Spain
Christianity

The metalworker Enrique de Arfe completes the great Monstrance of Toledo, a 10-foot sculpture in silver of a Gothic tower in which are embedded scenes from the life of Jesus of Nazareth. It had been commissioned seven years earlier by Cardinal Cisneros, who desired to possess a monstrance greater than that owned by Isabella, the queen of Castile and León. The Monstrance will be brought out annually for the celebration of the feast of Corpus Christi of Toledo (Spain).

1524

Europe: Sweden
Christianity

The brothers Olaus and Laurentius Petri speak out in favor of the Lutheran reformation of the Swedish church, which leads to their being excommunicated as heretics by the church leadership in Uppsala.

1524

Russia, Central Asia, and the Caucasus: Russia
Christianity

Czar Vasily III founds Novodevitchy (New Maidens) Convent in Moscow. It would become one of the most important monastic establishments in the country as females of the royal family and Russia's noble families chose to enter the religious life there. A large cathedral church is erected and dedicated to the Mother of God of Smolensk (a miraculous icon of the Blessed Virgin Mary).

1524

Southwest Asia and North Africa: Persia
Islam

Tahmasp (r. 1524–1576) succeeds his father Ismail I as the shah of Persia (Iran). Only 10 years old at the time, his first years are controlled by a regent, but he will emerge as the longest-ruling monarch of the Safavid Dynasty.

Modern Iran is essentially defined by the territory of Ismail's kingdom. He also took control of Mesopotamia (Iraq), a mixed Sunni/Shi'a land. He created a situation in which Sunnis and Shi'as in Iraq established a long-term hostile relationship. While taking control of the Shi'a holy sites, especially at Najaf and Karbala, he destroyed the major Sunni shrines in Baghdad including the tombs of Abbasid caliphs.

1524–1525

Europe: Germany
Christianity

The Peasant's Revolt erupts and Luther calls upon the German princes to restore order.

1524–1525

Southwest Asia and North Africa: Asia Minor
Christianity

Shortly after his election, the ecumenical patriarch Jeremias I made an extended visit to Egypt, the Sinai, and Palestine. While he is away from the city, church leaders in Istanbul conspire to depose him and select in his place Joannicios I (r. 1525), the metropolitan of Sozopolis. Jeremias responded to their action by calling together the three patriarchs of Alexandria, Antioch, and Jerusalem, and together they excommunicate Joannicius. His opponents in Istanbul back down, he is restored to office, and goes on to enjoy one of the longer tenures of any patriarch in the 16th century.

May 3, 1524

Europe: Italy
Christianity

On the feast of the Finding of the Holy Cross, Gaetano dei Conti di Tiene (1480–1547), a member of the Oratory of Divine Love, founds the Order of the Clerics Regular (popularly termed the Theatines) to assist the reformation of the priesthood and provide care for the ill. The founder would later be canonized as St. Catajen. Among the original members, Giovanni Pietro Carafa would later be known as Pope Paul IV. A month after its founding, on June 24, Pope Clement VII grants formal approval to the new Order of the Clerics Regular.

September 24, 1524

Europe: Switzerland
Christianity

From Basel, Erasmus issues *De Libero Arbitrio,* a treatise on free will in which he argues that the human will is not impaired by sin to the extent that humans cannot work out their salvation. This counters Luther assertion that the human will is bound until freed by God's gracious act of salvation.

The Zurich town council abolishes the Roman Catholic mass.

ca. 1525

Southwest Asia and North Africa: Maghreb
Islam

The Ottomans capture Algiers on the Mediterranean coast of what is now Algeria. It becomes the headquarters of Ottoman territory in the Maghreb, the Regency of Algiers. It becomes the base for further expansion and a home from which privateers (pirates) attack European shipping in the Mediterranean. From Algiers, Ottoman territory expanded east and west through the next half-century.

1525

Central America and the Caribbean: El Salvador
Christianity

Roman Catholic missionaries begin work in El Salvador.

1525

Central America and the Caribbean: Honduras
Christianity

Spanish forces under Hernán Cortés enter what is now Honduras as part of their attempt to overthrow the remnants of the Mayan Empire.

1525

Central America and the Caribbean: Mexico
Christianity

The Roman Catholic Diocese of Tlaxcala (Mexico) is erected.

1525

East and Southeast Asia: China
Buddhism

Gedun Gyatso, later to be designated the second Dalai Lama, the abbot of Drepung monastery, becomes the abbot of Sera Monastery, a monastery of the Gelupga school of Tibetan Buddhism.

1525

Europe: Denmark
Christianity

Catholic priest Hans Tausen initiates the reformation in Denmark through his preaching from the monastery of the Order of Saint John at Viborg in Jutland, and then, after being turned out at the monastery, at Saint John's Church at Viborg.

1525

Europe: Estonia
Christianity

Lutheran Protestants publish the first book ever printed in the Estonian language. Copies never reach the public, however, as Catholic authorities seize it and have it destroyed immediately after its publication.

1525

Europe: Germany
Christianity

The Catholic princes of Germany unite in the Dessau League in the hopes of suppressing Protestantism in the German lands.

1525

Europe: Norway
Christianity

From his base at the monastery of Antvorskov, the monk Hans Tausen begins spreading Lutheran doctrines in Viborg, from which they will begin to penetrate the country at large. He is protected from the Catholic majority who wish to suppress him by King Frederick I.

1525

Russia, Central Asia, and the Caucasus: Russia
Christianity

The scholar Maximus the Greek, residing in Moscow, has injected himself into a number of local issues. His opponents use the church assembly (*sobor*) of 1525 to accuse him of heresy and use mistakes in his translations to denounce him. He is exiled to the Joseph-Volokolamsk Monastery and not allowed to correspond with anyone concerning his predicament.

1525–1526

Europe: Germany
Christianity

British scholar William Tyndale completes his translation of the New Testament, the first complete New Testament in English, using Erasmus's Greek text, and sees to its publication in Worms. Copies will subsequently be smuggled into England. As copies begin to circulate, the Anglican bishop of London hires Augustine Packington as his agent in Antwerp to buy all the copies of Tyndale's translation, which are sent to London and burned. Packington passes the money from their sale to Tyndale, which supports him as he works on a new edition.

1525–1526

Europe: Hungary, Ottoman Empire
Christianity, Islam

The ongoing hostilities between France and the Holy Roman Empire lead to a major defeat of French forces in Lombardy and the capture and imprisonment of Francis I in Spain. In an attempt to have him released, Ottoman sultan Suleiman the Magnificent allies himself with the French king Francis, and in the summer of 1526, invades Hungary. The defeat of the Hungarian Christian army in the Battle of Mohács made the Ottomans the dominant force in eastern Europe. Meanwhile, Francis signs the Treaty of Madrid, surrendering his claims to land in Italy.

January 17, 1525

Europe: Switzerland
Christianity

In Zurich, Ulrich Zwingli holds an open debate on the question of infant baptism. As a result, on the following day, the city council issues an edict calling all parents to have their infants baptized within a week or face banishment.

In response, Anabaptist leader Conrad Grebal rebaptizes George Blaurock in protest and the Zurich Anabaptists leave the Roman Catholic Church and abandon belief in infant baptism. The event is followed by an attempt to spread their position among the general population of Switzerland. The Zurich council banishes any who submit to rebaptism.

In Zurich Bathasar Hubmaier openly opposes Zwingli by arguing that infant baptism is unknown in the New Testament. Zwingli responds that infant baptism is a Christian form of circumcision.

Authorities arrest Anabaptist Felix Manz and confine him in the Tower in Zurich.

May 1525

Europe: Germany
Christianity
Frederick the elector of Saxony, called the Wise, who had protected Luther through his position and political skill, dies. He is, fortunately for Luther and the reformers, succeeded by the new elector John, called the Steadfast, who proves a staunch ally of the Reformation.

May 15, 1525

Europe: Germany
Christianity
Thousands of peasants are killed by forces attempting to quell the Peasants' Revolt. As a result, many in the poorer classes feel betrayed, and for the time being, Martin Luther loses significant popular support.

The peasants issue a statement of Twelve Articles in which they ask for the right to elect their own pastors, to receive a fair wage, and to live under humane working conditions.

June 13, 1525

Europe: Germany
Christianity
The former monk Martin Luther marries a former nun, Catherine von Bora.

November 18, 1525

Europe: Switzerland
Christianity
Anabaptist Michael Spattler is banished from Zurich.

1526

Sub-Saharan Africa: Congo
Christianity
King Afonso, the Christian king of Congo, sends a letter to the ruler of Portugal complaining of the negative impact that the slave trade is having on his country. King John ignores him.

1526

Central America and the Caribbean: Mexico
Roman Catholic missionaries of the Dominican Order initially arrive in Mexico.

1526

South Asia: India
Hinduism
Future Hindu saint Tulsidas leaves his wife and life as a householder behind as he takes the vows of the renounced life to become a sadhu (a Hindu ascetic). He would through the rest of his life become well known as a saintly poet totally devoted to the god Rama. His most famous work is *Shri Ramcharitamanasa,* an epic poem in praise of the god Rama.

1526

Europe: Belgium
Judaism
Holy Roman Emperor Charles V invites Jews who had converted to Christianity but had nevertheless been expelled from Portugal to settle in Antwerp. There they will live in relative peace for a quarter of a century.

1526

Europe: France
Christianity
Anabaptist Hans Denck, having been banished from the city of Augsburg, baptizes Hans Hut who begins his career as an Anabaptist preacher. Denck, along with colleague Michael Sattler, settles in Strasbourg, and the Anabaptist movement begins to grow.

1526

Europe: Germany
Christianity
The Diet of Speiers sets aside the main rulings of the Diet of Worms, which had condemned Martin Luther.

1526

Europe: Germany
Unbelief

German humanist Martin Cellarius, a friend of Martin Luther's, advocates a Unitarian theology in his book *De operibus Dei* (i.e., *On the Works of God*).

1526

Europe: Germany
Christianity

The rulers of the Holy Roman Empire gather for the first Diet of Speyer. They offer a temporary suspension of the Edict of Worms, by which reformer Martin Luther was condemned as an outlaw, and generally agree to exercise some degree of tolerance until a council can be convened to discuss the differences between the Protestants and Roman Catholics. Their action, in fact, took pressure off the Protestants and allowed them a period for expansion.

1526

Europe: Holy Roman Empire, Italy
Christianity

Pope Clement VII takes the lead in organizing the League of Cognac, which includes France and several Italian states (Venice, Florence, and Milan), to oppose Holy Roman Emperor Charles V's territorial encroachments in northern Italy. As a result, a four-year conflict will ensue with Charles V emerging victorious.

1526

Europe: Hungary
Judaism

Maria of Habsburg expels the Jews from Pressburg, Hungary.

1526

Europe: Sweden
Christianity

As the Reformation spreads in Sweden, Swedish ruler Gustav I, aka Gustav Vasa (r. 1523–1560), having commissioned a new Swedish translation of the Bible, sees the New Testament published.

1526–1530

Europe: Italy
Christianity

The artist Correggio creates the huge fresco of *Assumption of the Virgin* on the interior of the dome of the cathedral of Parma, Italy.

April 26, 1526

South Asia: India
Islam

The First Battle of Panipat. Babur had led an army of central Asians and Afghanis in India and defeats Ibrahim Lodi, the last ruler of the Lodi Dynasty, which heads the Delhi Sultanate. Babur becomes the first ruler of the Mughal Dynasty and subsequently assumes his throne in Delhi.

August 26, 1526

Europe: Hungary
Christianity, Islam

The Battle of Mohács. The Ottoman forces led by Suleiman the Magnificent defeat the army led by Louis II of Hungary (1506–1526) who dies in the battle. As a result, Hungarian resistance collapses, the Ottoman Empire becomes the dominant power in Eastern Europe, and Vienna is threatened.

1527

South Asia: India
Islam

The Battle of Khanwa. Babur defeats Rana Sanga, the Rajput ruler and his allies, the remaining challenger to his control of north India, at Khanwa, Uttar Pradesh, some 40 miles west of Agra. His army subsequently demolished many Hindu temples at Chanderi. They enter Ayodhya, considered the ancient home of Rama, the incarnation of Vishnu, and destroy the Rama Janmabhoomi Temple. Mir Baqshi constructed the Babri Masjid (named for Emperor Babur). In the center of the mosque is a well that both the Hindus and Muslims believed to have miraculous properties.

1527

Europe: Denmark
Christianity

Ottoman miniature showing the First Battle of Mohács on August 26, 1526. Ottoman sultan Suleiman I (the Magnificent) defeated Hungarian forces under King Louis II. After massacring the prisoners, Suleiman laid waste to much of Hungary. (Fotosearch/Getty Images)

As a step in the gradual transition of Denmark from Catholicism to Protestantism, King Frederick I authorizes the closing of the Franciscan centers and monasteries found in some 28 Danish cities.

1527

Europe: England
Christianity

British king Henry VIII requests that Pope Clement VII annul his marriage to Catherine of Aragon, the daughter of the Spanish rulers. Fearing the further wrath of her nephew Charles V, the Holy Roman emperor, Clement delays his decision but eventually refuses.

1527

Europe: France
Christianity

The city council at Strasbourg moves against the Anabaptists and warns citizens to stay away from them. Many of their leaders are arrested, tortured, and banished.

1527

Europe: Germany
Christianity

Philip I, Margrave of Hesse, founds the first European university under Protestant sponsorship at Marburg. Converted to Protestantism in 1524, he had taken the lead to introduce reform in Hesse.

1527

Europe: Sweden
Christianity

The Reformation reaches Sweden and the Swedish Parliament moves to dissolve the Catholic monasteries. The Church of St. Nicholas, commonly known as *Storkyrkan* (the Great Church) or *Stockholms domkyrka* (Stockholm Cathedral) becomes a Lutheran church. The site at which many Swedish kings have been crowned, it is now the cathedral for the bishop of Stockholm of the Church of Sweden.

1527

Europe: Switzerland
Christianity

As part of the sweeping reforms and simplification of worship at Zurich, the large organ in the main church building is dismantled.

1527

Europe: Switzerland
Christianity

Anabaptists gather at Schleitheim and agree to a confession of faith outlining their free believers' church stance, largely written by Michael Sattler. Soon afterwards, Sattler is arrested and dies under torture.

1527

Southwest Asia and North Africa: Syria
Christianity

Pope Clement VII erects the Maronite Archeparchy of Damas, a further sign of the revival of the Maronite community based in Lebanon.

January 5, 1527

Europe: Switzerland
Christianity

Feliz Manz is sentenced to death by drowning for his rebaptizing followers, and he becomes the first of many executed for refusing to recant his Anabaptist views.

January 24, 1527

Europe: Germany
Christianity

Michael Sattler presides over a meeting at Schleitheim (Germany) where the first Anabaptist statement of faith, the Schleitheim Confession, is assembled. Soon after its promulgation, Ulrich Zwingli authored a refutation of it.

May 5, 1527

Europe: Italy
Christianity

In the midst of the war between the Holy Roman Empire and the Cognac League, forces of Holy Roman emperor Charles V enter Rome, sack the city, and force the pope to flee his residence. In the aftermath, the pope pays a sizable ransom for his own life and surrenders lands previously acquired for the Papal States.

The burial sites of popes Julius II and his uncle Sixtus IV are desecrated during the Sack of Rome. The destruction in Rome, including the burning of the libraries, is often used to date the end of the Renaissance.

During his time of confinement following the Sack of Rome, Pope Clement VII grows a beard as a sign of his mourning over the sacking of the city. He will wear the beard for the remainder of his papacy. Through the next century, all the popes follow his example and grow a beard, in spite of it being contrary to canon law, which prescribed that all priests be clean-shaven.

May 21, 1527

Europe: Austria
Christianity

Anabaptist Michael Sattler, having been arrested by Roman Catholic authorities, is executed by burning at the stake. His wife is executed a few days later.

August 1527

Europe: Germany
Christianity

A synod of Anabaptists gathers at Augsburg, later termed the "Martyrs' Synod." Most in attendance will be arrested and executed.

1528

Central America and the Caribbean: Mexico
Christianity, Judaism

The Inquisition emerges in Mexico and the first auto-da-fe (act of faith) is held in Mexico City. Dominican inquisitor Fray Vicente de Santa Maria orders two Jews (who had previously converted to Christianity), including conquistador Hernando Alonso, to be burned at the stake.

Juan de Zumárraga, having been designated bishop of Mexico, sails from Spain as bishop-elect with the title Protector of the Indians. Upon his arrival in Mexico City, he launches efforts to convert the Native population to Catholicism. His efforts will extend Catholicism throughout New Spain, but he almost immediately begins a struggle with the secular authorities over their treatment of the Native population.

1528

South Asia: India
Hinduism

Thirty-year-old Meerabai, a Vaishnava Hindu mystical singer and devotee of Lord Krishna, leaves her home in Rajasthan to journey to the lands associated with Krishna—Mathura, Vrindavan, and Dwaraka—where she will live the rest of her life. She will compose numerous poems built around her love of Krishna.

1528

Europe: France
Christianity, Islam

King Francis I appeals to Suleiman the Magnificent, the sultan of the Ottoman Empire, which ruled Palestine, to restore a church to the Christians residing in Jerusalem that had been taken and converted into a mosque. Suleiman turns back the request on the grounds that Islam did not allow the alteration of the purpose of a mosque, but he did offer to guarantee to the Christians the possession of all the other places currently occupied by them and further to defend them against any oppression. This interaction would later set the stage for a more inclusive treaty between France and the Ottoman Empire.

1528

Europe: Germany
Christianity
Given the negative reaction to his preaching Protestant ideas, Miles Coverdale leaves England and settles in Hamburg, Germany, where he begins to work with William Tyndale on Bible translation.

1528

Europe: Italy
Christianity
Pope Clement VII gives permission to Franciscan Matteo da Bascio to live as a hermit and continue his reformation activity among the Franciscans. Fr. Matteo claims the inspiration of God to institute the manner of life intended by Francis of Assisi, a life of solitude and primitive simplicity. His work will develop into the Capuchin order.

1528

Europe: Scotland
Christianity
Archbishop James Beaton of St. Andrews has Patrick Hamilton, an early Protestant reformer in Scotland, burned at the stake.

1528

Europe: Spain
Christianity
Construction begins on the Cathedral of Málaga, a Renaissance-style church in Málaga, Andalusia, Spain, following plans drawn up by architect Diego de Siloé.

1528

Europe: Switzerland
Christianity
Berthold Haller, a colleague of Ulrich Zwingli, issues the "Ten Theses of Berne," which brings the Reformation to Berne (French-speaking Switzerland). Like Zwingli, Haller denies the real presence of Christ in the Eucharist.

1528–1536

North America: United States
Two vessels carrying survivors of the ill-fated Narváez expedition wreck on or near Galveston Island. The few who survive the wreck are enslaved for a few years among the Native groups of the upper Gulf Coast. Only four men, three Spaniards—Cabeza de Vaca, Andrés Dorantes de Carranza, Alonso del Castillo Maldonado—and a Moroccan Berber named Esteban, eventually make their way to Mexico City. De Vaca will later pen a detailed account of the many Native Americans he had encountered. He will be recognized and practice as a shaman among the Coahuitecan.

March 21, 1528

Europe: Austria
Christianity
Balthasar Hubmaier (1480–1528) is tortured and burned at the stake by Roman Catholic authorities in Vienna after refusing to recant his Anabaptist activities.

1529

Sub-Saharan Africa: Ethiopia
Islam
Ahmad ibn Ibrahim al-Ghazi (aka Ahmad Gran), a Muslim imam, leads an army from the Islamic country of Adal, located east of Ethiopia on the Horn of Africa, into Ethiopia. He will for the next decade attempt to subdue the land and incorporate it into the Sultanate of Adal. In the process, he lays waste to many Christian churches and monasteries.

1529

Sub-Saharan Africa: Ethiopia
Islam, Christianity

Ahmad Gran leads a Muslim army into Ethiopia and has a major victory at the Battle of Shimbra Kure. He later ravages the countryside and destroys many Christian churches and monasteries.

1529

Sub-Saharan Africa: Ethiopia
Islam

Somali Muslim imam and general Ahmad ibn Ibrahim al-Ghazi (c. 1507–1543) (aka Ahmad Gran) invades Ethiopia.

1529

Europe: Austria
Christianity

Austrian authorities in the Tyrol arrest and torture Anabaptist leader George Blaurock. After weeks in prison, they execute him by burning at the stake. Meanwhile, Anabaptist leader Jacob Hutter arrives in Austerlitz and begins preaching. Those who respond would later form the communal group known as the Hutterian Brethren.

1529

Europe: England
Christianity

Henry VIII removes Cardinal Thomas Wolsey, who was unable to attain a papal annulment of his marriage, as lord chancellor. He is succeeded by Thomas More. Wolsey is subsequently arrested. Several days later, the pope named Henry a "Defender of the Faith" for Henry's defense of the seven sacraments against German Protestant leader Martin Luther.

1529

Europe: France
Christianity

Anabaptist preacher Melchior Hoffman begins preaching his apocalyptic notions at Strasbourg. He predicts that Christ will return and establish Strasbourg as the New Jerusalem. His followers will form a distinct group within the larger Anabaptist movement.

1529

Europe: France
Christianity

French lawyer Louis de Berquin rejects the authority of the pope and accuses the divinity professors at the Sorbonne of heresy. In response, authorities arrest him and burn him at the stake.

1529

Europe: Germany
Christianity

Reformer Martin Luther composes the anthem of the Protestant Reformation, "A Mighty Fortress Is Our God." True to basic Protestant understanding at the time, the hymn is based on a psalm, being a paraphrase of Psalm 46. Luther called for many new hymns to be written in the vernacular languages for use in worship.

Luther also writes two catechisms, a longer one for adults and a shorter one for children and youth. These will later be included in the collection of basic Lutheran confessional documents.

1529

Europe: Germany
Christianity

The ruling princes of Germany meet at the second Diet of Speyer and reverse all the decisions made at the Diet three years earlier. The outlaw ban again falls on Martin Luther. Meanwhile, Lutherans in Saxony, following the intention of the first Diet, draw up the Schwabach Articles to present to Holy Roman Emperor Charles I at the Diet of Augsburg (April 8, 1530), called to discuss the issues raised by the Reformation. These articles would later become the basis of the first part of the Augsburg Confession of Faith, the most representative summary of the Lutheran position.

1529

Europe: Germany, Denmark
Christianity

Danish scholar Christiern Pedersen, an ally of exiled king Christian II, publishes a new translation of the New Testament in Danish. At about the same time, he renounces Roman Catholicism and adheres to Lutheranism.

1529

Europe: Hungary, Austria
Islam, Christianity

When Christian forces of the Holy Roman Empire retake Buda (modern Budapest), Ottoman sultan Suleiman moves up the Danube, resumes control of Buda, and heads for Vienna, to which he lays siege. Suleiman suffers his first major defeat and has to retreat.

1529

Europe: Hungary
Christianity, Judaism

Authorities in Posing, Hungary, charge Jews with conducting a blood ritual and burn thirty at the stake.

1529

Europe: Italy
Judaism

The first of five main synagogues that will serve the Jewish ghetto in Venice, the Scuola Grande Tedesca, opens. As with the additional synagogues built over the next century, this one is constructed on the top of existing buildings, and hence largely unidentifiable as a distinctive sacred structure from the outside. It had been ordered that all the synagogues be higher than the surrounding buildings.

1529

Europe: Italy
Christianity

In Venice, Jerome Emiliani begins a religious and social reform movement focused on the care of the poor, orphans, abandoned youth, the sick, and others in extreme need. His effort will lead to the founding of the Somascan Fathers and the placement of a motherhouse at Somascha, a secluded hamlet near Milan.

1529

Europe: Portugal, Spain
Christianity

The Treaty of Zaragoza. The rulers of Spain and Portugal, at odds over possession of the Moluccas Islands, drew a line north and south through the Pacific and agreed that Portugal had hegemony west of that line, which left them with all of Asia and its neighboring islands and granted Spain hegemony over most of the Pacific Ocean.

September–October 1529

Europe: Austria
Christianity, Islam

The Siege of Vienna. Forces of the Ottoman Empire, led by Suleiman the Magnificent, approach the walls of Vienna, Austria, the last obstacle to their invasion of central Europe. After an unsuccessful attempt to storm the walls in early October, the army turns back.

October 1–4, 1529

Europe: Germany
Christianity

Ulrich Zwingli and Martin Luther meet at Marburg to reach an agreement that would unite the German and Swiss wings of the Protestant movement. At what has come to be known as the Marburg Colloquy, the two reformers agreed on everything except the Eucharist. Though both rejected the Roman Catholic doctrine of transubstantiation, Luther affirmed and Zwingli denied the real presence of Christ in the Lord's Supper. By the time John Calvin emerged with a third possible reconciling position, the Lutheran and Reformed movements were already on different trajectories.

ca. 1530

Central America and the Caribbean: Mexico
Christianity
Mexico

Monks working in what is now in Jalisco state, Mexico, having run out of the brandy that they had brought from Spain, began to distill a new drink from the agave plant (following a process initially learned from the local residents), which is variously termed mezcal wine, mezcal brandy, agave wine, or mezcal tequila. Over the next century the product evolves into tequila.

ca. 1530

East and Southeast Asia: Hong Kong
Chinese Religions

Residents of Tai O, an island off the coast of Lantau Island, establish a temple dedicated to Kwan Kung, the red-faced god of war in traditional Chinese religion.

ca. 1530

Europe: Italy
Christianity

Duke Francesco II Sforza commissions the building of a new cathedral church for Vigevano, a city of Lombardy in northern Italy. It will be dedicated to Saint Ambrose. The duke contributed a number of his personal possessions, which became the core of a rich treasury still owned by the cathedral.

1530

Central America and the Caribbean: Mexico
Christianity

The Roman Catholic diocese of Mexico is erected from territory previously assigned to the Diocese of Tlazcala. It will be elevated to an archdiocese in 1546.

An effort to convert and baptize the native population of Mexico through the next decade will bring some 9 to 10 million people into the Roman Catholic Church, one of the largest mass movements of people into Christianity ever.

1530

South Asia: India
Islam

December 25. The Mughal ruler Babar dies in Agra. He is succeeded by his son Humayun (r. 1530–1540, 1555–1556).

1530

East and Southeast Asia: China
Chinese Religions

Chinese emperor Jiajing separates the worship of heaven and of earth, the important rituals for keeping the country in connection with the spiritual world, previously conducted at the large temple southeast of the Forbidden City in Beijing, and constructs a new Temple to the Earth to the north and east of the Forbidden City. It becomes the site of elaborate

The Temple of Heaven in Beijing, China, built in the 15th century. This temple symbolizes the connection between Earth and Heaven and was dedicated to the god of Heaven. (Yong Hian Lim/Dreamstime.com)

summer solstice rituals each summer. At the earlier temple, constructed by the Yongle emperor a century earlier, he adds what is known as the "Earthly Mount." Now designated the Temple of Heaven, this temple remains the most important religious site in the city.

Simultaneously, Emperor Jiajing also saw to the construction of the Temple of the Sun in the eastern part of the city and the Temple of the Moon to the west. These two additional temples completed the sites that focused the annual ceremonies that maintained the spiritual unity of the country and assured its prosperity and protection.

Turning his attention to Beijing's Confucius Temple complex, Jiajing has the Chongsheng Temple built. It serves as the ancestral temple of the Confucius family. It will differ from the rest of the complex in that it will be covered with green tile, rather than the yellow tile (which is limited to the exclusive use of the imperial family) that comes to cover the other buildings in the 18th century.

1530

Europe: Belgium
Christianity

William Tyndale publishes his English translation of the Pentateuch (the first five books of the Christian Old Testament) and sends copies from Antwerp into England.

French theologian and biblical scholar Jacques Lefevre completes and publishes the first translation of the Bible into French. As with the Tyndale English translation, it is printed in Antwerp.

1530

Europe: Denmark
Christianity

As the Protestant Reformation spreads, Denmark adopts a Lutheran confession of faith. The Collegiate Church of St. Mary becomes a center for Roman Catholic resistance to the Reformation. The king orders that the church remain available to both Catholic priests and Lutheran ministers. Then on December 27 a mob enters the building, destroys every statue, and tears the choir stalls apart. They strip the 17 altars of valuables and smash them. Any reliquaries are opened and their contents destroyed. The church's name is changed from St. Mary's to Our Lady's Church, thus keeping the reference to Mary without calling her a saint. Protestants honor Mary but do not refer to her as a saint.

1530

Europe: Germany
Christianity

The lector John of Saxony had the theologians at Wittemburg draw up articles of faith to present to Charles I. The result of their work, the Tetrapolitan Confession, would later become the basis of the second half of the Augsburg Confession.

1530

Europe: Germany
Christianity

Luther's supporters present the Schwabach and Tetrapolitan documents, primarily authored by Philipp Melanchthon, to Charles I in an effort to reconcile with Roman Catholics. The two documents would later be edited and published as a single statement, the Augsburg Confession of Faith.

1530

Europe: Italy
Christianity

Three Italian noblemen found the Clerics Regular of Saint Paul (popularly called the Barnabites), a new Roman Catholic religious order with a particular emphasis on the study and exposition of St. Paul's Epistles.

1530

Europe: Russia
Christianity

After years of disappointment, a son and heir is born to Vasily III. In order to get to this event, he has defied the Russian Orthodox Church leadership by divorcing his first wife, sending her to a nunnery, marrying a second (a Roman Catholic), and allowing various native Pagan practitioners with reputed magical powers to assist the attempts to get his wife pregnant. As part of the celebration of the birth, he orders the construction of the Church of the Ascension at Kolomenskoye, the imperial estate near Moscow.

1530

Europe: Switzerland
Christianity

The Swiss cantons unite in a campaign to suppress the Anabaptist movement. They are condemned as advocates of revolution, destroyers of authority, and supporters of apocalyptic ideas.

1530–1531

Europe: Bohemia

Michel Weisse, a Franciscan monk who had converted to the Moravian Brethren, edits the first Moravian hymnbook, *Ein New Gesengbuchlen,* the first Protestant hymnbook.

1530–1531

Europe: Germany
Christianity

In the winter of 1530/1531, the residents of Ulm, Germany conduct a referendum and as a community affirm their allegiance to the Lutheran movement. They are in the midst of a lengthy project to build a large Gothic church building. Work on the building, including its tall church spire, would not be finished until 1890.

1531

Sub-Saharan Africa: Ethiopia
Islam

The Somali army of Ahmad ibn Ibrahim al-Ghazi defeats the Ethiopians at the Battle of Amba Sel and subsequently loots the Lake Hayq monastery and the stone churches at Lalibela. Upon reaching Axum, it destroys the Church of Our Lady Mary of Zion, originally built in the third century.

1531

Central America and the Caribbean: Mexico
Christianity

Juan Diego, a Native American from Tepeyac, a hill northwest of what is now Mexico City, sees an apparition of a lady who identifies herself as the Blessed Virgin Mary. She requests that a church be built on the site where she appeared. When Juan Diego informs the bishop of Mexico of the occurrence, the bishop asks for a sign to indicate its truth. The Virgin tells Juan Diego to go to the hill (it being mid-December) and gather roses to be taken to Bishop Juan de Zumarraga. He delivers the roses wrapped in a *tilma,* a poor-quality cloth made from the local cactus plants. Upon it was found an image of the Virgin, miraculously imprinted.

1531

South America: Venezuela
Christianity

The present Roman Catholic Archdiocese of Caracas was founded as the Diocese of Coro, Venezuela previously being territory assigned to the Archdiocese of Santa Domingo. The name was changed to the Diocese of Caracas, Santiago de Venezuela in 1537 and it was elevated to an archdiocese in 1803.

1531

Europe: Bosnia
Islam

Painting of the Virgin of Guadalupe, Shrine of the Guadalupe, Mexico City. According to tradition, in December 1531 the Virgin miraculously appeared before a shepherd and Christian convert named Juan Diego. (William Perry/Dreamstime.com)

Gazi Husrev-beg, the Ottomans' provincial governor of Bosnia, commissions architect Mimar Sinan to build the Gazi Husrev-bey Mosque in the city of Sarajevo, Bosnia and Herzegovina. Many came to view it as the most important Islamic structure in the country. Simultaneously, Gazi Husrev-beg also caused the very similar Hüsreviye Mosque in Aleppo, Syria, to be constructed.

1531

Europe: England
Christianity

Clergy and lawyers meet together and conclude that the English Parliament is not empowered to have the archbishop of Canterbury act against the pope's prohibition of a divorce between King Henry VIII and Catherine of Aragon. Bishop John Fisher, the bishop of Rochester, emerged as the pope's primary spokesperson in the deliberations.

Virgin of Guadalupe

According to Guadalupe's Mexican myth, early one morning in December 1531, the Virgin miraculously appeared before a shepherd and Christian convert named Juan Diego. This apparition occurred on Tepeyac, a hill just a few miles north of the center of Mexico City, or Tenochtitlan, the traditional center of the entire Mexica domain. As did the Juan Diego at Ocotlan, Tepeyac's Juan Diego heard strains of beautiful music and a lovely lady calling to him: "Juanito, Juanito! The least of my sons, where are you going?" He told her he was going to church. She then told him that she was the "Virgin Mary, mother of the true God," and that she wanted a church built for her right there on Tepeyac. She also promised to reward his faithfulness.

Juan Diego hurried to Mexico City to make the Virgin's request known to Bishop Zumarraga, but the good father dismissed the shepherd's story as nonsense and sent him away. Juan Diego went back to the lady at Tepeyac to explain the problem; she sent him back to the bishop, who again rebuffed him. Then he was sidetracked by his uncle who had fallen mortally ill with smallpox. On his way to find a priest to administer last rites, Juan encountered the Virgin again. She told him she had already cured his uncle. Then she directed him toward the normally dry, cactus-ridden hilltop, where he was to pick some unusually lush roses. After he had done so, she arranged the flowers carefully in his cloak, telling him to take them back to the bishop, for they were a sign. When Juan Diego opened his cloak at the cleric's house, the roses tumbled to the floor, revealing a lovely painting of the Virgin that had not been there before. The bishop carried this amazing cloak to the chapel and hung it on the wall. The next morning, he rode with Juan Diego to the latter's house, where they found his uncle in perfect health. His uncle reported that the Virgin had appeared to him the previous evening, had cured him, and had informed him that she wanted to be called Guadalupe. The bishop was finally convinced and had a chapel built to honor the Virgin of Guadalupe. As the story goes, the Indians had already been acquainted with this Lady for many years and called her Tonantzin, which means "Our Honorable Mother" in Nahuatl.

KAY ALMERE READ AND JASON J. GONZÁLEZ

Following a subsequent meeting between King Henry VIII and the clergy, Henry is declared the supreme head of the Church of England.

Robert Roose, the cook of John Fisher, the bishop of Rochester, attempts to poison Fisher and his family. He is arrested and as part of the reaction to the crime, a law is passed by Parliament equating such an act with treason. Upon conviction, Roose is boiled alive.

1531

Europe: Germany
Western Esotericism
German occultist Cornelius Agrippa publishes his monumental *Three Books of Occult Philosophy,* some two decades in the writing. It presents a systematic and comprehensive exposition of Esoteric wisdom as it existed at the time.

Mimar Sinan (c. 1489/1490–1588)

A member of an Eastern Orthodox family well known for its architectural works, Mimar Sinan became the most famous designer of royal buildings in the history of the Ottoman Empire. He lived from 1489/1490 to July 17, 1588, and served the famous sultans Suleiman, Selim II, and Murad III. After many years designing aqueducts, bridges, and other relatively banal yet useful structures for the Ottomans, Sinan became Suleiman's primary architect.

Among the many buildings designed by Sinan, the most magnificent is the Mosque of Suleiman, or "Suleimaniye," a gigantic compound in the heart of Istanbul. In his endowment papers, Suleiman expressed his desire that the complex be an inspiration to the population of Istanbul, placing religion at the center of public life. Along with a stunning mosque crowned with expansive domes, the Mosque of Suleiman had a public kitchen for the poor, a caravan rest stop, a Qur'anic school and six other schools, two mausoleums, a hostel, a hospital, a shopping plaza, and a bathhouse. That center, along with his many other public buildings, made Sinan the most famous of many architects who realized the Ottoman goal of imbuing public life in Istanbul with Islamic values and symbols.

ABC-CLIO

1531

Europe: Netherlands
Christianity

John Volkertsz Trijpmaker, who heads the Anabaptist congregation in Amsterdam and is an advocate of the millennial views of Melchior Hoffmann, is arrested and executed by beheading.

1531

Europe: Spain
Unbelief

Spanish physician Michael Servetus angers both Roman Catholics and Protestants with his publication of his first book, *De Trinitatis erroribus* (*On the Errors of the Trinity*), in which he denies belief in the Trinitarian perspective on God. His book will become the fountainhead of theological speculation that challenges the whole foundation of Christian theological development in the West and that leads to the founding of the Unitarian Church. The Trinity, which provides Christians with a means of affirming the worship of one God while affirming the divinity of Jesus of Nazareth, has been the distinguishing trademark of Christian thinking since the fourth century. Servetus follows his original book with two supplementary texts, *Dialogorum de Trinitate* (*Dialogues on the Trinity*) and *De Iustitia Regni Christi* (*On the Justice of Christ's Reign*), which are published together the next year.

Taken in one direction, Servetus's challenge to Christian theological hegemony will lead to Deism, a popular theological perspective in the 17th century and eventually to full-fledged atheism.

1531

Europe: Sweden
Christianity

King Gustav Vasa breaks with the Roman Catholic Church and declares Sweden to be Lutheran. He has been deeply influenced by Olaus and Laurentius Petri, who have openly advocated the Protestant cause for the last seven years, and he appoints Laurentius as the first Protestant archbishop of the Church of Sweden.

1531

Europe: Switzerland
Christianity

The Battle of Kappel. When Swiss reformer Ulrich Zwingli is killed in battle, Heinrich Bullinger succeeds him as head of the Zurich church.

1531–1532

Europe: Germany
Christianity

Philipp Melanchthon writes his *Apology of the Augsburg Confession* to counter Roman Catholic criticisms of the Confession.

Philip I, Landgrave of Hesse and John Frederick I, Elector of Saxony, take the lead in forming the Schmalkaldic League, an alliance of Protestant princes in Germany who pledge to defend each other in the event of Charles V, the Holy Roman emperor, moving against any one of them.

The formation of the league prompts Charles V, more concerned about Turkish advances along the Danube and threatening Vienna, to issue the Peace of Nuremberg, which grants the Protestants some toleration.

1532

South America: Peru
Traditional Religions, Christianity

Pizarro encounters Incan emperor Atahualpa at Cajamarca, the capital of the Inca Empire. The emperor declines Pizarro's suggestion that he convert to Christianity. Subsequently. Pizzaro and his soldiers kill several thousand Incas and take Emperor Atahualpa into custody. Though Atahualpa pays a considerable sum as a ransom, Pizarro orders his death by strangling and moves his forces into Cuzco.

1532

East and Southeast Asia: Japan
Buddhism

The Ikkō (Jodo Shinshu) Buddhist sect establishes Ishiyama as their headquarters.

1532

Europe: England
Christianity

William Warham, the archbishop of Canterbury, dies. He is succeeded by Thomas Cranmer (r. 1532–1555), who will lead the Church of England into the Protestant camp.

1532

Europe: France
Christianity

In France, John Calvin has a conversion experience that leads him from Catholicism to adherence to the Protestant cause.

1532

Europe: Germany
Christianity

In return for assisting in the defeat of the Turks at Vienna, Holy Roman Emperor Charles V grants the Lutherans the Peace of Nuremberg, which allows them time to consolidate their gains over the past two decades.

1532

Europe: Germany
Judaism

David Reuveni, a Jew from the East, appears in Europe in an attempt to create an alliance between the Jews and Christians against the Ottoman Empire. After almost a decade of activity that took him to Italy, Spain, Portugal, and France, he is arrested by the Holy Roman emperor, examined by the Inquisition, and condemned to be burned at the stake. Many saw him encouraging Jewish Christians to revert to their former Jewish faith.

Condemned along with Reuveni is Solomon Malcho, a son of Jewish Christian parents who reasserted his Jewish roots and attempted to assist Reuveni in creating a Jewish-Christian alliance. He had written materials suggesting that Jewish redemption was imminent.

1532

Europe: Hungary
Islam, Christianity

The Siege of Güns. Small forces of the Austrian Habsburg monarchy under the leadership of Croatian captain Nikola Jurišić defended the small fort of Kőszeg with less than a thousand soldiers. The Ottoman army of more than 100,000, heading for Vienna, is held up until the rains come. Having already lost a portion of his armament en route, Suleiman decides to retreat and abandon his immediate plans for capturing Vienna. Vienna remains a focus of interest of both the Holy Roman Empire and the Ottomans and there would be continued hostilities throughout the century.

1532

Europe: Switzerland
Christianity

Oswald Myconius, who succeeded the recently departed John Oecolampadius, revised the confession of faith written by his friend and presented it to the City Council at Basel (Switzerland). The council issued the statement, now known as the "First Confession of Basel," in 1534. It continues Zwingli's understanding of the Lord's Supper as a memorial meal kept as an ordinance of the church without sacramental import.

1533

Central America and the Caribbean: Mexico
Christianity

The first church is erected at the site where Juan Diego had an apparition of the Blessed Virgin Mary two years previously.

Juan de Zumárraga (1468–1548), the bishop elect of Mexico, returns to Spain under charges resulting from rumors spread by his enemies. After he vindicates himself, he is finally consecrated as the first bishop of Mexico, a post he has held since his nomination to office in 1527.

1533

South America: Peru
Traditional Religions, Christianity

The Inca Empire, weakened by a smallpox epidemic that had begun two years previously, was stripped of its power with the capture of the Inca leader Atahualpa at the Battle of Cajamarca. Subsequently, Francisco Pizarro, the head of the Spanish forces, transformed Cuzco into a Spanish settlement.

1533

Europe: England
Christianity

Soon after Archbishop Thomas Cranmer's declaration of his marriage to Catherine of Aragon as null and void, possibly as early as November 1532, English king Henry VIII marries Anne Boleyn. As a result of his marriage, Pope Clement VII excommunicates him. In June, Boleyn is crowned queen at Westminster Abbey, and three months after that ceremony, she gives birth to a daughter, who is named Elizabeth. The removal of Catherine sets off a series of actions that will eventually distance the British church from Roman authority.

The Act of First Fruits and Tenths transfers all taxes on ecclesiastical income, usually sent to Rome, to the English Crown. It is followed by the Peter's Pence Act, which stops the annual payment by landowners of one penny, which had also been sent to Rome.

The Act of Restraint of Appeals places an obstacle between the British clergy and the authority of Roman canon law in ecclesiastical matters. The clergy are forbidden to seek Rome's assistance on any rulings against them.

1533

Europe: France
Christianity

John Calvin writes a speech calling for a return to the pure gospel, which is delivered by his friend Nicholas Cop on the occasion of his inauguration as the rector at the University of Paris. The speech would be burned by the authorities, and both Cop and Calvin have to flee the city.

King Francis I is initially rather tolerant of the new Protestant movement, in part because it was causing disharmony in the lands under the control of his major rival, Holy Roman Emperor Charles V. This tolerance continued into the mid 1530s, and in 1533 Francis suggests to Pope Clement VII that he convene a church council at which Catholic and Protestant rulers could discuss their differences and reach some settlement. Both Pope Clement and Charles V reject the suggestion.

1533

Europe: France
Christianity

Apocalyptic Anabaptist Melchior Hoffman is arrested in Strasbourg and imprisoned for what becomes the rest of his life.

Monarchs of England and Great Britain, 1399–1820

Reign	Name
House of Lancaster	
1399–1413	Henry IV
1413–1422	Henry V
1422–1461	Henry VI
House of York	
1461–1470	Edward IV
House of Lancaster	
1470–1471	Henry VI
House of York	
1471–1483	Edward IV
1483	Edward V
1483–1485	Richard III
House of Tudor	
1485–1509	Henry VII
1509–1547	Henry VIII
1547–1553	Edward VI
1553–1558	Mary I
1558–1603	Elizabeth I
House of Stuart	
1603–1625	James I
1625–1649	Charles I
1649–1660	*Interregnum*
1660–1685	Charles II
1685–1688	James II
1689–1702	William III
1689–1694	Mary II
1702–1714	Anne
House of Hanover	
1714–1727	George I
1727–1760	George II
1760–1820	George III

1533

Europe: Italy
Christianity

Pope Clement VII gives formal approval to the Clerics Regular of Saint Paul, a new religious order popularly called the Barnabites.

1533

Europe: Netherlands
Christianity

Barber and surgeon Obbe Philipps converts to Anabaptism and soon emerges as the leader of the Dutch Anabaptist community out of which the Mennonite Church will emerge.

1533–1534

Europe: Portugal
Christianity

In a series of steps, Pope Paul III elevates the Diocese of Funchal (Portugal) to be an archdiocese and divides it by erecting the new dioceses of the Azores, Cape Verde, and Sao Tomé, which become its suffragan dioceses.

1534

Central America and the Caribbean: Guatemala
Christianity

The Roman Catholic Diocese of Guatemala is erected from territory previously incorporated in the Diocese of Santo Domingo.

1534

Central America and the Caribbean: Mexico
Christianity

Juan de Zumárraga, the first bishop of Mexico, returns from Spain and reassumes his task of converting the Native population. In that effort, he pens a catechism and manual of Christian doctrine for the missionaries and sees to the Bible being translated into the languages of the local population.

1534

Central America and the Caribbean: Nicaragua
Christianity

The Roman Catholic Diocese of León in Nicaragua is erected from territory previously assigned to the Diocese of Panama.

1534

South America: Colombia
Christianity

The Roman Catholic Diocese of Santa Marta (Colombia) is erected.

1534

South Asia: India
Christianity

Pope Paul III issues his bull *Quequem Reputamus,* which elevates the Diocese of Funchal (headquartered on the Madeira archipelago in the north Atlantic Ocean) to an archdiocese and designates the Diocese of Goa as a suffragan diocese. He assigns the new Diocese of Goa jurisdiction for Roman Catholic work in all of India, indeed ideally of all Portuguese lands between the Cape of Good Hope (Africa) and China. Pope Clement VII names Francisco de Mello as the first bishop of Goa.

1534

Europe: England
Christianity

The British Parliament passes the Act of Supremacy that names the king the "Protector and only Supreme Head of the Church and Clergy of England." In the wake of the abrogation of papal authority, the clergy are obliged to swear allegiance to Henry as the new head of the Church of England. The Act of Supremacy marks the official break of the Church of England with the Roman Catholic Church. The subsequent Act of Ecclesiastical Appointments gives the king of England hegemony over the British clergy.

1534

Europe: Germany
Christianity

Luther publishes his German translation of the complete Bible. It will influence the development of the German language over the next centuries.

1534

Europe: Italy
Christianity

Pope Clement VII dies. Shortly before his death, he commissions Michelangelo to create his rendition of *The Last Judgment* within the Sistine Chapel. He is succeeded by Pope Paul III (r. 1534–1550). Shortly after taking the throne, he names his several grandsons, whose grandmother had been his mistress, as cardinals.

1534

Europe: Poland
Judaism

Rabbi Anshel of Crakow publishes the first book in Yiddish (a language composed of elements of German and Hebrew), a concordance of the Hebrew Bible.

1534–1535

Europe: Germany
Christianity

The Siege of Münster. Apocalyptic Anabaptists led by Jan of Leiden take control of the town of Münster in Germany and reorganize it along socialist lines. The Bible was the only allowed reading material, and in the end, polygamy was introduced. Roman Catholic forces lay siege to recover the town, which fell in 1536. The leaders of the attempted reform were tortured and executed and their bodies placed on display. The Münster event joined the Peasants' Revolt in shaping strong negative images of the Anabaptist movement among both Protestants and Catholics and prompted the Anabaptists under their new leader Menno Simons to abandon apocalyptic views and abandon all ideas of using violence in any form to accomplish their goals.

1534–1535

Southwest Asia and North Africa: Tunisia
Islam

Under orders from Suleiman, the sultan of the Ottoman Empire, Hayreddin Barbarossa leads an Ottoman naval force in an attack on Tunis. Once conquered, Tunis could be used for raids throughout the region, especially nearby Malta. The victory was short-lived, as the very next year, a force under Holy Roman Emperor Charles V destroys the Ottoman navy force, captures Tunis, and drives the Ottomans from the area.

July 7, 1534

North America: Canada
Christianity

Explorer Jacques Cartier sails around the Gaspé Peninsula (Canada) where the first Catholic mass of record was celebrated.

August 1534

Europe: France
Christianity
Ignatius Loyola leads six other young men at the University of Paris in professing vows of poverty and chastity. The event is looked upon as the beginning of the Society of Jesus (popularly called the Jesuits).

October 17, 1534

Europe: France
Christianity

Portrait of Ignatius Loyola, founder of the Society of Jesus (the Jesuits) in the 16th century. The Jesuits dedicated themselves to missionary activities and the establishment of schools throughout the world. Loyola was canonized in 1622. (Library of Congress)

The Affair of the Placards. King Francis I's relatively tolerant attitude toward Protestantism changes almost overnight when a number of posters denouncing Catholic worship appear around Paris and several other major French cities. One such poster is found on the door to the king's room. The placards are traced to Antoine Marcourt, a Protestant minister. Francis begins to see Protestantism as a plot directed against him personally, and from this point turns on the movement and begins to persecute its adherents with increasing ferocity.

1535

Central America and the Caribbean: Mexico
Christianity
The rapid growth of the Roman Catholic Church in Mexico leads to a third diocese being named, the Diocese of Antequera, Oaxaca.

1535

South America: Peru
Christianity
On a trip by ship to Peru, the boat carrying Fray Tomás de Berlanga is carried by the ocean current to the Galápagos Islands, of which he thus counts as the discoverer.

1535

South America: Peru
Christianity
Pizarro founds the city of Lima (Peru) and initiates construction of the main church in the city, the Basilica (and later Cathedral) of Lima dedicated to St. John the Apostle and Evangelist.

1535

Europe: Denmark
Christianity
Hans Tausen, the leading Lutheran theologian of the Danish phase of the Protestant Reformation, published the first Danish translation of the Pentateuch (the first five books of the Hebrew Bible).

1535

Europe: England
Christianity

IGNATIUS LOYOLA (1491–1556)

Ignatius Loyola was the founder of the Society of Jesus, also known as the Jesuits. Loyola was born Iñigo de Oñez y Loyola in 1491 at the castle of Loyola in Azpeitia, Spain, in the Basque province of Guipúzcoa. In 1517, Loyola joined the army at a time when France and Spain were at war. In 1521, while fighting at the siege of the city of Pamplona, he was hit by a cannon ball, which broke one of his legs and injured the other. The long recovery forced the otherwise active Loyola to spend many hours lying down while his legs healed from the wounds. To pass the time, he was brought a book on the life of Christ and the saints. Having nothing else to read, Loyola decided to get through it and see if he could compete with the saints in all their trials and tribulations.

Loyola discovered that while he daydreamed about knights and adventures, his soul was restless, but when he focused on the lives of the saints, he found peace. One night, he had a vision in which the image of Mary and the Holy Child appeared to him. The experience profoundly affected him, and from then on he was a changed man.

For the next 11 years, Loyola underwent a rigorous education, which he had to start among the schoolboys in Barcelona since he did not know Latin, the language used at all universities. By 1526, he had mastered the language well enough to be able to enroll at the University of Alcalá in Madrid, where he studied philosophy. In Paris, Loyola met Francis Xavier and a few others, who became the core of his first "society of Jesus." In 1534, they all took vows of poverty and chastity, and Loyola became a priest three years later. Despite his idea of going to live in Jerusalem, Loyola decided to offer his services to the pope. He had the idea of designating his group the "Company of Jesus," taken from the military idea of a company around a captain, but it was eventually approved by the pope as the Society of Jesus.

Loyola died on July 31, 1556, in Rome of a fever. He was beatified by Pope Paul V on July 27, 1609, and canonized by Pope Gregory XV on May 22, 1622.

JOSE VALENTE

John Fisher, the bishop of Rochester and former tutor of King Henry VIII, opposes Henry's divorce and defends the actions of Pope Clement VII, who names him a cardinal. Henry has him arrested and executed.

Henry also has his lord chancellor Sir Thomas More executed. Like Fisher, More refuses to accept either Henry's divorce from Catherine of Aragon or his subsequent marriage to Anne Boleyn. The king charges him with treason.

1535

Europe: Estonia
Christianity
Protestants in Lithuania, whose first attempt to publish a book in the Estonian language was thwarted by its being confiscated and destroyed (1525), finally succeed in having the first book in the Lithuanian language printed. It is a bilingual German-Estonian translation of the Lutheran catechism by S. Wanradt and J. Koell.

1535

Europe: France
Christianity

In Paris, some two dozen Protestants are arrested and executed by being burned at the stake.

1535

Europe: France
Christianity

A revised edition of the French Bible originally published by Jacques Lefèvre d'Étaples in 1530 is published by Pierre Robert Olivétan. Olivétan's edition would become the foundation for an official French Catholic edition of the Bible, which is published at Leuven in 1550.

1535

Europe: Italy
Christianity

Angela de Merici founds a new religious order for women, the Ursulines, at Brescia, Italy. Its focus will be the education of girls and the care of the sick and needy. She adopts Saint Ursula, a Christian martyr who was killed in Cologne a millennium earlier, as the order's patron saint.

1535

Europe: Italy
Christianity

Pope Paul III commissions Michaelangelo to paint the wall above the altar of the Sistine Chapel. He will take some five years to execute *The Last Judgment,* one of several of his most important creations, which will be completed in 1541.

1535

Europe: Italy
Christianity

Angela de Merici (later St. Angela) organizes a group of women into the informal Company of St. Ursula, which meets for conferences and devotional practices, though the members do not live together. It will later become the seed from which a new Roman Catholic religious order, the Ursulines of the Roman Union, will emerge.

1535

Europe: Spain
Christianity

A young woman of a mystical temperament named Teresa enters the Carmelite Monastery of the Incarnation in Avila, but soon discovers to her consternation that the observance of the rules of the cloister are regularly ignored, which inspires her to launch a reformation of the Carmelite order.

1535

Europe: Switzerland
Christianity

Miles Cloverdale publishes the first complete English translation of the Bible. He dedicates it to King Henry VIII. It is the first complete edition of the Bible printed in English.

1535

Southwest Asia and North Africa: Maghreb
Judaism, Islam

The Hafsid Caliphate that controls much of the coast of North Africa from northeast Algeria to northwest Libya becomes the victim of the increasing competition between the Ottoman Empire and Spain. Spanish forces capture Tunis, which had fallen to the Ottomans only a year before. Also caught in the middle, the members of the Tunisian Jewish community attempt to flee, but many are taken prisoner and sold into slavery. Jews in Italy are able to ransom some 150 of their fellow believers.

1535–1536

Europe: Austria
Christianity

Following the expulsion of all Anabaptists from Moravia, Jacob Hutter returns to the Tyrol where Austrian authorities arrest him. Tortured and asked to recant, he refuses and is executed by burning at the stake. More than 350 of his fellow Hutterites will also be executed in the current push to suppress Anabaptist thought.

1535–1536

Europe: Belgium
Christianity

Authorities of the Holy Roman Empire in Antwerp arrest and imprison biblical scholar William Tyndale. After some months in jail, he is convicted of heresy on charges related to his English translation of the New Testament. He is executed by strangulation and his body subsequently burned at a stake.

1536

Central America and the Caribbean: Mexico
Christianity
The new Diocese of Michoacán is erected from territory previously a part of the Diocese of Mexico.

1536

South America: Peru
Christianity
Pope Paul III erects the Roman Catholic Diocese of Cuzco (Peru). Its jurisdiction includes Bolivia.

1536

Europe: England
Christianity
Lawyer Robert Aske leads the Pilgrimage of Grace, an uprising in York, to protest generally Henry VIII's break with the Roman Catholic Church and most particularly his move to dissolve the monasteries. As a result, Aske will be arrested and executed (1537).

1536

Europe: England
Christianity
Pope Paul III names Reginald Pole a cardinal and appoints him the papal legate to England.

1536

Europe: France
Christianity
The Diocese of Maguelonne (in southeastern France) is transferred to Montpellier to escape the piracy that afflicted the French Mediterranean coast. The church attached to the monastery of Saint-Benoît, which had been founded in 1364, is appropriated and designated as the cathedral for the new diocese. Within a few

decades, the church fell victim to the Religious War in France between the Huguenot Protestants and Roman Catholics and was severely damaged.

1536

Europe: France
Unbelief, Western Esotericism
Michael Servetus moves to Paris to continue his study of medicine. While there, he employs himself as an astrologer to pay his way. He comes into conflict with the dean of the Faculty of Medicine, Jean Tagault, and writes the *Apologetic Discourse of Michel de Villeneuve in Favour of Astrology and against a Certain Physician* as an answer to Tagault's attacks on him. He is ordered to withdraw his book.

1536

Europe: France
Christianity, Islam
Francis I, the king of France, and the sultan of the Ottoman Empire, Suleiman the Magnificent, conclude a treaty that establishes the Franco-Ottoman Alliance. From a French perspective, the treaty provided a significant ally in Francis's efforts to block further growth of the Habsburg Empire based in Germany and Austria. Francis justifies his making the alliance with the Ottoman Muslims because of his desire to provide protection for those Christians residing in Ottoman lands. The alliance includes a set of agreements, the so-called "Capitulations of the Ottoman Empire," that provide these protective measures.

From the Ottoman perspective, the treaty provided the Ottomans with further grounds for their invasion of Europe, which was at the time primarily directed toward Habsburg lands along the upper reaches of the Danube River in Hungary and Austria, and the treaty also provided some comfort after their loss of Tunis the previous year to the Habsburg emperor Charles V. The Ottomans allow the French to establish a permanent ambassador in Constantinople, the Ottoman capital.

1536

Europe: France, Switzerland
Christianity

John Calvin publishes (in Latin) the *Institutes of the Christian Religion*, the first systematic presentation of Protestant theology. He writes in part to inform the French king that people who were his subjects were unjustly being killed. He joins his colleague Guillaume Farel in Geneva, where a reformation of the church is proceeding.

1536

Europe: Germany
Christianity

Leaders of the Lutheran and Reformed churches attempt to resolve their difference over the Eucharist by signing the Wittenberg Concord. It affirms the real

---

JOHN CALVIN (1509–1564)

John Calvin was a French theologian and leader of the Protestant Reformation. Calvin was born Jean Cauvin on July 10, 1509, in Noyon, France. Calvin was educated at the University of Paris, where he first studied to be a priest. In 1533, he converted from Catholicism to Protestantism, endeavoring to become an instrument of God's will. Fleeing religious persecution, Calvin left France in 1534 and traveled to Basel, Switzerland, where he found other Protestants. In 1536, he first published *Institutes of the Christian Religion,* a work that put forth his beliefs about Christianity and that he would continue to revise until 1559.

In his work, Calvin opined that all men are flawed and corrupt and no one can ever know God or participate in his own salvation. God is omniscient and omnipotent and has preordained everything that will ever happen. In his merciful magnificence, God has already chosen which people will be saved and which will suffer eternal damnation. If man imagines that he can change the will of God through his actions, he has simply shown that he does not understand the greatness and glory of God. All people should strive to live a moral life in the hope that they are already among God's elect; their lives should not be lived just to become saved. If anyone protested this image of God, Calvin believed that human reason was too feeble to judge God's will.

Calvin also rejected the elaborate ceremonies and sacramental system of the Roman Catholic Church in favor of a more simplified and orderly worship. Likewise, he rejected any separation of church and state, seeing the state as an instrument to ensure people's strict morality. Calvin approved the use of force by the state against false teachings, including Catholicism—which in turn approved the use of force against such "false teachings" as Protestantism.

In Strasbourg, Calvin set about regulating every aspect of life in Geneva based on his own *Ecclesiastical Ordinances.* The church had the power to search everyone's home. Gambling, drunkenness, theater, and dancing were banned. Calvin declared that the punishment for adultery would be death. Under his dictatorial hand, Geneva became a model of order and cleanliness. At the same time, 58 people were executed and 76 banished to preserve the moral order. After a long illness, Calvin died on May 27, 1564, of tuberculosis. However, his strong influence on Protestant churches continues to the present.

ABC-CLIO

presence of Christ's body and blood in the Eucharist. Among the signers for the Lutherans were Martin Luther and Philipp Melanchthon, and for the Reformed Church community, Martin Bucer and Wolfgang Fabricius Capito.

1536

Europe: Greece
Christianity

Moni Starronikita, the last of the 20 monasteries on Mount Athos, is consecrated following its acquisition and rebuilding by the monk Gregorios Gerimeriatis. Jeremias, the patriarch of Constantinople, supports the rebuilding financially and is credited as its founder.

1536

Europe: Ireland
Christianity

The Irish Parliament declares British king Henry VIII to be the supreme head of the Church of Ireland, even though he will not officially become the king of Ireland for another five years. By this act, the former Roman Catholic Church in Ireland becomes the independent Church of Ireland, an Anglican body. Changes in belief and practice will occur in stages over the rest of the century, reflecting changes in England, though the majority of the laity maintain an allegiance to Catholicism.

1536

Europe: Netherlands
Christianity

Menno Simons leaves the Catholic Church and reorganizes scattered remnants of the Radical Reformation.

1536

Europe: Netherlands
Christianity

Dutch Catholic priest Menno Simons, having studied Anabaptist ideas for several years, rejects his priesthood and converts to Anabaptism. He will be ordained as an Anabaptist minister by Obbe Philips the following year and quickly join Philips as one of their major leaders.

1536

Europe: Switzerland
Christianity

The First Helvetic Confession resulted from the meeting of church leaders from both the French- (Berne) and German-speaking (Basel and Zurich) areas of Switzerland to prepare a joint statement. Among their concerns is the reconciliation of the Lutheran and Reformed wings of the Reformation, and in that regard they drop Zwingli's view of the sacraments and begin to develop John Calvin's view of the sacraments as vehicles for the spiritual reception of Christ by faith.

1536

Europe: Switzerland
Christianity

The Swiss Canton of Berne displaces the rule of the Italian House of Savoy over the Canton of Vaud and its primary city, Lausanne. Immediately after assuming control, it introduces Protestant reform, and in a sermon, reformer Guillaume Farel introduces Ten Articles designed to be discussed at a deputation already scheduled to be held in Lausanne the first week of October.

1536

Europe: Switzerland
Christianity

Five years after the Reformation was introduced into the French-speaking Canton of Switzerland, the church in Geneva published three documents representing the Reformed church as it then existed: a document outlining the church's governance, a catechism, and a confession of faith (the Geneva Confession of 1536). As promulgated the next year, the Geneva Confession represents the Calvinist perspective that would dominate the Swiss Reformation for the rest of the century.

1536–1537

Europe: Denmark, Norway
Christianity

The reformation in Denmark culminates at a meeting of the Diet of Estates of the Realms at which the country's Catholic bishops were officially deposed and a bill redistributing power between the church and the government passed. With Lutheranism now the officially designated religion, King Christian III promises to appoint new bishops. The following year he commissions reformer Johann Bugenhagen to consecrate new bishops for the Church of Denmark outside of any lineage of apostolic succession.

The Danish phase of the Reformation brings significant change to the wealthy and prominent Roskilde Cathedral on the island of Zeeland. The Diocese of Roskilde is relocated to Copenhagen and its bishop replaced with a Protestant superintendent. All of the bishop's property will be transferred to the king, now designated the head of the Church of Denmark. Later, it would be endowed with a variety of gifts from King Christian IV.

As Norway was under Danish hegemony at the time, it too experiences the change from Catholicism to Lutheranism.

1536–1537

Europe: Italy
Christianity

Pope Paul III appoints a committee of nine eminent prelates to prepare a report on the reformation of the church. They present their widely disseminated report, *Consilium de emendenda ecclesia,* which includes descriptions of significant abuses in the church's administrative apparatus and its worship life, and detailed steps to be taken for meaningful change. In Rome, no action was taken on the committee's recommendations.

1536–1541

Europe: England
Christianity

The Dissolution of the Monasteries. Under authority granted him in the Act of Supremacy two years previously, King Henry VIII moves against the monastic establishment in England, Wales, and Ireland. He disbands their centers (some 800) and appropriates their income, property, and treasures, all of which is deposited in his treasury. Various arrangements are made to relocate the former monks and nuns.

At Canterbury, a priory, a nunnery, and three friaries are closed. St. Augustine's Abbey, the oldest and one of the richest in England, is turned over to authorities. Its church and cloister are immediately destroyed, while the process of dismantling the abbey is begun.

January 25, 1536

Europe: Austria
Christianity

Jacob Hutter, who had previously been arrested and tortured, is burned at the stake in Austria. His wife suffered the same fate a short time later.

1537

Central America and the Caribbean: Dominican Republic
Christianity

Maria de Rojas y Toledo, Christopher Columbus's daughter-in-law, oversees the transfer of the remains of her husband Diego and his father from Spain to the cathedral in Santo Domingo (Dominican Republic) for burial.

1537

Central America and the Caribbean: Mexico
Christianity

Bishop Juan Zumárraga of Mexico submits a question to Rome concerning the format by which the Native converts have been baptized. In the wake of the apparitions of the Virgin Mary at Guadalupe (1531), millions of Natives have converted and a somewhat abbreviated format for more quickly baptizing the large numbers was adopted. When the legitimacy of this practice was questioned, the bishop asked Rome for a ruling. In the bull *Altitudo divini consilii,* Pope Paul III declares the baptism format valid, while ordering that it be avoided in the future except in cases of urgent need.

1537

South America
Christianity

Pope Paul III issues *Sublimis deus,* a papal bull in which he declares Native Americans to be rational beings who must not be robbed, enslaved, or otherwise abused.

1537

South America: Bolivia
Christianity
An initial Roman Catholic mission was established in Bolivia to work among the Parias and Charcas peoples.

1537

Europe: Austria
Western Esotericism
Swiss physician and alchemist Philippus Aureolus Theophrastus Bombastus von Hohenheim, better known as Paracelsus, publishes *Grosse Astronomie,* an astrology manual.

1537

Europe: Belgium
Christianity
Under the name Thomas Matthew, British Protestant John Rogers publishes an edition of the Bible using primarily the work of William Tyndale, who before his death had translated the New Testament and much of the Old Testament. He used Miles Coverdale's work of the remaining portions of the Old Testament and most of the Apocrypha. The edition included the Apocrypha, considered canonical by the Roman Catholics, though in the end it would be rejected by the Protestants.

What became known as Matthew's Bible was possibly printed in Antwerp, though the actual printer is unknown. Both it and Coverdale's Bible would be licensed for sale in England and appear under a variety of imprints.

1537

Europe: Denmark, Norway
Christianity
As the Lutheran Reformation spreads and becomes dominant in Scandinavia, King Christian III of Denmark disbands the Catholic hierarchy in the lands under his hegemony and designates Lutheranism as the established form of Christianity.

1537

Europe: Germany
Christianity
Martin Luther issues the Schmalkaldic Articles, a further statement of Lutheran faith.

1537

Europe: Germany
Christianity
Reformer Martin Luther prepares the Schmalkald Articles, a summary of the Lutheran position, for a gathering of the Schmalkaldic League (an alliance of Protestant princes), for their use at an impending Ecumenical Council of church leaders.

1537

Europe: Italy
Christianity
Consilium de emendenda ecclesia, a report of a papal commission, highlights abuses found in the operation of the Curia and the need for reformation throughout the Roman Catholic Church's organization, leadership, and worship. It is widely disseminated, but prompts no immediate changes of note.

March 1537

Europe: Italy
Christianity
Members of a committee, largely drawn from the Oratory of Divine Love and appointed by Pope Paul III, present a report, *Consilium de emendenda ecclesia,* which is a scathing exposé of the level of immorality that has invaded the priesthood. Never published, copies nevertheless circulate. Significant action on the report would await the arrival of a member of the oratory to the papal throne in the person of Pope Paul IV (r. 1555–1559)

June 2, 1537

Europe: Italy
Christianity
Pope Paul III issues a papal bull, *Sublimus Dei,* which denounces the practice of enslaving the peoples residing in the Americas.

June 24, 1537

Europe: Italy
Christianity

The original company of Jesus led by Ignatius Loyola, having received initial approval for their new order, are ordained as priests in Venice by the bishop of Arbe. An early goal to visit Jerusalem is prevented by the war that has begun between the Holy Roman Empire and the coalition of Italian states, including the Papal States.

August 15, 1537

South America: Paraguay
Christianity

Spanish adventurers, looking for Inca silver, begin the settlement of Asuncion, Paraguay. The city, begun on the day of the Feast of the Assumption of the Virgin Mary, is formally named for her.

1538

Central America and the Caribbean: Dominican Republic
Christianity

In the 1830s, the Dominicans stationed on the island of Hispanola created a seminary for the training of priests. In 1538, that school was reorganized as the University of Saint Thomas Aquinas under directions from a papal bull issued by Pope Paul III. The school was then officially sanctioned in 1558 by a royal decree from the king of Spain, who in 1551 had issued a similar decreee creating the Royal and Pontifical University of Mexico. The University of Saint Thomas Aquinas (aka Universidad Santo Tomás de Aquino and now known as the Universidad Autónoma de Santo Domingo) is the oldest university in the Western Hemisphere.

1538

Europe: England
Christianity

The shrine at Chichester Cathedral dedicated to Richard de la Wyche, the former bishop of Chichester (1245–1253), is destroyed, an early victim of the English phase of the Protestant Reformation.

1538

Europe: England
Christianity

Thomas Cromwell orders that an English Bible be made available to the public in every local church throughout England. Then under his direction, biblical scholar Richard Taverner makes a revision of Matthew's Bible, an English translation issued just two years before somewhere on the continent, and publishes it (1539). It is known as the Great Bible and enjoys brisk sales, as do reprints of Miles Coverdale's translation and Matthew's Bible.

1538

Europe: Greece
Islam, Christianity

The Battle of Preveza. Holy Roman Emperor and ruler of Spain Charles V challenges the growing power of the Ottomans in the Mediterranean. Sultan Suleiman appoints naval commander Khair ad Din, better known as Barbarossa, to rebuild and lead his Mediterranean fleet. Charles sends his fleet from Spain, which is met by Barbarossa off the coast of Greece. In defeating the Spanish, Barbarossa takes control of the eastern Mediterranean for the Ottomans for the next generation.

1538

Europe: Italy
Islam

The oldest edition of the Qur'an produced by printing with movable type is published in Venice. Publishers were responding to both the opportunity afforded by the new technology and the law in Venice's neighbor, the Ottoman Empire, which forbids the use of movable-type printing using Arabic characters. The project is not successful as the new printed edition proves unpopular, Muslims preferring hand-produced copies of the Qur'an.

1538

Europe: Switzerland
Christianity

Opposition to the reforms introduced to Geneva by John Calvin and Guillaume Farel force the pair to leave the city. Calvin settles in Strasbourg where he issues a revised edition in French of his *Institutes of the Christian Religion.*

ca. 1539

Europe: England
Christianity

Miles Coverdale, best known for his work on translating the Bible, publishes the first English hymn book, *Ghostly Psalmes and Spirituall Songes drawen out of the Holy Scripture.* Most of the songs were translations from the German Lutheran hymns. The circulation will be radically curtailed by Henry VIII placing the hymnal on a list of prohibited books.

1539

North America: United States
Christianity

Franciscan priest Fray Marcos de Niza, accompanied by two additional Franciscan brothers, leads an expedition north from Mexico into New Mexico where the Zuni people reside.

1539

Central America and the Caribbean: Mexico
Christianity

The new Diocese of Chiapas is erected with territory taken from the Diocese of Antequera, Oaxaca.

1539

South India: India
Sikhism

September 22. Guru Nanak, founder of the Sikh religion, dies. Shortly before his death, he designates Bhai Lehna, who took the name Guru Angad, as his successor. Among his many accomplishments, Guru Angad Dev authors 236 lines of inspirational poetic verse that would later be incorporated in the Sikh scripture, the Guru Granth Sahib.

1539

Europe: England
Christianity

Thomas Cromwell, the chief minister of King Henry VIII, initiates action to take control of the property of Glastonbury Abbey, the richest monastic center in England. Its abbot, Richard Whiting, resists the actions and is branded a traitor. Taken to Glastonbury

In the 1530s Thomas Cromwell was chief minister to English king Henry VIII and played a crucial role in the establishment of the royal supremacy. (Library of Congress)

Tor, he is executed by being hung and then drawn and quartered.

The monastery at St. Albans is closed and looted. It is later sold and its buildings dismembered for construction materials.

1539

Europe: England
Christianity

Pope Paul III issues the second and final excommunication of King Henry VIII of England.

As King Henry VIII moves forward with the process of dissolving the monasteries throughout England, he moves against the priory in Bath attached to the cathedral, one of the two cathedrals serving the Diocese of Bath and Wells. He finds Bath Cathedral redundant, and though it was recently the subject of extensive renovations, he sells it to the people of Bath who make it a parish church. The cathedral in Wells becomes the single cathedral of the continuing diocese.

1539

Europe: France
Christianity

King Francis of France decrees that henceforth all official documents in his realm will be written in French, rather than Latin.

1539

Europe: Germany
Christianity

As the Protestant Reformation proceeds in Germany, Philip of Hesse, a descendent of St. Margaret of Hungary, travels to Marburg where her relics are maintained and venerated. He removes her relics from her shrine and orders the discontinuance of pilgrimages to the church, which had centuries earlier been erected in her honor. He would keep them in his castle for the next decade.

1539

Europe: Iceland
Christianity

Christian III of Denmark begins to impose Lutheranism by force into Iceland. He meets significant resistance and it will take a decade to suppress Catholic forces that organize against changing the religion of the nation. The first book printed in Iceland, an edition of the Bible, appears in 1540.

1540

Central America and the Caribbean: Puerto Rico
Christianity

Construction begins on a new stone building for the Cathedral of San Juan Bautista, the Roman Catholic cathedral in Old San Juan. An initial cathedral made of wood had been erected in 1521, but it was destroyed on several occasions by passing storms.

1540

South Asia: India
Islam

The Battle of Kanauj. Sher Shah Suri (1486–1545), a Shi'a Muslim and founder of the Muslim-led Sur Empire with its capital at Delhi, defeats the Mughals, and soon afterward occupies the Mughal capital at Agra and largely gains control of India.

1540

Europe: France
Christianity

King Francis I's increasing paranoia relative to Protestantism leads to his issuing the Edict of Fontainebleau. He describes Protestantism as "high treason against God and mankind," hence its adherents deserve torture, loss of property, public humiliation, and death. The edict provides the initial codification of the persecution of the French Protestants (the Huguenots).

1540

Europe: Iceland
Christianity

The New Testament is translated and published by Oddur Gottskálksson. It is the first book ever printed in Icelandic.

1540–1542

North America: United States
Christianity

In search of the fabled Seven Cities of Cibola, Spanish explorer/adventurer Francisco Vasquez de Coronado leads an expedition into the interior of the Southwest that carries him across what are now Arizona, New Mexico, Texas, Oklahoma, and Kansas. Father Marcos de Niza, a Franciscan priest, accompanies the expedition.

September 27, 1540

Europe: Italy
Christianity

Paul III gives formal approval of the new Society of Jesus (the Jesuits) in his bull *Regimini militantis ecclesiae.*

1541

Central America and the Caribbean: Guatemala
Christianity

A massive lahar (mudflow) from the Volcán de Agua destroys the capital of Guatemala, and colonial authorities order the capital moved to the Panchoy Valley area where they found a new city that they name Santiago de los Caballeros. Construction soon begins on a new cathedral dedicated to St. Joseph.

1541

South America: Argentina
Christianity

Franciscan missionaries introduce Christianity to Argentina; however, local residents destroy Buenos Aires, and most Spaniards flee upriver to Asunción (Paraguay), which subsequently becomes the center of the Giant Province of the Indies, a new Spanish colonial jurisdiction that includes parts of Brazil, Paraguay, and Argentina.

1541

South America: Chile
Christianity

The first Roman Catholic priest arrives in Chile.

1541

South America: Peru
Christianity

The Roman Catholic Diocese of Lima (Peru) is erected, and the authority previously placed in the Diocese of Cuzco is largely transferred to it. It was elevated to an archdiocese in 1546. The Basilica of St. John is designated as the diocese's cathedral.

1541

Europe: Germany
Christianity

The Colloquy of Regensburg (aka the Colloquy of Ratisbon) brought Roman Catholic and Protestant church leaders together for a theological discussion of the issues raised by the Augsburg Confession. While consensus was reached on a variety of issues, the colloquy eventually failed and became the last significant attempt to bring the two parties together by means of theological discussion. Attendees at the conference included the emperor Charles V, Johann

Eck, papal legate Cardinal Contarini, Martin Bucer, and Philipp Melanchthon.

1541

Europe: Hungary
Christianity

János Sylvester, a professor at the University of Vienna, publishes the first full text of the New Testament in Hungarian.

1541

Europe: Italy
Christianity

Michelangelo completes his rendition of *The Last Judgment* in the Sistine Chapel of the Vatican Palace in Rome. It is officially unveiled on All Hallows Eve. He subsequently accepts the commission of Pope Paul III to paint the *Crucifixion of St. Peter* and the *Conversion of St. Paul* (1542–1550) in the Pauline Chapel at the Vatican.

1541

Europe: Italy
Judaism

The authorities in Venice, in an attempt to improve their economic condition, which includes trade with Jews from the East, grant Jews from Syria and Palestine the privilege of settling in the city. There is already a large Jewish community in the Venice ghetto, but it consists almost entirely of Ahskenazi Jews.

1541

Europe: Poland
Judaism

Rabbi Shalom Shakhna ben Joseph, Poland's new chief rabbi, establishes his court in Lublin, which emerges as a center of Jewish learning in the region over the next generation.

1541

Europe: Switzerland
Christianity

John Calvin is recalled to Geneva where he reestablishes the Reformed Church and where he will remain for the rest of his life.

1541–1542

Europe: England
Christianity

The dissolution of the monasteries leads to the creation of new dioceses for the Church of England, with some of the finest of the monastic sanctuaries being turned into cathedrals. The new Diocese of Gloucester is created from territory formerly a part of the Diocese of Worcester. John Wakeman, a former abbot at the monastery at Tewkesbury, is named as the first bishop. The church at the 11th-century Gloucester Abbey (dissolved in 1540) is appropriated as the diocese's new cathedral. It will come to be known as the Cathedral Church of St. Peter and the Holy and Indivisible Trinity.

The new Diocese of Oxford is created from territory formerly a part of the diocese of Lincoln (England). The church of St Frideswide's Priory, which had survived the dissolution of the monasteries in 1539 by having been selected by Cardinal Thomas Wolsey as the site of a new college, was designated as the cathedral for the new diocese.

The new Diocese of Peterborough is erected, and the church attached to the Benedictine Abbey, a victim of the dissolution of the British monasteries, is selected as the cathedral church for the new diocese. It will later be known as the Cathedral Church of St. Peter, St. Paul and St. Andrew.

The Diocese of Chester is created with territory reassigned from the dioceses of Lichfield and Coventry and of York. The former St. Werburgh's Benedictine abbey church, which had been dedicated to Christ and the Blessed Virgin Mary, is designated as the new diocese's cathedral.

The abbey church of St. Augustine's Abbey in Bristol, which had been closed three years earlier, is appropriated as the cathedral church for the newly formed Diocese of Bristol. It subsequently became known as the Cathedral Church of the Holy and Undivided Trinity. The church contains a shrine to King Edward II, who was assassinated at a nearby castle in 1327.

1541–1542

Europe: Ireland
Christianity

The Irish Parliament agrees to the change in status of the country from that of a Lordship to that of the Kingdom of Ireland and subsequently names Henry VIII as the king of Ireland. This change includes the official break between the church in Ireland and the Roman Catholic Church. Because of the widespread public support of the Catholic church, Henry's policy of dissolving the monasteries is resisted and he has difficulty in accomplishing his goal of taking over the monastic property and adding it to his coffers. Only those relatively close to Dublin are closed.

1541–1543

Sub-Saharan Africa: Ethiopia
Christianity, Islam

Portuguese forces under Christovan da Gama intervene on the side of Ethiopian forces to repel the attempt of Somali imam/general Ahmad ibn Ibrahim al-Ghazi to overrun Ethiopia. At the Battle of Waim Dega (February 21, 1543), al-Ghazi is killed.

1542

South America: Peru
Christianity

The recently formed Río de la Plata Province, which covers the modern countries of Paraguay, Argentina, Uruguay, and parts of Chile, Brazil, and Bolivia, is incorporated into the Viceroyalty of Peru, based in Lima, and unites Spain's South American territory.

1542

South Asia: India
Hinduism

Gopala Bhatta Goswami initiates the building of Sri Radha Raman Mandir, one of the 16th-century temples at the newly founded town of Vrindavan. It still houses the original saligram (a representation of Vishnu in the form of a spherical, black-colored stone, originating in a sacred river in Nepal) of Krishna, alongside a statue of Radha, Krishna's consort. Krishna is believed to have been an incarnation of the deity Vishnu. At about the same time, Srila Jiva Goswami led in the building of another Krishna-related temple, Radha Damodar Mandir. Damodar is another name for Krishna.

1542

South Asia: India
Christianity

Francis Xavier arrives in India to launch the Jesuit mission to the Indian people from the Portuguese outpost at Goa. The coming of Jesuits marks a significant turn in the role of the Catholic Church, which heretofore has primarily served the Portuguese settlers. For the next half century, the Jesuits are the only Roman Catholic missionaries in Asia.

1542

East and Southeast Asia: China
Chinese Religions
The Jiajing emperor of China survives an assassination attempt, after which he begins to pay increasing attention to his Taoist faith. He began to pay attention to Taoist alchemy and commissioned priests to gather rare materials to create elixirs that could prolong his life. It is hypothesized that some of these elixirs, containing mercury, may have ultimately contributed to his death.

1542

East and Southeast Asia: Japan, China
Christianity
The first contact of Japan with the European West occurs when a Portuguese ship that had been blown off its course to China lands in Japan at Tanegashima, a small island off the coast of Kyūshū. Japanese assist the three Portuguese to return to China where they inform other Westerners about the existence of Japan. As a result both Roman Catholic missionaries and traders will begin to arrive. Antonio da Mota, a Portuguese explorer, becomes the first European known to have entered Japan.

1542

Europe: Denmark
Christianity
In the wake of the success of the Protestant Reformation in Denmark, Hans Tausen, whose preaching had initiated the move toward Lutheranism, is named the bishop of Ribe.

1542

Europe: England
Western Esotericism

British law for the first time defines "witchcraft" as a felony and offers the possibility of death as the penalty. The law condemns the practice of malevolent magic, that is, the making of incantations that aim at harming another. The law also denies the condemned the right to "benefit of clergy," a legal loophole that spared accused persons from capital punishment if they were able to read a passage from the Bible.

1542

Europe: France
Christianity
Clement Marot, who had composed psalms in French while working at the court of Francis I, publishes a set of psalms designed to be sung in French. He is accused of heresy by Roman Catholic Church authorities, and he flees to Geneva where John Calvin and the Protestants welcome him and he continues his career. His work will be included in the *Geneva Psalter* (1562).

1542

Europe: Italy
Christianity
As part of his effort to counter the growth of Protestantism and the many new sectarian groups that had emerged around Europe, Pope Paul III established the Congregation of the Holy Office of the Inquisition and assigned it the tasks of maintaining and defending the integrity of the faith. It assumed hegemony over the various preexisting local inquisitions.

1542

Europe: Sweden
Christianity
The complete Bible in Swedish, originally commissioned by Swedish ruler Gustav Vasa, is published.

1542

Europe: Switzerland
Christianity
John Calvin publishes his revised Geneva Catechism, which has been simplified for the instruction of children in Reformed theology.

1543

South America: Paraguay
Christianity

A fire sweeps through Asunción. It damages the Cathedral of Asunción but the building is repaired and continues.

1543

South Asia: India
Islam

Mughal emperor Humayun, escaping his enemies, including a rival in his immediate family, finds refuge in the Safavid Empire in Iran. The Persia ruler, Tahmasp I I (1514–1576), offers support for his regaining his throne in return for his conversion to Shi'a Islam, and Humayan abandons his Sunni Islam.

1543

East and Southeast Asia: Japan
Christianity

The Portuguese land on Tanega-shima Island, Japan, and introduce rifles to the country.

1543

Europe: England
Christianity

In the context of the circulation of a variety of England translations of the Bible, Parliament moves to standardize the text used in churches. It designates the Great Bible (the 1539 text produced by Richard Taverner) as the official Bible of the Church of England. This act effectively banned William Tyndale's translation. At the same time Parliament forbade the lower classes from reading the Bible privately and prohibited any unlicensed person from reading the Bible and/or attempting to explain it to others in public settings.

1543

Europe: Germany
Judaism, Christianity

Reformer Martin Luther publishes his pamphlet "On the Jews and Their Lies." He advocates the burning of synagogues and the expulsion of Jews from Europe. The work has been credited with helping perpetuate anti-Semitism in modern Europe. It appears to have been a result of earlier efforts to convert German Jews, which the Jewish community had rebuffed.

1543

Europe: Italy
Christianity

Benedictine monk Benedetto Fontanini authors the most notable treatise on the theological position taken by the Spirituali, a reform movement within the Roman Catholic Church based in Italy. The *Beneficio di Cristo* (or the Benefit of Christ's Death) affirms salvation through faith in Christ alone, rather than through works or the church. In the context of the time, as Protestants and Catholics assume ever more radical positions both politically and doctrinally, the work is rejected by most Catholics as too Protestant, and distrusted by Protestants because of its source within the Roman Catholic Church.

1543

Europe: Poland
Christianity

Shortly before the death of astronomer Nicolaus Copernicus, his book *On the Revolutions of the Heavenly Orbs* (*De Revolutionibus Orbium Caelestium*), in which he offers proof of a heliocentric solar system, is published. He suggests that the earth moves (rotating once a day) and revolves around the sun annually.

1543

Europe: Portugal
Christianity

Jesuits in Coimbra, Portugal, begin construction of the church to serve their formation house. It will later become the main cathedral for the city.

1543

Europe: Scotland
Christianity

Mary Stuart, a devout Roman Catholic, is crowned Queen of Scotland at Stirling Castle.

1543

Europe: Switzerland
Islam

At the request of Martin Luther, a publisher in Basel reprints the Latin translation of the Qur'an. Issued under the title *Lex Mahumet pseudoprophete,* it is partially designed as a refutation of Islam. It also reproduces and hence perpetuates the errors and omissions of the Latin original.

1543–1544

Europe: France
Islam, Christianity

Toward the end of 1543, King Francis I of France expels the residents of Toulon in Provence from their city in order to provide living space for some 30,000 Turkish sailors under the command of the Ottoman-Barbary admiral Hayreddin Barbarossa, to whom Francis was indebted. While in Toulon, the Roman Catholic cathedral is transformed into a mosque for the sailors' use. In the spring, Francis pays the admiral a large sum of money to leave France.

1543–1544

Europe: Finland
Christianity

Michael Agricola, rector of the cathedral at Turku, publishes his first book, a primer for reading Finnish with an attached catechism. He follows it with a prayer book, *Rucouskiria.* Both books become foundational items of the Finnish written language.

1544

North America: United States
Christianity

Franciscan Andrés de Olmos, a veteran missionary in Mexico, struck northward into the Texas wilderness. After gathering a group of Indian converts, he will lead them back into Tamaulipas.

1544

Europe: Spain
Christianity

Thomas of Villanova, a friar of the Order of Saint Augustine, is named Archbishop of Valencia. During his decade in office, he became known for his oratorical skills, his austere lifestyle, and the care for the poor in his jurisdiction. He would later be canonized.

1545

South Asia: India
Islam

With Persian assistance, Mughal emperor Humayun begins his return to power by taking control of Kabul and eastern Afghanistan from his brother Kamran.

1545

Europe: France
Christianity

Catholic forces attack the Waldensians (French Protestants) residing near Merindol, Provence. They end what has been a period of persecution with a general massacre.

1545

Europe: Italy
Christianity

The Roman Catholic Council of Trent, which will attempt to consolidate the gains of the Counter-Reformation and further expand it, convenes at Trento, Italy. It will be one of 25 sessions stretching over 20 years.

The future pope Julius III serves as the first president of the council and opens its proceedings with a brief oration.

1545

Southwest Asia and North Africa: Morocco
Islam

Abu al-Abbas Ahmad ibn Muhammad (r. 1526–1545), a sultan of the Wattasid dynasty, is taken prisoner by Sadiyans, an Arab sultanate that ruled southern Morocco. Ali Abu Hassun, who comes to power in Morocco as the regent for Ahmad's son and successor Nasir al-Qasiri (r. 1545–1547), decides to pledge allegiance to the Ottoman Empire (which controlled neighboring Algeria) as a means of securing their support.

1545–1547

Europe: Holy Roman Empire
Christianity

Holy Roman Emperor Charles V attempts to find a resolution to his religiously divided realm by war. His Catholic army had pacified southern Germany by the end of 1546. In the spring of 1547, the forces of the Holy Roman Empire decisively defeat the Lutheran Protestant army of the Schmalkaldic League under the command of Elector John Frederick I of Saxony and Philip I of Hesse at the Battle of Mühlberg. The battle ended the Schmalkaldic War. As a result, John Frederick was forced to sign the Capitulation of Wittenberg, by which he lost his electorship and much of his territory. The victory temporarily slowed the Protestant cause, but did not stop it.

Meanwhile, Charles V quarrels with Pope Paul III, whose son is assassinated in 1547. The pope blames Charles for the death. Charles possesses the duchies of Parma and Piacenza, over which Paul's son was supposed to rule.

1546

Central America and the Caribbean: Mexico, Panama
Christianity

In creating the new Archdiocese of Mexico, Pope Paul III appoints Mexican bishop Zumárraga as the first archbishop and designates the dioceses of Oaxaca, Michoacán, Tlaxcala, Guatemala, and Ciudad Real de Chiapas as suffragan dioceses. The Diocese of Guadalajara is added in 1548. The bull authorizing all of these changes is forwarded to Mexico in 1548, but Bishop Zumárraga dies before it reaches him. Archbishop Zumárraga is succeeded by Alonso de Montúfar (r. 1551–1572).

The dioceses of Panama, Santiago de Cuba, and Puerto Rico are made suffragans of the new Archdiocese of Santo Domingo.

Drepung Monastery in Lhasa, Tibet. Founded in 1416, it is the largest monastery in Tibet. (Frank van den Bergh/iStockphoto.com)

1546

South America: Peru
Christianity

Pope Paul III makes significant changes in the Roman Catholic organization in the New World. The dioceses of Mexico City, Lima, and Santo Domingo are separated from the Archdiocese of Seville (Spain), elevated to archdioceses, and given metropolitan status over all the other dioceses in Spanish America. The new Archdiocese of Lima, which will extend along the Pacific coast from Central America to Chile, is assigned the new dioceses of Quito (Ecuador) and Popayán (Colombia) as suffragans. A year later, it also receives the new dioceses of Paraguay and Nicaragua as suffragans.

1546

East and Southeast Asia: China
Buddhism

The three-year-old later to become the third Dalai Lama is recognized as the reincarnation of Gedun Gyatso, the abbot of Sera Monastery in Tibet, who had passed away in 1542. The child was taken to Drepung Monastery, another center of the Gelugpa school of Tibetan Buddhism, where he would be trained and nurtured in Buddhist teachings and raised as a monk.

1546

East and Southeast Asia: Japan

The shogun Ashikaga Yoshiharu tires of his existence as a powerless monarch and retires. His 11-year-old son Ashikaga Yoshiteru (r. 1546–1565) succeeds him. Yoshiteru, though lacking financial and military resources, proves a capable diplomat and is thus able to operate by matching Japanese feudal lords (daimyos) against each other.

1546

Europe: England
Christianity

In light of the Great Bible, which had been created from the work of William Tyndale and Miles Coverdale, and which had been designated as the official English text to be utilized in the worship of the Church of England, authorities now explicitly ban Tyndale's and Coverdale's translations, which were popularly published and sold in England.

1546

Europe: Scotland
Christianity

Authorities burn George Wishart, a Protestant, at the stake in St. Andrews. Several weeks later, David Beaton, the archbishop of St. Andrews, is assassinated.

1546–1547

East and Southeast Asia: Indonesia
Christianity

Jesuit missionary Francis Xavier initiates a Roman Catholic mission in the Maluku Islands (which the Portuguese had originally colonized in 1534). During his two-year stay, he will travel among the islands of Ambon, Ternate, and Morotai, where he founds the original Catholic parishes.

February 18, 1546

Europe: Germany
Christianity

Protestant reformer Martin Luther dies.

1547

South America: Paraguay
Christianity

The Roman Catholic Diocese of Asuncion (Paraguay) is erected. It becomes an archdiocese in 1929.

1547

Europe: England
Western Esotericism

England repeals the antiwitchcraft law of 1542.

1547

Europe: France
Christianity

Francis I, the king of France, dies and is succeeded by his son Henry II (r. 1547–1559).

1547

Europe: France
Western Esotericism

The physician Michel de Nostredame (aka Nostradamus) (1503–1566) settles at Salon-de-Provence (southern France), where he marries and begins a second family, his first having been taken by the plague a decade earlier. He gradually withdraws from the medical profession and begins to devote himself to Esoteric topics. He soon begins work on what will become his first almanac that will include his first published predictions of the future.

1547

Europe: Germany
Christianity

The Battle of Mühlberg. Holy Roman Emperor Charles V defeats the Lutheran princes of the Schmalkaldic League. The battle launches an ongoing war.

1547

Europe: Italy
Islam

Andrea Arrivabene produces the first translation of the Qur'an into a modern European language—Italian. It is not made from the Arabic, rather Arrivabene uses the Latin text produced by Robertus Ketenensis in 1143. The Arrivabene text will subsequently become the basis of translations into additional European languages.

1547

Europe: Lithuania
Christianity

The first book in the Lithuanian language, a Christian catechism, is printed at Königsberg. Prepared by Martynas Mazvydas from Polish catechisms at the invitation of Prussian Protestant ruler Albert of Brandenberg, it had been designed to assist priests in teaching the language while spreading Lutheranism.

1547

Europe: Portugal
Christianity

The Inquisition in Portugal forbids possession of copies of the Bible in vernacular languages, only the Latin version being acceptable. It denounces António Pereira Marramaque, who previously championed the cause of vernacular translations and is known to own a Portuguese Bible. The operation of the Inquisition would stop the ongoing work of translation for the next century.

1547

Europe: Slovenia
Christianity

Primož Trubar, a Roman Catholic priest in Slovenia, begins to adopt Protestant views for which he is expelled from Ljubljana.

1547

Southwest Asia and North Africa: Morocco
Islam

Abu al-Abbas Ahmad ibn Muhammad (r. 1526–1545, 1547–1549), a sultan of the Wattasid Dynasty, who had been a prisoner of the Sadiyans who rule in southern Morocco, is released and returns to the throne of Morocco. He displaces his still minor son, Nasir al-Qasiri, who had ruled through a regent in his absence.

1547–1553

Europe: England
Christianity

King Henry VIII dies and is succeeded by his son who reigns as Edward VI (r. 1547–1553). He is but nine years old when he ascends the throne, and during his entire reign, the country is led by a regency council. During Edward's reign, every effort is made to Protestantize the church in England. The ban on the Tyndale and Coverdale versions of the Bible is lifted. The Church of England adopts the liturgy of the new Book of Common Prayer (1549) as its order of worship and abandons the Roman Catholic mass.

January 16, 1547

Russia
Christianity

Ivan IV is formally crowned as the ruler of Russia in a celebration at the Cathedral of the Dormition in

Moscow. He is the first to assert himself by adopting the title Czar (or Caesar).

1548

Central America and the Caribbean: Mexico
Christianity
Pope Paul III erects the Diocese of Guadalajara in Mexico. It includes California, then Spanish territory, within its boundaries.

1548

East and Southeast Asia: China
Chinese Religions
After many decades of relative peace, a Mongol army twice invades northern China (June, October) and on the second occasion threatens Beijing. Intermittent warfare would continue through the remainder of the Jiajing emperor's time on the throne.

1548

Europe: Finland
Christianity
Michael Agricola, having previously retired from his position as rector of the cathedral at Turku, completes his translation of the New Testament, which cements his position as the founder of Finnish literature.

1548

Europe: Germany
Christianity
The Augsburg Interim. Catholics and Protestants reach a temporary agreement to end hostilities.

The Holy Roman emperor Charles V orders Philip of Hesse to return the relics of St. Margaret of Hungary to the church in Marburg from which he had taken them in 1539. He complies, but does not reinter them in the golden shrine located in the church that had previously been erected in her honor. The relics are later dispersed to locations around Europe.

1548

Europe: Italy
Christianity

Pope Paul III formally approves the *Spiritual Exercises,* a form of meditation, prayer, and self-examination used by Jesuits to keep their personal spiritual life active and committed.

1548

Europe: Italy
Christianity, Islam
Having previously approved the open buying and selling of slaves by the inhabitants of Rome, Pope Paul III now authorizes specifically the purchase and possession of Muslim slaves within the Papal States.

1548

Europe: Italy
Christianity
In Rome, Philip Neri, a Roman Catholic layman, with the assistance of Fr. Persiano Rossa, founded the confraternity of the Santissima Trinita de' Pellegrini e de' Convalescenti, an association to assist the poor among the many pilgrims who journeyed to Rome each year, though especially targeting the many who would arrive in the jubilee approaching in 1550. Members also assisted those patients who were still too weak to care for themselves after spending time in the hospital.

Pope Paul III formally approves the *Spiritual Exercises* of Ignatius of Loyola and the book is published. The *Spiritual Exercises* offer a set of meditations, prayers, and mental exercises, with instructions on their use over a period of a month. They become an integral part of Jesuit life and find their way into the larger Christian world.

1548

Southwest Asia and North Africa: Palestine
Judaism
Sephardic scholar Moses ben Jacob Cordovero (aka the Ramak), a resident of Palestine, completes his first book, *Pardes Rimonim* (*Orchard of Pomegranates*), which summarizes and systemizes Kabbalistic thought of the time. Cordovero attempts to reconcile the variant interpretations of the Kabbalah and show their essential underlying unity.

1549

North America: United States
Christianity

The Dominican monk Fray Luis Cancer de Babastro attempts to initiate mission work among the Native people in the area around Tampa Bay, Florida, but is killed before establishing any permanent work.

1549

South America: Brazil
Christianity

Jesuits begin their first missionary work in the Americas at Bahia, Brazil. They will organize their converts into cooperative Native communities called reductions.

1549

East and Southeast Asia: Japan
Christianity

Jesuit priest Francis Xavier introduces Roman Catholicism to Japan. Landing at Kagoshima on the island of Kyūshū, he is accompanied by Anjiro, a Japanese convert he had met in Malaysia. He is received as a

FRANCIS XAVIER (1506–1552)

Francis Xavier, a first-generation Jesuit priest, was a pioneer Roman Catholic missionary to Asia. He established the church in India and Japan and prepared the way for the reentrance of Christianity into China.

Francis was born April 7, 1506, in Navarre. During the war that added Navarre to the new united Spain, the castle of Francis's family was destroyed in 1512. Sent to Paris for his college education, he met Ignatius Loyola while at the Sorbonne. Xavier became one of Loyola's close associates and was one of the original members of the Jesuit order (the Society of Jesus) who took their vows with him on August 15, 1534.

Meanwhile Xavier earned his doctorate and became a college professor. He settled at Venice and was ordained while there in 1537. In 1540, King John of Portugal called for priests to serve in India, where the Portuguese had been establishing colonies for several decades. Xavier volunteered to go and was named apostolic nuncio (papal ambassador with the authority of an archbishop) to Asia. He sailed for India in 1541 and reached Goa in 1542. He initially settled at Cape Comorin to work among the pearl-fishers. He assumed leadership of the Jesuit college, and in 1544 Loyola named him the first provincial of the Society of Jesus in Goa. In 1545, he further expanded his mission by moving to Malaysia (Malacca) and Indonesia (the Moluccas).

The most famous segment of his life began in 1547, when he encountered a Japanese man named Yajio. Yajio convinced Xavier to establish work in Japan and subsequently became his translator. He arrived in Japan in 1549 and was given some limited freedom to preach by the local ruler (daimyo) at Kagoshima. With Yajiro's help, he produced a catechism in Japanese.

While in Japan, Xavier developed a vision of evangelizing China. To that end, in 1552, he moved to Shangchuan, an island near Canton. He would die there December 3, 1552, while waiting to gain entrance into the Chinese kingdom. He was buried in the Good Jesus Church at Goa, India.

J. GORDON MELTON

representative of the king of Portugal. He had limited success as all Christian preaching and instruction was prohibited in 1550.

1549

Europe: England
Christianity

Anglican clergyman John Hopkins publishes a new edition of the metrical psalm book originally written by Thomas Sternhold (a groomsman in the household of Henry VIII) to which he adds additional psalms he had prepared for singing. It is the first metrical version of the Psalms to be widely used in both England and Scotland, and it attains a larger circulation than any work in the English language except the Bible and the Book of Common Prayer. It will remain in use until replaced by a new psalter at the end of the 17th century.

1549

Europe: England, Estonia
Christianity

A storm destroys the central tower of Lincoln Cathedral. The tower had made the cathedral the tallest building in the world (525 feet high). As a result of the lost tower, St. Olaf's Church in Tallinn, Estonia, at 521 feet, becomes the tallest building in the world, followed closely by St. Paul's Cathedral in London at 493 feet.

1549

Europe: Italy
Christianity

Pope Paul III dies toward the end of the year and is succeeded by Julius III (r. 1550–1555).

1549

Europe: Spain
Christianity

Church leaders in Gaudix, Spain, commission architect Diego de Siloé to design a new cathedral, which draws heavily on the designs of the cathedrals of Malaga and Granada. De Siloé had previously worked on the Malaga cathedral.

1549

Southwest Asia and North Africa: Morocco
Islam

Sultan Ahmad loses Fez and then Tlemcen to the emerging Saadian sultanate to the south. He dies and is succeeded by Ali Abu Hassun who again becomes Morocco's regent, but has to live in exile in neighboring Algeria, which is under Ottoman control.

ca. 1550

Central America and the Caribbean: Honduras
Christianity

Franciscan missionaries initiate work in Honduras, then part of Guatemala.

1550

South America: Brazil
Christianity

The first Africans arrive in Brazil as slaves to work on the sugar plantations.

1550

East and Southeast Asia: China, Tibet
Buddhism

The Sakyapa Buddhists establish a printing operation at Gengqing Monastery in Dege. It will publish a number of Buddhist works, including a new edition of the Buddhist scriptures.

1550

Europe: Belgium
Judaism

After a quarter of a century of relative peace under the protection of Holy Roman emperor Charles V, the Jewish community of Antwerp is expelled. Christian leaders in the city accuse the Jews, mostly New Christians who have moved to the city from Portugal, of favoring the Protestants and aiding the Reformation.

1550

Europe: Denmark
Christianity

The New Testament in Danish having been published in 1524, a complete Bible finally appears. It is the product of the translation work of Christiern Pedersen, a Danish scholar who had worked on a revised translation of the New Testament published in 1529. As with other northern European editions, the Danish Bible will have a strong role in the development of the Danish language and literature. It would be used as the primary translation in Denmark and Norway (Norwegian being very close to Danish) over the next century.

1550

Europe: England
Christianity
John Marbeck, an English church musician, compiles and publishes a concordance of the English-language Bible, the first such work of its kind.

1550

Europe: Italy
Christianity
Pope Julius III (r. 1550–1555) begins his reign. He succeeded Pope Paul III, who had died the previous year.

1550–1551

Europe: Switzerland
Christianity
Bible publisher Robert I Estienne (better known as Robert Stephens) moves from France to Geneva where he continues to publish editions of the Greek New Testament in Geneva. His 1550 edition is considered the epitome of Bible publishing in the century. It includes a critical notation apparatus noting the manuscripts from which the text is taken. His 1551 edition is, however, the better known as it is the first edition of the Greek New Testament to introduce the division of the New Testament into numbered verses. It also included the Latin translation of Erasmus and the Vulgate.

September 1550

Europe: Austria
Christianity

Leaders of the most radical wing of the Anabaptist movement gather in Vienna, Austria, and agree to a set of statements denying the Christian doctrine of the Trinity. The Council of Vienna becomes a significant step leading to the organization of the Polish Brethren, which adopts the non-Trinitarian Christianity of Laelius Socinus (d. 1562) and Faustus Socinus (d. 1604).

1551

Central America and the Caribbean: Mexico
Christianity
The Royal and Pontifical University of Mexico is created by a royal decree issued by Charles I of Spain. It has generally been considered the first university officially founded in North America and second in the Americas.

1551

South America: Brazil
Christianity
Pope Julius III erects the Diocese of Bahia, which relieves the Diocese of Funchal in Portugal of direct oversight of Portuguese holdings in South America.

1551

Europe: England
Christianity
Archbishop Thomas Cranmer published the 42 Articles of Religion, which provide the theological orientation of Anglican Protestantism.

1551

Europe: France
Christianity
King Henry II issues the Edict of Châteaubriant, one of a series of measures to attempt to slow the progress of Protestantism in his kingdom. The edict calls the courts to act by detecting and punishing heretics, and grants one-third of the property of convicted heretics to any who would inform on them. Much of the edict tried to suppress the spread of Protestant literature by prohibiting the publishing and sale of books disapproved by the Faculty of Theology at the University of Paris.

1551

Europe: Italy
Christianity

Ignatius of Loyola, the founder of the Society of Jesus, establishes a small college in Rome. It will grow to become the Pontifical Gregorian University.

1551

Russia
Christianity

Government authorities with the ruler's consent call a council of the Russian Orthodox Church, presided over by Macarius (r. 1542–1563), the metropolitan of Moscow and All Russia, and attended by Czar Ivan IV and representative nobles. The council, later known as the Stoglavy (or One Hundred Chapters) Sobor, produces a church code that unified church ceremonies and regulated church life, one goal being the improvement of the education of the clergy. The code was formatted as a set of questions from the czar with answers from the church. The questions would be organized into 100 chapters and published as the Synodal Code of the Russian Orthodox Church Synod. The Sobor establishes the jurisdiction of the church, with the czar, for example, abandoning any jurisdiction over the clergy, while the church in turn gives up a set of rights and privileges to the government. The One Hundred Chapters document would structure church-state relations in Russia for the next three and a half centuries.

1551–1552

Europe: Poland
Christianity

With the spread of the Reformation from Germany, the demand for a Bible in Polish was forthcoming and Jan Seklucjan, a Lutheran minister at Königsberg, prepares the first translation of the New Testament to be published and made available to the general public.

1552

South America: Bolivia
Christianity

The Roman Catholic Diocese of La Plata o Charcas (Bolivia) is erected from territory formerly under the Archdiocese of Lima (Peru). It became an archdiocese in 1609 and was renamed the Archdiocese of Sucre in 1924.

1552

South Asia: India
Sikhism

Before his death, Sikh Guru Angad Dev appoints Amar Das as his successor. Amar Das contributed some 7,500 lines of inspirational poetic verse to what would later become the Sikh scripture, the Guru Granth Sahib.

1552

Europe: Germany
Christianity

To end the conflict following the Interim of Augsburg of 1547, the war-weary emperor of the Holy Roman Empire, Charles V, signs the Peace of Passau, which guarantees a spectrum of freedoms to the German Lutherans.

1552

Europe: Italy
Christianity

Following the example of Ignatius of Loyola, Pope Julius III opens the German College in Rome, whose main purpose is the training of secular priests for German-speaking lands.

December 3, 1552

East and Southeast Asia: China
Christianity

Jesuit missionary Francis Xavier dies on Shangchuan Island off the coast of China while awaiting a boat that would take him to the mainland. He has left six of his Jesuit brothers to continue his work in Japan.

1553

Europe: England
Christianity

King Edward VI falls ill and the Regency Council creates a "Devise for the Succession" in a vain attempt to prevent a succession that could lead the country's return to Catholicism. Edward names his cousin Lady Jane Grey as his successor while specifically excluding his two half-sisters, Mary and Elizabeth. Jane is acknowledged as queen but a mere nine days later Mary is able to push her aside and is proclaimed queen. As Mary I (r. 1553–1558) she begins the process of returning England to the Roman Catholic fold.

1553

Europe: France
Unbelief
French physician Michael Servetus, who had published a book a decade earlier attacking the Christian doctrine of the Trinity, publishes *Christianismi Restitutio* (*The Restoration of Christianity*), a work that continues his unitarian views but also rejects the idea of predestination, that God saves and/or condemns souls by his grace, regardless of worth or merit. Protestant reformer John Calvin, who had championed the idea, begins a correspondence with Servetus that becomes ever more heated as it continues.

1553

Europe: Germany
Christianity
Pope Julius III suspends (but does not terminate) the work of the Council of Trent. The suspension will remain in place for nine years.

1553

Europe: Italy
Judaism, Christianity
Pope Julius III establishes a commission to examine the Talmud and, upon reviewing its report, orders its public burning.

October 17, 1553

Europe: Switzerland
Christianity, Unbelief
With John Calvin's approval, Michael Servetus, who had been arrested in Geneva, is burned at the stake as the author of a book, *On the Errors of the Trinity*, which challenged traditional concepts of the nature of the Christian deity. This action would become the major blemish on Calvin's record of accomplishments.

November 13, 1553

Europe: England
Christianity
Thomas Cranmer, the archbishop of Canterbury, and four others are tried for treason, convicted, and condemned to death.

1554

South America: Brazil
Christianity
The Jesuits found what becomes São Paulo, Brazil.

1554

South Asia: India
Islam
Shah Suri, the head of the Suri Empire in India, dies, leaving the empire in chaos. Mughal emperor Humayun, whom Suri had displaced in 1540, uses the opportunity to march on Delhi and reclaim his throne.

1554

East and Southeast Asia: Thailand
Two Dominican priests become the first Christian clergy active in Thailand. They are assigned as chaplains to Portuguese soldiers who serve the Thai king, but their job allows them time to seek converts from among the indigenous population.

1554

Europe: England
Christianity
Cardinal Reginald Pole, in exile in Italy, returns to England as papal legate to receive it back into the Roman Catholic fold.

1554

Europe: England
Christianity

Philip, the king of Naples and heir to the throne of Spain, marries Mary I, the queen of England, at Winchester Cathedral.

1554

Europe: France
Christianity
French Protestant theologian Sebastian Castellio questions the use of the sword to suppress heresy in his classic treatise on religious freedom, *Concerning Heretics.*

1554

Europe: Italy
Christianity
The constitution of the Jesuits is approved and promulgated. It emphasizes the virtue of obedience and outlines the unique obedience the order gives to the sitting pope.

1554

Europe: Switzerland
Christianity
Calvin writes *Defense of the Orthodox Trinity against the Errors of Michael Servetus* to answer the critics about his allowing Servetus to be executed.

1554

Southwest Asia and North Africa: Maghreb
Islam
The Zayyanid Dynasty, whose kingdom is based in Tlemcen, northwest Algeria, becomes a protectorate of the Ottoman Empire.

1554

Southwest Asia and North Africa: Morocco
Islam
Moroccan regent Ali Abu Hassun is killed in a battle for control of Morocco with the rival Saadians at the Battle of Tadla. Saadian sultan Mohammed ash-Sheik (r. 1554–1557) recaptures the city of Fez and takes charge of the country. Almost immediately, he opens discussions with Spain aimed at cooperation to oust the Ottomans from Algeria.

1554–1555

Europe: England
Christianity
John Hooper, the bishop of Gloucester, is arrested, removed from his office as bishop (because he was married), condemned for heresy (as an outspoken Calvinist), and eventually burned at the stake.

1555

Sub-Saharan Africa: Ghana
Islam
The Portuguese build Forte se Sao Tiago (now known as Fort Coenraadsburg) at Elmira, Ghana. It will become infamous as a slaving center.

1555

Central America and the Caribbean: Mexico
Christianity
The first provincial council of the Archdiocese of Mexico, presided over by Archbishop Alonso de Montufar, rules against ordination of any Native person or mestizo (a person of mixed racial birth).

1555

South America: Brazil
Christianity
Some 500 French colonists led by Admiral Nicolas Durand de Villegaignon build Fort Coligny on an island in Guanabara Bay, Brazil.

July 23, 1555

South Asia: India
Islam
Formerly deposed emperor Humayun (r. 1555–1556) finally takes Delhi and once again inhabits the Mughal throne after a 15-year absence.

1555

East and Southeast Asia: Cambodia
Christianity
Gaspar da Cruz, a Portuguese member of the Dominican order, arrives in Cambodia hopeful of establishing a Roman Catholic mission. He finds the country

has a closed religious system and the people are difficult to work among. He withdraws, and pronounces his effort a failure.

1555

Europe: France
Western Esotericism

The queen consort of France, Catherine de' Medici, summons Nostradamus to Paris to explain the predictions published in his almanac that seem to prophesy an unfavorable future for the royal family. Meanwhile, Nostradamus has begun composing a set of poetic verses, each containing predictions for the more or less long-term future. The publication of the first collection of *The Prophecies* would be followed by an additional volume in 1557 and a third published posthumously (1568). The prophecies are largely based upon Nostradamus's reading of astrology, his particular methods being largely denounced by contemporary astrologers.

1555

Europe: France
Christianity

French Protestants organize the first Huguenot congregation in Paris. It will soon attract a number of the wealthy, nobles, and even members of the French court.

1555

Europe: Germany
Christianity

The Peace of Augsburg gives the first legal recognition to Lutheranism and allows each ruler throughout Germany to choose between Lutheranism and Catholicism. The peace agreement does not recognize Reformed or Anabaptist Protestantism.

1555

Europe: Italy
Judaism

Pope Paul IV issues a papal ruling that had the effect of creating the Jewish ghetto in Rome. He forced all Jews to move their residence to a specified area of the city, which would be locked up each evening. The new Jewish regulations include the wearing of a distinctive item of clothing—a yellow hat for men and a veil or shawl for the women.

1555

Europe: Italy
Christianity

Pope Julius III dies. He has been the subject of a growing scandal surrounding his relationship with a young man, Innocenzo Ciocchi del Monte, whom his brother had adopted as his son. Some accused Julius of having an affair with the boy, who was promoted to office within the Vatican and given a number of benefices, all of which made him a wealthy man. Julius is succeeded by Pope Marcellus II, whose reign lasts less than a month. He is then succeeded by Pope Paul IV (r. 1555–1559), who had earlier been one of the co-founders of the Theatine order. Paul will use the new powers he has been granted to suppress the Spirituali, the popular reform group within the church, which he considers heretical. Some will be called to account before the Inquisition.

Paul IV issues a new church ordinance in which he proclaims that the Blessed Virgin Mary was a virgin before, during, and after the birth of Jesus of Nazareth. This doctrine of perpetual virginity is held by the Eastern Orthodox churches and Roman Catholicism, but denied by most Protestants who believe that while she was a virgin at the time of Jesus's birth, she later bore other children (Mark 6:3).

1555–1556

Europe: England
Christianity

Thomas Cranmer is officially deposed as the archbishop of Canterbury. He is succeeded by Reginald Pole, a layman, who was ordained as a Roman Catholic priest on March 20, 1556, and consecrated as the archbishop of Canterbury two days later.

Thomas Cranmer signs a confession of his errors but is still condemned to be burned at the stake. He subsequently retracts his confession and as he is about to be burned, he extends his hand in the fire and announces, "For as much as my hand offended, writing contrary to my heart, my hand shall first be punished."

October 16, 1555

Europe: England
Christianity

Bible publisher John Rogers becomes the first victim of the Roman Catholic backlash against British Protestants by Queen Mary I. Soon afterward, prominent Protestant leaders Hugh Latimer and Nicholas Ridley, the bishop of Rochester, are also burned at the stake at Oxford after they are denounced for heresy by British Catholic authorities.

1556

Central America and the Caribbean: Mexico
Christianity

The second archbishop of Mexico, Alonso de Montúfar, having reached a positive assessment of the apparitions of the Blessed Virgin Mary at Guadalupe, launches the construction of a new, more substantial church at the site.

1556

South Asia: India
Islam

The Second Battle of Panipat. Mughal emperor Humayun dies from a falling accident and is succeeded by his 13-year-old son Akbar (r. 1556–1605). Immediately after Akbar ascends the throne, Hemu (1501–1556), a Hindu king who rules a remnant of the former Suri kingdom in North India, challenges his authority. Mughal forces meet his army at the Second Battle of Panipat and soundly defeat him. Hemu was captured and brought to Delhi for execution. The battle proved to be a major step in the establishment of Mughal power across India.

Among the consequences of the battle, the Katra Mosque is erected on the site of the previous Keshava Deo Temple, the reputed birthplace of Krishna, a spot now marked by a small marble slab leading to a small room where the story of Krishna is told in pictures and text.

1556

East and Southeast Asia: China
Buddhism

The ninth karmapa, the head of the Karma Kagyu school of Tibetan Buddhism, is born Wangchuk Dorje

Akbar (1542–1605), the third Mughal emperor of India, consolidated an empire that extended over most of India and reformed the administration of the Mughal Empire. Gouache on paper, Indian School (17th century). (London Library, St James's Square, London, UK/The Bridgeman Art Library)

in eastern Tibet. As a child he declared his identity to his parents, and as news spread, a student of the former karmapa, who had died in 1554, took charge of the child and traveled with him to Kyamo Lhundrub Tse Monastery. The child subsequently went through a series of tests culminating in his meeting the shamarpa, another Karma Kagyu incarnated lineage holder who had been originally identified by the eighth karmapa, who accepted the child and became his teacher.

1556

East and Southeast Asia: China

A massive earthquake shakes Shaanxi Province, China. Killing hundreds of thousands of people, it is deemed the deadliest earthquake of all time.

1556

Europe: Bohemia
Christianity

A Spanish princess, Maria Manriques, marries Czech nobleman Vratislav of Pernstejn and brings as a wedding gift a statue of the infant Jesus of Nazareth. The statue would eventually find its way to the Church of Our Lady of Victory in Prague, a church managed by the Carmelites, and devotion offered the statue becomes entwined with the fortunes of the city.

Holy Roman Emperor Ferdinand I invites the Jesuits to Prague to counter the growing power of the Protestants and gives them the Collegium Clementinum (later the Catholic University of Prague).

1556

Europe: England
Christianity

Joan Waste, a relatively poor woman who objected to the Latin mass and denied the doctrine of transubstantiation, is tried for heresy at All Saints Church in Derby, England. Upon being convicted, she is executed.

1556

Europe: England
Christianity

Cardinal and papal legate Reginald Pole is ordained as a Roman Catholic priest and named the new archbishop of Canterbury (r. 1556–1558). He already served as the chancellor of both Oxford and Cambridge universities. As a member of the Spirituali reform group, he will remain in England in spite of attempts of Pope Paul IV to recall him and place him under investigation for his reformist views.

1556

Europe: Italy
Christianity

Philip Neri, a priest in Rome, founds an informal society, the Congregation of the Oratory, an association of clergy who undertake a variety of evangelical and charitable works throughout the city. Later named the Oratory of Saint Philip Neri, the group evolves into a community of Roman Catholic priests and lay brothers who live together without formal vows, bound only by the bonds of charity. They are popularly referred to as Oratorians. Unlike most religious orders, the society would not develop a central authority and each center is essentially autonomous.

1556

Europe: Italy, Spain
Christianity

Holy Roman Emperor Charles resigned to spend his last days in retirement in a Spanish monastery. He bequeaths the Spanish throne to his son Philip II, but turns the Holy Roman Empire over to his brother Ferdinand I. Ferdinand I will become Holy Roman emperor without being crowned by the Pope.

Philip II (r. 1556–1598), already the king of Naples, becomes the king of Spain. By virtue of his marriage to Mary I, he is also king of England. He will reign from his hometown of Valladolid, which briefly serves as the Spanish capital.

1556

Europe: Malta
Islam, Christianity

Forces of the Ottoman Empire attack the strongholds of the Knights Hospitaller (now reorganized as the Knights of Malta). They secure early success in the Great Siege of Malta over the summer months. As victory seems to be in their grasp, however, Spanish forces arrive to relieve the Maltese and drive the Ottomans away with heavy losses.

1556

Europe: Switzerland
Christianity

With Mary I's assumption of the throne of England, many British Protestants flee the country and settle in Geneva. In 1556, the Reformed congregation they had formed issues the "Confession of Faith of the English Congregation of Geneva," reflecting their continued belief in the doctrine of the early church as seen in the Nicene Creed of the fourth century, and detailing their differences with the Roman Catholic ruler then in control in England.

1556

Europe: Switzerland
Christianity
John Calvin sanctions the execution of Michael Servatus for denying the Trinity.

1556

Southwest Asia and North Africa: Maghreb
Islam
The Zayyanid Dynasty in western Algeria comes to a formal end as its territory is officially absorbed into the Regency of Algiers, the territory of the Ottoman Empire in the Maghreb. The regency would remain Ottoman territory until the early 19th century.

January 22, 1556

Europe: Poland
Christianity
Piotr of Goniądz, a Polish student, denies the doctrine of the Trinity during the general synod of the Reformed churches of Poland meeting in Secemin, Poland.

March 21, 1556

Europe: England
Christianity
Thomas Cranmer, the former archbishop of Canterbury, who had been removed from office and defrocked, is executed by being burned at the state.

June 16, 1556

South America: Brazil
Christianity
The Caytes people of coastal Brazil kill Pedro Fernandes Sardinha, the first bishop of Bahia (Brazil), following his being shipwrecked at a point between the rivers São Francisco and Cururipu.

Portuguese missionary priests arrive in what is now the state of Espírito Santo, Brazil, and found the cities of Serra, Nova Almeida, and Santa Cruz.

July 31, 1556

Europe: Italy
Christianity
Ignatius Loyola dies. By this time the Jesuit order he founded has become a global organization. In Europe it has founded a number of colleges, which will become major assets of the church as it attempts to recover territory largely taken over by Protestants.

1557

East and Southeast Asia: China, Macau
Christianity
The Portuguese are finally able to establish a permanent settlement in Macau, and for the foreseeable future they will pay an annual rent for that privilege. The next year they erect the first church, St. Anthony's, a small building constructed of bamboo and wood.

1557

East and Southeast Asia: Japan
Shinto
The main buildings at Munakata Taisha, a fourth-century Shinto shrine on Oshima Island in Fukuoka Prefecture, seven miles off the coast of the Sea of Japan, burn. They will be rebuilt over the next 20 years.

1557

Europe: England
Christianity
Mary I, the ruler of England, charters the Stationers' Company as a structure to assist in the suppression of Protestant and other dissenting books. The right to print books is limited to two universities and the 21 existing printers in the city of London. Through the Stationers' Company, the Crown took control of all 53 printing presses then to be found in England.

1557

Europe: France
Christianity
The Edict of Compiègne strengthens the Edict of Châteaubriant (1551) by making heresy a capital crime. It also calls attention to printers, viewed collectively as radical and rebellious individuals.

1557

Europe: Lithuania
Christianity

Martynas Mažvydas, an early Protestant, compiles and publishes the first book in Lithuanian, *The Catechism,* which also contains translations of several biblical passages—the Ten Commandments, two psalms, and extracts from the Gospels and the Epistles.

1557

Europe: Serbia
Christianity

Ottoman sultan Suleiman the Magnificent allows the restoration of the Serbian patriarchate. Makarije Sokolović, a close relative of Suleiman's Grand Vizier Mehmed-paša Sokolović, becomes the new patriarch in Peć. Peé, a city in the Serbian province of Kosovo, is home to a complex of churches that serves as the spiritual seat of the Serbian church leadership.

1557

Europe: Switzerland
Christianity

A group of British Protestant exiles residing in Geneva, under the leadership of William Whittingham, prepare a new English edition of the Bible based on the edition of William Tyndale (which had appeared in 1525) and including an introduction by Calvin. The New Testament appears in 1557.

1557

Southwest Asia and North Africa: Morocco
Islam

Moroccan ruler Mohammed ash-Sheikh is assassinated by agents of the Ottoman Empire as he attempts to create an alliance with Spain against the Ottomans. He is succeeded by his son Abdallah al-Ghalib (r. 1557–1574). He makes Marrakesh his capital, refurbishes and enlarges the several mosques, and transforms the 12th-century Ben Youssef Medrassa into one of the largest Islamic colleges in North Africa.

December 3, 1557

Europe: Scotland
Christianity

A group of Protestant noblemen in Scotland covenant together to maintain and defend the Reformed faith. They become known as the "Lords of the Congregation."

1558

South America: Brazil
Christianity

Pedro Palácios founds Penha Convent in Vila Velha, Brazil. The convent will later house the miracle-working statue of Our Mother of Penha (the Blessed Virgin Mary), and it becomes a major pilgrimage site of the region.

1558

South America: Paraguay
Christianity

Jesuits launch a mission among the native peoples of Paraguay. They move converts into a set of Christian settlements following a pattern already at work in Argentina, Brazil, and Bolivia.

1558

South Asia: India
Hinduism

Muslim forces from Bengal take control of Orissa. As part of the attempt to preserve sacred objects from destruction, the priests at the main Puri temple remove the statue of Lord Jagannath and hide it, while the priests at Konark similarly conceal the sun deity statue. The removal of the Konark statue leads to the abandonment of the temple as a place of worship; it falls into ruin and a forest soon envelops it.

1558

South Asia: India, Sri Lanka
Christianity

Pope Paul IV erects the Roman Catholic Diocese of Cochin, which covers the island of Sri Lanka (Ceylon) and Portuguese settlements along the coast of India on the Bay of Bengal. Both the new Diocese of Cochin and of Malacca (in Malaysia) are made suffragans of the newly elevated Archdiocese of Goa.

1558

East and Southeast Asia: China
Buddhism

Sonam Gyatso, later to be named the third Dalai Lama and already the abbot of Drepung Monastery, additionally becomes the abbot of Sera Monastery, and thus head of two of the most important centers of the Gelugpa school of Tibetan Buddhism.

1558

East and Southeast Asia: Malaysia
Christianity

Pope Paul IV erects the Roman Catholic Diocese of Malacca, which covers the southern half of the Malay Peninsula. It is under the authority of the Archdiocese of Goa. Jorge de Santa Luzia, a Dominican, is named as the diocese's first bishop.

1558

Europe: England
Christianity

John Foxe issues the first edition of his *Book of Martyrs,* a history of Christian martyrdom with a special emphasis on the sufferings of the Protestants under Mary. The book will go through numerous editions and continue in print over succeeding centuries. It will contribute to popular anti-Catholicism in the English-speaking world well into the 20th century.

1558

Europe: Germany
Christianity

Holy Roman Emperor Charles had attempted to abdicate in 1556 in favor of his younger brother Ferdinand I (r. 1558–1564). The Imperial Diet, however, refused to accept the abdication and did not act until the beginning of 1558. Ferdinand becomes the new emperor but does not inherit the rule of Spain, which has already been passed to Charles's son Philip.

1558

Europe: Switzerland, Scotland
Christianity

From Geneva, Scottish reformer John Knox issues *The First Blast of the Trumpet against the Monstrous*

Engraving of John Foxe (1517–1587), English historian and martyrologist. Foxe was the author of the *Book of Martyrs,* the most widely read volume in Elizabethan England. (Georgios Kollidas/Dreamstime.com)

Regiment of Women, a work directed at the rule of Catholic monarchs Mary I in England and Mary, Queen of Scots. Meanwhile, in Scotland, Walter Mylne becomes the last Protestant to be executed by burning at the stake in St. Andrews.

November 17, 1558

Europe: England
Christianity

Mary I of England dies and is succeeded by her half-sister Elizabeth I (r. 1558–1603). Elizabeth's increasing concern with Roman Catholic schemes to remove her from the throne sets the stage for a resurgent Protestant movement in both England and Scotland (where Mary, Queen of Scots, a Roman Catholic, has made her claim to the British throne known).

About 12 hours after the death of Mary I, Reginald Pole, the archbishop of Canterbury, also dies of an illness. Following his death, the office will be left vacant for over a year.

During the reign of Queen Elizabeth I, England consolidated its position as a European power and embarked on becoming a colonial power. A shrewd and forceful monarch, Elizabeth encouraged the spread of English influence throughout the world. (Corbis)

December 18, 1558

South Asia: India
Christianity

During the celebration of the mass on a hill outside Madras, the location assigned by tradition of the martyrdom of the Christian apostle Thomas, a stone into which a cross had been engraved is seen to ooze blood. Over the next century and a half, reoccurrences of the phenomenon on December 18 are frequently reported.

1559

South Asia: India
Christianity

The Roman Catholic Archdiocese of Goa commissions Goncalo da Silveria as a missionary to Zimbabwe and Mozambique. In Africa he will have initial success, but will soon be denounced by the Native people as a sorcerer (practitioner of malevolent magic) and executed (1661). His work will be supplemented the next year by Jesuit missionaries.

1559

Europe: England
Western Esotericism

Esoteric astrologer John Dee carefully calculates the day and time of the coronation ceremony of Queen Elizabeth I of England, which occurs at noon on January 15.

1559

Europe: England
Christianity

Matthew Parker (r. 1559–1575) is named the archbishop of Canterbury; however, church leaders have a problem locating the four bishops necessary for the consecration to occur. Finally, the ceremony is held on December 19. Parker will emerge as one of the major architects of modern Anglicanism as he steers the church away from Roman Catholicism, but refuses to accept Calvinist demands for the full adoption of Reformed theology and ecclesiology.

1559

Europe: France
Christianity

French Calvinist Protestants (Huguenots) gather for a first national synod. Protestantism had spread through France and gained the support of many nobles.

1559

Europe: France, Switzerland
Christianity

Through the 1540s and 1550s, Protestantism permeates all sections of France in spite of the more visible early reformers being driven into Switzerland. Persecution of the church, especially in Paris, led John Calvin and others in Switzerland to write a confession designed to assist their fellow believers in France. Relatively persecution-free years at the very end of the 1550s offer the occasion for the Parisian Protestants to publish their statement. Now known as the "French Confession of Faith," it is addressed to the king of France.

1559

Europe: Italy
Christianity

Pope Paul IV responds to the coronation of England's Queen Elizabeth I by calling for the overthrow of those sovereigns that support heresy (that is, Protestantism). England ignores the papal pronouncement and issues a new Act of Supremacy defining Queen Elizabeth as the supreme governor of the Church of England.

1559

Europe: Italy
Christianity

After issuing a initial list of prohibited books and quickly withdrawing it, Pope Paul IV issues a new edition of the *Index Librorum Prohibitorum* (i.e., *List of Prohibited Books*), a list of publications prohibited by the Roman Catholic Church. It bans the entire corpus of approximately 550 authors plus a number of individual titles that are proscribed. It specifically includes all books written by Protestants and all translations of the Bible into German and Italian. A new edition will be issued after the approval of the Council of Trent.

1559

Europe: Italy
Christianity

Pope Paul IV dies and is succeeded by Pope Pius IV (r. 1559–1565), born Giovanni Angelo Medici, a distant relative of the more famous branch of the Medici family who were so prominent in the history of Florence.

Before his death, Paul IV establishes new archdioceses in France (Cambrai), the Netherlands (Utrecht), and Belgium (Mechelen).

1559

Europe: Italy
Judaism

Pope Paul IV adds to the restrictions on the Jews of Italy by placing the Talmud on the list of prohibited books. He allows the publication of a revised version of the Talmud under an alternate name, which will be edited and all passages deemed opposed to or insulting Christianity will be deleted.

Paul IV will allow the first printing of the *Zohar* (*The Book of Splendor*), an important Jewish mystical text, which he has determined contains no anti-Christian statements.

1559

Europe: Spain
Christianity

Teresa of Avila has her first encounter with Jesus Christ, who, she is convinced, presents himself to her in bodily (if invisible) form. These encounters will continue for some two years.

1559

Europe: Spain
Christianity

King Philip II of Spain (r. 1556–1598) designates Juan Bautista de Toledo as his royal architect and with him begins to plan the royal and ecclesiastical complex known as El Escorial outside of his capital of Madrid, as a monumental statement of Spain's position in the center of the Christian world. Among the purposes of the complex would be a commemoration of the Spanish victory at the Battle of St. Quentin (1557) against France, a place of burial for the past and future rulers of Spain, and a center for the Counter-Reformation effort against Protestantism. The final design seems to have been influenced by the description of the Jewish Temple in Jerusalem in the writings of Flavius Josephus. The center of the complex is the Basilica of San Lorenzo el Real, a Gothic structure.

1559

Europe: Switzerland
Christianity

John Calvin dies and is succeeded as head of the Reformed church movement by theologian and Bible scholar Theodore Beza. Beza becomes moderator of the company of pastors and a teacher in Calvin's academy.

1559–1560

Europe: France
Christianity

Henry II, the king of France, dies an untimely death from wounds inflicted during a jousting tournament he had organized to celebrate the Peace of Cateau-Cambrésis, which for the moment had ended a lengthy war with the Habsburgs, then the dominant power in Europe. He is succeeded by his 15-year-old son, Francis II (r. 1559–1560), who died of an illness still not fully understood the next year. He was succeeded by his 10-year-old brother, Charles IX (r. 1559–1574). His time on the throne was largely dominated by his mother, Catherine de' Medici, who initially emerged as regent.

1559–1560

Europe: France
Christianity

Delegates representing Protestant churches across France (the Huguenots) meet secretly in Paris where they approve a Constitution of Ecclesiastical Discipline and a Reformed Confession of Faith, based on one that John Calvin in Geneva had approved and sent to France. The final confession, which would the next year be presented to King Francis II, would become known as the Gaelic Confession.

1559–1560

Europe: Scotland
Christianity

Upon his return to Scotland from exile in Geneva, authorities declare John Knox an outlaw. With his Protestant followers, he retreats to the walled city of Perth, and at the city's church of St. John the Baptist he preaches a sermon that leads to a major riot. The Protestants ransack the church and then attack two friaries that are looted. They also smash Catholic statues and destroy an array of artifacts.

Knox later returns to St. Andrews where a sermon in the cathedral also leads to a riot with resulting vandalism and looting. The Protestant revolt spread to Edinburgh where Mary of Guise, the queen regent, is forced to promise freedom of conscience on religious matters. The issues raised by the Protestant strength in Edinburgh brought both Protestant England and Catholic France into the situation, which took a decisive turn following the sudden death of Mary of Guise in June 1560.

Within weeks, the Scottish Parliament met to settle religious issues and approved the new Scots Confession of Faith authored by Knox and several other Protestant ministers. A week later, Parliament abolished the jurisdiction of the pope in Scotland, condemned all doctrine and practice deemed contrary to the Protestant Reformed faith, and forbade the celebration of the Catholic mass throughout the land. Knox and his colleagues were then assigned the task of reorganizing the Church of Scotland along Presbyterian lines, and they set about writing a *Book of Discipline.*

1559–1563

Europe: England
Christianity

Following her coronation, Elizabeth I outlines a *via media* between Puritanism and Roman Catholicism by issuing the Act of Uniformity (1559), publishing a new edition of the Book of Common Prayer (1959), and promulgating a revised doctrinal statement, the Thirty-Nine Articles of Religion (1563).

1560

South Asia: India
Hinduism

Vishwanatha Nayak submits a design to rebuild Meenakshi Amman Temple, the ancient Hindu temple located in Madurai, Tamil Nadu, to Nayak, the king of Madurai, who had just taken the throne the year before. It will take a century to begin to bring the temple, which had been thoroughly destroyed in 1310, back to a state approaching its former grandeur; however, once rebuilt it will again become one of India's most important Hindu centers.

1560

East and Southeast Asia: China
Buddhism

The third Dalai Lama Soinam Gyamco initiates construction of the Tar Monastery (aka "Holy Place for the 100,000-Body Maitreya Buddha") at Lotus Flower Mountain, Qinghai Province, Yunnan. It is built to honor Tsongkhapa, the founder of the Gelugpa school of Tibetan Buddhism. The large monastery, one of the largest Tibetan Buddhist centers, is one of six major Gelugpa monasteries and the place for training many of the next generation of Tibetan monks.

1560

East and Southeast Asia: Japan
Christianity

A Jesuit missionary (one of approximately a dozen) meets in Kyoto with the shogun Yoshiteru who issues orders that the missionaries are to be well treated and not taxed. He sanctions their work in Kyoto.

1560

Europe: England
Christianity

British Protestant exiles in Geneva finish their work on the new translation of the Christian Old Testament and publish a complete edition of the Bible (the New Testament having been published three years previously). It becomes known as the Geneva Bible or more popularly as the Breeches Bible due to a misprint in the text of Genesis 3:7, where reference is made to Adam and Eve covering themselves with "breeches" made from fig leaves.

The Bible was dedicated to Queen Elizabeth, who hesitated in accepting the dedication, but allowed the volume to be distributed. It would become the most popular edition of the Bible in England, replacing the Great Bible, which had become the standard text for the Church of England in 1543 until superseded in the next century by the King James Version.

1560

Europe: France
Christianity

The Amboise Conspiracy. Huguenot Protestants attempt to abduct the young king, Francis II, and simultaneously arrest Francis, Duke of Guise, a leading Catholic layman, and his brother, Charles de Lorraine, the archbishop of Rheims and a Roman Catholic cardinal. The event would provoke retaliation by the Catholic community and the Guise family and lead directly to the Wars of Religion that would divide France for a generation (1562–1598).

1560

Europe: France
Christianity

Jeanne III, the queen of the small independent kingdom of Navarre in the southwest corner of France immediately north of the Pyrenees Mountains, converts to Protestantism and identifies with the French Huguenots. She would commission the translation of the Bible into the Basque language, one of the first books published in the language, and with her son, Henry III of Navarre, become a leader among the Huguenots during the French Wars of Religion.

1560

Europe: Germany
Christianity

Lutherans in Magdeburg initiate publication of a new chronicle/history of Christianity with a decided anti-Catholic perspective arranged in a century by century format. Because of the format they adopt, they come to be known as the Centuriators.

1560

Europe: Ireland
Christianity

The Irish Act of Uniformity establishes compulsory worship according to the (Anglican) Church of Ireland, while Irish church officials had to swear the Oath of Supremacy, which recognized Queen Elizabeth as head of the church. Attendance at Church of Ireland services became obligatory, though initially continuing Roman Catholic worship was tolerated.

1560

Europe: Scotland
Christianity

In a confrontation between the queen regent of Scotland, Mary of Guise, and the Protestant "Lords of the Congregation," Mary backs down and signs a peace agreement, which leads to a meeting of the Scottish Parliament at which a set of proposals were considered relative to reforming the church. Among the items adopted by the Parliament (August 24) is the "Scottish Confession of Faith," a landmark document in the move to transform the Church of Scotland into a Presbyterian church in the theological tradition of the Reformed Church of Geneva. After the confession is adopted, the Parliament moved to abolish the Catholic mass and renounce the jurisdiction of the pope in the country.

1560

Europe: Spain
Christianity

In his book *Tizon de la nobleza de Espana* (*The Blot on the Spanish Nobility*), Cardinal Mendoza, the archbishop of Burgos, claims that almost all of the Spanish aristocracy had Jewish or Moorish blood. He concludes that the Inquisition's campaign to prevent anyone with Jewish blood from rising to a significant position in the royal government was wishful thinking in the extreme.

1560–1561

Europe: Bosnia
Islam

Hadim Ali-pasha, the former Ottoman governor of Bosnia, endows and constructs Ali Pasha's Mosque in Sarajevo. It is modeled on mosques in Istanbul.

1561

Central America and the Caribbean: Honduras
Christianity

The Roman Catholic Diocese of Comayagua (Honduras) is erected. It will be elevated as an archdiocese and its name changed to the Archdiocese of Tegucigalpa in 1916.

1561

Central America and the Caribbean: Mexico
Christianity

Construction begins on the Cathedral de San Idelfonso in Merida, Mexico. It is located on the site of a former Mayan temple and designed as a center for the new Spanish ruler in the effort to pacify and convert the Maya. It will take a generation to complete.

1561

South America: Chile
Christianity

The Roman Catholic Diocese of Santiago (Chile) is erected. Chile had previously been in the Archdiocese of Lima, and the new diocese is created as a suffragan of Lima. The Diocese of Chile will become an archdiocese in 1840.

1561

East and Southeast Asia: Timor

Portuguese Roman Catholic missionaries on Timor convert the ruler of the island to Christianity.

1561

Europe: France
Christianity

Increasing persecution of the French Protestant community is temporarily halted by the Edict of Orléans, though high tension levels between Protestants and Catholics continued, occasionally breaking out in violent incidents.

Huguenots (French Protestants) severely damage the Cathedral of Saint John the Baptist of Bazas (Gironde, France), necessitating a complete rebuilding (1583–1635). The church, parts of which date from the 11th century, is an important stop for pilgrims making their way to Santiago de Compostela in Spain. The rebuilt church combines Gothic and several pre-Gothic patterns of architecture.

Acting on the edict, Catherine de' Medici, then the regent of France, calls the Colloquy of Poissy to effect Protestant-Catholic harmony. She orders the Protestants (the Huguenots) to return any Catholic property they have seized.

1561

Europe: France
Western Esotericism

Authorities arrest Nostradamus, whose almanacs with their many predictions have become quite popular. He is charged with publishing his volumes without obtaining the prior sanction of his bishop.

1561

Europe: Germany
Christianity

Lutherans in Tübingen begin to publish the first volume of a New Testament in the Croatian language for the use of recent converts to Lutheranism. They use the text as translated by Anton Dalmata and Stipan Consul as their source. The second volume would be released in 1564. This is the only Bible published in one of the Balkan languages before the 19th century.

1561

Europe: Netherlands
Christianity

A statement of beliefs written for Reformed Christians in the Low Countries was written in 1559 by Guido de Brés, assisted by Adrian Saravin and H. Modetus, using the French confession of 1559 as a model. As the church was experiencing severe repression, what became known as the "Belgic Confession of Faith" was published in France in 1561. As the church emerged from persecution, the confession gained support and eventually was accepted as the doctrinal standard by the Netherlands Reformed Church.

1561

Europe: Russia
Christianity

St. Basil's Cathedral, officially the Cathedral of the Intercession of the Virgin by the Moat, is completed after eight years of work. Russian czar Ivan the Terrible ordered the construction of the cathedral to commemorate his victory over the Mongols and the taking of the town of Kazan. The cathedral will attain its popular designation from Basil the Blessed, a Muscovite holy man who had been buried at the Trinity Cathedral that the new church replaced. It is located just outside the Kremlin in Moscow on what is now Red Square.

1561

Europe: Scotland
Christianity

Mary, Queen of Scots arrives in Scotland after several years' absence and five days later attends a Roman Catholic mass that is being celebrated in the royal chapel at Holyrood Palace. This being against the decrees of Parliament, Protestants protested, and Mary proclaims that the religious status quo, that is, the Protestant control of religious affairs throughout the land, is still in effect. Mary's statement prompts a confrontation with Protestant leader John Knox, but they reach an uneasy agreement to disagree, with additional confrontations as Mary continues to attend Catholic masses in contradiction to the law of the land. Catholicism remains strongest in the northern regions of Scotland.

1561

Europe: Spain
Christianity

King Philip II transfers the capital of Spain from Toledo to Madrid, though the focus of the Spanish church remains in Toledo.

1562

Central America and the Caribbean: Colombia
Christianity

The Roman Catholic Diocese of Santafé en Nueva Granada is erected from territory previously in the Diocese of Santa Marta, reconstituted as an archdiocese two years later, and in 1998 renamed the Archdiocese of Bogota (Colombia).

1562

Central America and the Caribbean: Nicaragua
Christianity
Nicaragua

Don Lorenzo de Ahumada y Cepeda, the brother of the future saint and doctor of the church Teresa of Avila, brings a statue of the Virgin Mary as the Immaculate Conception on a trip to South America. While delayed in Nicaragua due to a storm, he takes shelter with the Franciscan friars in El Viejo. Grateful for their hospitality, he donates the statue to them. Years later, the statue becomes the focus of veneration of the Immaculate Conception of the Blessed Virgin named as the Patroness of Nicaragua. The statue would come to reside at the National Shrine of the Immaculate Conception of El Viejo.

1562

Europe: England
Western Esotericism

Parliament passes *An Act against Conjurations, Enchantments and Witchcrafts,* which reinstitutes laws against the practice of malevolent magic. It demands the death penalty in cases in which the magical act causes significant harm, with lesser cases punished by imprisonment.

1562

Europe: France
Christianity

The Edict of Saint-Germain provides formal recognition of the French Protestant community for the first time. They are granted permission to hold public communal worship in locations apart from the towns and to worship privately in their homes within the towns' limits.

1562

Europe: Germany
Christianity
Pope Pius IX reconvenes the Council of Trent, whose last session had been in 1553.

1562

Europe: Netherlands
Christianity
French Reformed scholar Franciscus Junius edits a copy of the *Confession of Faith* authored by the Dutch Reformed minister Guido de Brès, sends it to various churches for approval, and forwards a copy to King Philip II of Spain in 1562. This statement would later become known as the Belgic Confession of Faith.

1562

Europe: Switzerland
Christianity
Reformed church leaders in Geneva publish the *Genevan Psalter*, a metrical French translation of the Psalms.

1562–1563

Spain
Christianity
Teresa of Avila founds a new Carmelite cloister named for St. Joseph. She overcomes initial negative reaction by gaining the approbation of the local bishop. After finally gaining a papal sanction, she leaves her former residence and moves into the new cloister, which she demands should follow a strict rule of absolute poverty and the renunciation of property. The constitution she eventually installs calls for, among other austerities, ceremonial flagellation in the weekly divine service, and the acceptance of discalceation (shoelessness). Teresa spends the first five years in her new home in pious seclusion, where she writes intensely.

The founding of the convent becomes the first act in organizing a new Discalced Carmelite Order.

1562–1598

Europe: France
Christianity
The French Wars of Religion. Following the Massacre of Vassy, when French troops under Francis, Duke of Guise murder Huguenot (Protestant) worshipers in Wassy, France, a variety of attacks and counterattacks are initiated by both Roman Catholics and Protestants. The conflict involves all levels of society from some of the aristocratic families to farmers and laborers, and both sides suffer the destruction of ecclesiastical properties and loss of life. The wars are brought to an initial end by the issuance of the Edict of Nantes (1598), which granted Protestants toleration.

Protestants inflict severe damage on the Cathedral of St. Maurice at Vienne, France, as an early reaction to the murder of Protestants at Wassy.

1563

Central America and the Caribbean: Honduras
Christianity
Construction begins on the Cathedral of the Immaculate Conception on the main square at Comayagua, the main city of Honduras into the 19th century. Construction will be intermittent for more than a century.

1563

East and Southeast Asia: Indonesia
Christianity
Javanese Muslims burn down a fort built the previous year by Dominican priests on Solor Island, one of the Lesser Sunda Islands of Indonesia. The Dominicans rebuild, using more durable materials, and continue their work of converting the local population.

1563

Europe: Austria
Christianity
Construction is completed on the Hofkirche (or Court Church) at Innsbruck. Ferdinand I has spent a decade building this memorial to his grandfather, Maximilian I, the late Holy Roman emperor. He has

installed a magnificent organ that will survive to become the oldest two-manual organ in the world. The church is otherwise famous for the 28 large bronze statues of his ancestors that surround Maximilian's cenotaph.

1563

Europe: Belarus
Judaism

Forces of Czar Ivan the Terrible capture Polotsk, a town in Belarus then controlled by the Polish-Lithuanian Commonwealth. The Jews who reside there are forced to accept Eastern Orthodox Christianity. The Russians drown those who refuse in the nearby river. The survivors return to Judaism when the city is returned to Polish Lithuania 15 years later.

1563

Europe: England
Christianity

The Canterbury Convocation sets the doctrinal stance of the Elizabethan Church of England by revising the 42 Articles of Religion. The resulting 39 Articles adopt a Calvinist Protestant theology with specific anti-Catholic provisions, while leaving a traditional episcopal church organization in place. The combination becomes unique to Anglicanism.

The Sternhold and Hopkins Psalter provides the Church of England with a metrical translation of the Psalms.

The term Puritan is initially applied to the British Protestants who in one degree or another wish to further purify the Church of England. The largest group will be Anglicans who wish to revitalize the spiritual, theological, and pastoral life of the church, followed by the Presbyterians who wish to rid the church of bishops and install a thoroughgoing Calvinist theological perspective. The Congregationalists and Baptists are smaller Puritan communities.

1563

Europe: France
Christianity

The Peace of Amboise ends the first phase of the Wars of Religion with the Huguenots being promised some limited level of tolerance.

1563

Europe: Germany
Christianity

Reformed church leaders in Germany publish the Heidelberg Catechism, one of the most influential statements of Reformed theology. It originated out of the request of Frederick II of the Palatinate for the theological faculty of the University of Heidelberg to compose a new catechism for use in the Reformed church throughout his land. The authors sought to find common ground between Lutheran, Calvinist, and Zwinglian perspectives.

1563

Europe: Poland
Christianity

A group of Polish and foreign theologians and scholars commissioned and financed by the Lithuanian prince Nicholas Radziwill, a staunch adherent of Reformed Protestantism, completes six years of work on a translation of the Bible into Polish. The first complete Bible in the Polish language, it is published at Brest-Litovsk and comes to be known as the Brest Bible.

1563

Europe: Scotland
Western Esotericism

Mary, Queen of Scots signs the Scottish Witchcraft Act. It makes the use of malevolent magic and the consultation with practitioners of magic a capital offense. The new law will sanction numerous witch trials across Scotland for the next two centuries.

1563

Europe: Switzerland
Christianity

John Calvin dies and leadership of the church in Geneva passes to Theodore Beza. Calvin's passing will mark the beginning of the relative decline of Geneva's role as the center of the Reformed church as new centers emerge in Germany (Heidelberg) and Holland and as Presbyterianism gains strength in Scotland and England.

1563–1564

Europe: Italy
Christianity

Michelangelo Buonarroti adapts a section of the remaining structure of the Baths of Diocletian on the Quirinal Hill in Rome to create the Basilica of St. Mary of the Angels and the Martyrs. The finished church becomes somewhat of a memorial to Pope Pius IV, whose tomb is located within it.

1564

North America: United States
Christianity
A Huguenot (French Calvinists) settlement, Ft. Caroline, is established on the St. Johns River in Florida. It is destroyed by the Spanish from St. Augustine the following year.

1564

South Asia: India
Hinduism, Islam
Akbar (r. 1556–1605) abolishes the *jizya* tax on non-Muslims and lifts the ban on Hindus building new temples and making pilgrimages to their holy site throughout the Mughal Empire.

1564

Europe: Germany
Christianity
The work of the Council of Trent concludes, and Pope Pius IV issues a papal bull confirming its various final decrees and actions. The council will publish the Tridentine Creed, an authoritative expression of Roman Catholic belief.

1564

Europe: Germany
Christianity
Holy Roman Emperor Ferdinand I dies and is succeeded by his son Maximilian II (r. 1564–1576). Influenced by Sebastian Pfauser, a Catholic court preacher who manifested tendencies toward Lutheranism, Maximilian was believed by many to be a candidate for conversion to Protestantism. In fact, Ferdinand was so concerned that he cajoled Maximilian's consent to Pfauser's banishment and his agreement to remain a Roman Catholic, at least outwardly, as a condition of his inheriting the throne. Prior to becoming emperor, Maximilian began to attend the Catholic mass, a practice he had earlier discontinued.

Prior to his coronation, Maximilian assured the Catholic electors of his faithfulness to Catholicism while promising the Protestant electors that he would at a later date publicly acknowledge the Augsburg Confession, the primary statement of Lutheranism. He did not carry through on his promise to the Protestant electors, but did increase the level of toleration of Lutheranism throughout his realm. He also prevented the pronouncements of the Council of Trent from being promulgated in the empire.

1564

Europe: Germany
Christianity
German Anabaptists publish a hymnal under the title *Etliche schöne christliche Gesäng wie dieselbigen zu Passau von den Schweizer Brüdern in der Gefenknus im Schloss durch göttliche Gnade gedicht und gesungen warden* (or *Genuinely Beautiful Christian Songs Which Were Written and Sung Through God's Grace by the Swiss Brethren in the Passau Castle Prison*). Many of the songs were composed by prisoners at Passau Castle in the 1530s. The Ausbund hymnal remains in use in some Mennonite and Amish congregations.

1564

Europe: Italy
Christianity
Pius IV names his nephew Charles Borromeo (r. 1564–1584), already a highly placed cardinal, as the new archbishop of Milan. He would have an outstanding two decades in office, working to reform his archdiocese, which had been leaderless for over half a century, completing the work of the Council of Trent, and founding a set of institutions of higher learning.

1565

North America: United States
Christianity
Pedro Menendez de Aviles leads a Spanish expedition designed to secure Spanish claims to Florida in the establishment of the first permanent European

colony in what is now the United States—St. Augustine, Florida. The colony inhabits the site of the Timucuan village of Seloy. Allying with the Timucuan people, several weeks later, the Spanish destroy a settlement of French Protestants (Huguenots) that had recently been established at Fort Caroline, Florida.

1565

South America: Brazil
Christianity

The Portuguese found the city São Sebastião do Rio de Janeiro, named for St. Sebastian, the patron saint of the Portuguese king, on Guanabara Bay, Brazil. They destroy the previously founded French colony in the bay.

1565

East and Southeast Asia: China
Buddhism

Karma Tseten assumes control of lands formerly in the hands of the Rinpungpa Dynasty of central Tibet and founds the Kingdom of Upper Tsang in west central Tibet. The new Tsangpa Dynasty continues in power until the emergence of the fifth Dalai Lama in 1642. His dynasty is aligned to the Karma Kagyu school of Tibetan Buddhism and develops a growing dislike of the Gelugpa school after its leaders are designated as the Dalai Lama and establish close ties to the Mongolians.

1565

East and Southeast Asia: Japan
Buddhism

Two feudal lords, Matsunaga Hisahide and Miyoshi Yoshitsugu, lay siege to the residence of the shogun Ashikaga Yoshiteru. As the troops overrun the palace, Yoshiteru commits suicide. The office of shogun will remain vacant for three years.

1565

East and Southeast Asia: Philippines
Christianity

The Augustinian order initiates work in the Philippines.

1565

Europe: Austria
Christianity

Peter Riedermann's (d. 1556) apology for the Hutterite Anabaptist community, *Account of Our Religion,* is published.

1565

Europe: Bosnia
Christianity

The Emperor's Mosque in Sarajevo (Bosnia and Herzegovina) having been destroyed at the end of the 15th century, it is rebuilt as a stone structure, which becomes the largest single subdome mosque in the country. Originally dedicated to the sultan, Muhammad al-Fatih, the conqueror of Constantinople, the new mosque is dedicated to Suleiman the Magnificent.

1565

Europe: Italy
Christianity

Pope Pius IV dies and is succeeded by Pope Pius V (r. 1565–1572).

1565

Europe: Malta
Christianity

With heavy loss of life, the Knights Hospitaller, a Christian martial order, repulse the invasion of Malta by forces of the Ottoman Empire. An important battle in the century-long conflict between the Muslim and Christian forces for control of the Mediterranean, the Ottoman defeat, which followed the successful defense of Vienna, gave Christians hope that they could stop the advance of Islam into Europe.

1565

Europe: Poland
Christianity

Following a theological debate set up by King Sigismund II Augustus of Poland, the non-Trinitarian faction within the Reformed churches of Poland breaks ties with those who continue to hold a Trinitarian theology and organize a separate synod, which had its initial meeting at Brzeziny, Poland, on June 10. The non-Trinitarian group becomes known as the Polish Brethren.

1565

Europe: Switzerland
Christianity

John Calvin dies and is succeeded by Theodore Beza. Beza releases a new edition of the Greek New Testament (with an accompanying Latin text) in the tradition of the prior texts published by Erasmus and Robert Entienne.

1566

North America: United States
Christianity

A short-lived attempt to build a mission to the native people of Florida was launched by the Jesuits in 1566, but abandoned six years later.

1566

East and Southeast Asia: Japan
Buddhism

Buddhists pressure the Japanese emperor to expel the Christian missionaries from Kyōto, and they quickly relocate to Kyūshū and Sakai.

1566

East and Southeast Asia: Laos
Buddhism

Laotian king Setthathirat moves his capital from Luang Prabang to Vientiane and orders the reconstruction of Pha That Luang ("Great Stupa in Lao"), originally built in the third century as a Hindu temple. The new enlarged and elaborate structure, reaching some 150 feet in height, is covered in gold and surrounded by 30 stupas. Each level of the building is construed to represent a new level of Buddhist attainment toward enlightenment.

1566

Europe: Belgium
Christianity

Reformed church leaders meeting in a clandestine synod in Antwerp approve the Belgic Confession, a classic restatement of the Reformed church position.

1566

Europe: Italy
Christianity

Charles Borromeo (later canonized), the Roman Catholic archbishop of Milan and nephew of the late Pope Pius IV, launches an effort at his cathedral to implement the promulgations of the Council of Trent. His reforms included simplifying the interior of the cathedral, instituting educational programs for the archdiocese's clergy, suppressing Protestantism, and crusading against the practice of magic and witchcraft.

Roman Catholic Church leaders issue the Roman Catechism, the first official catechism published by the church.

1566

Europe: Netherlands
Christianity

A *Beeldenstorm* ("statue storm"), an outbreak of destruction of religious images, sweeps through Amsterdam and a mob attacks the Oude Kirk, the oldest church in the city. Most of the church art is lost, including an altarpiece decorated by Jan van Scorel and Maarten van Heemskerck. The only surviving art would be that on the ceiling that the mob could not reach.

1566

Europe: Switzerland
Christianity

Most of the Swiss cantons adopt as their statement of belief and publish the Second Helvetic Confession. The Confession had originally been composed by Swiss reformer Heinrich Bullinger, who had succeeded Zwingli as leader of the movement in Zurich. An expanded version of the First Helvetic Confession, of which Bullinger was a co-author, it had first been circulated to Frederick II of the Palatinate, who sought a document to use to defend the Reformed position in the face of aggressive advocates of Lutheranism in his land.

1567

Central America and the Caribbean: Mexico
Christianity

Construction begins on the Metropolitan Cathedral of the Assumption of Mary in Mexico City. It will be located on the site of the former Aztec sacred precinct near the Templo Mayor, which had been destroyed in 1521. It will take some 250 years to complete.

1567

South Asia: India
Islam

Mughal emperor Akbar orders the exhumation of the body of a prominent Shi'a Muslim, Mir Murtaza Sharifi Shirazi, which had been buried in Delhi relatively close to that of Amir Khusrau, a prominent Sunni leader. In citing his rationale for his action, he referred to Shi'a Islam's heretical status.

1567

East and Southeast Asia: China
Chinese Religions

The Jiajing emperor in China dies and is succeeded by his son, the Longqing emperor (r. 1567–1572). He would spend much of his reign dealing with the national chaos caused by his father's lack of attention to his governmental duties. Among other changes, he dismissed from the court the large number of Daoist priests to whom the Jiajing emperor had looked in the hope of extending his own life and secondarily of improving the situation throughout the empire. Toward the end of his regime, he would reverse his policy and recall many of the Taoist priests to the Forbidden City.

1567

Europe: France
Christianity

A second attempt to end the fighting between Protestants and Roman Catholics leads to the promulgation of the Peace of Longjumeau, which temporarily suppresses hostilities.

1567

Europe: France
Christianity

The church at Boulogne, France, dedicated to the Blessed Virgin Mary is designated as the cathedral for a newly created diocese. The church has been a popular pilgrimage site as it houses what is believed to be a miraculous statue of the Virgin called Our Lady of the Sea.

1567

Europe: Scotland
Christianity

Elizabeth I discovers a plot being carried out by Sir Anthony Babbington to have her assassinated, which also involved Mary, Queen of Scots. As a result, Mary was arrested and executed. She was succeeded by her son, who would reign as King James VI, though he was but 13 months old. At the first Parliament meeting after his crowning, the Scottish Confession of Faith (1560), a Presbyterian creedal statement, was officially ratified. Though ruling a country following a Presbyterian Protestant faith, James was raised as a Roman Catholic.

1567

Europe: Spain
Christianity

Teresa, who has organized a new reformed Carmelite convent in Avila, comes out of seclusion after receiving the approbation of the head of the Carmelites, Rubeo de Ravenna, to establish additional new centers following the reformed Carmelite order she had created. She travels the length and breadth of Spain. Having also been granted permission to establish houses for men, she reaches out to two Carmelite brothers, John of the Cross and Anthony of Jesus, to assist her. Together, they found the first convent of Discalced Carmelite Brethren at Duruello. John later becomes second only to Teresa in his impact with the Reformation (or more properly Catholic Counter-Reformation) movement she has begun.

1567–1568

Europe: Scotland
Christianity

Scottish nobleman Lord Bothwell abducts Mary, Queen of Scots and forces her into a marriage, an action rejected by both Protestants and Catholics. After raising an army, a group of Scottish nobles drive Bothwell into exile and imprison Mary at Loch Leven Castle where she is forced to abdicate in favor of her one-year-old son James. Five days later, the infant is crowned King James VI at the Church of the Holy Rude beside Stirling Castle.

After months in custody, Mary escapes and makes her way to England, where Elizabeth I has her taken into protective custody.

June 20, 1567

South America: Brazil
Christianity

Brazilian regent Don Henrique expels the Jews from Brazil.

September 9, 1567

Europe: Netherlands
Christianity

The lengthy struggle of the Dutch to overthrow Spanish rule in the Low Countries opens with Dutch Protestant forces winning the costly Battle of Heiligerlee. Shortly thereafter, under orders from King Philip II of Spain, the Duke of Alba moves into the Netherlands with orders to suppress the Protestants. Among his first actions is the creation of a tribunal, the Council of Troubles. It begins to try the leaders who have been agitating on behalf of the Protestant cause throughout the region.

1568

South Asia: India
Hinduism

Ramachandra Deb is able to wrest a portion of Orissa from Muslim control and establishes an independent kingdom with its capital at Khurda. His territory includes Puri, the site of the famous Jaganath Temple. He is able to refurbish the temple and reinstall the deities, which had been taken into hiding as the Muslim forces approached a decade earlier.

1568

South Asia: India
Judaism

On a small piece of land given by the Raja of Kochi, the Malabar Yehudan people (aka the Jewish community in the Kingdom of Cochin) erect a synagogue in Old Cochin (now Kochi). It is located next to the Mattancherry Palace temple, with which it shares a common wall. The Pazhayannur Bhagavathy Temple is dedicated to the ancestral deity of the Cochin royal family. The Paradesi Synagogue has emerged as the the oldest active synagogue in the (British) Commonwealth of Nations.

1568

East and Southeast Asia: Japan
Buddhism

Three years after the death of the shogun Ashikaga Yoshiteru, a cousin, Ashikaga Yoshihide, is installed as shogun. Within a few months, however, he becomes ill and dies. His death becomes the occasion for Oda Nobunaga, who had emerged as a powerful daimyo (feudal lord) in Japan, to march on Kyoto and take charge of the capital. He subsequently installs Ashikaga Yoshiaki, the brother of the former shogun, Ashikaga Yoshiteru, as the new shogun.

1568

Europe: Belgium
Christianity

Authorities in Brussels execute by beheading Lamoraal, Count Egmont, prince of Gavere; Philips van Montmorency, Comte d'Horn; and 18 other leaders of the Flemish opposition to the work of the Spanish Inquisition. Spain then rules the Low Countries, and its Catholic leadership is in the process of attempting to suppress the Reformed church, which had gained strong support.

1568

Europe: England
Christianity

Archbishop Matthew Parker leads a group of British bishops in an effort to publish a new English edition of the Christian scriptures, which came to be known as the "Bishops' Bible." It is designed to supersede the popular Geneva Bible, the favorite of the Puritans, most of whom were Calvinists. The bishops objected to the many footnotes to the Geneva Bible, all of which pushed Calvinist theology. A minor revision, it deleted the offensive footnotes, but never gained a popular audience.

1568

Europe: France
Christianity
The Cathedral of the Holy Cross in Orleans, France, is severely damaged in the French Wars of Religion between the Huguenots and Catholics.

The as yet uncompleted Cathedral of Saint Peter at Saintes in southwestern France, upon which construction began in 1450, is sacked by Huguenot Protestants.

1568

Europe: France
Christianity
William Allen and a group of British Roman Catholic exiles found an English College at Douai.

1568

Europe: Italy
Christianity
Construction begins in Rome on the Chiesa del Santissimo Nome di Gesù all'Argentina (or the Church of the Most Holy Name of Jesus at the "Argentina"), popularly known simply as the Church of the Gesù, the mother church of the Society of Jesus. It will be completed and consecrated in 1584 and subsequently become the model of Jesuit churches worldwide. It will be constructed on the site of the former church of Santa Maria della Strada.

1568

Europe: Italy
Christianity
Members of the Society of Jesus, popularly known as the Jesuits, begin construction of Il Gesù, their headquarters' mother church in Rome.

1568

Europe: Italy
Christianity
Pope Pius V names four great doctors of the Eastern church—John Chrysostom, Basil the Great, Gregory of Nazianzus, and Athanasius of Alexandria. They join the four great doctors of the Western church—Saint Ambrose, Saint Augustine, Saint Jerome, and Pope Gregory I—named in 1298, and are thus recognized both for their personal sanctity and as having particular importance because of their contribution to theology. In the Catholic Church, only people who have previously been canonized may be considered for the additional status as a doctor of the church. The same year that Pius V names the four Eastern doctors, he also names his fellow Dominican Thomas Aquinas as a doctor of the church.

1568

Europe: Italy
Christianity
Aonio Paleario, a Protestant poet, is burned at the stake for writing a satirical poem directed at Pope Pius IV. He had posted the poem for public reading on one of Rome's statues. It read:

> You'd think it was winter the way Pius is burning Christians, like so many logs on the fire. He must be getting himself ready to enjoy the flames of Hell.

1568

Europe: Netherlands
Christianity
The Holy Office of the Inquisition issues a blanket condemnation of (Protestant) heretics against all the inhabitants of the Netherlands. Only a few individuals, specifically named in the condemnation, are excepted from the sentence.

1568

Europe: Poland, Hungary
Christianity
Urged on by his minister, Unitarian Francis David, King John II Sigismund of Poland issues the Edict of Torda, designed to guarantee religious toleration throughout his kingdom. That same year, the non-Trinitarian Unitarian Church of Transylvania is founded with a primarily Hungarian-speaking membership.

The Orthodox Church is allowed to establish worship, but not allowed to construct churches of stone, only wood.

1569

South Asia: India
Islam

In celebration of several victories on the battlefield, Mughal emperor Akbar, a disciple of Salim Chishti, a Sufi holy man of the Chisti Sufi order, moves his capital to a site just west of Agra near the Salim Chishti's residence. Here he launches a new city named Fatehpur (or "town of victory"). The town came to be known as Fatehpur Sikri. It would be the home of a mosque especially built for Salim Chishti and the site of future discussions Akbar had with religious leaders from the many faiths practiced in his realm.

1569

East and Southeast Asia: Japan
Christianity

After a meeting with the feudal lord Oba Nobunaga and the shogun Yoshiaki in Kyoto, the Jesuit missionaries are allowed back in the capital to preach.

1569

East and Southeast Asia: Myanmar, China
Buddhism

A Burmese princess of the Toungoo Dynasty marries the leader of the Dai people, one of China's ethnic minority groups, who reside in Yunnan Province. The marriage serves as a catalyst for the spread of Theravada Buddhism in Yunnan.

1569

Europe: France
Christianity

Pontigny Abbey, a Cistercian abbey in Pontigny, France, is severely damaged in the French Wars of Religion between the Huguenots and Catholics.

1569

Europe: Italy
Judaism

With the exception of the cities of Rome and Ancona (where ghettos had been established), all Jews are

Mughal emperor Akbar's pavilion, known as Ibadat Khana (House of Worship), at Fatehpur Sikri, India. From 1556 to 1605, Akbar was the third emperor of India's Mughal Empire. (Cyril Bele)

ordered to leave the Papal States, including the papal territory in France around Avignon.

1569

Southwest Asia and North Africa: Maghreb
Judaism, Islam
The Ottomans again conquered Tunis, which they are able to hold for four years.

December 12, 1569

Russia
Christianity
Phillip, the outspoken former metropolitan of Moscow, dies, and many believe him to have been murdered by Czar Ivan IV as part of an attempt to silence opposition to his regime.

1570

Central America and the Caribbean: Mexico
Christianity
Dominicans establish themselves in Oaxaca, Mexico, and begin construction of the Church and Monastery of Santo Domingo de Guzmán, a massive ecclesiastical building complex in the Spanish baroque style.

1570

South America: Peru
Christianity
The Inquisition sets up operation in Lima.

1570

Europe: France
Christianity
The Peace of St. Germain ends the third phase of the French Wars of Religion. Huguenots take control of four fortified towns as safe havens from attack.

1570

Europe: Italy
Christianity
Pope Pius V implements the decision of the Council of Trent and issues a standardized text of the Roman Catholic mass, the liturgy for worship (including the celebration of the Eucharist), through the publication of the new edition of the Roman missal. He further directs that the new missal would be mandatory for Latin rite Catholic congregations throughout the world. The only exceptions allowed were liturgies that had been in use prior to the year 1370. The Tridentine liturgy would dominate the church until the implementation of the reforms of the Second Vatican Council in the 1960s.

1570

Europe: Poland
Christianity
Polish Protestants—Lutherans, Calvinists, and Moravian Brethren—put aside their differences in the Consensus of Sendomir to ally against the Jesuits in Poland.

1570

Europe: Spain
Christianity
Archbishop of Mexico Montufar commissions an oil-painted copy of the image of Our Lady of Guadalupe and sends it to King Philip II of Spain.

The first complete translation of the Bible is published in Switzerland. Its popular designation, the Biblia del Osa, refers to a picture of a bear eating honey that appears on the title page.

1570–1571

North America: United States
Christianity
Spanish Jesuits establish the Ajacan mission on the York River in what will become the state of Virginia. In 1571, Native people wipe out the settlement and kill the priests. The Jesuits abandon the effort.

April 27, 1570

Europe: England
Christianity
Pope Pius V formally declares Queen Elizabeth I of England a heretic and releases her subjects from their allegiance to her. Elizabeth had previously tolerated Catholic worship, at least in private, but answers the pope's action by actively suppressing Roman Catholicism in her realm.

Pius's action will be the last time a Roman pontiff attempts to interfere in the affairs of a nation by releasing believers from their national allegiances.

1571

Central America and the Caribbean: Mexico
Christianity
The Inquisition sets up operation in Mexico City.

1571

South Asia: India
Islam
Mughal emperor Akbar builds the Jama Masjid at Fatehpur Sikri, his new capital city near Agra. It remains one of the largest mosques in India.

1571

East and Southeast Asia: Japan
Buddhism, shinto
In his effort to unite the country, Oda Nobunaga moved against the increasing opposition of the Tendai Buddhist warrior monks residing on Mt. Hiei. He attacked the mountain site and destroyed Enryaku-ji, the main Tendai temple. The death of so many of the monks ended the power and influence they had accumulated over the last few centuries.

Nobunaga also destroys Hiyoshi Taisha, a Shinto shrine on the eastern slope of Mt. Hiei facing Lake Biwa. The shrine will be rebuilt in stages through the 1580s and 1590s.

1571

East and Southeast Asia: Mongolia
Buddhism
Altan Khan, who had been able to unite a group of the Mongol tribes, receives the title Shunyi Wang ("Obedient and Righteous King") from the Longqing emperor, the ruler of Ming China. He subsequently turns to Tibet and renews efforts to spread the Gelugpa school of Tibetan Buddhism among the Mongolians.

1571

East and Southeast Asia: Philippines
Christianity
The era of Spanish colonization of the Philippines begins with Miguel López de Legazpi's expedition, which settles on the Bay of Manila on the island of Luzon and establishes a town later to be known as Manila. The Spanish introduce Roman Catholicism, later to become the dominant religion of the islands. Work is initiated by Augustinians who had arrived in Spain with Legazpi.

The Philippines are added to the territory that had been designated as the Viceroyalty of New Spain, which is administered from Mexico City from 1565 until the early 19th century.

In occupying Manila Bay, the Spanish challenge the local Kingdom of Tondo, whose residents follow a local indigenous religion. It will take some two decades to conquer Tondo.

1571

Europe: Cyprus
Islam, Christianity
After a siege lasting a year, Ottoman forces capture Famagosta, the last Venetian stronghold on Cyprus, and will control the island for the next 300 years. They transform St. Sophia Cathedral in Old Nicosia into the Selimiye Mosque.

The Muslim victory succeeds in providing the alcoholic sultan with direct access to his favorite wine.

1571

Europe: Cyprus
Christianity, Islam
The Ottomans take control of Cyprus, with significant results for both Roman Catholics and the Orthodox Church. The main cathedral dedicated to St. Nicholas, which had been used by the Crusader knights that had been ruling the island, is transformed into a mosque. The Ottomans recognize the Orthodox Church as the only legitimate Christian church on the island, and suppress Roman Catholicism, which had been given a leadership role by the Crusaders. The Orthodox bishops, who previously had to work under the supervision of a Catholic bishop, become independent. The head of the Orthodox Church of Cyprus begins to accumulate power as he has a position in the occupation government as the head of the Christian community.

1571

Europe: England
Christianity

Queen Elizabeth I approves a slightly revised text of the 39 Articles of Religion for the Church of England prepared by the 1563 Canterbury Convocation (to replace the abandoned 42 Articles) and imposes them on the clergy.

1571

Europe: France
Western Esotericism

Trois-Echelles, a defendant accused of witchcraft, tells the court that he knows of some 100,000 fellow witches roaming the country. His remarks raise a wave of antiwitchcraft panic, and French judges respond by eliminating normal legal protections for any accused of witchcraft.

1571

Europe: Germany
Christianity

Anabaptists from across southern Germany, Moravia, and Holland attend a three-week disputation on Anabaptist issues held in Frankenthal. Afterwards, authorities banish the Anabaptists and confiscate their property.

1571

Europe: Germany, Netherlands
Christianity

Twenty-nine exiled Protestant church leaders gather in Emden, Germany to establish rules and doctrines for what will become the Dutch Reformed Church. The church's history is usually dated from the Synod of Emden.

1571

Europe: Italy
Christianity

Pope Pius V creates the Sacred Congregation of the Index, to which is assigned the task of investigating questionable books and regularly updating the list of books included on the *Index Librorum Prohibitorum* (i.e., List of Prohibited Books), a list of those books that the Catholic Church ordered the faithful to refrain from reading. Priority would be given to books deemed immoral or containing significant theological errors.

October 7, 1571

Europe: Greece
Islam, Christianity

The Battle of Lepanto. The fleet assembled by the Holy League, a coalition of Roman Catholic European states with a stake in the Mediterranean, decisively defeats the main fleet of the Ottoman Empire. The battle was fought off the coast of Greece not far from the Turkish naval base at Lepanto. This battle has been seen as a turning point in Mediterranean history for the long-term loss of control of the Eastern Mediterranean experienced by the Ottomans in its aftermath.

Admiral Doria carries a copy of the image of the Virgin of Guadalupe aboard his ship during the battle of Lepanto and afterward imputes the victory over the Ottoman Empire forces to the Virgin. Subsequently, Pope Pius V institutes a new Roman Catholic feast day for Our Lady of Victory, which over the centuries will evolve into the present Feast of Our Lady of the Rosary.

1572

South America: Peru
Christianity

Construction of a third building to be used as the Cathedral of St. John in Lima, Peru. Workers demolish the adobe walls of the older cathedral, but soon afterward the lack of financial resources forces the abandonment of the new cathedral. Work will later resume and the project will be completed early in the next century.

1572

East and Southeast Asia: China
Buddhism

The Longqing emperor of China dies and is succeeded by his 10-year-old son who reigns as the Wanli emperor (r. 1572–1620). His lengthy rule saw a steady decline of the Ming Dynasty's rule.

1572

Europe: Italy
Christianity
Pope Pius V dies and is succeeded by Pope Gregory XIII (r. 1572–1585).

1572

Europe: Scotland
Christianity
The clergy of Scotland are required to subscribe to the Scottish Confession of Faith of 1560.

August 22, 1572

Europe: France
Christianity
In Paris for the wedding of Henry, King of Navarre and Marguerite de Valois, Protestant leader and French admiral Gaspard de Coligny (1519–1572) is shot and wounded, though not fatally so.

August 24, 1572

Europe: France
Christianity
St. Bartholomew's Day Massacre. French Catholics in Paris, fearing a Huguenot retaliation for the attempt on Gaspard de Coligny's life, decided to preemptively assassinate the Huguenot leadership. The assassination began on what is the feast day for the apostle Bartholomew with the murder of the recuperating Coligny. The assassinations that began on August 24 multiplied over the next couple of weeks and spread to other parts of France. This permanently crippled the Huguenot movement, while enraging the Protestant majorities in other countries. Many Catholics saw the massacre as an act of divine retribution, and Pope Gregory XIII had a medal struck with himself on one side and an angel bearing a cross and sword next to slaughtered Protestants on the obverse side.

November 1572

Europe: Denmark
Christianity
Danish astronomer Tycho Brahe observes what is now known to be a supernova in the constellation known as Cassiopeia, about which he wrote a book, *De Nova Stella.* The event lasted for some 16 months and was bright enough for several weeks that it could be seen in broad daylight. Bache, a Protestant residing in a Protestant country, pays little attention to the denial of his observations by Roman Catholic clerics.

The supernova of 1572 is one of some eight supernovas known to have been visible to the naked eye through world history. It would become the focus of a variety of apocalyptic predictions. In England, Queen Elizabeth consulted her astrologer Thomas Allen as to the significance of the new star.

1573

South Asia: India
Sikhism
Sikh guru Ram Das initiates construction on the holy water tank for ritual baths at Amritsar, Punjab.

1573

East and Southeast Asia: Japan
Buddhism
Oda Nobunaga, who had established Ashikaga Yoshiaki in power as shogun, drives him from office. Yoshiaki becomes a Buddhist monk under the religious name Sho-san. Whatever power had remained to the Ashikaga shogunate ends, though Yoshiaki officially remains shogun until 1588. In the meantime, Oda Nobunaga continues his drive to unite Japan under his leadership.

1573

Europe: Italy
Judaism
Construction begins on the Cinque Synagogue in the middle of the Jewish ghetto in Rome. Papal regulations allow only one synagogue for Roman Jews, but the large new synagogue is able to accommodate five separate sanctuaries with space for the various different linguistic and ethnic factions of the community to hold their own Sabbath services.

1573

Europe: Italy
Christianity

Greek residents of Venice complete construction of the Church of San Giorgio dei Greci, considered the oldest and most important church of the modern Greek Orthodox Diaspora. It will become the ethnic and religious focus of Hellenistic life in Venice and the larger Venetian realm. Soon after its completion, noted Cretan artist Michael Damaskinos paints the iconostasis for the church.

1573

Europe: Poland
Christianity

Nobles of the Poland-Lithuanian Commonwealth gather at Warsaw and issue a declaration by which representatives of all the major religions in the land pledge to each other their mutual support and tolerance. The declaration of the Warsaw Confederation stands as a landmark in the history of religious liberty, reaching not only various ethnic groups but beyond Christianity to include Muslims and Jews.

1573–1574

Southwest Asia and North Africa: Maghreb
Islam

Spanish forces recapture Tunis, and the Hafsids again are forced to accept their status as a Spanish vassal state to offset the Ottoman threat. Muhammad IV (1373–1374), the last caliph of the Hafsid Empire, is taken to Istanbul and executed because he had attempted to negotiate his status with Spain. It is also the case that Ottoman sultan Selim II, who inherited the title Caliph from his father, Suleiman the Magnificent, wanted to do away with any competitors who were also using the title.

1574

Central America and the Caribbean: Mexico
Christianity

Church officials representing the Inquisition hold the first auto-da-fe (act of faith) at which two people convicted of heresy are burned at the stake.

1574

South Asia: India
Sikhism

Shortly before his death, Sikh guru Amar Das appoints his daughter's husband, Jetha, as the fourth Sikh guru and names him Raam Das.

1574

East and Southeast Asia: China
Buddhism

Sonam Gyatso, already the abbot of both Drepung Monastery and Sera Monastery, two of the most important centers of the Gelugpa school of Tibetan Buddhism, founds Phende Lekshe Ling, later known as Namgyal Monastery, which would come to be the personal monastery and school overseen by successive dalai lamas.

1574

East and Southeast Asia: Japan
Buddhism

Oda Nobunaga, in his drive to unite a badly divided Japan, defeats the forces of the Ikkô sect in a protracted siege of their strongholds at Nagashima. He accomplishes this by offering peace and then massacring 40,000 believers when they accept.

1574

Europe: France
Christianity

King Charles IX dies and is succeeded by Henry III (r. 1574–1589).

1574

Europe: Netherlands
Christianity

Eight years after the end of the unsuccessful but costly Spanish siege of Leiden, William the Silent founds the University of Leiden, which will emerge as one of the major Protestant centers of learning in Europe.

1574

Southwest Asia and North Africa: Morocco
Islam

Sultan Abdallah al-Ghalib dies and is succeeded by his son Abdallah Mohammed (r. 1574–1576).

Nineteenth-century woodblock print depicts 16th-century Japanese feudal warlord Oda Nobunaga battling another warrior. Oda Nobunaga allied with Toyotomi Hideyoshi and Tokugawa Ieyasu to overthrow the Ashikaga shoguns of the Sengoku period and secure Japan's military reunification. (Library of Congress)

1575

South Asia: India
Islam

At his new capital city, Fatehpur Sikri, Mughal emperor Akbar builds the Ibadat Khana (House of Worship), a hall at which he stages discussions and debates, originally among Muslims and later including intellectuals of various religious traditions.

1575

East and Southeast Asia: Japan
Buddhism

Nobunaga defeats the Ikkô sect in Echizen and Kaga Provinces and again massacres some 40,000 believers.

1575

Europe: England
Christianity

Matthew Parker, the archbishop of Canterbury, dies and is succeeded by Edmund Grindal (r. 1575–1583) who had previously served as the bishop of London and the archbishop of York. He is a Protestant who favors Calvinist theology and during his term of office emphasizes the use of the Geneva Bible.

1575

Europe: Italy
Christianity

As part of the Holy Year activities in the city of Rome, Veronica's Veil, believed by many to show a representation of the face of Jesus of Nazareth, is placed on display for the pilgrims who travel to Rome.

Church authorities publish the Book of Bamberg, the first official Roman Catholic hymnbook.

1576

East and Southeast Asia: China
Buddhism

Ming empress dowager Li, a devout Buddhist, commissions the building of the Cishou Buddhist Temple. Along with the adjacent 150-foot-high Yong'anwanshou Pagoda (patterned after the Tainning Temple Pagoda), it is erected at Balizhuang, a western suburb of Beijing.

1576

East and Southeast Asia: China
Christianity

Pope Gregory XIII erects the Diocese of Macau. Previously, the area that includes Macau had been tentatively assigned to the Diocese of Malacca (Malaysia) though no work had developed in that part of China. Gregory also appoints a Jesuit priest, Melchior Miguel Carneiro Leitão, as the first bishop of the newly erected Diocese of Macau. In a bull issued the year before, anticipating the erection of the new diocese, Pope Gregory XIII assigned Japan to the Diocese of Macau, thus giving the Portuguese, in fact the Portuguese Jesuits, leadership of the missionary efforts in the country.

1576

Europe: Belgium
Christianity
Spanish troops overrun and sack Antwerp. Protestants respond by signing a new alliance agreement, the Pacification of Ghent.

1576

Europe: France
Christianity
King Henry III signs the Edict of Beaulieu, which grants a set of concessions to the Protestants in his kingdom (the Huguenots). The leading Catholic activist, Henry I, Duke of Guise, counters his action by forming the Catholic League. Catholic reaction forces Henry to rescind the concessions that he had made to the Protestants.

1576

Europe: Germany
Christianity, Western Esotericism
Maximilian II, emperor of the Holy Roman Empire of the German Nation, dies. He had worked for reform in the Catholic Church, but was unable to get the church to allow the marriage of the clergy, or to offer communion in both kinds (it being the common practice to offer laypeople only the bread and not the wine in the Roman Catholic Eucharist). In the end, Maximilian refuses to receive the last rites of the Catholic Church, but is buried in St. Vitus Cathedral in Prague.

Maximilian is succeeded by his son Rudolf II (r. 1576–1612), who also holds the titles of King of Hungary and Croatia, King of Bohemia, and Archduke of Austria. Rudolf had become a student of Esotericism and became versed in both astrology and alchemy. Rudolf never married and was rumored to be homosexual, though he had several affairs and fathered several children.

1576

Europe: Italy
Christianity
An epidemic of the bubonic plague strikes Milan. Archbishop Charles Borromeo leads the effort to minister to the ill and bury the dead. He continually risks his own life to visit parishes where the disease rages and freely uses the church treasures to finance the care of the sick. He punishes the clergy he finds backing off from serving those entrusted to their care.

1576

Europe: Scotland
Christianity
Edinburgh publisher Thomas Bassandyne prints an edition of the New Testament based on the text of the Geneva Bible (the English Bible prepared by British Protestants in exile in Switzerland). It is the first Bible published in Scotland. Bassandyne dies the following year and the complete Bible is later published by Alexander Arbuthnet.

1576

Europe: Spain
Christianity
Members of the Carmelite order organize opposition against the reforms of the order instituted across Spain by Teresa of Avila. They order her to cease founding convents, demand that she retire from public activity, and actually institute proceedings of the Inquisition against her. Her movement is temporarily suppressed, until King Philip II steps into the controversy on her side. The Inquisition drops all investigations of her, and the king, acting with Pope Gregory XIII, sets up structures to assist the continuing reform activity.

1576

Southwest Asia and North Africa: Morocco
Islam
Abu Marwan Abd al-Malik I (r. 1576–1578), with Ottoman assistance, takes the Moroccan throne from his brother Abdallah Mohammed.

1577

Sub-Saharan Africa: Mozambique
Islam
Dominicans land on the coast of Mozambique and make their way to the interior. They burn Muslim mosques as they explore the region.

1577

South Asia: India
Sikhism

Sikh guru Raam Das begins construction of the site of the future Golden Temple, the central place of worship for the Sikh religion, in Amritsar, northern Punjab, India.

1577

East and Southeast Asia: China
Buddhism

Sonam Gyatso, the abbot of Drepung Monastery and Sera Monastery, and the most prominent lama of the Gelugpa school of Tibetan Buddhism, accepts the invitation of Mongolian leader Altan Khan to visit Mongolia. Once in Mongolia, Sonam Gyatso publicly claims to be a reincarnation of Drogön Chögyal Phagpa, the Sakya Buddhist monk who had worked with Kublai Khan, and names Altan Khan a reincarnation of Kublai Khan, the former Mongolian emperor of China. He proclaimed that the two had come together to propagate Buddhism.

Altan Khan refers to Sonam Gyatso as the "Dalai" (or "ocean"), a simple translation of his name in Mongolian, but which results in Sonam Gyatso becoming entitled the Dalai Lama, a title that would commonly be translated as "Ocean of Wisdom." Sonam Gyatso then asks that the title be posthumously conferred on his predecessors, Gendun Drup and Gendun Gyatso. Thus, Sonam Gyatso became officially known as the third Dalai Lama.

Sonam Gyatso remains in Tibet spreading Buddhism among the Mongolian elites. Altan Khan memorialized the site of their meeting with the construction of Thegchen Chonkhor, Mongolia's first Buddhist monastery. Sonam Gyatso urged Altan Khan to abolish the more objectionable aspects of traditional Mongolian religion—animal sacrifices, the statues of the old gods, and the immolation of women on the funeral pyres of their husbands.

1577

East and Southeast Asia: Japan
Buddhism

Nobunaga troops defeat Ikkô forces in Kii Province, thus cutting off supply routes to their main center, Ishiyama Hongan-ji.

1577

Europe: France
Christianity

Construction begins on the Ajaccio Cathedral, dedicated to Our Lady of the Assumption on the island of Corsica in the Mediterranean. It will be completed in 1593.

1577

Europe: France
Christianity

In the midst of the French Wars of Religion, the Huguenots attack the Cathedral of Our Lady of Alet in the town of Alet-les-Bains in Languedoc (southeastern France). It is largely destroyed and never rebuilt. The Diocese of Alet was eventually absorbed into the Diocese of Carcassonne.

1577

Europe: Germany
Christianity

Lutheran theologians create the last of a series of 16th-century Lutheran statements of faith, the Formula of Concord.

1578

East and Southeast Asia: China
Buddhism

Ming empress dowager Li oversees the construction of the Wanshou Buddhist Temple in Beijing along the Changhe River (a mile from the Zhenjue Temple originally built in the early 1400s). It would later become a royal temple especially favored by several powerful empresses.

1578

East and Southeast Asia: Philippines
Christianity

Pope Gregory XIII issues a papal bull that invokes the patronage of *La Purisima Concepción* (the Immaculate Conception of the Blessed Virgin Mary) for Catholics in the Philippine Islands. It is the earliest designation of a national patronage relative to the Immaculate Conception.

Franciscans arrive in the islands to supplement the work already underway by the Augustinians.

1578

Europe: Italy
Christianity

The shroud believed to be the burial cloth of Jesus of Nazareth, owned by the royal House of Savoy in northern Italy, is taken to Turin where it will be housed to the present. The archbishop of Milan Charles Borromeo will travel to Turin to view it.

1578

Europe: Italy
Christianity

Over the centuries since the Christianization of Rome, the catacombs used for Christian burials in the first centuries of the Common Era were abandoned, the relics of the martyrs transferred to churches above ground, and the location of the ancient burial sites lost to memory. Accidentally rediscovered, they will become the subject of historical research, with an initial volume based on decades of personal exploration and investigation being produced by Antonio Bosio in 1632.

1578

Europe: Netherlands
Christianity

The first meeting of the Dutch National Synod (of the Dutch Reformed Church) gathers at Dordrecht. A major item of business is the request of refugees from the Spanish suppression of Protestantism in the south (what is now Belgium) and the organization of Walloon congregations. The synod approves the formation of separate French-speaking parishes, which would then be organized in a separate classis (the Reformed equivalent of a diocese). The new classis was set up as an autonomous unit that would manage its own affairs, provided it remained doctrinally in the Reformed tradition.

1578

Southwest Asia and North Africa: Morocco
Islam, Christianity

The Battle of Alcazar-el-Kebir (aka the Battle of the Three Kings) at Qasr al-Kabir in Morocco. A crusade against the Moors of Morocco is stopped abruptly when King Sebastian of Portugal and 8,000 of his soldiers are killed, along with the king of Fez and the Moorish Pretender. Sebastian is succeeded by his uncle Henry, then a cardinal in the Roman Catholic Church.

Though defeating the Portuguese, Moroccan ruler Abu Marwan Abd al-Malik I dies in the climactic battle. He is succeeded by his brother Ahmad al-Mansur (r. 1578–1603), who will prove to be one of the country's most notable sultans. He built his power by making a set of alliances and trade relations with various European powers, most notably France and England.

1578–1583

Europe: France
Christianity

The English college founded by British Roman Catholics at Douai moves to Rheims, where it will be located for five years. During this time, Gregory Martin, a professor, completes a translation into English of the Latin Vulgate. The New Testament is published in Rheims in 1582.

1579

North America: United States
Christianity

Sir Francis Drake, sailing on the *Golden Hind,* lands near present-day San Francisco and claims California (which he calls Nova Albion) for Queen Elizabeth I and England. While there, he holds a worship service using the Book of Common Prayer of the Church of England.

1579

South Asia: India
Islam

Mughal emperor Akbar issues a declaration (or *mazhar*) signed by all major Muslim legal authorities (the *ulema*) naming him as the Khalifa of the age. As the ruler of an empire in which sharia law is acknowledged, he now outranks any of the *Mujtahid,* the specialists in sharia law, especially in cases

The Disrobing of Christ, El Greco, 1577–1579, Cathedral of Toledo, Spain. The painting depicts the scene just prior to Christ's crucifixion, with onlookers arguing over which of them should have his clothing. El Greco combined the painting style of the Venetian Renaissance with the religious intensity of the Spanish Catholic Reformation. (Toledo Cathedral, Castilla y Leon, Spain/The Bridgeman Art Library)

where their rulings conflicted. The declaration had the added effect of asserting Akbar's status relative to the emerging power of the Ottoman caliphate.

1579

East and Southeast Asia: China
Buddhism

Buddhists in Huhhot, Inner Mongolia, build the Da Zhao Temple, a Buddhist temple/monastery, the oldest in the region.

1579

East and Southeast Asia: Philippines
Christianity

Pope Gregory XIII erects the Diocese of Manila, with hegemony over Spanish colonies in Asia. Its first episcopal leader, Bishop Domingo de Salazar, a Dominican, will arrive two years later.

1579

Europe: Bosnia
Islam, Christianity

The Bosnian Sanjak-bey Ferhat-paša Sokolović commissions the building of the Ferhat Pasha Mosque in the city of Banja Luka. Financial resources for the mosque reportedly came from the ransom paid for the head of the Habsburg general Herbard VIII von Auersperg and for the general's son. The general had lost a battle at the Croatian border in 1575, in which Ferhat-paša was triumphant. He was executed by beheading and his head subsequently placed on display.

1579

Europe: Spain
Christianity

The artist El Greco completes his large painting, *The Disrobing of Christ* (also called *El Expolio*), which is placed above the high altar of the sacristy of the Cathedral of Toledo. That same year, he also completes his nine commissions for the church of Santo Domingo el Antiguo in Toledo, including his famous *Assumption of the Virgin*.

1579–1593

Europe: Moravia
Christianity

Scholars of the Moravian church (the United Brethren) begin publishing the fruits of their translation activity, the first edition of the Bible in the Czech language translated directly from Greek and Hebrew texts. The final work would not be completed until 1593, but the first of the six volumes of the new Bible (named from the place of printing, Kralitz, Moravia) appears in 1579 (and the last in 1593). The Kralitz Bible would be reprinted into the 19th century and become the standard Bible used by both Czech-speaking and Slovak-speaking Protestants.

1580

South America: Argentina
Christianity

The Spanish establish the first permanent colony in Argentina (part of the Viceroyalty of Peru) on the site of modern-day Buenos Aires.

1580

South Asia: India
Islam

Mughal emperor Akbar suppressed a rebellion in the eastern part of his empire. The leaders were Muslims and justified their action by reference to several *fatwas* (legal opinions) that had been issued that declared the emperor a heretic. Akbar dealt harshly with those who authored the fatwas.

1580

East and Southeast Asia: Japan
Buddhism

With no supplies, no relief in sight, the Ikkô Buddhist fortress of Ishiyama Hongan-ji surrenders to the army of Oda Nobunaga. This ends the power of the Ikkô sect and survivors integrate back into the mainstream of the Jodo Shinshu sect.

1580

East and Southeast Asia: Mongolia
Buddhism

With resources from the Chinese government, Buddhists in Inner Mongolia build Dazhao Temple (aka Wuliang Si or Infinite Temple), the oldest and largest Vajrayana Buddhist temple in Hohhot. It is also referred to as the Silver Buddha Temple for the rare eight-foot silver statue of Sakyamuni Buddha housed there.

1580

East and Southeast Asia: Vietnam
Christianity

Franciscan missionaries initiate Roman Catholic missions in Vietnam.

1580

Europe: England
Christianity

English Jesuits persuade Pope Gregory XIII to suspend the bull *Regnans in Excelsis,* issued by Gregory's predecessor in 1570, which in excommunicating Queen Elizabeth I had released Roman Catholics in England from their allegiance to her. He now advises Catholics to obey the queen outwardly in all civil matters, at least for the time being.

1580

Europe: Germany
Christianity

Lutherans gather the various doctrinal statements they have produced over the century into *The Book of Concord,* which remains the major sourcebook for Lutheran theology to the present. First published in Dresden, it will contain several of the ancient creeds of the undivided church (the Apostles' Creed, the Nicene Creed, and the Athanasian Creed), the Augsburg Confession (1530), the Defense of the Augsburg Confession, the Smalcald Articles (1537), the Treatise on the Power and Primacy of the Pope, Luther's Small Catechism, Luther's Large Catechism, the Epitome of the Formula of Concord (1577), and the Solid Declaration of the Formula of Concord.

1580

Europe: Spain
Christianity

Henry I, the king of Portugal, dies. Philip II of Spain claims the Portuguese throne and leads his army into the country. The Portuguese Empire comes under Spanish control.

1581

North America: United States
Christianity

The Rodríguez/Chamuscado *entrada* (expedition), led by Franciscan friar Agustin Rodriguez, explores the area around El Paso and enters New Mexico.

1581

South Asia: India
Sikhism
Shortly before his death Sikh guru Raam Das names his youngest son, Arjun Dev, as the fifth Sikh guru.

1581

East and Southeast Asia: Philippines
Christianity
The Jesuits become the third religious order to launch missionary work in the Philippines. They will be joined by the Dominicans in 1587.

The first Cathedral-Basilica of the Immaculate Conception (aka the Manila Cathedral), two years under construction, is consecrated by Bishop Domingo de Salazar, the first bishop of Manila.

1581

Europe: England
Christianity
Jesuit priest Edmund Campion, who had arrived in England to serve British Catholics, is arrested for treason—the pope having excommunicated Queen Elizabeth and having suggested that Catholic believers did not owe her allegiance as the country's monarch.

1581

Europe: Scotland
Christianity
Scottish Presbyterian leader John Craig draws up what is termed the King's Confession or National Covenant in opposition to the efforts of Roman Catholics to gain control again in Scotland. The General Assembly of the Church of Scotland adopts the covenant, which is based on the Scottish Confession of Faith of 1560 and is highly critical of Roman Catholicism. Subsequently, King James signs the covenant and presses it upon the population at large.

1581

Europe: Ukraine
Judaism
The Jewish community of Lvov (Ukraine) erects the Nachmanowicz Synagogue (aka the Golden Rose Synagogue). It is the oldest synagogue in Ukraine. It will remain in use until destroyed by the Nazis in 1942.

1582

South Asia: India
Islam
Frustrated with the acrimonious atmosphere of the debates at the Ibadat Khana ("House of Worship") he has arranged, Mughal emperor Akbar discontinues them. At about this same time, he begins to expound a new spiritual ethical perspective that came to be called Din-i-Ilahi and expresses doubts about his faith in Muhammad and Islam. His new perspective attempted to rely on the particular strengths and best insights from the different religions of his empire, and to serve as a means of reconciling religious differences and thereby uniting the people of his realm. At its heart, Din-i-Ilahi proposed a new ethical system that sought purity through intense yearning for God. It considered lust, sensuality, slander, and pride as major sins and advocated piety, prudence, abstinence, and kindness as primary virtues. Din-i-Ilahi provoked strong opinions with some religious leaders backing it and others, especially Muslims, condemning Akbar as a heretic attempting to become a prophet.

Mughal emperor Akbar moves his capital from Fatehpur Sikri near Agra to Lahore.

1582

East and Southeast Asia: China, Macau
Christianity
Italian Jesuit missionary Matteo Ricci, accompanied by Michele Ruggieri, arrives in Macau to begin a major Christian effort to convert China to Christianity. Both men apply themselves to mastering Chinese language and customs.

Jesuits in Macau begin building St. Paul's Cathedral, which when completed (1802) was one of the largest Catholic churches in Asia. It would also house St. Paul's College, the first Christian college in Asia.

1582

East and Southeast Asia: Japan
Christianity
Japanese Christian youth delegates start for Rome.

1582

East and Southeast Asia: Japan
Buddhism

In the midst of his campaign to unite Japan, Oda Nobunaga briefly stays at Honnō-ji, a Buddhist temple
in Kyoto. While there, a supposedly loyal general in
his army, Akechi Mitsuhide, turned on Nobunaga and
attacked the temple. As the temple burned, Nobunaga
was slain. Mitsuhide's success was short-lived and
within two weeks, Nobunaga's successor, Toyotomi
Hideyoshi, caught up with Mitsuhide, who was killed
during the Battle of Yamazaki. Toyotomi Hideyoshi
would complete the reunification of Japan that Oda
Nobunaga had initiated.

During the campaign, Oda Nobunaga also burned
down Erin-ji, a temple of the Myoshin-ji sect of
Rinzai Zen in Koshu, Yamanashi Prefecture. Rinzai
master Kaisen and a hundred temple members died
in the flames.

Oda Nobunaga also attempted to eliminate the
last of the Ikkô believers now in Saginomori, but the
campaign fell short when Nobunaga was unexpectedly assassinated. He was succeeded by Toyotomi
Hideyoshi (c. 1536–1598). Hideyoshi sees to the
burial of Nobunaga at Daitoku-ji, the prominent Zen
Buddhist temple in Kyoto.

1582

Europe: Italy
Christianity

By papal decree, Pope Gregory XIII introduces a new
calendar he has worked on with Jesuit astronomer
Christopher Clavius. The new calendar has a more accurate measurement of the length of the year. It begins
by dropping 10 days from the month of October in
this first year of its operation. Later named the Gregorian calendar after the pope, it will replace the Julian
calendar in the Roman Catholic countries of Europe
immediately and later spread to Protestant lands.

The Netherlands becomes the first Protestant
country to adopt the new calendar. The number of
countries using it would grow century by century
through the 19th century, but in the 20th century
evolve into the much more precise Common Era calendar, now the world's standard. The Common Era
calendar would, in turn, become the basis of several
new calendars including the revised Julian calendar

used by many Eastern Orthodox churches and countries and the Saka calendar in India.

1582

Europe: Netherlands
Christianity

British Puritan Robert Browne, whose work would
lead to the formation of Congregationalism, publishes two books, *A Treatise of Reformation without
Tarying for Anie,* and *A Booke which sheweth the life
and manners of all True Christians,* which outline the
basic theory of Congregational independency, while
in exile in Middelburg. He had previously attempted
unsuccessfully to found some independent congregations. His ideas would initially be successfully developed in Massachusetts in the next century.

1582

Europe: Scotland
Christianity

The Church of Scotland rejects an episcopally led
government and adopts Presbyterianism (church government under the leadership of presbyters or elders)
as well as the Reformed theology of John Calvin.
Those who wish to remain in a church led by bishops
with apostolic authority form the Scottish Episcopal
Church. The church will generally receive the support
of the Scottish monarch over the next century and survive as the Scottish affiliate of the Church of England
and representative of the Anglican tradition.

1582

Europe: Switzerland
Christianity

Theodore Beza releases a second edition of the Greek
New Testament (the original was issued in 1565).

1582–1583

North America: United States
Christianity

Two Franciscan friars, Fray Bernadino Beltran and
Fray Antonio de Espejo, lead an expedition to New
Mexico to look for any survivors of the Rodriguez
expedition that had left Mexico two years earlier.

1583

North America: Canada
Christianity
Episcopal priest Erasmus Stourton settles in St. John's, Newfoundland.

1583

East and Southeast Asia: China
Jesuit missionaries Matteo Ricci and Michele Ruggieri move to Zhaoqing, where they begin work on a Portuguese-Chinese dictionary, the first of its kind. Their host, Wang Pan, the governor of Zhaoqing, admires the pair's skill as mathematicians and cartographers. For Wang Pan, Ricci will draw the first European-style map of the world in Chinese.

1583

East and Southeast Asia: Japan
Shinto
A new hondan, the major shrine room at the Kamosu Jinja in Shimane Prefecture, is reconstructed in the *taisha-zukuri* (or grand shrine style). It is the first building erected in the new style, which will become increasingly popular for the rebuilding of Shinto shrines.

1583

East and Southeast Asia: Philippines
Christianity
Only two years after it is completed and consecrated, the cathedral in Manila is destroyed by a fire that started in another church during the funeral mass for the Spanish governor, but then spread and consumed most of Manila. A new cathedral, made of stone, would be built in 1592.

1583

Europe: Czech Republic
Christianity
Rudolf II, the emperor of the Holy Roman Empire, moves his capital from Vienna to Prague. Here, he supported the arts and sciences, and turned Prague into a leading intellectual center. He also funded efforts to seek the philosopher's stone, the primary goal of alchemy, and invited a spectrum of Esoteric teach-ers to his court, most notably Edward Kelley and John Dee. Rudolf performed his own experiments in his personal alchemy laboratory.

1583

Europe: England
Christianity
Edmund Grindal (r. 1575–1583), the archbishop of Canterbury, dies and is succeeded by John Whitgift (r. 1583–1604), formerly the bishop of Worcester. Grindal finished his tenure in conflict with Queen Elizabeth for his leniency in suppressing the activities of the nonconforming Puritans. He was under pressure to resign at the time of his death.

1583

Europe: Italy, Switzerland
Western Esotericism
During the year before his death, Archbishop of Milan Charles Borromeo visits the cantons of Switzerland in his archdiocese and launches a Counter-Reformation to turn back the spread of Protestantism. While visiting Switzerland, he uncovers widespread practice of witchcraft and sorcery (malevolent magic), which included among its practitioners some Catholic priests. Some hundred people are arrested, and at Roveredo the parish rector and 10 women are executed by being burned at the stake.

1584

South America: Chile
Christianity
Roman Catholics open a seminary for the training of priests in Santiago.

1584

South America: Peru
Christianity
A major synod meeting in Lima sets rules for the Roman Catholic Church in the Americas. It rules that the native people must be treated as free men and women, and their languages utilized in the church. They order the production of a trilingual catechism, move to set up schools for the training of indigenous clergy, and set standards for ordination of native priests.

1584

Europe: France
Christianity

Francis, Duke of Anjou, the brother of Henry III and next in line to the French throne dies. His death leaves Henry III of Navarre, a descendant of St. Louis IX and a Protestant, as the heir apparent. The activist Catholic duke of Guise puts pressure on King Henry to take further measures against the French Protestant community and issue a decree that annuls Henry of Navarre's claim to the throne.

1584

Europe: Iceland
Christianity

Guðbrandur Þorláksson, a Protestant (Lutheran) bishop at Hólar, oversees the printing of the first complete edition of the Bible in Icelandic.

1584

Europe: Italy
Christianity

Pope Gregory oversees the establishment of a new college in Rome to serve the needs of Syrian Maronite Catholics, most of whom live as a minority community under the rule of the Ottoman Empire.

Camillus de Lellis founds the Order of the Ministers of the Sick (popularly known as the Camillians). Members of the order dedicate themselves to caring for plague victims. Two years later, Pope Sixtus V confers his official approbation. The founder would later be canonized as a saint.

1584

Europe: Scotland
Christianity

King James VI of Scotland forces the Parliament of Scotland to pass the Black Acts, which provide for two bishops to lead the Church of Scotland. He meets staunch opposition and is in the end forced to return control of the church to the General Assembly, which favors Presbyterianism, including church leadership by the elders (presbyters) rather than bishops.

1584

Europe: Slovenia
Christianity

The first complete Bible printed in Slovenian is published. Protestants smuggle the Bible into the country to prevent its confiscation by the Roman Catholic authorities.

1585

Europe: France
Christianity

French Protestants under their local military leader François de Bonne, duc de Lesdiguières, pillage the cathedral at Embrun in southern France. The cathedral had been the focal point of an effort to suppress the Waldensian movement a century earlier.

1585

Europe: Italy
Christianity

Pope Sixtus V (r. 1585–1590) begins his reign. During his relative brief time in office, he carried out an ambitious renovation of the church's facilities in Rome. He had the Lateran Palace demolished and replaced with a new building. He also saw through to completion the dome of St. Peter's Basilica; laid out new streets that connected the major Roman basilicas; erected four obelisks, including one in Saint Peter's Square; and added a chapel to the Church of Santa Maria Maggiore.

Sixtus also renewed the excommunication of Queen Elizabeth I of England, and backed his pronuncement with action by making a grant to the armada of Philip II, which he promised to deliver as soon as the army it carried landed in England. When it failed to make landfall, his obligation to Philip dissolved.

In the meantime, a British spy stole a copy of a document condemning Queen Elizabeth, which was designed to be released in England if the Spanish succeeded in establishing a beachhead. The document, authored by British cardinal William Allen, is entitled *An Admonition to the Nobility and Laity of England*. After the destruction of Spain's armada, Allen destroyed all his copies, and the stolen copy remains the only one to survive.

Toyotomi Hideyoshi was instrumental in the 16th-century unification of Japan after a century of civil war. He also implemented administrative reforms and laid the groundwork for the prosperous Tokugawa period that followed his death. (Library of Congress)

1585–1586

East and Southeast Asia: Japan
Buddhism
As part of his campaign to assume control of Japan, Toyotomi Hideyoshi brings his army to Mount Koya, the mountain home of Shingon Buddhism. Mokujiki Ogo, a revered Shingon priest, is able to persuade Hideyoshi not to attack the monastic complex. He becomes a trusted associate of the future chancellor/ruler of Japan, and the next year, when Hideyoshi founds Hoko-ji Temple in Kyoto, an attempt to rival Nara's famous Todaiji Temple, he places Ogo in charge of constructing the Great Buddha Hall.

1586

East and Southeast Asia: China
Following the adoption of the Gelugpa school of Tibetan Buddhism as the state religion of Mongolia, Abtai Sain Khan, a Mongol leader who was present at the 1577 meeting of Altan Khan and the Dalai Lama, leads in the construction of the expansive Erdene Zuu monastery at Karakorum, the former Mongol capital. Over the first years of its existence, the site grew to include some 60 temples and house some 10,000 monks.

1586

East and Southeast Asia: Japan
Buddhism
Having largely completed the reunification of Japan, Toyotomi Hideyoshi assumes the title of chancellor of Japan. He would never take the title of shogun.

Toyotomi Hideyoshi will lavish much attention on Kyoto, his new capital. He will realign the streets and create a set of new rectangle blocks that supersede the ancient square blocks. In the process, he relocates several temples along Teramachi Street in central Kyoto, which transforms into a Buddhist temple quarter. Among the temples rebuilt here will be the Honno-ji temple, where Hideyoshi's predecessor Oda Nobunaga died.

1586

Europe: England
Christianity
Sir Anthony Babington, a British nobleman of Catholic faith, organizes a plot against Queen Elizabeth, a Protestant, to replace her with Mary, Queen of Scots, a Catholic. Implicated in the plot, Mary is arrested and tried for treason. Elizabeth hesitates for months following her conviction to sign the death warrant, but finally does so, and Mary died by beheading. She wore a pair of dark red sleeves on her arms, a color associated with martyrdom.

1586

Europe: Germany
Christianity
Primož Trubar, a Protestant exile from Slovenia, dies. He has lived in Germany for almost 40 years during

which time he publishes the first books ever printed in Slovenian, his *Catechismus* and *Abecedarium,* both published in 1555. Operating out of Tübingen, he will author some 25 books in Slovenian and produce a translation of the New Testament.

Jurij Dalmatin, a Slovenian Lutheran minister who had assisted Trubar, worked on the translation of the Old Testament, which culminated in the publication of a complete edition of the Bible in Slovenian in 1584.

1586

Europe: Italy
Christianity, Western Esotericism
In a papal bull, Pope Sixtus V condemns magic along with all forms of divination, including the various kinds of astrology. As a result, Italian astrologer Jerome Cardan is accused of violating the pope's order, and the Inquisition detains him under house arrest.

1586

Europe: Italy
Christianity
Pope Sixtus V issues a papal declaration establishing the maximum number of cardinals at 70, a number that remains firm until the last half of the 20th century.

Two years later he further reorganizes the church's administration around some 15 congregations (or departments), which would remain in place until the reorganization by the second Vatican Council in the 1960s.

1587

North America: United States
Christianity
The first Anglican services in the British American colonies are held at the Roanoke Colony in Virginia.

1587

East and Southeast Asia: China, Macau
Christianity
Dominican monks in Macau found St. Dominic's Roman Catholic church.

1587

East and Southeast Asia: Japan
Christianity
Hideyoshi reverses his predecessor's policy and issues an order officially banning Christianity and expelling Jesuit missionaries from Japan. The order went into immediate effect, but was not energetically enforced until 1597.

1588

East and Southeast Asia: China
Buddhism
Sonam Gyatso, the Dalai Lama, dies. A search ensued for his reincarnation who was discovered to be Yonten Gyatso, the great-grandson of Altan Khan, the late Mongolian ruler.

1588

East and Southeast Asia: Japan
Christianity
Pope Sixtus V erects the Diocese of Funay (or Funai, i.e., Nagasaki) under the hegemony of the Portuguese Jesuit missionaries.

1588

Europe: England, Spain
Christianity
Naval forces of Queen Elizabeth I of England defeat the Spanish Armada sent to avenge the insults to Henry VIII's Spanish wife Catherine of Aragon and their child, later Queen Mary I, and to reimpose Catholicism on the country. The defeat of the fleet would severely limit Spain's influence in Europe for the next century.

1588

Europe: Italy
Christianity
The Lateran Obelisk, the largest freestanding obelisk in the world, had been placed in the Circus Maximus in Rome in 357 by the emperor Constans. At a later date, it broke and was buried in the Circus Maximus close to where it had fallen. In the 1500s it was rediscovered and dug up, and in 1588, it was re-erected on a new pedestal located on the square in front of the Lateran Palace.

1588

Europe: Italy
Christianity

Pope Sixtus V, a Franciscan, names St. Bonaventura, also a Franciscan, as the 10th person designated a doctor of the church.

Pope Sixtus issues the papal bull *Effraenatam* (Without Restraint), in which he makes the use of any form of contraception and abortions at any stage in fetal development a violation that requires the added penalty of excommunication. Previously, there had been arguments about the moment in the birth process at which God had infused the fetus with a human soul, with some arguing that it occurred as late as 20 weeks into the pregnancy (that is, when the mother could discern the fetus's movement in the womb). Sixtus builds on earlier statements condemning both the use of contraceptive devices and abortion.

1588

Europe: Poland
Christianity

The Counter-Reformation grows in Poland with the appointment of Piotr Skarga as the court preacher by Polish ruler Sigismund III.

1588

Europe: Spain
Christianity

Spanish Jesuit theologian Luis de Molina, professor of moral theology in Madrid, completes his four-volume *De liberi arbitrii cum gratiae donis, divina praescientia, praedestinatione et reprobatione concordia*, in which he attempts to defend human free will by reconciling the Augustinian doctrines of predestination (now popularized by Protestants) and efficacious grace with the Renaissance ideal concerning the nature of humans' free will. Contrary to the thought of John Calvin, the Molinist position holds that humans are able to resist God's grace.

May 12, 1588

Europe: France
Christianity

The Day of the Barricades. Culminating an ongoing rivalry between Henry I, Duke of Guise, the leader of the hardline Catholic community in France, and King Henry III, perceived by many to be soft on French Protestants, the duke of Guise returns to Paris. The citizenry of Paris welcome him, rise up in a demonstration against the king, and barricade the streets of the city. Outmanuvered politically, Henry feels threatened and flees the city.

Several months later, the king has the duke of Guise and his brother Louis II, Cardinal of Guise, murdered and the duke's son imprisoned. The Catholic majority in the country, especially in Paris, will now turn against the king.

1589

Europe: France
Christianity

A young Dominican friar, Jacques Clément, gains access to King Henry III, ostensibly to deliver important documents. Drawing close to the king, he is able to plunge a knife into his abdomen. Clément is killed by the king's guards, but Henry dies from the wounds.

Henry III of Navarre (a small independent country in southwestern France) becomes the king of France (r. 1589–1610). At the time of his ascension to the throne he is a Protestant, and his formal coronation is delayed for four years.

1589

Europe: Greece
Christianity

Ottoman authorities in Athens enter the nunnery established by Philothei, a nun from a prominent Athenian family, accost her, and beat her to the point that she dies a few days later. She had provided a haven for a number of Muslim women seeking to escape their life as multiple wives of abusive men. She would later be canonized by the Greek Orthodox church, named a patron of the city of Athens, and have her relics interred in the Metropolitan Cathedral of Athens.

1590

South America: Brazil
Christianity

The Dominicans settle in Rio de Janeiro where they will found the abbey of Sao Bento and the church of Nossa Senhora de Montserrat. The church carries on the tradition of the 11th-century Benedictine monastery at Montserrat, Spain.

1590

South Asia: India
Hinduism

General Raja Man Singh, who served under the emperor Akbar, financed the Govinda Deo temple, one of the oldest temples in Vrindavan, built at an extravagant cost to serve the Vaishnava Krishna believers. Reputedly, Emperor Akbar donated some of the red sandstone from the Red Fort at Agra to be used in its construction.

1590

East and Southeast Asia: Japan
Shinto

Toyotomi Hideyoshi lays siege to Odawara, the castle of the Hojo clan, the major obstacle to his complete control of Japan. After the castle falls, Hideyoshi stops in Kamakura to visit the shrine to the deity Hatchiman, where there is a shrine dedicated to Minamoto no Yoritomo (r. 1192–1198), the first shogun of the Kamakura shogunate of Japan. The Hojo clan whom he had just defeated has provided the governors of Kamakura during the century of the Kamakura Shogunate. Hideyoshi identified with Yoritomo, whom he saw as the only other Japanese ruler who had arisen from obscure roots.

Hideyoshi rebuilds the central shrine at Yoshida Jinja in Yoshida, which was challenging Ise as the most prominent Shinto shrine in Japan.

1590

Europe: France
Christianity

Some years after the bishop of Nice, France, had abandoned the Cimiez Cathedral located on a hill overlooking the city and moved his headquarters to the Church of Saint Reparata in the city proper, Luigi Pallavicini, the bishop of Nice, and Charles Emmanuel I, Duke of Savoy, attend a ceremony in which the church is declared to be a cathedral.

1590

Europe: Hungary
Christianity

Gáspár Károli, a Hungarian Calvinist (Reformed church) pastor, completes and publishes the first complete edition of the Bible in Hungarian. It would remain the standard Protestant translation of the Bible in Hungarian through the 20th century and is still widely used.

1590

Europe: Scotland
Christianity

The Church of Scotland reaffirms its allegiance to the National Covenant, a statement originally promulgated in 1591 voicing the church's allegiance to Presbyterianism in belief and practice and staunch opposition to Roman Catholicism.

1591

East and Southeast Asia: Japan
Buddhism

Sen no Rikyu, a Zen Buddhist and tea master successively for Oda Nobunaga and, Toyotomi Hideyoshi, dies by ritual suicide. According to one story, Hideyoshi ordered the suicide following Sen no Rikyu's completion of the two gates for Daitoku-ji, the large Zen temple in Kyoto. He placed a statue of himself on top of the second gate, and Hideyoshi, who regularly entered the temple by way of the gate, saw himself as having to always look up to the statue. He subsequently ordered the offending statue removed and Sen no Rikyu to commit *seppuku*.

1591

East and Southeast Asia: Japan
Shinto

The main hall at Dazaifu Tenmangu in Dazaifu-shi, Fukuoka Prefecture, is rebuilt. It is the primary Shinto shrine at which the scholar Sugawara no Michizane is venerated. He had died in Dazaifu-shi in 903.

1591

East and Southeast Asia: Japan

Sen-no-rikyu (b. 1520), founder of the Tea Ceremony, dies. Both Oda Nobunaga and Toyotomi Hideyoshi have been devotees of tea.

Toyotomi Hideyoshi builds Nishi Honganji (or West Honganji) in Kyoto, the new headquarters of the largest Nishi Hongwangi, one branch of Jodo Shinshu Buddhism, and the largest Buddhist group in Japan. Their earlier headquarters, Ishiyama Honganji in Osaka, had been destroyed by Oda Nobunaga as retribution for the group's involvement in Japanese politics. The Kyoto complex includes Goeido Hall, which is dedicated to Shinran, the founder of Jodo Shinshu Buddhism, and Amidado Hall, dedicated to the Amida Buddha, the Buddha upon whom Jodo Shinshu is focused. The Jodo Shinshu have some 10,000 subtemples across the country.

1591

East and Southeast Asia: Macau
Christianity
Augustinian monks in Macau establish St. Augustine's Roman Catholic Church.

1591

Europe: Italy
Christianity
Pope Gregory XIV dies. He is succeeded by Innocent IX (r. 1591), who dies before the year is out.

1591

Southwest Asia and North Africa: Morocco
Islam
Fall of the Songhai Empire: Attracted by its wealth, the armies of al-Mansur of Morocco overran the Songhai capital of Gao.

1592

Central America and the Caribbean: Trinidad
Christianity
Almost a century after Columbus first visited Trinidad, a successful Spanish settlement is planted at San José de Oruña (now known as St. Joseph).

1592

East and Southeast Asia: China, Macau
Chinese Religions
Residents of Macau erect the Temple of the Lotus, one of the oldest temples in the region, dedicated to Kun Lam (Guan Yin), the ubiquitous Chinese goddess of mercy. The statue in the main hall occupies a large elaborate altar.

Through the centuries, Lin Fung Miu serves as a stopping place for Chinese mandarins from Guangdong Province when visiting Macau.

1592

East and Southeast Asia: Japan, Korea
Buddhism
Hideyoshi, the chancellor of Japan, having united the country, deploys 200,000 Japanese troops to invade Korea, then a vassal state of China. Seoul is occupied with only token resistance. The effort to occupy all of Korea and use it as a beachhead for an invasion of China would stall, however, as China dispatches its army into Korea to reclaim its territory. Eventually, Japan withdraws its forces.

1592

East and Southeast Asia: Malaysia
Christianity
Sir James Lancaster, captain of the British ship *Edward Bonadventure,* arrives at the island of Penang off the coast of Malaysia and lays claim to the island for Britain. It will come to be valued for the sheltered harbor it possesses.

1592

Ireland
Christianity
Queen Elizabeth I of England founds Trinity College in Dublin.

1592

Europe: Italy
Christianity
Pope Clement VIII (r. 1592–1605) begins his reign. He succeeds Pope Innocent IX, who had died the

previous year after only a few months in office. As one of his first accomplishments, Clement publishes a new corrected edition of the Latin Vulgate Bible. It will become the standard authoritative Roman Catholic version of the Bible into the 20th century.

1593

East and Southeast Asia: Japan
Buddhism

Toyotomi Hideyoshi founds Kongobuji, the large Shingon Buddhist temple to memorialize his recently deceased mother. It would later become the head temple of Shingon Buddhism, the Japanese version of Vajrayana Buddhism, introduced to Japan from China by Kobo Daishi in the ninth century.

1593

East and Southeast Asia: Japan
Christianity

In spite of the order banning Christianity, Franciscan missionaries initiate new missionary work in Kyoto and Osaka, Japan.

1593

Europe: Bohemia
Christianity

A century after the first complete Bible in the Czech language had been published at Prague (1488), a new translation (the Kralice Bible) appears. It has been translated from the Hebrew and Greek Bible now available and is the first Czech Bible translated directly from the original languages.

1593

Europe: France
Christianity

King Henry IV (previously known as King Henry III of Navarre) formally converts to Roman Catholicism, a necessity for gaining the support of the majority of his subjects, and is finally crowned as king of France in ceremonies at the Cathedral of Chartres.

1593

Europe: Italy
Judaism

The Medici rulers of Tuscany invite the Jews expelled from the Papal States by Pope Clement to settle in Leghorn, the province's main port. Through the next century several thousand will settle there and the only nonghettoized Jewish community in Italy will emerge.

1593

Europe: Spain
Christianity

Holy Cross Cathedral in Cadiz, Spain, is destroyed by a fire.

1593

Europe: Sweden
Christianity

Nationally, Sweden adopts the Augsburg Confession and officially becomes a Lutheran Protestant nation.

1594

Europe: England
Christianity

Anglican apologist Richard Hooker publishes *Of the Lawes of Ecclesiastical Politie,* a summary of the rationale of Anglican church organization (and of episcopal government in general), as an answer to the challenges to the role and rule of bishops made by the English Puritans, who are operating out of the Reformed theological tradition initiated by John Calvin.

1595

North America: United States
Christianity

Initial missionary efforts by the Franciscans to convert the native populations along the South Atlantic coast (Florida, Georgia, South Carolina), begun as early as 1577, did not bear fruit until Fray Juan de Silva established a series of missions along the coast. Though the South Carolina and Georgia missions were soon abandoned, the Florida ones flourished in the first half of the new century.

1595

South Asia: India
Hinduism, Islam

A Mughal general, Man Singh, starts construction of a Hindu temple without getting formal permission from the emperor, and he is ordered to convert it into a mosque.

1595

South Asia: India
Hinduism

Maloji Bhosale, a general in the army of the the Ahmadnagar sultanate, is named raja by Bahadur Nizam Shah II, the sultanate's ruler, and assigned territory in Maharashtra. As raja, he builds Grishneswar temple dedicated to Lord Shiva as one of the 12 Jyotirlingas, the sacred abodes of Shiva. Maloji Bhosale's grandson Shivaji would become the founder of the Maratha Empire.

1595

East and Southeast Asia: Japan
Buddhism

Ceremonies are held at Hoko-ji, the Buddhist temple built by Toyotomi Hideyoshi in Kyoto, to commemorate the completion of the large new statue of the Buddha. By this time, the statue had become a bone of contention among Buddhist leaders, especially the Nichiren priests. Nichio, the head of Myokaku-ji, a Nichiren temple in Kyoto, protests any Nichiren in the statue's dedication, believing that donations should neither be given to nor received from Hideyoshi, whiom he considers an unbeliever. The majority of the Nichiren priests ignore Nichio and participate.

1595

East and Southeast Asia: Philippines
Christianity

Pope Clement VIII elevates the Diocese of Manila to an archdiocese and divides the work in the islands by erecting three new dioceses—Nueva Caceres, Cebu, and Nueva Segovia.

1595

Europe: England
Christianity

Archbishop of Canterbury John Whitgift approves the nine Lambeth Articles originally drafted by Dr.

William Whitaker, the Regius Professor of Divinity at Cambridge, as a means to define and settle controversy on the Calvinist position relative to predestination. In their final form, they were signed by Archbishop Whitgift, Richard Fletcher, the bishop of London, Richard Vaughan, the bishop-elect of Bangor, and other church leaders. They represent a peak of Calvinist influence in the Church of England. Their promulgation without the consent of Queen Elizabeth would lead to her demanding that the archbishop recall and suppress the Articles. They never became an official Anglican statement.

1595

Europe: Spain
Christianity

A new diocese is erected in Valladolid, the birthplace of King Philip II of Spain. The previously built Collegiate Church is designated as the Cathedral of Our Lady of the Holy Assumption. Plans to turn the church into a large building rivaling other Spanish cathedrals were abandoned once the city lost its political importance to Madrid.

1595

Europe: Ukraine
Christianity

The Union of Brest. The Ruthenian Church of Rus ends its relationship with the patriarch of Constantinople, comes into communion with the pope of Rome, and becomes a semiautonomous Eastern rite church within the larger Roman Catholic church. At this point in time, the church includes Ukrainians and Belarussians who live within the Polish-Lithuanian Commonwealth, a kingdom led by Roman Catholic rulers. Led by the archbishop-major of Kiev-Halych and All Russia, the church is known today as the Ukrainian Greek Catholic Church.

1596

South Asia: India
Hinduism

Puran Mal, an ancestor of the maharaja of Giddhour, initiates the building of the temple of Lord Baidyanath (Shiva) at Deoghar (aka Baidyanath Dham) in what is now the state of Jharkhand, India. It is one of the 12 jyotirlingas, that is, a shrine dedicated to Lord Shiva, who appears in the form of a lingam, and one of the 51 Shakti peethas, worship centers dedicated to the goddess Shakti (who can appear under a variety of names such as Parvati, Sati, or Durga). The Baidyanath Temple is the only temple that has the double designation as both a jyotirlinga and a Shakti peetha. In many places, however, a Shiva lingam, interpreted as symbol of male creative energy, is juxtaposed with the yoni, a symbol of the female energy, thus symbolizing the inseparable nature of the male and female principles in the totality of creation.

1596

East and Southeast Asia: Indonesia
Christianity
The Dutch captain Cornelius Houtman sails around the Cape of Good Hope and makes his way to Sumatra. He opens the era of Dutch activity in southeast Asia. While their activity is primarily commercial, their entrance will lead to the introduction of Protestant Christianity in its Reformed mode into the region, especially in what will become the Dutch East Indies (today known as Indonesia).

1596

East and Southeast Asia: Japan
Buddhism
Hoko-ji, the large new Buddhist temple built by Toyotomi Hideyoshi in Kyoto, is destroyed by an earthquake. It is rebuilt but only the enormous bell its founder had donated remains to certify its short-lived prominence.

1596

Europe: Scotland
Christianity
The Church of Scotland again reaffirms its allegiance to the National Covenant, a statement originally promulgated in 1581 voicing the church's allegiance to Presbyterianism in belief and practice and staunch opposition to Roman Catholicism.

1597

Sub-Saharan Africa: Sao Tomé and Principe
Islam

An illustration from a Chinese manuscript of the Italian Jesuit missionary to China, Matteo Ricci (1552–1610), and his first convert, Li Paul. Ricci was instrumental in the introduction of Catholicism and Western science to China during the Ming Dynasty. (Hulton Archive/Getty Images)

The Dutch attack on Sao Tomé and Principe opens a six-decade era of hostilities known as the Dutch-Portuguese War. The Dutch hope to assume control of the trade networks that the Portuguese had established with the Asian spice-producing regions as well as the West African slave trade.

1597

East and Southeast Asia: China
Christianity
Alessandro Valignano, Matteo Ricci's superior in the Roman Catholic China mission and himself a former missionary in China, appoints Ricci as the major superior of the mission with the rank and powers of a provincial (i.e., an archbishop).

1597

East and Southeast Asia: China
Christianity

Jesuit missionary Giovanni Aroccia (1566–1623) begins his quarter of a century of work in the interior of China—much in Nanjing.

1597

Europe: Italy
Christianity

Pope Clement establishes the Congregatio de Auxiliis to deal with a theological controversy that had erupted between the Dominicans and the Jesuits concerning the role of divine grace versus that of free will in human salvation. The Dominicans tended toward an emphasis on divine grace and the Jesuits toward an emphasis on free will. The debate had been affected by some personal animosities between individual members of the two orders. Discussions would continue through Clement's pontificate.

February 5, 1597

East and Southeast Asia: Japan
Christianity

Hideyoshi orders 26 Christians, known as the Twenty-six Martyrs of Japan, publically executed by crucifixion in Nagasaki. The group included 5 European Franciscan missionaries, 1 Mexican Franciscan missionary, 3 Japanese Jesuits, and 17 Japanese laymen. Then in October, Hideyoshi reaffirms his earlier order to expel all Christians from the country, with the exception of a few who serve the small Portuguese community in Nagasaki. Most of the remaining missionaries go underground rather than leave and clandestinely continue to serve their estimated 300,000 converts.

1598

North America: United States
Christianity

Don Juan de Oñate, the governor of New Mexico, leads an expedition from Santa Barbara, Chihuahua, Mexico, to the Rio Grande Valley and at a site that will become San Elizario, Texas, formally claims the land for King Philip II of Spain. The ceremony conducted by Oñate, known as "La Toma," marks the beginning of over 200 years of Spanish rule in Texas. The Native people that the expedition initially encounters are called Mansos. As Oñate establishes Spanish hegemony in New Mexico, El Paso becomes a major stopping point for travel between New Mexico and Old Mexico.

1598

East and Southeast Asia: Japan
Confucianism

Emperor Go-Yôzei orders what becomes the first work printed by the Japanese from movable type, a printing of the *Analects* of Confucius.

1598

East and Southeast Asia: Japan
Buddhism

Shortly before his death, Toyotomi Hideyoshi reconstructs and expands Daigo-ji, a Shingon Buddhist temple located on a mountainside southeast of Kyoto. It will become the site for a famous cherry blossom–viewing party he holds. The temple manifests the lavish style that emerged in the new wealth of a united Japan.

1598

Europe: France
Christianity

King Henry IV of France, who prior to becoming king had been raised as a Protestant and become a leader of the Huguenots (French Protestants), issues the Edict of Nantes, which guarantees religious liberties to the Protestant community and effectively ends the Religious Wars in France, which had raged for a generation.

1598–1600

East and Southeast Asia: Japan
Christianity

Hideyoshi, the chancellor of Japan, dies. He has an heir who could succeed him, but his son is still a minor. He had also established a Council of Five Elders made up of the five most powerful daimyo (noblemen). However, in the power void accompanying his death, another general who had served under Oda Nobunaga emerges as the most powerful man in the country.

Hideyoshi is enshrined at Daigengu, the main building at the Yoshida Jinja, one of the main Shinto shrines in Japan, which Hideyoshi had rebuilt after taking power.

Immediately after the death of Hideyoshi, Tokugawa Ieyasu begins to consolidate his power, a process that culminates in the Battle of Sekigahara, after which Ieyasu secures the title of shogun from Japanese emperor Go-Yōzei and establishes the Tokugawa shogunate that would rule Japan until the Meiji Restoration in the 19th century.

Shingon Buddhist priest Mokujiki Ogo, the head priest of Hoko-ji Temple, who had previously been placed in charge of the Hideyoshi shrine, Tyokuni Jinga, in Kyoto, presides over Hideyoshi's funeral. He then retires from the spotlight to a small rural temple to spend the rest of his life composing poetry.

Among the victims of the rise of the shogunate is the Rinzai priest Ekei, a capable leader who rose to power during Hideyoshi's reign as the head priest at Tofuku-ji, a Rinzai Zen temple in Kyoto, which he had rebuilt. He opposed the rise of the new shogun, and in 1600 is arrested, executed, and later vilified as an evil priest.

The Urabe clan, which controls the Yoshida Jinja, continues in control of the *jingikandai* (which had superseded the *jingikan*) (the Council of Kami Affairs).

1599

South America: Argentina
Christianity

The Jesuits receive a plot of land in Córdoba upon which they construct a massive complex of buildings that includes several churches and monastic establishments as well as a university. It will become the focal point of a number of centers established throughout the region.

1599

South Asia: India
Christianity

The Synod of Diamper, held at Udayamperoor (Diamper), incorporates the Christian Church of the Malabar Coast (in what today is Kerala state) into the Roman Catholic Church. Under pressure from Aleixo de Menezes, the Roman Catholic archbishop of Goa, the Indian archdeacon George (of the Cross) is forced to submit to Rome and separate from the jurisdiction of

the Church of the East. The Indian Archdiocese of Angamale is transformed into the suffragan Diocese of Goa (1600) and becomes subject to the Portuguese. A process of westernization of the Malabar Christians will follow quickly on the heels of the synod, and a variety of Indian customs are condemned and suppressed.

1599

South Asia: India
Christianity

Pope Clement VIII erects the Archdiocese of Alagamale (aka Cranganore). This action culminates a set of events that had begun with the death of Archdeacon Abraham, the leader of the Saint Thomas Christians two years earlier. Archbishop of Goa Menezes moves to incorporate the Saint Thomas groups into the Catholic Church. He gains the submission of Archdeacon George, the highest remaining member of the Saint Thomas church hierarchy. Menezes also convenes the Synod of Diamper, which approves the necessary changes to bring the church into alignment with the Latin rite of the Catholic Church. After the synod concludes its work, Menezes consecrates Francis Ros, a Jesuit, as the first archbishop of the newly erected Archdiocese of Aagamale, which has jurisdiction over the former Saint Thomas Christians. Algamale is designated a suffragan see to the Archdiocese of Goa. While most of the believers accept the change, a strong minority does not and will eventually break away and assert their independence.

1599

East and Southeast Asia: Japan
Shinto

Maeda Toshinaga, the head of the powerful Maeda clan, builds the Oyama Shrine (aka Oyama Jinja), which he dedicates to his predecessor Maeda Toshiie. It is located on Mount Utatsu, Ishikawa Prefecture.

1599

East and Southeast Asia: Japan
Buddhism

Tenkai, the most powerful Tendai Buddhist priest of his generation, becomes abbot of Kita-in Temple in Kawagoe near Edo (Tokyo). He transforms Kita-in into the lead temple of the Tendai temples in the region.

1599

Europe: Sicily
Christianity

Having outgrown their cemetery, the monks of the Capuchin monastery in Palermo dig out a crypt beneath the monastery for future interments. The first body is that of the recently deceased Brother Silvestro of Gubbio, whose body was mummified. Other bodies were subsequently added and the environment of the crypt led to their dehydration and preservation. It was originally limited to members of the order, but later some of the city's prominent Roman Catholic citizens were allowed space in the crypt. Having one's body displayed along with the brothers in the crypt became a matter of honor among the Sicilian devout.

1599–1600

Europe: Italy
Christianity

Pope Clement VIII names Robert Bellarmine as a cardinal and names him a cardinal inquisitor. In this capacity, his first task is to sit as a judge at the trial of Dominican priest Giordano Bruno, who had emerged as a prominent astronomer and offered a variety of conclusions based on his speculations growing out of the data concerning the heliocentric nature of the solar system.

Arrested in 1592, Bruno had undergone a lengthy imprisonment and numerous interrogations. He will eventually be condemned for departing from the Roman Catholic faith on a variety of points, asserting the existence of a plurality of worlds, believing in metempsychosis (reincarnation) and the transmigration of human souls into less than human animal bodies, and dealing in magic and divination. Following his conviction, the pope pronounces the death sentence, and he is turned over to the secular authorities who carry out the sentence. Bruno is burned at the stake as a heretic.

1600–1699 CE

Introduction: 1600s

The 1600s opened with three large and relatively stable empires in control of large blocs of Asia. The Ming Dynasty controlled China; the Mughal Dynasty controlled the northern half of the Indian subcontinent; the Ottomans based at Istanbul (formerly Constantinople) controlled southwestern Asia, all of North Africa except Morocco, and south central Europe from Hungary to Greece. Meanwhile, rival Europeans, now divided not just by nationality but by religion, had turned their attention westward across the Atlantic. Catholic France looked to Canada.

Protestant/Anglican England looked to the eastern coast of the future United States, while Spain looked to enlarge its realm of control centered upon Mexico and the Caribbean into the American southwest and South America. Once present in the Americas, England looked to enlarge its sphere of influence at the expense of both France and Spain, toward whom they maintained a religious animosity. Thus along with their major settlements along the North American Atlantic coast, they began to explore and search out remaining available territory in the Caribbean and to challenge the Spanish both directly and indirectly.

The French, who had explored North America in the previous century, began to settle Canada with the arrival of Samuel de Champlain in 1605. Quebec, established three years later, will become the center of New France, which will grow along the St. Lawrence River through the remainder of the century. Catholic priests will arrive to both serve the French settlers and begin the process of Christianizing the native population.

The London Company, an entrepreneurial endeavor, financed the first permanent English settlement in what became British North America at Jamestown, Virginia, from which Anglican history in the new world begins. As the additional colonies are designated, the losers in the British religious conflict of the Elizabethan era would all play a role.

On one side are the Catholics, who will make their appearance in Maryland in 1634, where they dedicate their settlement to the Blessed Virgin and create a haven for their fellow church members, who have no legal status in England. Puritans—Calvinist Protestants who have failed in their program to "purify" the Church of England of episcopal leadership—have divided among Presbyterians (who vest church authority in elders or presbyters), Congregationalists (who vest church authority in the congregations), and Independents (who have largely rejected the idea of a state church establishment and the universal religious membership of the country's population). They also lack legal standing in England.

One group of Independents who had left England for Holland will found the original Plymouth colony in 1620. They will be followed to Massachusetts a decade later by Puritan Congregationalists who found the Massachusetts and then the Connecticut colonies, and eventually control all of New England. Later in the century, a member of the Society of Friends, a radical new Christian group founded by John Fox, which had had trouble negotiating a place in the British religious community, received a boon when one of their leaders, William Penn, received a land grant that allowed him to form a haven for both the Quakers and a spectrum of small dissenting groups on the European continent to settle what is now Pennsylvania.

Other countries—most notably the Dutch in New Amsterdam and the Swedes in Delaware—attempted to settle amid the British North American colonies, but were soon forced out, but not before introducing Swedish Lutheranism and the Dutch Reformed Church into the land.

The Spanish push into North America begins in 1598 with the arrival of Juan de Oñate in New Mexico. Twelve years later the city of Santa Fe is established and becomes the center of Spanish life and the spread of Roman Catholicism for most of the century, until the Native revolt of 1680 drives the Spanish out and they are forced to move their operation to what is now El Paso.

Throughout the 17th century, Spain remained the dominant force in the Caribbean. That hegemony will be challenged by both the British and the French. The British have their first major success in Jamaica when they drive the Spanish out in 1655. The French gain control of the western half of Santo Domingo in 1697. The Dutch will claim a vacant part of the South American coast and establish Suriname in 1683. The British and Dutch provide the original openings for Protestantism to enter the region.

Spain was largely unchallenged in its settlement of South America, the primary barrier to taking control of the whole being the continent's easternmost coast, which by treaty had been given to Portugal and will become Brazil. Actually, from 1580 to 1640, the kingdoms of Spain and Portugal were unified under Spanish rule. In both cases, however, Roman Catholicism comes to dominate the land and Catholic missionaries work hard to bring the native population into the Catholic fold.

In 1630, the city of Recife becomes the target in ongoing Dutch-Spanish rivalry, and the Protestant Dutch, then arguably the most religiously tolerant nation of Europe, attack and occupy the Brazilian coastal city.

The city had become home to a number of Jews, many of whom had at least formally converted to Christianity. Once the Dutch took control, they came out, founded the first openly Jewish community in the Americas, and opened the first Jewish worship center, Kahal Zur Israel Synagogue.

The Dutch surrender of the city in 1654 creates a crisis for the Jewish community, and it will be dispersed to other Dutch settlements, most notably Curacao and New Amsterdam (now New York).

The conflict in the Americas reflects the conflicts of Europe where Protestants who have separated themselves from papal authority have struggled for control in England, Scotland, the Netherlands, and most of Germany. The religious wars of the 1500s will continue in the 1600s and be especially vicious in France where a strong Protestant minority has arisen in a land that still remains basically Catholic. The issue has been temporarily resolved by granting Protestants toleration (Edict of Nantes, 1598), but never goes away. European relations are marred by intense Protestant-Catholic antipathy marked by hostility, recriminations, and distrust. The bitter feelings left from the mutual hatred generated by the Reformation will remain strong until the 1960s.

Both Protestantism and Catholicism have now also become international movements tied to the rise and fall of their home countries. Treaties made to end wars in Europe will henceforth carry provisions for the change of leadership in far-off places around the world and change the religion of lands as colonial leadership is passed around.

This issue of religious hegemony becomes vividly illustrated in the fight over the Spice Islands where the Portuguese, Spanish, and Dutch vie for control and where economic issues become an additional factor, with businessmen not wishing religious interests or ethics to become an obstacle or compete for their attention as they drive for profits from the spice trade.

Meanwhile, as the European nations move to enlarge their global empires, Christianity enters a significant growth phase. This is particularly evident in Asia where Jesuits have taken the lead in developing a Roman Catholic presence in India and China.

Matteo Ricci emerges as the leader of the China missionaries and in his thought and behavior raises the issue of how much the missionaries can "go native" in their desire to communicate the faith and identify with those whom they are attempting to convert. Missionary executives in Europe remain distrustful of indigenization efforts and increasingly identify and justify the spread of Christianity with the spread of civilization.

Eastern Orthodoxy is somewhat pushed aside in the global spread of Christianity through the 17th century. Its traditional centers of power—Alexandria, Jerusalem, Antioch, and now Constantinople (Istanbul)—are all under Muslim control and their leadership efforts directed toward adjusting to their loss of cultural hegemony. The one bright spot is Russia where the patriarchate is experiencing a decided ascent along with the rise of modern Russia.

The large Ming Dynasty, which had begun the century in control of most of East Asia, began to show signs of decline after several centuries in power. During the latter half of his reign, the Wanli emperor (r. 1572–1620) showed signs of boredom and disinterest in his job and internal dissension became rife at court. That internal turmoil at the highest levels had a religious/philosophical dimension with the disagreements over the teachings of Wang Yangming, whose dissenting opinions, propounded a century earlier, challenged some of the primary views of the reigning neo-Confucianism, which controlled much of court life.

Problems multiplied through northern China due to both disease and agricultural problems stemming from climate change. Simultaneously, a new Manchurian leader named Nurhaci (r. 1616–1626) emerged in Ming-controlled lands in the far northeast of China and eventually succeeded in uniting all the Manchurians. Once united, the Manchurians declared their independence from Ming rule and then began to eat away at the border of Ming territory in Mongolia and Korea. By the 1640s, a second center of dissent from Ming rule developed in the Southwest, where rebels under Li Zicheng, based in Henan Province, march on Beijing. In 1644, Li marched on Beijing, overthrew the Ming Dynasty (whose last emperor committed suicide as his government was overthrown), and established the short-lived Shun Dynasty.

Li's success quickly ran up against the emerging Manchus, and within a month of taking the throne, Li was forced from Beijing. Within a year his army was defeated and he died. The Shun Dynasty came to an end and the Qing Dynasty established Manchurian rule over the Han Chinese. A loyalist Ming government survived in Southern China for almost 20 years, but it too eventually fell and its territory was absorbed into the Qing lands.

Shunzhi, the first Qing emperor, had an affection for Western learning and briefly showed himself open to Christianity, as represented by several Jesuit intellectuals who were welcomed to the Chinese court and funded in some of their scientific exploits. However, in the 1659s, Shunzhi experienced a conversion to Chan Buddhism and crushed the hope of the Jesuit leadership that they might be able to woo China into the Christian world.

As the century comes to a close, the Chinese Qing Dynasty would anchor a large Buddhist world that stretched from Korea in the northeast to Burma in the southeast, while the Ottoman Empire anchored a Muslim world that reached from northern Africa to India, where Hindus and Muslims were fighting for the allegiance of the masses. Christianity (in its Roman Catholic form) had, however, by this time become a decidedly missionary-oriented religion and its representatives were active on every continent where they hoped to subvert the dominant faiths of the lands in which they had taken up residence.

ca. 1600

East and Southeast Asia: Indonesia
Islam
Sheikh Abdur Ra'uf al-Fansuri from the Aceh sultanate completes a first translation of the Qur'an into the classical Malay language. This language will later evolve into modern Indonesian on the one hand and modern Malaysian on the other.

ca. 1600

Europe: Bohemia, Moravia
Judaism
The Jewish community emerges as Polish Jews begin to settle there. Rabbi Judah Loew ben Bezalel emerges as the leader. He is best remembered as the creator of the legend of the Golem, a mysterious creature who may be brought to life to protect the Jewish community in times of need.

FUJIWARA SEIKA (1561–1619)

As the first Zen monk to abandon Buddhist orders and become a professional neo-Confucian scholar, Fujiwara Seika marks an important turning point in the history of Japanese spirituality.

Born in 1561, Fujiwara first entered a monastery at the age of seven. After his father and elder brother were killed and the family estate destroyed in a military conflict in 1578, he entered Sokokuji, one of the Gozan Zen temples in Kyoto. Distinguishing himself in both Zen practice and Confucian studies, he soon rose to the position of chief seat, second in rank only to the abbot. It was probably in 1598 that Fujiwara withdrew from the monastic order, inspired in part by his meetings with visiting Korean Confucian scholars in 1590. From 1598 to 1600, he enjoyed a close relationship with another Korean Confucian, Kang Hang, brought back as a captive by Hideyoshi, and the two worked on preparing neo-Confucian editions of the Confucian classics. In 1600, Ieyasu summoned Fujiwara to an audience in Kyoto, where, clad in the robe of a Confucian scholar, Fujiwara engaged in a vehement debate with some representatives of the Buddhist establishment.

Fujiwara declined Ieyasu's subsequent invitation to enter government service, but in 1604 he met Hayashi Razan and accepted him as a disciple. In 1607, Razan entered Ieyasu's service as an expert on Chinese books and the composition of legal and diplomatic documents. He continued to serve the next two shoguns for another 50 years, gradually establishing a position for himself and his descendants as the leading Confucian teacher and historian in direct shogunal service. Fujiwara remained inclined toward a reclusive life, but he was avidly sought out as a teacher by a number of powerful men.

Fujiwara laid a broad and solid foundation for Japan's Edo-period turn to Confucian learning, presenting Confucianism as something fully capable of competing with Zen in the realm of spirituality but also as something much more capable than Zen of development in the direction of political philosophy and practical learning.

BARRY D. STEBEN

ca. 1600

Southwest Asia and North Africa: Asia Minor
  Christianity
Patriarch Matthew transfers the patriarchal see from its temporary location in the Church of St. Demetrius Xyloportas to the Church of St. George in the Fanar, the Fatih district of Istanbul. This church will become the patriarchate's permanent headquarters to the present.

1600

East and Southeast Asia: Japan
Buddhism

Tokugawa Ieyasu (r. 1600–1616) defeats his opponents at the battle of Sekigahara. He goes on to found and become the first shogun of the Tokugawa shogunate of Japan. The shogunate will rule until the Meiji Restoration in 1868. Ieyasu was able to take power in the wake of the inability of the previous shogun to complete the invasion of Korea and successfully attack China.

Tenkai, a Tendai priest who leads a ritual ceremony to protect the nation from Ieyasu's enemies, wins the new shogun's favor and is eventually appointed high priest at Mount Hiei, Tendai's main temple. He regularly advised the shogun and helped write policies relative to Buddhist temples during his reign.

1600

East and Southeast Asia: Japan
Buddhism

Nichiren priest Nichio, the head of Myokaku-ji, a temple in Kyoto, had continued to advocate his belief that Nichiren Buddhists should neither give nor receive money from unbelievers, including the Japanese ruler. After Shogun Tokugawa Ieyasu come to power, he exiles Nichio, but is unable to prevent the priest from founding the No Alms Accepting school of Nichiren Buddhism, based upon his separatist doctrine.

1600

East and Southeast Asia: Japan
Christianity

The Jesuits ordain two Japanese priests—Lewis Niabara from Nagasaki and Sebastian Kimura from Hirado. Kimura, who had been born into a Christian family, would ultimately be martyred for his faith.

1600

Europe: Italy
Christianity

Pope Clement VIII hosted some 3 million pilgrims who arrived in Rome for the Jubilee Year celebrations. The pope led the primary ceremonial in which the Holy Doors of the four major churches of Rome were unsealed at the beginning of the Jubilee and closed again at the end of the year.

1600

Europe: Poland
Christianity

Court preacher Piotr Skarga, a Jesuit, convinces Polish ruler Sigismund III to found the Church of SS. Peter and Paul in Krakow. He will use the main Jesuit church in Rome, Il Gesú, as the model for the new church.

1600

Europe: Spain
Christianity

At the height of his fame as a creator of ecclesiastical art, the painter El Greco completes three paintings for the Colegio de Doña María de Aragon, an Augustinian monastery in Madrid.

February 19, 1600

South America: Peru
Traditional Religions

Huaynaputina, a volcano in southern Peru, explodes, producing catastrophes globally. It is the largest volcanic explosion in South America to have occurred in historic times.

1601

North America: United States
Christianity

New Mexico's governor Juan Oñate leads an expedition to the Canadian River, which runs through the Texas Panhandle. It ends in a battle with the Apaches he encounters.

1601

South Asia: India
Sikhism

Guru Arjan completes the compilation of the Sikh Holy Book, the Adi Granth, and the construction of the Harmandir, now commonly known as the Golden Temple.

1601

East and Southeast Asia: China
Buddhism

Twelve-year-old Yonten Gyatso, who had earlier been recognized as the reincarnation of Sonam Gyatso, the third Dalai Lama, is escorted from Mongolia to Tibet. He is the grandson of Altan Khan, the Mongolian ruler who had originally bestowed the title "Dalai" on Sinam Gyatso.

1601

East and Southeast Asia: China
Christianity

In 1601, the Wan Li emperor invites Jesuit missionary Matteo Ricci to become an adviser to the imperial court. Ricci subsequently becomes the first Westerner invited into the Forbidden City in Beijing. While in Beijing, he will establish the Cathedral of the Immaculate Conception, the oldest Catholic church in the city.

1601

Europe: Bulgaria
Christianity
Bachkovo, Bulgaria's second largest monastery, is rebuilt after being left in ruins during the Ottoman invasion in the middle of the 15th century. Its main church, Sweta Bogorodica, would be rebuilt three years later.

1601

Europe: France
Christianity
Reconstruction of the cathedral of the Holy Cross in Orleans, France, largely destroyed in 1568, began. King Henry IV of France was present to lay the first stone.

1601–1603

Russia, Central Asia, and the Caucasus: Russia
Christianity
Russia suffers a massive famine caused by several years of poor crops. Some 2 million, about one-third of the entire population, perish. Climatologists blame the problem on the 1600 eruption of Huaynaputina, a volcano in southern Peru.

1602

East and Southeast Asia: China
Chinese Religion
Li Yingshi, a Chinese military officer with a reputation as a mathematician, astrologer, and *feng shui* expert, converts to Christianity under missionaries Matteo Ricci and Diego de Pantoja. The Jesuit missionaries had developed an appreciation for the Confucian classics but at the same time had denounced Chinese occult divinatory practices. Ricci and de Pantoja subsequently were allowed to go through Li's large personal library, from which they removed and burned all Esoteric texts. Li Yingshi remained a zealous member of the Roman Catholic Church for the rest of his life.

1602

East and Southeast Asia: Japan
Buddhism
Japanese shogun Tokugawa Ieyasu orders the division of the Jodo Shinshu beginning with Hongan-ji, the major temple in Kyoto. Kyonyo, the monshu (chief priest) of Hongan-ji, becomes the first monshu of the new Higashi Honganji (Eastern Temple of the Primal Vow). Meanwhile, his younger brother Junnyo becomes the chief priest of the original Hompa-Honganji (Western Temple of the Primal Vow). The Jodo Shinshu will become the largest Buddhist sect in Japan.

1602

Europe: Ireland
Christianity
While copies of the Bible in the Irish language had existed for centuries, the first published edition of the New Testament, to which a number of scholars and church leaders contributed, finally appears as *A Modern Irish New Testament.* The work of translation had been sponsored by Queen Elizabeth and initially handled by Nicholas Walsh, the bishop of Ossory, but continued by Archbishop Nehemiah Donnellan after Walsh's murder in 1585.

1602

Southwest Asia and North Africa: Bahrain
Islam
Safavid Persian ruler Shāh Abbās expels the Portuguese, who had been in the Persian Gulf for a century, from Bahrain.

1602–1603

Southwest Asia and North Africa: Asia Minor
Christianity
Ecumenical Patriarch Matthew retires from his office and moves to Mount Athos. He is succeeded by the tyrannical Neophytos II (r. 1602–1603), who is on the throne for a year before being pushed aside and Matthew again resumes office. His third tenure as patriarch lasts less than a month before he dies and is succeeded by Raphael II (r. 1603–1607).

1603

Sub-Saharan Africa: Ethiopia
Christianity
After six years in prison in Yemen, Spanish Jesuit priest Pedro Paez makes his way to Ethiopia. His arrival opens a new era of Roman Catholic presence in the country.

1603

South Asia: India
Mughal emperor Akbar issues a decree granting the Jesuit priests with whom he had visited permission to make willing converts within his realm.

1603

Europe: England
Christianity
Queen Elizabeth I dies without an heir. The British crown goes to James VI, the king of Scotland (a Presbyterian land), who also becomes the king of England (an Anglican land) and of Ireland (a Roman Catholic land). He will rule over the three otherwise independent kingdoms, which are only united in his person. He also moves to England and exercises his authority from London.

Puritan clergy present the Millenary Petition in which they call for the abolition of the rite of confirmation and the use of wedding rings, and call for the abandonment of the term "priest" when referring to clergy. They also ask that the wearing of cap and surplice by clergy become optional. The petition will lead to the Hampton Court Conference of January 1604, at which King James I will meet with a number of leaders of the Church of England, which includes among its number a number of English Puritans. The most substantive action to result from the conference would be the king's commissioning a group of church leaders to create a new translation of the Christian Bible into English. That version would later be known as the Authorized Version, commonly called the King James Version.

1603

Europe: Netherlands
Christianity
Jacob Arminius receives an appointment as professor of theology at Leiden University. His appointment will lead to a major controversy as he has been on a search for a Calvinist theology that emphasizes free grace and free will and downplays the belief in predestination. He will initially be opposed by Franciscus Gomarus, a member of the faculty who holds to a more traditional Reformed theology.

1603

Southwest Asia and North Africa: Asia Minor
Islam
Ottoman sultan Mehmed III dies and is succeeded by his 13-year-old son Ahmed I (1603–1617). He did not follow the example of his father and execute his brothers, all potential rivals. One of his brothers, Yahya, reportedly converted to Christianity and spent much of his life traveling in Europe conspiring against Ahmed.

1604

Sub-Saharan Africa: Sierra Leone
Christianity
After more than a decade in Angola, the Portuguese Jesuit priest Balthazar Barreira moves to Sierra Leone as the country's first Roman Catholic missionary. He will argue for local indigenization of the faith, which he demonstrates by establishing real local communities, treating the people with respect, and honoring local languages and cultures.

1604

South Asia: India
Sikhism
Sikh guru Arjun Dev opens the Golden Temple and culminates the opening by formally installing the Adi Granth in the temple on September 1. He then appoints a member of the faith named Baba Buddha as the caretaker of the scripture.

1604

East and Southeast Asia: China
Buddhism
The future 10th karmapa, the head of the Karma Kagyu school of Tibetan Buddhism, is born as Choying Dorje in the northeast of Tibet. The task of recognizing

him as the reincarnation of the ninth karmapa fell to Chokyi Wangchuk, the sixth shamarpa, considered to be the bearer of a second lineage of reincarnated tulkus in the Karma Kagyu school. The shamarpa would become the teacher of the new karmapa and pass to him the full Kagyu transmission.

1604

Kobori Masakazu (aka Kobori Enshu) receives his inheritance and goes on to become the leading tea ceremony master and Zen garden designer in the country. Among his creations are the tea houses at Daitoku-ji and the garden for Kōdai-ji in Kyoto. From his residence at Raikyu-ji, a Rinzai Zen temple in Takahashi, he will be invited to instruct Shogun Tokugawa Iemitsu on the tea ceremony.

East and Southeast Asia: Japan
Buddhism
Japanese aristocrat

1604

Europe: England
Christianity
John Whitgift, the archbishop of Canterbury, dies and is succeeded by Richard Bancroft (r. 1604–1610), formerly the bishop of London. Bancroft comes to the office just as the Church of England is dealing with a set of problems that have been detected in the currently used translations of the English Bible, that is, the Great Bible that dated from the reign of King Henry VIII and the Bishop's Bible of 1568. Bancroft is placed in charge of a new authorized translation that will finally appear in 1611. The translation was done under the authority of the British monarch, King James I, and will be popularly known as the King James Version.

1604

Europe: England
Christianity
Elizabethan antiwitchcraft legislation (1563) is strengthened by making the mere invoking of evil spirits or communing with familiar spirits a capital offense. The act would undergird the practice of witchhunting and witch trials in Great Britain and its overseas possessions through the next century. Except where treason was associated with the act, convicted witches were to be hung rather than burned at the stake. This law would remain in effect until 1735.

1604

Europe: Ukraine
Christianity
A monk, Job of Pochayiv, becomes abbot of the Monastery of the Dormition at Pochayiv. He would develop and introduce to the monks a new strict rule, which would transform Pochayiv into the center of the resistance to the attempts to spread Roman Catholicism in the Ukraine.

1604

Southwest Asia and North Africa: Palestine
Islam, Judaism
Members of the Druze (Shi'a Muslim) community attack the Jewish community at Safed, plunder it, and force many to flee.

1604

Southwest Asia and North Africa: Palestine
Christianity
Henry IV of France negotiates a treaty (capitulation from Ottoman sultan Ahmed I) that allows France to play a role in protecting pilgrims journeying to the Holy Land, especially in visits to the Church of the Holy Sepulchre in Jerusalem. The treaty also allows the entrance of members of various religious orders who may reside, move about, and carry out their religious duties without hindrance or threat. The French are able to receive these considerations as they are not part of the Holy Roman Empire's effort to drive the Ottomans from Europe. Over the next decades, members of several religious orders (most notably the Capuchins, Carmelites, Dominicans, Franciscans, and Jesuits) will establish themselves at places throughout the Ottoman Empire, initially as chaplains to the representatives of the French government. In the Ottoman cities from Alexandria to Constantinople and throughout the Levant, they assemble, organize Catholics, and create new communities.

1605

South Asia: India
Christianity

Italian Jesuit priest Roberto de Nobili arrives in Goa and launches a notable missionary career. He masters Sanskrit, Telagu, and Tamil; adopts the appearance of a Hindu holy man; and translates major Catholic texts into local languages. He becomes the first European Christian to model the process of indigenization of an Asian culture in his attempt to evangelize the people. His own writings in Tamil will contribute to the development of the language.

1605

South Asia: India
Islam
Mughal emperor Akbar dies and is succeeded by his son Jahangir (r. 1605–1627).

1605

East and Southeast Asia: China
Judaism
A member of the Jewish community at Kaifeng contacts Matteo Ricci, the Christian Jesuit missionary then residing in Beijing. Ricci later corresponds with the chief rabbi of the group and, according to his own account, almost converts him to Christianity. Ricci refuses to give up the eating of pork. The Kaifeng Jews, whose origin is ultimately unknown, are members of a small community in Henan Province that had assimilated into Chinese society and had been able to preserve many Jewish traditions and customs. As early as 1163, they had constructed a synagogue, the Temple of Purity and Goodness, with an accompanying study hall, ritual bath, communal kitchen, and kosher butchering facility.

1605

East and Southeast Asia: China
Chinese Religions
Taoists in Shaanxi construct the White Cloud temple at Baiyan Mountain in Jaixian on the banks of the Yellow River. It will become one of the largest Taoist temple complexes in the region.

1605

East and Southeast Asia: Indonesia
Christianity

Ambon Island, one of the Maluku Islands of Indonesia, is taken from the Portuguese by the Dutch East Indies Company, leading to the conversion of the population from Roman Catholicism to the Protestantism of the Dutch Reformed Church.

1605

East and Southeast Asia: Japan
Buddhism
Japanese shogun Tokugawa Ieyasu formally abdicates his position in favor of his son Tokugawa Hidetada (r. 1605–1632), though he, in fact, retains the power of the office until his death in 1616. While living in "retirement" in Sunpu Castle, he carries out a variety of building programs including the construction of the monumental Edo Castle and the rebuilding of the Shizuoka Sengen Jinja, three closely related Shinto shrines located at Mount Shizuhata, Shizuoka Prefecture.

Toyotomi Hideyori, the son and designated successor of Toyotomi Hideyoshi, who was unable to claim the Japanese throne that was snatched away from him by Shogun Tokugawa Ieyasu, builds the Mikumari Shrine (aka Yoshino Mikumari Jinja) dedicated to the kami (god) of water, fertility, and safe childbirth in Yoshino.

1605

Europe: England
Christianity
In what becomes known as the Gunpowder Plot, a group of English Roman Catholics led by one Robert Catesby attempt to assassinate King James I of England (aka King James VI of Scotland). The investigation of the plot would lead to the principal Jesuit priest in England at the time, Father Henry Garnet, who was arrested, tried, and executed.

The British celebrate the anniversary of the failed plot as Guy Fawkes Night (November 5), a reference to one of the leaders of the conspiracy. Since agents of the pope were believed to be involved in the plot, the burning of an effigy of Pope Paul V became part of the annual celebration of the plot's failure.

In the wake of the discovery of the plot, King James orders his subjects to swear an oath supportive of him and declarative of the pope's powerlessness to order subjects of a monarch to withdraw their allegiance to him. His hastily drawn up oath offends many Catholics who see it as not only a political response to the plot on the king's life, but an attack on their faith. A controversy involving Catholic leaders both in England and Italy would keep the issue before the public for a decade.

1605

Europe: Italy
Christianity

Pope Clement VIII dies and is succeeded by Alessandro Ottaviano de' Medici, who rules as Pope Leo XI (r. 1605) for less than four weeks. He is then succeeded by Pope Paul V (r. 1605–1621).

Pope Paul moves to end an ongoing controversy between the Dominicans and Jesuits. Through the pontificate of his predecessor, a number of discussions, some quite heated, have been held on the subject of the respective roles of grace and free will in human salvation with the Dominicans emphasizing grace and the Jesuits free will. Pope Paul ends the discussions and grants each group the privilege of continuing to defend its own doctrine but without critiquing the other, while he and his associates make a final decision.

Pope Paul V founds the Bank of the Holy Spirit, which becomes the bank of the Papal States, and as such the first national bank established in Europe.

1605

Europe: Poland
Christianity

The Racovian Catechism, a work expressive of the non-Trinitarian Socinian movement, the Polish Brethren, is published in Polish but quickly translated and published in other languages.

1605

Russia, Central Asia, and the Caucasus: Russia
Christianity

Russian ruler Boris Godunov dies and is succeeded by his son Feodor II. Boris, his wife, and their children are later buried together near the entrance of the Assumption Cathedral at Trinity–St. Sergius Lavra. His death begins a period of instability in Russian life known as the Time of Troubles.

Feodor inherits a country in crisis and his reign is short as a group of dissident nobles depose him and replace him with a person claiming to be Dmitriy, the son of Ivan the Terrible. Dmitriy had been assassinated in 1591, but during the chaos that ensued following Godunov's death, three such imposters appeared and briefly ruled the country. Among the few actions of the first false Dmitriy was to recall the disgraced nobleman (boyar) Feodor Nikitich Romanov, who had been forced to take vows as a monk, back to Moscow, where he was made the bishop of Rostov.

1605–1606

Russia, Central Asia, and the Caucasus: Russia
Christianity

Dmitriy I [Ioannovich] (r. 1605–1606), an imposter who briefly claims to be the czar during the period known as the Time of Troubles in Russia, raises an army and assumes control of Moscow. He asserts his right to rule by claiming to be the youngest son of Czar Ivan the Terrible, whose real son Dmitriy had died at the age of nine. Shortly after taking Moscow, armed supporters of Dmitriy enter the Cathedral of the Dormition and declare the patriarch Job a traitor. Job is immediately exiled to a monastery in Staritsa. Dmitriy names a new patriarch, a Greek cleric named Ignatius, who as Archbishop of Ryazan had supported Dmitriy. He officiates at the coronation of the would-be czar.

Among those present at the coronation is Hermogenes, the archbishop of Kazan. While in Moscow, he learns that Czar Dmitriy plans to marry a woman who is a Roman Catholic. He opposes the marriage and is banished from the city.

1605–1610

Europe: Germany
Christianity

Lutheran theologian John Arndt issues his principal work, *True Christianity,* in four volumes. Inspired by the likes of Johannes Tauler and Thomas à Kempis, he adds a mystical and devotional element to the Lutheran tradition, and his work will provide a foundation for numerous devotional works written by both Protestants and Roman Catholics in future generations. Arndt emphasizes the mystical union between the believer and Christ.

Kōdai-ji, a Rinzai Buddhist temple in Kyoto, Japan, founded by the shogun Tokugawa Ieyasu in 1606. (Vin Photo/Dreamstime.com)

1606

South America: Bolivia
Christianity
The Roman Catholic Diocese of La Paz (Bolivia) is erected from territory previously assigned to the Diocese of La Plata o Charcas.

1606

South Asia: India
Christianity
Pope Paul V erects the Diocese of St. Thomé de Meliapur, which includes Roman Catholic work in Bengal.

1606

East and Southeast Asia: India
Islam

Khusrau Mirza (1587–1622), the son of Mughal emperor Jahangir (r. 1605–1627), claims to be the true heir to the Mughal throne of Akbar and rebels against his father. On a trip to build a supporting army, he met Sikh guru Arjan Dev, who gave him a blessing. After Khusrau was defeated and arrested by his father's forces, Guru Arjan Dev was also arrested as part of the revolt.

When the Muslim emperor Jahangir (r. 1605–1627), the son of Akbar, requested Sikh guru Arjun Dev, who had been arrested as an accomplice to the attempted revolt of Khusrau Mirza, to alter a passage in the Sikh scripture, the Adi Granth, that mentioned Islam, the guru refused, and Jahangir had the guru tortured for five days. At the end of the five days, Arjun Dev died, and Sikhs came to see him as the first Sikh martyr. That day is now commemorated annually by Sikhs worldwide. Before his death, he designates his 11-year-old son, Har Govind, as the sixth Sikh guru.

Sikh guru Har Gobind adopts two symbolic swords, one for religious affairs and another for worldly affairs.

1606

East and Southeast Asia: Japan
Shinto

Shogun Tokugawa Ieyasu gives land to Fujisan Hongu Sengen Taisha, a Shinto shrine at the base of Mount Fuji, Japan's most sacred mountain. The land is used to build the *okumiya,* the remote shrine that sits as close to Fuji's crater as possible. At the same time, the whole of the shrine goes through a process of renovation and expansion. Ieyasu had come to Fuji to claim the inspiration and support of the kami before the decisive Battle of Sekigakama, during his rise to power. He had vowed that if he won the battle he would rebuild the shrine.

1606

East and Southeast Asia: Japan
Buddhism

Shogun Tokugawa Ieyasu Kodaiji funds Kōdai-ji, a new Rinzai Buddhist temple in Kyoto. It is built as a memorial to his predecessor, Toyotomi Hideyoshi, and his wife is also enshrined at the temple. The temple's buildings feature elaborately decorated interiors set within a surrounding Zen garden.

1606

Europe: England
Christianity

The British Parliament passes the Popish Recusants Act, which requires any citizen whose allegiance is in doubt to take an Oath of Allegiance that denies any papal authority over the king. King James continues to appoint former Catholics who take the Oath of Allegiance to high office, aware that their oath might very well be insincere and would likely be revoked prior to the individual's death.

1606

Europe: Hungary
Christianity

Working with Melchior Klesl, the bishop of Vienna, and his chief advisor, Matthias, the archduke of Austria and future emperor of the Holy Roman Empire, issues the Peace of Vienna, which guaranteed religious freedom to Protestants in Hungary and allowed the Transylvanians the right to elect their own independent princes.

1606

Europe: Italy
Christianity

In the midst of a struggle over state hegemony over church affairs, Pope Paul V excommunicates the government of Venice and places the city-state under an interdict. Most of the city's clergy sides with the government, and the city expels those who favor the pope—namely the Jesuit, Theatine, and Capuchin orders. After the governments of Spain and France intervene to mediate the situation, the pope backs down and withdraws the interdict.

1606

Europe: Ukraine
Christianity

Jesuits confiscate the Nachmanowicz Synagogue in Lviv (Ukraine). The Jewish community has to pay a large sum to regain possession.

1606

Russia, Central Asia, and the Caucasus: Russia
Christianity

The pretender Dmitriy I [Ioannovich] (r. 1605–1606), who seized Moscow and had himself crowned as czar, is assassinated. Those who supported him are either killed or forced to flee. Vasili IV (r. 1606–1612) becomes the czar of Russia.

Czar Vasili deposes Patriarch Ignatius and imprisons him in Chudov Monastery. The new czar also puts his weight behind the selection of Hermogenes (r. 1606–1612) as the new patriarch of Moscow and All Russia. The former archbishop of Kazan is credited with inspiring the popular uprising that brought the Time of Troubles to an end.

1607

North America: United States
Christianity

Captain Christopher Newport leads a group of British settlers in the founding of Jamestown, a new settlement in what is now the state of Virginia. They will construct the first Anglican parish church in the Americas and hold the first Protestant church services. Rev. Robert Hunt serves as the first minister.

1607

South Asia: India
Hinduism
Swami Haridas, a poet and classical Indian musician, dies at Vrindavan. He founds the Haridasi school of mysticism focused on the Hindu deities Krishna and Radha (to the exclusion of other deities). He has operated out of an ashram he built at Nidhivan, Vrindavan, where he will also be buried.

1607

South Asia: India
Islam
The future Mughal emperor, Prince Khurram (later known as Shah Jahan), marries a Persian bride, Arjumand Banu Begum, upon whom he bestows the title Mumtaz Mahal (or Jewel of the Palace). His constant companion, she would bear him 14 children.

1607

East and Southeast Asia: Japan
Shinto
Date Masamune, a Japanese feudal lord, orders the construction of Osaki Hachimangu at Sendai. The shrine is dedicated to the worship of Hachiman, the Shinto god of war, whom Date considered to be a guardian/protector of the city.

Toyotomi Hideyori, the son and designated successor of Toyotomi Hideyoshi, who lost his throne to the first Tokugawa shogun, initiates the construction of Kitano Tenmangu, a Shinto shrine in Kyoto. It emerges as the head shrine of the several thousand Tenjin shrines dedicated to the deified scholar Sugawara no Michizane (aka Tenman Tenjin) scattered across Japan. The building of this shrine in Kyoto gave a significant boost to the veneration of Tenjin, whose worship had previously been focused in Kyushu, where he is buried.

1607

Europe: France
Carthusian monks at the Grande Chartreuse monastery, located in the Chartreuse Mountains near Grenoble, first produce a distinctive liqueur created by aging distilled alcohol with a mixture of 130 herbal extracts. The green and yellow herbs give the liqueur its unique color.

1607

Europe: France
Christianity
Having been nominated to the office of Bishop of Luçon, the underage Armand Jean du Plessis (later the duc de Richelieu) journeys to Rome where he receives a special dispensation from Pope Paul V and is consecrated. He will be the bishop in France who initiates the various institutional reforms promulgated by the Council of Trent 50 years previously.

1607

Europe: Italy
Christianity
Giovanni Diodati publishes what is the third Italian translation of the Bible by a Protestant. It has been preceded by those of Antonio Brucioli (1530) and Massimo Teofilo (1552), and it becomes the standard Protestant translation into the 20th century. It will be revised and republished several times in the 18th and 19th centuries.

1607

Russia, Central Asia, and the Caucasus: Russia
Christianity
A second pretender also claiming to be Dmitriy, the youngest son of Czar Ivan the Terrible, gains some support during what is a lengthy time of political instability in Russia. He would on two occasions march toward Moscow with his supporters, but would be turned back.

1607

Southwest Asia and North Africa: Asia Minor
Christianity, Islam

Ecumenical Patriarch Raphael II reverses the policy of most of his predecessors and voices some hope for a reunion with the Roman Catholic Church. He even begins a secret correspondence with Pope Clement VIII. His hopes are dashed when he runs afoul of Sultan Ahmed I who deposes him and sends him into exile. He is succeeded by Neophytus II (r. 1607–1612).

1608

North America: Canada
Christianity

A French Roman Catholic priest introduces Roman Catholicism into Canada by founding a mission among the Micmac, part of the Algonquin people of eastern Canada.

1608

Central America and the Caribbean: Mexico
Christianity

An earthquake strikes Oaxaca and extensively damages the massive Santo Domingo monastic complex, which had been built by the Dominicans. They rebuild and continue their work.

1608

South America: Bolivia
Christianity

Pope Paul V elevated the Diocese of La Plata o Charcas, Bolivia to the status of archdiocese.

1608

South Asia: India
Sikhism

Though only 13 years old, Sikh guru Har Govind leads in the building of the Akal Takht, the Seat (or Throne) of the Timeless One (God). Located in Amritsar, near the Golden Temple, it is one of the five seats of temporal physical religious authority of the Sikh community.

1608

East and Southeast Asia: Japan
Buddhism

Nichiren Buddhists in Tokyo build the Honmonji Temple. Beside the temple, a five-storied pagoda will be built. The temple will become the site of an annual festival, the Oeshiki service, held each October in honor of the sect's founder, Nichiren.

1608

East and Southeast Asia: Japan
Buddhism

Suden, a Rinzai Zen priest and head of Nanzen-ji Temple in Kyoto, is summoned into the service of the retired Japanese shogun Tokugawa Ieyasu and begins his rise to power that would see his being placed in charge of religious affairs in Japan.

1608

Europe: Ireland
Christianity

William Bedell, the bishop of Kilmore of the (Anglican) Church of Ireland, completes and publishes a translation of the Book of Common Prayer into Irish Gaelic.

1608

Europe: Italy
Christianity

The chapel in St. Peter's Basilica that houses Veronica's Veil, a piece of cloth believed by many to picture the face of Jesus of Nazareth, is destroyed and rebuilt, in part to provide better security for it.

1608

Europe: Netherlands
Christianity

Puritan Separatists from the Church of England move to Holland and eventually establish themselves in Leiden.

1609

North America: United States
Christianity

The French challenge the control of the St. Lawrence River valley by the Five Nation confederation of Iroquois people (i.e., the Haudenosaunee or People of the

Longhouse), which included the Mohawk, Oneida, Onondaga, Cayuga, and Seneca people. The lengthy conflict would reach out to include the other nearby Native people such as the Algonquin and Huron.

1609

Central America and the Caribbean: Bermuda
Christianity
The British who originally settle Bermuda are Anglican, and over the next decades as new towns are created, an Anglican church is erected.

1609

East and Southeast Asia: Japan
Buddhism
Date Masamune, the feudal lord at Matsushima, a town north of Sendai located in what is considered one of Japan's most beautiful scenic areas, revives and rebuilds the ninth-century Zuigan-ji, originally a Tendai temple that had been transformed into a Zen temple several centuries earlier. After years of neglect, Zuigan-ji reemerges as the Date clan temple and has remained a prominent Zen temple to the present.

1609

Europe: France
Christianity
A young British Catholic residing in northern France, Mary Ward, founds the Institute of the Blessed Virgin Mary (aka the Loreto Sisters), a new religious order for women. It is unusual for its day as Ward eschews the contemplative life for an active ministry in the world. The order modeled much of its life on the Jesuits and operated free from the authority of the local bishop. The women did not adopt a uniform habit. Controversial at first, over the years it will enjoy great success and the church's eventual approbation.

1609

Europe: Netherlands
Christianity
John Smythe, who leads a small group of Protestant Puritan Separatists in Amsterdam, comes to believe in believer's baptism (waiting until a person can make a rational choice of faith in Christ before baptism) and discards the idea of infant baptism. On this point he agrees with the groups that formed the Radical Reformation such as the Mennonites, and disagrees with most of the established Protestant churches (such as the Lutherans, Dutch Calvinists, and the Church of England). The idea further separates him from the greater community of Puritans, and his Dutch congregation is generally considered to be the first Baptist church. Those who agree with Smythe will later expand their understanding of the mature baptism into the mature Baptist position.

1609

Russia, Central Asia, and the Caucasus: Russia
Christianity
The monk Filarat, a member of the soon to be ruling Romanov family, who had served as the metropolitan of Rostov (1605) during the brief reign of the pretender Dmitriy I, is named the Patriarch of Moscow and All Russia by the pretender Dmitriy II. His appointment is generally ignored by most Russians. The next year, he would be taken prisoner by the Poles, who also did not recognize his ecclesiastical status.

1609

Southwest Asia and North Africa: Asia Minor
Islam
The Ottoman sultan initiates construction of the large Sultan Ahmed Mosque (also known as the Blue Mosque) in Istanbul. It will take seven years to complete and will feature six minarets and eight domes. The construction of six minarets created a controversy, as four was the maximum commonly accepted, being the number of minarets at Al-Masjid al-Harām (the Grand Mosque) at Mecca. The problem was not solved until three more minarets were added to the Mecca mosque (1629).

1609–1610

Europe: France
Christianity
The faculty at the English college at Douai publishs the complete Bible in English following the translation of Professor Gregory Martin from the Latin

Vulgate. The Douai Bible, as it came to be known, would be the principal English Catholic translation of the Bible until the mid-20th century.

1610

South America: Brazil, Paraguay
Christianity

Jesuit missionaries working in South America found the first "reduction," a settlement in which converted Native people can reside in a community and live their new Christian life. Eventually more than 30 such communities will be created.

1610

East and Southeast Asia: China
Christianity

Jesuit missionary Matteo Ricci dies and is succeeded as superior general of the China mission by Nicolò Longobardo. Longobardo sees to the editing of Ricci's papers, which will be published in Latin as *De Christiana expeditione apud Sinas* (1615). It becomes a popular work and is subsequently translated and published in several other European languages.

1610

Europe: England
Christianity

Richard Bancroft, the archbishop of Canterbury, dies and is succeeded by George Abbot (r. 1610–1633).

1610

Europe: France
Christianity

Francis de Sales, the Roman Catholic bishop of Geneva (Switzerland), publishes his devotional classic "Introduction to the Devout Life," which he directs to the lay public with whom he hopes to develop a pious vision of the Christian life.

About the same time, de Sales joins with Jane Frances de Chantal to found the Order of the Visitation of Holy Mary (aka the Visitandines), a new religious order for women. Its mission combines a dedication to the prayerful life with an active presence in the world.

1610

Europe: France
Christianity

King Henry IV of France, who had granted toleration to the Protestant community in the Edict of Nantes (1598), is assassinated by François Ravaillac, a devoted Roman Catholic layman. He is succeeded by his nine-year-old son Louis XIII (r. 1610–1643), whose mother, Marie de Medici, assumes power as regent.

1610

Europe: Italy
Christianity

Galileo Galilei makes two observations through his telescope that call the accepted view of an earth-centered universe into question—the moons of Jupiter and the phases of Venus. The confirmation of the existence of the moons of Jupiter makes him famous, and he is welcomed with honor when he travels. His observations of Venus lead to widespread abandonment of traditional Aristotelian and Ptolemaic views of the solar system, but do not lead to any full acceptance of the Copernican view of heliocentrism. Prominent resistance to the implications of the new finding comes from a strict reading of the Christian scriptures, which have previously been interpreted as teaching an earth-centered universe.

1610

Europe: Netherlands
Christianity

Following the death of Dutch theologian Jacob Arminius, followers of his revised Calvinism issue a document that emphasizes five points of disagreement with mainstream Calvinism. Entitled *Five Articles of the Remonstrants* (1610), it is the first systematized and formalized presentation of his perspective and gives its name to Arminius's students, the Remonstrants.

1610

Europe: Poland
Western Esotericism

After a visionary experience in which he comes to understand the unity of the cosmos and out of which he develops a belief that he had received a vocation from God, shoemaker Jacob Böhme begins to write various works offering a mystical and esoteric interpretation of Christianity. When a copy of an unfinished first book, *Die Morgenroete im Aufgang* (*The Rising of Dawn*), popularly dubbed Aurora, falls into the hands of Gregorius Richter, the Lutheran pastor at Görlitz, he is accused of heresy, and he ceases writing for several years. He has, however, by this time built a small following for his Esoteric ideas.

1610

Russia, Central Asia, and the Caucasus: Russia
Christianity

Czar Vasili is deposed when his former supporters turn on him. He is not killed, but is forced to become a monk and is confined to the Chudov Monastery. Russia falls under the leadership of seven boyars (noblemen) who then invite the Poles into Russia. They plan to have the teenaged Polish prince Władysław as the next czar of Russia. Hermogenes, the patriarch of Moscow and All Russia, assumes a leadership role in the campaign to stir up popular opposition to Prince Władysław (a Roman Catholic). He is arrested and confined along with the former Czar Vasili in Chudov Monastery.

1610

Russia, Central Asia, and the Caucasus: Russia
Christianity

Filaret, the patriarch of Moscow and All Russia, is sent as an ambassador to Poland, with which Russia has been in conflict, but instead of being received, he is imprisoned by the Polish ruler.

1611

North America: Canada
Christianity

Jesuits initially arrive in Canada, but their first mission is short-lived.

1611

North America: United States
Christianity

Presbyterian minister Alexander Whitaker settles in Virginia and establishes two churches near the James-town colony. American Presbyterianism dates itself from his work, though the first congregation in direct lineage to a Presbyterian synod will not be founded for a half century.

1611

East and Southeast Asia: Philippines
Christianity

Dominican missionaries found the University of St. Thomas.

1611

Europe: England
Christianity

Forty-seven scholars, all members of the Church of England working under the general oversight of the late Richard Bancroft, the archbishop of Canterbury, complete a new translation of the Christian Bible, including the Apocrypha, into English and present it to King James I. Once approved, its text replaced the text of the Great Bible produced a century earlier in the reading of the Bible in Anglican church services. It would become the dominant Christian Bible in use by English-speaking Christians for the next 400 years, and continues into the 21st century to be the official Bible for a variety of Christian denominations.

1611

Europe: England
Christianity

Thomas Helwys founds the first Baptist church in England. This radical Puritan Separatist congregation rejects infant baptism and the state's religious establishment.

1611

Europe: France
Christianity

French priest and mystic Pierre de Bérulle founds the Congregation of the French Oratory in Paris. The congregation becomes his vehicle for spreading the mystic spirituality with which he has become identified. In opposition to forms of mysticism that ignored Christ's humanity, he offered a spirituality based on a mystical journey through the Blessed Virgin Mary

Imam Mosque in Isfahan, begun by Persian shah Abbas I in 1612 and completed in 1638. The mosque is renowned for its calligraphic inscriptions and colorful mosaic tiles. (Matejh Photography/iStockphoto.com)

to Christ, and then through Christ to the Trinity. He would draw support from a number of leading clerics of his day including Vincent de Paul and Francis de Sales.

1611

Europe: Germany, Austria
Christianity

In the wake of his brother's loss of popular support, Matthias, the archduke of Austria, forced Rudolf, the emperor of the Holy Roman Empire, to cede his position as the king of Bohemia to him, and with it took what remained of Rudolf's power. Rudolf would die a year later.

1611

Europe: Italy
Christianity

Pope Paul, unwilling to make a definitive decision on the theological differences that had divided the Do-

minicans and Jesuits, and led to heated discussions over the previous decades, settles the dispute with a decree issued through the office of the Inquisition. It forbids any publications concerning the subject of efficacious grace until there is further word from the pope. However, there is no further statement by successive popes and the prohibition will remain in force through the century. While both orders abide by the structure, the Dominicans were able to circumvent it through the publication of commentaries on the works of Thomas Aquinas, the Dominican theologian who had been named a doctor of the church, hence one to be read and studied.

1611

Europe: Spain
Christianity

Residents at the Monastery of the Holy Face on the outskirts of Alicante, Spain, build a chapel to house a piece of cloth believed to picture the face of Jesus of Nazareth dating to the week of his crucifixion.

Safavid Emperors of Persia, 1587–1722

Reign	Ruler
1587–1629	Abbas I
1629–1642	Safi I
1642–1667	Abbas II
1667–1694	Safi II
1694–1722	Husain

Soon after the cloth's arrival in Spain from Rome, it was associated with a miracle that ended a severe drought. The chapel will subsequently be decorated with paintings that depict the miraculous end to the drought.

1611

Russia, Central Asia, and the Caucasus: Russia
Christianity

Amid the war between Poland and Moscow, Polish forces finally capture Smolensk, culminating a two-year siege. As Polish forces pour into the city, 3,000 Russian citizens blow themselves up in the Cathedral Church of the Assumption. The roof collapses, killing all the people inside.

1611

Southwest Asia and North Africa: Persia
Islam

Persian shah Abbas I commissions his chief architect Shaykh Bahai to initiate construction of the Imam Mosque, designed as the major religious site in the new capital city of Isfahan. It will take 18 years to complete and features four towering gateways, one on each side of the mosque, that challenge the importance, architecturally, of the main prayer hall. The mosque has four minarets, indicative of its royal origins.

The Imam Mosque supersedes the older Jameh Mosque of Isfahan as the main mosque of the city.

1612

East and Southeast Asia: Japan
Christianity

Luis Sotelo, a Spanish Franciscan friar, leaves the territory of the shogun, who had begun his effort to suppress Christianity in his realm, and flees to northern Japan where he continues his missionary endeavors. While there, he attempts unsuccessfully to found a new Japanese Roman Catholic diocese that would operate apart from the hegemony of the Japanese Jesuits, all of whom were Portuguese.

1612

East and Southeast Asia: Japan
Buddhism

Shogun Tokugawa Ieyasu moves the Osu Kannon Temple from the neighboring Gifu Prefecture to central Nagoya, the capital of Aichi Prefecture, where it will emerge as one of the most popular temples on Japan's main island of Honshu.

1612

East and Southeast Asia: Malaysia
Christianity

A Dutch trader, Albert Cornelisz Ruyl, translates the Gospel of Matthew into Malay. It will be printed in 1629, the first translation of a Bible portion into an Eastern Asian language.

1612

Europe: England
Christianity

Convicted as heretics, Bartholomew Legate, an anti-Trinitarian Christian, and Edward Wrightman, an Anabaptist, who both denied the Trinity and believed that he was the coming messiah, in two separate incidents are burned at the stake. They are the last two persons to suffer such punishment in England.

1612

Europe: England
Christianity

Baptist minister Thomas Helwys publishes *A Short Declaration of the Mistery of Iniquity* in which he argues that the king has no power over the souls of his subjects and should not make laws that invade their spiritual life. He sends a copy to King James I who responds by having Helwys arrested. He will remain in Newgate Prison until his death around 1616.

1612

Europe: Germany
Christianity

Rudolf II, the emperor of the Holy Roman Empire of the German Nation, who had grown unpopular due both to his involvement of his subjects in a lengthy undecisive war and his religious views, dies. Although nominally a Catholic, Rudolf was most tolerant of both Protestantism and other religions (Judaism). Through the years of his reign, he largely discontinued attendance at mass and saw himself as the instigator of religious unity. He tended to see the agents of the Catholic Counter-Reformation as partisans in the extreme.

Rudolf is succeeded as Holy Roman Emperor by Matthias of Austria (r. 1612–1619), who had the year before assumed control of his realm.

1612

Russia, Central Asia, and the Caucasus: Russia
Christianity

The Polish attempt to take control of Russia prompted a popular revolt and an army forms under Prince Pozharsky, which marches on Moscow. Upon learning of the army, Patriarch Hermogenes offers them his blessing, for which he is beaten and then starved to death.

Czar Vasili was carried to Poland by the retreating Polish army and died there. Prince Pozharsky ruled a caretaker government until a new Czar was selected the next year.

1612

Russia, Central Asia, and the Caucasus: Russia
Christianity

During the midst of the post-Godunov unrest, Germogen (r. 1606–1612), the patriarch of Moscow and All Russia, dies while in captivity by Polish forces. His place is temporarily assumed by Arsenius, a Greek bishop. Arsenius receives word of a vision received by Serge, the founder of Holy Trinity Monastery in Zagorsk, who promised victory for Russia under the protection of the Virgin Mary. Subsequently, Arsenius rallied the Russian forces under the banner of the icon of Our Lady of Kazan. Following the victory, which focused on retaking possession of Moscow, Russian prince Dmitry Pozharsky named Our Lady of Kazan

the liberator of Russia, and church leaders designated a feast day to commemorate the victory (October 22). Subsequently, Prince Dmitry, who had prayed to our Lady of Kazan during the Time of Troubles, used his private funds to finance the construction of a church to the Virgin of Kazan on Red Square in Moscow.

1612

Southwest Asia and North Africa: Asia Minor
Christianity

As was his predecessor, Ecumenical Patriarch Neophytus II is deposed and the ecumenical patriarchate is temporarily placed under the authority of Cyril Lucaris, the Greek patriarch of Alexandria. Cyril, a candidate to become the new ecumenical patriarch, runs into stiff opposition, with the eventual appointee, Timothy II (r. 1612–1620) offering Sultan Ahmed I a substantial increase in the annual fee paid by the patriarchate to the sultan.

1612

Southwest Asia and North Africa: Egypt
Christianity

Friends and supporters in Crete of St. Catherine's Monastery, located in the Sinai Desert, create a new iconostasis, a wall of illustrations of the major saints, which separates the chancel area of an Eastern Orthodox church from the space where worshippers gather for the liturgy. It is sent to the Sinai and installed in the monastery's chapel.

1612

Southwest Asia and North Africa: Maghreb
Islam

The Ottoman rulers of Algiers construct the Ketchaoua Mosque inside the Casbah (walled city) at the city's center. It originally served the powerful and wealthy element in the Ottoman regency.

1612

Southwest Asia and North Africa: Persia
Islam

The outstanding Persian philosopher Mulla Sadra settles in Shiraz to teach at a new madrassa and begins to write a set of innovative philosophical texts. He will propose several "proofs" for the existence of God, not unlike similar arguments circulating in the West, based on his basic theological propositions.

1613

East and Southeast Asia: Japan
Christianity

Roman Catholic missionaries in Kyoto, Jesuits, publish selections of the New Testament in Kyoto for liturgical use. Unfortunately, when Christianity is banned a short time afterward, copies are destroyed and none survive.

1613

Europe: Luxembourg
Christianity

Jesuit priests begin construction of a large church in Luxembourg as part of their efforts on behalf of the Counter-Reformation. The church would eventually be elevated by Pope Pius IX to become the Cathedral of Notre-Dame at the time of the creation of the Diocese of Luxembourg (1870).

1613

Europe: Spain
Christianity

Construction begins on the new Church of San Nicolas in Alicante, Spain, which will be built over the site formerly occupied by the city's mosque. It would be elevated to the status of a cathedral in 1959.

1613

Russia, Central Asia, and the Caucasus: Russia
Christianity

Mikhail I Fyodorovich (r. 1613–1645) is selected as the new czar of Russia. He initiates the Romanov family, which will rule Russia into the 20th century. He is the son of Feodor Nikitich Romanov, who had become a monk, taking the name Filaret, and is at the moment in confinement in Poland.

1613

Russia, Central Asia, and the Caucasus: Russia
Christianity

After a period of chaos, the Russian nobility place the 16-year-old Mikhail I Fyodorovich (aka Michael Romanov, r. 1613–1645), on the throne as the czar of Russia. He is the grandson of the first wife of the brother of Ivan the Terrible. Both of his parents had been forced to enter the religious life. His father, Feodor Nikitich Romanov, then a prisoner of the Polish king, had as a monk taken the name Filaret. As Mikhail matures, he will stabilize and bring central control to Russia. He will rule for more than three decades as the first czar of the Romanov lineage.

1613–1620

Europe: Spain, Italy
Christianity

Hasekura Rokuemon Tsunenaga, a representative of the feudal lord Date Masamune of Sendai, Japan, travels on a diplomatic mission to Europe, the first such mission from Japan to the West. Hasekura crosses the Pacific to Mexico, travels by land from Acapulco to Veracruz, and hence by ship to Spain. While in Spain, he accepts baptism as Roman Catholic at the hands of Bernardo de Sandoval y Rojas, the archbishop of Toledo, at which time he is given the Christian name Francisco Felipe Faxicura. The entourage then travels to Rome, where Hasekura presents Pope Paul V (November 1615) two letters, which request trade between Japan and Mexico and asks the pope to send Christian missionaries to Japan.

Hasekara and his associates depart for home by the route they had previously taken and reach Japan in 1620. The mission would prove a failure as Japan was at the beginning stages of a widespread suppression of Christianity. The government is unwilling to receive missionaries, and Europe's rulers refuse the trade overtures.

1614

North America: United States
Christianity

The daughter of the Native American chief Powhatan, Pocahontas, is baptized as a Christian and marries tobacco planter John Rolfe.

1614

East and Southeast Asia: Japan
Christianity

Shogun Ieyasu initiates a full-scale suppression of Christianity throughout Japan that leads to the destruction of many churches. The Christian Expulsion Edict, written by the Rinzai Zen priest Suden, which he signs, bans Christianity, expels all Christians and foreigners, and forbids Christians from practicing their religion. As a result, missionaries are ferreted out and imprisoned while many Kirishitans (the early Japanese Christian converts) flee either to Macau (under Portuguese control) or the Philippines (ruled by the Spanish).

1614

Europe: Netherlands
Christianity

Dutch theologian and jurist Hugo Grotius inserts himself into the growing controversy between the Remonstrants, the followers of the theology of Jacob Arminius, and the Calvinists when he drafts an edict reflecting the government's intention of toleration (and hence lack of favoritism) toward both sides. Grotius had come to believe that the state should advocate only the most basic of religious affirmations (such as belief in God) that he felt were necessary for preserving social order and should leave most theological issues in the realm of individual conscience. The edict enflames the controversy, and Calvinists, a distinct majority, turn on Grotius.

1614

Europe: Spain
Christianity

Lightning strikes the tower of the cathedral in Segovia, Spain. Made of mahogany wood, the tower, the tallest in Spain, burns and is replaced with a new stone tower.

1614–1616

Europe: Germany
Western Esotericism

Lutheran pastor Andrae Valentin anonymously issues the three original Rosicrucian documents: *The Fama*, which introduced the world to Christian Rosencreutz and told the story of his travels and the origin of the Rosicrucian order; *The Confessio*; and *Chemical Wedding of Christian Rosencreutz*.

1615

North America: Canada
Christianity

Friars of the Augustinian Recollect order begin mission work among the Native people of the St. Lawrence River valley. The Recollects are a branch of the Franciscans that emerged out of a reform movement within the order in 16th-century Spain.

1615

East and Southeast Asia: China
Chinese Religions

The emperor Wan Li constructs the Assembled Religions Hall (aka the Three Religions Temple) on Emeishan, one of the four sacred mountains of China, located some 100 miles southwest of Chengdu. The temple is designed to bring together the worship of Confucianism, Taoism, and Buddhism. He installs there a new bronze statue of the Celestial Master Zhang Ling, the founder of the Way of Five Bushels of Rice sect of Taoism. The monastery also becomes home to the Shengli Bell, the second largest bell in China, which is covered in writing. (The temple would evolve into the present-day Baoguo Monastery.)

1615

Europe: Ireland
Christianity

The Convocation of the Church of Ireland adopts a new statement of faith, largely written by James Ussher (soon to become the archbishop of Armagh) in the form of 104 articles known as the Irish Articles. They represent a turn toward Calvinism as a theological position, while maintaining an episcopal polity.

1615

Europe: Italy
Christianity

Paul V meets with a delegation from the Empire of Japan headed by Hasekura Tsunenaga, a samurai. Hasekura requests the sending of Christian missionaries to Japan, to which the pope agrees.

1615

Europe: Netherlands
Judaism

RVIT *HORA.*

HVGO GROTIVS,
*Reginæ Regnique Suedici Consiliarius, eorundemque ad
Regem Christianissimum Legatus. ordinarius. quondam
Syndicus Roterodamensis, ejusdemque Urbis in Conventu
Ordinum Hollandiæ & Westfrisiæ Delegatus?*

Dutch philosopher Hugo Grotius (1583–1645) was one of the most important legal theorists in the history of the West. His works on international law remain the theoretical basis of relations between countries, and his writings on "natural law" were even more important during his life. (Library of Congress)

Jurist Hugo Grotius leads a commission to consider the status of Jews in Holland, most of whom are fleeing Spain and Portugal. The commission decides to admit the Jews and allow them religious freedom. The main prohibitions concern mixed marriages and numbers. Three hundred Jews may reside in Amsterdam and 200 in the surrounding provinces. Rabbi Isaac Uziel, a former resident of the Maghreb, emerges as the leader of the Jewish community as the rabbi of the Neveh Shalom congregation.

1615

Europe: Serbia
Islam

With the Ottoman Muslim Empire in control of Serbia, Sofi Sinan Pasha, the bey (governor) of Budim, builds the Sinan Pasha Mosque in the city of Prizren in the Serbian province of Kosovo. He uses stones taken from the nearby Saint Archangels Monastery.

1616

South America: Uruguay
Christianity
Jesuit and Franciscan missionaries arrive in Uruguay to begin work.

1616

East and Southeast Asia: China
Buddhism
Shabdrung Ngawang Namgyal, the primary lineage holder of the Drukpa Kagyu school of Tibetan Buddhism, comes into conflict with the tsang desi (or regent) who ruled over central Tibet. The desi favored a rival claimant to the lineage. Facing possible arrest and incarceration, Shabdrung Rinpoche leaves Tibet and establishes himself in western Bhutan, where he founds Cheri Monastery. Bhutan had been dominated by Tibetan Buddhism for several centuries with the Drunpa dominating the western half and the Nyingmapa the eastern half.

1616

East and Southeast Asia: China
Chinese Religions
Nurhachi, the chieftain of a relatively minor tribe of the Jurchen people of northern China (Manchuria), has led a successful movement to unify the Jurchen tribes and proclaims himself Khan of the Great Jin (assuming the name of an earlier Jurchen dynasty).

1616

East and Southeast Asia: Japan
Buddhism
Japanese shogun Ieyasu dies. His body is taken to Kunō-zan Tōshō-gū, a Shinto shrine in the city of Shizuoka in Shizuoka Prefecture, Japan. He was quickly recognized as a divine being and given the title Tōshō Daigongen, or the "Great Gongen, Light of the East." A gongen is a buddha who has appeared on earth in the form of a *kami* (divine being) in order to assist

sentient beings. (On the first anniversary of his death, his remains were transferred to Nikkō Tōshō-gū, a shrine in Nikkō, Tochigi Prefecture, where they remain to the present.)

Tokugawa Hidetada now comes into his own as the shogun of Japan. Among his first acts, he reaffirms the policy of banning and suppressing Christianity. He favors Pure Land Buddhism and makes Zojoji, the main Jodoshu temple in Edo, the Tokugawa family temple and has his own mausoleum constructed there.

1616

Europe: England
Christianity
William Laud, later to become archbishop of Canterbury, is named dean of Gloucester Cathedral.

1616

Europe: France
Christianity
King Louis XIII appoints the still youthful bishop Armand Jean du Plessis (later the duc de Richelieu), who had emerged as the spokesperson of the French clergy, as his secretary of state and assigns him responsibility for foreign affairs.

1616

Europe: Germany
Islam
Solomon Schweigger of Nuremberg produces the first German translation of the Qur'an. It is translated from the Italian edition of 1547, which in turn is based on an earlier Latin translation.

1616

Europe: Italy
Christianity
As controversy grows about Copernicus's notion that the earth traveled around the sun, not the reverse, Galileo Galilei travels to Rome in hopes of persuading the Catholic Church leadership to remain open to Copernicus's ideas. Roberto Cardinal Bellarmine, a prominent theologian and head of the Supreme Sacred Congregation of the Universal Inquisition, informs Galileo that the idea set forth by Nicolas

Copernicus that the earth moves around the immobile sun (heliocentrism) had been declared false and condemned. Bellarmine orders him to abandon the notion, to which Galileo submits, for the moment.

1616

Europe: Italy
Christianity
Pope Paul V limits the making of copies of Veronica's Veil, a piece of cloth believed by many to picture the face of Jesus of Nazareth. Henceforth, copies can only be created by a canon of Saint Peter's Basilica. P. Strozzi, the secretary of Pope Paul V, makes six copies of Veronica's Veil, one of which will survive among the relics at the Hofburg Palace in Vienna, Austria.

Carlo Maderno completes six years of work on the façade of St. Peter's Cathedral, which establishes its current appearance, including the placement of the statues of the 12 apostles on the balustrade.

1617

East and Southeast Asia: Japan
Shinto
Shogun Hidetada fullfills the wish of his father to be enshrined at Nikko, a town north of Edo (Tokyo), and founds Nikko Toshogu, a Shinto shrine from which the late shogun Ieyasu could continue to lead the nation. The shrine, originally a relatively small complex of buildings, will over the next few decades expand to become one of the main Shinto sites in the Kanto region.

Ieyasu's body is removed from Kunō-zan Tōshō-gū, the Shinto shrine in Shizuoka Prefecture, and carried in great ceremony to Nikko. Along the way, the procession stops at Kita-in, the Tendai temple in Kawagoe, where the prominent priest Tenkai presided over a four-day ceremony in Ieyasu's honor.

1617

Europe: England
Christianity
King James I issues the Declaration of Sports (aka the Book of Sports) dealing with the sports and recreational activities that are permitted on Sundays and other holy days. Permitted activities include archery and dancing, while bowling is prohibited. Puritan Nonconformists considered the regulations far too

lax. The declaration condemned both the Puritans who were seen as too strict as well as those who did not attend their local parish church. Sunday recreation was intended for church attenders.

1617

Europe: England
Christianity

John Traske, a wandering preacher who described himself as a Jewish-Christian, espoused sabbatarianism (the keeping of Saturday as a holy day) and adopted various practices derived from the law presented in the Hebrew scriptures. He is arrested in London and after a lengthy judicial process is convicted of attempting to lead the Christian people of England astray. He is sentenced to be fined a substantial amount, expelled from the ministry, whipped, have his ears nailed to the pillory, and finally be branded on the forehead with the letter J (a reference to his Jewish opinions). He eventually will be released from jail when he agrees to recant his opinions.

1617

Europe: England, Scotland
Christianity

To assist King James I in converting Scotland to an episcopal form of church governance, Lancelot Andrewes, the Anglican bishop of Chichester, accompanies the king to Scotland, where he is dean of the Chapel Royal, and then is transferred from Chichester to become the bishop of Winchester.

1617

Europe: Italy
Christianity

Pope Paul V culminates a decade-long process of development by giving official approval to the new Congregation of the Pious Schools, dedicated to educating the poor youth of Rome. Founded by Joseph Calasanza, it is the first religious institute dedicated essentially to teaching. The order would later expand across Europe.

1617–1618

Southwest Asia and North Africa: Asia Minor
Islam

Ottoman sultan Ahmed I dies and is succeeded by his brother Mustafa I Deli (r. 1617–1618, 1622–1623). Unfit to rule due to a mental illness, he was sultan in name only. A year after being given the title, he was removed from office and replaced with his 14-year-old nephew Osman II (r. 1618–1622).

1618

East and Southeast Asia: Japan
Buddhism

Nichiren Buddhists erect a five-story pagoda that rises more than 100 feet in the air at Myojo-ji, the head temple of Nichiren Buddhism. It is located adjacent to a large statue of Nichizo, a direct disciple of Nichiren and the temple's founder.

1618

Europe: England
Christianity

Henry Jacob moves to London after a time among Puritan separatists in Holland. He forms a religious society in Southwark, now considered to have been the first Congregational congregation in England.

1618

Europe: Netherlands
Christianity

Maurice of Nassau, Prince of Orange, who supports the Calvinists in what had become a major theological controversy in the Netherlands, moves against the Remonstrants, who advocated the anti-Calvinist perspective originally put forth by the late theologian Jacob Arminius. Due to events *De Imperio* would not be published until 1647 (two years after Grotius' death). What forestalled the publication was Maurice's ordering the arrest of Oldenbarnevelt and Grotius on August 29, 1618. Ultimately, Oldenbarnevelt was executed, and Grotius was sentenced to life imprisonment, which was met with the approval of King James's representatives who were in attendance.

A synod convenes at Dordrecht in the Netherlands to respond to the Remonstrants, followers of Jacob Arminius, whose theology opposed ideas of predestination and by extension other basics of Reformed Church thought. The synod suggested five basic pillars of Calvinist theology: total predestination, utter depravity, limited atonement, irresistible grace, and perseverance of the saints. In the end, the synod declared Armenian theologian Conrad, who now held the chair formerly occupied by Arminius at the University of Leiden, to be unworthy of the professorship.

The synod attaches the five Canons of Dort to two other popular statements of Calvinist Protestantism, the Belgic Confession and the Heidelberg Catechism, which are offered to Reformed churches as the Three Forms of Unity, a widely accepted standard for full communion.

The Arminian perspective, while largely losing out in Holland, would later be embodied in the Methodist movement.

1618

Europe: Scotland
Christianity

King James I of England (also ruling as King James VI of Scotland) has worked to move the Church of Scotland from its Presbyterian stance and transform it into an Anglican body. With his strong backing, the church's General Assembly adopted the Five Articles of Perth, which provided for kneeling during communion, private baptism, private communion for the sick or infirm, confirmation of youth by a bishop, and the observance of the festivals of Christmas and Easter. The Scottish Parliament delayed ratification for several years, but finally passed the articles in 1621. Though widely disregarded, the articles will remain church law until 1690.

1618–1619

Europe: Netherlands
Christianity

Calvinist theologians in the Netherlands gather in Dort determined to respond to the teachings of theologian Jacob Arminius and his followers, called Remonstrants, who have developed a revised form of Calvinism that emphasizes free grace and de-emphasizes predestination. The Synod of Dort condemns Arminius, anathematizes the Remonstrants, and advocates what comes to be known as the five points of Calvinism. They used the state's apparatus to attempt to suppress the Arminian perspective and those who held it.

The five points of Calvinism, which later became somewhat definitive of the tradition, affirmed belief in total human depravity, unconditional election, limited atonement, utter predestination, and perseverance of the saved. Calvinists believe that sin is so destructive that it destroys human ability to do anything that assists in the process of salvation, but that God chooses to save some and sent Christ to die for those individuals. The Arminians or Remonstrants affirm that Christ died for all, that his death spread what is termed prevenient grace to all and created a situation in which any can turn and develop faith in Christ that brings salvation.

1618–1619

Russia, Central Asia, and the Caucasus: Russia
Christianity

Following the signing of the Truce of Deulino (signed on December 11, 1618), Metropolitan Filaret, the Russian Orthodox patriarch of Moscow and All Russia, who had been a prisoner of the Polish king for a decade, returns to Moscow where his son Michael Romanov has become the czar. He will become the power behind the throne and virtually rule Russia until his death in 1633. As the leader of the church, he ordered all of his archbishops to establish a seminary, a school for the formal training of the clergy.

1619

North America: Canada
Christianity

Rasmus Jensen, a Danish Lutheran minister, travels to Hudson Bay aboard an expedition sent out by Danish king Christian IV. The expedition lands at the mouth of Churchill River near the present site of Churchill, Manitoba, where on Christmas Day, Jensen leads a worship service, the first Lutheran service held in North America.

1619

South Asia: India
Sikhism

The sixth Sikh guru Har Gobind is freed after a year of imprisonment in the fort of Gwalior by Indian Mughal emperor Jahangir. The two men were subsequently able to develop a more friendly relationship.

THIRTY YEARS' WAR

The Thirty Years' War, which raged from 1618 until 1648, embroiled most of Europe in a conflict that dramatically changed not only the map but also the balance of European power. By the end of the war much of Germany was in ruins, the Habsburgs were no longer masters of the continent, and the wars of religion that had ravaged Europe since the early 16th century were finally over. The immediate cause of the conflict was a crisis within the Habsburg family's Bohemian branch, but the war also owed much to the religious and political crises caused by the Reformation and the competition between monarchs, particularly the Habsburgs of the Holy Roman Empire, various German princes, and the monarchs of Sweden and France.

ABC-CLIO

1619

East and Southeast Asia: Japan
Buddhism
Jodo-shu (Pure Land) Buddhists add a new gate to Chionin Temple, the head temple of Jodo Buddhism, located in Kyoto. The two-story gate stands 79 feet tall and is Japan's largest temple gate. A few years later, the temple would acquire a new 74-ton temple bell, the heaviest in Japan.

1619

East and Southeast Asia: Japan
Shinto
The Kashima Shrine, a seventh-century Shinto shrine in northeast Tokyo, is rebuilt. The shrine will continue under the patronage of the Tokugawa family.

1619

Europe: Austria, Hungary
Christianity, Judaism
Matthias, the emperor of the Holy Roman Empire, dies. He has followed a policy in agreement with his chief advisor, the bishop of Vienna, Melchior Klesl, of seeking reconciliation with the Protestants who formed a significant portion of his realm. He is succeeded by his brother, the archduke of Austria Ferdinand II (r. 1619–1637) who had been trained by the Jesuits, then at the height of their Counter-Reformation enthusiasm, and who believed that the

Catholics should reign supreme. He moved to retract the freedoms granted the nobles and people by his predecessors. His intransigent attitude directly contributed to the series of conflicts that became known as the Thirty Years' War, which kept his and the neighboring realms in a state of war and destruction from 1618 to 1648.

Ferdinand II will become known for his open policy toward the Jews in his realm, especially in Vienna where he will move to establish a new Jewish community just outside the city's walls. He will gradually expand their privileges throughout his time on the throne.

1620

North America: Canada
Christianity
Recollect friars brew the first beer known to have been consumed in New France.

1620

North America: Canada
Christianity
George Calvert purchases land in Newfoundland and establishes a settlement he calls Avalon, named for the spot where tradition placed the entrance of Christianity into Britain. Calvert subsequently obtains a charter for his settlement as the "Province of Avalon," to be under his personal rule. He introduces religious

Fort Dansborg, established 1620 in the former Danish colony on the South Eastern coast of India, in Tranquebar, Tamil Nadu. (Ajay Bhaskar/Dreamstime.com)

tolerance to Avalon, meaning open worship for both Protestants and Catholics.

1620

North America: United States
Christianity

The Pilgrims (independent Separatists) residing in Leiden, Holland, accept an invitation from the Virginia Company to move to North America. Their ship, the *Mayflower,* lands at Plymouth, Massachusetts. Before going ashore, the Pilgrim leaders make an agreement, the "Mayflower Compact," detailing their plan of government and separate church organization.

1620

South America: Argentina
Christianity

Pope Paul V divides the Diocese of Asunción (Paraguay) and establishes the Diocese of Buenos Aires (Argentina). The main church in the city, which had been rebuilt in 1618, is designated as the first cathedral.

1620

South Asia: India
Christianity

The Danish East India Company established their headquarters for trade with India at Fort Dansborg at Tranquebar, Tamil Nadu, on India's southeast coast.

1620

East and Southeast Asia: China
Buddhism

The Wanli emperor, the Ming ruler of China, dies and is succeeded by his son, the Taichang emperor. The Taichang emperor, however, dies only a month after assuming office. He is succeeded by his son Zhu Youxiao, who becomes the Tianqi emperor (r. 1620–1627).

1620

East and Southeast Asia: Japan
Buddhism

Chinese Buddhist priest Shin-en builds Kofuku-ji, the first temple of the Obaku sect, the form of Zen just recently introduced from China. It will be built at the foot of a hill in Nagasaki's Teramachi (or "temple town").

1620

Europe: Bohemia
Christianity

The Battle of White Mountain. Catholic forces led by Ferdinand II, the Holy Roman emperor, defeat the largely Protestant forces under Christian of Anhalt. The battle marks both the end of the Thirty Years' War in Bohemia and Moravia, and the beginning of the Counter-Reformation in the region.

Ferdinand gives Charles College to the Jesuits, who already manage the Collegium Clementinum in Prague.

1620

Europe: Italy
Islam

Turkish (Muslim) forces) attack the coastal city of Manfredonia in southeastern Italy and largely destroy it, including its cathedral.

1620

Europe: Spain
Christianity

Pope Paul V creates the title of titular bishop of Merida (Spain). The main church at Merida has been in the hands of the Order of Santiago, a religious military order. The new bishop of Merida was chosen from the order's members and he subsequently named the Church of Santa María in Merida as the new cathedral church of the diocese.

1620

Europe: Wales
Christianity

While several translations of the Bible in the Welsh language had been in existence, a new edition from the Greek, following the translation of William Morgan, is published. It will become the standard Welsh Bible for the next four centuries. The first printing, a large volume intended for use in church liturgies, will be followed (1630) by smaller-size editions, which allow it to be circulated for personal use by the laity.

1620

Russia, Central Asia, and the Caucasus: Russia
Christianity

The Diocese of Tobolsk, Siberia, is elevated to an archdiocese and becomes the center for the spread of the Russian Orthodox Church in the region.

1620

Southwest Asia and North Africa: Asia Minor
Christianity

Ecumenical Patriarch Timothy II dies, possibly as a result of poison. Cyril I Lucaris, the Greek patriarch of Alexandria, who had been a candidate for the patriarchy in 1612, is appointed to succeed him.

1621

East and Southeast Asia: China
Buddhism

A bronze Buddhist pagoda is cast for placement in the Amitayus Hall at the Wanshou temple, which is located along the Changhe River outside Beijing. The temple is a favorite place to stop on the long boat trip between the Forbidden City and the summer palace of the Chinese emperors. The pagoda is decorated with over 400 small sculptures of Buddhist holy figures.

1621

East and Southeast Asia: Japan
Buddhism

Yoshiminedera, Tentai Buddhist temple of the Tendai sect located in the mountains west of Kyoto, is rebuilt. It had been destroyed over a century earlier during the Onin War (1767). Surviving the earlier destruction are two statues of Kannon (Guan Yin), the goddess of mercy, one carved by the temple's 11th-century founder Gesan and the second a gift to the temple by Emperor Gosuzaku (1042), which remain the main objects of worship.

1621

Europe: England
Christianity

Poet John Donne, who had reluctantly been ordained as a Church of England priest, is appointed the dean of St. Paul's Cathedral in London.

1621

Europe: France
Christianity

Benedictine monks establish the Congregation of St. Maur (aka the Maurists), which will become renowned for scholarship and intellectual endeavors. The congregation is named for Saint Maurus (d. 565), a disciple of Saint Benedict who introduced Benedictine life into Gaul.

1621

Europe: Italy
Christianity

Pope Paul V dies in Rome and is succeeded by Gregory XV (r. 1621–1623).

Early in his pontificate, Gregory knights the 23-year-old Gian Lorenzo Bernini, soon to become the leading Roman artist of the next generation. Bernini will go on to work on a variety of projects for a succession of popes—most notably Urban VIII, Alexander VII, and Clement IX.

1621–1622

Sub-Saharan Africa: Ethiopia
Christianity

Ethiopian emperor Susenyos, who has listened to the advocacy of Jesuit missionary Pedro Paez, grants land on Gorgora Peninsula north of Lake Tana for the construction of a Roman Catholic church. The following year, Emperor Susenyos makes a public confession of faith in the teachings of Roman Catholicism, though most of his subjects remain members of the Ethiopian Orthodox Tewahedo Church.

1622

South America: Peru
Christianity

Work on the new cathedral in Lima, Peru, is finally completed after a half century of intermittent work and the first mass is said in what is the third cathedral to grace the site.

1622

Europe: France
Christianity

The Diocese of Paris (France), already a focus of much informal power within the church, is elevated to an archdiocese, representative of its further ascension in the Roman Catholic hierarchy. It is also by this act removed from its traditional subordination to the Archdiocese of Sens.

Bishop Armand Jean du Plessis (later the duc de Richelieu), already a power at the court, begins a swift rise in the esteem of King Louis XIII, beginning with Pope Gregory XV naming him a Roman Catholic cardinal, which will be followed by his being appointed to the French royal council of ministers (1624), and then named president of the council (1629). He made the centralization of power within France and the assertion of French power internationally over against Habsburg rule in Spain and Germany the main goals of his lengthy time in office.

1622

Europe: France
Christianity

Francis de Sales, founder of the Visitation Order, dies. His heart is removed from his body and placed in a silver container, which will be kept in the Church of the Visitation in Lyon, where he passed away. His body is returned to Annecy, where he is interred in the first monastery of the order he had founded. Francis will later be canonized and in 1877 named a doctor of the church.

1622

Europe: Italy
Christianity

Pope Gregory XV founds the Congregation for the Propagation of the Faith, the missionary arm of the Roman Catholic Church.

1622

Southwest Asia and North Africa: Persia
Islam, Christianity

Aligning with the British, the Safavid Persian shah Abbas I takes control of the island of Hormuz off the coast of Persia, which holds a commanding position at the entrance of the Persian Gulf from the Indian Ocean. His expelling the Portuguese culminates two decades of effort to open the Persian Gulf to a broad spectrum of trade with European nations now operating in the area.

1622

Southwest Asia and North Africa: Persia
Judaism, Islam

Persian shah Abbas I initiates a program of forced conversion of Jews to Islam that will remain in place through the decade. The new Muslim converts practice Islam outwardly, but similar to Jews living in Christian lands, continue to practice Judaism in the privacy of their homes.

1622–1623

Southwest Asia and North Africa: Asia Minor
Islam

Ottoman emperor Osman II attempts to curb the power of the Janissary soldiers (units made up of individuals selected from the non-Turkish nations of the Turkish-led empire), who had emerged as a power unto themselves within the Ottoman Empire. His actions provoke an uprising and lead to his assassination and the return of his mentally ill uncle Mustafa I (r. 1622–1623) to the throne. Mustafa's utter inability to rule led the royal family to turn to Osman II's 11-year-old half-brother Murad IV (1623–1640) to depose Mustafa and seize the throne.

March 12, 1622

Europe: Italy
Christianity

Pope Gregory XV canonizes a set of the more renowned of Catholic saints—Teresa of Avila, Francis Xavier, Ignatius Loyola, Philip Neri, and Isidore the Farmer. The acknowledgement of Teresa of Avila culminates a series of honors bestowed on her in Spain in the years since her death, including the Spanish legislature naming her patroness of Spain (1617) and the University of Salamanca granting her a posthumous diploma as a "doctor ecclesiae."

1623

Central America and the Caribbean: St. Kitts and
Nevis
Christianity

The British settlement of the island of St. Kitts and Nevis coincides with the arrival of members of the Church of England who establish the church that is now an integral part of the province of the West Indies.

1623

East and Southeast Asia: China
Buddhism

A court eunuch named Wei Zhongxian leads the effort to restore and renovate what was then known as the Yugong Temple, located near the recumbent Buddha Temple in Beijing. Originally built as a mansion for a Yuan Dynasty official, the impressive temple complex was transformed into a nunnery and is now renamed Biyun (or azure cloud) Temple. Wei Zhongzian will eventually be buried at the temple.

1623

East and Southeast Asia: Japan
Buddhism

Shogun Hidetada formally resigns as shogun in favor of his son, Tokugawa Iemitsu (r. 1623–1651). As his father had done, Hidetada becomes the Retired Shogun, and as such retains effective power until his death in 1632.

1623

East and Southeast Asia: Taiwan
Christianity

The Portuguese occupy southwest Taiwan and introduce Roman Catholicism.

1623

Europe: Italy
Christianity

Gregory XV dies and is succeeded by Pope Urban VIII (r. 1623–1644).

1623

Europe: Lithuania
Christianity

Sigismund III Vasa, who serves as both king of Poland and grand duke of Lithuania, initiates construction of the Saint Casimir chapel attached to the

Cathedral at Vilnius. The new structure of Swedish sandstone symbolizes the prosperity that the Polish-Lithuanian union brought to both countries. Saint Casimir Jagiellon, whose body rests within an ornate sarcophagus in the chapel, had been the crown prince of Poland and Lithuania. He has been canonized in 1602 by Pope Clement VIII and was named a patron saint of Lithuania and Poland.

1624

South America: Brazil
Christianity
The Dutch conquered Salvador, Brazil.

1624

East and Southeast Asia: China
Christianity
The Chinese attack the Dutch settlement on the Penghu archipelago. The Dutch abandon the archipelago, but the Chinese recognize their settlement on Taiwan and the two nations establish initial trade relations.

1624

East and Southeast Asia: Japan
Christianity
All Spaniards (including both Roman Catholic priests and laymen) are banned from Japan, and the public is prohibited from having any contact with them.

1624

Europe: Austria
Judaism
Jews in Vienna build a synagogue in the new separate district that has been set aside for them. They had previously not been allowed to have their own place of communal worship. With royal protection, the community flourishes.

1624

Europe: Belgium
Christianity
Cornelius Jansen, a theologian at the University of Leuven (Belgium), is named bishop of Ypres with the approval of the Spanish who control the country

Detail of *David* by Gian Lorenzo Bernini, completed 1624. Galleria Borghese, Rome, Italy. Bernini's baroque sculptures are famous for capturing their subjects in moments of highest drama. (Araldo de Luca/Corbis)

at the time. Jansen had opposed the Jesuits who had been attempting to evangelize the local Protestant community. He had begun work on a large book on St. Augustine of Hippo, which he hoped would be a tool in assisting the conversion process in a manner more fruitful than that pursued by the Jesuits.

1624

Europe: Italy
Christianity
Sculptor Gian Lorenzo Bernini completes his statues of the biblical youthful future-king *David,* showing him prior to his defeat of the giant Goliath, a masterful example of the Baroque attention to dynamic

movement and emotion, which had superseded the classical Renaissance attention to form.

1624

Europe: Moravia
Christianity

As Roman Catholics regain control in Prague, the Carmelites assume control of the large Church of Our Lady Victorious in Prague.

1624

Europe: Netherlands
Judaism

Jewish leaders in Amsterdam turn on Uriel de Costa and burn his book examining the Jewish intellectual traditions. He denies rabbinic authority and the biblical basis for the belief in the immortality of the soul. Though in continual conflict with the rabbis, the now disfellowshipped de Costa is allowed to remain in Amsterdam within the Jewish community but is excommunicated from religious participation.

1624

Europe: Norway
Christianity

A great fire sweeps through Oslo and destroys much of the city, including the city's 400-year-old cathedral. King Christian IV decided to rebuild several miles west of the old city. Construction of the new cathedral was begun in 1632 and completed seven years later.

1624

Europe: Poland
Western Esotericism

Jacob Böhme, who has been writing and privately circulating his Esoteric texts among friends, sees the first publication of a selection of his writing under the title *Weg zu Christo* (*The Way to Christ*). In reaction, some Lutherans complain and he is forced to appear before the Town Council of Görlitz, which forces him to leave town. He settles in Dresden, where he finds some support among the faculty at the university. He begins work on his last book, *177 Theosophic Questions,* but falls ill and dies. He leaves behind a small

but enthusiastic following among German pietists and the intelligentsia.

1624–1625

North America: United States
Christianity

An initial group of Dutch settlers arrive on Noten Eylant (now Governors Island) to take possession of the area bounding the Hudson River, which had been designated New Netherlands. They establish themselves in locations as far away as Verhulsten Island (now Burlington Island) in the South River (now the Delaware River), Kievitshoek (now Old Saybrook, Connecticut) and north up the Hudson River to what is now Albany. They build a fort at Noten Eylant, but shortly thereafter many move to Manhattan Island where a new Fort Amsterdam was being constructed to protect the mouth of the river. Many of these first settlers were members of the Dutch Reformed Church, and the American branch dates its history from their arrival.

1625

North America: Canada
Christianity

Jesuits, in the person of Jean de Brébeuf, initiate work among the Huron and Algonquin people of the St. Lawrence River valley. Brébeuf initially takes up residence among the Huron Native people near Lake Huron, studies their customs and language, and will compile the first dictionary of the Huron language.

1625

North America: United States
Christianity

The Dutch introduce slavery into New Netherlands. Some Africans later joined the Reformed Church.

1625

Central America and the Caribbean: Haiti
Christianity

French buccaneers establish a settlement on the island of Tortuga off the coast of Haiti, which becomes a fabled center for pirates of varied background who target Spanish shipping.

1625

Central America and the Caribbean: Virgin Islands
Christianity

The Dutch East India company recognizes Joost van Dyk, who organized a settlement on one of the Virgin Islands, as the patron of Tortola. The Dutch and Spanish begin a half-century of conflict over the islands.

1625

East and Southeast Asia: Japan
Shinto

In Kyoto, the Hirano Jinga, a Shinto shrine destroyed during the Onin War, is finally rebuilt. The shrine is home to four kami (gods): Imaki-no-kami (a kami of revitalization), Kudo-no-kami (the kami of the cooking pot), Furuaki-no-kami (a kami of new beginnings), and Hime-no-kami (a kami of fertility).

1625

East and Southeast Asia: Japan
Buddhism

Tenkai, a prominent Tendai Buddhist who has received a gift of land from Shogun Hidetada (1622), builds what he conceives to be a guardian temple for Edo and a large regional temple for Tendai believers that would rival the lead temple on Mount Hiei. He erects Toeizan Kanei-ji on Keno Hill on the northern edge of Edo to be the main Tendai temple in eastern Japan. It joins Zojo-ji, the Pure Land temple, one of the family temples of the Tokugawa family. Most of the Tokugawa shoguns will be enshrined either at Toeizan Kanei-ji or Zojo-ji.

1625

Europe: England
Christianity

Following George Calvert's resignation as secretary of state, King James I confirms his place on the Privy Council and appoints him Baron Baltimore in County Longford, Ireland, in recognition of his years of service. Immediately after resigning, Calvert also converts to Roman Catholicism, which leads James's successor, Charles I, to drop him from the Privy Council.

1625

Europe: England
Christianity

King James I dies and is succeeded by his son who as Charles I (r. 1625–1649) rules over the three kingdoms of England, Ireland, and Scotland. Charles was accused of attempting to move the Church of England toward Roman Catholicism, a charge initially leveled following his marriage to a Roman Catholic princess, and increased as he aligned himself with two high church clergymen—Richard Montagu, the bishop of Chichester, and William Laud, the archbishop of Canterbury.

1625

Europe: France
Christianity

The nuns of the Cistercian Abbey of Port-Royal des Champs move to a new abbey in Paris known as Port-Royal de Paris. The nuns have recently gone through a reformation of their life under the leadership of their abbess Mother Marie Angelique Arnauld (1591–1661).

Pope Urban VIII elevates the Diocese of Paris to the status of an archdiocese.

1625

Europe: Estonia
Christianity

A lightning strike ignites a fire in the spire of St. Olaf's Church in Tallinn, Estonia. The spire had made it the tallest building in the world at 521 feet. It would be replaced by St. Mary's Church, located in Stralsund, northern Germany. Its spire was 495 feet tall.

1625

Europe: Ireland
Christianity

James Ussher (r. 1625–1656) is named to succeed Christopher Hampton as the archbishop of Armagh and primate of All Ireland, the leader of the Anglican Church of Ireland.

1626

Sub-Saharan Africa: Ethiopia
Christianity

Alfonso Mendez, as head of the Roman Catholic mission in Ethiopia and with the backing of the emperor, moves to suppress the Ethiopian Orthodox Church, including its liturgical calendar, and replace its rites with Roman Catholic worship. His reordering of church life leads to the reordination of priests and the rebaptism of laypeople.

1626

Central America and the Caribbean: Barbados
Christianity
The first British settlers on Barbados were largely Anglican and included several priests among their number. During the first decade of their settlement, a half-dozen parishes are created.

1626

East and Southeast Asia: China, Tibet
Christianity
Antonio del Andrade, a Jesuit missionary in Tibet, begins construction of a Christian church, the first in the land.

1626

East and Southeast Asia: Taiwan
Christianity
Spanish forces assert a claim to Taiwan and construct Fort Santo Domingo on the northern coast of the island.

1626

Europe: England
Christianity
Nicholas Ferrar, a priest of the Church of England, retires from London with his extended family and moves to the village of Little Gidding in Huntingdonshire where the family attempts to live a Christian life following the teachings and piety of the Book of Common Prayer interpreted in a high church manner. Their experiment in communal self-sufficiency becomes well known throughout the land and many visitors arrive to observe and learn.

1626

Europe: Hungary
Christianity

György Káldi completes his translation and publishes the first complete translation of the Bible for the use of Roman Catholics in Hungary.

1626

Europe: Netherlands
Christianity
Painter Rembrandt Harmenszoon van Rijn, who will be remembered primarily for his secular subjects, completes two important works of a religious nature, *Judas Repentant,* and *Returning the Pieces of Silver.*

1626

Southwest Asia and North Africa: Lebanon
Christianity
Capuchin missionaries establish work in Lebanon. They work primarily among the Maronite Eastern rite Catholics and launch an educational effort, which is later joined by the Jesuits. Through the rest of the century a school will open next to each parish church, thus making basic education available to the Maronite minority.

1627

South Asia: India
Islam
Mughal emperor Jahangir dies and is succeeded by his son Prince Khurram, better known by his later title Shah Jahan (r. 1628–1658).

1627

East and Southeast Asia: China
Chinese Religions
The Tianqi emperor dies without an heir and is succeeded by his brother Zhu Youjian, who ruled as the Chongzhen emperor (r. 1627–1644), the last emperor of the Ming Dynasty. He inherited a government nearly bankrupt and in chaos.

1627

East and Southeast Asia: China
Buddhsim
Shabdrung Ngawang Namgyal, the primary lineage holder of the Drukpa Kagyu school of Tibetan

Buddhism, builds Simtokha Dzong, a monastery at the entrance to Thimphu Valley, which provides him with significant control of a large part of western Bhutan.

1627

East and Southeast Asia: China
Christianity
Two Portuguese Jesuits, Estevao Cacella and João Cabral, visit Bhutan on their way to Tibet. Shabdrung Ngawang Namgyal attempts to convince them to stay and agrees to provide sanction for their missionary efforts. The pair refuse the request as they have been commissioned to find a legendary lost Nestorian church, which they believe has possibly survived in Tibet.

1627

East and Southeast Asia: China, Macau
Buddhism
The 13th-century Kun Lam Tong, a Buddhist temple dedicated to Kam Lun (Guan Yin), the goddess of mercy, is rebuilt. As Macau grows into a large city, it will become one of the largest and wealthiest temples in the city.

1627

East and Southeast Asia: Japan
Shinto
Tomioka Hachimangu, the main shrine dedicated to the god Hachiman in Tokyo, is founded. Here, later in the century, the first sumo wrestling bouts following the lifting of the ban imposed on sumo wrestling in 1648 were held, from which modern sumo develops.

Todo Takatora, a prominent Japanese feudal lord (daimyo) most famous for his ability to design castles, founds Ueno Toshogu, a Shinto shrine on the northern edge of Edo (Tokyo). Here the first Tokugawa shogun Ieyasu is enshrined.

1627

Europe: Bohemia, Poland
Christianity
Pastor and educator John Amos Comenius leads the Moravian Brethren into exile when the Roman Catholic Counter-Reformation threatens to suppress Protestantism throughout Bohemia. Under Comenius, the Brethren arrive in Leszno in Poland, where he assumes leadership of the Bohemian and Moravian churches.

1627

Europe: Germany
Western Esotericism
Astronomer-astrologer Johann Kepler published the Rudolphine Tables containing a new catalogue of stars and more accurate tables of planetary positions, which greatly improve the accuracy of astrological prediction and interpretation.

1627

Europe: Sweden
Christianity
Swedish king Gustavus Adolphus decrees a tax equal to a barrel of grain, the proceeds of said tax to be used for church construction.

1627

Southwest Asia and North Africa: Persia
Islam
Shi'a reformer Muhammad Amin al-Astarabadi dies. He had emerged as an advocate of Muslim sources, especially the Hadith, out of belief that the tradition had been corrupted by the accumulation of commentaries over the years.

1627–1629

Europe: France
Christianity
Cardinal Richelieu leads a successful effort to suppress a rebellion among French Huguenots based at their stronghold of La Rochelle. He lays siege to the fortified city, which eventually falls, and then defeats their army led by Henri, duc de Rohan. The Protestants were forced to accept the Peace of Alais, which continues their right to religious toleration (that had been granted in the edict of Nantes), but abolishes their political rights and protections.

1627–1630

East and Southeast Asia: Vietnam
Christianity

French Jesuits Alexander de Rhodes and Antoine Marquez create the first successful Roman Catholic mission in what is now Vietnam. De Rhodes creates an alphabet for the Vietnamese language, still in common use. He begins with Latin script and adds diacritic marks. The new alphabet will not, however, lead to the translation of the Bible into Vietnamese until the 19th century.

1628

North America: United States
Christianity

Dutch Reformed minister Jonas Michaelius organizes the Collegiate Reformed Protestant Dutch Church of the City of New York, now known as the Marble Collegiate Church, the oldest continuously existing Christian congregation in the United States. It is affiliated with the Dutch Reformed Church, a Calvinist church based in the Netherlands.

1628

North America: United States
Christianity

The Rev. John White, a Puritan minister from Dorset, forms the New England Company (soon superseded by the Massachusetts Bay Company) to set up a colony and trading enterprise in Massachusetts. The company creates a settlement at Salem (Naumkeag). The following year a group of Puritans associated with the company sign the Cambridge Agreement to emigrate to the New World.

1628

North America: United States
Christianity

Puritan settlers establish plantations along the southern shore of what is now known as Isle of Wight in Virginia. They erect a wooden chapel that in 1632 is replaced with a stone Gothic-style church, the only original Gothic church erected in what is now the United States.

1628

South Asia: India
Sikhism

Sikh guru Har Govind is victorious in the first-ever Sikh conflict with the forces of the Mughal Empire.

1628

South Asia: India
Islam

Shah Jahan (r. 1628–1658) succeeds his father, the emperor Jahangir, as the ruler of the Mughal Empire in India.

1628

East and Southeast Asia: Japan

Shogun Hidetada has moved to complete the eradication of Christianity begun by his father. He bans all Christian books, forces Christian daimyo (nobles) to commit suicide, orders all other remaining Christians to apostatize, and executes the 55 Christians (including both Japanese citizens and foreigners) who refuse to renounce Christianity (and would not escape by going into hiding).

1628

Europe: Albania
Christianity

Roman Catholics establish a small initial community of Byzantine Catholic Albanians at a small mission along the coast of Epirus.

1628

Europe: England
Christianity

Cyril I, the patriarch of Constantinople, gives the Codex Alexandrinus, a rare fifth-century manuscript copy of the text of the Bible (both Old and New Testament) in Greek, to King Charles I of England. Considered the oldest and best text of the New Testament, it will become the first manuscript used by textual critics in any extensive reconsideration of the text produced by Erasmus in the 16th century.

1628

Europe: Italy
Christianity

Antonio Barberini, a cardinal, a member of the Capuchin order, and the brother of Pope Urban VIII, initiates a new practice within the order when he begins to have the remains of the deceased members placed on display in the crypt of the Church of Santa Maria della Concezione della Cappucini in Rome. Over the centuries, the decoratively arranged bones of some 4,000 monks decorate the crypt. Other Capuchin churches and monasteries will follow the example set in Rome.

1629

North America: United States
Christianity
Samuel Skelton is selected as the pastor of the first Congregational church in America, located at Salem (Naumkeag), Massachusetts.

1629

North America: United States
Christianity
Roman Catholic missionary priests Francisco de Porras, Andrés Gutierrez, Cristobal de la Concepcion, and Francisco de San Buenaventura settle at Awatobi (Arizona) among the Hopi people and establish the mission of San Bernardino.

1629

East and Southeast Asia: Japan
Buddhism
Japanese shogun Tokugawa Hidetada banishes Takuan, a prominent Rinzai Buddhist priest and abbot of the Daitoku-ji Temple in Kyoto, due to his protesting government interference in the appointment of priests to Buddhist temples. Takuan had opposed his fellow Rinzai priest Suden, who had been placed in charge of Buddhist affairs and had drafted legislation that allowed the imperial court to make appointment of the purple robe, the symbol of the priestly office, to Buddhist priests only with the shogun's approval.

1629

East and Southeast Asia: Japan
Buddhism
Chinese immigrants residing in Nagasaki construct Sofuku-ji, an Obaku Zen temple, unique for its Chinese architecture. The Obaku sect had only recently been introduced into Japan.

1629

Europe: France
Christianity
Pierre de Bérulle, founder of the Congregation of the French Oratory, dies. He is succeeded as the general of the Oratory by Charles de Condren, who had been active in spreading the work of the Oratory throughout France. Under his leadership, the French school of spirituality advocated by the Oratory would spread through the Roman Catholic Church internationally, calling laypeople to a personal experience of the person of Jesus and setting them on a quest for personal holiness.

1629

Europe: Germany
Christianity
In the midst of the conflicts of the Thirty Years' War, Ferdinand, the Holy Roman emperor, issues the Edict of Restitution, which revoked the 1552 Peace of Passau, stripped the Lutherans of their rights, and attempted to return control of religion throughout the empire to the Roman Catholics. This action would lead directly to the intervention of the Protestant king of Sweden, Gustavus II Adolphus, in the conflict.

1629

Europe: Germany, Denmark
Christianity
The Peace of Lubeck. King Christian IV's unsuccessful intervention in the Thirty Years' War leads to his defeat and the end of Denmark's role as a major power in Europe. In the wake of the Danish defeat and other Catholic successes in the Thirty Years' War, Holy Roman emperor Ferdinand II issues the Edict of Restitution, which orders German Protestants to return all the property seized from Roman Catholics over the last 70 years. The Protestants do not accept the edict, which also becomes the excuse for the French to enter the war.

1629

Europe: Italy
Christianity

TOKUGAWA IEMITSU (1604–1651)

Tokugawa Iemitsu was the third shogun from the Tokugawa family. He outlawed Christianity in Japan and closed the country to foreigners, a policy that stood for 200 years.

Iemitsu was born on August 12, 1604. He was the eldest legitimate son of Tokugawa Hidetada. His mother was a younger sister of the concubine of Toyotomi Hideyoshi, and his wet nurse was Kasuga No Tsubone, a noblewoman of considerable influence. Iemitsu journeyed with his father to Kyoto to the court of the emperor and was officially confirmed as shogun on August 23, 1623.

After his father's death, Iemitsu used his brother's mistreatment of his vassals as an excuse to strip him of his large fief. Applying further pressure, he drove Tadanga to suicide, probably not only to rid himself of a rival but also to demonstrate the power of the shogunate. Iemitsu quickly issued additional decrees to weaken the power of the daimyos who controlled most of Japan. In 1633, Iemitsu ordered that the *hatamoto* (lesser vassals) under the shogun were to continue their military practice. They were to have no other profession like merchant or farmer. The military contribution each daimyo was to make to the shogun's army was planned. Such matters as the number of men with firearms, horsemen, and normal foot soldiers were all specified. For each fief, the amount of stipend that would be paid to the vassal by the shogun was also determined.

Iemitsu sought to keep Japanese society as stable as possible. Iemitsu recognized that Japanese religions like Shinto and Buddhism could instill a sense of duty and responsibility in the people. Distrusting Christianity, he stepped up the persecution of Christians and forbade missionaries from entering the country. Such measures resulted in the Shimabara Revolt in southern Kyushu, which was seen by Iemitsu as a direct challenge to his power. He ordered the local daimyos to raise a large army and destroy the rebels. After a lengthy siege, the daimyos were successful.

Believing Portuguese missionaries played a role in the revolt, Iemitsu ordered the Portuguese deported and ceased trade with them. A ship that arrived after he made that decree was taken into custody. Most of the Portuguese crew were beheaded and the rest sent home with a warning. New decrees were also issued that forbade Japanese ships from trading with other countries. By 1641, Iemitsu was largely successful in shutting out the world, and for more than 200 years, Japan remained isolated. Iemitsu died in Edo on June 8, 1651. He was succeeded by Tokugawa Ietsuna.

TIM WATTS

Pope Urban VIII prohibits further reproductions of Veronica's Veil, a piece of cloth believed by many to picture the face of Jesus of Nazareth, and orders all existing copies to be destroyed. He also demands that anyone who has a copy must bring it to the Vatican or face excommunication.

1629

Southwest Asia and North Africa: Arabia
Islam
In 1621 and again in 1629, the Grand Mosque in Mecca suffered severe weather-related damage.

Ottoman sultan Murad IV initiates a massive renovation project that includes rebuilding the Kaaba and adding three minarets. The new minarets bring the total to seven, one more than the Blue Mosque in Istanbul, and stops the criticism directed at the Ottoman sultans for having a mosque with six minarets.

1629

Southwest Asia and North Africa: Asia Minor
Christianity

Patriarch Cyril I publishes his *Confessio,* a volume declaring his incorporation of the Reformed theology into his Eastern Orthodox faith. Long a devotee of Protestant thinking, he had attempted to bring reform to the Orthodox Church and had been responsible for sending a number of priests to Western Europe for training. Cyril finds strong support in Europe, but creates a controversy throughout the Eastern Orthodox world. He would be briefly deposed and replaced as patriarch due to the opposition to him among the Orthodox, but would in each case be reinstated.

1629

Southwest Asia and North Africa: Persia
Islam

Persian shah Abbas I, fearful that his sons were plotting against him, had each in succession killed or blinded. Thus, as his end approached, he chose Sam Mirza, the son of Mohammed Baqir Mirza, as his heir. When Abbas dies, Sam Mirza comes to the throne as Shah Safi (r. 1629–1642).

1629–1630

Europe: France, Italy
Christianity

Mary Ward, who had founded the Institute of the Blessed Virgin Mary (aka the Loreto Sisters), a new Catholic order for women modeled on the Jesuits, is allowed to plead her case for the church's approval of the order before a group of cardinals appointed by Pope Urban to examine the situation. The controversial noncloistered order is not approved, and in 1630 it is suppressed, but not destroyed. It will slowly recover from the cardinals' action, but eventually revives and finds approval.

ca. 1630

East and Southeast Asia: Japan

Shogun Iemitsu issues the first of what will be a series of edicts that will largely end Japan's interactions with foreign countries. He forbids Japanese citizens from leaving the country, or if they leave, from returning, which now becomes a capital offense. He expels all Europeans from the country, with the exception of a few associated with the Dutch East India Company, whom he restricts to Dejima, a manmade island in Nagasaki harbor.

1630

North America: United States
Christianity

Eleven ships associated with the Massachusetts Bay Company sail for America. Those aboard settle along the coast of Massachusetts north of Plymouth. Here they set up a colony with a Congregational church establishment. Puritan leader John Winthrop settles at Shawmut, Massachusetts, and renames it after his hometown in England, Boston.

1630

East and Southeast Asia: China
Christianity

Jesuit priest Johann Adam Schall von Bell, accompanied by Giacomo Rho, travels to Beijing as successor of the late Johann Schreck. Schall von Bell begins work on a new reformed Chinese calendar, which among other improvements is designed to provide greater accuracy in predicting the eclipses of the sun and moon. When completed it is named for the Chongzhen emperor.

1630

East and Southeast Asia: Japan

The Japanese government issues a prohibition against books propagating Christianity, especially those translated by Jesuit missionaries into Chinese and hence more accessible to the Japanese public.

1630

East and Southeast Asia: Laos
Christianity

Catholics from Thailand initiate missionary efforts in Laos in areas close to the border.

1630

Europe: France
Christianity

King Louis XIII names Cardinal Armand Jean du Plessis to be the new duc de Richelieu and welcomes him as a new peer of France. He will henceforth be known simply as Cardinal Richelieu.

1630

Europe: Italy
Judaism

When forces of the Holy Roman Empire overrun Mantua in northern Italy and sack the Jewish community, the Jews of Vienna intervene and the emperor Ferdinand orders the reestablishment of the Mantua community.

1630

Europe: Scotland
Christianity

In Scotland, King Charles I "touches" around 100 people to demonstrate his power to cure the "King's Evil" (i.e., scrofula, a usually not-fatal form of tuberculosis of the bones and lymph nodes). The power to cure had been associated since medieval times with the divine right of monarchs to rule, especially in France and England. Though the practice had fallen from favor somewhat in England following the Reformation, the original Book of Common Prayer used by the Church of England contained a liturgy for carrying out the ceremony.

1631

South America: Brazil
Christianity, Judaism

The Dutch capture Recife, Brazil. Their policy of religious toleration attracts many Jews from other parts of Brazil and they begin to live openly, observe the Sabbath, and open synagogues. They prosper financially.

1631

East and Southeast Asia: Japan
Buddhism

Tenkai, a prominent Tendai Buddhist priest and favorite of the Tokugawa shoguns, builds Kiyonizu Kannon-do, a temple dedicated to Kannon (Guan Yin), the goddess of mercy, and meant to rival the famous Kyoto temple, Kiyomizu-dera. It is erected in northern Edo (Tokyo) near the Kaneiji Temple that Tankai had also been responsible for building.

1631

Europe: Germany
Christianity

As the Swedish Protestant army under Gustavus II Adolphus, who has entered the war following the defeat of the Danes, marches through Germany toward Austria, the Roman Catholic forces of the Holy Roman Empire suffer two of their most important defeats of the Thirty Years' War in the Sack of Magdeburg and the First Battle of Breitenfeld (near Leipzig). The Swedish army had been supported by finances supplied by French Roman Catholic cardinal Richelieu, whose enemies denounce him as a traitor to the Catholic Church. He is able, however, to reorient the Thirty Years' War from a battle between Protestants and Catholics to one between emerging national states and the dominant influence and rule of the Holy Roman Empire. He also saps much of the strength of the Habsburg rule and severely limits their hegemony over much of Europe.

1631

Southwest Asia and North Africa: Morocco
Christianity

In 1631, Pope Urban VIII erects the Prefecture Apostolic of Morocco and names its first incumbent, Giovanni da Prado, a Franciscan priest. Before the end of the year he is killed at Marrakesh and the prefecture is suppressed. Roman Catholic missionaries remain active in the country. They operate out of Spanish-controlled bases along the coast.

June 17, 1631

South Asia: India
Islam

The wife of Shah Jahan, ruler of the Mughal Empire, Mumtaz Mahal (1593–1631), a Shi'a Muslim, dies. Out of his love for her, Shah Jahan has the Taj

March of the Swedish Army in 1631 through Frankfurt, Germany, during the series of devastating political and religious conflicts in central Europe known as the Thirty Years' War. (Anton Gindley, *History of the Thirty Years' War,* 1884)

Mahal constructed as her mausoleum. He would later also be laid to rest within it. The whole complex of the monument would take some 20 years to complete (ca. 1632–ca. 1653). At the western part of the complex is a mosque whose floor is notable for outlines for the placement of 569 prayer rugs in black marble.

1632

Sub-Saharan Africa: Ethiopia
Christianity

Fasilides (r. 1632–1657) begins his lengthy rule of Ethiopia. He immediately launches a revival of the Ethiopian Orthodox Church, which he restores to its official status and sends a request to the patriarch of Alexandria of the Coptic Orthodox church for a new abuna (archbishop). He also initiates the construction of a new monastery of Debre Berhan Selassie (Holy Trinity of the Mountain of Light). He also moves against the growing power of Roman Catholicism, initially by confiscating the lands that had been granted to the Jesuits and then banishing them entirely from the country.

1632

North America: United States
Christianity

George Calvert, the first Lord Baltimore, a Roman Catholic, having given up in his attempt to found a colony in Newfoundland, receives a land grant from British king Charles I for land north of the Potomac River upon which he founds the colony of Maryland. He dies just as the charter is issued, and his son Cecilius Calvert, second Baron Baltimore, takes control of the family's possessions and actually founds the new colony north of Virginia. As the charter did not limit settlers to Protestant Christians, he was able to invite fellow Catholics to his colony and offered religious toleration to all.

1632

North America: United States
Christianity

Roger Williams, a Separatist minister in Massachusetts, authors a tract that questions the right of the Puritans to Massachusetts as they did not buy it from the Native residents. In the tract he also charges King

James with lying in his assertion that he was the first Christian monarch to have discovered the land. Summoned by the authorities, he agrees to let the matter drop.

1632

North America: United States
Christianity

John Eliot inaugurates his ministry as the pastor of the Congregational church in Roxbury, Massachusetts. While there he will develop a mission toward the Pequot tribe of the Iroquois people and learn to speak their language.

1632

North America: United States
Christianity

Anglicans in Virginia construct St. Luke's Church, aka the Old Brick Church, a Gothic-style church that survives as the oldest still-existing church in North America.

1632

North America: United States
Christianity

The first Roman Catholic mission in Texas is established near present-day San Angelo. It was a follow-up effort to an initial 1629 missionary trip to the area at the request of the Jumano People, which was the first journey into Texas specifically for Christian evangelization. The Spanish Franciscans spent only a short time there in 1629 but promised to return. The 1632 mission existed for only six months before it was abandoned because of its remoteness from the Franciscan home base in New Mexico.

1632

East and Southeast Asia: Japan
Buddhism

Retired shogun Hidetada dies and his son, Shogun Tokugawa Iemitsu, comes into his own power.

1632

Europe: Netherlands
Christianity

Mennonites issue their basic statement of faith, the Dordrecht Confession.

1632

Europe: Poland
Christianity

The original Polish publication of the Bible, the Brest Bible of 1563, was called into question by the intense polemic between the Protestant Christians and the non-Trinitarian Socinian Christians (the Polish Brethren), and both groups produced new translations favoring their particular theological perspectives. Thus in 1600, a proposal for a new Bible translation into Polish was well received and the work turned over to a Reformed minister, Martin Janicki. After editing and revision by a committee representing the Reformed, Lutheran, and Moravian Protestant communities, the New Testament would be published in 1606. The complete Bible finally appears in 1632. Termed the Danzig Bible, it will become the Bible common to non-Catholic groups in Poland for the next centuries.

1632

Russia, Central Asia, and the Caucasus: Russia
Christianity

The Kazan Cathedral of Moscow, located on Red Square, is completed. It honors the icon of Our Lady of Kazan and commemorates the 1612 victory of Czar Michael (r. 1613–1645) over the Poles at the end of the Time of Troubles.

1632

Russia, Central Asia, and the Caucasus: Russia
Christianity

Czar Michael I orders the rebuilding of the church dedicated to Our Lady of Kazan on Red Square in Moscow. It had been destroyed by a fire. The new brick church is dedicated in 1636.

1632

Southwest Asia and North Africa: Asia Minor
Islam

The Ottoman sultan Murad IV comes of age and takes control of an empire in chaos. Through the remainder of the decade, he will deal with foreign entities who had tried to take advantage of the perceived weakness of the imperial rule, suppress challenges to the central authority of the sultan within the empire, and instill discipline in the city of Istanbul proper.

1632–1633

Europe: Italy
Christianity

After staying away from his ideas on heliocentrism, the idea that the earth moves around the sun, Galileo publishes *Dialogue Concerning the Two Chief World Systems*. He had the authorization from the Inquisition, and Pope Urban VIII had requested that Galileo present the arguments for and against heliocentrism, but so as not to appear to advocate any condemned opinion. The way the book was finally edited, however, made it appear to many that Galileo was advocating for the heliocentric idea. He was ordered to Rome to stand trial. In his hearing, he defended himself by claiming that since 1616 he had faithfully adhered to his promise not to hold any of the condemned opinions, but finally admitted that a reader of his book could easily come to the conclusion that he favored heliocentrism.

In the end, the Inquisition pronounces its sentence. It finds Galileo suspected of heresy and calls for him to make a new complete statement abjuring the idea that the earth travels around the sun. He is then ordered confined to house arrest for the rest of his life and his book is banned. After the trial, the Inquisition also quietly orders that none of his books were ever to be published again, including any new ones he might write.

1633

Sub-Saharan Africa: Ethiopia
Christianity

The German Lutheran Church sends Peter Heyling as first Protestant missionary to Ethiopia.

1633

East and Southeast Asia: Japan
Buddhism

Tenkai, a Tendai Buddhist priest who has served as an advisor to the various shoguns over the last 30 years, completes work on a new edition of the Buddhist canon, which appears as the Tenkai edition.

Shogun Tokugawa Iemitsu orders the complete reconstruction of Kiyomizu-dera, a prominent and influential eighth-century temple of Hossō Buddhism in Kyoto. The temple is noted for its construction without the use of any nails, and for the waterfall that flows beneath the main hall, the water of which is believed to have wish-granting powers.

1633

Europe: England
Christianity

George Abbott, the archbishop of Canterbury, dies and is succeeded by William Laud, the former bishop of London. His election motivates the migration of many Puritans to New England.

King Charles I issues a slightly modified version of the Book of Sports (originally issued in 1618) as *The King's Majesty's declaration to his subjects concerning lawful sports to be used.* It reiterates the activities in which people can lawfully participate on the Sabbath.

1633

Europe: England
Christianity

Nicholas Ferrar edits and publishes the collected poems of his fellow Church of England priest George Herbert in *The Temple: Sacred Poems and Private Ejaculations. The Temple* becomes a bestseller and goes through numerous editions, while many of the poems are set to music and become popular hymns.

1633

Europe: England
Christianity

Several members leave the Separatist congregation that Henry Jacob had founded in London in 1616 and form a new congregation that baptizes only believers. They continue a Calvinist theological perspective and baptize by immersion. This congregation is considered the first Particular Baptist church, the term "particular" referring to a belief that Jesus Christ died only for those "particular" persons, the elect, whom God predestined to be redeemed. General Baptists asserted that Christ died for all.

1633

Europe: Sweden
Christianity

Construction begins on a new church for the recently founded city of Gothenburg, Sweden. It will eventually (1665) be designated as the cathedral for the bishop of the (Lutheran) Church of Sweden's Gothenburg diocese.

1633

Europe: Switzerland
Christianity

Cyril Lucaris, the patriarch of Constantinople, publishes a Confession of Faith drawing heavily on Calvinist Protestant themes, most notably justification by faith alone. The confession will split Orthodox believers in Constantinople and throughout the eastern Mediterranean and contribute directly to the several movements of Cyril in and out of office.

1633

Russia, Central Asia, and the Caucasus: Russia
Christianity

Filaret, the patriarch of Moscow and All Russia, dies. He has largely ruled the country and the church for the last 14 years. As patriarch, he is credited with raising the educational level of the clergy and founding schools for their training across Russia, He is succeeded by Joasaphus (r. 1634–1640), the archbishop of Pskov and Velikiye Luki.

1634

North America: United States
Christianity

The first group of colonists arrives in Maryland and celebrates the first mass.

Jesuit priest Andrew White, with fellow Jesuits John Altham Gravenor and Thomas Gervase, land on St. Clement's Island, Maryland, hold the first Roman Catholic mass in what became the original 13 English colonies, and launch a mission to the Native people of Maryland. Their landing day, March 25, is considered the birthdate of Maryland and is celebrated annually as Maryland Day.

1634

North America: United States
Christianity

A group of German Protestants from Salzburg Province (Austria), Lutheran Protestants who had survived for several centuries in what was otherwise a Roman Catholic environment, finds their way to Georgia and establishes a Lutheran colony near Savannah.

1634

Central America and the Caribbean:
  Netherlands Antilles
Christianity

The Dutch expel all Roman Catholic priests from the islands of the Netherlands Antilles and prohibit Catholic worship.

1634

Europe: France
Christianity

Jean du Vergier de Hauranne, Abbé de Saint-Cyran, becomes the spiritual director of the Abbey of Port Royal de Paris. He was a friend and disciple of the controversial Cornelius Jansen, the bishop of Ypres (Belgium), and brings Jansenism to France. Under his direction, the abbey becomes the main center of the pietist Jansenist movement in France.

1634

Europe: Germany
Christianity

Believing that God has spared them from the bubonic plague then at epidemic proportions through the area, the citizens of Oberammergau hold the first performance of the Passion Play that will become famous throughout Europe. In keeping with the vow they made, the play will in the future be performed every 10 years.

1634–1636

East and Southeast Asia: Japan
Shinto

Shogun Tokugawa Iemitsu and Tenkai, a Tendai Buddhist priest who had emerged as possibly the most powerful Buddhist priest in Japan, combine to expand in a significant manner the Nikko Toshogu Shinto Shrine, where the first Tokugawa shogun had been enshrined. The work is completed in time for the 20th anniversary of Shogun Ieyasu's death.

1635

North America: United States
Christianity

Roger Williams, who arrived in Massachusetts in 1631 and eventually became the pastor of the church at Salem, is banished after his criticism of the structure of the government and his suggesting that the Salem congregation separate from the other congregations.

Puritan minister Richard Mather arrives in Boston in the midst of a catastrophic hurricane that had struck New England. He survives and becomes the pastor of the church at Dorchester, which he leads until his death in 1669.

1635

Central America and the Caribbean: Martinique, Guadeloupe
Christianity

Cardinal Richelieu creates the Compagnie des Îles de l'Amérique (Company of the Isles of America) to direct French interests in the Caribbean. Before the year was out, settlement and the initiation of work by Roman Catholic priests had begun on several islands over which the French claimed hegemony, most notably Martinique and Guadeloupe. Missionary work was largely placed in the hands of several religious orders, most notably the Dominicans, Jesuits, and Capuchins.

1635

South Asia: India
Hinduism, Islam

To suppress a rebellion by Jhujhar Singh, the ruler of Bundela, a small independent Hindu state, Ashah Jahan launched an attack against Orchha, the capital city (located in what is now Madhya Pradesh). Notable actions included demolishing the large Bir Singh Dev Temple and replacing it with a new mosque.

1635

East and Southeast Asia: China
Buddhism

The Battle of Five Lamas. Shabdrung Ngawang Namgyal, the primary lineage holder of the Drukpa Kagyu school of Tibetan Buddhism, who had settled in Bhutan some two decades earlier, wins over forces opposed to his leadership and unites Bhutan into a single country. He establishes a distinctive dual system of government in which control is shared by a spiritual leader (called the Je Khempo) and a temporal leader (the Druk Desi, or regent).

1635

East and Southeast Asia: China
Buddhism

As the Chinese Ming Dynasty continues to decline, the Manchurian people, now united under Hong Taiji and allied with the Mongols, drive the Ming forces from southern Manchuria. Hong Taiji's reign adopts the name "Manchu" for the united Jurchen people.

1635

East and Southeast Asia: Japan
Buddhism

Shogun Iemitsu places all religious structures under the authority of the Jisha Bugyō (aka the commissioner of temples and shrines).

1635

Europe: Spain
Christianity

Construction begins on the Santiago Church, dedicated to the biblical apostle James, located on the Plaza de la Catedral in Cadiz, Spain. It faces the same square as the former cathedral, which had been destroyed by a fire in 1596.

1636

North America: United States
Christianity

After spending the winter with the Native people, Roger Williams negotiated the sale of land upon which he founded the town of Providence.

The Massachusetts legislature establishes Harvard University in Cambridge, Massachusetts, primarily for the training of Puritan ministers. It is the first college chartered in what is now the United States, second in North America only to the university in Mexico City.

1636

East and Southeast Asia: China
Buddhism
Hong Taiji, the leader of the united Manchu people, is presented with the imperial seal of the former Yuan Dynasty, the Mongol-led dynasty that had formerly ruled China. Hong Taiji changed the name of his regime from "Great Jin" to "Great Qing" and elevated his own status from khan to emperor.

1636

East and Southeast Asia: Japan
Christianity
Portuguese traders with Japan are confined to Deshima Island off Nagasaki.

1636

Europe: Italy
Christianity
The image of Mary at the Basilica of Santa Maria in Aracoeli (Rome) is crowned.

1636

Europe: Netherlands
Judaism
Manasseh ben Israel, a Jewish scholar in Amsterdam, releases his book, *The Creation Problem,* a volume in Latin aimed at a non-Jewish audience. His Christian colleague Caspar Barleus contributes a preface in which he argues that Jews are a pious people and proposes that Jews and Christians can live together as mutual friends before God. The book is not well received, but there is no negative reaction toward the Jewish community.

1637

North America: United States
Christianity

Congregationalist minister John Davenport and merchant Theophilus Eaton found the Colony of New Haven (Connecticut). He would be the pastor of First Church in New Haven for the next 30 years. During that time he emerges as an opponent of the Half Way Covenant that would open the Congregational churches to the children of members who had no profession of faith.

1637

North America: United States
Christianity
Rev. John Davenport, a Congregational minister, established the town of New Haven. Other towns were established nearby, which in 1841 united in the colony of New Haven and adopted the Mosaic law as the basis of its legal system.

Roger Williams facilitates the purchase of a place called Pocasset (now the site of the town of Portsmouth, Rhode Island) by a group of followers of Anne Hutchinson who had been forced into exile by the General Court of Massachusetts. They began settling the area in the following spring.

1637

South America: Venezuela
Christianity
Roman Catholics erect the Diocese of Caracas, Santiago de Venezuela.

1637

Europe: England
Christianity
Presbyterian lawyer William Prynne, an outspoken critic of Archbishop of Canterbury Laud and generally of policies of the Church of England, and having already lost his ears in a previous conviction, is sentenced to be branded on his cheeks with the letters SL (for seditious libeler).

1637

Europe: England
Christianity
Eccentric Anglican cleric William Chillingworth publishes *The Religion of Protestants a Safe Way*

Anne Hutchinson (1591–1643) led the first organized attack on the male-dominated Puritan religious establishment. Banished from the Massachusetts Bay Colony for her independent views, she has been hailed as one of America's earliest feminists. Illustration from *Harper's Monthly,* v. 102, 1901. (Library of Congress)

to Salvation in which he attempts to vindicate the sole authority of the Bible in spiritual matters and the exclusive right of the individual conscience to interpret it.

1637

Europe: Germany
Christianity

Holy Roman Emperor Ferdinand II dies. He is succeeded by his son Ferdinand III (r. 1637–1657). He moved immediately to end the Thirty Years' War, but it would drag on through the first half of his reign.

1637

Europe: Netherlands
Christianity

The first official Bible translation into the Dutch language from the original Greek and Hebrew, the *Statenvertaling,* is published. A few decades in the making, it had been originally ordered by the Dutch parliament meeting at the time of the Synod of Dort (1618/1619).

1637–1638

East and Southeast Asia: Japan
Christianity

Christians assume a leading role in the Shimabara Uprising on the Shimabara Peninsula, Kyūshū, Japan. It is brutally suppressed with only 100 people surviving of the estimated 37,000 participants.

1637–1638

Europe: Scotland
Christianity

King Charles I, as part of a long-term effort to transform the Church of Scotland (a Presbyterian church) into an Anglican body, commissions the bishops of the Scottish Episcopal Church and William Laud, the archbishop of Canterbury, to produce an edition of the Book of Common Prayer, the Anglican book of worship, for Scotland. Published in 1637, the book is rejected by Scottish church authorities and never authorized for use in the churches. The conflict over the book will lead to what are known as the Bishops' Wars that saw Charles challenging the Scottish Parliament.

Reacting to the prayer book controversy, Archibald Johnston (aka Lord Warriston) initiates a move to reaffirm the National Covenant, a statement of loyalty to Presbyterian belief and practice along with a staunch denunciation of Catholicism, originally signed into law in 1581 and reaffirmed in 1590 and 1596. Johnston and his supporters signed a slightly revised National Covenant and circulated it for signatures. The document would become the rallying point for those opposed to the reforms in the Church of Scotland introduced by King Charles in his attempt to move the church toward Anglicanism.

ANNE HUTCHINSON (1591–1643)

Anne Hutchinson led the first organized attack on the male-dominated Puritan religious establishment. Banished from the Massachusetts Bay Colony for her independent views, she has been hailed as one of America's earliest feminists.

She was born Anne Marbury in Alford, Lincolnshire, England in July 1591, the daughter of a dissenting Anglican clergyman, Francis Marbury, who a year before her birth lost his ministry because of his liberal views. The oldest daughter and the second of 13 children, Hutchinson received her religious instruction from her father and absorbed his penchant for conscientious dissent. In 1605, the family moved to London, where Hutchinson remained until her marriage in 1612 to William Hutchinson, an Alford businessman of means.

Over the next 20 years, Hutchinson was drawn to the preaching of John Cotton, vicar of St. Botolph's Church in Boston, Lincolnshire. Cotton was a former Anglican minister with nonconformist Puritan leanings, holding that redemption could only come through the gift of God's grace; Cotton did not, however, accept elements of Puritan Covenant theology, especially what was known as the Covenant of Works, which holds that an individual's redemption is best manifested through a person's behavior or works.

When Hutchinson discovered that most Boston women believed in the Covenant of Works, she began holding weekly meetings in her home to exchange views. At first the meetings were limited to restatements of Cotton's sermons, but gradually Hutchinson began to add her own interpretations. Although in interpreting sermons Hutchinson was assuming the role of a minister—unheard of for a woman—her meetings did not generate open controversy until the Rev. John Wilson joined Cotton in the pulpit. Dismayed by Wilson's views, she began criticizing his sermons at her meetings. Wilson then denounced her teachings in his sermons, accusing her of trying to upset the dominant role of men in the family.

Then in August 1637, a synod of the churches was organized to deal with heresies in the colony. It condemned Hutchinson and declared her meetings disorderly. Hutchinson was brought to trial for "traducing the ministers and their ministry." Brilliantly holding her own against her accusers, claiming her right to discuss sermons in her home, she made the mistake of announcing that God had revealed to her that he would destroy her persecutors. The horrified court promptly banished her. In the custody of Cotton, and under stress, she was partially convinced of her theological error; when placed on trial again in March 1638, she publicly recanted. Her inquisitors were unconvinced of her sincerity and so formally excommunicated her.

WILLIAM MCGUIRE AND LESLIE WHEELER

1638

Sub-Saharan Africa: Ghana
Christianity

As part of the African phase of the Dutch-Portuguese War, the Dutch successfully capture the king of Elmina on the west coast of Africa.

1638

North America: United States
Christianity

Rev. Thomas Hooker, who has led a group of Congregationalists from Massachusetts to Hartford, Connecticut, leads in the founding of the city's First Congregational Church.

1638

North America: United States
Christianity

Swedish Lutherans establish Fort Christiana on the Delaware River.

1638

East and Southeast Asia: Japan
Buddhism

Fire destroys Kita-in, the head temple of Tendai Buddhism in the Kanto region of central Japan, and the adjacent Toshogu Shinto Shrine. To assist in the rebuilding, Shogun Iemitsu orders several palace buildings to be moved from Edo Castle from Tokyo to Kawagoe. Kita-in is reborn (1340) and flourishes under the leadership of Tenkai, a Tendai priest who became a trusted advisor of three shoguns of the era. Because of the later destruction of Edo Castle in the 20th century, the buildings at Kawagoe are its only surviving buildings. The temple also houses the 540 Gohyaku Rakan, stone statues of the enlightened disciples of the Buddha.

Shogun Tokugawa Iemitsu invites Zen master Takuan to become the first abbot of Tokai-ji Temple, which had been constructed especially for the Tokugawa family in Edo.

1638

East and Southeast Asia: Japan
Christianity

Portuguese priests and traders are forced out of Japan, and future trade with the Portuguese prohibited. Christianity all but disappears in Japan.

1638

South Asia: Sri Lanka
Christianity, Buddhism

The Buddhist king of Sri Lanka, Rajasinghe II, who rules from Kandy, concludes a treaty with the Dutch from whom the Sri Lankans had been seeking assistance to throw off Portuguese control of their coastal area. The Dutch will drive the Portuguese off the island, return the land to Sri Lankan control, and receive exclusive international trading rights on the island.

1638

Europe: England
Christianity

John Spilsbury, who had withdrawn from a Separatist church in London in 1633, joins with William Kiffin in forming a Calvinist Baptist congregation. Spilsbury later will publish two important works on the Baptist understanding of the traditional Christian sacraments: *A Treatise Concerning the Lawfull Subject of Baptisme* (1643) and *God's Ordinance, The Saints Privilege* (1646). He discards the idea of sacraments and opts for the church maintaining what he considers two scripturally based ordinances, baptism for adults and the Lord's Supper.

1638

Europe: Italy
Christianity

Pope Urban VIII issues a papal bull relative to the Jesuits. He forbids the enslavement of natives who take up residence in one of the Jesuit mission communities functioning in various parts of South America, thus ensuring the community's integrity. Simultaneously, he removes the Jesuit monopoly on work in China and Japan, both countries now becoming the target of missionary efforts by other Catholic orders.

1638

Europe: Italy
Judaism

Rabbi Simone Luzzatto, the long-time head of the Venice Jewish community, releases his *Essay on the Jews of Venice,* in which he argues for religious toleration based on the economic service provided by the Jews to Italy.

1638

Europe: Poland
Christianity
Roman Catholics begin suppression of Socinianism in Poland and other countries under their control.

1638

Southwest Asia and North Africa: Asia Minor
Christianity
The Ottoman sultan Murad IV accuses the controversial ecumenical patriarch Cyril I of subversive activities and finally sends the Janissaries to kill him. He is succeeded by Cyril II (1638–1639), who had been among those who opposed Cyril I's rule. Cyril had briefly taken the throne on two occasions as his predecessor fought to keep his position.

France declares its intention of protecting all Roman Catholic believers residing in the bounds of the Ottoman Empire. Above and beyond the many Latin-rite Catholics throughout the empire, their declaration includes Greeks in the Greek Islands, Maronite Catholics in Lebanon, and Melkite Catholics in Syria, all of whom follow an Eastern rite.

March 1638

North America: United States
Christianity
After several years of conflict, Anne Hutchinson was tried for sedition and contempt, charges growing from her voicing ideas that challenged the standard interpretation of Calvinism that dominated the Massachusetts colony at the time. Excommunicated, she left the colony.

Roger Williams accepts the idea of believer's baptism and the small group that has been meeting in his home gives up infant baptism. Ezekiel Holliman baptizes and the group around him forms what becomes the first Baptist church in America. Interestingly, Williams's ideas on baptism continued to evolve. Within months of the formation of the church,

he concludes that the true Christian ordinances had been lost through the centuries and could be validly restored only through a special divine commission. Thus, he decided that there was no regularly constituted church of Christ on earth. He thus resigns from the church he had led in founding. Though he remains active in preaching and the attempt to live the Christian life, he never again formally affiliated with a church organization.

1639

North America: Canada
Christianity
The first Ursuline sisters arrive in Quebec. One of their number, Marie de l'Incarnation, with the assistance of a wealthy laywoman, Madame Marie-Madeline de Chauvigny de la Peltrie, founds the Ursuline Convent of Quebec City, the oldest institution of learning for women in North America.

1639

South America: Peru
Christianity
More than 80 New Christians (Jews who converted to Christianity) were burned at the stake after the Inquisition caught them holding regular Jewish services in Lima, Peru.

1639

East and Southeast Asia: Japan
Buddhism
Doi Tishikatsu, the great elder at the Kaneji Temple, a Tendai temple in Tokyo that had been designated a family temple for the ruling Tokugawa shoguns, had helped in the building of a prominent five-story pagoda adjacent to the temple. The wooden structure, unfortunately, burns to the ground a few years after its construction and Doi Tishikatsu is forced to gather the resources to have it rebuilt.

1639

Europe: Netherlands
Judaism
The Sephardic community of Jews in Amsterdam, which had previously met in three separate

synagogues, merge their religious life and construct a new large synagogue to serve the whole community.

1639

Southwest Asia and North Africa: Asia Minor
Christianity
After a third brief tenure as the ecumenical patriarch, Cyril II is succeeded by Parthenius I (r. 1639–1644).

1639–1640

Europe: Scotland
Christianity
King Charles I's attempts to force an episcopal church polity on the Church of Scotland (a Presbyterian church) leads to the Bishops' Wars, a set of conflicts that pitted Charles against the Scottish parliament. They are seen as a prelude to the soon to follow English civil wars of the 1640s.

1640

North America: United States
Christianity
Presbyterians on Long Island, New York, organize the first Presbyterian congregation in the British American colonies at South Hampton.

1640

North America: United States
Christianity
Lutheran minister Rev. Reorus Torkillus arrives at Fort Christina, the recently founded Swedish settlement on the Delaware River.

1640

East and Southeast Asia: China
Buddhism
Mongolian leader Gushi Khan invades Tibet and conquers Kham (southeastern Tibet), which has the effect of bringing the leadership of the Sakya school of Tibetan Buddhism under their hegemony.

Both the Panchen Lama and the Dalai Lama recognize Zanabazar, the son of one of the khans of the Khalkha Mongolian people, a reincarnated lama. He is designated the head of the Gelug tradition in Mongolia

and makes his headquarters at Örgöö. Termed the Jebtsundamba Khutuktu, his successors will become the head of Tibetan Buddhism for all of Mongolia.

1640

East and Southeast Asia: Japan
Buddhism, Shinto
All Japanese citizens are ordered to register at the temple of their choice.

1640

Europe: Netherlands
Judaism
Eriel de Costa, who has been disfellowshipped from the Jewish religious community of Amsterdam, is readmitted, but must undergo a humiliating public flogging in the synagogue. The experience leads to his suicide.

1640

Europe: Scotland
Christianity
The Scottish Parliament adopted the revised National Covenant drawn up by Archibald Johnston (aka Lord Warriston) in 1637. The action includes a demand that Scottish citizens subscribe to both its pro-Presbyterian and anti-Catholic provisions. With the Parliament's backing, the Covenanters raise an army to oppose any attempts by King Charles I to impose religious reforms aimed at transforming the Church of Scotland into an Anglican institution. They are able to defeat Charles's invading army in what is termed the Bishops' Wars, a prelude to the several civil wars in England that would later in the decade end Charles's regime.

1640

Russia, Central Asia, and the Caucasus: Russia
Christianity
Joasaphus I, the patriarch of Moscow and All Russia, dies. His office will remain vacant for a year and a half.

1640

Southwest Asia and North Africa: Asia Minor
Islam

Ottoman sultan Murad IV dies at the age of 27. He is succeeded by his brother Ibrahim I (r. 1640–1648), who like another recent Ottoman sultan suffered from a mental illness that greatly hampered his ability to rule effectively.

1641

Sub-Saharan Africa: Angola
Christianity
The (predominantly Protestant) Dutch take control of Luanda (Angola) from the (largely Roman Catholic) Portuguese.

1641

East and Southeast Asia: Malaysia
Christianity
The Dutch conquer Malacca, which is taken from the Portuguese. The Dutch proscribe Roman Catholicism and convert existing churches into Dutch Reformed churches. St. Paul's Church, the Catholic church on the summit overlooking the city, is transformed into the Bovenkerk (or High Church) and henceforth became the main parish church of the Dutch Reformed community.

1641

Europe: England
Two members of Parliament, Henry Vane the Younger and Oliver Cromwell, the latter a dedicated Puritan, present the Root and Branch Petition. It calls the English Parliament to abolish episcopacy thoroughly, to its "roots and branches." Parliament voted it down, but then passed the Bishops Exclusion Act, which blocked the bishops of the Church of England from their seats in the House of Lords.

1641

Europe: France
Christianity
Jean-Jacques Olier, a member of the congregation of the French Oratory, which had been working to revive and reform the Roman Catholic Church in France, accepts the offer to take charge of the Church of St. Sulpice in Paris. He initially intends to revive the parish, establish a seminary, and Christianize the

nearby Sorbonne, then very secular in its instruction. His work would attract young students of the priesthood from across France and become the basis of the new order of St. Sulpice, a fellowship of diocesan (i.e., secular) priests who share a common life but are bound by no special religious vows. Olier hoped his priests would actualize the ideal of life as a secular priest.

1641

Europe: Netherlands
Islam
The first Dutch translation of the Qur'an is published. It has been translated from the German translation of 1616, which in turn is based on the Italian translation of 1447.

1642

Sub-Saharan Africa: Ghana
Christianity
The Dutch take Axim (Ghana) from the Portuguese.

1642

North America: United States
Christianity
The new director-general of New Amsterdam, Willem Kieft, initiates the process of building a stone church for Reformed believers within the settlement's fort. It would take several years to carry out and the new building was not finished until 1645.

1642

South America: Brazil
Judaism
The first Jewish colony in the New World is established in Recife, Brazil. It grows quickly with the immigration of several hundred Jews from Amsterdam.

1642

South Asia: India
Buddhism
Sengge Namgyal (r. 1616–1642), the ruler of Ladakh (now a part of Kashmir, India), dies and is succeeded by his son Deldan Namgyal (r. 1642–1694).

Dalai Lama V, Lobsang Gyatso (1617–1682). As the secular and religious leader of Tibet, he established a strong relationship with China and built the Potala Palace of Lhasa. (Rubin Museum of Art/Art Resource, NY)

He will survive by keeping back the attempts of both Tibet and the Mughal kingdom of India (led by Aurangzeb) to take control of his country. To keep the Indian Muslims away, he agrees to the building of the first of several mosques that will be erected at his capital, Leh. He will himself eventually convert to Islam.

1642

East and Southeast Asia: China
Buddhism

Mongolian leader Gushi Khan conquers western Tibet, which both unifies the country and places the karmapa, who heads the Karma Kagyu school of Buddhism, under his control. Gushi Khan then establishes the fifth Dalai Lama as the new ruler of united Tibet. The karmapa moves into involuntary exile in Yunnan. In the aftermath, the Kagyu Karma school

is significantly weakened and many of the monks are forced to join the Gelugpa school, formally headed by the Dalai Lama.

1642

East and Southeast Asia: China
Buddhism

Lobsang Gyatso (b. 1617), whose identity had been kept quiet as Tibet moved through turbulent political times, is finally enthroned as the fifth Dalai Lama in the main hall of Tashilhunpo Monastery at Shigatse (Tibet). In the process, Karma Tenkyong, who had ruled much of Tibet since 1620 and who privileged the Karma Kagyu school of Tibetan Buddhism, was overthrown. The Dalai Lama is now recognized as both the spiritual and political leader of the country. He appoints a regent, called the desi, to manage the temporal affairs of the government and provide continuity during the hiatus between the death of successive Dalai Lamas and the recognition and maturing stages of the next holder of the office.

The fifth Dalai Lama moves to unite as much of Tibet as possible under his leadership. In that process his supporters invade the neighboring kingdoms of Bhutan and Ladakh. The two countries form an alliance against Tibet. Shabdrung Ngawang Namgyal, who heads Bhutan, sends Choje Mukzinpa as his representative to Ladakh. He will found Tagna (or "Tiger's Nose") Monastery, which becomes the headquarters of the Southern Drukpa Kagyu tradition in Ladakh.

1642

East and Southeast Asia: China
Judaism

Chao Ying-Cheng helped rebuild the synagogue in Kai Fen after the Yellow River flooded the area. He also served in the government, helped build schools, and quashed marauding bandits.

1642

East and Southeast Asia: China
Chinese Religions

Li Zicheng leads a rebel force that takes control of Shaanxi Province and declares Li as the king of the Shun Dynasty.

1642

Europe: France
Christianity
Jean-Jacques Olier, a Roman Catholic priest in charge of the Church of Saint-Sulpice in Paris, founds the Society of Saint-Sulpice, a priestly society dedicated to the education of priests and the improvement of their parish work. The Sulpicians come to be known for the academic attainment and spiritual formation of their members.

1642

Europe: Italy
Christianity
Galileo dies. Pope Urban stops the plans of the Grand Duke of Tuscany, Ferdinando II, who had planned to have his body interred in a prominent spot in the Basilica of Santa Croce (Church of the Holy Cross) in Florence. Urban argued that it would not be right to have a person suspected of rank heresy so honored. Thus Galileo is buried in a small out-of-the-way spot in the church. He would be moved to a prominent position only in 1737.

1642

Russia, Central Asia, and the Caucasus: Russia
Christianity
A year and a half after the former patriarch of Moscow had died, a new patriarch is selected. He is chosen by a lottery in which the candidate is chosen randomly from a list of acceptable church leaders submitted by the czar. Joseph (r. 1642–1652), an archimandrite from the Simonov Monastery, emerges as the new patriarch.

1642

Southwest Asia and North Africa: Persia
Islam
Persian shah Safi dies and is succeeded by his 10-year-old son Shah Abbas II (r. 1642–1666).

1643

East and Southeast Asia: China
Buddhism

The Manchurian Qing emperor Hong Taiji dies. The Manchu leaders select his five-year-old son Fulin to succeed him and name his half-brother Dorgon as regent.

1643

Europe: England
Christianity
After much debate, the British Parliament appoints a group of British church leaders to meet for the purpose of restructuring the Church of England. The Westminster Assembly of Divines consisted of 121 clergymen and 30 laymen (no women being included) and were appointed from four groups recognized as having a voice in the decisions—the Episcopalians who favored the current structure, the Presbyterians who wanted a Reformed theology and a Presbyterian polity imposed on the church, the independents who wanted a Reformed church but one free of state control, and the Erastians who wanted a church plainly subordinate to state control. Also included in the assembly were several Scottish Presbyterians.

The assembly would meet over the next six years, during which time it would draw up the major statements of British Presbyterianism—the Westminster Confession of Faith, the Westminster Larger Catechism, the Westminster Shorter Catechism, and the Directory of Public Worship.

The British Parliament burns the hated *Book of Sports* which the Anglicans had circulated as a list of approved recreational activities on the Sabbath. The next year, Parliament will follow up and ban Christmas celebrations.

1643

Europe: Scotland
Christianity
The leadership of the English Parliament, seeking help from Scotland in its civil war with the forces supporting King Charles I, adopt a treaty that came to be called "Solemn League and Covenant." The treaty guaranteed the preservation of the Reformed faith, including the Presbyterian polity, of the church in Scotland, and the future reformation of the Church of England and Ireland in the Scottish model. Following its approval by the English Parliament, the Scottish Covenanters (Scots who had already defeated

Charles's attempts to introduce Anglican reforms in their land) send an army south to England, which is instrumental in the Parliament's eventual victory over the king.

1643

Europe: Scotland
Christianity
King Louis XIII dies, and his son, Louis XIV (r. 1643–1716), begins what will become the longest reign in European royal history, lasting for 72 years and 110 days.

1643–1645

Europe: England
Christianity
John Milton, having been deserted by his wife, writes a set of pamphlets advocating divorce on the grounds merely of the incompatibility of the couple. He is harshly criticized by his Puritan colleagues and eventually abandons the idea in favor of polygamy.

1644

North America: United States
Christianity
Roger Williams was granted a charter to found the colony of Rhode Island, which united several independent settlements that had been made around Narragansett Bay.

1644

South America: Brazil
Christianity, Judaism
The Portuguese attack Dutch-controlled Recife where an openly Jewish community has emerged. When the city falls, almost all the the Jews, some 5,000 in number, scatter to other settlements, especially Curacao and Suriname.

1644

South Asia: India
Sikhism
Har Rai (r. 1644–1661) succeeds his grandfather Har Govind to become the seventh guru of the Sikhs.

1644

South Asia: India
Islam
The large Jama Mosque is erected by Mughal emperor Shah Jahan and dedicated to his favorite daughter, Jahanara Begum, who was born to the love of his life, Mumtaz Mahal.

1644

East and Southeast Asia: China
Chinese Religions
Rebels led by Li Zicheng overrun and sack Beijing, leading the Chongzhen emperor, the representative of the Ming Dynasty, to commit suicide. The Ming Dynasty comes to an end, and Li proclaims himself as the first emperor of the new Shun Dynasty. His success is short-lived, however, as the Manchurians to the north have now risen in strength. Moving south, the Manchurians defeat Li at the Battle of Shanhai Pass, take control of Beijing, and drive Li from the scene.

On October 30, Manchurian Qing officials make sacrifices at the mound of the altar of the Temple of Heaven, to the southeast of the Forbidden City in Beijing, a ceremony symbolizing their assumption of the mandate of heaven, deemed by the Chinese as the right to rule the nation. Ten days later, the six-year-old Manchu leader Fulin is installed as the new ruler of China as the Shunzhi emperor (r. 1644–1661). Through his regent, he will immediately begin the lengthy process of bringing the whole of the lands of the former Ming Dynasty under his hegemony.

Jesuit priest Johann Adam Schall von Bell, who has worked on astronomical projects for the former emperor, is able to establish a relationship with the new emperor and is appointed head of the Chinese Bureau of Astronomy. His favorable position at court provides an environment that allows Catholic missionaries to convert many Chinese at various locations throughout the realm.

1644

Europe: England
Christianity
Seven Particular Baptist churches in London associate together and issue their First Confession of Faith. The confession advocates a Calvinist doctrinal

perspective with a strong statement on Christ's death as a "particular" atonement for the elect alone (rather than all humankind).

1644

Europe: England
Christianity
Though possessing no formal training in military tactics or warfare, Oliver Cromwell leads a cavalry unit in the Battle of Marston Moor, in which the forces of the Parliament (heavily Puritan in its sympathies) defeat the forces loyal to King Charles (and to the episcopally led Church of England).

1644

Europe: England
Christianity
John Lightfoot, a Puritan cleric and scholar at St. Catharine's College, Cambridge, publishes the first volume of a multivolume work entitled *The Harmony of the Four Evangelists among Themselves, and with the Old Testament,* in which he calculates the creation of the world to have begun at nightfall near the autumnal equinox, in the year 3929 BCE. His calculations would soon be forgotten due to the success of similar speculations proposed a few years later by Irish bishop James Ussher.

1644

Europe: England
Christianity
Puritan writer John Milton publishes his book *Aeropagitica* in which he argues for a freedom of conscience between the various Christian sects then operating in England (though not extending that right to those professing atheism, Judaism, Islam, or Catholicism). He concludes that disestablishment (the government cutting its ties to the established Church of England) is the only way of achieving broad religious toleration.

Leader of the Rhode Island colony Roger Williams publishes *The Bloody Tenent of Persecution, for Cause of Conscience* in London. This is his most famous work, and was a clear and able statement and defense of the liberty of conscience (and of religion). It plainly outlined the thinking undergirding the colony's policies on religious toleration and later

provided a foundation for the Bill of Rights of the U.S. Constitution.

1644

Europe: France
Christianity
Workers uncover the body of Germaine, a saintly laywoman who had been buried in 1601 in the village church at Pibrac (near Toulouse), as they prepare a place for the body of a relative. The body of Germaine is found to be incorrupt and becomes the object of miracle stories and pilgrimages.

1644

Europe: Italy
Christianity
Pope Urban VIII dies. He is extremely unpopular in Rome at the time of his demise, having been a lavish spender who almost doubled the papal debt. Soon after his death, his detractors destroy a bust of him located beside the Palace of the Conservators on the Capitoline Hill. The famed sculptor Gian Lorenzo Bernini has been commissioned to carve the altarpiece for his tomb. Urban is succeeded by Cardinal Giovanni Battista Pamphili who takes the name Innocent X (r. 1644–1655).

1644

Southwest Asia and North Africa: Asia Minor
Christianity
In the midst of an extremely unstable time for the Ecumenical Patriarchate, Parthenius II (r. 1644–1646) succeeds Parthenius I in the patriarch's office. The controversies within the Greek Orthodox community that gave birth to the frequent changes in the patriarch's office were allowed and at times even encouraged by the financially strapped sultans of the Ottoman Empire, as the appointment of each new patriarch was accompanied by a fee to the sultan, above and beyond the annual fee the patriarchate paid simply to exist.

The constant change of the holders of the patriarch's office also serves to keep attention on the office itself while diverting attention from policy decisions, the development of programs, and accomplishments that were generally expected from those who held the position. The overall effect of the periodic changes was to weaken the patriarchate.

March 2, 1644

South Asia: India
Sikhism

Sikh guru Har Gobind, known for arming the Sikh community in the face of a growing hostile environment, dies at Kiratpur Rupnagar, Punjab. He is succeeded by the 14-year-old Har Rai (r. 1644–1661) who becomes the seventh guru of the Sikhs.

July 12, 1644

Russia, Central Asia, and the Caucasus: Russia
Christianity

Russian czar Michael I dies. He is succeeded by his 16-year-old son Alexei I (r. 1645–1676).

1645

South Asia: India
Jainism

Mughal prince and future emperor Aurangzeb, a Muslim, desecrates the Chintamani Parshvanath Temple, which had been constructed by Jain devotee Shantidas Jhaveri, a wealthy merchant in gold and jewels. He caused a cow to be killed in the temple premises, lopped the noses off all the temple's statues, and then converted the building into a mosque, which he named the "Might of Islam." Shantidas used his access to the Mughal court to complain directly to the emperor Shah Jahan, Aurangzeb's father. The emperor forced his son to return the building.

1645

East and Southeast Asia: China
Buddhism

Chinese regent Dorgon issues an imperial edict requiring all Han Chinese males to adopt a Manchu appearance, including most notably shaving the front of their heads and combing their remaining hair into a queue. Noncompliance was a capital offense. This ordinance met stiff resistance as it ran counter to Chinese patterns of filial piety.

1645

East and Southeast Asia: China
Buddhism

The Dalai Lama initiates the building of what becomes the Potala Palace on the Red Hill in Lhasa, the site where the king of Tibet Songtsen Gampo had once constructed a red fort. The palace, which would take almost half a century to complete, would become the home of the Dalai Lama.

1645

East and Southeast Asia: Philippines
Christianity

The Roman Catholic cathedral in Manila is destroyed by an earthquake. A new cathedral whose construction begins in 1654 is completed and consecrated in 1671.

1645

Europe: England
Christianity

As the British Parliament and King Charles I continue their conflict, the imprisoned archbishop of Canterbury William Laud is executed by beheading. He had been arrested in 1640 under charges of treason because of his support of the king. He was finally brought to trial in 1644, but no verdict was reached, there being little evidence of any specific treasonable acts. Subsequently, Parliament passed a bill of attainder, an act declaring Laud guilty and authorizing his execution without benefit of trial.

At the time of Laud's death, the Church of England was under the control of the Puritans, who favored a Presbyterian form of ecclesiastical government. The office of the archbishop of Canterbury was thus not filled for the next 15 years.

1645

Europe: England
Christianity

Parliament approves of the first document produced by the Westminster Assembly, *The Directory for Public Worship*. This guide to worship following a Reformed Presbyterian pattern is published and sent to the local churches to replace the Book of Common Prayer, which had been in use since the reign of

Queen Elizabeth. King Charles I denounces the Parliament's action, but to no avail.

ca. 1646

North America: United States
Christianity

Lutheran minister John Campanius, pastor of the Swedish church in Philadelphia, translates Luther's catechism in the language of the Delaware Native people. It would exist only in manuscript for a half century before finally being published in Stockholm in 1696.

1646

East and Southeast Asia: Japan
Buddhism, Christianity

The local feudal lord of Matsushima, Date Terumune, builds Entsuin Temple adjacent to the area's most prominent temple, Zuigan-ji. The new temple houses the remains of Date Mitsumune, Date Terumune's son who had died suddenly at the age of 19. It is dedicated to Kannon (Guan Yin), the Buddhist goddess of mercy. The temple grounds feature a statue of the deceased son on a white horse surrounded by his devoted followers, who had committed ritual suicide in their grief. The mausoleum is decorated in gold leaf and contains Western symbols of Latin crosses and the oldest Japanese image of a rose. These symbols point to the Date clan's interest in Christianity. They had recently dispatched envoys to the pope in Rome.

1646

East and Southeast Asia: Malaysia
Chinese Religions

Chinese residing in Malacca erect Cheng Hoon Teng Temple, a traditional Chinese temple, now the oldest standing in Malaysia.

1646

Europe: England
Christianity

The Westminster Assembly completes and sends to Parliament for approval the Westminster Confession of Faith, a statement of belief in the Reformed theological tradition of John Calvin. Adopted by Parliament, it becomes the major standard of doctrine for English-speaking Presbyterians worldwide. Sent to Scotland, it is approved by the Church of Scotland (which already had its own similar statement of faith), and has subsequently been recognized as its "subordinate standard" of doctrine.

1646

Europe: Scotland
Christianity

The Battle of Philiphaugh. Civil war in Scotland between the Scottish Royalists, who support King Charles, and the Covenanters, Presbyterians who oppose Charles's attempts to lead the Church of Scotland into Anglicanism, results in a major victory for the Covenanter forces.

Charles I's surrender to the Scots effectively ends the first English civil war.

1646

Europe: Slovakia
Christianity

Responding to Roman Catholic missionary work among its largely Eastern Orthodox population, 63 Orthodox priests in eastern Slovakia formally join the Catholic Church. The Union of Uzhorod swings the population into the Roman Catholic camp.

1646

Europe: Slovenia
Christianity

Augustinian monks in Ljubljana initiate construction of a Baroque church and monastery, which would in the next century be transferred to the Franciscans. It is part of a larger movement of members of various religious orders through the centuries to recapture territory for Roman Catholicism from the Protestants who had become a majority in the area in the previous century.

1646

Russia, Central Asia, and the Caucasus: Russia
Christianity

Czar Alexei I appoints the monk Nikon (later to become the patriarch of Moscow) as the archimandrite (prior) of the wealthy Novospassky Monastery in Moscow.

1647

Sub-Saharan Africa: Madagascar
Christianity
The Discalced Carmelites begin work on Madagascar.

1647

North America: Canada
Christianity
Construction begins on the first Canadian Roman Catholic cathedral to serve the Diocese of Quebec. It is dedicated to the Blessed Virgin Mary.

1647

North America: United States
Christianity
Peter Stuyvesant (r. 1647–1664) becomes director-general of New Amsterdam, the capital of New Netherlands, the Dutch colony in North America.

1647

South Asia: India
Hinduism
Bhakta Ramadas, a devotee of Lord Rama (an incarnation of the god Vishnu), constructs a temple to Sri Rama at Bhadrachalam, Andhra Pradesh, India. It is second in size only to Ayodhya as a pilgrimage site to Lord Rama. The area once formed the Dandakaranya forest, which, according to tradition, Rama, his spouse Sita, and his brother Lakshmana visited during a time in exile. Murtis of these three are commonly placed together in Vaishnava temples.

1647

East and Southeast Asia: Mongolia
Buddhism
Zanabazar, the first Jebtsundamba Khutuktu, the spiritual head of Tibetan Buddhism and lineage holder of the Gelugpa tradition, founds Shankh Monastery, the oldest Buddhist monastery in Mongolia. It is located in the Övörkhangai Aimag, Central Mongolia.

1647

Europe: England
Christianity

After four years of work, the Westminster Assembly completes the text of the Westminster Longer Catechism, a detailed, exact, and comprehensive document to be used in catechizing the faithful. It had been developed after a major decision by the assembled church leaders that they needed two catechisms, a shorter one to be used for beginners in the faith and a longer one that was more precise and exacting. The completed Longer Catechism was approved by Parliament and the following year adopted by the General Assembly of the Church of Scotland. It has since joined the Westminster confession of faith as a primary statement of belief for English-speaking Presbyterians.

Its oft quoted first question is: "What is the chief and highest end of man?" to which the answer is "Man's chief and highest end is to glorify God, and fully to enjoy him forever."

1647

Europe: England
Christianity
Puritan theologian John Owen publishes *The Death of Death in the Death of Christ*, a study of the meaning of the death of Jesus of Nazareth espousing the idea of a limited atonement, that is, that Christ's death was not for all humanity but for the elect alone.

1647

Europe: England
Christianity
After several years of intense religious turmoil culminating in a series of resolutions and insight, George Fox begins public preaching. A group of followers gather around him, which evolves into the Society of Friends, popularly called the Quakers.

1647

Europe: England
Unbelief
John Biddle, already in jail for his heretical views, publishes a pamphlet, *Twelve Arguments Drawn Out of Scripture,* which present his non-Trinitarian views. It is publicly burned by the hangman. Biddle appears to be the first person in England publicly to espouse what would later be termed Unitarianism.

1647

Europe: France
Islam

André du Ryer publishes the first French translation of the Qur'an. It would later become the basis of various retranslations, including the first in English.

1647

Europe: Germany
Christianity

A fire destroys the spire of St. Mary's Church in Stralsund, Germany, then the tallest building in the world. With the loss of the spire (reaching some 341 feet), the Cathedral of Our Lady in Strasbourg (France) becomes the tallest building (at a height of 341 feet).

1648

North America: United States
Christianity

American Congregationalists define their stance in the "Cambridge Platform." Boston minister John Cotton further defines the "New England Way" in his "The Way of the Congregational Churches Cleared," in which Calvinist theology is mixed with a congregational polity.

1648

Europe: England
Christianity

The British Parliament approves the last of the several statements of Presbyterian faith produced by the Westminster Assembly of Divines—the Westminster Shorter Catechism. Developed from the Longer Catechism produced the previous year, the Shorter Catechism was designed for use among youth and others perceived to not yet be ready to master the details of Reformed theology. It would become, next to the Westminster Confession of Faith, the most widely used presentation of the Presbyterian position on belief and practice throughout the English-speaking world.

1648

Europe: England
Unbelief

Gerrard Winstanley publishes *The Mysterie of God Concerning the Whole Creation, Mankinde,* the first modern text espousing a belief in universal salvation (which includes a denial of the standard Christian belief in damnation and hell for the unsaved). In his own time, Winstanley is better known for his reformist activity and advocacy of egalitarianism. He is one of the founders of the True Levellers, a group believing in a form of Christian communalism, who are derisively called the Diggers as they would take over public land and dig it up to plant food crops.

1648

Europe: France
Judaism

France annexes Alsace and Lorraine, where unlike in the rest of France, many Jews reside. After due consideration, Louis XIV grants letters patent, taking the Jews under his special protection, although his unique policy here does nothing to open France to a Jewish presence elsewhere.

1648

Europe: Holy Roman Empire
Christianity

The Peace of Westphalia is the name given to a set of peace treaties signed in 1648 and designed to bring an end to several long-standing hostilities, most notably the Thirty Years' War (1618–1648) and the Eighty Years' War (1568–1648).

1648

Europe: Netherlands
Judaism

The Ashkenazi Jews of Amsterdam construct a synagogue. The community is in a growth trajectory as many Jews fleeing the Khmelnytsky Uprising in Ukraine begin to arrive in town. Artist Rembrandt van Rijn, who has many Jewish friends, etches his view of *The Jews in the Synagogue.*

1648

Russia, Central Asia, and the Caucasus: Russia
Christianity

PEACE OF WESTPHALIA (1648)

The Peace of Westphalia refers to a set of treaties drafted at the conclusion of the Thirty Years' War and the Eighty Years' War. These treaties made significant alteration in national boundaries and altered religious allegiance among the participating countries. Most notably, Roman Catholic Spain recognized the independence of the Dutch Republic, which had become predominantly Reformed Protestant. Both the Netherlands and Switzerland were dismissed from inclusion in the Holy Roman Empire.

The treaties were signed in two especially designated German cities, Münster, a Roman Catholic city, and Osnabrück, a city divided between Lutheran and Catholic believers, though the leadership was Lutheran.

The Peace of Westphalia revived recognition of the Peace of Augsburg (1555) and affirmed the right of each prince to determine the religion of his own state. While the Peace of Augsburg offered only two choices—Catholicism or Lutheranism—the new agreement allowed for a third choice, the Reformed (or Calvinist) church. Provisions were added for believers who resided in a state in which their particular form of Christianity was not the one chosen by the ruler. The Peace of Augsburg had lost much of its power toward the end of the 16th century with the rise of the Reformed Church, the desire of many Catholics to regain the territory lost to Protestants, and the conversion and subsequent swing of votes in various parts of the Holy Roman Empire.

France gained control of the area covered by the Catholic bishoprics of Metz, Toul, and Verdun (near Lorraine), and the cities of the Décapole in Alsace.

Sweden, a Lutheran country, received not only a large cash settlement, but control of the territories of Western Pomerania (aka Swedish Pomerania), Wismar, and the prince-bishoprics of Bremen and Verden.

The Peace of Westphalia represented a political setback for the Habsburg rulers of the Holy Roman Empire. It finally ended the idea that Europe could be considered a single Christian empire under the spiritual governance of the pope and the temporal leadership of the Holy Roman emperor. The Habsburg family, which controlled what was left of the empire, solidified their realm in southern Germany, Austria, Hungary, and Bohemia, but lost control elsewhere. The popes, having never accepted the Peace of Augsburg, found a voice in Pope Innocent X, who denounced the new peace agreement.

J. GORDON MELTON

Czar Alexei I appoints Nikon, the archimandrite (prior) of Novospassky Monastery in Moscow, as the metropolitan of Great Novgorod.

1648

Southwest Asia and North Africa: Asia Minor
Islam

Though mentally ill, if not deranged, Ottoman sultan Ibrahim I married and fathered children by his several wives. When he dies in 1648, his six-year-old son Mehmed IV (1648–1687) comes to the throne. The events of reigns of recent sultans have, however, changed the environment in the royal palace, and the sultan has been stripped of much of his power, which has now been transferred to his grand vizier.

The Jews in the Synagogue, 1648, etching by Dutch artist Rembrandt van Rijn (1606–1669). (Rob Crandall/Time Life Pictures/Getty Images)

1648–1649

Europe: England
Christianity

The Second Civil War. Ongoing conflict between King Charles I and the British Parliament leads to a second outbreak of hostilities resulting in Charles's capture. Parliamentary authorities subsequently try him, and following his conviction, execute him for high treason. With Charles's death, the monarchy is abolished and a republic declared. The British Parliament passes "An Act declaring England to be a Commonwealth."

In the midst of the conflict, Johanna and Ebenezer Cartwright, British Baptists residing in Amsterdam, submit what will become the first petition to readmit Jews to England. Due in part to the execution of King Charles and other priorities, Parliament refuses the petition a hearing.

1648–1657

Europe: Ukraine
Christianity, Judaism

The Khmelnytsky Uprising. A coalition of Cossacks and various peasant groups, mostly of Eastern Orthodox faith, revolt against the Polish-Lithuanian Commonwealth, the Roman Catholics who controlled their land. The rebels also target Jewish communities, as many of the Polish agents exercising some authority are Jewish. The revolt leads to the Pereiaslav Agreement and the incorporation of Ukraine into Russia. The Cossacks swear an oath of allegiance to the czar. Russian Orthodoxy becomes the dominant religion of the country. Some 300 Jewish communities are destroyed during the uprising and as many as 100,000 Jews die. Many additional Jews migrate eastward to Poland and Germany.

1649

North America: Canada
Christianity

After more than two decades of work among the Native people, Jean de Brébeuf dies when the Iroquois attack and destroy his mission station, which operated among the Huron people.

1649

North America: United States
Christianity

A Toleration Act for the colony of Maryland promised religious toleration to all who professed a Trinitarian Christian faith.

1649

North America: United States
Christianity

The Maine colony passed an act granting all orthodox Christians who led a non-scandalous life the right to form churches.

1649

Central America and the Caribbean: Mexico
Christianity

In the largest auto-da-fe ever held in the New World, 109 crypto-Jews were accused of Judaizing, and all but nine were burned alive in Mexico City.

1649

East and Southeast Asia: Japan
Shinto

The 14th-century Asakusa Shrine, dedicated to two fishermen, the Hinokuma brothers, and a friend, Hajino Matsuchi, who were later deified, is rebuilt. It is located in Tokyo adjacent to the Sensori Buddhist Temple.

The two fishermen had caught a statue of Kannon, the goddess of mercy, in their nets, and Hajino Matsuchi had realized the significance of the statue and originally enshrined it. The statue would later be the main deity worshipped at the Sensori Temple. Centuries later, the three men responsible for discovering and recovering the Kannon statue were themselves enshrined at the nearby shrine.

1649

Europe: England
Islam

Alexander Ross, chaplain to King Charles I, translates the Qur'an into English using the French translation that had been published in 1647.

1649

Europe: France
Christianity

Having found the church adopted in 1590 as the new cathedral for Nice, France, to be too small, the Roman Catholic bishop of Nice proposes the construction of a new larger cathedral. Work began the next year and was completed in 1699.

1649

Europe: Germany
Christianity

The 495-foot spire of St. Mary's Church, located in Stralsund, northern Germany, the tallest building in the world, is struck by lightning and burns. When rebuilt, it is considerably shorter. As a result of the fire, the Cathedral of Our Lady of Strasbourg (France), at 466 feet, becomes the tallest building in the world. It would maintain that distinction until 1874.

1649

Europe: Italy
Christianity

A project is launched for the enlargement of the Cathedral of St. John the Baptist in Turin, Italy, occasioned by a desire to create a suitable home for the cathedral's main treasure, the Shroud of Turin, which the faithful believe to be the burial shroud in which Christ was entombed. The project led to the construction of the Shroud Chapel located immediately behind the cathedral.

1649–1650

England
Christianity

George Fox, the founder of the Society of Friends, experiences his first stay in jail following his arrest by authorities disturbed by his preachings. On one of his later encounters with the law, a judge in Derby makes fun of Fox's adminition to him to "tremble at the word of the Lord," and initially refers to the group gathered around him as "Quakers."

1649–1653

East and Southeast Asia: China
Buddhism

The fifth Dalai Lama makes an extensive visit to Beijing, the capital of China, at the invitation of the Sunzhi emperor, who rules China. The visit begins with a formal military escort from the Chinese province of Ningxia to the capital. While in Beijing, the Dalai Lama resides at the Yellow Palace, which the emperor had built for him.

ca. 1650

Europe: England
Christianity

Discussions on the keeping of the seventh-day Sabbath (worship on Saturday rather than Sunday) among Protestant Christians in England lead some to conclude that it is a requirement of biblical Christianity. Reacting to the dominant Sunday worship in the Christian community, they separate themselves and found the Mill Yard Church in London.

1650

North America: United States
Christianity

Dutch attacks on the French in Quebec force the Jesuits to abandon their missions to the Hurons and other Native people in the St. Lawrence River valley.

1650

Central America and the Caribbean: Granada
Christianity

Roman Catholic missionaries begin work on the island of Granada.

1650

South America: Peru
Christianity

An earthquake strikes Cuzco and destroys the Jesuit church of La Compañía de Jesús in the city center. They rebuild and in the process create a large new Baroque-style building that features a new elaborate altar with a gold leaf–covered sun motif.

1650

South America: Suriname
Christianity

A new attempt to settle in Suriname is made by the British, who establish a policy of religious toleration for settlers who will join their adventure.

1650

East and Southeast Asia: China
Buddhism

The Chinese regent Dorgon dies, and the youthful Shunzhi emperor assumes full imperial powers. He will choose to include among his close advisors a German Jesuit priest, Johann Adam Schall von Bell, a man knowledgeable about both astronomy and contemporary technologies.

As prince regent, Dorgon had resided in a palace that had been built over the site of a former temple to the god of the North Pole that stood during the Yuan Dynasty.

1650

Europe: England
Christianity

The postmonarchy government of England, the Commonwealth, retains and maintains the state-controlled church, that is, the Church of England, but its episcopal leadership is abandoned and replaced with a presbyterian polity. The Act of Uniformity is repealed, which allows the legal existence of independent churches not directly controlled and supported by the government. Citizens, no matter their personal religious affiliation and identification, are expected to pay taxes that were used to support the state-established church.

1650

Europe: England
Christianity

Anglican cleric Jeremy Taylor issues his devotional classic *The Rule and Exercises of Holy Living,* produced at a time when he is without a parish due to the disfavor of the Commonwealth with his Anglicanism. He will later be appointed as the bishop of a diocese in Ireland.

1650

Europe: Ireland
Christianity

Irish scholar and bishop James Ussher publishes his most famous work, *The Annals of the Old Testament, deduced from the first origins of the world,* in which he calculates the date of Creation to have begun at night-fall preceding October 23, 4004 BCE. It is not a work of trivial speculation; Ussher worked through and mastered a considerable amount of contemporary scholarship in ancient history to arrive at his conclusion.

1650

Europe: Italy
Christianity

Pope Innocent X leads in the celebration of a Jubilee Year, which brings many pilgrims to Rome.

1650

Europe: Netherlands, England
Judaism

Amsterdam scholar Manasseh ben Israel releases *The Hope of Israel,* a volume advocating the readmission of Jews to England. He integrates into his argument the accounts of Antonio De Montezinos, a Jewish traveler who had visited South America and claimed to have discovered native people in Ecuador who were aware of Jewish rituals and could repeat the Shema. He identifies them as remnants of the Ten Lost Tribes of Israel (which had disappeared from history after being carried into captivity by the Assyrians). Manasseh ben Israel argues for the global dispersion of the Jews throughout the world and hence that England is the only country of note without a Jewish presence. His argument is well received in England and he is invited to visit. Meanwhile, Amsterdam Jews, seeing the economic possibilities of opening markets in England, provide additional support to their rabbi.

1650–1651

Europe: England
Christianity

Anglican clergyman Jeremy Taylor, later to be named Bishop of Down and Connor (Ireland), while living in semiretirement during the years of the Commonwealth, produces two devotional texts, which become long-term best-sellers, *The Rule and Exercises of Holy Living* (1650) and *The Rule and Exercises of Holy Dying* (1651).

1651

North America: United States
Christianity

Massachusetts fines and banishes three Baptists from their midst.

1651

North America: United States
Christianity

After several years of evangelizing the several groups of Native people, Congregational minister John Eliot created the first of more than a dozen communities of "Praying Indians" at Natick in the Massachusetts Bay Colony. These communities, which eventually included more than 1,000 converts, survived until decimated by King Philip's War in 1675. To further enrich the life of his converts, Eliot translates the Bible into their language and publishes it in 1663.

1651

South America: French Guiana
Christianity

A quarter-century of work by French Roman Catholic priests in French Guinea leads to the creation of the Prefecture Apostolic of French Guiana-Cayenne. That office becomes the Vicariate Apostolic of French Guiana-Cayenne in 1933 and finally the Diocese of Cayenne in 1956.

1651

East and Southeast Asia: China
Buddhism

Shabdrung Ngawang Namgyal, the lineage holder of the Drukang Kagyu school of Tibetan Buddhism, who has unified the nation of Bhutan, dies. In order to keep the government together and prevent the country from returning to its former divided state, his successors will keep his death a secret and continue to issue orders in his name for the next half century.

1651

East and Southeast Asia: China
Buddhism

On the highest point of an island west of the Forbidden City, Chinese Qing Dynasty officials erect a

Tibetan-style temple, the White Temple Pagoda (now known as the Yong'an Temple). A monastery would be built below the pagoda at a later date.

1651

East and Southeast Asia: Japan
Shinto

Shortly before his death, Shogun Iemitsu orders the complete rebuilding of Ueno Toshogu, a Shinto shrine in Edo (Tokyo).

Shogun Iemitsu dies. He is succeeded by his 10-year-old son, Tokugawa Ietsuna (1651–1680).

1651

East and Southeast Asia: Vietnam
Christianity

French Jesuit missionary Alexandre de Rhodes culminates his decades of work by producing the *Dictionarium Annamiticum Lusitanum et Latinum,* a trilingual (Vietnamese/Portuguese/Latin) dictionary, which is published in Rome.

1651

Europe: Bohemia
Christianity

The monks of the Capuchin Church of the Holy Cross in Brno adopt the practice initiated by the Capuchin Church in Rome a generation earlier of decorating the crypt of the church by artistically arranging the bodies of the deceased members of the Order, still clad in their habits, and making the crypt available for public viewing.

1651

Europe: England
Christianity

Dr. Peter Chamberlen, a noted physician of the day, leads the first known Seventh Day Baptist congregation, which meets at the Mill Yard Church in London. The church espouses the keeping of the Sabbath on Saturday rather than Sunday.

1651–1652

East and Southeast Asia: China
Buddhism

Gelugpa Tibetan Buddhists erect two temples in Beijing to the north of the Forbidden City The initial construction is termed the East Yellow Temple (the yellow referring to the color of the hats worn by the Gelugpa priests) and the latter the West Yellow Temple. Included in the West Yellow Temple complex is one of the four five-pagoda temples of Beijing, the main structure being a large building with a square base upon which five pagodas rest.

1652

Sub-Saharan Africa
Christianity

The Dutch establish a colony at Cape of Good Hope, South Africa, and colonizing Boers ("farmers"), or Afrikaners, mostly attached to the Dutch Reformed Church, begin settling large farms at the expense of the San and Khoikhoi peoples, non-Bantu speakers of the region.

1652

Europe: England
Christianity

George Fox founds the Society of Friends (also known as "Quakers") at Pendle Hill, England.

1652

Europe: England
Christianity

Margaret Fell, the wife of Thomas Fell, the vice chancellor of the Duchy of Lancaster, converts to Quakerism. Her home, Swarthmore, becomes a popular stopping place for George Fox as he travels the countryside, and Fell is able to assist Fox in some of his encounters with the legal authorities.

1652

Europe: Italy
Christianity

Gian Lorenzo Bernini completes his impressive *St. Theresa in Ecstasy,* the centerpiece for the Cornaro Chapel attached to the Church of Santa Maria della Vittoria in Rome. Bernini had also designed the entire chapel, a commission from the Cornaro family. St. Theresa was a Spanish mystic and a popular leader of the 16th-century Counter-Reformation.

August 1, 1652

Russia, Central Asia, and the Caucasus: Russia
Christianity

Nikon (1605–1681), the metropolitan of Great Novgorod, is elected patriarch of Moscow. He appears reluctant to assume the position and accepts only after the assembled archbishops pledge obedience to his future rulings on matters concerning dogmas, canons, and church observances. He immediately opens conversations with Greek Church leaders on the liturgy and worship of the church.

Patriarch Nikon persuades Russian czar Alexis to bring the relics of the former patriarch Philip (1507–1569), believed to have been murdered by Czar Ivan IV, to Moscow, where he is glorified (proclaimed a saint by the Russian Orthodox Church).

1653

East and Southeast Asia: China
Buddhism

The Dalai Lama founds the Tse school, located within the Potala Palace in Lhasa, for the training of civil servants to work in the Tibetan government.

1653

Europe: England
Christianity

In the wake of the death of King Charles I, England accepted a new governing document, the Instrument of Government, which named Oliver Cromwell as the country's lord protector for life. He was assigned the office of chief magistrate to administer the government.

Soon after coming to office, Cromwell designates a number of "triers" whose job is to examine future parish ministers and pass on their suitability to fulfill their duties, and a set of "ejectors" who are given the power to dismiss any ministers and/or schoolmasters who are found to be unsuitable for their position. These two new sets of officials form a vanguard in what will be Cromwell's plan to reform parish worship.

1653

Europe: France
Christianity

Pope Innocent X issues a papal bull, *Cum Occasione,* which condemns five propositions drawn from *Augustinus,* a theological work written in Latin by Cornelius Jansen, the Catholic bishop of Ypres (Belgium). The work is considered too aligned with Lutheranism.

Following Jansen's death and the publication of his book on Augustine, theologians at the University of Paris extract five propositions from it that they consider heretical. Pope Innocent's agreeing with their work would set off the Jansenist controversy and ultimately lead to the destruction of the Jansenist community centered on Port Royal, a monastic community of nuns near Paris.

1653

Russia, Central Asia, and the Caucasus: Russia
Christianity

Patriarch Nikon of the Russian Orthodox Church erects the Church of the Twelve Apostles, a cathedral located within the Kremlin in Moscow. It was originally designed as part of his residence and in 1656 was dedicated to the apostle Philip. In building the new church, Nikon strove to show his equality with the czar in status if not power.

1654

North America: United States
Christianity

Maryland's Toleration Act of 1649 was rescinded, leaving Catholic believers without any legal protection.

1654

North America: United States
Judaism

Jacob Basimon, the first Jewish settler in New York, arrives (July) in New Amsterdam, with additional Jews arriving in August. Then, in September, a group of 23 Portuguese Jews from Recife arrive in New Amsterdam. Soon after their arrival they found Congregation Shearith Israel (the first Jewish worshipping community in America). New Amsterdam's governor Peter Stuyvesant openly opposes their settlement in his colony to the Dutch West Indies Company, but he is overridden and the Sephardim are granted permanent residency.

1654

East and Southeast Asia: Japan
Shinto, Buddhism
Shogun Ietsuna throws his support behind the major renovation of Yasaka Jinja, a Shinto shrine in Kyoto. A large stone *tori* (gate) had recently been added (1646). The reconstructed building includes the main temple (*honden*), the most massive of any shrine in the country. At the time of its reconstruction, it was under the control of the Tendai Buddhists headquartered on Mt. Hiei, and it has remained a *miyadera* (a shrine where Buddhist rites are also performed). Further renovations are required in 1666, following an earthquake in Kyoto. Yasaka Jinja is the site of the annual Gion Matsuri, a huge festival held each July that attracts tens of thousands.

1654

East and Southeast Asia: Japan
Buddhism
Ingen, a Chinese priest, founds the Obaku sect of Zen Buddhism in Japan. It integrates the practice of reciting the Nembutsu, commonly associated with Pure Land Buddhism, into Zen practice.

1654

Europe: Bohemia
Christianity
The Jesuits merge Charles College into the Collegium Clementinum in Prague and begin extensive reconstruction and expansion of the college in the new Baroque style. It will emerge as a center of scientific research and learning.

1654

Europe: France
Christianity
French intellectual Blaise Pascal has an intense mystical experience that leads him to identify with the controversial Jansenist movement. Largely abandoning his scientific work, he devotes his time to theological issues and writes his *Lettres provinciales,* which deals with the Jansenist conflict with the Jesuits.

1654

Europe: Germany
Christianity
To accommodate the growing number of pilgrims who want to visit the miracle-working statue of the Blessed Virgin Mary at Altotting, Bavaria, the prince-bishop of Regensburg founds the monastery of St. Anna for the Franciscans who oversee the needs of the many pilgrims.

1654

Russia, Central Asia, and the Caucasus: Russia
Christianity
Russian patriarch Nikon summons a church synod to consider revising the liturgical format of the church in line with what he has learned of the divergence of the Russian from the Greek Orthodox tradition. The synod votes to follow the Greek church over its own traditions.

April 26, 1654

South America: Brazil
Judaism
Jews are again expelled from Brazil.

1655

North America: United States
Judaism
The Dutch West India Company overrides Peter Stuyvesant's objections and allows Jewish settlers to reside permanently in New Amsterdam. It orders the Jews to support any poor among them rather than having them be a burden on the larger Christian community.

1655

Central America and the Caribbean: Barbados
Judaism
The first Jews arrive on the island of Barbados as refugees from Brazil. Over the next years some 300 will settle there.

1655

Central America and the Caribbean: Jamaica
Christianity

The British take Jamaica from the Spanish. They subsequently suppress the Roman Catholic Church, which, as in England, was officially prohibited until the early 19th century.

1655

East and Southeast Asia: China
Buddhism
Upon the death of Gushir Khan, the Mongolian ruler who had placed the Dalai Lama on the throne of Tibet, the fifth Dalai Lama appoints Gushir Khan's son Tenzin Dorjee as the new Mongol ruler.

1655

East and Southeast Asia: Japan
Buddhism
Tetsugen, a Jodo Shin priest, travels to Nagasaki, where he meets Ingen, the founder of Obaku Zen Buddhism. He subsequently becomes his close disciple.

1655

Europe: England
Christianity
Lord Protector Oliver Cromwell prohibits Anglican worship in the parishes across England. In three acts, Parliament prohibits all of the forms of recreation previously advocated in the infamous *Book of Sports,* promulgated earlier in the century by the Anglicans.

1655

Europe: England
Judaism
Oliver Cromwell hosts Amsterdam scholar Manasseh ben Israel who visits England. Cromwell is open to the return of Jews to England and organizes a conference at Whitehall to consider the idea. He has to dismiss the conference, however, when he runs into staunch opposition from merchants in London who feel threatened by a Jewish presence. He sidesteps their opposition and arranges for the Jews' presence on a more informal level.

1655

Europe: Italy
Christianity

Pope Innocent X dies and is succeeded by Pope Alexander VII (r. 1655–1667).

Queen Christina of Sweden (r. 1632–1654) converts to Christianity. In 1654 she abdicates and subsequently moves to Rome. Alexander VII confirms her baptism during ceremonies on Christmas Day, 1655.

Pope Alexander becomes a patron of sculptor Gian Lorenzo Bernini and commissions him to design the piazza and colonnade in front of St. Peter's Basilica. He would later do other significant work within the Vatican including the *Cathedra Petri* (the Chair of Saint Peter) located in the apse at St. Peter's.

1656

North America: United States
Christianity
The Massachusetts court forbade Quakers to live in the colony or hold meetings, and set a penalty of death on any Quakers who returned after being banished.

1656

South America: Brazil
Christianity
Jesuit missionary Antoinio Vieira obtains a set of decrees from King John IV of Portugal that grants the Jesuits hegemony over the Catholic missions in northern Brazil, appoints Vieira as the superior, and prohibits the enslavement of the Native people. He will subsequently organize a vast mission enterprise, though eventually encountering stiff opposition from settlers who wanted more slaves and members of other orders who were jealous of the monopoly the Jesuits had received.

1656

South Asia: India
Jainism
Future Mughal emperor Aurangzeb, then the governor of Gujarat, grants the village of Palitana to the prominent Jain Shantidas Jhaveri, a wealthy merchant in gold and jewels. Jhaveri had spent much of his wealth protecting and maintaining Jain temples. The Shatrunjaya Hills near Palitana will become the most prominent of Jain pilgrimage sites as the Jain faithful construct some 3,000 temples in relatively close proximity. It is considered by some as the largest temple complex in the world.

1656

East and Southeast Asia: China
Christianity

After completing his studies in the Philippines, Luo Wenzao becomes the first Chinese convert to be ordained as a Roman Catholic priest. He subsequently returns to Xiamen to begin his pastoral career.

1656

East and Southeast Asia: China
Chinese Religions

Wang Changyue, a master of Quanzhen Taoism, comes to Beijing at the request of Qing emperor Shunzhi and begins teaching at the Baiyun (White Cloud) Temple. He wrests control of the temple from the Zhengyi Taoists, who had controlled the temple through the years of the Ming Dynasty.

1656

East and Southeast Asia: China
Buddhism

Katok Monastery, originally founded in 1159 in eastern Tibet but long since fallen into disuse, is rebuilt through the efforts of Tertön Düddul Dorje (1615–1672) and Rigdzin Longsal Nyingpo. It is the first of six major monastic institutions created in the last half of the 17th century that helped organize and define the Nyingmapa school of Tibetan Buddhism. The six monasteries are Dorje Drak and Mindrolling in the upper region, Shechen and Dzogchen in the center, and Kathok and Palyul in the lower part of Tibet. From these six come a large number of Nyingmapa monasteries throughout Tibet, Bhutan, Nepal, and China.

1656

South Asia: Sri Lanka
Christianity

Almost two decades of struggle culminate in the Dutch finally capturing the Portuguese stronghold of Colombo, which leads quickly to their gaining hegemony over the whole island. The Dutch, Reformed Protestants, turn on the Roman Catholic converts, but largely leave the Buddhists, Hindus, and Muslims to themselves. The Sri Lankans soon come to dislike the Dutch as much as the Portuguese whom they replaced.

1656

Europe: England
Christianity

Puritan minister Richard Baxter publishes *The Reformed Pastor,* a volume detailing the reforms he had promoted and accomplished during his lengthy pastorate at Kidderminster, including the formation of a ministerial association that had united Presbyterians, Episcopalians, and Independents into a common fellowship.

1656

Europe: England
Judaism

Jews who have quietly settled in England petition for the right to worship openly. The Council of State approves the petition. This action marks the beginning of the unbroken presence of Judaism in England to the present.

While on his visit to England, Amsterdam scholar Manasseh ben Israel writes *Vindictiae Judaeorum,* an apologetic work defending the Jewish community against the common accusation of, most notably, the blood libel, while emphasizing the benefits that the emerging Jewish community will have on England.

1656

Europe: England
Christianity

On Palm Sunday, pioneer Quaker leader James Nayler reenacts Jesus of Nazareth's entry into Jerusalem by coming into Bristol riding on a donkey. He claims that "Christ is in him," a reflections of his Quaker belief in the Inner Light, but his followers had seen him as a figure of messianic authority, while authorities saw only a blasphemer, and they arrest and imprison him. Convicted, he is pilloried, branded with a "B" on his forehead, whipped, and imprisoned for two years.

George Fox, the founder of the Quakers, disavows Nayler and his actions, but critics continue to challenge the idea of the Inner Light as a doctrine that obscures the line between God and his human creatures.

1656

Europe: Netherlands
Judaism, Unbelief

The Jewish community in Amsterdam excommunicates philosopher Baruch Spinoza. Spinoza, who has already withdrawn from Jewish religious life, is accused of denying the inspiration of the Jewish scripture, the existence of angels, and the immortality of the soul. He becomes the first person known to have withdrawn from Judaism who did not adopt another religion. Unbelievers of Jewish heritage will later see him as the fountainhead of Jewish Unbelief.

1656

Europe: Poland
Christianity

Polish king John II Casimir Vasa credits the icon of the Blessed Virgin Mary known as Our Lady of Częstochowa with saving the country from an invasion of Swedish forces. He has the image temporarily removed to the cathedral of Lviv (Ukraine), where he crowns it as the queen and protector of Poland.

1656

Russia, Central Asia, and the Caucasus: Russia
Christianity

Nikon, the patriarch of Moscow, builds Novy Ierusalem (or New Jerusalem) Monastery at Istra, which he uses as his official seat. The monastery would include a new spectacular Cathedral of the Resurrection (built 1656–1685) designed to rival the Church of the Holy Sepulchre in Jerusalem. Tikon would ultimately be buried there, and construction would continue through the end of the century.

1656

Russia, Central Asia, and the Caucasus: Russia
Christianity

A synod of the Russian Orthodox Church led by the patriarch Nikon votes to revise the church's liturgy in light of changes suggested by consultation with the Greek Orthodox Church. Dissidents tie the changes to the arrival of the plague in the country. Changes include the introduction of new icons drawn with stricter concern for removing innovative art that had been introduced into Russian icon-making over the centuries. With the support of the monarchy, Nikon's reforms are quickly and forcefully imposed on the church rather than allowing a period for the majority of believers to become aware of them and accept them.

Among the changes introduced by Patriarch Nikon's reforms is the introduction of a new edition of the *Jerusalem Typicon,* the guidebook for the monastic life. The *Jerusalem Typicon* had been originally introduced in the 13th century, but had subsequently gone through numerous changes while in use.

1656

Russia, Central Asia, and the Caucasus: Russia
Christianity

Having become convinced that the service books used in worship and the icons being created for the veneration of the saints had departed from the Orthodox tradition, Patriarch Nikon of Moscow, the head of the Russian Orthodox Church, calls a church council at which a broad reform program is initiated. He uses the bishops' earlier pledge of obedience to move them behind the reforms and pronounces anathemas on any who oppose him. He is backed by Czar Alexis I, who has been his enthusiastic supporter over the previous decade.

Those who oppose Nikon's reforms, which they see as innovations, become known as Old Believers. Just as dedicated to maintaining the status quo as Nikon is to reform, they form a large enough minority to create a permanent rift in the Russian Orthodox Church.

1656

Southwest Asia and North Africa: Asia Minor
Christianity

Ecumenical Patriarch Joannicius II, now serving his fourth term in the patriarch's chair, is deposed and sent from Istanbul to the western Cyclades as the bishop of the islands of Kea and Thermia. During his brief times in power, he had encouraged Roman Catholic missions in the territories of the Ottoman Empire as a means of creating allies, but refused overtures to sign a statement of submission to the pope.

1656

Southwest Asia and North Africa: Persia
Judaism

Jews who refuse to convert to Islam are expelled from Isfavan, the capital of Persia. A generation earlier, they had been allowed to settle in Persia by the former shah Abbas I.

1657

North America: Canada
Christianity
Roman Catholic priests of the Sulpician Order arrive and take up residence in Ville-Marie (i.e., Montreal).

1657

North America: United States
Christianity
William Robinson and Marmaduke Stevenson, two Quakers formerly banished from Massachusetts, were upon their return executed by hanging.

1657

North America: United States
Judaism
The first Jews gain the rights of citizens in America.

1657

East and Southeast Asia: Japan
Buddhism
A great fire erupts in Edo (Tokyo) that burns the city to the ground. It takes some two years to rebuild, at which time Shogun Ietsuna presides over the ceremonies celebrating the resettlement of the city. Most of the temples and shrines burn to the ground; among the few surviving are the recently reconstructed (1649) Asakusa Jinga.

1657

Europe: England
Judaism
Antonio Fernandez Carajal, a Jewish merchant, leads his colleagues in financing the purchase of land for a Jewish cemetery and leasing a house that will be converted into a synagogue, the first for the reborn Jewish community of London.

1657

Europe: Germany
Christianity
Ferdinand II, the Holy Roman Emperor, dies. He is succeeded by his son Leopold I (r. 1657–1705). Like his immediate predecessors, he had been trained as a youth by the Jesuits and was a staunch Roman Catholic. Along with his theological training, he also had acquired a knowledge of and interest in astrology and alchemy. His rule, which paralleled the lengthy rule of Louis XIV in France, was dominated by balancing the efforts of the Ottoman Turks to his east and France to his west.

Lutheran pastor Paul Gerhardt moves to Berlin to become the deacon (associate pastor) of the Nikolai-kirche. By this time, he has already gained a reputation as a hymn writer. While in Berlin he becomes an important voice for Lutheranism at a time when the Protestants are strongly divided between Lutheran and Reformed, the latter favored by the ruler, Elector Friedrich Wilhelm I of Brandenburg.

1657

Southwest Asia and North Africa: Asia Minor
Christianity
Ecumenical Patriarch Parthenius II, now serving his third term as patriarch, initiates correspondence with a bishop in Russia. As Russia is an enemy of the Ottoman Empire, Sultan Mehmed IV views the correspondence as subversive of his authority and orders a public hanging for Parthenius. His body remained on display for three days at the "Gate of the Hook" in Istanbul and was then thrown into the sea.

Parthenius II is succeeded by Gabriel II (r. 1657) who is in office for one week. The Holy Synod refuses to confirm his appointment as he is deemed unfit for the job. After his deposition, he is named Metropolitan of Prousa (i.e., Bursa), where he runs into problems with the Jewish community. Some Jews accuse him of baptizing a former Muslim who had converted to Christianity, a capital offense in many Muslim countries. He would be arrested and eventually hung (1659) for the offense.

Gabriel II is succeeded as patriarch by Parthenius IV (r. 1657–1662). Parthenius would serve five terms as the patriarch, the last time being 1684–1685.

1658

North America: Canada
Christianity
A group of sailors from Breton are shipwrecked at Beaupré, Quebec, and credit St. Anne, the mother of the Blessed Virgin Mary, with their deliverance. They erect a small chapel, which will grow to become the Basilica of St. Anne de Beaupré. Miracles are reported at the chapel and they will multiply over the years.

1658

North America: United States
Judaism

Jews in Newport, Rhode Island, form a Jewish community and establish a cemetery.

1658

South Asia: India
Islam

The Masjid-i Jahān-Numā, more commonly known as the Jama Masjid, originally commissioned by Mughal emperor Shah Jahan, is completed. It took more than a decade to construct and is, at the time of its completion, the largest mosque in India.

Mughal emperor Shah Jahan fell ill in 1658. His several sons vie for his throne, and his third son, Aurangzeb, emerges as the winner. Meanwhile, though Shah Jahan recovers from his illness, Aurangzeb (r. 1658–1707) declares him incompetent to rule, exiles him to the Agra Fort, and assumes the throne as the new emperor. Aurangzeb was a follower of the Naqshbandi-Mujaddidi Sufi order and a direct disciple of Khwaja Muhammad Masoon, the third son and successor of the founder of the order, Shaykh Ahmad Sirhindi (1564–1624). Ahmad Sirhindi was credited with rejuvenating Islam during the time of the Mughal emperor Akbar. Khwaja Muhammad Masoon sent his scholarly fifth son, Khwaja Saif ad-Din Sirhindi, to live at Aurangzeb's court as advisor to the new emperor.

1658

East and Southeast Asia: Japan
Buddhism

Ingen, the Chinese Zen priest who developed the Obaku sect, gains an audience with the Shogun Ietsuna, whose patronage he obtains. Ietsuna grants him land in Yamashiro Province, where he builds Obakusan Mampuku-ji, the lead temple of the Obaku Zen sect.

1658

East and Southeast Asia: Vietnam
Christianity

After a generation of missionary work, Roman Catholics appoint Bishop Pierre Lambert de la Motte as the first vicar apostolic of Cochin and Bishop François Pallu as the first vicar apostolic of Tonkin.

1658

Europe: England
Christianity

Congregationalists, British Puritans who accept the Reformed belief and practice of the Presbyterians but favor a Congregational polity over the Presbyterian polity advocated by the Westminster Assembly, adopt a slightly refined version of the Westminster Confession of Faith (the major statement of British Presbyterian belief and practice) published as the Savoy Declaration.

1658

Europe: England
Christianity

Aurangzeb was the last of the great Mughal emperors of India, and it was during his reign (1658–1707) that the empire reached its zenith. (Library of Congress)

Oliver Cromwell, the lord protector of England, dies. He is succeeded by his son Richard.

1658

Europe: Poland
Unbelief

The Polish Diet passed a decree banishing all residents who professed the Socinian heresy (which denied the Christian doctrine of the Trinity). Once a powerful minority position in the country, Unitarian belief would never again gain a significant following in Poland.

1658

Russia, Central Asia, and the Caucasus: Russia
Christianity

People who opposed Patriarch Nikon's reform convince Czar Alexius that the patriarch was eclipsing his sovereign position. Alexius turns on Nikon, publicly divests him of the patriarchal vestments, and confines him to the Ascension Convent.

1658–1659

North America: Canada
Christianity

In Paris, the papal nuncio Piccolomini consecrates François-Xavier de Montmorency-Laval as the titular bishop of Petra and sends him to Quebec as the pope's representative with the title of vicar-general. He arrives in the summer of 1659 and takes the spiritual leadership of the Roman Catholic population of New France, which numbers some 2,000 persons.

July 19, 1658

Russia, Central Asia, and the Caucasus: Russia
Christianity

Having lost the support of Czar Alexis, Russian patriarch Nikon removes his patriarchal vestments (the symbols of his office) and retires to the Ascension Convent, a cloister primarily for female religious in the Kremlin in Moscow.

1659

East and Southeast Asia: China
Buddhism

Rigzin Ngagi Wangpo founds Dorje Drag, a monastic university of the Nyingmapa school of Tibetan Buddhism in Central Tibet.

1659

Europe: England
Christianity

Lacking the power base and abilities of his father, Richard Cromwell, the lord protector, resigns after only a year in office. His resignation effectively ends the Commonwealth and sets the stage for the restoration of the monarchy under Charles II the following year.

1659

Europe: England
Christianity

Massachusetts Congregational minister John Eliot publishes *The Christian Commonwealth: or, The Civil Policy of the Rising Kingdom of Jesus Christ,* in which he proposes a new system of government, an elected theocracy, based upon a biblical model and used to organize the Native communities he had established. He was inspired by Exodus 18 and the government developed by Moses for the Israelites. Embarrassed by Eliot's utopian notions, the Massachusetts colony bans the book, orders the destruction of all copies, and forces Eliot to make a public retraction of its proposal.

1659

Europe: France
Christianity

Missionary Alexandre de Rhodes, who has spent much of his life in Southeast Asia, dedicates his last years to recruiting successors to his pioneering work. Unable to find support in Portugal or Rome, he motivates the formation of the Paris Foreign Missions Society, which sends its first missionaries, François Pallu and Pierre Lambert de la Motte, to Asia. Pope Alexander VII appoints them as apostolic vicars.

1659

Europe: Iceland
Christianity

Lutheran minister and poet Hallgrímur Pétursson publishes his most notable work, *Passion Hymns,* a collection of some 50 hymns designed to be sung, one on each working day, during the seven weeks of Lent. The title of each hymn refers to an event during Christ's passion.

1660

North America: United States
Christianity
In their attempt to keep Massachusetts religiously uniform, the Congregationalists in Boston hang Mary Dyer, a Quaker.

1660

South America: Peru
Christianity
Jesuit father Francisco del Castillo develops a new devotional practice built around the three hours of agony experienced by Jesus Christ on the cross, which he introduces on Good Friday to the Escuela de Cristo of the Church of Nuestra Señora de los Desamparados in Lima.

1660

East and Southeast Asia: China
Christianity
The Vicariate Apostolic of Nanking (Nanjing) is carved out of territory previously assigned to the Roman Catholic Diocese of Macau.

1660

East and Southeast Asia: Thailand
Christianity
A century after the first Roman Catholic priest arrives in Thailand, Pope Alexander VII establishes the Vicariate Apostolic of Siam. By this time, both Portuguese and French missionaries are active in the region.

1660

Europe: England
Christianity
Quaker Margaret Fell pioneers women's leadership role in matters religious in her pamphlet *Women's Speaking Justified, Proved and Allowed by the Scripture.*

1660

Europe: France
Christianity
The large library created by Cardinal Richelieu is given to the Sorbonne (University of Paris). As the *proviseur* of the Sorbonne, he had supervised a major renovation of its buildings and the construction of its chapel. He had been buried in the chapel in 1642.

1660

Russia, Central Asia, and the Caucasus: Russia
Christianity
A Russian Orthodox Church synod held at Moscow strips the former patriarch Nikon of his archiepiscopal rank and defrocks him from priestly orders. Before the synod attendees take the further step of electing a new patriarch, they are halted in their resolve by questions of the appropriateness of their actions in ecclesiastical law. They do not elect a patriarch, and the office remains open.

May 29, 1660

Europe: England
Christianity
The monarchy is restored in England as King Charles II (r. 1660–1685) celebrates his 30th birthday by entering London to public acclaim. At this time, William Juxon (r. 1660–1663), the former bishop of London, who had been forced into retirement during the years of the Commonwealth, was named as the new archbishop of Canterbury. He assumed office in time to officiate at King Charles's coronation. Puritan Richard Baxter moves to London where he receives an appointment as the chaplain to Charles II.

A decade earlier, following the death of Charles II's father (1649), the Parliament of Scotland had proclaimed Charles II to be the king of Great Britain and Ireland, but soon afterward the English Parliament passed a statute nullifying such proclamations. King Charles II always considered his official rule to have begun with that proclamation.

Following the Restoration, the British Parliament passes the Indemnity and Oblivion Act of 1660, which limited persecution of those who had acted against the monarchy during the years of the Commonwealth to those who had been directly involved in the killing of former king Charles I. The act had the additional effect of freeing a variety of people who had been arrested for a spectrum of offenses growing out of their religious differences with the established church.

Clerics of both Anglican and Puritan persuasion meet to review the Book of Common Prayer, the main book used to order worship in the Church of England. The new edition is approved by convocations at Canterbury and York.

July 20, 1660

Europe: Poland
Christianity

Poland expels the Polish Brethren, the non-Trinitarian group that had survived in the country over the last century.

1661

North America: United States
Christianity

William Leddra, a Quaker, is executed in Boston. Shortly thereafter, orders from England arrived commanding that all Quakers who had been arrested and sentenced be sent to England for trial. The colony released all the prisoners and ordered them to leave the colony.

1661

South Asia: India
Sikhism

Shortly before his death at the relative young age of 31, Sikh guru Har Rai names his younger son, then but five years old, as the next Sikh guru—Guru Har Krishan. He had passed over his older son, Ram Rai, who had attempted to appease the Mughal emperor Aurangzeb by agreeing to change a reference to Muslims in a verse of Sikh founder Nanak's poetry (then already incorporated into the Sikh holy book, the Adi Granth). Har Rai never spoke to his elder son after that incident.

1661

East and Southeast Asia: China
Chinese Religions

The rule of the Shunzhi emperor of China comes to an end. In what is an ill-defined period, it is undetermined whether he died or retired to become a Buddhist monk in his later years. He is succeeded by

his young son, the seven-year-old Kangxi emperor (r. 1661–1722), who would enjoy a lengthy rule.

The Kangxi emperor will support the development of Taoism during his regime. Among the major accomplishments will be the construction of the Taiqing Temple in Shenyang, Liaoning Province. It is the largest Quanzhen monastery in northeastern China.

1661

East and Southeast Asia: Japan
Buddhism

Chinese Zen priest Ingen, the founder of the Obaku Zen sect in Japan, founds Mampuku-ji, which will become the Obaku head temple.

1661

Europe: France
Western Esotericism

French astrologer Jean Baptiste Morin publishes his *Astrologica Gallica,* which provides a new philosophical and rational basis for astrology as well as a comprehensive system of interpretation.

1661

Europe: France
Christianity

Under scrutiny for possible heretical tendencies, the monastic community of nuns at Port Royal de Paris, which has become identified with the condemned pietist movement known as Jansenism, is forbidden to accept any new novices. This all but ensures the soon demise of the community.

1661

Europe: Italy
Christianity

Pope Alexander VII issues the Apostolic Constitution *Sollicitudo Omnium Ecclesiarum* in which he states the doctrine of the Immaculate Conception of the Blessed Virgin Mary and, without condemnation of those who oppose it, states the papacy's preference for it.

1661

Europe: Netherlands
Judaism

In Amsterdam, Joseph Athias prints an edition of the Jewish Bible, the first to have the modern inclusion of numbered verses.

1661

Europe: Scotland
Christianity

Following the restoration of the monarchy, the Scottish Parliament passes the Recissory Act, which replaces the Presbyterian church government and re-institutes episcopal leadership. Only one bishop who served before the year of the Commonwealth remains alive, Thomas Sydserf, and he is appointed Bishop of Orkney. Several British bishops gather to consecrate four additional bishops for Scotland.

1661

Russia, Central Asia, and the Caucasus: Russia
Christianity

A copy of the famous icon called the Three-Handed Mother of God (the original is kept at Hilander Monastery on Mount Athos in Greece) is taken to Moscow. It would become the source of a number of copies over the next centuries.

1661

Southwest Asia and North Africa: Persia
Judaism

Following a campaign to force Jews to convert to Islam, the Jews remaining in Persia are allowed to practice Judaism openly if they pay a special tax and wear a distinctive patch on their clothing.

January 6, 1661

Europe: England
Christianity

Some 50 believers in what was termed the Fifth Monarchy, under the leadership of Thomas Venner, attempt to assume control of London in the name of "King Jesus." The group had formed their beliefs from reading the biblical book of Daniel, which in chapter 2 speaks of an idol made of four metals and having feet of mixed iron and clay. The idol is interpreted as a series of four successive kingdoms that in the end are destroyed and replaced by God's kingdom (i.e., the fifth monarchy).

Two weeks after the initial unsuccessful effort to take control of London, Venner and 10 of his followers were hung, drawn, and quartered for high treason. The authorities then turned on the remaining Fifth Monarchists and while totally suppressing what remained of the group, also moved against other nonconforming groups such as the Quakers.

1662

Sub-Saharan Africa: South Africa
Christianity

Dutch colonial administrator Jan van Riebeeck, representing the Dutch East India Company, establishes a resupply camp at Table Bay north of the Cape of Good Hope, This camp will evolve into Cape Town, which becomes a major stopping point for ships sailing between Asia and Europe and an entry point for European settlers attempting to colonize the land, now the residence of the Native Khoikhoi people.

1662

East and Southeast Asia: China

Lobsang Chökyi Gyaltsen, the Panchen Lama and abbot of Tashilhunpo monastery, dies. The fifth Dalai Lama has given him both the leadership of the monastery and his title. He also recognized him as an incarnation of Amitabha Buddha. Immediately after his death, the Dalai Lama began a search for his next incarnation and since this time, the Panchen Rinpoche has become a new lineage of reincarnated tulkus, like the Dalai Lama. In the future, the Panchen Lamas and Dalai Lamas would play an important role in recognizing and legitimizing each other's successors. Lobsang Chökyi Gyaltsen is considered the fourth Panchen Lama, the title being applied posthumously to his predecessors.

1662

East and Southeast Asia: Japan
Shinto

On land donated by Shogan Tokugawa Ietuna, believers in Edo (Tokyo) found a shrine honoring the 10th-century scholar Sugawara Michizane who died in disgrace and exile, only to be rehabilitated posthumously and his title and office restored. He subsequently became an object of veneration and worship. Kameido Tenjinsha also enshrines the deity

Amenohohi no mikoto, whom the members of the powerful Hajo clan considered their ancestor.

Matsuyama Sadanaga, head of the Hisamatsu Matsudaira clan, which rules Ehime Prefecture, makes a vow to the deity Hachiman that if he is victorious in an upcoming archery contest at Edo Palace, he will rebuild Isaniwa Jonja, the local Hachiman shrine. He wins and is true to his vow.

1662

East and Southeast Asia: Taiwan
Chinese Religions

A group of people still loyal to the deposed Ming Dynasty, led by Cheng Ch'eng-kung (aka Koxinya), drive the Dutch from Taiwan and establish a base of operation. Many of these Ming loyalists are from the southern coast of China and worship Tianhou (Matsu) whom they credit with their victory.

Koxinya dies only a few months after his victory. He is honored in death and quickly goes from hero to deity status. His Chinese followers erect an initial shrine that becomes a breeding ground for myths and legendary stories.

1662

East and Southeast Asia: Thailand
Christianity

A century of growth by the Roman Catholic Church in Thailand leads to the establishment of the Vicariate Apostolic of Siam (which will evolve into the Archdiocese of Bangkok).

1662

Europe: England
Christianity

The British Parliament passes the Quaker Act, requiring all to swear an oath of allegiance to the king. The act passes in the knowledge that members of the Society of Friends, that is, the Quakers, could not swear an oath because of their religious convictions. Parliament also passes the Act of Uniformity, which mandates the use of the new Book of Common Prayer in church services. The Act of Uniformity leads to several thousand nonconforming clergy being removed from their pastoral position. Included in that number is the Puritan Richard Baxter, who had unsuccessfully

argued for a broad church that could include both Presbyterians and independents.

1662

Europe: England
Christianity

Portuguese princess Catherine of Braganza, a Roman Catholic, marries King Charles II of England. In her dowry, she brings to England gifts of Tangier (the port city on the coast of Morocco) and the Seven Islands of Bombay (England's first territory in India). Portugal also grants the British religious freedom in Portugal.

Catherine is granted freedom to continue her Catholic worship while in England, a privilege that will erupt on several occasions as Charles's political enemies attempt to involve her in various plots occasioned by the widespread anti-Catholic sentiments in England.

1662

Europe: Scotland
Christianity

Once he was established on the throne of England, Ireland, and Scotland, Charles II denounced the National Covenant, a statement originally adopted by the Scots in 1581 that upheld Presbyterian faith and practice while strongly denouncing Roman Catholicism. He made the abandonment of the covenant a requirement for all who held public office and ordered any minister unwilling to accept episcopal oversight expelled from his parish. He designated James Sharp as the new archbishop of St. Andrews and primate of Scotland.

1663

North America: Canada
Christianity

Bishop François-Xavier de Montmorency-Laval founds the Séminaire de Québec, which will evolve into Laval University. It is the oldest institution of higher learning in Canada, the fourth oldest in North America, and the first in North America to offer instruction in French.

1663

North America: United States
Christianity

A new charter for Connecticut guaranteed religious freedom for residents.

1663

North America: United States
Christianity

Plockhoy Community, founded by a group of Dutch Mennonites, formed in rural Delaware.

1663

North America: United States
Christianity

Amid his work with the Native people of Massachusetts, Puritan minister John Eliot translates the Bible into Algonquin, the first of the Native languages to be reduced to written form and have a Bible.

1663

East and Southeast Asia: China
Buddhism

The Kangxi emperor has the Avalokitesvara Nunnery (aka the Cibei Nunnery), located on the Central Isle at Taoran Park in Beijing, renovated and rebuilt. The nunnery had originally been established during the Yuan Dynasty.

1663

Europe: England
Christianity

William Juxon (r. 1660–1663), the archbishop of Canterbury, dies and is succeeded by Gilbert Sheldon (r. 1663–1677), the former bishop of London.

1663

Europe: England
Christianity

Only three years after becoming an Anglican priest and accepting the duties of the pastor at Bemerton, a rural parish in Wiltshire, George Herbert dies. He leaves behind a collection of poems, which will be published posthumously as *The Temple: Sacred poems and private ejaculations.* Many of the poems will later be set to music and become popular hymns, among the most highly regarded of the era. A few,

such as "Let All the World in Every Corner Sing," are still included in Protestant hymnbooks.

1663

Europe: France
Judaism

Jews in Amsterdam petition King Louis XIV of France to allow them to settle in Dunkirk. They demand the right to practice their faith openly. In spite of his desire to gain from the Jewish presence in his kingdom, Louis rejects the petition as he cannot tolerate Jews openly worshipping in his domain.

1664

South Asia: India
Sikhism

The eighth Sikh guru, Har Krishan (1661–1664), still only eight years old, dies of smallpox after only three years in office. He had been summoned to Delhi by the Mughal emperor Aurangzeb at a moment when a smallpox epidemic had spread through the city. Guru Har Krishan, moved by the ill, began to assist them as he could, but while he helped to heal many, the contact with so many sick people led to his contracting the disease himself. He was succeeded in office by his granduncle, Guru Tegh Bahadur. A Sikh house of worship, the Gurudwara Bangla Sahib, was later built over the spot where Har Krishan died.

1664

North America: Canada
Christianity

The members of the Sulpician Order are given both temporal and spiritual control of Ville-Marie (i.e., Montreal). They will remain in charge of the settlement until 1840.

1664

North America: United States
Christianity, Judaism

The British take control of New Amsterdam and rename it New York (after the brother of King Charles II). Richard Nicholls, the new British governor, grants freedom of worship and various privileges of English citizenship to the Jewish residents of the colony.

1664

North America: United States
Christianity

Rhode Island approves a law stating that "Every man who submits peaceably to civil government in this Colony shall worship God according to the dictates of his own conscience without molestation."

Increase Mather, the son of Richard Mather, the pastor at Dorchester, is ordained as a Congregationalist minister and becomes pastor of the North Church. His parishioners include many of Boston's elite. He will remain in his post for the rest of his life.

1664

Europe: England
Christianity

Blind Puritan poet John Milton completes and publishes his *magnum opus,* the epic *Paradise Lost,* which retells the biblical story of the temptation of Adam and Eve, the fall of humanity into sin from their interaction with the fallen angel Satan, and their expulsion from the Garden of Eden.

1664

Europe: England
Christianity

In its further attempt to impose Anglican worship following the new Prayer Book, Parliament passes the Conventicles Act, which forbids gatherings of more than five people for the purpose of worship except in the format of the Church of England. The act serves to further inhibit worship among the Nonconformists (from Presbyterians to Baptists).

1664

Europe: France
Christianity

The Cistercian monk Armand Jean le Bouthillier de Rancé, reacting to laxity among the Cistercians, initiates a reform movement at La Trappe Abbey in Normandy. The reform will lead (1692) to the formation of the Trappist contemplative order, officially the Order of Cistercians of the Strict Observance. Among the distinctives developed at La Trappe, the monks learned to speak only when necessary and developed a Trappist sign language that largely rendered speaking unnecessary.

1664

Europe: Germany
Christianity

Having sponsored a series of conferences with the intent of finding a way of reconciling the Lutheran and Reformed clergy in his realm, Prussian ruler Friedrich Wilhelm I of Brandenburg vents his frustration at their lack of success and ends the conference by issuing an edict that offers a "syncretistic" solution. The edict, however, disallows the Formula of Concord, one of the key Lutheran Confessions of Faith included in the Lutherans' doctrinal standard, the Book of Concord. As a result, many Lutheran clergy refuse to assent to the edict and lose their pastoral appointments. Among those removed from their position is the Lutheran hymn-writer Paul Gerhardt.

1664

Europe: Ukraine
Christianity

A large number of Orthodox priests and believers unite with the Roman Catholic Church in ceremonies held at Mukaèevo in the Transcarpathia region of Ukraine, including Orthodox from the Hungarian Diocese of Hajdúdorog.

1665

North America: United States
Christianity

Fray García and Fray Benito de la Natividad establish the missions of San Francisco de la Toma for the Sumas people and La Soledad for the Janos people. Guadalupe de los Mansos, situated at a strategic location at the pass of the Rio Grande, becomes the mother church for El Paso. At the church's dedication ceremony in 1668, 400 Mansos were present. By 1680, the mission ministers to some 2,000 Native people.

1665

Central America and the Caribbean: Haiti
Christianity

The French establish their first settlement on the western half of the island of Hispanola to further their claim to what becomes the nation of Haiti.

The mission of Guadalupe de los Mansos, established in 1659, depicted in the painting *The Plaza and Church of El Paso*, by A. de Vauducourt, 1850s. (Library of Congress)

1665

South Asia: India
Sikhism

The new Sikh guru Teg Bhadur, whose choice for office was originally challenged, visits the Golden Temple for the first time since assuming his new role and is denied entry by its priests.

1665

East and Southeast Asia: China
Buddhism

Rigzin Kunsang Sherab founds Palyul, a monastic university of the Nyingmapa school of Tibetan Buddhism, in Kham province in southeastern Tibet.

1665

East and Southeast Asia: China
Buddhism

Losang Choeki Gyaltsen, the Panchen Lama, the second most important leader of the Gelugpa school of Tibetan Buddhism, having died three years earlier, the leaders of Tashilhunpo Monastery petition the fifth Dalai Lama to recognize his successor. The Dalai Lama verifies the candidate that had been found as the new Panchen Lama and gives him the name Lobsang Yeshi. The Dalai Lama had already predicted that the late Panchen, who had been his teacher, would reappear as a recognizable child-successor, and the child would grow up to become the new Panchen Lama and serve as the abbot of Tashilhunpo Monastery. At this point, the office of the Panchen Lama, previously given to a leading scholar/monk at Tashilhunpo, would be given to the child believed to be the reincarnation of the former Panchen Lama. Over the next three centuries, the successive Panchen Lamas and the Dalai Lamas would have a reciprocal relationship recognizing/designating the successors to the other's office.

1665

Europe: England
Christianity

Parliament again steps up pressure on Nonconformists with the Five Mile Act, which forbids nonconforming clergy from coming within five miles of former parishes or of incorporated towns. The act tends to drive them to isolated towns and rural villages.

1665

Europe: Moravia
Christianity

The 19-inch statue of the Infant Jesus of Prague is formally crowned by the bishop of Prague on the Sunday after Easter.

August 18, 1665

Sub-Saharan Africa: South Africa
Christianity

The first Dutch Reformed Church congregation is founded at Cape Town, and Johann van Arkel is appointed the first minister.

1665–1666

Southwest Asia and North Africa: Palestine
Judaism

Shabbetai Zevi, a Jew from Smyrna (Asia Minor), visits Nathan of Gaza, a noted Kabbalist and mystic, from whom he seeks healing. Instead, Nathan encourages Shabbetai to proclaim himself the expected Jewish Messiah. Nathan arouses a wave of enthusiasm for the new messianic figure.

Within weeks, news of the possible Messiah sweeps through the Jewish communities of Europe and delegates are dispatched to Palestine to pay homage to the "king." Christians, reacting negatively to the new messianism, riot and Jews have to seek protection from authorities.

Islamic authorities in Asia Minor summon Shabbetai to Istanbul and demand that he convert to Islam or face execution. He denies that he has made any messianic claims and converts. News of his conversion dashes Jewish hopes, and the messianic fervor quickly dies, though a small Shabbetai following will survive for another century.

1666

Sub-Saharan Africa: South Africa
Christianity

The first Dutch Calvinist church is built in Cape Colony, South Africa.

1666

Central America and the Caribbean: Mexico
Christianity

After 90 years of work, though yet to be completed, the Metropolitan Cathedral of the Assumption of Mary of Mexico City is considered ready for use and is dedicated. It is the largest ecclesiastical building in Latin America.

1666

South America: Venezuela
Christianity

Construction begins on the Romanesque-style Cathedral of Caracas on the site of a small church that had been destroyed in an earthquake in 1641. Construction would be completed in 1674.

1666

South Asia: India
Islam

Former Mughal emperor Shah Jahan, having spent an eight-year confinement in the Agra Fort, dies. He is buried beside his beloved wife at the Taj Mahal.

1666

South Asia: India
Sikhism

Guru Tegh Bahadur founds Amritsar, the city that will come to surround the site of the Golden Temple, the holiest of Sikh sites.

1666

Europe: England
Christianity

A great fire consumes most of London. Buildings lost include St. Paul's Cathedral, which is completely gutted, and some 87 parish churches. Actually, prior to the fire, the replacement of the cathedral was already under discussion, and after the fire plans are implemented to erect a completely new building. Architect Christoper Wren is appointed Surveyor General for Rebuilding the Cathedral Church of St. Paul (1669). Wren would later be responsible for the building of more than 50 churches in London.

As a result of the fire, the world's tallest structure became Strasbourg Cathedral in Strasbourg, France (466 feet).

1666

Europe: Germany
Christianity
Philipp Jacob Spener becomes pastor of the large Lutheran Church at Frankfurt. While there he publishes his two major books, *Pia desideria* (1675) and *Allgemeine Gottesgelehrtheit* (1680). He organizes Bible study and prayer groups, the College Pietatis, among church members in which he promotes a life of Christian piety that gives the emerging movement he leads its name, Pietism.

1666

Christianity
Russia, Central Asia, and the Caucasus: Armenia
Though the Bible existed in the Armenian language since the fifth century, the first Bible in Armenian to be printed and generally circulated was that of Bishop Oskan of Erivan, published in Amsterdam.

1666–1667

Southwest Asia and North Africa: Persia
Islam
Persian shah Abbas II dies and is succeeded by Shah Suleiman I (r. 1666–1694). A cluster of military and natural disasters that occur in his first year in office convince the court astrologers that he was crowned on an inauspicious day, and they hold a second coronation ceremony in 1667.

November 18, 1666

Russia, Central Asia, and the Caucasus: Russia
Christianity
A synod of the Russian Orthodox Church opens with Czar Alexis in attendance. After weeks of deliberation, the earlier pronouncements against the former patriarch Nikon are affirmed. The synod deprives him of all sacerdotal functions and rules that he is henceforth to be known simply as the monk Nikon. They order him sent away to be confined in Ferapontov monastery, far to the north of the city. The sentence was carried out immediately.

At the same time, in what appeared as a contradictory action, the same council that imposes its sentence on Nikon confirms all the reforms he initiated and all the anathemas pronounced on those who refused to accept them. Those opposed to the changes he has introduced begin to separate from the Russian Orthodox Church. They come to be known as the "Old Believers." The Old Believers feel that the Russian Orthodox Church has fallen into heresy, while the synod of the church anathematizes those who do not accept the reforms. Many leaders of the Old Believers are arrested and executed, though in some parts of Russian they emerge in the majority.

1667

South America: Suriname
Christianity
The Treaty of Breda is signed to end the second Anglo-Dutch War. The Dutch are granted hegemony over Suriname and relinquish claims to New Netherlands to the British, who had already occupied New Amsterdam, which they renamed New York. New Netherlands included territory in the present states of New York, Connecticut, and New Jersey. Before leaving New York, the Dutch free the slaves who become the core of New York's Free Black community.

Shortly after taking control of Suriname, the Dutch government founds the Dutch Reformed Church in the territory. An initial multipurpose building is erected at Oranjetuin (Orange Garden) in the center of Paramaribo, which serves as a church for both the Reformed and Lutheran residents as well as the Town Hall and Court of Police.

1667

South Asia: India
Christianity
Ignazio Arcamone, an Italian Jesuit working in Goa, translates and publishes parts of the Bible in the Konkani language.

1667

East and Southeast Asia: China
Chinese Religions
Taoists in Liaoning Province construct the first buildings of the Qianshan Wuliang Temple at the mountain city of Anshan. It will expand through succeeding

centuries following the topology of the mountain, with walkways connecting the different halls.

1667

Buddhism

The Chinese government moves to reorganize the government of Inner Mongolia. Seven Mongolian lamas are designated Banner Lamas and granted the authority of a feudal lord. One of the seven, the Changkya Khutukhtu, is recognized as the spiritual head of the Gelugpa lineage of Tibetan Buddhism in Inner Mongolia. In steps, he and his successors will be further empowered and enriched over the next century.

1667

Europe: Italy
Christianity
Pope Alexander VII dies and is succeeded by Pope Clement IX (r. 1667–1669).

1667

Russia, Central Asia, and the Caucasus: Russia
Christianity
Nine years after the office was vacated, a new patriarch of Moscow and All Russia is elected. The new patriarch Joasaph II (r. 1667–1672) had previously served as the archimandrite (prior) of the Trinity–St. Sergius Lavra, the church's most important monastic establishment.

1668

Sub-Saharan Africa: Mali
Islam
The Songhai (or Songhay) Empire, centered at Gao, dominated central Sudan after Sunni Ali Ber's army defeated the largely Tuareg contingent at Tombouctou (or Timbuktu, site of the famous University of Sankore, center of Islamic learning and book trade) and captured the city. An uncompromising warrior-king, Ali Ber extended the Songhai empire by controlling the Niger River with a navy of war vessels. He also refused to accept Islam, and instead advanced African traditions.

1668

North America: United States
Christianity
First Congregational Church in Boston invites John Davenport of New Haven to become their pastor. He moves to Boston and is installed as pastor, but a minority oppose his appointment because of his opposition to the Half-Way covenant. They leave and found a new church that will become known as the Old South Church.

1668

South Asia: India
Islam
Mughal emperor Aurangzeb issues a decree banning music throughout the empire.

1668

East and Southeast Asia: Japan
Buddhism
Tetsugen, an Obaku Zen priest, is inspired to create a new printed edition of the Buddhist canon. He begins a campaign to raise money and settles in Osaka to begin the work of creating the printing blocks. Work will be delayed on two occasions by famines that hit Japan. He uses all the money he has raised for famine relief and has to start over with fundraising for the new edition, which finally appears in 1681.

1668

Europe: England
Christianity
Samuel Morland publishes his volume on *The History of the Evangelical Churches of the Valleys of the Piedmont,* which details the sufferings of the Waldensians in their dissent from Roman Catholicism. The book argues for the pre-Reformation origin of the Baptists, who are placed in a lineage of groups beginning with the Donatists in North Africa in the fourth century who have separated and demanded rebaptism for their members.

1668

Europe: Scotland
Christianity

Covenanters, partisans of Presbyterianism in Scotland, attempt unsuccessfully to assassinate James Sharp, the archbishop of St. Andrews and primate of Scotland, whose authority they reject.

ca. 1669

Europe: England
Christianity

While in France, the future king of England, James II, secretly converts to Roman Catholicism while continuing to operate publically as an Anglican.

1669

Central America and the Caribbean: Guatemala
Christianity

Saint Joseph Cathedral located in the then capital of Guatemala (now known as Antigua Guatemala), which had been damaged on several occasions by earthquakes, is demolished. Construction begins on a new larger cathedral, which by the middle of the next century will emerge as one of the largest in Central America.

1669

South Asia: India
Hinduism

Rebuilt following its destruction in 1351 and in 1585, the Kashi Vishwanath Temple, one of the Jyotirlingas temples to Shiva in Benares, is again destroyed, on this occasion by Mughal emperor Aurangzeb, who proceeds to build the Gyanvapi Mosque on the site of the former Hindu temple.

1669

Europe: Crete
Christianity

The fifth-century Arkadi Monastery, later famed as a center for resistance to Turkish rule, is destroyed by invading Muslim Ottoman forces who have invaded the island. It is subsequently rebuilt and continues.

1669

Europe: England
Christianity

Margaret Fell, a long-time Quaker whose husband had died, marries Quaker founder George Fox.

1669

Europe: France
Judaism

Somewhat against his better judgment, Louis XIV allows a small Jewish community to develop in Marseilles. His hope is to stimulate trade throughout the Mediterranean.

1669–1670

Europe: Italy
Christianity

Pope Clement IX dies at the end of the year, his death partly attributed to his remorse over the fall of the Venetian fortress of Candia (Crete) to the Muslim forces of the Ottoman Empire. He is succeeded by Pope Clement X (r. 1670–1676).

July 30, 1669

Europe: England
Christianity

Sir Christopher Wren formally receives the commission to design the new St. Paul's Cathedral in London.

1670

North America: United States
Christianity

Solomon Stoddard becomes the pastor of the Congregationalist Church of Northampton, Massachusetts, succeeding the late Eleazer Mather. While there he becomes concerned about the children of church members who by church rules could not join the church and partake of the sacraments as they had no profession of personal faith. He supports what is termed the half-way covenant, which allowed a form of church membership to the children and grandchildren of full church members. Any who accept the church's creed within the church could participate in the Lord's Supper. Crucially, the half-way covenant provided that the children of full members could be baptized into the church, though they were not able to participate in the communion service or vote on church matters.

1670

North America: United States
Christianity

The first association of Baptists in Rhode Island, later known as the Six-Principle Baptists, is organized.

1670

Central America and the Caribbean: Puerto Rico
Christianity

Roman Catholics construct a small chapel in the center of the town of Ponce on the south coast of Puerto Rico. It will be designated a parish church in 1692 and eventually be replaced by the present Cathedral of Ponce in the 19th century.

1670

South Asia: India
Hinduism, Islam

The Mughal emperor Aurangzeb attacks Vrindavan and inflicts severe damage on a number of the Hindu temples that had been erected for the worship of Krishna. The original image of Lord Madan Gopal (Krishna as a child) is moved to Rajasthan for safekeeping prior to Aurangzeb's attack. It was not returned and a replica would later be installed at the Vrindavan Temple. The nearby Govinda Deo Temple, to which Aurangzeb's grandfather had donated much of the building material, was among the temples completely destroyed in the invasion of the city.

Kesava Deo Temple, a Vaishnava temple that commemorates the birthplace of Lord Krishna in Mathura, had been targeted for destruction on several occasions by passing armies. Muslim emperor Aurangzeb has moved in 1666 to have a carved stone railing installed in the temple by Prince Dara Shukoh removed. Now, four years later, he has the temple destroyed.

A short time later, he has the Kashi Vishwanath Temple in Varanasi, Uttar Pradesh, one of the 12 Jyotirlingas, and hence one of the holiest of Shiva temples, destroyed. He uses the materials to build the Gyanvapi Mosque (aka the Alamgiri Mosque) on the old site.

1671

North America: United States
Christianity

Samuel and Tacy Hubbard, both members of the First Baptist Church of Newport, Rhode island, withdraw and join with Stephen Mumford, a Seventh Day Baptist from England, and four additional brothers and sisters, and begin meeting together for worship on Saturday. They describe themselves as Sabbatarian Baptists. They constitute the first Seventh Day Baptist church in North America, though other congregations will soon emerge around New England.

1671

Central America and the Caribbean: Jamaica
Christianity

Quaker founder George Fox visits Jamaica and initiates the presence of the Society of Friends on the island. He travels around holding meetings and visits on two occasions with the governor.

1671

Central America and the Caribbean: Panama
Christianity

Pirate Henry Morgan attacks and destroys Panama Viejo, the capital of Panama. A new city is begun on a site some five miles away. It arises inside a high wall designed to protect residents from any future attacks. Roman Catholic believers erect several churches including the new Metropolitan Cathedral of Our Lady of the Assumption. A distinctive golden altar, which had been saved from Morgan's pirates by being buried in mud during the siege, will be dug up and become the central feature of the Church of St. Joseph.

1671

Europe: Spain
Christianity

Much of the monastery of the Escorial, residence of the King of Spain near Madrid, burns. The fire, which continues unabated for two weeks, destroys the monastery's collection of artworks, books, and manuscripts.

Pope Clement X canonizes King Ferdinand III, the 13th-century Spanish monarch who played a significant role in the Christian reconquest of the Iberian Peninsula from Islam.

1671

Southwest Asia and North Africa: Syria
Christianity

Sergius Risi, the Roman Catholic archbishop of Damascus, oversees the first publication of the Bible in Arabic. It is printed in Rome. Though the Bible had existed in Arabic for many centuries, Risi has a new translation prepared. It will be the last translation until the 19th century.

1671–1672

Southwest Asia and North Africa: Asia Minor
Christianity

Dionysios IV (r. 1671–1673) takes office as the ecumenical patriarch. He will join fellow Orthodox bishops at the Synod of Jerusalem in condemning the *Confession of Cyril Lucaris* (1629). The controversial book and its author (a former ecumenical patriarch) had initiated an attempted reform of Orthodoxy from the standpoint of Protestantism, a move heavily opposed by Orthodox leaders. The synod specifically reaffirmed its opposition to the use of the *filioque* clause in the church's creed and affirmed their belief that the Holy Spirit proceeds from God the Father and not from both the Father and the Son.

Dionysios IV will serve five times as the patriarch, the last being 1693–1694.

The gathering of prominent Orthodox leaders for the Synod of Jerusalem becomes the occasion for the reconsecration of the Church of the Nativity in Bethlehem.

1671–1673

North America: United States
Christianity

George Fox visits Quaker families in the American colonies.

April 12, 1671

South America: Peru
Christianity

Pope Clement X canonizes Rose of Lima (Peru) as the first person from the Americas to be recognized as a saint. Unable to receive her father's permission to become a nun, she joined the Third Order of St. Dominic as a lay sister. August 30 was originally set as her feast day, but it was changed in 1969 to August 23.

1672

North America: Canada
Christianity

The members of the Sulpician Order in Montreal found a parish dedicated to the Holy Name of Mary and erect the parish church of Notre-Dame. The church would briefly serve as the first cathedral for Montreal following the erection of the Diocese of Montreal in the 1820s.

1672

Central America and the Caribbean: Virgin Islands
Christianity

The Third Anglo-Dutch War begins and the British take control of the Dutch settlement on Tortola, Virgin Islands. They maintain possession when the war ends, and with additional associated islands organize the British Virgin Islands.

1672

South Asia: India
Sikhism

The Satnamis, a Sikh religious group whose members were concentrated near Delhi, assumed control of Narnaul, where the Mughal emperor Akbar had established his mint. The revolt, led by a man named Bhirbhan, grew so severe, the emperor Aurangzeb personally intervened in suppressing it. Many Satnamis were killed.

1672

South Asia: India
Hinduism

In an attempt to prevent its destruction by Mughal emperor Aurangzeb, believers remove the image of Shrinathji, a form of the Hindu deity Krishna as a seven-year-old child, from Govardhan Hill near Mathura to Agra. Six months later it is moved again to Mewar. Here a temple was built to house it under the protection of the maharana Raj Singh of Mewar, Rajasthan.

1672

East and Southeast Asia: China
Buddhism

The Dalai Lama, who now rules Tibet, welcomes the formerly exiled 10th karmapa, Chöying Dorje, the head of the Karma Kagyu school of Tibetan Buddhism, at the Potala Palace in Lhasa and works out a reconciliation, thus ending 20 years of conflict between the Karma Kagyu school and the now dominant Gelugpa school headed by the Dalai Lama.

1672

Russia, Central Asia, and the Caucasus: Russia
Christianity
Joasaph II, the patriarch of Moscow and All Russia, dies. He is succeeded by the aged Pitirim of Krutitsy (r. 1672–1673), Metropolitan of Novgorod.

1673

North America: United States
Christianity
Jesuit priest Pere Jacques Marquette (1637–1675) joins fur trader Louis Joliet on an exploratory journey around the Great Lakes and down the Mississippi River. The trip highlights the rivalry between the interests of the king of France and the pope (whose interests in the Americas were most represented by the Jesuits).

1673

South Asia: India
Islam
The Badshahi Mosque in Lahore (Pakistan), commissioned by Mughal emperor Aurangzeb in 1671, is completed. From 1673 until 1986, it was the largest mosque in the world, and today is still the fifth largest.

1673

East and Southeast Asia: China
Buddhism
Lobsang Yeshe, the fifth Panchen Lama of Tibet, begins his religious career by receiving his vows as a novice monk from the fifth Dalai Lama. Following the death of the fourth Panchen Lama in 1662, the Dalai Lama had instituted a search for his reincarnation. Once found, the child was installed at Tashilhunpo Monastery, the seat of the Panchen Lama.

1673

Europe: Denmark
Christianity
Thomas Kingo, pastor of a congregation of the Church of Denmark at Slangerup, publishes the first volume of his *Spiritual Song Choir* book (with Volume Two appearing in 1681) and emerges as the first of the great Danish hymn writers. His hymns remain popular in the Danish church to the present.

1673

Europe: England
Christianity
The harsh measures instituted over the previous decade against Nonconformists by the Church of England are somewhat mitigated by Charles II's Royal Declaration of Indulgence, which suspends the execution of penal laws against the Nonconformists and allows a few Nonconformist chapels to be constructed, staffed with pastors approved by the authorities.

1673

Europe: England
Christianity
Continuing fear of an emerging Catholic influence in the offices of the government lead the Parliament to pass the Test Act in 1673, which requires all civil and military officials to take a religious oath. Office holders must disavow the doctrine of transubstantiation (an essential Roman Catholic belief concerning the Eucharist) and subsequently receive the Eucharist in an Anglican setting. The person designated as heir to the British throne, James II, who had secretly converted to Roman Catholicism several years earlier, refuses to take the oath. He is forced to relinquish his office as lord high admiral, and his conversion becomes public.

With his conversion public, James, a widower, marries Mary of Modena, an Italian princess, in a Catholic ceremony. Even though the couple later go through an Anglican ceremony led by Nathaniel Crew, the bishop of Oxford, public sentiment begins to turn against James and his bride, the latter being considered an agent of the pope.

Badshahi Mosque in Lahore, Pakistan, built by the Mughal emperor Aurangzeb in the 16th century. It is one of the largest mosques in the world. (Naiyyer/Dreamstime.com)

1673

Europe: Italy
Christianity

Clement X beatifies the 19 Martyrs of Gorkum, who died in the Netherlands on July 8, 1572, at the hands of Protestants. The 19 include 11 Franciscan priests, 2 from other orders, 4 parish priests, and 2 laymen.

At the request of Charles II, the king of Spain, Clement X declares the Spanish Franciscan nun Mary of Agreda as Venerable and opens the discussion of her beatification. Mary had died in 1665. Two years after her death, her body had been exhumed and found to be incorrupt.

Her cause would become most controversial. A mystic and visionary, she had authored a six-volume book on the Blessed Virgin Mary based on revelations reportedly from the Virgin directly. The text of *The City of God* would advocate doctrines not yet confirmed by the church including the Immaculate Conception and the Assumption of Mary. Also, a faulty translation into French would cause the work to be placed on the Index of Forbidden Books for a brief period beginning in 1681. Ultimately, *The City of God*

would become a classic work enjoyed by devotees of the Virgin Mary, though Mary of Agreda's cause would not proceed to beatification and sainthood.

1673

Europe: Italy
Christianity

Clement X receives a delegation from Russia seeking his approbation over the Russian monarch in Moscow having assumed the title of czar (or caesar). The monarch is a Christian, but of the Eastern Orthodox faith rather than a Roman Catholic. The czar is also a rival of the Roman Catholic ruler of Poland. While treating the ambassadors graciously, the pope does not respond to their request.

1673

Russia, Central Asia, and the Caucasus: Russia
Christianity

Pitirim, the patriarch of Moscow and All Russia, dies. He is succeeded by Joachim (r. 1673–1690), Metropolitan of Novgorod.

1674

North America: Canada
Christianity
Pope Clement X transforms the Vicariate Apostolic of New France (Nouvelle-France) into the Diocese of Quebec. He names François de Laval de Montmorency as the first bishop.

1674

South Asia: India
Hinduism
Shivaji Bhosle (r. 1674–1680) is crowned as the sovereign (chhatrapati) of the independent Hindu-led Maratha kingdom. He designates Raigad, a hill fortress in Maharashtra, India, as its capital, though he later moves it to Poona (or Pune). Shivaji had led a resistance movement to free the Maratha people from the Adilshahi sultanate of Bijapur and the Mughal Empire and to establish *Hindavi Swarajya* ("self-rule of Hindu people").

A devout Hindu, he had a special devotion to the prominent Marathi saint and poet Ramdas (born Narayan Suryajipant Kulkarni Thosar). He gave Ramdas a fort, later called Sajjangad, and Ramdas responded with one of his most famous poems, *Shivastuti* ("Praise of King Shivaji"). While privileging Hinduism, he also followed a broad policy of religious toleration and opposed forced conversion.

Shivaji is considered a national hero in India, especially in Maharashtra.

1674

Europe: England
Christianity
Thomas Ken, an Anglican priest (and later bishop) teaching at Winchester College, publishes a book of private devotions for students, the *Manual of Prayers for the Use of the Scholars of Winchester College.* For the students he composes three hymns, important for their not being based on the Psalms, and famous as they were each followed by a four-line poem that became known as the "Doxology," one of the most ubiquitous songs in Protestant church liturgies:

> Praise God from whom all blessing flow;
> Praise Him, all creatures here below.

> Praise Him above, ye heavenly host;
> Praise Father, Son, and Holy Ghost. Amen.

1674

Russia, Central Asia, and the Caucasus: Russia
Christianity
The Cathedral Church of the Assumption, which had been heavily damaged in 1611 when the city fell to the Polish army, is demolished, and construction begins on a totally new building. It will take a century to complete as the architectural plans are flawed.

1675

South Asia: India
Sikhism
In Delhi, Mughal emperor Aurangzeb orders the execution of Sikh guru Tegh Bahadur (r. 1665–1675), the ninth guru of the Sikhs.

1675

North America: United States
Christianity
Louis Hennepin (1626–ca. 1701), a priest of the Augustinian Recollects (a order seen as aligned with the interests of the king of France), joined explorer Robert de La Salle in an exploration of the Great Lakes region (then known to him as western New France). Besides preparing the area for Roman Catholic expansion, hopefully apart from the Jesuits, Hennepin is remembered as the first European to see and describe Niagara Falls.

1675

North America: United States
Christianity
Franciscan friar Juan Larios accompanies Fernando del Bosque's expedition into southwest Texas, which will lead to the founding of four missions to serve the Coahuitecan people.

1675

North America: United States
Christianity

The Spanish authorities in New Mexico arrest 47 Native religious leaders from the northern Pueblos and charge them with "witchcraft." All are whipped and imprisoned, and three are executed. One commits suicide. The survivors are sentenced to be sold into slavery. Before the sale, 70 Pueblo warriors appear at the governor's office to seek the survivors' release, to which the governor agrees. Among the survivors is Popé, who will later lead a successful anti-Spanish revolt.

1675

Europe: England
Christianity
After six years of planning, construction begins on St. Paul's Cathedral in London. Its design draws on both the Pantheon and St. Peter's Basilica in Rome.

1675

Europe: Germany
Christianity
Pietist leader Philipp Jakob Spener (1635–1705), the chief pastor in the Lutheran Church at Frankfurt, publishes *Pia desideria* or *Earnest Desires for a Reform of the True Evangelical Church* in which he calls for reviving church life through a new emphasis on Bible study, devotion, and heartfelt preaching. The book will launch what is termed the Pietist movement.

1675

Europe: Netherlands
Judaism
Sephardic Jews in Amsterdam erect a new synagogue to replace the one they had formerly erected in 1639. Seating some 1,200 worshippers, it is at the time the largest synagogue in the world. Printer David de Castro Tartas celebrates the occasion by printing a volume of seven sermons preached at the new synagogue.

1675

Europe: Switzerland
Christianity
Johann Heinrich Heidegger of Zurich assumes the leadership of a loose association of Swiss Reformed clergy by drawing up a statement of belief in several doctrines that they believe were under attack within the larger Reformed Church. The finished document, termed the Helvetic Consensus, consisting of 25 statements, would be added to the Helvetic Confession, the Reformed confession of faith most in use in Switzerland. The consensus affirms the divine inspiration of the scriptures, the doctrines of election and predestination, and the total incapacity of man to believe in the Gospel by his own powers.

1676

South America: Brazil
Christianity
The Diocese of São Salvador da Bahia, the first erected in the Portuguese colony of Brazil, becomes the seat of a new archdiocese. Simultaneously, Pope Clement X elevates the Territorial Prelature of São Sebastião do Rio de Janeiro to become the Diocese of São Sebastião do Rio de Janeiro and erects a new diocese based in Recife.

1676

East and Southeast Asia: China
Buddhism
Rigzin Terdag Lingpa founds Mindroling (aka Minling Terchen Gyurmed Dorje), a monastic university of the Nyingmapa school of Tibetan Buddhism, in Central Tibet.

1676

Europe: Italy
Christianity
Pope Clement X dies and is succeeded by Pope Innocent XI (r. 1676–1689).

1676

Europe: Scotland
Christianity
Scottish Quaker Robert Barclay, who has emerged as the most learned of apologists for the fledgling Society of Friends, publishes his most significant work, *An Apology for the True Christian Divinity,* in Latin (an English translation appears two years later). He argues for the spectrum of Quaker principles, most notably the current revelations offered via the Inner Light.

1676

Russia, Central Asia, and the Caucasus: Russia
Christianity

Russian czar Alexei dies. He is succeeded by his 15-year-old son Feodor III (r. 1676–1682). Feodor has been well educated by his tutor Simeon Polotsky, a Slavonic monk, but suffers from a disabling condition that left him disfigured and partially paralyzed.

1676

Southwest Asia and North Africa: Yemen
Judaism, Islam

The imam of Yemen launches an effort to make the country a totally Islamic land. He expels all Jews and destroys their synagogues. The effort will continue through the rest of the decade. Jews were finally allowed to return to the homes they had abandoned around 1680.

1677

North America: United States
Christianity

The Roman Catholic mission of Santa Rosa de Nadadores is established north of Coahuila (Mexico).

1677

North America: United States
Judaism

The Jewish residents of Newport, Rhode Island, open a cemetery, a site later celebrated in a poem by Henry Wadsworth Longfellow.

1677

Europe: England
Christianity

Gilbert Sheldon, the archbishop of Canterbury, dies and is succeeded by William Sancroft (r. 1677–1691), a churchman not yet serving as a bishop but who had the trust and support of King Charles II.

1677

Europe: England
Christianity

Amid a growing wave of anti-Catholicism in England, the future king James consents to his daughter Mary marrying William of Orange. William is a Protestant and a relatively close relative, being James's nephew, the son of his sister Mary. James had acquiesced to the marriage under pressure from his brother, King Charles.

1677

Europe: Germany, Austria
Judaism

Leopold, the Holy Roman emperor, expels the Jewish community from Vienna and celebrates by renaming the former Jewish section of the city Leopoldville. The celebration is blunted by the action of Frederick William I, the elector of Brandenburg, who issues an edict announcing his offer of special protection for 50 families of the expelled Jews.

1677

Europe: England
Christianity

Henry Compton, the recently elected Anglican bishop of London, has a church erected in London to serve the Greek Orthodox community. Unfortunately, the church will be closed five years later and another will not be opened until after the successful Greek Revolution in the 1820s.

1677

Europe: Ukraine
Christianity

Pope Innocent XI erects a new eparchy (diocese) to serve the Orthodox believers who had become Roman Catholics. The Ukrainians will retain their slightly revised Eastern rite and emerge as the Ruthenian Catholic Church.

1678

East and Southeast Asia: Vietnam
Christianity

The Vicariate Apostolic of Tonkin is divided and a new Vicariate Apostolic of Western Tonkin created.

1678

Europe: England
Christianity

John Bunyan completes and publishes the first edition of *The Pilgrim's Progress from This World to That Which Is to Come,* a Christian allegorical novel of the Christian life, representative of the Puritan Nonconformist perspective at a time when the British government was attempting to enforce conformity to the worship of the Church of England and its Book of Common Prayer upon the whole of the English population. Bunyan had conceived the book while in prison. Once published, it enjoys great success and becomes a standard work of British literature.

1678

Europe: France
Christianity

Richard Simon, a biblical scholar and Roman Catholic priest with the Oratory of Saint Philip Neri, publishes his monumental work on the Hebrew scriptures, translated into English as *A Critical History of the Old Testament.* Startling for his day, he claims that Moses could not have written most of the material traditionally ascribed to him. The volume would become a landmark in modern biblical criticism.

1678

Europe: Italy
Christianity

Sculptor Gian Lorenzo Bernini completes the tomb of his late patron, Pope Alexander VII, located at St. Peter's Basilica.

1679

Europe: France
Christianity

French Roman Catholic priest Jean-Baptiste de La Salle founds a school for the poor in Rheims, which evolves to become the foundation for a new religious order, the Institute of the Brothers of the Christian Schools, popularly referred to as the De La Salle Brothers (aka the Christian Brothers). His institute is sometimes confused in the English-speaking world with another group also called the Christian Brothers founded in Ireland in the 19th century.

1679

Europe: Scotland
Christianity

James Sharp, the archbishop of St. Andrews and primate of Scotland, who survived an assassination attempt in 1668, is killed by Presbyterian Covenanters who reject his authority over the Church of Scotland. He was succeeded by Alexander Burnet (r. 1679–1684), the former archbishop of Glasgow.

1679–1681

Europe: England
Christianity

Fearing the possibility of a Catholic king, the Earl of Shaftesbury, legislation is introduced into Parliament to exclude James, the heir apparent to the throne, from the line of succession. Fearing the possibility that it might pass, King Charles dissolves Parliament. New Parliaments are elected in 1680 and 1681, but Charles dissolves them also. The elections lead to the development of two political parties—the Whigs, who support James's exclusion, and the Tories, who oppose it. The debate forces James to withdraw from significant government involvement. Charles appoints him lord high commissioner of Scotland and James moves to Edinburgh.

ca. 1680

Southwest Asia and North Africa: Morocco
Islam

During the lengthy reign of Sultan Moulay Ismaïl Ibn Sharif (r. 1672–1727) at Marrakesh, Morocco, with Sufism experiencing a heightened popularity, the sultan requests Sufi writer Abu Ali al-Hassan al-Yusi (1631–1691) to begin the annual celebration of the festival of the seven (Sufi) saints, a practice that continues to the present.

1680

Sub-Saharan Africa: Benin
Christianity

Portuguese Catholics establish a chapel at Ouidah, along the coast of Dahomey (now Benin). They will expand the work along the coast but not move into the interior until the 19th century.

1680

North America: United States
Christianity, Traditional Religions

Popé, a Tewa Native religious leader from Ohkay Owingeh (aka the San Juan Pueblo), leads the Native population around Santa Fe, New Mexico, in a massive revolt against Spanish rule. He has emerged as the leader of a revitalization movement calling for the overthrow of the Spanish and a return to pre-Spanish peace and prosperity.

Spanish settlers flee to the El Paso area. Along with the Spanish come friendly Natives who settle along the Rio Grande. Here, the Franciscans begin the missions of Corpus Christi de la Isleta (Ysleta), Nuestra Señora de la Limpia Concepción del Socorro, and San Antonio de Senecú.

The 1680 revolt has a significant role in given Native peoples access to horses for the first time. From this time, horses spread among the Plains Indians

Statue of Popé, Tewa spiritual leader and organizer of the Pueblo Revolt in New Mexico in 1680. No image or written description of Popé is known to exist. This depiction, by New Mexican artist Cliff Fragua, shows him holding the knotted cord which was used to determine when the revolt would begin. (Architect of the Capitol)

population and change their life, including their interaction with Europeans, in a variety of dramatic ways.

1680

South America: Uruguay
Christianity
The Portuguese found Colónia do Sacramento, Uruguay.

1680

South Asia: India
Hinduism
Sambhaji Bhosale (r. 1680–1689) succeeds his deceased father Shivaji as the new ruler of the Maratha Empire, centered on Maharashtra.

1680

East and Southeast Asia: China
Christianity
Pope Innocent IX names Bishop François Pallu as the first vicar apostolic of the Vicariate Apostolic of Fo-Kien (later the Diocese of Fuchow), China.

1680

East and Southeast Asia: Japan
Buddhism
Shogun Tokugawa Ietsuna dies. He is succeeded by his younger brother, Tokugawa Tsunayoshi (r. 1680–1709). Among the first actions of the new shogun is the founding of Gokoku-ji, a Shingon Buddhist temple in Tokyo, which he dedicates to his mother. (It will become one of the few buildings of historical note to survive the American air raids during World War II.)

1680

East and Southeast Asia: Japan
Buddhism
Eku, a scholar of the Higashi Hongwangi Pure Land Buddhist sect, begins work at Saifuku-ji, a temple in Kyoto, and begins his career lecturing on Pure Land Buddhism. He would make numerous contributions to the study of Pure Land practice, ethics, belief, and history.

1680

Europe: Ireland
Christianity

After almost a century of work, the Irish Gaelic translation of the Old Testament is finally published. It had been initially completed by William Bedell, the bishop of Kilmore, and then further revised by Narcissus Marsh, the archbishop of Dublin.

1680

Europe: Germany
Christianity

German Reformed pastor Joachim Neander dies. Only 30 years old, he has emerged as the first great German Reformed hymn writer, especially remembered for his "Praise to the Lord, the Almighty, the King of Creation." He is one of several notable hymn writers to be inspired by the Pietist movement.

1681

Sub-Saharan Africa: South Africa
Islam

Deported Islamic religious leaders arrive in South Africa from Batavia, later to become the Cape Malay community.

1681

North America: United States
Christianity

King Charles II grants William Penn, a member of the Society of Friends (Quakers), a charter for a colony in British America, which will later become the state of Pennsylvania. As a haven for the persecuted Quakers, it will become a bastion of religious toleration and freedom, and its founder will actually recruit members of various sectarian groups in Germany to populate the colony.

1681

North America: United States
Christianity

Quakers in Easton, Talbot County, Maryland, construct the Third Haven Meeting House, which survives as the oldest meetinghouse of the Religious Society of Friends in North America.

1681

East and Southeast Asia: Japan
Buddhism

Tetsugen, an Obaku Zen priest, completes work on the new printed edition of the Buddhist canon. It is the first complete woodcut edition of the Chinese Buddhist sutras in Japan and appears in some 6,771 volumes. The work has been delayed by Tetsugen's involvement in famine relief. In 1682, Tetsugen dies while again working to overcome a famine that had hit the countryside.

1681

Europe: France
Christianity

An army of King Louis XIV of France occupies Strasbourg, a longtime center of Protestantism, and returns the city to Roman Catholic control. The old cathedral, formerly a Protestant church, becomes the site of a Catholic mass, which the king attends.

1681

Europe: Ireland
Christianity

Oliver Plunkett, the Roman Catholic archbishop of Armagh and primate of All Ireland, is executed for treason. He is the last victim of a wave of anti-Catholic hysteria that has swept through England for several years, generated initially by a 1677 pamphlet (issued anonymously) that claimed knowledge of a plot initiated by the pope, who had plans to change the British government. This Popish Plot found resonance in England where a high level of anti-Catholicism continued from the time of the Protestant Reformation. Plunkett will be remembered by Catholics as a martyr/saint.

1681

Russia, Central Asia, and the Caucasus: Russia
Christianity

Fifteen years after being exiled from the city, the former Russian patriarch Nikon is granted permission to return to Moscow. He heads for Moscow, but dies before reaching the city.

1682

North America: United States
Christianity

William Penn founds Philadelphia and designs a simple plan of square blocks and straight streets along the Delaware River. Among the first settlers will be a group of Welsh settlers who will several years later construct the Merion Friends Meeting House, the second oldest Friends meetinghouse in the United States (an earlier one having been built in Maryland) and the oldest church building in Pennsylvania.

1682

North America: United States
Christianity

Antonio de Otermín, the new governor of New Mexico, now headquartered in El Paso, Texas, founds the missions of Corpus Christi de la Ysleta (Ysleta del Sur) for the Tiguas, San Antonio de Senecú for the Piros and Tompiros, and Nuestra Señora de la Limpia Concepción del Socorro for the Piros, Tanos, and Jemez. Corpus Christi de la Ysleta becomes the first permanent European settlement in what is now Texas.

1682

East and Southeast Asia: China

The fifth Dalai Lama dies, but his death is kept a secret from most monks and the general population of Tibet while the construction of the Potala Palace is brought to completion.

1682

East and Southeast Asia: Japan
Confucianism

Shortly after assuming the throne, Shogun Tokugawa Tsunayoshi became a devotee of the neo-Confucianism identified with the Chinese scholar Zhu Xi. He initiates the annual reading of the *Analects* of Confucius to the nobles that gather at his court in Edo (Tokyo). He would also frequently lecture on Confucian ideas to the daimyo (regional lords), most of whom were followers of either Buddhism or Shinto.

1682

Russia, Central Asia, and the Caucasus: Russia
Christianity

Shortly before his death, Russian czar Feodor III (r. 1676–1682) signs the charter of the Slavic Greek Latin Academy, Russia's first liberal arts institution of higher learning. It will be formally opened several years later on the premises of the Zaikonospassky Monastery in Moscow. The academy is the product of the movement to Moscow of various religious and secular intellectuals following the ascent of Feodor to the throne.

1682

Europe: England
Western Esotericism

Temperance Lloyd, a senile woman from Bideford, is executed for practicing witchcraft, the last execution of someone on such charges in England. Following Lloyd's death, Lord Chief Justice Sir Francis North, already a critic of witchcraft trials, investigates the case and denounces it as deeply flawed. His criticism of the incident discourages further prosecutions.

1682

Europe: France
Christianity

King Louis XIV calls together an assembly of the French clergy, which adopts the four statements known as the Gallican Liberties. These statements represent a next step in what has been a long-standing conflict over the relationship of papal power and that of secular monarchs. The Gallic position emphasizes the limitations of papal power in the face of that of the local ruler. Innocent XI denounced the four articles and in effect blacklisted all the clerics who participated in the assembly, refusing in the future to confirm them in any episcopal office to which they were nominated.

Over the next centuries the relationship of the church in France to the papacy would be cast in terms of ultramontanism (favoring papal authority) and gallicanism (favoring the authority of the local ruler). The conflict often focused on church revenue and its flow from dioceses either into the national coffers or to Rome.

1682

Europe: France
Judaism

Louis XIV, who has benefited economically from allowing a Jewish community to develop in Marseilles, but otherwise has persistently banned Jews from his domains, asserts his Roman Catholic faith and expels the Jews from the city.

April 27, 1682

Russia, Central Asia, and the Caucasus: Russia
Christianity

Russian czar Fyodor III (r. 1676–1682) dies without leaving an heir. Forces supporting relatives of his two wives emerge, and after the patriarch of Moscow names Peter (r. 1682–1725), the son of Czarina Natalia Naryshkina, as the new czar, the supporters of Czarina Maria Miloslavskaya revolt, creating the Moscow Uprising. The rebels, with strong support from the Russian Old Believers, succeed in having Czarina Sophia's son Ivan (r. 1682–1696) named czar, and he, as Ivan V, and Peter reign together, though Ivan's influence was blocked by his poor health. Peter I, later referred to as Peter the Great, will become known for the massive reforms of Russian life and culture he will initiate.

Prince Ivan Andreyevich Khovansky, a Russian boyar and leader of the Moscow Uprising, forces the Russian Orthodox patriarch Joachim to stage a public debate with Nikita Pustosvyat, a leading spokesperson of the Old Believers. After Joachim refuted the Old Believer position, Pustosvyat was arrested and executed. In September, Khovansky, a supporter of the Old Believers, was arrested as a mutineer and the patron of heretics and executed by decapitation.

1683

North America: United States
Christianity

Thirteen German Mennonite families arrive in Pennsylvania; they purchase 43,000 acres of land and found Germantown.

1683

North America: United States
Christianity

Anglicans complete construction of Bruton Parish Church in eastern Virginia. Bruton Parish had been created in 1674 when Marston Parish in York County merged with Middletown Parish. It will later become part of the city of Williamsburg.

1683

North America: United States
Christianity

Czars of Russia, 1462–1796

Reign	Name
House of Rurik	
1462–1505	Ivan III (the Great)
1505–1533	Vasily III
1533–1584	Ivan IV (the Terrible)
1584–1598	Fyodor I
1598	Irina Godunovna
House of Godunov	
1598–1605	Boris Godunov
1605	Fyodor II
Usurpers	
1605–1606	Dimitri III
1606–1610	Vasily IV
1610–1613	*Interregnum*
House of Romanov	
1613–1645	Michael I
1645–1676	Alexis I
1676–1682	Fyodor III
1682–1696	Ivan V and Peter I (the Great)
1696–1725	Peter I (the Great)
1725–1727	Catherine I
1727–1730	Peter II
1730–1740	Anna Ivanovna
1740–1741	Ivan VI
1741–1762	Elizabeth Petrovna
1762	Peter III
1762–1796	Catherine II (the Great)

Francis Makemie arrives in the British colonies from Ireland and begins his career founding Presbyterian churches, which leads to the founding of the first Presbytery. Among his first actions is the founding of the Rehoboth Presbyterian Church in Maryland.

1683

North America: United States
Christianity

Members of the Society of Friends open the first Quaker meetinghouse in Philadelphia.

1683

Central America and the Caribbean: Martinique
Judaism

Louis XIV expels the Jews from his newly acquired colony of Martinique. This policy reflects his long-standing policy relative to Jews in French domains.

1683

East and Southeast Asia: China, Taiwan
Chinese Religions

Forces of the Qing Dynasty in China take control of Taiwan and drive the last remnants of the Ming from power. The next year, in recognition of the divine role of the deity Tianhou (Matsu) in the conquering of Taiwan, the Kangxi emperor names her Empress of Heaven. His recognition of her gives her followers a boost and leads to further expansion of her worship. Temples already exist in a number of locations across Fujien and Guangzhou, usually adjacent to bodies of water, and an initial temple at Joss House Bay on Hong Kong Island has opened.

The mansion of a Ming prince in Tainan, Taiwan, is appropriated as a temple to Tianhou. The Da Tianhou Gong serves as the official temple for the Qing government officials, who conduct twice monthly rituals on behalf of the emperor.

1683

Europe: Austria
Christianity

The Battle of Vienna. The forces of the Ottoman Empire lay siege to Vienna where the Holy Roman emperor Leopold lives and which is the gateway along the Danube to the rest of Europe. Joined by a Polish-Lithuanian army, the Holy Roman Empire is able to inflict a decisive defeat on the Ottomans. The battle would destabilize Eastern Europe, which had largely been under Ottoman control (with lands ruled by a Christian vassal). The victory would launch a century-long campaign against Ottoman Muslim control of central Europe.

Prior to the final battle, the Christian troops had been given over to the protection of the Blessed Virgin Mary. After the victory, the feast of the Holy Name of Mary, celebrated annually in thanksgiving for the victory, would be added to the liturgical calendar of the Roman Catholic Church, with Pope Innocent XI extending the feast to the entire church.

1683

Europe: England
Christianity

Anglicans, who had been fearful of a rising presence of Catholicism in the country, are surprised by revelations of a plot to assassinate King Charles and his brother James (who had converted to Catholicism) as part of a scheme to reestablish a republican government like the one that reigned during the years of the Puritan Commonwealth.

The Rye House Plot causes public sympathy to turn in favor of the king. Taking advantage of the situation, Charles names James (who had been excluded from the government) to the Privy Council. While some remained concerned that a Catholic could become the king, the possibility of excluding James from the line of succession to the throne had disappeared.

1683

Russia, Central Asia, and the Caucasus: Russia
Christianity

Construction begins on the Cathedral of St. Sophia in the relatively new city of Tobolsk, the capital of Russian Siberia.

September 12, 1683

Southwest Asia and North Africa: Asia Minor
Christianity, Islam

The Battle of Vienna. Ottoman vizier Kara Mustafa leads a large army through Hungary and lays siege to Vienna. Christian forces (Austrians and Poles) hand the forces of the Ottoman Empire a devastating defeat, which drives them from the city. The Ottomans retreat into Hungary, and then abandon it. Austrian forces reoccupy Hungary in 1686.

1684

North America: United States
Christianity

Joseph Gatchell of Marblehead, Massachusetts, was convicted in court for teaching Universalism.

1684

East and Southeast Asia: Japan
Shinto

Ikazuchi Gondayu, a ronin (a samurai who had no master), convinces the shogunate to lift the ban on sumo wrestling and allow him to hold an eight-day sumo event at the Hachiman temple in Tokyo. He argues that he has introduced innovations into sumo that will stop the violence, and that he intends to deepen the linkage between the wrestling and Shinto.

1684

Europe: Estonia
Christianity

A fire sweeps Toompea Hill in Tallinn, where the 13th-century St. Mary's Cathedral is located. It is the only building to survive, though greatly damaged. Its interior furnishings, all of wood, are destroyed. Restoration begins soon afterwards and Estonian sculptor and carver Christian Ackermann creates a new pulpit with figures of the apostles and an altarpiece for the renovated structure.

1684

Europe: Scotland
Christianity

Following the death of Alexander Burnet, Arthur Rose (r. 1684–1689), the archbishop of Glasgow, becomes the third and last archbishop of St. Andrews and primate of the Church of Scotland.

1685

North America: United States
Christianity

Robert Cavelier, Sieur de La Salle, establishes Fort St. Louis at Matagorda Bay (between present-day Houston and Corpus Christi). This action will later become the basis of French claims to Texas. Also with La Salle are seven priests (four Recollects and three Sulpicians), who initiate the work of the Roman Catholic Church in Texas.

1685

East and Southeast Asia: China
Buddhism

Dzogchen Pema Rigzin founds Dzogchen, a major monastic university of the Nyingmapa school of Tibetan Buddhism in Kham Province in southeastern Tibet (now in Sichuan Province, China).

1685

East and Southeast Asia: China
Christianity

Lou Wenzao, the first Chinese convert to become a Roman Catholic priest, becomes the first Chinese priest to be consecrated as a bishop. Pope Innocent XI had appointed him to the episcopal office in 1679.

1685

East and Southeast Asia: Japan
Christianity

The Japanese government reaffirms the ban against books that propagate Christianity.

1685

Europe: England
Christianity

Charles II, king of England, Ireland, and Scotland, dies and being without a legitimate heir, is succeeded by his brother who reigns as James II (r. 1685–1688) and as James VII in Scotland. Charles formally converts to Roman Catholicism on his deathbed. In spite of continuing anti-Catholicism throughout the country, James is initially welcomed into his new role. He does have to deal almost immediately with two armed rebellions, one in south England and one in Scotland, but both are quickly suppressed and their leaders executed.

1685

Europe: England
Christianity

The Scottish Parliament votes down a measure that would have favored the Roman Catholic Church, but King James, who had publicly declared his adherence to Catholicism, approves the measure by royal fiat and invites the Jesuits to establish work at Holyrood.

1685

Europe: France
Christianity

King Louis XIV revokes the Edict of Nantes and declares Protestantism illegal in France. Some 400,000 Protestants leave the country, primarily settling in England, Holland, Prussia, Switzerland, South Africa, and French territory in what would become the United States, where they would be absorbed into various Reformed and Presbyterian churches.

1685

Europe: France
Christianity

King Louis XIV of France issues the Edict of Fontainebleau, which replaces and has the effect of revoking the Edict of Nantes that had guaranteed religious toleration to the Protestant community of France. It was his intent to bring religious uniformity back to his country.

In the wake of the Edict of Fontainebleau, the residents of Montauban, which had been a stronghold of French Protestantism, agree to build a new Roman Catholic cathedral, which will be dedicated to Our Lady of the Assumption. Work begins a few years later, with the cornerstone laid in 1692. It would be finished and consecrated in 1739.

1685

Europe: Ireland
Christianity

The first edition of the Hebrew scriptures (the Christian Old Testament) is published in the Irish language. A New Testament had been printed in 1602, after which William Bedel, the bishop of Kilmore, began work on translating the Old Testament. Completed in mid-century, it is later revised by Narcissus Marsh, the archbishop of Dublin, and finally published.

1685

Europe: Latvia
Christianity

Lutheran minister Johann Ernst Glück initially translates the Bible into the Latvian language. It will be reprinted and/or used as a basis for revised editions of the Latvian Bible into the 20th century.

1685

Russia, Central Asia, and the Caucasus: Russia
Christianity

A period of persecution of Old Believers begins in Russia. Over the next years, a number of the most conservative leaders are arrested, tortured, and executed. Some Old Believers flee to Ukraine and Romania. In spite of persecution and discrimination, they maintain a significant presence with more than 20 percent of the population reporting as adherents.

1685–1687

Europe: England
Christianity

Once securely on the throne and enjoying a relatively heightened level of popularity, British king James II attempts to make a place for Catholicism throughout his realm. Initially, he enlarges the standing army over which he appoints Catholics as regimental commanders, allowing them to ignore laws demanding that they renounce their Catholic beliefs relative to the Eucharist and receive communion from an Anglican priest. He also dismisses Parliament and refuses to call it back into session.

In 1686, James publishes two short pieces of writing by the late King Charles II. Charles presents his reasons for accepting Catholicism and argues for its superiority over Anglicanism. James then challenges the reigning archbishop of Canterbury to respond. Archbishop William Sancroft refuses, claiming such a debate would show disrespect for the late ruler.

James also openly opposes laws in Scotland that have been designed to suppress any dissent from the Presbyterian Church of Scotland. James sends a letter to the Scottish Parliament in which he declares his wish for new penal laws against refractory Presbyterians. He expresses indignation that men had the impudence to advocate repeal of the penal laws against Protestants, and laments that there is no one to promote new laws.

Parliament responds to James by passing an act that stated, "Whoever should preach in a conventicle under a roof, or should attend, either as preacher or as a hearer, a conventicle in the open air, should be punished with death and confiscation of property."

James also lobbies the Scottish Privy Council to provide toleration for Catholics, while agreeing that dissenting Presbyterian Covenanters should be persecuted. The Privy Councillors agree to grant relief to Catholics only if similar relief would be provided for the Covenanters. Negotiations finally break down

The first king of Great Britain (England and Scotland) and Ireland, King James I founded the ill-fated Stuart royal dynasty in the early 17th century. (Library of Congress)

with James stating his belief that Protestantism is a false religion. He could not privilege a false religion.

James receives the papal nuncio Ferdinando d'Adda at his court, the first papal representative since the reign of Mary I in the previous century. As James continues to appoint Catholics to high positions in his kingdom, he loses additional support. Further losses come when he seeks agreement with his actions that bypass Parliament and dismisses any who oppose him.

His actions culminate in his issuing the Declaration of Indulgence, in which he abolishes the effect of the laws attempting to suppress Catholics and Protestant Dissenters. He subsequently orders the declaration to be read from the pulpits of all Anglican churches. Further Anglican opposition emerges as he reduces the Anglican monopoly on education by allowing Catholics to hold important positions in Christ Church and University College, two of the University of Oxford's most prestigious colleges.

1686

North America: United States
Christianity

British king James revokes the Charter of Massachusetts, which he replaces with the Dominion of New England, over which he names Edmund Andros as governor. Upon his arrival in Massachusetts, Andros immediately demands space at Boston's Old South Meeting House for Anglican worship. In 1688 he had a new church constructed, the first Anglican church in New England, known as King's Chapel.

1686

Europe: Estonia
Christianity

The New Testament is translated into the southern dialect of Estonian and published, with a copy in the northern dialect appearing in 1715.

1686

Europe: Netherlands
Christianity

French Protestant philosopher Pierre Bayle, a professor of philosophy and history at the École Illustre in Rotterdam, publishes the initial volumes of his *Philosophical Commentary,* in which he makes a plea for religious toleration. He notes his rejection of the use of the Bible to justify persecution of religious groups.

1687

Sub-Saharan Africa: South Africa
Christianity

A group of Huguenots (French Calvinist Protestants) arrive at the Cape of Good Hope from the Netherlands. They had originated in France, which they left to flee Catholic attempts to suppress them. As the international Dutch enterprise expanded, the Dutch East India Company sought skilled farmers and artisans to populate their settlement at the Cape while the Dutch Government saw the Cape as a place where the Huguenot refugees could permanently settle.

1687

North America: United States
Christianity

The Congregational Church at Salem Village (now Danvers, Massachusetts, not to be confused with present-day Salem) hires Samuel Parris as its minister.

1687

Central America and the Caribbean: Trinidad
Christianity

Capuchin monks open missionary work among the Native people of Trinidad.

1687

South America: Peru
Christianity

Jesuit priest Alonso Messia Bedoya develops the "Three Hours of Agony of Christ Devotion," built around the "Seven Last Words" of Christ on the cross, which had been introduced in Lima in 1660, by adding music to the liturgy and publishing a book about the new devotional practice.

1687

East and Southeast Asia: China
Buddhism

The Changkya Khutukhtu, a Gelugpa lama and spiritual head of the Gelugpa lineage of Tibetan Buddhism in Inner Mongolia, arrives in Beijing after being summoned by the Kangxi emperor. He reports on a mediation mission he successfully completed between two rival local Mongolian leaders. He greatly impressed the Buddhist leadership of the city.

1687

East and Southeast Asia: China
Islam

Muslims in Gansu Province build the Grand Xiguen Mosque in Lanzhou City.

1687

East and Southeast Asia: Japan
Shinto

Members of the Nabeshima clan erect Yutoku Inari Jionja, a Shinto shrine that in the shadow of Mount Sekiheki in rural Saga Prefecture becomes the clan's family shrine. The Nabeshima clan formed the traditional ruling elite of Saga. The head of the clan at the time the temple is built, Nabeshima Mitsushige, was the subject of a popular book holding him up as an exemplar of *bushido,* the way of the Samurai warrior.

1687

Europe: England
Christianity

King James II excuses Quakers from swearing oaths (which they refused to do on religious grounds) and from any fines resulting from such refusal. Members of the Society of Friends have emerged as advocates of pacifism, refuse to take oaths in legal settings, and will not take off their hat to acknowledge nobles or even the king. They adopt plain clothing, eschewing any unnecessary ornament or decoration.

1687

Europe: Hungary
Christianity, Islam

The Second Battle of Mohács. A coalition of forces from various Christian nations of Europe unites to defeat the army of Ottoman sultan Mehmed IV. Within a few years the Ottomans are completely pushed out of Hungary.

1687

Europe: Italy
Christianity

Pope Innocent XI adds his opinion to that of the Inquisition in condemning 68 propositions attributed to Miguel de Molinos. Molinos followed a position labeled Quietist, which emphasized intellectual stillness and interior passivity in the spiritual life while downplaying the value of works of love and kindness. The controversy around Molinos had larger implications, as he was a friend of Pope Innocent and had been called out by the Jesuits. Molinos would find favor among some Protestants, especially the Society of Friends and the Moravians.

1687

Europe: Scotland
Christianity

King James, who had assisted the Roman Catholic Church to gain a foothold in Scotland, issues a decree granting freedom of public worship to all Nonconformists, including the Roman Catholics, Presbyterians, and even the Quakers. The Church of Scotland is, at the time, Anglican in belief and polity.

1687

Europe: Spain
Christianity

Pope Innocent XI condemns the writings of Miguel de Molinos, a Spanish mystic who seemed in his teaching of Quietism to make the role of the church superfluous in human salvation.

1687

Southwest Asia and North Africa: Asia Minor
Islam

Ottoman sultan Mehmed IV is deposed in a palace coup and his brother Suleiman II (r. 1687–1691) is placed on the throne.

1687–1688

North America: United States
Christianity

On March 19 French explorer La Salle is killed by one of his own men near the site of present Navasota, Texas. The next year, Henri de Tonti searches for survivors of the expedition, but instead encounters a group of Caddo people and during their visit is taken to their temple where he experiences a brief ceremony before his interview with their chief (who was a woman).

1687–1688

Europe: England
Christianity

King James commands the reading of his Declaration of Liberty of Conscience, which grants a level of toleration to Roman Catholics, Presbyterians, and even the Quakers, in all congregations of the Church of England. Feeling this declaration to be an offense to the authority of the Anglican establishment, the archbishop of Canterbury and seven other English bishops refuse. Charging them with seditious libel, James has the bishops imprisoned in the Tower of London. When they are subsequently tried, however, they are acquitted, an action that severely undermines James's authority and ability to rule.

He issues a statement to uphold Anglican rights and privileges, but it is too little, too late. William, Prince of Orange, lands at the head of an army in Devon and forces James to flee to France.

1688

Sub-Saharan Africa: South Africa
Christianity

French Huguenot refugees (Calvinist Reformed Protestants) arrive in Cape Town, South Africa, after the revocation of the Edict of Nantes.

1688

North America: United States
Western Esotericism

In Boston, Goody Glover is arrested and tried for witchcraft and is subsequently tried, convicted and hung. Congregational minister Cotton Mather subsequently publishes his account of magic and witchcraft, *Memorable Providences, Relating to Witchcrafts and Possessions.*

1688

North America: United States
Christianity

Philadelphia Quakers begin their history of antislavery activities with an initial formal protest.

1688

East and Southeast Asia: China
Buddhism

A young boy, born in 1682 in northern India, is brought to Nankartse, near Lhasa, Tibet, and educated quietly as the possible successor to the late fifth Dalai Lama (d. 1682), whose death has been kept a secret from the general population.

1688

East and Southeast Asia: Japan
Buddhism

Shogun Tokugawa Tsunayoshi grants the petition of the Jodo Buddhist priest Daitsu for the practitioners of what is termed "mutually inclusive Nembutsu" to separate from the Jodo sect and establish themselves as a separate Pure Land Buddhist group. Daitsu, finding his fellow Jodo believers existing in a lax atmosphere, has led a revival of Nembutsu practice with the added belief that the repetition of the Nembutsu (the name of Amida Buddha) has benefit not just for the individual practitioner, but for the whole world.

1688

Europe: France
Christianity

The ongoing power struggle between Pope Innocent XI and King Louis XIV of France becomes visible after Innocent appoints Joseph Clement, a candidate favored by Holy Roman emperor Leopold I, as archbishop of Cologne rather than Cardinal William Egon of Fürstenberg, the bishop of Strasbourg, the candidate favored by King Louis XIV of France. Disapproving of Innocent's choice, Louis XIV takes control of the papal enclave at Avignon, imprisons the papal nuncio, and calls for a general council to mediate the situation. He hints at the possibility of the church in France breaking communion with Rome. Innocent remains undeterred by Louis's threats and eventually Louis backs off.

1688

Europe: Romania
Christianity

The brothers Radu and Şerban Greceanu complete and publish the first complete translation of the Bible into Romanian. It is known as the Biblia de la Bucureşti.

1688

Europe: Serbia
Christianity, Islam

The forces of Holy Roman emperor Leopold I follow up the battle of Mohacs by taking Belgrade from the Ottomans. The Ottoman Empire will now come under steady pressure from both the Holy Roman emperor based in Vienna and the Russians and will slowly but steadily be pushed back from all its European conquests of the 15th and 16th centuries.

1689

North America: United States
Christianity

An uprising in Maryland overthrows the colonial government and petitions the king to assume control. Maryland was subsequently named a royal province and in 1692 the Church of England was formally established.

1689

North America: United States
Christianity

Reacting to La Salle's arrival at Matagorda Bay, Mexican explorer Alonso de Leon, with the goal of establishing a Spanish presence in Texas, arrives at Fort St. Louis and finds it uninhabited. Fray Damian Martinez (or Marzanet) from the Franciscan Apostolic College of Santa Cruz at Querétaro (Mexico) accompanies him on this expedition.

1689

Central America and the Caribbean:
    St. Pierre and Miquelon
Christianity

French Catholics initiate work on the islands of St. Pierre and Miquelon in the Atlantic off the coast of Canada, but the work is abandoned in 1713 while the British and French pass the island back and forth for the next century.

1689

South Asia: India
Hinduism, Islam

Maratha ruler Sambhaji is captured by the Mughal forces during what had been ongoing hostilities throughout his time on the throne. He is presented to Mughal emperor Aurangzeb, who after giving thanks to Allah for his capture, questions him on charges of war crimes. Sambhaji responds with insults directed at the emperor, but then adds an insult to the Prophet Muhammad, which sealed his fate. He was sentenced to death for the slaughter of innocent people.

Sambhaji is succeeded by his younger brother Rajaram Bhonsle (r. 1689–1700).

1689

East and Southeast Asia: China
Christianity

Jesuit fathers Jean-François Gerbillon and Thomas Pereira serve as translators for the negotiations of the Treaty of Nerchinsk, the first treaty between Russia and China. The Chinese acquire land north of the Amur River. The authoritative version of the treaty was written in Latin, with translations made into Russian and Manchu (rather than Chinese).

1689

Europe: England
Christianity

Following the flight of King James II, the British Parliament declares the throne to be vacant, and then offers the crown to William of Orange, who ruled as William III (r. 1689–1702) and his wife Mary II (r. 1689–1694), who ruled with him as joint sovereign.

William encourages Parliament to pass the Act of Toleration (1689), which will guarantee religious toleration to Protestant dissenters, most notably Presbyterians, Congregationalists, and Baptists. The act excludes from its provisions Roman Catholics, non-Trinitarian Christians (including the Unitarians and some Baptists), and any who follow a faith other than a form of Christianity (most notably the Jews). The Act of Toleration has the effect of repealing the Conventicle Act (1664) and Five Mile Act (1665), both of which had been directed against Nonconformists.

1689

Europe: England
Christianity

Those British Baptists who adhered to a Calvinist theological perspective issue the Second London Baptist Confession. The statement, a modified form of the Congregationalists' Savoy Declaration (which in turn was developed from the Westminster Confession of Faith), places the Baptists in the same Puritan theological tradition as the English Presbyterians, but like the Congregationalists, calls for a congregational form of government. The Baptists disagree with the Congregationalists in their rejection of any ties to the government. At this time, the Church of England is thoroughly Anglican in theology and headed by bishops. The Presbyterians, Congregationalists, and Baptists form a contingent of Nonconforming dissenters. They are united by their basic theology, but deeply divided by issues of ecclesiology.

1689

Europe: England
Christianity

Philosopher John Locke publishes his *Letter Concerning Toleration,* in which he advocates the granting of full civil rights to people of all religious communities, including the various dissenting Protestant sects, the Roman Catholics, and even the Jews. A rise in anti-Catholicism in England appears to be the occasion for the *Letter.*

1689

Europe: Italy
Christianity

Innocent XI dies. He is later beatified, but has yet to be canonized (the final step in his being recognized as a saint). He is succeeded by Pope Alexander VIII (r. 1689–1691).

1689

Europe: Scotland
Christianity

The Scottish Parliament rejects Anglicanism and reverts to Presbyterianism. The offices of bishop and archbishop are discontinued and the then serving bishops removed from their positions. Arthur Rose, the archbishop of St. Andrews and former primate of the church, continues informally to exercise authority among the minority of ministers and parishes that favor Anglicanism.

1690

Europe: Scotland
Christianity

The Articles of Perth, forced upon the Presbyterian Church of Scotland by King James I in 1618 as part of an effort to move the church toward Anglicanism, are repealed by the passing of the Confession of Faith Ratification Act. The Church of Scotland again becomes Presbyterian in organization.

Even as Presbyterianism was restored to the church in Scotland, a dissenting group that adhered to a strict literal reading of the Solemn League and Covenant, a 1643 agreement reached by Scottish Presbyterians, refused to accept the new status of the Church of Scotland. They formed the Reformed Presbytery and continued as an independent fellowship, popularly known as "the Covenanters."

ca. 1690

North America: United States
Christianity

German Pietist Conrad Beissel immigrates to America and joins the German Baptist Brethren.

1690

North America: United States
Christianity

Alonso de Leon returns to Fort St. Louis accompanied by Father Damian and four additional Franciscans who establish the mission of San Francisco de los Tejas in eastern Texas among the Tejas Indians on the Trinity River.

1690

North America: United States
Christianity

Franciscan missionaries travel along El Camino Real into the Piney Woods, just west of the Neches River in Texas, where they found San Francisco de los Tejas on San Pedro Creek east of present-day Augusta and a few miles west of Mission Tejas State Park, which is near Weches in Houston County. Fray Francisco Casana de Jesus Maria establishes the Santisimo Nombre de Maria on the Neches River.

1690

East and Southeast Asia: China
Christianity

Pope Alexander VIII elevates the Roman Catholic Vicariate Apostolic of Nanking (or Nanjing) to become the Diocese of Nanking, with Bishop Gregor Lo(u) Wen-tsao, the vicar apostolic, named as the first bishop of Nanking. At the same time, the Vicariate Apostolic of Peking is carved out of territory previously assigned to the Diocese of Macau.

1690

Russia, Central Asia, and the Caucasus: Russia
Christianity

Shortly before his death, Joachim, the patriarch of Moscow, calls upon the czar (and his successors in office) to not subvert the Orthodox faith by allowing foreigners with whom the czar develops relationships to come into the country and preach their heresies (among which he numbers the Roman Catholics, Lutherans, and Reformed Protestants). He is especially concerned with the "godless" Tatars, who should be avoided at all costs. These remarks, offered as a testament of his faith, are put forth in the midst of the westernizing reforms being made by Czar Peter the Great.

Following the death of Joachim, the patriarch of Moscow, Adrian (r. 1690–1700), the metropolitan of Kazan and Sviyazhsk, is chosen to succeed him. A traditionalist like his predecessor, he would also oppose many of the reforms introduced by Peter the Great and notably rebuked the monarch's decree making the shaving of beards mandatory.

1691

North America: United States
Christianity

Reacting to the French presence in Texas, Domingo de Teran, the new governor of the Province of Coahuila (Mexico), heads for Texas. He is accompanied by nine Franciscan fathers—Francisco Hidalgo, Nicolas Riccio, Miguel Estelles, Pedro Fortuny, Pedro Garcia, Ildefonso Monge, José Saldona, Antonio Miranda, and Juan de Garayuschea. These priests explore the possibility of establishing missions along the Red River, the Neches, and the Guadalupe for the Native population, but plans are abandoned when the French threat is seen as far less than expected.

1691

North America: United States
Christianity

A group of Spanish explorers and Roman Catholic missionary priests arrive at a Native settlement (inhabited by the Sun Otter people of the Lipan Apaches) along a river in south central Texas. It is June 13, the feast day of St. Anthony of Padua, and thus they name the site and the river San Antonio.

1691

South Asia: India
Islam

Sultan Bahu (ca. 1628–1691), a Sufi Muslim poet, writer, and saint, dies. He had founded the Sarwari Qadiri Sufi order in India. Following his death, a large mausoleum/shrine is built over his grave and remains as a popular pilgrimage site. He was a strong supporter of the Sufi Muslim Mughal emperor Aurangzeb (1658–1707).

1691

East and Southeast Asia: Japan
Shinto

Kokei, a Shinto priest, leads in the rebuilding of the Tamukeyama Hachiman Shrine in Nara, which had burned to the ground in 1691. It functioned as a guardian shrine of Todaiji Temple, which houses the giant Buddha statue. Tamukeyama Hachiman was the first Hachiman branch shrine and had initiated Hachiman's integration into Buddhist lore.

1691

East and Southeast Asia: Japan
Buddhism

Adherents of Obaku Zen Buddhism among the Mori clan in Hagi, Yamaguchi Prefecture, build Tokoji Temple. The most recently introduced form of Buddhism, the temple still reflects its Chinese heritage. The Mori clan leadership had also recently renovated the nearby older Daishoin Temple, and the Mori daimyos (feudal lords) would alternate their burials between the two. The third, fifth, seventh, ninth, and 11th lords (and their consorts) are buried at Tokoji, and the fourth, sixth, eighth, 10th, and 12th daimyos are buried at Daishoin. The Mori clan will later play a central role in overthrowing shogunate rule of Japan in the 19th century.

1691

Europe: England
Christianity

Benjamin Keach, pastor of the Particular Baptist Church in Southwark (London), writes *The Breach Repaired in God's Worship; or Singing of Psalms, Hymns & Spiritual Songs Proved to Be a Holy Ordinance of Jesus Christ,* which opens a debate among the Baptists over the practice of hymn singing, which he has introduced to the congregation he pastors. That same year he also publishes *Spiritual Melody,* a collection of some 300 original hymns. By the end of the century, most Particular Baptists have accepted hymn singing.

1691

Europe: England
Christianity

Representatives of the Presbyterians and Congregationalists, rivals within the Puritan movement, seek to acknowledge their common Reformed theological unity and sign a brief statement, the "Heads of Agreement," on several points of ecclesiology, the main issue that divides them, which lessens the tensions between the two churches.

1691

Europe: England
Christianity

William Sancroft, the archbishop of Canterbury, retires from office two years prior to his death. He is succeeded by John Tillotson (r. 1691–1694), who had served as dean of Canterbury during Sancroft's episcopacy. Tillotson is known as a capable orator and identified as anti-Catholic.

Thomas Ken, the bishop of Bath and Wells, is deposed from office for refusing to swear an oath of allegiance to the new king, William. He had previously sworn an oath to King James II and felt as James was still alive (having been deposed in 1688), he could not in good conscience switch allegiance. He thus takes his place among the nonjurors (or nonswearers).

1691

Europe: France
Christianity

During the Nine Years' War between France and the Holy Roman Empire, General Nicolas Catinat leads French forces in the capture of the city of Nice in southeastern France. In the process of accomplishing his goal, the cathedral church of the city was severely damaged. Rather than rebuilding, the cathedral was demolished in 1706.

1691

Europe: Germany
Christianity
Philipp Jakob Spener, founder of the Pietist movement, becomes the rector of St. Nicholas Church in Berlin, which gives him access to the Brandenburg court and new prominence in national life. It also multiplied his critics who resisted his emphasis on personal religious life rather than the defense of Lutheran doctrinal purity.

1691

Europe: Hungary
Christianity
Arsenije III Čarnojević (r. 1691–1706), the archbishop of Peć of the Serbian Orthodox Church, who had led many Serbs to leave the Muslim-controlled territory of the Ottoman Empire into that controlled by the Holy Roman Empire, becomes the metropolitan of Szentendre. Szentendre, a town near Budapest, would become the center of an autonomous Serbian Orthodox Church enclave in largely Roman Catholic Hungary.

1691

Europe: Italy
Christianity
Pope Alexander VIII dies and is succeeded by Pope Innocent XII (r. 1691–1700).

1691

Southwest Asia and North Africa: Asia Minor
Islam
Suleiman II dies and is succeeded by his brother Ahmed II (r. 1691–1695).

1692

North America: United States
Christianity

The Church of England forces the opening of King's Chapel in Puritan-dominated Boston, Massachusetts.

Massachusetts receives a new charter. It grants home rule and enfranchises all freeholders, that is, all who own land (not just males who are members of the church).

1692

North America: United States
Christianity
Quakers on Long Island construct the first meetinghouse of the Society of Friends in New York. At this site in 1716, the first public meeting to advocate the end of slavery in the British American colonies would be held.

1692

North America: United States
Western Esotericism
The witch trials in Salem are initiated when Thomas and Edward Putnam, Joseph Hutchinson, and Thomas Preston swear complaints against Tituba, a servant in the Rev. Parris's household, and two townswomen in Salem Village, Sarah Good and Sarah Osborne, which leads to the arrest of the three for suspicion of witchcraft. A young girl, Abigail Williams, then accuses Rebecca Nurse of witchcraft. As accusations and arrests mount, Massachusetts governor William Phips establishes a Court of Oyer and Terminer to investigate the witchcraft allegations. Bridget Bishop, the first to be tried, is found guilty and hung. As the trials proceed, Cotton Mather writes a letter to the court suggesting that it not use spectral evidence otherwise unconfirmed as the evidence to convict anyone accused of witchcraft. He is largely ignored.

The wife of Governor Phips becomes one of the accused, and he moves to stop further proceedings. Before the trials end, however, some 19 people have been convicted and executed. One who refuses to plead is pressed to death.

1692

North America: United States
Christianity
New Mexico governor Diego de Vargas leads an army of Spanish soldiers and pro-Spanish Pueblo warriors

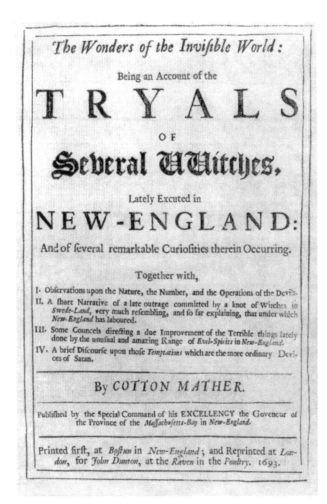

The Wonders of the Invisible World:

Being an Account of the

TRYALS

OF

Several Witches,

Lately Excuted in

NEW-ENGLAND:

And of several remarkable Curiosities therein Occurring.

Together with,

I. Observations upon the Nature, the Number, and the Operations of the Devils.

II. A short Narrative of a late outrage committed by a knot of Witches in *Swede-Land*, very much refembling, and fo far explaining, that under which *New-England* has laboured.

III. Some Councels directing a due Improvement of the Terrible things lately done by the unusual and amazing Range of *Evil-Spirits in New-England*.

IV. A brief Difcourfe upon thofe *Temptations* which are the more ordinary Devices of Satan.

By COTTON MATHER.

Publifhed by the Special Command of his EXCELLENCY the Governcur of the Province of the *Maffachufetts-Bay in New-England*.

Printed firft, at *Bofton* in *New-England*; and Reprinted at *London*, for *John Dunton*, at the *Raven* in the *Poultry*. 1693.

A 1693 publication by Puritan leader Cotton Mather describing the Salem Witch Trials. During the trials in Salem, Massachusetts, 150 people were tried for witchcraft and 20 were executed. (Library of Congress)

in a reconquest of the land taken by the Pueblo people in the revolt of 1680. Their leader, Popé, had died in 1688 and the alliance he had constructed fell apart. Most Natives accept the return of the Spanish, including the Roman Catholic missionary priests, over the next few years. The Hopi, based in neighboring Arizona, are the main group to retain their autonomy.

1692

North America: United States
Christianity
Jesuit missionary priest Eusebio Francisco Kino founds the mission San Xavier du Bac, one of a chain of Spanish missions in Arizona's Sonoran Desert. The mission serves the Tohono O'odham (aka the Papago), a group of Native American people who had settled in the desert lands of southeastern Arizona and northwest Mexico.

1692

East and Southeast Asia: China
Christianity
Jesuit priest Thomas Pereira, who has ingratiated himself with the Kangxi emperor, requests tolerance for Christianity throughout the land. The emperor responds to the request and issues the Edict of Toleration, which recognizes Roman Catholicism, forbids attacks on their local churches, and legalizes the following of Christianity by his subjects.

The Chinese feel indebted to the Jesuits. Kangxi was grateful to the Jesuits for their contributions to improving Chinese military prowess with innovations they had provided in gun manufacturing and artillery. At the same time they had a facility with many languages including Chinese, which they spoke well. Though foreigners, they dressed in a Chinese manner and moved around unobtrusively.

1692

Europe: Holy Roman Empire
Christianity
Leopold, the Holy Roman emperor, names a ninth elector to the electoral college that will choose his successor in the person of the duke of Hanover.

1693

North America: United States
Western Esotericism
Massachusetts governor Phips pardons the remaining people who have been accused of witchcraft at Salem Village.

1693

North America: United States
Christianity
Having secured a charter, Anglicans in eastern Virginia found William and Mary College at Williamsburg (also named for King William). The college is an Anglican school. Governors have to be members

of the Church of England, and professors have to suscribe to the Thirty-Nine Articles of Religion.

1693

North America: United States
Christianity

In Texas, the Roman Catholic mission of Santa Rosa de Nadadores was moved to a location further north to better serve the native people. The Franciscans abandon the missions San Francisco de los Tejas on San Pedro Creek and Santisimo Nombre de Maria on the Neches River.

1693

Central America and the Caribbean: Cuba
Christianity

Construction is initiated on La Catedral San Carlos de Borromeo (or the Cathedral of St. Charles Borromeo). It will be completed and ready for use in 1735.

1693

East and Southeast Asia: China
Buddhism

Six years after his original visit to Beijing, the Changkya Khutukhtu, the spiritual head of the Gelugpa lineage of Tibetan Buddhism in Inner Mongolia, returns to Beijing. The Kangxi emperor orders him to settle at Fayuan Temple (one of the oldest Buddhist temples in the city) and names him Jasag Lama, the administrative head of all the temples in Beijing. He will remain a favorite Buddhist leader and over the next decade will be given a variety of honorific titles and additional administrative posts.

1693

East and Southeast Asia: China
Islam

Muslims who have settled in Inner Mongolia erect the Grans Huhlot Mosque to serve what was becoming a significant minority community.

1693

Europe: Malta
Christianity

A large earthquake hits the island of Malta and destroys the cathedral at Mdina. Four years later construction begins on the new cathedral, which will be dedicated in remembrance of the apostle Paul's shipwreck on the island during his journey to Rome in the first century. The cathedral stands on the spot where, according to tradition, the local governor Publius met the shipwrecked apostle. The Christian New Testament (Acts 28:7–10) records Paul's curing of Publius's father of dysentery. Publius reputedly later converted to Christianity and became the first bishop of Malta.

1693

Europe: Switzerland
Christianity

A leader among the Swiss Brethren, Jakob Amman, and several associated church leaders issue an open letter to the Swiss Brethren asking clarification on three issues: shunning socially any who have been banned by the church; lying as a cause for excommunication; and the place of the good people who have assisted them but have not chosen to accept baptism. The letter will lead to a meeting to discuss these and other issues, during which Amman and his followers tend to take the more strict side of the matters under discussion. The discussions made visible disagreements within the body of believers and led to mutual pronouncements of excommunication. Those who sided with Amman would later be known as the Amish.

1694

North America: United States
Western Esotericism

Rosicrucians arrive in Germantown, Pennsylvania, and form the Chapter of Perfection.

1694

East and Southeast Asia: China
Buddhism

The future Yongzheng emperor, who has been named the Kangxi emperor's successor, builds a new palace in Beijing. A half century later it will be converted into a lamasery (temple for the worship of Tibetan Buddhists).

The former palace, which had been constructed earlier in the century for the use of the prince regent Dorgon, and which had been built over the site of a former Yuan Dynasty temple to the god of the North Pole, was rebuilt as the Maha Gela (or big black god) Temple.

1694

Europe: England
Christianity

John Tillotson, the archbishop of Canterbury, dies and is succeeded by Thomas Tenison (r. 1694–1715), formerly the bishop of Lincoln.

1694

Europe: France
Christianity

The Roman Catholic Church establishes the Diocese of Alès in southern France and work begins on a new cathedral dedicated to John the Baptist.

1694

Europe: Germany
Christianity

In the midst of battles with the more rationalistic defenders of Lutheran orthodoxy, from his base in Berlin, Pietist leader Philipp Jakob Spener influences Frederick III, elector of Brandenburg, to fund the University of Halle, which subsequently becomes the center of the central European Pietist movement.

Spener's younger colleague, August Hermann Francke, who was also having trouble from the opponents of Pietism, accepts the chair of Greek and Oriental languages in the new university, and later becomes its leading professor of theology, while remaining the pastor of the nearby church at Glaucha. His early text, *A Guide to the Reading and Study of the Holy Scriptures,* circulated throughout Germany, was translated into several languages, and helped spread Pietism to both Denmark, where it led to the Danish Halle Mission to India, and England, where it influenced Methodism.

1694

Europe: Italy
Christianity

The Royal Chapel is completed adjacent to the cathedral at Turin, Italy, as the permanent home of the Shroud of Turin, believed by many to be the burial shroud of Jesus of Nazareth.

1694

Europe: Norway
Christianity

The Roman Catholic cathedral in Oslo, Norway, again burns to the ground only 50 years after being rebuilt. The foundation stone for what would become the still-existing cathedral (now a Lutheran church) would be laid in 1694 and the church consecrated three years later.

1694

Southwest Asia and North Africa: Persia
Islam

Persian shah Suleiman I dies and is succeeded by his elder son, Sultan Husayn. Husayn, as a practicing Muslim, moves swiftly to deal with what he sees as a spectrum of moral problems that had emerged in his realm and initially empowers a Muslim cleric, Mohammed Baqer Majlesi, to assist in correcting them. Husayn's father had been a problem drinker, and he issues new prohibitions on alcohol and opium consumption and restricts the movement of women in public. He also issues a series of decrees aimed at suppressing the various Sufi orders active in the country. Finally, he orders the governors in the various districts to enforce sharia law.

ca. 1695

East and Southeast Asia: Japan
Buddhism

Shogun Tsunayoshi's religious sentiments lead him to issue a series of edicts, the *Edicts on Compassion for Living Things,* granting protection to animals. Having been born in what astrologically was the year of the dog, he concluded that he should offer special protection to canines. The residents of Edo are ordered to protect the dogs in the city, which includes many ownerless strays. The edicts create a problem as the number of animals increase and finally, the stray dogs are rounded up and housed outside the city.

1695

North America: United States
Western Esotericism
Quaker Thomas Maule's book, *Truth Held Forth and Maintained,* condemns the handling of the Salem witchcraft trials by the Puritan leaders and concludes, "It were better that one hundred Witches should live, than that one person be put to death for a witch, which is not a Witch." As a result, Maule was arrested and imprisoned for a year awaiting trial, only to be found not guilty.

1695

East and Southeast Asia: China
Buddhism
The Shechen Monastery, one of the primary monasteries of the Nyingmapa school of Tibetan Buddhism, is founded in Derge, Dêgê County, in Sichuan Province, China.

1695

Europe: England
Christianity
Philosopher John Locke publishes *The Reasonableness of Christianity,* in part a response to John Toland's Deistic separation of reason and faith. Locke argues that reason could achieve knowledge of the essential articles of the Christian faith and that understanding those tenets could lead reasonable men to assent to the Christian revelation. Though it is published as a defense of Christian faith, the unanswered aspects of the essay lead some Christian critics to accuse Locke of being a Deist himself.

1695

Europe: France
Christianity
Madame Guyon (aka Jeanne-Marie Bouvier de la Motte-Guyon), a French mystic and writer of devotional literature, is arrested and imprisoned for advocating heretical views in her book *A Short and Easy Method of Prayer.* Her opinions were associated with the condemned Quietism previously advocated by Spanish mystic Miguel de Molinos.

1695

Europe: Netherlands
Christianity
French Protestant philosopher Pierre Bayle, currently residing in the Netherlands, publishes the first two volumes of his *Historical and Critical Dictionary,* an encyclopedic work in which he attempts to compile a summary of human knowledge and in which he argues that much that was considered to be truth by society's influentials was simply popular opinion, and that society suffers from a high level of gullibility and stubbornness.

1695

Europe: Switzerland
Christianity
Controversy over the strictness of behavior leads to separation of the Amish from the Mennonites in Switzerland.

1695

Russia, Central Asia, and the Caucasus: Russia
Christianity
Russian co-czar Ivan dies, and Peter I comes fully into power as czar. Rising to the top in his vision for a greater Russia is a need for an ice-free port. He sets his vision on the Black Sea, which immediately sets him at odds with the Ottoman Empire and its vassal states that controlled the Crimea.

1695

Southwest Asia and North Africa: Asia Minor
Islam
Ottoman sultan Ahmed II dies and is succeeded by Mustafa II Ghazi (r. 1695–1703), a son of former sultan Mehmed IV (r. 1648–1687).

1695–1696

East and Southeast Asia: China, Mongolia
Buddhism
Following a meeting with Mongolian leaders, the Kangxi emperor agrees to build a monastery as a memento of the gathering and chooses Dolonor, Inner Mongolia, as the site. He orders the building of Dolonor

Monastery (later renamed Huizong Monastery), which will become one of the most heavily endowed of Mongolian Buddhist religious sites. Over the next years, the Dolonor Monastery will spawn more than a dozen additional monasteries in the region.

1696

North America: United States
Christianity, Western Esotericism
As part of the day of fasting held at Boston's South Church relative to the events surrounding the Salem witchcraft trials four year earlier, Rev. Samuel Willard reads an apology penned by Samuel Sewall, one of the judges, for his role in the deaths, and a number of the jurors also ask forgiveness.

1696

North America: United States
Christianity
The bishop of London appoints Thomas Bray commissary for the American colonies. He subsequently founds the Society for Promoting Christian Knowledge (1689) and the Society for the Propagation of the Gospel in Foreign Parts (1701).

1696

Central America and the Caribbean: Mexico
Christianity
Construction begins on what will become a new stone sanctuary at Guadalupe, the site of a 1531 apparition of the Blessed Virgin Mary. It will be the third church erected on the site.

1696

East and Southeast Asia: China
Christianity
Pope Innocent XII expands the Catholic hierarchical presence in China by erecting a set of vicariates apostolic, including ones in Kuiceu, Chekiang (Zhejiang), Houkouang (Changsha), Se-Ciuen (Chengdu), Yunnan, and Kiam-Si (Kiangsi, Jiangxi).

1696

Europe: England
Christianity

Nahum Tate, England's poet laureate, and Anglican cleric Nicholas Brady collaborate on the *New Version of the Psalms of David,* a metrical version of the Psalms designed as a hymnal. It would largely replace the widely used mid-16th-century psalter written by Thomas Sternhold and John Hopkins. In a supplemental volume published in 1700, *A Supplement to the New Version of the Psalms by Dr. Brady and Mr. Tate,* they include the now famous Christmas carol "While Shepherds Watched Their Flocks by Night."

1696

Europe: England
Christianity
Henry Compton, the bishop of London, commissions the Rev. Thomas Bray to travel to America and report on the condition of the church in the colony of Maryland.

1696

Europe: France
Christianity
French king Louis XIV nominates Francois Fénelon, a Sulpician priest who is the tutor of his son and heir, to be the new archbishop of Cambrai.

1696

Russia, Central Asia, and the Caucasus: Russia
Christianity
Ivan V (r. 1682–1696), co-czar of Russia, dies and his half-brother Peter I (r. 1682–1725) becomes the sole ruler.

1696–1698

Europe: Ukraine
Christianity
Construction on the All Saints Church at the Kiev Lavra, one of the two main monastic complexes in Ukraine, is completed. The church is an outstanding example of Ukrainian baroque architecture.

July 19, 1696

Russia, Central Asia, and the Caucasus: Russia
Christianity

All Saints Church, at the Kiev Pechersk Lavra Orthodox Monastery in Kiev, Ukraine. (Dmitry Ometsinsky/Dreamstime.com)

Russian forces under the command of Peter I finally capture Azov, a fortress outpost of the Ottoman Empire located on the lower Don River just north of the Sea of Azov. Subsequently, Peter founds the city of Taganrog, the first Russian naval base. This action will set up several centuries of conflict between the Muslim Ottoman Empire and the Christian Russian nation.

1697

North America: United States
Christianity
Anglicans in New York found Trinity Church, which will become one of the most prominent congregations in the city.

1697

North America: United States
Christianity

Lutherans in Philadelphia begin construction of Gloria Dei (or the Old Swedes') Church. The congregation had been founded in 1677 (the Swedes then being strong in neighboring Delaware). Their building survives as the oldest church building in Pennsylvania (though there is an older Quaker meetinghouse in the city). The congregation will remain Swedish Lutheran until 1845 when it affiliates with the Episcopal Church.

1697

Central America and the Caribbean: Haiti
Christianity
In the Treaty of Ryswick, Spain officially cedes the western third of Hispaniola (now known as Haiti) to France.

1697

East and Southeast Asia: China
Buddhism
Fifteen years after the death of the fifth Dalai Lama, Tibetan leaders who had withheld the news of his death announce it to the general population of Tibet and inform the emperor of China. At the same time, they announce the previous discovery of the sixth Dalai Lama, a teenage boy who had been born in India and had been quietly residing for the past decade at Nankartse near Lhasa, Tibet. The country's regent then invites the Fifth Pachen Lama, the abbot of Tashilhunpo monastery, where he leads the ceremonies officially welcoming the youth, now given the name Tsangyang Gyatso, into his new office. Tsangyang Gyatso is subsequently enthroned as the sixth Dalai Lama in a ceremony attended by officials from the three major Gelugpa school monasteries—Sera, Gaden, and Drepung—and a variety of political notables from Tibet and neighboring China and Mongolia.

1697

Europe: France
Christianity
The just completed collegiate church of Saint-Solenne in the city of Blois (France) is designated the seat of a new diocese, and the church is elevated to the status of a cathedral. Seven years later French

king Louis XIV presented the new cathedral with an organ loft, at which time the cathedral was dedicated to Saint Louis (i.e., Louis IX, 1214–1270), the only French king to have been formally canonized by the Roman Catholic Church.

1697

Europe: Ireland
Christianity

The Irish Parliament passes the Banishment Act and sends all of the Irish bishops of the Roman Catholic Church into exile, believing such a measure will protect the (Anglican) Church of Ireland.

1697–1698

Russia, Central Asia, and the Caucasus: Russia
Christianity

Traveling incognito, Peter I of Russia makes a lengthy tour of Europe in hopes of organizing a Christian coalition against the Ottoman Empire. The Grand Embassy, as it was called, failed on its primary mission but the tour allowed Peter to become familiar with many Western European advances, which he subsequently attempted to introduce to his country.

1698

North America: United States
Christianity

Presbyterians in Philadelphia organize the first church of their denomination in the city and six years later construct their first church building.

1698

East and Southeast Asia: China
Christianity

The Jesuits in China, who had developed a close relationship with the Kangxi emperor, petition Pope Innocent XII to sanction Chinese converts continuing to pay respects to their ancestors, and for a mass (worship) to be said in Chinese rather than Latin. Ultimately these petitions are denied.

1698

Europe: England
Christianity

Prior to his departure to the British American colonies on a mission from the bishop of London, Thomas Bray meets with four close friends and associates who resolve to organize a society to facilitate the continuance of the many projects in which Bray was involved. Foremost in their discussion was the perceived growth of vice and immorality in the country, which they believed was caused by widespread ignorance of Christianity. They planned a countermeasure in the encouragement of education and the production and distribution of Christian literature. To that end, they form the the Society for Promoting Christian Knowledge (SPCK).

1698

Italy
Islam

Ludovico Marracci, an instructor at the Sapienza University of Rome, publishes a new Latin translation of the Qur'an, notable for its accuracy relative to the older one, which had been completed in the 12th century. The published work includes both the Arabic text and the Latin translation, and thus will serve as the starting point of translations into additional European languages for the foreseeable future.

1698

Europe: Malta
Christianity

Russian czar Peter I sends a delegation to Malta. The delegates visit with the Knights of Malta and discuss possible coordinated action against the Ottomans.

1698

Russia, Central Asia, and the Caucasus: Russia
Judaism

On a visit to Holland, Czar Peter I receives a petition from the mayor on behalf of the Jewish community, asking for the readmission of Jews to imperial Russia. Peter, claiming the time has not yet arrived, refuses.

1699

North America: United States
Christianity

Father Francisco Kino establishes Mission San Xavier del Bac a few miles south of what will become Tucson, Arizona.

1699

North America: United States
Christianity

Virginia leaders act on a plan to create a new capital for the state on land known as Middle Plantation. They lay out a village, which is named Williamsburg in honor of King William III of England. The new town includes the recently founded William and Mary College and the older Bruton Parish Church (Anglican).

1699

North America: United States
Christianity

Priests of the Sulpician Order establish a mission at Cohokia (East St. Louis), part of the French effort to secure their claims to the Mississippi River Valley.

1699

North America: United States
Christianity

At the request of the Bishop of London, Thomas Bray spends 10 weeks in Maryland surveying the state of the Church of England in the colony. He develops a deep concern for the neglected state of the church in the colonies. He has a special concern for the poor education of the clergy and the lack of instruction offered laypeople, including the children. As a result of his visit, he will found 39 free libraries in Maryland and an additional number of schools.

1699

East and Southeast Asia: China, Hong Kong
Chinese Religions

Residents of Tai O, an island off the coast of Lantau Island, construct a temple to Prince Marquis Yang Liang Chieh, originally an official of the Song Dynasty who was later deified.

1699

Europe: England
Christianity

Politician Joseph Addison publishes his collection of poems and hymns, *Devotional Poems*. Addison's hymns would become quite popular through the next century.

1699

Europe: France
Christianity

Pope Innocent XII formally condemns 23 propositions he determined to be unorthodox in the *Explication des Maximes des Saints* (*Maxims of the Saints*), a text written by François Fenelon, the bishop of Cambrai (France). The book was written in partial defense of Madame Guyon, then sitting in prison for writing a heretical text earlier in the decade. Following the publication of the papal ruling, Fenelon quickly makes a public abjuration of his book and complete submission to Rome, and is allowed to stay at his post. His work is translated and published in English and becomes popular in Protestant countries while completely forgotten in the French-speaking world.

French archbishop François Fenelon further angers King Louis XIV by publishing *Les aventures de Télémaque* (*The Adventures of Telemachus*), a novel set in ancient Greece in which he denounces war and excessive luxury, and advocates a more equitable society. He calls it a constitutional monarchy in which the ruler is assisted by a council of advisers.

1699

Europe: Germany
Christianity, Judaism

Johann Andreas Eisenmenger, a Christian and professor of Hebrew at Heidelberg University, writes *Judaism Unmasked*. It revives arguments that the Jews caused the Black Death and that the blood libel is true. The Jewish community moves quickly and petitions the Holy Roman emperor to prevent its publication, and initially succeeds. (It will finally appear in 1711.)

1699

Europe: Hungary
Christianity

The Treaty of Karlowitz. Following defeats suffered by the Ottoman Empire, the forces of the

Habsburg-led Holy Roman Empire finally gain control over almost all of the whole of Hungary (including the largely Serbian province of Vojvodina, which is home to a Serbian Orthodox Church community). In the Ottoman Empire's signing away its claims to Hungary, the treaty is usually seen as the beginning of the empire's long decline. Cistercian life begins anew in Hungary. Heinrichau Monastery in Selicia (Poland) comes into possession of the charter for the Abbey of Zirc (among the many monastic centers destroyed in the Ottoman overrunning of Hungary in 1526) and dispatches a group of monks to rebuild it.

1699

Russia, Central Asia, and the Caucasus: Russia
Christianity

Russian czar Peter I makes an important calendar change in his country. He discards the old Russian calendar based on a traditional date for the creation of the world and installs the Julian calendar, believed to have started with the traditional date of the birth of Jesus of Nazareth. The change has the immediate effect of changing the celebration of New Year's Day from September 1 to January 1.

March 30, 1699

South Asia: India
Sikhism

Sikh guru Govind Singh creates the Khalsa, a Sikh military order, and baptizes its members in the original Amrit Sanchar (initiation) ceremony. In the Amrit Sanchar the new member takes the surname Singh (lion) and adopts the "five Ks," five items that members will possess/wear at all times in the future—Kesh (uncut hair), Kanga (a comb), Kara (a bracelet), Kachera (underwear), and Kirpan (a sword). The Khalsa is born out of a century of tensions with the Muslim rulers of northern India that was punctuated with the martyrdom of two of the Sikh gurus. At a later date, the Khalsa will evolve into the collective body of all baptized Sikhs. Women initiated into the order take the surname Kaur.

Initial negative reaction to the formation of the Khalsa will cause a rift within the Sikh community among the vast majority of Sikhs who are not yet members.

1700–1799 CE

Introduction: 1700s

The late 17th century marked the end of Ottoman expansion, especially in Europe, where the Turks were turned back at Vienna (1683) as they tried to extend themselves into central Europe along the route provided by the Danube River. The 18th century would mark the beginning of the decline of Ottoman power as slowly Christian European forces began step by step to push the Turkish Muslims away from the gates of Vienna and out of Hungary. Budapest quickly returned to European Christian hands and through the century Belgrade would become the contested city and fortress after Austrian forces initially captured it in 1717. It would take more than two centuries to complete the process of returning the Balkans to European control, but decade by decade Christian rule would be reasserted in the lands east and north of Istanbul.

Meanwhile Europe proper, which had settled into its division between Catholic and Protestant rulers, with the Protestants divided between Lutherans in the far north (Germany and Scandinavia), the Reformed Church (Switzerland, the Netherlands, Scotland), and Anglicanism (England, Ireland), would see its national churches settle into their control of the land. Simultaneously, the large national churches would be challenged on the one hand by a wave of skepticism among intellectual leaders who had come to doubt traditional Christian affirmations, and on the other by new advocates of devotional formats that demanded the spiritual response of the churches' administrative leaders.

Building on what seemed like two centuries of more or less isolated voices who challenged some of the basic identifying beliefs of traditional Christianity—the Trinity, and with it the full deity of Jesus of Nazareth—a new set of voices, building on a new wave of interest in learning from observation of the natural order, sought to open social space for those who no longer believed in the church nor adhered to its teachings. While not ready to give voice to a full-blown atheism, the thinkers of what came to be called the Enlightenment differed from the earlier Unitarians, who seemed content to become a new sect of Christians. The new Deists united to challenge the basic building blocks of Christianity—a God who cared about and was active in the affairs of the human community and who could thus answer prayer and work miracles. Proposing an alternative to orthodoxy, the Deists offered a God who created the world and the laws that governed it (and hence a moral order), but who was basically unavailable for religious succor.

The challenge to the metaphysical underpinnings of the Christian West, the ideal of a society united around Christian theological assertions and managed by an integrated church-state authority, eventuated in a serious counterproposal, a secular society that separated religion and state. That new possibility would be initially realized in the United States but later gain popular support in Europe (beginning in France) and find some support from rulers eager to push aside any obstacles posed by the churches to their plans as king (or queen).

Even as Deism challenged traditional structures, the large churches faced more or less hostile charges of dead religiosity from new revitalization movements that attempted to recover a more vital, emotionally alive, and intense spirituality. In Germany, a new Pietist movement initiated in the previous century by Philipp Jakob Spener and carried into the next by August Hermann Francke spread across Europe, bringing new life to German Lutheran and Reformed churches while spawning a set of new Pietist churches. In England, the brothers John and Charles Wesley launched the Evangelical Awakening within the Anglican church that toward the end of the century emerged as the new Methodist church. In the British American colonies, the Wesleys' colleague evangelist George Whitefield led what became known as the First Great Awakening, which brought many of the socially and religiously detached colonists into the church community. Meanwhile, the Catholic countries would see the rise of numerous new religious orders, many offering new avenues of piety and devotion, mixed with care of the poor, ill, and/or neglected.

Even as new waves of piety and devotion swept through the Protestant world, a new vision of the world was being supplied by the developing exploration of the globe and the attempts of European nations to colonize the Americas, Africa, Asia, and the South Pacific. The colonization process, primarily an economic enterprise, also inspired a new Protestant world missionary movement, which joined the Roman Catholic missionary effort initiated in the 16th century. Protestant missions began with the Lutheran Pietist mission in India sponsored by the Danes and

Anglican responses to the church's spread among African Americans. It was followed by the Moravians and Methodists in the Americas and climaxed by the Baptists joining in as the century ended. In the next century, most European and then American Protestant groups would add their strength to the world missions enterprise.

The 18th century found imperial Russia on an upward trajectory most clearly symbolized in the lengthy reigns of Peter the Great (r. 1682–1725) and Catherine the Great (r. 1762–1796). As Russia had struggled to overthrown Mongol rule, the Russian Orthodox Church had emerged in strength, and both Peter and Catherine moved to bring it into the emerging country's overall structure and put it under their control. Peter built a new capital that showcased the church with magnificent cathedrals and parish churches. At the same time he moved to reorganize the church and assume control of the church's hierarchy, and Catherine followed by reorganizing church finances in ways that diverted substantial income to her coffers. All the while, the Orthodox Church remained strong and relatively wealthy, and its hegemony over the religious life of the nation was substantially unchallenged. At the same time, Muslims and Jews received new privileges, and Catherine granted them economic opportunities that they had traditionally been denied. Russia, unfortunately, remained home to intense anti-Semitism, a problem found in almost all of Europe, where it seemed somewhat randomly to flare up and to lead to actions against Jewish communities—from denial of rights to expulsions and purges to outright massacres.

Though facing a mounting attempt against its European territory by both Austria and Russia, the Ottoman Empire remained largely stable and strong. Its Indian counterpart, the Mughal Empire, now showed itself to be past its prime. It entered the century fighting with the rising new power, the Maratha kingdom, a Hindu regime that sought to regain control of the land from the Muslims who had shown themselves more often to be hostile to the Hinduism of the majority of their subjects. The Marathas scored a major victory in 1707 that signaled a significant change in the balance of power across the subcontinent. Though the Mughal Empire would last another 30 years, it was repeatedly defeated on the battlefield and steadily lost territory. By the end of the 1730s, the Marathas dominated northern and central India, and would remain in control until the arrival of the British in force in the early 19th century.

The 18th century would be the Qing century in China. The Qing Dynasty had erupted from Manchuria in the previous century and claimed the mandate of heaven, the consent of the people to the rightfulness of the current regime, by the beginning of the new century. Buddhism would remain the largest religion, though the persistence of Confucianism, Taoism, popular local religions, and even Christianity would prevent it from becoming the majority faith.

Christianity had found an opening in China in the previous century, but Roman Catholic leaders in faraway Europe exercised their control over the Chinese church by denying it the right of indigenization. The ruling on the "Chinese rites" controversy in 1704 left the Christian community vulnerable to being targeted as an unwanted agent of Western influence, and opened Christians to persecution for their faith.

In Japan, Buddhism had emerged as the dominant faith—one sponsored by the ruling shogunate, which privileged Rinzai Zen, but also favored the spectrum of Buddhist sects over the Shinto alternative backed by the imperial court. In Korea, Buddhism struggled to find a place in the national life after its leadership had been banished to the mountains by the Korean rulers, who sought to establish neo-Confucianism as the land's dominant teachings.

Over 200 years after Columbus revolutionized Europe's understanding of the world as a globe inhabited by lands few even imagined to exist prior to his bringing information back on their life and wealth, Europeans now navigated the world's seaways with relative freedom. While Europeans now left home in increasing numbers to establish new colonies on every continent, the main movement was across the Atlantic from Europe to the Americas, where indigenous peoples and their religions were being swept aside and new countries and new forms of Christianity were planted in their stead. The rise of Christianity in the Americas was possibly the most notable religious event of the 18th century, heralding as it did the even more massive spread of Christianity in the next century, when it would become the world's first global faith.

The movement across the Atlantic would also include the forced migration of hundreds of thousands of African peoples to all parts of the Americas. Their traditional religions would survive, though efforts to suppress them by Christian missionaries would be strong and persistent. Where they survived through the crucible of the slave culture, they would be transformed into new eclectic Americanized religions that now go under names such as Voudou, Santeria, and Umbanda.

The century would climax with the American and then the French Revolution, both products of the emerging challenge to traditional religious and political patterns that had dominated history for millennia. The two first revolutions would initiate a process that would continue in the 19th century with the throwing off of European control in most of the Americas even as colonialism spread to Africa and Asia. Religiously, the revolutions marked the coming era of new freedoms as people of no religious faith and adherents of new forms of old faiths demanded recognition and space to exist in what would be transformed into a radically pluralistic world.

ca. 1700

East and Southeast Asia: Japan
Shinto
Shogun Tokugawa Tsumayoshi orders major renovations and rebuilding of the ancient Katori Shrine, a seventh-century Shinto shrine located in Katori, Chiba Prefecture. It had regularly been rebuilt according to a prearranged schedule over the centuries of its existence, but the system was discontinued in the 16th century. At the time of the last rebuilding, a new gate was also added to the shrine. Katori is the head shrine of some 400 Katori shrines scattered throughout Japan, most located in the Kantō region, in and around Tokyo.

1700

North America: United States
Christianity, Traditional Religions
Eusebio Francisco Kino, who has been working among the Native people of Arizona, begins construction of the mission church of Saint Xavier del Bac, which combines Mexican and native American motifs. The church is dedicated to Jesuit missionary Francis Xavier. Shortly after completing the building, Kino turned over his work to the Franciscans. Toward the end of the century, Native artists would decorate the interior with many unique illustrations of traditional Roman Catholic themes.

The Tewa people, who have rejected the return of the Spanish to northern New Mexico, accept the invitation of the Hopi at Walpi Pueblo in Arizona to settle nearby. They establish the pueblo of Hano where they are able to maintain their traditional religious beliefs and practices.

1700

North America: United States
Christianity

The Roman Catholic mission of San Francisco Solano is established along the Rio Grande River.

1700

North America: United States
Western Esotericism

Robert Calef, a Baptist and a merchant in Boston, unable to get his book published in Massachusetts, has his *More Wonders of the Invisible World* printed in England. Highly critical of the recent witch trials in Salem Village, with particularly stinging remarks on the role of Congregational minister Cotton Mather, it provokes a new debate on the practice of witchcraft, indeed of its very existence.

1700

South Asia: India
Hinduism

Maratha ruler Rajaram dies. His minor son, Shivaji II, is too young to lead the nation. Rajaram's wife, Tarabai, assumes control and rules the empire as regent for her young son, Shivaji II.

1700

Europe: Austria
Christianity

Berthold Dietmayr (r. 1700–1739) begins his tenure as abbot of Melk Monastery, famous for the reform movement that began there early in the 15th century. He will devote his year to the renovation, expansion, and rebuilding of the monastic complex, which turns it into Austria's largest Baroque monastic establishment. Dominating the complex is the abbey church whose interior is decorated with frescoes by the prominent artist Johann Michael Rottmayr. Dietmayr also builds one of the most significant libraries of the era, noted for its collection of some 1,800 manuscripts and 750 pre-1500 first editions.

1700

Europe: Austria, Germany
Christianity

Leopold, the emperor of the Holy Roman Empire, now consisting of Austria, Hungary, and Bohemia, elevates the prestige of the elector of Brandenburg by naming him the king of Prussia. The action gains him temporary support but costs him in the long run by further weakening the authority of the empire.

1700

Europe: Germany
Christianity

Jacob Hamberger (r. 1700–1739) begins his lengthy tenure as the abbot of the ninth-century Niederaltaich Abbey of Bavaria during which he will lead a complete renovation of the Benedictine monastic complex in the new Baroque style. Featured among the new additions would be a frescoed ceiling and an elaborate high altar.

1700

Europe: Hungary, Romania
Christianity

The Romanian Orthodox bishop of Transylvania Atanasius leads a synod that formally agrees to come into full communion with the Roman Catholic Church. This act culminates a decade of missionary activity that followed Habsburg Holy Roman emperor Leopold I assuming control of Transylvania from the Ottoman Turks in 1689. Jesuits entered the area in 1693. The new Catholics will follow a slightly modified Eastern rite and become the nucleus of the Romanian Catholic Church.

1700

Europe: Italy
Christianity

Pope Innocent XII dies and is succeeded by Pope Clement XI (r. 1700–1721).

October 16, 1700

Russia, Central Asia, and the Caucasus: Russia
Christianity

Russian Orthodox Church archbishop Adrian (1627–1700), the patriarch of Moscow and All Russia, dies. The czar sees an opportunity to implement reforms and refuses to name an immediate replacement. The office remains vacant for the next 21 years, and then Czar Peter appoints Archbishop Stephen Yavorsky (1658–1722) as the custodian of the spiritualities of the patriarchal see.

1701

North America: United States
Christianity
The General Court of the Colony of Connecticut passes an act to create a new institution of higher learning to train ministers and the future leadership for Connecticut. The effort finds support among a group of 10 Congregationalist ministers who pool their personal libraries to create the school's library. The new Collegiate School opens in the home of Abraham Pierson, who served as rector, in Killingworth. The school evolves to become Yale College and then Yale University.

1701

North America: United States
Western Esotericism
Robert Calef's book, *More Wonders of the Invisible World,* with its rehashing of the case of the Salem witches from a highly skeptical position and its criticism of Congregational minister Cotton Mather, provokes an angry reaction. Mather issues a defensive response, *Some Few Remarks upon a Scandalous Book,* and his father, Increase Mather, leads a public burning of the book. The ensuing debate severely damages Mather's reputation, is a factor in his being denied the presidency of Harvard, and turns him into one of the more controversial figures in American history.

1701

South Asia: India
Hinduism
The Somnath Temple, a prominent Shiva temple located on the western coast of Gujarat, one of the 12 Jyotirlinga shrines and a favorite target of Muslims who have become a significant power in the region, is destroyed by Mughal emperor Aurangzeb. This time

it is not rebuilt, however, as Aurangzeb has a mosque erected on the site of the Somnath temple, using the stones from the temple, whose Hindu sculptural motifs remain visible.

1701

East and Southeast Asia: China
The sixth Dalai Lama renounces his office and spends the rest of his rather short life in secular pursuits, neglecting both his political and religious duties.

1701

Europe: England
Christianity
The Act of Settlement. Given the large number of Roman Catholics in the official line of succession to the British throne, the British Parliament decreed that succession would favor the descendants of the electress Sophia of Hanover (who was a granddaughter of King James I). To be eligible for the throne, the candidate must be a Protestant and not married to a Roman Catholic. Further, if not already a member, any new monarch shall immediately become a member of the Church of England. Originally effective for the throne of England and Ireland, its provisions were applied to Scotland in 1707 when it merged with England to form the Kingdom of Great Britain. In more recent years, the law passed to the British Commonwealth.

1701

Europe: England
Christianity
Having returned from his visit to Maryland and having found the Society for the Promotion of Christian Knowledge thriving, Anglican minister Thomas Bray takes the lead in founding the Society for the Propagation of the Gospel (SPG), a foreign missions sending agency.

1701

Europe: England
Christianity
Parliament passes the Act of Settlement, which bans Roman Catholics and even those married to a Catholic from ascending the British throne.

1701

Europe: England
Judaism

The London Jewish community erects a new synagogue. The Bevis Marks synagogue is located just beyond the city limits of London, it still being against the law for them to hold property within the city, and on a side street, as they were not allowed to erect a synagogue on a main street.

1701

Southwest Asia and North Africa: Egypt
Christianity

Over a century after it is attacked and the site abandoned, the monastery of St. Paul in the Egyptian desert is reinhabited by monks and begins its revival as a viable community.

1702

East and Southeast Asia: Japan
Buddhism

Forty-seven ronin, samurai warriors without a feudal lord, are buried at Sengaku-ji, a small Soto Zen temple in Tokyo. Their death by *seppuku,* ritual suicide, one of the most heralded stories in Japanese history, followed their successful revenge on Kira Hozukenosuke, the feudal lord of Edo Castle. He had been the cause of their former lord Asano Takuminokami being forced to kill himself.

1702

Europe: England
Christianity

King William III dies of pneumonia, which developed while recovering from following a fall from his horse. He is succeeded on the throne by Queen Anne (r. 1702–1714), the daughter of former King James II, who rules England, Ireland, and Scotland. Unlike her Roman Catholic father, Anne is a practicing Anglican.

During Anne's reign, the two main British political parties evolved with the Tories generally aligned religiously to the Church of England and the Whigs more aligned with dissenting Protestant groups (Presbyterians, Congregationalists, and Baptists). Anne's Anglicanism manifested in her tendency to appoint Tories to high offices.

1702

Europe: France
Christianity

The Camisards, French Protestants (Huguenots) who reside in the somewhat isolated Cevennes region in south-central France, lead an insurrection against the increasing attempts to suppress Protestantism in the years following the revocation of the Edict of Nantes (1685). The revolt begins in 1702, but will last more than a decade.

1702

Russia, Central Asia, and the Caucasus: Russia
Christianity

Filofey Leschynsky begins his tenure as Philotheus, the metropolitan of Tobolsk. He will become known

Portrait of Queen Anne by the studio of John Closterman, ca. 1702. Located in the National Portrait Gallery, London, England. The second daughter of James II and granddaughter of Charles I, Anne ruled Great Britain during a time of tremendous change. (Corbis)

as the apostle of Siberia and will found the theological school for the training of the archdiocese's priests.

1702–1703

Europe: England
Christianity

Queen Anne comes to power as the Tories are supporting the Occasional Conformity Bill, an attempt to close a loophole in the legislation establishing the Anglican Church. At the time, members of dissenting groups could become eligible for public office if they took communion from an Anglican priest at least once annually. The bill would come up in both 1702 and 1703, but the Whigs were able to keep it from passing. Queen Anne supports the law, but does so with a lack of energy as her husband, a Lutheran, retains his government position due to his annual conformity to the law.

After its initial defeat, the bill would be revived in 1703 following the Great Storm of 1703, the most severe natural disaster known to have ever struck southern England. The roofing was blown off Westminster Abbey, and major damage was reported from the cathedrals at Wells and Cardiff. Queen Anne referred to it as a judgment from God and called for a general fast. Tying the bill to the storm did not assist it, however, and it again failed to pass.

1703

North America: United States
Christianity

Jesuit priests establish a mission at the mouth of the Kaskaskia River (near present-day Chester, Illinois).

1703

East and Southeast Asia: Japan
Buddhism

Jodo Shinshu Buddhists in Kyoto build Higashi Honganji (or East Honganji), the headquarters temple of Higashi Hongwangi (or Otani) Buddhism, one of the largest Buddhist groups in Japan. The main hall, the Goeido, dedicated to Shinran, the founder of Jodo Shinshu Buddhism, is Kyoto's largest wooden structure. It rests adjacent to Amidado Hall, dedicated to the Amida Buddha.

1703

Europe: France
Christianity

After seven years' work, a new church for the Abbey of St. Sulpice in Cambrai, France, is completed during the archbishopric of François Fénelon (r. 1696–1715). It would survive the French Revolution and later be designated as the cathedral church for the diocese.

1703

Europe: France
Christianity

A former lawyer turned priest, Claude-François Poullart des Places, forms a new religious order designed to receive young men who felt called to the priesthood, but lacked the resources to obtain the necessary training. He opens the Seminary of the Holy Ghost in Paris, which will evolve into the Congregation of the Holy Spirit under the protection of the Immaculate Heart of Mary, whose members are usually called Spiritans or Holy Ghost Fathers. Initially focused on service to the poor, the Spiritans soon added a missionary emphasis to serve in the developing French colonies.

1703

Russia, Central Asia, and the Caucasus: Russia
Christianity

Russian czar Peter I founds the city of Saint Petersburg (named for the apostle Peter) on land taken in war from Sweden. It is designed to become his new capital.

1703

Southwest Asia and North Africa: Asia Minor
Islam

Ottoman sultan Mustafa II attempts to take back some of the power that been transferred to the grand vizier in the middle of the previous century. When the attempt fails, he is deposed and replaced with his brother Ahmed III (r. 1703–1736).

1704

South Asia: India
Sikhism

Sikh guru Gobind Singh issues a final edition of the Sikh Holy Book, the Adi Granth, and simultaneously announces that the line of succession of human gurus that had led the movement since its founding would come to an end. Henceforth, the Adi Granth would be considered the new guru and would find expression in the *Panth* (i.e., the collective will of the Sikh community).

1704

East and Southeast Asia: China
Christianity

Pope Clement XI rules against the Jesuit petition to allow Chinese converts to continue honoring their ancestors in a matter resonant with past practices following traditional Chinese religion. The ruling has the effect of supporting Franciscans and Dominicans, rivals of the Jesuits.

1704

Europe: Germany
Christianity

Based on a recommendation of the pope, the Ratgar Basilica, which serves as the abbey church of the prominent Fulda Monastery in Germany, is demolished, and construction begins on a new Baroque-style church modeled somewhat on St. Peter's Basilica in Rome.

1705

Central America and the Caribbean:
  Netherlands Antilles
Christianity

Jesuits are allowed access to the island of the Netherlands Antilles and permitted to reestablish Roman Catholic worship.

1705

South Asia: India
Christianity

Frederick IV (r. 1699–1730), the king of Denmark and Norway, launches the era of Protestant foreign missions. He is inspired by the founding of both the Society for Promoting Christian Knowledge and the Society for the Propagation of the Gospel in Foreign Parts in England and by his contact with the Pietists at the university at Halle in Germany. He initially funds two Halle students, Bartholomew Ziegenbalg

and Heinrich Plutschau, and commissions them to begin work at the Danish East India Company's headquarters at Tranquebar, Tamil Nadu. The work will in turn inspire the two British societies, which will offer some support to what became known as the Danish-Halle mission.

During his lengthy tenure, Ziegenbalg will compile a Tamil dictionary and grammar and translate the New Testament into Tamil, though he will die before finishing the Old Testament.

1705

Europe: Austria, Germany
Christianity

Leopold I (r. 1658–1705), the Holy Roman emperor, who also held the titles of King of Hungary and King of Bohemia, dies. He is succeeded by his son Joseph I (r. 1705–1711).

1705

Europe: Netherlands
Christianity

In their attempt to curb the growing influence of Jansenism in Holland, the Jesuits accuse Peter Codde, the archbishop of Utrecht, of espousing Jansen heresies. Though he is absolved of any heresy, Pope Innocent XII suspends and deposes Codde. The action has the effect of encouraging those who oppose papal power. The dioceses of Utrecht and Haarlem refuse to recognize the pope's appointment of Theodore de Cock as pro-vicar-apostolic to replace the deposed archbishop, and the Dutch government banishes de Cock from Holland.

1705

Russia, Central Asia, and the Caucasus: Russia
Christianity

Archimandrite Martinia, a monk of the Russian Orthodox church, arrives on the Kamchatka Peninsula (Siberia) to begin the work of Christianizing the Pagan population.

1705–1706

East and Southeast Asia: China
Buddhism

With the approval of the emperor of China and occasioned by the scandalous behavior of the then Dalai Lama, Lha-bzang, head of the Oirat Mongols, invades Tibet, deposes the Dalai Lama from his office, and sends him to China. The Dalai Lama dies before reaching Beijing, and Lha-bzang sees to the installation of Ngawang Yeshey Gyatso as the new Dalai Lama without the approval of Tibetan religious leaders.

1706

North America: United States
Christianity

Francis Makemie, joined by six other ministers, organizes the first presbytery of the Presbyterian Church in the British American colonies. The organizing meeting is held in the "Old Buttonwood" Church in Philadelphia.

1706

South Asia: India
Christianity

Bartholomew Ziegenbalg and Heinrich Plutschau, two young Lutheran Pietists from Halle University, arrive in the Danish colony at Tranquebar, Tamil Nadu, to launch the first Protestant mission in India. Ziegenbalg, who showed great facility at learning new languages, learns Portuguese and then Tamil (with the assistance of a local assistant named Eliapar). During his first two years in India, he compiles an annotated bibliography of 161 Tamil books he had read, the *Biblithece Malabarke.*

1706

East and Southeast Asia: China
Chinese Religions

The Kangxi emperor orders a major renovation and reconstruction of the White Cloud Temple in Beijing, originally built in 733.

1706

East and Southeast Asia: Japan
Shinto

Nezu Jinga, a Shinto shrine in Edo (Tokyo), is rebuilt in honor of future shogun Ienobu on orders of the present shogun Tsunayoshi. The shrine is dedicated to Susano-o no Mikoto, the brother of the goddess Amaterasu in Shinto mythology; Oyamakui, a descendent of Susano-o; and Homudawake no Mikoto (aka the legendary Japanese emperor Ojin).

1707

East and Southeast Asia: China
Christianity

Roman Catholic work in China is slowed by the issuance of a decree at Nanjing on January 25 by Papal Legate Maillard De Tournon (1668–1710) calling upon all Catholic priests to cease the use of the so-called Chinese rites, developed as a means of creating links between Christianity and the indigenous culture. As a result, Maillard De Tournon was arrested and banished to Macau. Missionary work suffered severely across the country.

1707

North America: United States
Christianity

Baptists in Pennsylvania form the Philadelphia Baptist Association, the first association of Baptist congregations in what becomes the United States.

1707

North America: United States
Christianity

Presbyterian minister Francis Makemie is arrested by New York's governor Lord Cornbury for preaching without a license. At his subsequent trial, he is acquitted of all charges in a case now considered a landmark on the road to religious liberty in America.

1707

North America: United States
Christianity

Anglicans make further inroads into the Congregational hold on New England by establishing St. Michael's Church in Marblehead, Massachusetts, whose original members include a number of sailors whose work had brought them to the area in recent years.

1707

South Asia: India
Islam, Hinduism

Mughal emperor Aurangzeb, now in his late 70s, dies. Two of his sons battle for the throne. Prince Muazzam wins, kill his brother Prince Azam Shah, and becomes the next Mughal emperor as Bahadur Shah I (r. 1707–1712). He moves to moderate the harsh policies of his father relative to non-Muslim religious life. He all but drops the effort to collect the *jizya* tax, frequently imposed on non-Muslims by Muslim rulers; he provides support for the revival of music (which his father had banned); and he ceases further destruction of Hindu temples.

Following the death of Mughal emperor Aurangzeb, Shahuji (r. 1707–1747), the son of the former Maratha ruler Sambhaji, is released from his captivity by the Mughals. He pushes aside the regent Tarabai and her son, Raja Shivaji, and takes his father's throne as the new Maratha ruler. He immediately sets about the rebuilding of the Maratha Empire, which had fallen into an extremely weakened condition. He will build it into the largest nation on the subcontinent.

1707

East and Southeast Asia: China
Buddhism

The sixth Dalai Lama accepts the invitation of the emperor of China for a visit, but dies while traveling to Beijing.

1707

East and Southeast Asia: Japan
Buddhism

Hotan, a Tendai priest, follows his study of Kegon Buddhism with the authorship of *Notes on the Kegon Five Teachings,* through which he announces his conversion to Kegon beliefs and intention to revitalize Kegon Buddhism in Japan. His books provoke several responses and launch his career as a polemicist and promoter of Kegon.

1707

Europe: England
Christianity

Isaac Watts, the pastor of Mark Lane Independent Chapel in London, initiates a new era of ecclesiastical music with his publication of *Hymns and Spiritual Songs,* which initiates his effort to persuade Calvinist Protestants to abandon the idea of including only metrical psalms in their worship. He especially seeks the emphasis of hymns that celebrate the life and work of Christ. His first book of hymns includes what will become his most popular Protestant hymns such as "When I Survey the Wondrous Cross" and "Alas! and Did My Savior Bleed."

While Lutherans had previously been singing hymns apart from the Psalms, Watts had the effect of opening the churches of the Calvinist tradition to modern hymnody. He would prepare the way for Charles Wesley, the hymnist of the Wesleyan movement, who emerges in the next generation.

1707

Europe: England, Scotland
Christianity

The Act of Union. The heretofore independent kingdoms of England and Scotland, which had shared the same monarch for several centuries, are united as a single sovereign state, the Kingdom of Great Britain.

1707

Europe: Spain
Christianity

In the midst of the War of the Spanish Succession, which had divided Spain, King Philip V issues the Nueva Planta decrees, which centralize Spanish rule and abolish the charters of the independently administered kingdoms within Spain. That same year Philip's troops capture the city of Lleida in Catalonia. As the cathedral, located on the highest point in the city, had assumed a prominent role in the city's defense, Philip orders its destruction. That order is never implemented; however, the cathedral is secularized and transformed into a military citadel. Later in the century, a new cathedral would be built at a different location.

1707

Russia, Central Asia, and the Caucasus: Russia
Christianity

Czar Peter I celebrates his victory over Sweden in the battle at Poltava by building the Alexander Nevsky Monastery in St. Petersburg. It is placed on the banks of the River Neva at the place identified as the site of Nevsky's defeat of the Swedes in 1240. The monastery includes a cathedral honoring Prince Nevsky, the seat of the metropolitan archbishop of St. Petersburg, and Peter has his relics transferred there.

February 20, 1707

South Asia: India
Islam

Mughal emperor Aurangzeb dies and, true to his life as a Muslim Sufi believer, is buried in the courtyard of the shrine of the Sufi saint Shaikh Burham-u'd-din Gharib (d. 1331), who was in turn a disciple of Chishti Sufi saint Nizamuddin Auliya (1238–1325) of Delhi. Aurangzeb is succeeded by his son Bahadur Shah I.

1708

South Asia: India
Sikhism

The tenth and last Sikh guru Gobind Singh is assassinated by agents of the Muslim-led Mughal Empire.

1708

Europe: France
Christianity

Pope Clement XI condemns the book of French writer Pasquier Quesnel entitled *Abrégé de la morale de l'Evangile* ("Morality of the Gospel, Abridged") as containing all the errors of Jansenism. Clement's statement proves unacceptable in France and many high-ranking church officials refuse to accept it. King Louis XIV and others request that the pope issue a bull, a more authoritative document, so they can disregard the earlier document. The pope responds positively to the request and appoints a Vatican commission to do the necessary research.

Pope Clement issues a bull formally dissolving the community of nuns at Port Royal de Paris, which has been the major center of Jansenism for several generations. The following year all the remaining nuns are forcibly removed from the premises, and later the buildings are pulled down. The chapel, containing the body of Mother Angélique, who had led a reformation among the nuns a century earlier, is preserved and survives to be integrated into the maternity hospital that is later erected on the site.

1708

Europe: Germany
Christianity

Having been influenced by the Pietist movement that had spread throughout Germany, a miller named Alexander Mack organizes a small group to pray and study the Bible in Schwarzenau, Bad Berleburg. By 1708, the group, consisting of Mack, four additional men, and three women had arrived at the conclusion that believers' baptism was the proper form of baptism and was for each of them a necessity. Thus the group decides to baptize themselves, and they choose one of their number to facilitate their baptism by lottery. The baptisms, led by Mack, occur in the nearby Eder River.

The initial group becomes known as the Schwarzenau Brethren and later evolves into the Church of the Brethren. Beginning with believers' baptism, they will adopt many of the beliefs of the Radical Reformation, including pacifism.

1708

Europe: Italy
Christianity

Pope Clement XI makes the Feast of the Immaculate Conception of Mary a Holy Day of Obligation.

1709

North America: United States
Christianity

Experience Mayhew, a Congregationalist minister sponsored by the (Anglican) Society for the Propagation of the Gospel, publishes his translation of parts of the Bible (the Psalms and John's Gospel) in the Martha's Vineyard dialect of the Wampanoag language of the Massachusetts Algonquian Native people, among whom he had worked for many years.

1709

North America: United States
Christianity

Father Antonio de San Buenaventura y Olivares, a Franciscan priest, visits San Antonio and makes the founding of a mission station there a primary objective.

1709

Central America and the Caribbean: Mexico
Christianity
The new sanctuary of the church at the site of the 1531 apparition of the Blessed Virgin Mary is completed and consecrated at Guadalupe.

1709

East and Southeast Asia: China
Buddhism
The first holder of the Jamyang Zhaypa lineage of tülkus (reincarnated Tibetan Buddhist lamas), Ngawang Tsondru, founds Labrang Monastery in Xiahe County in Gansu province. Labrang Monastery is home to the largest number of Tibetan Buddhist monks outside of the Tibet Autonomous Region. One of the six great Gelugpa Buddhist monastic extablishments, it is Tibetan Buddhism's most important monastery outside the Tibetan Autonomous Region.

1709

East and Southeast Asia: Japan
Buddhism
The shogun's wife murders Tokugawa Tsunayoshi who is about to name a young man in whom he has developed sexual interest as his successor. He is thus succeeded by his nephew, Tokugawa Ienobu (1709–1712). In continuity with his predecessor, he had been well trained in the Chinese classics and Confucianism.

During his reign, he moved to improve relations with the Japanese emperor who resided in Kyoto. As an institution, the imperial court had continued over the centuries of shogun rule, but had little power and shoguns generally ignored it. Tokugawa Ienobu removed many of the administrative regulations under which it lumbered along. Ienobu ended the rules forcing the younger sons of emperors to enter the priesthood and allowed the emperor's daughters to marry.

1710

East and Southeast Asia: Malaysia
Christianity
Roman Catholics in what is now Dutch Protestant–controlled Malacca build St. Peter's Church. St. Paul's Church, the original Catholic church erected in 1521,

had been lost to the Protestants in 1641. St. Peter's is the oldest Roman Catholic church in Malaysia.

1711

East and Southeast Asia: China
Christianity
Matteo Ripa, an Italian priest representing the Congregation for the Evangelization of Peoples, begins a decade of work as a painter and copper-engraver at the Chinese court in Beijing.

1711

China, Mongolia
Buddhism
The Kangxi emperor builds Koke Monastery in Inner Mongolia for the Changkya Khutukhtu, the spiritual head of the Gelug lineage of Tibetan Buddhism in Inner Mongolia. Two years later, he declares that the affairs of the Yellow Sect (the Gelugpa) to the east of Tibet are to be entirely handled by the Changkya Khutukhtu.

1711

Europe: England
Christianity
Construction begins on the Church of Saint Philip in Birmingham, England, originally designed as a new parish church for a growing community. In 1905, it became the cathedral for the newly designated Diocese of Birmingham.

December 25. Parliament officially declares the completion of St. Paul's Cathedral in London. It again is recognized as the tallest structure in the city, passing Southwark Cathedral. It remained the tallest structure in the city until the erection of a variety of skyscrapers in the later 20th century. It remains the tallest house of worship in the city.

1711

Europe: England
Christianity
Parliament passes an "Act for the Building of Fifty New Churches in the Cities of London and Westminster or the Suburbs thereof," and establishes a commission to implement its provisions. Of the 50

proposed churches, only 12 will be constructed due to financial limitations. Of these, six are designed by Nicholas Hawksmoor, a student of Christopher Wren. They include St. Alfege's Church, Greenwich; St. George's Church, Bloomsbury; Christ Church, Spitalfields; St. George in the East, Wapping; St. Mary Woolnoth; and St. Anne's, Limehouse.

1711

Europe: Germany
Judaism

The heirs of the late Johann Andreas Eisenmenger (d. 1704), the former professor of Hebrew at Heidelberg University, finally secure the publication of *Judaism Unmasked.* The book repeats arguments that the Jews caused the Black Death and that the blood libel is true, and feed the anti-Semitism already present in the empire. In spite of its being repeatedly denounced for its inaccuracies, it will continue to be periodically reprinted and used by anti-Semites to the present.

1711

Europe: Holy Roman Empire
Christianity

Joseph I, the Holy Roman emperor, dies of smallpox. Having left no heirs, he is succeeded by his brother Charles VI (1711–1740).

1711

Europe: Netherlands
Judaism

Jacques Christian Basnage, a Protestant Christian theologian, completes his *History and Religion of the Jews from the Time of Jesus Christ to the Present,* the first modern history of Judaism.

1711

Russia, Central Asia, and the Caucasus: Russia
Christianity

Philotheus, the metropolitan of Tobolsk, Siberia, retires and is succeeded by the wonderworker, John Maximovitch, remembered as an effective missionary among the Pagan Siberians. Metropolitan John is an unpretentious, saintly figure, who maintains a close relationship with the monks of Mount Athos and is the author of numerous books.

1712

East and Southeast Asia: Japan
Buddhism

Shogun Tokugawa Ienobu dies. He is succeeded by his son, Tokugawa Ietsugu, still a small child. Confucian scholar Arai Hakuseki, who had advised the two previous shoguns, assumes rule as regent.

1712

Europe: England
Christianity

In one of several occasions on which she practiced the Queen's Touch, Queen Anne "touches" a two-year-old infant who grew up to become the famous Dr. Samuel Johnson. Johnson suffered from scrofula, a usually nonfatal form of tuberculosis. The touching was done with a gold coin given to the person as part of the ceremony. The act appears to have had no effect on Johnson. He later recovered but was left severely scarred and blind in one eye. He continued to wear the gold coin, however, for the remainder of his life in the belief that it would prevent the reappearance of the disease.

Touching the sick had been done by English monarchs for centuries, but the practice had fallen into disrepute. Anne's immediate predecessor refused to do it, and Anne would be the last known to have attempted it.

1712

Russia, Central Asia, and the Caucasus: Russia
Christianity

Russian czar Peter I married his mistress Martha Skavronskaya, who had converted to the Russian Orthodox Church and taken the name Catherine (the future Elizabeth I) at the newly constructed Saint Isaac's Cathedral in St. Petersburg. St. Isaac's Cathedral is the first of the four large churches planned by the czar as part of his new capital city.

Czar Peter initiates construction of the Peter and Paul Cathedral, a Russian Orthodox church built within the central fortress of the new city of St. Petersburg, Russia, on Zayachy Island in the Neva River. The cathedral features the world's tallest Orthodox bell tower, which leads the church to be considered by some as the highest Orthodox church in the world.

The cathedral replaces a church hastily erected soon after the founding of the city and dedicated in 1704.

1712–1713

South Asia: India
Islam
Mughal emperor Bahadur Shah I dies and is succeeded by his son Jahandar Shah (r. 1712–1713). The empire is in decline and Jahandar Shah is overthrown after only a short time on the throne. He is defeated at the battle of Agra by his nephew Farrukhsiyar (r. 1713–1719), who assumes the throne. As he is a weak monarch, the power of running his kingdom falls to the Sayyid brothers—Syed Hassan Ali Khan Barha and Syed Hussain Ali Khan Barha, two Mughal generals.

1713

Europe: Netherlands
Christianity
The Treaties of Utrecht, a set of agreements ending the War of Spanish Succession, include provisions recognizing Portugal's sovereignty over Brazil and leading to the return of Colonia del Sacramento (Uruguay) by Spain.

France cedes to Great Britain its surviving claims relative to Rupert's Land, Newfoundland, and Acadia, but retains, for the time being, Île-Saint-Jean (Prince Edward Island) and Île Royale (Cape Breton Island) with its Fortress of Louisbourg.

1713

South Asia: India
Christianity
Lutheran missionary Bartholomew Ziegenbalg acquires a printing press for the Danish Halle Mission based in Tranquebar and prints a first book in Portuguese. He soon adds a type-making factory and a paper mill to the mission's acquisitions. The printing facility continues in operation for the next century.

1713

East and Southeast Asia: China
Islam
Sufi master Qi Jingyi (aka Hilal al-Din and Qi Daozu, i.e., Grand Master Q) dies. He has worked to spread the Qadiriyyah Sufi movement among Chinese Muslims.

1713

Europe: France
Christianity
After several years of work by a commission especially appointed to the task, Pope Clement XI issues the papal bull *Unigenitus,* which condemns 101 propositions attributed to Pasquier Quesnel. The work begins by suggesting that his book *Abrégé de la morale de l'Evangile* ("Morality of the Gospel, Abridged") is most dangerous in that it teaches error in the guise of promoting piety. Many of the ideas condemned, such as irresistible grace and the idea that Christ died for the elect only, resonate with Calvinist Huguenot theology. Also condemned is the Protestant notion that the reading of sacred scripture is for all.

Once he receives it, King Louis XIV passes the bull immediately to Louis-Antoine de Noailles (r. 1696–1729), the bishop of Paris and a cardinal, who had earlier praised the condemned book. By this time, church leaders in France had come to view the matter as an issue of the rights of the French church over papal authority.

1713

Europe: Germany
Christianity
Maurus Bachl (r. 1713–1743) begins his tenure as the abbot of Wehtenburg Abbey, a Benedictine monastery in Bavaria, originally constructed along a picturesque bend in the Danube River. Having become the monastery's leader at a time of great prosperity, he leads the brothers in the complete rebuilding of the complex of buildings in the Baroque style that would come to characterize the leading Benedictine centers in southern Germany.

1713

Europe: Holy Roman Empire
Christianity
Holy Roman emperor Charles VI, who came to the throne because his brother and former emperor had had no male heirs, and facing a similar situation, issues the Pragmatic Sanction of 1713, which decrees

an end to the male-only succession that had been the policy in most Habsburg-led realms, and also declares the perpetual wholeness of the lands he ruled, thus demanding that they remain under one ruler.

1713

Europe: Romania
Christianity

The majority of the Eastern Orthodox believers in the county of Maramures in northern Romania adhere to the Roman Catholic Church. They will become part of what is the Ruthenian Catholic Church.

1714

North America: United States
Christianity

The founding of the Community of True Inspiration in Germany. It would later relocate to the state of Iowa and build the community at Amana.

1714

South Asia: India
Christianity

Bartholomew Ziegenbalg, a Lutheran missionary in southern India, publishes a Tamil translation of the Christian New Testament.

1714

Europe: Austria
Christianity

Gottfried Bessel (r. 1714–1749) begins his tenure as abbot of Stift Gottweig, an 11th-century Benedictine monastery. Following a massive fire in 1718, he is able to initiate a new building program that turns the center into a model of the new Baroque style. The very supportive Holy Roman emperor Charles VI is depicted on the massive ceiling as the ancient deity Apollo-Helios driving a sun chariot. Simultaneously with the rebuilding of the monastery, Bessel transforms it into a major European center of learning.

1714

Europe: England
Christianity

Queen Anne dies without an heir. The person designated to follow her, the electress Sophia of Hanover, had died two months earlier, hence her son, George I, Elector of Hanover (r. 1714–1727), becomes the new king.

1714

Europe: England
Judaism

Enlightenment philosopher John Toland anonymously publishes *Reasons for Naturalizing the Jews in Great Britain and Ireland* in which he argues that increased Jewish immigration to Great Britain will bring an increase in prosperity. His tract is largely met with indifference.

1714

Europe: Germany
Judaism

King Frederick William I of Prussia authorizes the construction of the Heidereutergasse synagogue in Berlin and attends its dedication ceremonies.

ca. 1715

Southwest Asia and North Africa: Persia
Islam

The leading Muslim cleric in Persia, Mohammed Baqer Majlesi, and his grandson and chief mullah, Mohammed Hosein, have sparked a revival of Shi'a Islam throughout the country. It had an unintended consequence—a rise of intolerance toward Christians (many of whom were Georgians or Armenians), Sunni Muslims, and Jews. The shah's new law ordering the forced conversion of Zoroastrians only increased the intolerance. While by no means the primary cause, the loss of support from religious minorities soon contributed to the fall of Sultan Husayn's rule and with it Persia's Safavid dynasty.

1715

North America: United States
Christianity

Anglicans in Radnor, Pennsylvania, outside of Philadelphia, found St. David's Church.

1715

East and Southeast Asia: China
Buddhism

With what most Tibetans considered an illegitimate person holding the Dalai Lama post in Lhasa, Tibetan religious leaders confirm Kelzang Gyatso as the true Dalai Lama. He was formerly residing at Litang Monastery for training; in 1715, the Qing ruler, the Kangxi emperor, sponsors his move to Kumbum Monastery, an act accompanied by ceremonies that signal the public challenge to the reigning Dalai Lama in Lhasa.

1715

East and Southeast Asia: China
Christianity

Pope Clement XI issues the papal bull *Ex illa die* in which he condemns a set of specific Chinese rites that are forbidden to Catholic converts. Among those activities forbidden to Christians are the honoring of Confucius on the first and 15th of each month and the veneration of ancestors. This decision is received very unkindly in China and will greatly hamper the progress of the church's work.

1715

East and Southeast Asia: Japan
Shinto

Kirishima Shrine, which had been destroyed on several occasions by volcanoes, is most recently rebuilt. The shrine is devoted to the deity Ninigi no Mikoto, grandson of the sun goddess Amaterasu. According to legend, he descended from heaven to the mountains of Kirishima and from there intended to rule over the earth. When he alighted on Mt. Takachiho-no-mine, he had with him three items of the imperial regalia: a sword, a mirror, and a gem. These are now symbols of the imperial family. He subsequently married a local princess, became mortal, and established the lineage of Japanese emperors.

1715

Europe: England
Christianity

Thomas Tenison, the archbishop of Canterbury, dies and is succeeded by William Wake (r. 1715–1737), formerly the bishop of London. Duruing his tenure, Wake

Kirishima Shinto shrine, Kirishima, Japan. It is dedicated to the god Ninigi no Mikoto, grandson of the sun goddess Amaterasu. (Koichiro Ohba)

will unsuccessfully try to negotiate a reunion of the Church of England and the Roman Catholic Church.

1716

North America: United States
Christianity

In and around Nacogdoches County, Texas, Spanish Franciscans establish the Mission Nuestra Señora de la Purísima Conception de Acuna near present-day Douglas; the Mission San José de los Nazonis near present-day Cushing; and the Mission Nuestro Padre San Francisco de los Tejas on the Neches River near present-day Alto, all to serve the Tejas Native people.

1716

East and Southeast Asia: Japan
Buddhism

The six-year-old Shogun Togugawa Ietsugu dies of complications of a cold. He has no brothers or heirs to succeed him, so the new shogun is a cousin, Tokugawa Yoshimune (r. 1716–1751), from another branch of the family.

Once assuming control of the government, Yoshimune dismisses the conservative Confucian adviser Arai Hakuseki, who had served the last three shoguns, and launches a set of changes that would be known as the Kyōhō Reforms. The reforms challenged some of the basic negative Confucian attitudes about money that had dominated Japanese thinking about the economy but which Yoshimune considered inhibited the country's development of a money-centered economic culture.

1716

Europe: England
Christianity

Mary Hicks and her daughter Elizabeth, who are executed in England, become the last to be killed as a result of accusations of witchcraft. Other countries will continue to persecute witches but most will refrain from executing people by the end of the century.

1716

Europe: Germany
Christianity

Count Nicolas von Zinzendorf feels a call from God to settle down as a landowner and spend his life on behalf of the tenants who work the land. Greatly influenced by the Pietists, he plans to create an association of devoted Christians who would work for the awakening of the spiritual life of the German Lutheran Church. The initial association consists of himself; Johann Andreas Rothe, the pastor on his estate, Berthelsdorf; Melchior Schäffer, the pastor at Görlitz; and an old friend, Friedrich von Watteville.

1716

Europe: Greece
Christianity, Islam

Forces of the Ottoman Empire attack the Greek island of Corfu, then ruled by Venice. While ably defended, the salvation of the island from the invaders is largely attributed to the action of Spyridon the Thaumaturgist (miracle worker). According to the story, the Ottomans panicked and fled after seeing Spyridon approaching with a cross in one hand and a flaming torch in the other. Spyridon is later canonized as a saint and named the patron of the island.

1716

Russia, Central Asia, and the Caucasus: Russia
Christianity

Peter the Great summons Feofan Prokopovich to Moscow to advise him on ecclesiastical affairs. Having brought widespread reforms to Russia, Peter turns his attention to the Russian Orthodox Church, and Feofan becomes one of the leading voices in its future restructuring.

1716

Russia, Central Asia, and the Caucasus: Russia
Islam

Pyotr Posnikov, having been commissioned by Czar Peter, makes a translation of the Qur'an into Russian. He does not use the Arabic version, but rather works from the French translation of 1647 published by André Du Ryer in Paris.

1716

Southwest Asia and North Africa: Asia Minor
Christianity

Jeremias III (r. 1716–1726), the archbishop of Caesarea (Sappadocia), succeeds Kosmas III (r. 1714–
1716) as the ecumenical patriarch. He is the first
patriarch in a century to serve more than one or two
years in office.

1717

North America: United States
Christianity
Congregational minister Ebenezer Gay receives
a call to become pastor of the church at Hingham,
Massachusetts, and he is ordained and installed in
his position.

1717

South America: Colombia, Venezuela
Christianity
The Spanish create the Viceroyalty of New Granada,
a new colonial jurisdiction that includes what would
later emerge as the countries of Colombia, Ecuador,
Panama, and Venezuela.

1717

East and Southeast Asia: China
Dzungar Mongols invade Tibet. They claim to be responding to the earlier deposition of the Dalai Lama
by Lha-bzang Khan, head of the Oirat Mongols in
1706. Taking control of Lhasa, they kill Lah-bzang
and depose the Dalai Lama that he had placed in
power. Their bad behavior, including attempts to suppress the Nyingma school of Buddhists and the Bon
religion, however, soon costs them the support of the
Tibetan people.

1717

East and Southeast Asia: China, Hong Kong
Chinese Religions
Residents of Tung Tau Wai in what is now the New
Territories found a temple dedicated to Hung Sing
Yeh, one of the Chinese deities especially related to
fishermen, and to Che Kung, a god of protection. As
the temple has expanded over the years, the number
of deities has grown and the two original deities take
second place to Dai Wong, the god of rain and guardian of the farmers.

1717

Europe: Poland
Christianity
Pope Clement XI sends a golden crown to adorn the
icon of Our Lady of Czestochowa at the Jasna Gora
Monastery.

1717

Russia, Central Asia, and the Caucasus: Russia
Christianity
As the original St. Isaac's Cathedral had been destroyed by floods (being located too close to the river
in St. Petersburg), Czar Peter I initiates construction
of a new building, the second of four that would rise
on the site.

Archimandrite Martinia, a monk of the Russian
Orthodox Church who has converted a number of Pagans of the Kamchatka Peninsula (Siberia) during his
decade of work, is murdered. He will subsequently be
honored as a martyr/saint of the church.

June 14, 1717

Europe: England
Western Esotericism
Modern constituted Freemasonry begins as four Ma-
sonic lodges in London affiliate together as a grand
lodge, which evolves to become the Grand Lodge of
England.

September 29, 1717

Central America and the Caribbean: Guatemala
Christianity
A massive earthquake hits Antigua, Guatemala,
which is essentially destroyed. In light of the damage to the city, authorities consider moving the capital
elsewhere.

1718

North America: United States
Christianity
The mission of San Francisco Solano is moved to
San Antonio (Texas) and renamed Mission San Anto-
nio de Valero (aka the Alamo). A short distance away,
the Spanish governor erects the Presidio San Antonio

de Béxar from which the city of San Antonio will develop.

1718

India
Christianity
Lutheran missionary Bartholomew Ziegenbalg leads his small congregation in the construction of a church building, the first Protestant church erected in India. He then turns to the founding of a seminary to train local leadership.

1718

Russia, Central Asia, and the Caucasus: Russia
Christianity
Peter the Great names Feofan Prokopovich the bishop of Pskov.

1719

North America: United States
Christianity
Schwarzenau Brethren first arrive in colonial America at Philadelphia under the leadership of Elder Peter Becker.

Mennonites in Lancaster County use the home of Christian Herr as their first meetinghouse.

1719

Central America and the Caribbean: St. Lucia
Christianity
French Catholic missionaries establish work on the Caribbean island of St. Lucia.

1719

South Asia: India
Islam
The Sayyid brothers who are administering the Mughal Empire tire of the emperor Farrukhsiyar's activities that attempt to undermine their authority. They have him blinded, deposed, and subsequently murdered. They establish his first cousin Rafi ud-Darajat as the new emperor, but he dies weeks later and they move on to his elder brother Rafi ud-Daulah, who also sickens and dies a few weeks later. Finally, they

choose Muhammad Shah (r. 1719–1748), who is able to enjoy a lengthy tenure on the Mughal throne with the Sayyid brothers as his regents from 1719 to 1722.

1719

Europe: England
Christianity
Hymnist Isaac Watts initiates a new format for adapting the Psalms, which at the time remained the major source for hymns in Protestant worship in the Calvinist tradition, in his *Psalms of David Imitated in the Language of the New Testament.* Included in his adaptations of the Psalms is what would become a popular Christmas song, "Joy to the World," adapted from Psalm 96. Also included in the 1719 hymnal is "O God, Our Help in Ages Past."

1719

Russia, Central Asia, and the Caucasus: Russia
Christianity
A first wooden church, named after the birth of John the Baptist, is erected adjacent to the Obvodny Canal in St. Petersburg, Russia. It will later go through several rebuildings and emerge in the 1790s as the Church of the Exaltation of the Cross.

1719

Russia, Central Asia, and the Caucasus: Russia
Christianity
Czar Peter I banishes the Jesuits, who had been active in Russia since the mid-17th century, from his realm. He finds their support of Roman Catholicism undermining the Russian Orthodox Church.

1719–1720

Europe: Bohemia
The tomb of the honored martyr John of Nepomuk is exhumed. The flesh of his body had melted away, except for his tongue, which is declared to be "incorruptible." It prompts the initiation of a new church in his honor at Zelena Hora, and the pope beatifies him (a step to his canonization). The tongue becomes a valued relic kept in the St. Vitus Cathedral in Prague, as are the future saint's bones.

1720

North America: United States
Christianity

Alexander Mack leads the Schwarzenau Brethren (later the Church of the Brethren) to join a similar group led by Peter Becker in a migration to Germantown, then a suburb of Philadelphia, Pennsylvania, as a new home, safe from the attempts to suppress them in Germany.

1720

North America: United States
Christianity

Friar Antonio Margil de Jesus petitions the governor of Coachuila, Texas, Miguel de Aguayo, for permission to found a second mission in San Antonio, which he plans to name after the governor. His request leads to the founding of the Mission San José y San Miguel de Aguayo.

1720

South Asia: India
Jainism

The Anandji Kalyanji Trust is founded to administer the temples in the Shatrunjaya Hills near Palitana, Gujarat, a complex of thousands of Jain temples, most of the Shvetambara Jain tradition.

1720

East and Southeast Asia: China
Buddhism

Due to the conflict between the Oirat and Dzungar Mongols, the long-delayed enthronement of the seventh Dalai Lama as the spiritual and religious leader of Tibet finally occurs at the Potala Palace in Lhasa. The Panchen Lama took the lead in the installation ceremony. At the same time, he took the novice vows of monkhood and began an intense period of study of Tantric Buddhism in which he became a recognized scholar.

1720

East and Southeast Asia: Japan
Christianity

Tokugawa Yoshimune ends the ban on foreign books that had been established in 1640, and the resulting influx of new texts initiates the emergence of Western studies. The ban on books relating to and/or referring to Christianity continues.

1720

Europe: England
Christianity

Pope Clement XI proclaims Anselm, the 11th-century British theologian and former archbishop of Canterbury, a doctor of the church.

1720

Europe: Italy
Christianity

Italian mystic Paul of the Cross (born Paolo Francesco Danei) concludes from a set of experiences in his prayer time that God wanted him to form a community whose members would promote by precept and example the love of God as revealed in the Passion of Jesus. He also was given the new order's uniform, a black habit with a cross atop a white heart. On the heart the words "the Passion of Jesus Christ" are written. The actualization of the mission begins when Pope Benedict XIII ordains Paul and his brother John in 1727 in St. Peter's Basilica in Rome, and they launch a preaching mission.

1720

Europe: Ukraine
Christianity

The famed Pochayiv Monastery, long known as a bastion of Eastern Orthodoxy, is turned over to Uniate converts to Roman Catholicism who follow the Greek Catholic rite.

1720

Southwest Asia and North Africa: Asia Minor
Christianity

Ecumenical Patriarch Jeremias III obtains permission from Sultan Ahmed III to rebuild the Orthodox Patriarchal Cathedral of St. George, which had previously been destroyed by fire. It had remained in its burned condition due in large part to the instability in the patriarch's office over the preceding decades. The cathedral serves as the headquarters church of the patriarchate in Istanbul.

1720–1721

East and Southeast Asia: China
Buddhism

A Chinese army sent by the Qing emperor drives the Dzungar Mongols from Tibet. They bring Kelzang Gyatso with them from Kumbum to Lhasa, and in ceremonies at the Potala Palace, Tibetan religious leaders enthrone him as the seventh Dalai Lama.

1720–1730

Europe: Spain, England
Judaism

The Inquisition in Spain turns renewed attention to the Jewish Christians of the land, which leads many to migrate. Over the next decade, upwards of 1,000 Spanish Jews will swell the Jewish community of England. At the same time, a steady flow of Jews from Germany and Poland is also reaching England.

1721

North America: United States
Christianity

Smallpox begins to spread in Boston, and Congregationalist minister Cotton Mather supports the exploration of inoculation as a means of prevention. The idea causes an intense controversy, though its demonstrated efficacy finally would win the day.

1721

South Asia: India
Sikhism

Bhai Mani Singh becomes the head priest and administrator of the Sikh Golden Temple complex in Amritsar, Punjab. His appointment represents the return of control of the Golden Temple to the Sikh community after a century of conflict with the Muslim Mughal rulers of India. Members of the Sikh community are, however, still prohibited from visiting the temple.

1721

East and Southeast Asia: China
Christianity

The Kangxi emperor issues a decree reacting to the Christian ban on allowing converts to continue to practice various Chinese rites, especially the honoring of Confucius and of ancestors. He bans all Westerners from preaching in his realm.

1721

Europe: England
Christianity

After his original design was rejected, architect James Gibbs oversees the building of St. Martin-in-the-Fields, located in Trafalgar Square, London, according to a second set of plans. The church honors St. Martin of Tours. The design of the church would prove quite popular and would become the model of numerous churches in both England and the United States. Among the most famous of the noncathedral churches in England, it serves officially as the parish church for the British royal family.

1721

Europe: Germany
Christianity

A lecture "On the Practical Philosophy of the Chinese" by Christian Wolff, professor of mathematics and natural philosophy at the University of Halle, initiates a storm of criticism from the Lutheran Pietists who control the university. His harshest critics label him an atheist. In the lecture he praises the moral precepts of Confucius as evidence of the power of human reason. The controversy will lead to his firing (1723) and immediate hiring by the University of Marburg. The firing brought him fame and some 200 separate publications appeared over the next decade attacking and defending him.

1721

Europe: Ireland
Christianity

Irish philosopher George Berkeley, a lecturer at Trinity College, Dublin, is ordained a priest in the Church of Ireland and receives his doctorate in divinity. A decade earlier, he had published his *Treatise Concerning the Principles of Human Knowledge,* the work for which he is best known, in which he argues what has been called subjective idealism, the theory that nothing exists outside the mind.

1721

Europe: Italy
Christianity
Clement XI dies and is succeeded by Pope Innocent XIII (r. 1721–1724).

1721

Europe: Romania, Hungary
Christianity
A jurisdictional conflict with the Latin rite Roman Catholic bishop in Transylvania leads Pope Innocent XIII to formally erect the Eastern rite Diocese of Far-argas and name John Patachy as the first bishop ordinary of the Eastern rite Catholics in Romania.

1721

Russia, Central Asia, and the Caucasus: Russia
Christianity
The patriarchate of the Russian Orthodox Church, having existed for 21 years without a patriarch, becomes the subject of reforms instituted by Czar Peter I. The czar creates the Holy Synod, consisting of 10 archbishops, to lead the church rather than leaving it in the hands of the patriarch alone. He then names Stephen Yavorsky (1658–1722), who had in the interim served as the custodian of the spiritualities of the patriarchal see, as the first president of the newly erected Holy Synod with the title of Metropolitan and Archbishop of Moscow. Yavorsky is assisted by Feofan Prokopovich, the bishop of Pskov, in shaping the Holy Synod.

As part of his attempt to reform the church, Russian czar Peter I promulgates a law preventing Russian men from joining a monastery before reaching the age of 50. He hoped, in part, to make more men eligible to serve in the army. Since few men reached the age of 50 at the time, the number of monastic men dropped steadily during the remainder of Peter's regime.

1722

Sub-Saharan Africa: Mauritius
Christianity
The Lazarist Fathers, members of a Roman Catholic religious order, launch an evangelization effort in Mauritius. The French takeover of the island kingdom provides the opening. They will continue their effort into the 19th century.

1722

Europe: Greenland
Christianity
Danish Lutheran missionary Hans Poulsen Egede arrives in Greenland where he establishes a mission among the Inuit people. His work has the unintended consequence of reviving Danish interest in the island. Egede would found Greenland's capital, Godthåb (now called Nuuk).

1722

North America: United States
Christianity
Spanish Franciscans establish the mission Espiritu Santo de Zuniga on Garcitas Creek, Victoria County, Texas, to serve the Karankawa.

The Spanish establish the Presidio Nuestra Senora de Loreto de la Bahía del Espíritu Santo, the fort that will grow to become the city of Goliad.

1722

South Asia: India
Islam
Mughal emperor Muhammad Shah is finally able to throw off the behind-the-scenes rule of the Sayyid brothers—Syed Hassan Ali Khan Barha and Syed Hussain Ali Khan Barha—the two Mughal generals who had run the empire for the last decade. He orders their assassination.

1722

East and Southeast Asia: China
Buddhism
The Kangxi emperor has the large Huguo Monastery in northeast Beijing renovated and rebuilt.

1722

Europe: Austria
Christianity
Pope Innocent XIII elevates the Diocese of Vienna to an archdiocese.

Portrait of China's Yongzheng emperor. The Yongzheng emperor was the third ruler of the Qing Dynasty and reigned from 1722 to 1735. (RMN-Grand Palais/Art Resource, NY)

1722

Europe: Czech Republic
Christianity

Refugee Moravian families from Bohemia and Moravia settle on the estate of German count Nicholas von Zinzendorf and found the community of Herrnhut. Zinzendorf encourages them to achieve spiritual renewal in the Pietist tradition, leading to their launching a global missionary movement. As Herrnhut grows, its reputation as a place of religious tolerance and freedom spreads across Europe attracting a variety of individuals from a spectrum of groups and perspectives, some of whom became a cause of tensions over their advocacy of extreme and questionable opinions.

1722

Russia, Central Asia, and the Caucasus: Russia
Christianity

Stefan Yavorsky, the first president of the Most Holy Synod of the Russian Orthodox Church, dies. He is succeeded by Feofan Prokopovich, the bishop of Pskov. A confidant of Czar Peter I, he is a major spokesperson for the reforms Peter introduced. He also became a co-founder of the St. Petersburg Academy of Sciences (now the Russian Academy of Sciences).

1722

Southwest Asia and North Africa: Persia
Islam

Ghilzai Afghans under the leadership of Mahmud Hotaki, having earlier broken free of Safavid rule, invade Persia and lay siege to Isfahan. After a six-month siege, the city surrenders and Sultan Husayn abdicates in favor of Mahmed (r. 1722–1725), who becomes the new shah of Persia and the founder of the Hotaki Dynasty.

December 20, 1722

East and Southeast Asia: China

The Kangxi emperor of China dies and is succeeded by his son Yinzhen, who rules as the Yongzheng emperor (r. 1722–1735).

1723

North America: United States
Christianity

Anglicans in Boston, many former Congregationalists from First Church Boston, found the Old North Church (officially known as Christ Church in the City of Boston). Timothy Cutler, a Congregationalist minister who had served as rector of Yale College before converting to the Church of England, is named as the church's first pastor.

1723

South America: Brazil
Christianity

The Church of Sao Francisco (Roman Catholic) in Salvador, Brazil, with walls lined with gold, is completed.

1723

East and Southeast Asia: China
Buddhism

A private school built in the previous century for the training of the emperor's son, adjacent to the Forbidden City, is converted into a Tibetan Buddhist temple and renamed Fuyuo Temple. In the late 20th century, it would become the headquarters of the Panchen Lama in the city.

1723

Europe: England
Christianity

Philip Dodderidge becomes pastor of an independent Nonconforming congregation at Northampton. While there, he will write his most influential book, *The Rise and Progress of Religion in the Soul,* later credited with being the catalyst for leading William Wilberforce, the champion of the antislavery cause, to accept Christianity. Doddridge also writes some 400 hymns, most written as learning tools to summarize the teachings in his sermons.

1723

Europe: France
Judaism

The granting of legal residence to the Jews of Bordeaux signals the gradual changes occurring in the toleration of a Jewish presence in France. Though without legal sanction, a Jewish community is emerging in Paris and individual Jews are emerging in the French court.

1723

Europe: Italy
Christianity

Matteo Ripa, an Italian priest who has spent time in China as a missionary, returns to Naples. Accompanying him are four young Chinese converts whom Ripa plans to educate as priests and send back to China. Pope Clement XII sanctions the founding of the Collegio dei Cinesi, dedicated to the propagation of Christianity in China. The first school of sinology in Europe, the college will evolve to become the Instituto Orientale and more recently the Naples Eastern University.

1724

East and Southeast Asia: China
Christianity

Claiming that Christians supported his rival for the throne, the Yongzheng emperor orders the expulsion of all Christian (i.e., Roman Catholic) missionaries from his realm.

1724

Europe: Italy
Christianity

Pope Innocent XIII dies and is succeeded by Pope Benedict XIII (r. 1724–1730). During his first year in office, he gives official approbation to the new order, the Brothers of the Christian Schools (aka the Christian Brothers), founded in France by Saint Jean-Baptiste de la Salle.

1724

Russia, Central Asia, and the Caucasus: Russia
Christianity

Feofan Prokopovich, the bishop of Pskov, who has assumed a leading role in reforming the Russian Orthodox Church, is named archbishop of Novgorod.

1724

Southwest Asia and North Africa: Syria
Christianity

Athanasius III, the patriarch of Antioch, dies. Two factions in the church each elect a successor. Those favoring union with Rome select Cyril IV. Those opposed to Rome select Silvester, and he is consecrated by the ecumenical patriarch in Constantinople. The authorities of the Ottoman Empire choose to support Silvester, and Cyril had to move into exile. He came to reside at a remote Maronite monastery in Lebanon.

Pope Benedict XIII recognizes Cyril's election as the patriarch of Antioch (1729), an action that formalizes the schism in the Syrian church with the Catholic segment of the population becoming known as the Melkite Greek Catholic Church. It maintains a separate existence as it follows a slightly modified Eastern rite, rather than the Latin rite used by most Roman Catholics.

ca. 1725

Europe: Ireland
Western Esotericism

Freemasons in Ireland organize the Grand Lodge of Ireland.

1725

South Asia: India
Hinduism

Peshwa Balaji Baji Rao I, prime minister of the Maratha Empire, builds a temple to the goddess Annapurna, the goddess of happiness and prosperity, at Varanasi. According to the legend, Annapurna was sent to earth by Vishweswar to make sure that Varanasi's residents would never be hungry. Her name means "completely filled with food."

1725

Europe: Netherlands
Christianity

Following the death of deposed archbishop Peter Codde (1710), the Archdiocese of Utrecht, which has refused to accept the deposition, moves to select a new archbishop, but communication with Rome is blocked. After more than a decade of unsuccessful attempts to resolve the issue, the archdiocese elects Cornelius Steenhoven to be the new archbishop. Dominique Maria Varlet, the bishop of Babylon (a diocese in Persian territory) who had been suspended from his duties for confirming youth in Holland, consecrates Steenhoven. The Archdiocese of Utrecht continues in an irregular status as it appeals its situation to a church council.

The consecration of Steenhoven is generally considered the founding point of the Old Catholic movement that would emerge full blown in the 19th century, which protests what it sees as innovations in the Roman Catholic Church that depart from traditional faith. The Archdiocese of Utrecht considers itself as one with Rome in belief and practice, but protests what it sees as the wrongful assertion of absolute papal power in managing local jurisdictions (dioceses and archdioceses).

1725

Russia, Central Asia, and the Caucasus: Russia
Christianity

Catherine I (r. 1725–1727), the second wife of Peter I, is crowned as Empress of All Russia. Shortly thereaf-

ter, Peter I dies, and she reigns as Emperor of Russia. She is the first female to rule imperial Russia.

1725

Southwest Asia and North Africa: Persia
Islam

Just three years after conquering Persia, Shah Mahmed dies and is succeeded by his cousin Shah Ashraf Hotaki (r. 1725–1730).

ca. 1726

Europe: England
Christianity

Anglican minister William Law, a former teacher at Cambridge who has lost his position for his refusal to swear allegiance to King George I, becomes the private tutor to the son of Edward Gibbon. While there, he writes two classic texts of English devotional literature, *A Practical Treatise upon Christian Perfection* (1726) and *A Serious Call to a Devout and Holy Life* (1728). Above and beyond their popularity with the general public, they have a strong influence on John Wesley, the founder of Methodism.

1726

North America: United States
Christianity

The Mission Espiritu Santo de Zuniga moves to a site across the Guadalupe River from Goliad (Texas) to focus on the Aranama people (of the Coahuitecan).

1726

East and Southeast Asia: China
Buddhism

The fifth Panchen Lama, Lobsang Yeshi, who gave the name Kelzang Gyatso to the seventh Dalai Lama, leads the ceremony conferring full ordination on him. The Panchen Lama has been involved in each step of the development of the new Dalai Lama.

1726

Southwest Asia and North Africa: Asia Minor
Christianity

After a decade on the throne, Ecumenical Patriarch Jeremias III is pushed aside and Callinicus III (r. 1726) replaces him. Callinicus pays a record amount (several thousand pounds of gold) to the Muslim sultan to secure the patriarch's throne, only to die several weeks later from a heart attack. The very day his body is found, Paisius II (r. 1726–1732), the metropolitan of Nicomedia, is named to replace him, the quick election occurring to prevent the return of Jeremias.

1727

North America: United States
Christianity

Twelve Ursuline sisters arrive from France, landing in what is now New Orleans with the approval of Pope Pius III and King Louis XV of France. They are the first Roman Catholic nuns in what is now the United States. They soon establish a convent and a school, the Ursuline Academy, which continues today as the oldest continually operating Catholic school in the United States and the oldest girls' school in the United States. The Old Ursuline Convent, located in New Orleans' French Quarter, is the oldest building in the Mississippi River Valley.

1727

North America: United States
Christianity

The first Baptist congregation in North Carolina is founded as the Shiloh Church in Chowan Precinct.

Paul Palmer founds the first free-will Baptist Church in Perquimans, North Carolina.

1727

North America: United States
Christianity

Presbyterian minister William Tennent establishes a school for training ministers in a log cabin in the countryside north of Philadelphia. It is initially derisively called the Log College, but facilitates the education of a number of preachers who contribute to the religious revival termed the First Great Awakening and evolves to becomes Princeton Theological Seminary and University.

1727

North America: United States
Christianity

Construction begins on Christ Church, a Church of England congregation in Philadelphia. The construction will take a decade, in part due to the decision to construct the church with bricks brought from England. Benjamin Franklin becomes a financial backer of the edifice and holds a lottery to raise money for its bells.

1727

Central America and the Caribbean: Virgin Islands
Christianity

Quakers begin to settle in the British Virgin Islands where they agitate for the end of slavery.

1727

Europe: England
Christianity

King George I dies and is succeeded by his son, George II (r. 1727–1760). George I's reign marks a significant transition of power in England, as the prime minister gained real power, a shift facilitated in part by George's inability to speak fluent English and his seeming lack of interest in domestic policy.

1727

Europe: Germany
Christianity

The *St. Matthew Passion,* possibly the most acclaimed work of sacred music written by composer Johann Sebastian Bach, is initially performed at vespers on Good Friday at St. Thomas Church in Leipzig. At this time, Bach serves as the Cantor of the Thomas School in Leipzig.

1727

Europe: Germany
Judaism, Christianity

Lutheran theologian Johann Heinrich Callenberg, a professor at the University of Halle, establishes the Institutum Judaicum, the first German Protestant mission dedicated to the conversion of Jews to

Christianity. He would, through the institute, issue a spectrum of Christian literature especially designed for a Jewish audience.

1727

Europe: Germany
Christianity

Following a time of study, discussion, and prayer, the diverse community that had formed at Herrnhut, on the estate of Count Nicolas von Zinzendorf, adopts the Brotherly Agreement, a statement of self-discipline for their Christian community, many of whom had migrated from what is now the Czech Republic. The agreement, along with the rules pressed on the community by Zinzendorf (The Manorial Injunctions), will evolve into the Moravian Covenant for Christian Living. The signing ceremony would initiate a religious revival and lead to an experiment in communal Christian living. In the meantime, Zinzendorf had read and found significant agreement between his own prior conclusions on theology and those of Moravian bishop John Amos Comenius.

1727

Europe: Scotland
Western Esotericism

Janet Horne, a resident of Dornoch, Scotland, is accused by her neighbors of witchcraft, including consorting with the devil. Convicted, she is stripped, covered with tar, marched through the town, and executed by being burned alive. She is the last person executed after being charged with witchcraft in the British Isles.

1727

Russia, Central Asia, and the Caucasus: Russia
Christianity

Catherine I, the empress of Russia, dies. She is succeeded by Czar Peter III (r. 1727–1730), the grandson of Peter the Great.

1728

East and Southeast Asia: China
Buddhism

The Yongzheng emperor of China's Qing Dynasty involves himself in the border war between the provinces of U and Tsang in central Tibet. As part of the settlement, the emperor requests the Panchen Lama to assume hegemony over a large section of west central Tibet (and to give up some territory further east to the authorities in Lhasa). He initially refuses, but in the end consents to the new arrangement.

1728

East and Southeast Asia: China, Macau
Christianity

Roman Catholics in Macau erect St. Joseph's Seminary to train priests in the missionary endeavor in the region. St. Joseph's Church would be established next door to the seminary in 1758.

1728

Europe: Denmark
Christianity

A massive fire that burned for four days sweeps through Copenhagen. Along with about one-third of the city, the 14th-century Our Lady's Church burns down. Lost in the fire are commemorative markers for many of Denmark's most prominent citizens. A new red brick church rises on the site over the next decade. The new higher tower is modeled after the spire of the now famous church in London, St. Martin-in-the-Fields.

1729

North America: United States
Christianity

Alexander Mack and other Brethren emigrate to America from Rotterdam.

1729

South Asia: India
Hinduism

Marthanda Varma (r. 1729–1758) assumes the throne as king of Travancor, a kingdom in southern Kerala. Under his rule, Travancore emerges as a powerful military state. A more than capable military leader, Varma also emerges as a devout disciple of Lord Padmanabha, a form of the Hindu deity Vishnu, especially as embodied at the Padmanabhaswamy Temple located at Thiruvananthapuram, the capital of Kerala.

Early in his reign (1731), the platforms in front of the tower at the Padmanabhaswamy Temple are carved from a single massive stone from Thirumala, brought to the temple, and put in place before the temple's deity statues. To perform *darshan* and *puja* (worship), the believer has to ascend to the platforms. Following the installation, the deity statues are reconsecrated.

1729

Southwest Asia and North Africa: Persia
Islam

Tahmasp II (r. 1730–1732), the son of the Safavid shah of Persia, Husayn, had escaped from Isfavan during the 1722 siege. He subsequently establishes a government-in-exile in Tabriz through which he slowly regains control of Persia. By 1729, he could claim legitimately to have reestablished the Safavid Dynasty.

1730

North America: United States
Judaism

Sephardic Jews in New York open Congregation Shearit Israel, the first synagogue in North America.

1730

North America: United States
Christianity

Former general James Oglethorpe, who has chaired a Parliamentary committee on prison reform, and a group of fellow members, offer a petition to form the Trustees for the Establishment of the Colony of Georgia in America. It will be approved two years later.

1730

North America: United States
Western Esotericism

Daniel Cove is appointed Provincial Grand Master of the Masonic lodges in New York, Pennsylvania, and New Jersey.

1730

East and Southeast Asia: China, Hong Kong
Chinese Religions

Residents of Kowloon construct a temple to Yang Liang Chieh, also called Hau Wong (or Marquis Prince). Yang was a Chinese official of the Southern Song Dynasty who was honored as a hero and eventually deified.

Residents of Tung Chung, a town on Lantau Island, construct a temple dedicated to Hau Wong, a local court official of the late Sung Dynasty who lived in the 1270s and was later deified.

1730

Europe: England
Unbelief

Anglican Deist author Matthew Tindal publishes *Christianity as Old as the Creation; or, the Gospel a Republication of the Religion of Nature,* in which he argues that religion must be eternal, universal, simple, and perfect, and consists of the essential duties that humans owe to God, that is, the practice of morality, and that true Christianity consists of nothing more than the eternal religion whose truths can be deduced from nature. The work provokes numerous replies by leading British theologians and greatly influences German intellectual thinking.

1730

Europe: Italy
Christianity

Pope Benedict XIII dies and is succeeded by Pope Clement XII (r. 1730–1740).

1730

Russia, Central Asia, and the Caucasus: Russia
Christianity

Czar Peter III dies. He is buried in Moscow, and is thus the only czar to follow Peter the Great on the throne who is not buried in Peter and Paul Cathedral in Saint Petersburg. He was succeeded by Anna Ivanovna (r. 1730–1740), the daughter of former czar Ivan V (Peter the Great's half-brother). During her regime, she would exile tens of thousands of Old Believers to Siberia.

1730

Southwest Asia and North Africa: Asia Minor
Islam

Ottoman sultan Ahmed III's indulgent lifestyle steadily increased his unpopularity, and he is forced to resign in favor of his nephew Mahmud I (r. 1730–1754). Ahmed led an informal ceremony transferring power. As part of the changes accompanying the end of his reign, Ahmed's grand vizier, İbrahim Pasha, who was blamed for many of the reverses suffered by the empire, was executed.

1731

North America: United States
Christianity

Residents from the Canary Islands who have settled in San Antonio found the San Fernando Catholic Church, which will later be designated as the cathedral church when the Diocese of San Antonio is established. The government of New Spain offers a generous grant to complete construction of the first church building.

The Spanish Franciscans move the three missions—Nuestra Señora de la Purísima Conception de Acuna, San José de los Nazonis, and Nuestro Padre San Francisco de los Tejas—to three new sites near San Antonio. Nuestro Padre San Francisco de los Tejas is renamed San Francisco de la Esoada, and San José de los Nazonis becomes San Juan Capistrano.

1731

South America: Suriname
Christianity

Missionaries of the Moravian church organize their first congregation in Suriname.

1731

East and Southeast Asia: China, Mongolia
Buddhism

The Yongzheng emperor commits a large gift of gold for the building of Shanyin Monastery in Inner Mongolia as the new residence of the Changkya Khutukhtu, the spiritual head of the Gelug lineage of Tibetan Buddhism in Inner Mongolia.

1731

Europe: Austria
Christianity

Archbishop Firmin of Salzburg drives all of the Protestants out of his territory. Most take refuge in southern Germany.

1731

Europe: Germany
Christianity

The Moravians publish the first edition of their annual devotional manual, *Watchwords*. A new edition continues to appear annually to the present.

1731

Europe: Italy
Christianity

Pope Clement XIII, responding to the growing popularity of the devotion centered on the Passion of Christ known as the Stations of the Cross, in which believers imaginatively reimage the suffering of Christ immediately before, during and after his crucifixion, standardizes the number of stations at 14.

1731

Europe: Italy
Christianity

Alphonsus Maria de Liguori is ordained to the Roman Catholic priesthood and begins work among the homeless and marginalized youth of Naples, where he begins to establish chapels. He founds the Evening Chapels, which were managed by the young people themselves. These chapels were centers of prayer and piety, preaching, community, social activities, and education.

1731

Europe: France, Netherlands
Western Esotericism

Francis I, the duke of Lorraine and future husband of the Holy Roman empress Maria Theresa, is initiated into Freemasonry as a member of the Grand Lodge of England at a lodge in The Hague (Netherlands) convened for that singular purpose at the home of the British ambassador, Philip Stanhope, fourth earl of Chesterfield. Subsequently, Francis would visit England, at which time he was made a Master Mason while visiting Houghton Hall, the estate in Norfolk of Robert Walpole, the British prime minister.

1732

North America: United States
Christianity, Judaism

George Oglethorpe receives a charter to found the colony of Georgia. The charter grants religious freedom to all Protestant groups. The founders of the first settlement, Savannah, prohibit the import of slaves. The Sephardic Jewish community in London provides financial support for 42 Jews to migrate to the new colony.

1732

North America: United States
Christianity

Conrad Beissel moves to Ephrata, where he establishes a communal experiment emphasizing celibacy, mysticism, and separation from the world's evil influences.

1732

Central America and the Caribbean: Curacao
Judaism

Sephardic Jews in Willemstad erect the Mikve Israel synagogue.

1732

Central America and the Caribbean: Virgin Islands
Christianity

Two missionaries of the Moravian Church, Leonard Dober and David Nitschmann, arrive on Saint Thomas, Danish West Indies (the Virgin Islands) to begin their mission to those trapped in slavery. From the original mission, the work spread to Jamaica (1754), Antigua (1756), Barbados (1765), St. Kitts (1777), Tobago (1790), and throughout the West Indies.

1732

East and Southeast Asia: China
Buddhism

Vajrayana Buddhists in Huhhot, Inner Mongolia, construct the large Temple of the Five Pagodas, a Tibetan-style temple whose interior walls are decorated with some 1,500 figures of the Buddha.

1732

Europe: Germany
Christianity

The Moravians residing at Herrnhut are visited by a former slave, Anthony Ulrich, who shares with them his story of the horrible conditions under which the slaves of the West Indies exist and pleads for Christian missionaries to minister to them. Count von Zinzendorf uses his relations with the Danish king Christian VI to gain an opening for missionaries from Herrnhut to begin work in the Caribbean. The Moravian effort will initiate a global missionary movement.

The success of the work in the Caribbean would lead over the next generation to the sending of Moravian missionaries to Greenland (1733), the British American colonies, Livonia (Latvia), Suriname, Tranquebar (India), the Nicobar Islands in the East Indies, Egypt, Labrador, and the west coast of South Africa.

1732

Europe: Hungary
Christianity

Work begins on the massive renovation and rebuilding of Zirc Abbey at Veszprém, one of Hungary's most prominent Benedictine centers, all of which had been destroyed in the early 16th century. The rebuilt monastery will boast an organ created by the noted organ builder Johann Ignaz Egedacher and a new library devoted to the natural sciences.

1732

Southwest Asia and North Africa: Asia Minor
Christianity

Former ecumenical patriarch Jeremias III (r. 1732–1733), deposed in 1726, is able to force his return to his office and force the deposition of Paisus II, who would later himself return and serve two different terms as patriarch.

1732

Southwest Asia and North Africa: Persia
Islam

Shah Tahmasp II is deposed in favor of his son Abbas II, who becomes the shah of Persia.

1732–1733

North America: United States
Christianity

James Oglethorpe leads a group across the Atlantic and settles at what is now Savannah, Georgia. He negotiates with Chief Tomochichi of the local Yamacraw people for land upon which he will lay out his new colony. He arranges for the banning of slavery and plans to invite debtors who now languish in prison to inhabit the land. The colony's charter makes space for believers of the wide variety of Protestant sects, but not Roman Catholicism. In this case, the exclusion of Roman Catholic settlers is partly based on the close proximity to Florida, controlled by Spanish Catholics.

1733

North America: United States
Western Esotericism

Shortly after Georgia's establishment, Oglethorpe opens Solomon's Lodge No. 1, F. & A. M., the first Masonic lodge in Georgia. About the same time, Henry Price, the provincial grand master representing the Grand Lodge of England, grants a charter to a group of Freemasons in Boston who open what becomes St. John's Lodge. These are the first duly constituted lodges in North America, though in 1730, Benjamin Franklin had posted an item in the *Pennsylvania Gazette* that makes note of several lodges of Freemasons already in operation there, and there is some evidence of Freemasonry in Philadelphia as early as 1715. Franklin will adhere to St. John's Lodge in Philadelphia in 1731 and become the junior grand warden of the Grand Lodge of Philadelphia in 1732. Over the next few years (1733–1737), additional lodges will be chartered in New York, Pennsylvania, and South Carolina.

1733

Europe: Greenland
Christianity

Danish monarch Christian VI sends three Moravian missionaries led by Christian David to support the Danish Lutheran mission in Greenland. Hans Egede assists them to settle in and learn the Greenlandic language; however, differences soon arise. As a result, the Moravians move away from the Lutheran station at Zuuk and create a new mission station, which they call Neu Herrnhut. The mission work is further disturbed by a smallpox epidemic that strikes before the year is out and kills more than 2,000.

1733

South Asia: India
Islam

Muslim reformer Shah Waliullah returns to India after making his pilgrimage to Mecca. He gathers and trains a growing number of pupils to assume roles in a new Islamic leadership, and Emperor Muhammad Shah builds a new madrassa for his work. He also authors a number of books on Islamic teachings.

1733

East and Southeast Asia: China
Chinese Religions

The Yongzheng emperor orders a massive renovation of the seventh-century Fayuan Temple located on the southwest of Beijing. He also builds the Juesheng Temple (now called the Big Bell Temple) just outside the city to the west in a secluded location.

1733

Russia, Central Asia, and the Caucasus: Russia
Christianity

The Peter and Paul Cathedral, located inside the confines of the Peter and Paul Fortress in St. Petersburg, Russia, is completed after 20 years of work. It is designed, in part, as a burial site for future Russian monarchs. The cathedral's bell tower is the tallest bell tower in the world of Eastern Orthodoxy, and the church is thus considered by many as the tallest Orthodox church in the world.

1733

Southwest Asia and North Africa: Asia Minor
Christianity

Ecumenical Patriarch Jeremias III becomes ill and is forced to retire from office. He is followed by Seraphim I (r. 1733–1734) and then Neophytos VI (r. 1734–1740), the metropolitan of Caesarea in Cappadocia.

1734

East and Southeast Asia: China
Buddhism

The Yongzheng emperor orders a massive renovation of the seventh-century Recumbent Buddha Temple located at the foot of Mount Shou'an on the northwest edge of Beijing. The layout of the renovated temple follows that of the Fayuan Temple, which had undergone a similar renovation the year before.

1734

Europe: England
Islam

George Sale, a lawyer and linguistic scholar, produces the first English translation of the Qur'an directly from Arabic.

1734

Europe: Ireland
Christianity

Idealist philosopher George Berkeley is appointed bishop of Cloyne in the Church of Ireland. Shortly thereafter he publishes a polemic work against Deism, *Alciphron, or The Minute Philosopher.*

1734

Europe: Italy
Judaism

Fearing another wave of messianism in their midst, Italian rabbis move to suppress the teachings of Moshe Chaim Luzzatto, the kabbalist and philosopher. He had received divine instruction from a mystical spirit being and identified one of his followers as the Messiah while assigning himself the role of Moses. He claimed to be the biblical Moses's reincarnation. The opposition of the Jewish leadership drives Luzzatto out of Italy and he eventually settles in Amsterdam.

1734

Russia, Central Asia, and the Caucasus: Russia
Christianity

The Russian government issues an edict against the Iconoclasts, those who denounce the use of icon

John Wesley (1703–1791), Anglican cleric and theologian who co-founded the Methodist movement. (Linda Steward/iStockphoto.com)

images in the church. The edict offers the first written evidence of the existence of a dissenting sect group, the Doukhobors. One of a spectrum of sectarian groups to appear in 18th-century Russia, the Doukhobors were pacifists who rejected government authority. They also rejected the necessity of priests, church rituals, the Bible, and the divinity of Jesus Christ—all opinions that would continue to bring them into tension with both the secular government and church authorities.

1734–1735

East and Southeast Asia: China
Christianity

Culminating a generation of survey work in China, originally instigated as part of a mission to gather astronomical data, Jesuit priest Jean Baptiste Bourguignon d'Anville publishes a map of China (Paris, 1734) and Jean-Baptiste Du Halde publishes his four-volume *Description géographique, historique, chronologique, politique et physique de l'empire de la Chine et de la Tartarie chinoise* (Paris, 1735), which provides the West with detailed knowledge of China and its land.

1735

North America: United States
Christianity
The first Amish migrate to North America.

1735

North America: United States
Christianity
Anglican priest John Wesley and his brother Charles sail to Savannah, Georgia, where John will become the minister of the newly formed Church of England parish and Charles becomes the secretary of Indian affairs and the chaplain to the garrison at nearby Fort Frederica, St. Simon's Island. On the voyage to Georgia, they make the acquaintance of fellow traveler and Moravian bishop August Gottlieb Spangenberg, with whom John Wesley had a memorable conversation about Wesley's personal appropriation of the Christian message.

On the trip over, John Wesley begins to learn German to understand the hymns sung by the Moravians in their daily worship. By the time the voyage concludes, he is making his initial translations of the hymns into English.

1735

North America: United States
Christianity
Johann Conrad Beissel founds the Ephrata Cloister, an ordered communal society espousing sabbatarian Christian ideals. Members live a celibate highly disciplined life. The community, located at Ephrata, Lancaster County, Pennsylvania, has roots in the German Baptist Brethren movement led by Alexander Mack in Germantown, Pennsylvania.

1735

North America: United States
Christianity, Judaism

Judah Monis, the instructor of Hebrew at Harvard College, publishes *A Grammer of the Hebrew Tongue.* Though not a product of the Jewish community, it is the first book to use the Hebrew alphabet published in North America.

1735

South America: Suriname
Christianity
Missionaries of the Moravian church establish their first congregation in Suriname.

1735

East and Southeast Asia: China
Chinese Religions, Buddhism
The Yongzheng emperor who ruled the Chinese Qing Empire dies suddenly, most likely from an overdose of medicines he took in the belief that they would prolong his life. He is succeeded by his young son, who will enjoy a lengthy rule as the Qianlong emperor (r. 1735–1796). During his reign the total number of temples (Buddhist, Taoist, traditional Chinese) in Beijing, now the one undisputed capital of China, would exceed 1,300.

During his time on the throne, the emperor would order the carving of a set of printing blocks from which a new edition will be published of the Tripitaka (ca. 1738), the Buddhist sacred texts. The *Qianlong Tripitaka* of 7,173 volumes, is the only official publication of the Tripitaka in Chinese produced during the Qing Dynasty. Approximately 150 copies are produced, and they are distributed to the major monastic centers throughout the country. A copy will be placed in the Zhihua Temple in Beijing.

1735

Europe: England
Christianity
At the command of King Charles I, Francis White, the Anglican bishop of Ely, writes and publishes his *Treatise of the Sabbath-Day.* The book grows in part out of his discussions with Theophilus Brabourne, who espoused the keeping of a Saturday Sabbath, an opinion that led to his confrontation with the authorities. The issue had also become a matter of discussion between Anglicans (the Church of England) and Puritans (Pres-

byterians), the latter demanding a rather strict keeping of the Sabbath as a day of rest when the public should be ordered to refrain from both work and most frivolous recreational pursuits. White's book is dedicated to Archbishop of Canterbury William Laud.

1735

Europe: England
Christianity

The talented orator and Anglican minister George Whitefield has an intense religious awakening, which sets him on his career as an evangelist.

1735

Europe: England
Western Esotericism

The Witchcraft Act of 1735 supersedes former anti-witchcraft laws (1604). The crime of witchcraft is dropped in favor of penalties for pretending to be a witch. With the public no longer believing that witchcraft was possible, penalties are now directed against any who claim to be able to practice witchcraft by calling up spirits, casting spells, or foretelling the future. Engagement in these acts is considered evidence of fraud, and any found guilty are subject to imprisonment.

1735

Europe: Lithuania
Christianity

A group of Lithuanian scholars complete their work of translation and publish the first complete edition of the Bible in Lithuanian.

1735

Europe: Netherlands
Christianity

Jacobus Capitein, an African from what is now Ghana, arrives in the Netherlands as a slave, is baptized in the Dutch Reformed Church, and lets his desire to return to Africa as a missionary be known.

1736

South Asia: India
Hinduism

Srimant Raanojirao Shinde Maharaj Scindias initiates the rebuilding of Mahakaleshwar Jyotirlinga, a temple dedicated to Lord Shiva. One of the 12 Jyotirlingas considered to be sacred abodes of Shiva, it is located in the city of Ujjain, Madhya Pradesh. The temple complex had been destroyed by Sultan Iltutmish of the Delhi sultanate in 1234–1235.

1736

East and Southeast Asia: China, Hong Kong
Chinese Religions

Residents at Fong Ma Po in what is now the New Territories of Hong Kong construct a temple to Tianhou (Matsu), one of the oldest temples in the area. Its popularity is boosted by the presence of a tree adjacent to the temple proper, which is known as the Wishing Tree. Its reputation as a place of miracles came after a seaman who had been sick for some time prayed before it and reported being healed.

1736

Europe: England
Christianity

Joseph Butler, the head chaplain of Caroline, the wife of King George II, publishes his Christian apologetic work, *Analogy of Religion, Natural and Revealed,* in which he draws an analogy between the divine government pictured in the Bible and nature, concluding that their likeness suggests but a single author of both. Two years later he would be named the Anglican bishop of Bristol and eventually become the bishop of Durham (1750).

1736

Europe: Holy Roman Empire
Christianity

Francis I, the duke of Lorraine, marries Maria Theresa, the future empress of the Holy Roman Empire.

1736

Europe: Scotland
Western Esotericism

Freemasons in Scotland organize the Grand Lodge of Scotland.

1736

Southwest Asia and North Africa: Persia
Islam

Shah Abbas II, the shah of Persia, owed his position to Nadar Khan, a military leader who had assisted in the deposition of Shah Tahmasp Abbas's father. In 1736 he deposed Abbas, ended for a second time the Safavid Dynasty of Persia, and took the throne as Nadar Shah. Four years later he had both Tahmasp and Abbas murdered.

Though seemingly not a religious man, Nadar Shah was moved by the religious problem he had inherited in the Shi'a Islam of the people he ruled. Their religion was in many ways offensive to Sunni Muslims in the lands surrounding Persia, especially the Ottoman Empire. He thus suggested a more moderate form of Shi'a faith, which he termed Ja'fari after the sixth Shi'a imam, Ja'far al-Sadiq. He moved to suppress those Shi'a practices that had proved most objectionable to Sunnis, such as using derogatory references about the first three caliphs. He also introduced a hat with four peaks, each of which was said to symbolize one of the first four caliphs.

Along with having the Ottomans accept Ja'farism as something compatible with Sunni Islam, possibly even a fifth school of Sunni jurisprudence, he wanted Persian Muslims admitted to the *hajj* (the pilgrimage to Mecca that all Sunni Muslims are supposed to make at least once in their lifetime). The Ottomans only partially approved of Nadar's reformed Islam, but did allow Persian pilgrims to Arabia.

1737

Sub-Saharan Africa: South Africa
Christianity

Moravian missionary George Schmidt establishes a mission station at Baviaanskloof (which he names Genadendal or Valley of Grace) near Cape Town. After seven years of working among the Native people, conflict with the Boer farmers of the area and the dominant Dutch Reformed Church force him out of South Africa.

1737

North America: United States
Christianity

Anglican minister John Wesley issues the first hymnbook published in America, *A Collection of Psalms and Hymns*. These include hymns from the several hymnbooks he had brought from England, many by Isaac Watts, as well as several German hymns he had translated from the Moravian hymnbook.

1737

South Asia: India

Bhai Mani Singh, the administrator in charge of the Sikh Golden Temple in Amritsar, Pubjab, receives permission from the Mughal governor Zakariya Khan to celebrate the annual Indian Diwali festival at Amritsar. A large number of Sikhs arrive for the festival, but the celebration is broken up by the arrival of a Mughal army sent to intimidate the attendees. Unable to receive an offering from attendees, Bhai Mani Dingh is unable to pay the promised sum to the governor and he is killed by being hacked to death (1738).

1737

Europe: England
Christianity

Scottish biblical scholar Alexander Cruden presents the first edition of his concordance of the King James Version of the Bible to Queen Caroline (the wife of British king George II). He had hoped for a financial reward for his work, but she dies a few days later and none is forthcoming. He goes into debt to finance the printing. This first carefully prepared concordance enjoys some limited success, but it would not reach a large audience until after the second edition (1761).

1737

Europe: England
Christianity

William Wake, the archbishop of Canterbury, dies and is succeeded by John Potter (r. 1737–1747), formerly the bishop of Oxford.

1737

Europe: Germany

Two Moravian bishops, David Nitschmann der Bischof and Daniel Ernst Jablonski, consecrate Count Nicolas von Zinzendorf as bishop in a ceremony held at Berlin.

1737

Europe: Italy
Christianity
The Roman Catholic Church having revised its stance relative to heliocentrism, the idea that the earth travels around the sun, the body of Galileo is removed from its obscure burial site in the Basilica of Santa Croce (Church of the Holy Cross) in Florence to the main sanctuary where a monument in his honor had been erected.

1737

Europe: Italy
Christianity
After a year of preaching activity during which a following has gathered around Paul of the Cross, he opens the first retreat (i.e., monastery) on Monte Argentario and begins the formation of the Passionist order, officially the Congregation of the Passion of Jesus Christ.

1737

Russia, Central Asia, and the Caucasus: Russia
Christianity
A wooden church is erected on Stable Square (Konyushennaya Ploshchad) in St. Petersburg, Russia. It will later be replaced by a stone building and become the home of a copy of a famous Orthodox icon, the "Savior Not Made by Human Hand."

1738

North America: United States
Christianity
Anglican minister George Whitefield visits Savannah, Georgia, the first of many trips across the Atlantic. While there, he concludes that one of the primary needs of the new colony is an orphan house, and he returns to England to raise funds for it.

1738

North America: United States
Christianity
The first Reformed Presbyterian congregation in North America, aligned with the Reformed Presby-

tery of Scotland, the Covananter Church, is organized in Lancaster County, Pennsylvania.

1738

Europe: Germany
Christianity
Frederick Augustus II, Elector of Saxony and King of Poland, commissions the building of the Catholic Church of the Royal Court of Saxony, a Roman Catholic cathedral in the city of Dresden, Germany. It would take 13 years to complete.

1738

Europe: Italy
Western Esotericism
Pope Clement XII issues the first papal decree directed against the Freemasons.

May 24, 1738

Europe: England
Christianity
Having returned from a disastrous time as the Church of England parish minister in Georgia, John Wesley finds his way to a religious society meeting on Aldersgate Street in London where, while listening to a person read from Martin Luther's preface to the Epistle to the Romans, he has an intense spiritual awakening, which he describes as having his "heart strangely warmed."

Since his return from Georgia, John Wesley has spent much time with Peter Böhler, a Moravian minister in London to learn English as he prepares to go to the British American colonies as a missionary to the African American slaves. Böhler organizes a religious society on Fetter Lane, which Wesley joins. Shortly after his awakening, he will travel to Germany to spend time with the Moravians at Herrnhut and return to England to found the Methodist movement.

Shortly after John's awakening, his brother Charles also experiences a similar awakening. Once John returns from Herrnhut, the two will join forces in developing Methodism. Charles, a poet, will become most known for the many hymns he wrote and published.

JOHN WESLEY (1703–1791)

John Wesley, a priest in the Church of England, founded the Methodist movement in the 1740s. The Methodists would expand across the Atlantic during his long life and in the 19th century from their bases in England and the United States would become a global community.

John Wesley was born June 17, 1703, in the rectory at Epworth, England. He was the 15th of 19 children born to Samuel and Susannah Wesley. The seriousness with which John pursued a religious quest was shown at Oxford, where he assumed leadership of an informal organization dubbed the Holy Club. After graduation and ordination, he accepted an invitation from James Oglethorpe to help build the religious life of his new colony of Georgia. On the voyage to America, John had his first encounter with members of the Moravian Church, who impressed him with their personal faith. Some years later, Wesley broke with the Moravians over several issues, and the first Wesley-led "Methodist" religious societies began to take shape.

Methodism evolved as a revitalization movement within the Church of England. In the 1760s the first classes and societies were organized in the American colonies. Wesley commissioned a number of preachers to travel through the colonies and build the movement; however, as the American Revolution began, all but one of those preachers, Francis Asbury, would return to their homeland. The success of the Revolution presented Wesley with a hard decision—what to do with the American Methodists. Unable to persuade the Anglican authorities to assume responsibility for them, he assumed the office of a bishop and "set aside" two men, Thomas Coke and Richard Whatcoat, as Methodist "superintendents," assigning them the task of setting up American Methodism as an independent movement. At a conference held at Barrett's Chapel in Delaware, they oversaw the consecration of Asbury as the first American Methodist bishop and the organization of the independent Methodist Episcopal Church (now the United Methodist Church).

Wesley itinerated throughout the British Isles for some four decades, and during that time delivered more than 40,000 sermons (many of his sermons being repeated multiple times to different audiences). He remained active until close to the end of his life on March 2, 1791 in London. One of his last actions was to pen a letter to William Wilberforce in support of Wilberforce's work to end slavery.

J. GORDON MELTON

1739

Europe: England
Anglican minister Charles Wesley, the brother of John Wesley, the founder of Methodism, publishes his first collection of *Hymns and Sacred Poems.*

1739

South Asia: India
Islam
The Mughal authorities negotiate a peace with the Sikhs in the Punjab.

Persian ruler Nadir Shah demonstrates the weakness of the Mughal Empire by invading and looting its capital, Delhi. This event would come to mark the beginning of the end of Mughal rule. In the process of marching on Delhi, Nadir Shah passes through Amritsar and attacks the Sikh Golden Temple.

1739

Europe: England
Christianity

John Wesley, who had allied with the Moravians following his awakening experience the year before, breaks ties with them over the issue of quietism, the question of waiting until one has been awakened before engaging in an active Christian-motivated life. He forms the small group around him into a religious society from which the Methodist movement will develop. He makes the Foundry, a former government building in surbaban London where cannons had been cast, his new headquarters.

Wesley is also invited to Bristol by his friend George Whitefield who introduces him to preaching out-of-doors to the miners as they exit the mines each day. As Whitefield leaves for a preaching tour in the British American colonies, Wesley accepts responsibility for the work in Bristol.

In his absence, a layman has taken on responsibility for leading worship and preaching to Wesley's followers in London. Wesley reevaluates his prejudices against lay preaching and embraces it as an additional resource for his movement.

With the publication of John Wesley's *Hymns and Sacred Poems,* the Wesley brothers signal the integration of music into their evangelistic activity, a trademark of the Evangelical Awakening that will become the major religious change in the British Isles in the next generation and North America by the end of the century. They choose hymn tunes that people find easy to sing and remember, while the words carry the Arminian theological message of Christ's redemption of all humankind.

1739

Europe: Estonia
Christianity

Anton Thor Helle, who is largely credited for uniting the southern and northern dialects of the Estonian language into the common modern language, also publishes the first edition of the complete Bible in Estonian.

ca. 1740

North America: United States
Unbelief

Ebenezer Gay, pastor of the Congregational Church at Hingham, Massachusetts, begins to speak about his non-Trinitarian theological speculations. He would go on to become a pioneering voice of Unitarianism in New England.

1740

North America: United States
Christianity

Anglican minister George Whitefield returns to Savannah where he founds the still existent Bethesda Orphanage (now known as Bethesda Academy), the oldest extant charity in North America. Following a short stay in Savannah, he launches a preaching tour of the British American colonies that takes him north to New England, the first religious event shared by all the colonies simultaneously. He ignites a religious awakening through the colonies that came to be known as the Great Awakening of 1740. He would continue to preach in the colonies over the next decades as he makes five additional trips across the Atlantic.

Whitefield represents the most Calvinist wing of Anglicanism, which brings him into theological conflict with John and Charles Wesley, who are staunch Arminians. Wesley preaches free grace and universal atonement while Whitefield believes in predestination and a limited atonement. The disagreement causes them to gradually separate and go their separate ways, though they maintain a relationship throughout their lives (Wesley would preach at Whitefield's funeral in 1770). Whitefield develops a relationship with Selina, Countess of Huntingdon, who becomes his patron and appoints him as her chaplain. Whitefield's followers in England will form the Countess of Huntingdon's Connexion, a form of Methodism that follows his Calvinist theology, which will eventually merge into Presbyterianism.

1740

North America: United States
Christianity

Members of Old North Church in Boston add a 190-foot wooden tower to the church, with a large elaborate weathervane on its top.

1740

South Asia: India
Hinduism
Nanasaheb Peshwa is appointed the prime minister (or peshwa) of the Maratha Empire. During his two decades in office he will greatly expand the city of Pune. Among his contributed structures is the Parvati temple, placed on a hillock overlooking the city. He also builds the new structure housing Shiva's lingam at Trimbakeshwar at Trimbak, Maharashtra, one of the 12 Jyotirlingas, one of the holiest of sites to Saivite Hindus. Trimbak is near the origin point of the Godavari River, the second longest in India. The temple's Shiva lingam is adorned with the large Nassak Diamond (43 carets).

1740

South Asia: India
Missionary Johann Phillip Fabricius arrives in India and assumes leadership of a small Lutheran congregation in Madras. While serving as the church's pastor, he also learned Tamil, produced the first Tamil to English dictionary, and worked on a new translation of the Bible into Tamil. Fabricius picked up the original work of pioneer missionary Bartholomew Ziegenbalg, improving his translation where necessary and making altogether new translations of those sections of the Bible on which Ziegenbalg had not worked.

1740

Europe: Austria, Germany
Christianity
Charles VI, the Holy Roman emperor, dies. Having no male heirs, he is succeeded by his daughter Maria Theresa (r. 1740–1780) who is forced to take up arms to maintain her place on the throne—a coalition of states that had earlier agreed to recognize a female inheriting the emperor's throne reneging at the last minute. She lost land to Poland and Prussia, but remained in power otherwise.

1740

Europe: Germany
Christianity
Frederick William, the king of Prussia and elector of Brandenburg, dies. During his reign, he had seen to the firing of philosopher Christian Wolff from the University of Halle. He is succeeded in office by his son Frederick II (r. 1740–1786), who greatly admires Wolff and recalls him to Halle. Wolff not only returns, but eventually becomes chancellor of the university.

1740

Europe: Italy
Christianity
Pope Clement XII dies and is succeeded by Pope Benedict XIV (r. 1740–1758).

1740

Europe: Netherlands
Judaism
Kabbalist philosopher Moshe Chaim Luzzatto, now residing in Amsterdam, completes his book, *The Path of the Upright,* a book of ethics that will gain a significant readership in the Jewish, especially the Hasidic, communities of Eastern Europe.

1740

Europe: Ukraine
Judaism
Israel Ba'al Shem, who will launch the new movement of Hasidism, takes up residence at Medzibezh, Podolia, in what is now the Ukraine, where he will teach for the rest of his life. He meets with his growing number of students in a relatively small, simple building where they learn to cultivate a simple life of mystical prayer and inner cultivation.

1740

Russia, Central Asia, and the Caucasus: Russia
Christianity
Anna Ioannovna, the empress of Russia, dies and is succeeded by the one-year-old czar Ivan VI (r. 1740–1741). When he is but eight weeks old, Anna, his grand-aunt,

adopts Ivan and declares him the successor to Russia's throne.

1740

Southwest Asia and North Africa: Arabia
Islam

Mohammad ibn Abd-al-Wahhab launches his movement to purify and revive Islam, and settles in Diriyah where he makes an accord with the local ruler, Muhammad ibn Saud. Ibn Saud agrees to implement Ibn Abd-al-Wahhab's teachings, and as they are enforced, ibn Saud and his family are designated the temporal "leaders" of the movement. Over the next four centuries, ibn Saud's family would take control of much of the Arabian Peninsula which they would organize into the modern state of Saudi Arabia.

1740

Southwest Asia and North Africa: Palestine
Judaism

Rabbi Haim Abulafia accepts the invitation of Sheikh Daher-al-Omar to settle in Tiberias and cooperate with the sheikh's plan to revive the city. He leads an effort to build a new synagogue, construct houses and shops, and rebuild the wall around the city's Jewish quarter. He not only revives the spiritual life, but assists in the rebuilding of the community's economic viability.

1741

North America: United States
Christianity

Isaac Backus is converted to evangelical Christianity and becomes an independent preacher. His evolving views will lead him to identify with the Baptists, among whom he is ordained. He will eventually represent the Baptists before the Continental Congress as the American Revolution begins. He is best known for his advocacy of separation of church and state.

1741

North America: United States
Christianity

David Nitschmann and Count Nicolaus von Zinzendorf lead a small group of Moravians to Pennsylvania where on Christmas Eve they found the town of Bethlehem, which they name after the birthplace of Jesus of Nazareth. Meanwhile, Moravians who had been working in Pennsylvania with Anglican evangelist George Whitefield purchase the land, previously named the Barony of Nazareth, from him and transform it into a Moravian settlement.

1741

North America: United States
Christianity

Two factions develop within the Presbyterian Church over support for the revivalist activity of the First Great Awakening, leading to their dividing into separate synods. The New Light faction supports the revival and the Old Lights oppose it. The schism lasts for 17 years.

1741

North America: United States
Christianity

In March and April, a set of fires erupt in Lower Manhattan. The Reformed Church built in 1645 is among the buildings destroyed. Authorities arrest a 16-year-old Irish servant, Mary Burton, who tells of a conspiracy of poor whites and blacks to burn the city as a first step in a revolt. Two slaves are executed by being burned at the stake, but not before confessing to burning the fort and naming dozens of co-conspirators. In the end, some 152 blacks and 20 whites are tried and convicted. John Ury, suspected of being a Roman Catholic priest, is accused of leading the plot. Among those convicted, 17 blacks and four whites (including John Ury) are hung, 13 blacks are burned at the stake, and 70 blacks and seven whites are banished from New York.

1741

South America: Suriname
Christianity

Lutherans in Suriname, which had previously worshipped with the Reformed Church, receive permission to form a separate congregation in the capital city, Paramaribo, and establish a congregation under the jurisdiction of the Lutheran Consistory in Amsterdam, Holland. It is the oldest Lutheran congregation in South America.

1741

South Asia: Afghanistan
Islam
Ahmad Shah is chosen as a new king by the Afghani tribes and begins to build a new Afghani kingdom centered on Kandahar.

1741

East and Southeast Asia: Myanmar
Christianity
Bishop Pio Gallizia becomes the first vicar apostolic of Ava e Pegù.

1741

Europe: Netherlands
Christianity
After attending the University of Leiden where he studies theology, former slave Jacobus Capitein is ordained as a minister in the Dutch Reformed Church. He is subsequently appointed as the minister of the fort of Elmina, from where the Dutch organize their slave trade activity.

1741

Russia, Central Asia, and the Caucasus: Russia
Christianity
Elizaveta Petrovna (r. 1741–1762), the daughter of Peter the Great, orchestrates a coup and takes the throne from the infant czar Ivan VI. Ivan is placed in confinement, and will never rule. The infant was deposed, but no one was executed following the coup. Elizabeth rules for the next 21 years.

1742

North America: United States
Christianity
The Philadelphia Baptist Association issues a formal statement of belief. The Philadelphia Confession of Faith is a slightly edited version of the Second London Confession of Faith (1689), which has originated from a Calvinist theological tradition.

1742

North America: United States
Christianity

Pietist German Lutheran minister Henry Melchior Muhlenberg arrives in Philadelphia and becomes the pastor of Augustus Lutheran Church, a congregation at Providence (now Trappe), Pennsylvania. He builds the new church building for the congregation (now the oldest Lutheran church in continuous use since its founding in the United States). He organizes Zion Lutheran church in Philadelphia. Subsequently, he begins to function as the overseer of various congregations along the Mid-Atlantic and leads in efforts to secure qualified pastors and found new congregations.

1742

Europe: England
Christianity
Messiah, an oratorio composed by George Frideric Handel, utilizing scriptural texts compiled by Charles Jennens from the King James Bible and the Book of Common Prayer, premieres in London. Initially receiving but modest public acclaim, it will grow in popularity over succeeding decades to become one of the most frequently performed choral works in all of Western music. The oratorio is designed as a celebration of the life of Jesus of Nazareth, beginning with the prophecies of his birth and continuing through his Incarnation, Passion, Resurrection and ultimate glorification in heaven and coming kingdom.

An interesting tradition is created by King George II who attends the premiere and stands to leave as the sounds of the "Hallelujah Chorus" begin. The audience also stands as was customary, and the respect originally paid the king is later transferred to the chorus itself. It has been customary to the present for the audience listening to the *Messiah* to stand as the "Hallelujah Chorus" begins.

1742

Europe: Italy
Christianity
A decade after Clement XIII standardizes the images for the Stations of the Cross devotional activity (1731), Pope Benedict XIV recommends that all churches establish a set of the images of the Stations of the Cross on the interior walls of their sanctuary. This request has the effect of bring the devotional activity inside, as previously it had been primarily an outside activity, as most of the events described in the devotion originally occurred out-of-doors.

1742

Europe: Netherlands
Peter Jan Meindaerts, who has succeeded to the leadership of the independent archdiocese of Utrecht, revives the vacant Diocese of Haarlem, which becomes a suffragan diocese, and consecrates the first bishop of a new lineage.

1742

Russia, Central Asia, and the Caucasus: Russia
Judaism
Empress Elizabeth of Russia reiterates the 1727 policy against Jews residing in Russia and attempts to ban all Jews from her realm, including Ukraine and Belarus, except for those who might formally convert to the Russian Orthodox Church. She pays more attention to this policy than her predecessors, which leads to the displacement of thousands of Jews.

1742

Russia, Central Asia, and the Caucasus: Russia
Christianity
Unmarried and childless Empress Elizabeth of Russia chooses her nephew, Peter, the duke of Holstein-Gottorp in Germany, as her heir and brings him to St. Petersburg, where he becomes a member of the Orthodox Church and is publicly proclaimed her heir. In choosing Peter, she rejects the imprisoned Ivan VI.

1743

North America: United States
Christianity
The first resident of the Aleutian Islands is baptized as a Christian by missionaries of the Russian Orthodox Church.

1743

North America: United States
Christianity
Lutheran minister Henry Melchior Muhlenberg arrives in the British American colonies.

1743

North America: United States
Christianity

The Sauer Bible, the first printed in America, emphasizes Universalist themes.

1743

Central America and the Caribbean: Guatemala
Christianity
The Roman Catholic Diocese of Guatemala (Santiago de Guatemala) is elevated to become the Archdiocese of Guatemala. The Diocese of Nicaragua is added to the new province.

1743

East and Southeast Asia: India, Persia
Islam
The life of the financially strapped and weakened Mughal Empire is extended a few years by its alignment with the Ottoman Empire against their common enemy, Persia. Ottoman sultan Mahmud I uses Persian ruler Nadir Shah's campaign against the Mughal Empire as the rationale for initiating the Ottoman-Persian War (1743–1746). The Mughal emperor Muhammad Shah cooperates with the Ottomans.

1743

East and Southeast Asia: China
Buddhism
The White Pagoda temple in Qionghua Park in Beijing undergoes a major renovation and is renamed Yong-an Temple. The roofs of the buildings of the adjacent monastery are covered with yellow glazed tiles (yellow being exclusive to the imperial family), and dragons, also associated with the emperor, added to the decorations.

Emperor Chengzu has a gigantic bell transferred from the Wanshou Temple in Beijing to the recently built Juesheng Temple just outside the city to the west. The bell is covered in numerous incantation formulas.

1743

Europe: France
Christianity
King Louis XV lays the first stone for the new church at Versailles, France, which, when completed and consecrated (1754), will serve as the local parish church for the king. It will be elevated as the cathedral of the new Diocese of Versailles in 1801.

Rulers of France, 1422–1799

Ruler	Name
House of Valois	
1422–1461	Charles VII
1461–1483	Louis XI
1483–1498	Charles VIII
1498–1515	Louis XII
1515–1547	Francis I
1547–1559	Henry II
1559–1560	Francis II
1560–1574	Charles IX
1574–1589	Henry III
House of Bourbon	
1589–1610	Henry IV
1610–1643	Louis XIII
1643–1715	Louis XIV
1715–1774	Louis XV
1774–1792	Louis XVI
1793–1795	Louis XVII
First Republic	
1792–1795	French National Convention
1795–1799	French Directory

1743

Southwest Asia and North Africa: Asia Minor
Islam

Shortly after coming to the throne, Sultan Mahmud places the royal architect Atik Sinan in charge of the new construction project in Istanbul, the large Fatih Mosque (aka Mosque of the Conqueror), which will rise on the site of the former Church of the Holy Apostles. The Church had been a victim of the Fourth Crusade (when Crusaders had invaded and sacked Constantinople) early in the 13th century.

1743–1744

Europe: England
Christianity

Anglican minister John Wesley takes major steps to shape the Methodist movement. He issues a set of General Rules for the several Methodist societies (congregations) that have been formed. Initial affiliation with the Methodists is open to all who desire "to flee from the wrath to come, and to be saved from their sins" (hence to be a seeker rather than a believer), who agree to show that desire for salvation by agreeing to do no harm and avoid evil of every kind, especially that which is most generally practiced in society such as public drunkenness, slaveholding, fighting, borrowing with no thought of repayment, and so on.

Wesley also meets with those who have come to share leadership with him in the Methodist movement, during which they confer with him on a variety of questions. These annual gatherings evolve into the Methodist conference of ministers and lay preachers that continues to guide the movement.

1744

South Asia: India
Christianity

In his bull *Omnium sollicitudinem,* Pope Benedict XIV rules against the accommodation of the prospective converts to Christianity in India by denying the privilege of using familiar local words for naming God and the continuance of aspects of Native culture, which had the possibility of continuing what was thought of as non-Christian patterns of worship. The bull has the effect of stopping the accommodationist practices of the Jesuit missionaries.

1744

East and Southeast Asia: China
Buddhism

The palace in Beijing built just east of the forbidden city for the Yongzheng emperor late in the 17th century, when he was still Prince HeZe, is transformed into the Yonghe Temple (or Palace of Eternal Harmony), a lamasery (temple for the worship of Tibetan Buddhists). It becomes the base for the Gelugpa School of Tibetan Buddhism in the imperial capital. The temple and monastery complex not only have a unique design, given its original purpose as a palace, but it emerges as one of the largest temple complexes in Beijing, rivaling the Temple of Heaven.

Among the treasures added to the lamasery is the Wandala Buddha, a 50-foot statue carved from a single piece of sandalwood, which the seventh Dalai Lama had presented as a gift to the Qianlong emperor.

Yonghe Temple, a Tibetan Buddhist temple in Beijing, China. Also known as the Palace of Eternal Harmony Lama Temple, it was built during the Qing Dynasty and has been used as an imperial palace and a monastery. (Anzeletti/iStockphoto.com)

1744

East and Southeast Asia: Japan
Shinto

The hondan (main hall where the deities are enshrined) at the Izumo Taisha in Shimane is rebuilt. It is one of the earliest buildings in what will become the *taisha-zukuri* (or grand shrine) style. It appears to have originally been some 157 feet high, making it one of the tallest structures in Japan (most notably, taller than the great Buddha hall at Todai-ji in Nara, considered the tallest wooden building in the world).

1744

Europe: Germany
Christianity

A lightning strike destroys the 14th-century Ettal Abbey, a Benedictine monastery in Bavaria. It would be rebuilt in the High Baroque style, of which it would become a notable example.

1744

Southwest Asia and North Africa: Arabia
Islam

The daughter of Islamic reformer Muhammad bin Abdul-Wahhab' marries Abdul Aziz, son and successor of Muhammad ibn Saud, who was in the process of creating the modern state of Saudi Arabia. The wedding confirmed the alliance between Wahhab and ibn Saud made in 1740.

The wedding is also seen as the founding date of the first Saudi state, evolving from the emirate of Diriyah, ibn Saud previously holding the title of Emir of Diriyah. The government subsequently moved to rid Saudi territory of a spectrum of what were considered heretical practices—offering prayers and/or veneration to saints (especially Sufi leaders whose bodies were usually enshrined at tombs where the faithful gathered), or the veneration of trees, caves, and stones (remnants of pre-Islamic polytheistic practices).

1744

Southwest Asia and North Africa: Asia Minor
Christianity

Neophytus VI, the ecumenical patriarch, is deposed from office and exiled to the island of Patmos in the Aegean Sea. For the third time, Paisius II (r. 1744–1748) returns to the office.

1745

South America: Brazil
Christianity

The Roman Catholic Diocese of São Sebastião do Rio de Janeiro, Brazil is divided, and several new dioceses, including the Diocese of São Paulo, are created.

1745

South Asia: India
Christianity

Benjamin Schultze, a German Lutheran missionary who has worked in India since 1719, sees the fruits of his labor published as the first translation of a portion of the Bible into Hindi, the book of Genesis, along with a grammar for the Hindi language as he had encountered it in Madras.

1745

East and Southeast Asia: Japan
Buddhism

Adopting a practice used by many shoguns in the past, Tokugawa Yoshimune formally retires and has his eldest son, Tokugawa Ieshige (1745–1761), invested with the shogun's office. The retired shogun retained the power of the office until his death in 1751. Though somewhat lessened during the period of economic reform, Confucian thought remained powerful in the shogun's court as evidenced in the choice of the new ruler. Shogun Yoshimune cites the Confucian principle of primogeniture as the rationale for overlooking his younger sons, who appeared to be better candidates for the job. As it turned out, Ieshige will be a poor choice as he has little concern for his responsibilities and leaves important decisions to others. Government corruption rises significantly, and through the 1750s, the power of the shogun reaches a new low.

1745

Europe: Germany
Christianity

Prussian ruler Frederick II (r. 1740–1786) cooperates in the erection of the first Roman Catholic church to open in Prussia since the 16th-century Reformation. Construction begins on St. Hedwig's Cathedral in Berlin in 1747, and it is completed in 1773, when the bishop of Warmia leads the ceremonies at which it is dedicated.

1745

Europe: Holy Roman Empire
Christianity

Francis I (r. 1745–1765), the husband of Empress Maria Theresa, is formally crowned Holy Roman emperor, though his wife retains the power in her hands.

1745

Europe: Sweden
Western Esotericism

Emanuel Swedenborg, one of Sweden's outstanding scientists, has gone through a period of spiritual awakening that culminates in his experiencing a visionary encounter in which he is appointed by the Lord to reform Christianity. Having had his spiritual eyes opened, he was now able freely to visit heaven and hell, talk with angels, and understand the spiritual truth in the Christian scriptures. He would go on to write numerous books and propose a new Reformed Church, the Church of the New Jerusalem.

1745

Europe: Ukraine
Christianity

Construction of the Great Lavra Belltower at Kiev Lavra is completed. The tallest free-standing belltower at the time of its construction, it becomes a prominent feature of the Kiev skyline.

1745

Russia, Central Asia, and the Caucasus: Russia
Christianity

Empress Elizabeth of Russia chooses a bride for her nephew and heir, the future czar Peter III. She selects Princess Sophie of Anhalt-Zerbst, who is brought to St. Petersburg and formally converts to the Russian Orthodox Church, at which time she receives the name Catherine, the same received by Elizabeth's mother when she had converted.

1746

East and Southeast Asia: China
Christianity
The Qianlong emperor orders all foreign missionaries to leave his realm and demands that all Christian converts recant and return to their previous religion. Two years later he bans Christianity in China altogether.

1746

Europe: Germany
Islam
A translation of the Qur'an into German is made utilizing the English edition made by George Sale.

1747

North America: United States
Christianity
German congregations in Pennsylvania form the Coetus of the Reformed Ministerium of Pennsylvania, later the Reformed Church in the United States.

1747

North America: United States
Unbelief
Jonathan Mayhew is ordained minister of the West Church in Boston. From the pulpit he begins to preach his Unitarian perspective that affirms the strict unity of God (as opposed to the Trinity), the subordinate nature of Jesus Christ, and salvation by character rather than an act of God.

1747

North America: United States
Christianity
Construction begins on the Basilica Cathedral of the Assumption of the Blessed Virgin Mary at Leon, the former capital of Nicaragua. Work would continue

for many decades and it would finally be consecrated by Pope Pius IX in 1860. The cathedral will become the largest cathedral in Central America, its massive structure allowing it to survive the destructive forces (both natural and manmade) of the area.

1747

South Asia: India
Islam
The chiefs of the Abdali tribes of Afghanistan meet to choose a new leader and select Ahmad Shah Durrani, who adopts the title of king and over the next decade establishes an Afghani Empire that reaches into Persia and India, including what is now Pakistan.

1747

Europe: England
Christianity
John Potter, the archbishop of Canterbury, dies and is succeeded by Thomas Herring (r. 1747–1757), formerly the archbishop of York.

1747

Europe: Germany
Christianity
Moravian bishop Johannes de Watteville, seeking a way to explain Christmas to children, devises what would become the Christingle when he gives each child a lighted candle wrapped in a red ribbon upon which are the words, "Lord Jesus, kindle a flame in these dear children's hearts." The Christingle eventually emerges as an orange with a candle, ribbon, and dried fruit attached.

1747

Europe: Sweden
Western Esotericism
Spiritual seer Emanuel Swedenborg resigns from his job with the Swedish Bureau of Mines to devote his life to spiritual work. He will now turn his attention to the Bible with the goal of interpreting the spiritual meaning of every verse. Time will not allow him to complete the task, but he does extensive commentary on the books of Genesis, Exodus, and Revelation.

1747

Southwest Asia and North Africa: Persia
Islam

Some Persian officers, fearing that the shah is about to execute them, plot his death. They carry out their plot and assassinate Nader Shah at Fathabad in Khorasan. He is surprised in his sleep by his captain of the guards Salah Bey and stabbed with a sword. Nader is able to kill two of his would-be assassins before he dies.

Nader is succeeded by his nephew Ali Qoli, who reigns as Adil Shah ("righteous king"), seemingly one of those involved in the assassination plot. A power struggle in the royal family leads to Adil Shah being deposed within a year. The struggle—between Adil Shah, his brother Ibrahim Khan, and Nader's grandson Shah Rukh—provides an opportunity for almost all of the provincial governors to declare independence. As they establish their own autonomous states, the entire empire of Nader Shah falls into anarchy. Finally, Karim Khan emerges to found the Zand Dynasty. By 1760 he rules Iran, while Ahmad Shah Durrani, who proclaims independence in the east, marks the foundation of modern Afghanistan.

1748

North America: United States
Christianity

Henry Melchior Muhlenberg leads in the formation of the first Lutheran church body in North America, the Ministerium of North America (changed to the Ministerium of Pennsylvania and Adjacent States in 1792).

1748

Central America and the Caribbean: Cuba
Christianity

Jesuits initiate the construction of the new Catedral de la Virgen María de la Concepción Inmaculada de La Habana (or the Cathedral of the Virgin Mary of the Immaculate Conception), built over the site of a previous church in Havana. It will take some 30 years to complete. The church is also dedicated to St. Christopher.

1748

South America: Chile
Christianity

Construction begins on a new cathedral for Santiago, Chile. It will take a half century to complete and will supersede the several cathedrals that had been destroyed by earthquakes.

1748

South Asia: India
Islam

Mughal emperor Muhammad Shah dies. His greatly weakened empire is inherited by his son Ahmad Shah Bahadur (r. 1748–1755).

1748

South Asia: India
Islam

Having absorbed most of Afghanistan under his control, Ahmad Shad Durrani crosses the Indus River for the first time and overruns Lahore, which is added to his kingdom.

1748

East and Southeast Asia: China
Buddhism

Expansion occurs at the Biyun (or azure cloud) Temple in Beijing by the addition of the somewhat unique Diamond Throne Pagoda (consisting of a large square base that supports five pagodas, similar to the earlier pagoda at Zhenjue Temple) and a large new hall for the veneration of the *arhats* (enlightened beings).

1748

East and Southeast Asia: Hong Kong
Chinese Religions

Residents of Tai O, an island off the coast of Lantau Island, construct a temple to Hung Shing Yeh, a god of the sea especially favored by sailors and fishermen.

1748

Europe: England
Christianity

Anglican minister John Wesley writes *A Plain Account of the People Called Methodists* to describe the groups that have responded to his preaching and gathered in the religious societies he has founded.

The term Methodist is a derisive term used by others, a reference to Wesley's methodically organized daily life and the disciplined lifestyle that the members of the societies try to adopt. Critics often see it as fanaticism. Wesley tries to allay any fears of the Methodists as people who simply follow the gospel message and try to live an upright and moral life in which they support, admonish, and assume responsibility for each other.

1748

Russia, Central Asia, and the Caucasus: Russia
Christianity

A wooden church dedicated to the Vladimir Icon of the mother of God is erected in St. Petersburg. The day following its dedication, Empress Elizabeth visits the church for a special liturgy commemorating the new church's opening.

1748

Southwest Asia and North Africa: Asia Minor
Christianity

Ecumenical Patriarch Paisius II began with inheriting the debt that had been accumulated by the patriarchate. In his attempt to reduce the debt, he raised taxes on the Christian community (i.e., the Christian millet), which tipped popular opinion against him. Desirous of the office, the metropolitan of Nicomedia Cyril V Karakallos (r. 1748–1757) replaces him in the patriarchal office, though in 1751–1752 he would have to fight off a return by Paisius.

At issue between the two patriarchs, apart from taxation, was the growing presence of the Roman Catholic Church in Ottoman lands. Cyril is strongly opposed and refuses to recognize Roman Catholic baptism as valid. Paisius has a more moderate opinion concerning the Catholics and does not, for example, require Catholics who convert to Orthodoxy to be rebaptized. Since the Ottomans forced Roman Catholics into the Christian millet ruled by the ecumenical patriarch, many Catholics chose to convert.

1748–1749

North America: United States
Christianity

The press at Ephrata Cloister issues the first American edition of the *Martyr's Mirror,* a Mennonite martyrology.

1749

North America: Canada
Judaism

Following the British assuming control of Halifax, Nova Scotia, Jews, previously banned by the previous French government, organize a Jewish community and purchase a cemetery (1750).

1749

North America: Canada
Christianity

Presbyterians and Congregationalists begin settlement of British Nova Scotia.

1749

North America: United States
Christianity

The Spanish move the Presidio La Bahia and the associated Roman Catholic Mission Nuestra Señora del Espíritu Santo de Zúñiga from its location along the Guadalupe River to a new site along the San Antonio River. The new settlement will later (1829) become known as Goliad.

1749

North America: United States
Judaism

The Jewish community in Charleston, South Carolina, found Congregation Kabat Kadosh Beth Elohim, later to become one of the leading Reform congregations in the United States.

1749

South Asia: India
Islam

To save Delhi from attack, the young and just enthroned Ahmed Shah Bahadur (r. 1748–1775), the emperor of the now declining Mughal Empire, cedes the Sindh and all of the Punjab to the Afghan forces of the Durrani Empire.

1749

South Asia: India
Hinduism

Maratha ruler Shahuji dies and is formally succeeded by his adopted son, Rajaram II (r. 1749–1777). He proved to be highly incompetent; however, during his time in office Shahuji had created the office of peshwa (prime minister) whose office was filled by a succession of most competent government servants. In the future, they assumed the power in the empire and the rulers became largely figureheads.

1749

East and Southeast Asia: China, Mongolia
Buddhism
Several decades of work culminates in the Wudang-zhao Monastery located in Wudang Valley northeast of Baotou, Inner Mongolia. It is the largest Tibetan-style Buddhist monastery in what is now the Inner Mongolia Autonomous Region (Inner Mongolia, for short).

1749–1756

Europe: Sweden
Western Esotericism
Emanuel Swedenborg publishes the *Arcana Coelestia,* a multivolume commentary on Genesis and Exodus using his spiritual (allegorical) interpretation of Christian scripture.

ca. 1750

North America: United States
Christianity
The Eastern Apaches find themselves caught between the Spanish to the South and the Comanches, their rivals on the Plains. They will evolve to become what will be known as the Lipan Apaches and begin to move southwest from their earlier homeland.

1750

South America: Paraguay
Christianity
Portugal secretly cedes the land upon which the Jesuits have established a set of Native communities (reductions) to Spain. Spain subsequently orders the removal of the Native residents, who resist to the point of causing a war. The Jesuits, caught in the middle of the international agreements, become scapegoats as Spain blames them for the hostilities.

1750

South Asia: India
Christianity
Christian Friedrich Schwarz, a Lutheran missionary, arrives in Tiruchirapalli to begin what would become a half-century of Christian evangelism in Tamil-speaking India.

1750

South Asia: India
Hinduism
Marthanda Varma, the king of Travancore in southern Kerala, offers his kingdom to Padmanabha and then begins to rule as Padmanabhadasa, the Lord's servant. Since then, the name of all Travancore kings will include the title Padmanabha Dasa, while the female members of the royal family would be called Padmanabha Sevinis.

1750

Europe: France
Christianity
A new large church of red sandstone, under construction for a quarter of a century, is opened for worship in the city of Belfort (France). The church had been commissioned by a businessman, Henri Schuller, and dedicated to Saint Christopher. In the 20th century, it would become the cathedral for the newly formed Diocese of Belfort.

1750

Russia, Central Asia, and the Caucasus: Russia
Christianity
One of the original wooden churches erected on Vasilevskiy Island, the original center of St. Petersburg, is replaced with a stone church that evolved into the Church of the Annunciation, the oldest of several churches dedicated to the biblical event of the Blessed Virgin Mary being informed by the angel that she was to bear Jesus.

1750

Southwest Asia and North Africa: Persia
Islam
After a period of turmoil, former general Karim Khan Zand (r. 1750–1779) emerges as the new ruler of Iran,

the first Iranian to rule after centuries of Turkish shahs on the throne. His reign will be a time of relative peace and prosperity. As part of his building program, he will erect the Vakil Mosque in Shiraz. The mosque includes a unique *minbar* (pulpit) fashioned from a single solid piece of green marble.

November 1750

East and Southeast Asia: China
Buddhism
Two Manchurian officials assassinate Gvurme Nam-gyal, the regent of Tibet, and widespread rioting spreads through Lhasa. Qing forces enter the country to restore order. The Dalai Lama, who headed the Gelug school of Tibetan Buddhism, was alienated from the assassinated regent and did not support the riot. He allied with the Qing emperor, a patron of Tibetan Buddhism, and the emperor confirmed the Dalai Lama role as the ruler of Tibet and left a Qing force in Tibet to maintain Chinese hegemony.

1751

North America: United States
Christianity
Georgia, which had banned slavery in its original charter, legalizes the buying and selling of slaves. One factor in the change was the support given it by Anglican minister George Whitefield, who like his colleague John Wesley had originally written against slavery. Whitefield, however, altered his stance in the controversy he had raised, and went on to own slaves the rest of his life.

1751

South Asia: India
Sikhism
With Sikhs occupying the city of Lahore which he claimed as his own, Afghani Ahmad Shah returns to reestablish his rule.

1751

East and Southeast Asia: China
Buddhism
The Qianlong emperor celebrates the birthday of his mother by having the Wanshou Temple, a favorite stopping point along the Changhe River for members of the imperial household traveling between the Forbidden City in Beijing and the summer palace, refurbished and expanded. The temple is some 200 years old at the time, having been originally built by the 16th-century empress dowager Li. The Qianlong emperor would again expand the Wanshou Temple in 1761. A palace is added, so his mother could stop for an extended visit to the temple.

1751

East and Southeast Asia: China
Buddhism
The seventh Dalai Lama abolishes the post of desi (or regent), who served as the top secular government official and provided continuity during the periods in which the office of the Dalai Lama was vacant or held by a youth. The Dalai Lama claims that too much power has been focused in the office and replaces it with a ruling council called the Kashag.

1751

East and Southeast Asia: Malaysia
Christianity
Dutch authorities in Malacca complete work on a new large church to replace the old Bovenkerk, which had served as the Reformed Protestant church in the city since 1541. The striking red stone building, later converted into an Anglican church, is the oldest functioning Protestant church in Malaysia.

1751

Europe: France
Christianity
Jesuit priest and mystic Jean-Pierre de Caussade dies. He has spent years as a spiritual counselor, most famously to the nuns of the visitation at Nancy. His life is lived during the controversy over Quietism, which the Catholic Church would officially denounce. As his approach to the spiritual life has the possibility of being confused with Quietism, to avoid controversy, de Caussade does not publish his work. His most famous work would only appear in 1861, *Abandonment to Divine Providence* (aka *The Sacrament of the Present Moment*). He taught that the present moment should be considered a sacrament from God, hence self-abandonment to it and its needs constitutes a

holy state. His approach continues to find followers to the present.

1751

Russia, Central Asia, and the Caucasus: Russia
Christianity

The Elizabeth Bible, commissioned by the empress Elizabeth of Russia, the authorized version of the Russian Orthodox Church, is published. It brings to fruition an effort initiated by Czar Peter I in 1723 to produce a printed edition of the Bible in Church Slavonic. The translation was completed, and Peter ordered its printing, but died before the order could be carried out. The effort lay moribund until 1744 when Elizabeth revived the project. Further checking and revision of the text took another six years and the finished work finally appeared. The additional editions would be printed in 1756, 1757, and 1759. Since the 1750s, all reprints of the Russian Church Bible are based on the second edition (1756) of the Elizabeth Bible.

1751

Southwest Asia and North Africa: Palestine
Judaism

Kabbalist Shalom Sharabi assumes leadership of Yeshiva Bet El in Jerusalem. He will acquire a large student following as his reputation for piety grows and stories of miraculous occurrences involving him circulate.

1752

Sub-Saharan Africa: South Africa
Christianity

Thomas Thompson, the first Anglican missionary commissioned by the Society for the Propagation of the Gospel for Africa, arrives at the slaving castle at Cape Coast in what is now Ghana. While there, he serves as the garrison's chaplain and makes initial missionary efforts among the Native people by starting a small school in the castle. He had previously worked among African Americans in the British colony of New Jersey in North America.

1752

Central America and the Caribbean:
Netherlands Antilles

Christianity

Revival of the Roman Catholic Church in the Netherlands Antilles is signaled by the establishment of the Prefecture Apostolic of Curaçao. The prefecture becomes a vicariate apostolic in 1842 and the Diocese of Willemstad in 1958.

1752

South America: Argentina
Christianity

The nave of the cathedral in Buenos Aires collapses. Work on a new, larger building begins shortly thereafter and continues off and on for over a century, only being completed in the 1860s.

1752

South Asia: India

Afghani ruler Ahmad Shah captures Kashmir and moves on to overrun Turkmenistan, Uzbekistan, and Tajikistan.

1752

East and Southeast Asia: Myanmar
Buddhism

Alaungpaya becomes king of Burma, founds the Konbaung Dynasty, and unites the country under a single rule. In the process, he founds the city of Yangon (aka Rangoon).

1752

Europe: England
Christianity

The British government adopts the Gregorian calendar and makes it standard for all of Great Britain, Ireland, and the British colonies.

1752

Europe: Germany
Christianity

The new Diocese of Fulda is erected in Germany by the Roman Catholic Church. The large abbey church of the Fulda Monastery is designated as the cathedral for the bishop. The abbey, which had entered a period of decline, would be dissolved in 1802.

1753

North America: United States
Christianity

Moravian bishop August Spangenberg purchases land in North Carolina and leads a group of the faithful from Bethlehem, Pennsylvania to the land they call Wachovia, where they found the town of Old Salem.

1753

North America: United States
Unbelief

Dr. George de Benneville, who has spent the previous decade spreading the belief in universal salvation in the British American colonies, sees to the translation and publication of a German book espousing Universalism, *The Everlasting Gospel* by Georg Klein-Nicolai. The book would contribute significantly to the creation of the first generation of converts to the idea and later to the formation of the Universalist Church.

1753

South Asia: Sri Lanka
Buddhism

King Kirti Sri Rajasinha of Sri Lanka invites bhikkhus from the Thai court to reinstate the bhikkhu ordination line in his country. Their actions lead to the formation of a new Buddhist sangha, the Siyam Nikaya.

1753

Europe: England
Christianity

Evangelist George Whitefield opens a new tabernacle in the London suburb of Moorfields, not far from the Methodist headquarters, the Foundry. He also issues a new hymn book, *Hymns for social worship, collected from various authors, and particularly design'd for use of the Tabernacle Congregation in London.* A Calvinist, he freely altered the Arminian text of some of Charles Wesley's hymns, which further stressed the already tense relations between him and his former colleagues.

1753

Europe: France
Christianity

Physician and biblical scholar Jean Astrue publishes his anonymously written essay on the accounts of Moses's reception of the law in the Bible. In his attempt to reconcile the variant texts, which use different Hebrew names for God, he suggests that in composing the law, Moses utilized some older texts that had variant names for God. Astrue becomes the first to turn the techniques of textual analysis, already commonplace in studying classical writings, to the biblical Book of Genesis and to arrive at what today is termed the documentary hypothesis of its origin.

1753

Europe: Portugal
Christianity

After a two-century hiatus in work on a Portuguese translation of the Bible, a complete translation (apart from the deuterocanonical books, i.e., the Apocrypha, considered canonical by Roman Catholics but not by Protestants) appears. This version is the work product of a Portuguese Protestant, João Ferreira de Almeida, who worked on it for almost half a century. He initially collaborated with scholars in the Reformed Church in Holland to translate the Bible into Portuguese using the Spanish edition as his basic text. Later as a Reformed minister in Indonesia, he learned Greek and Hebrew, which he used to assist his final editing work. The revised New Testament was finally published posthumously in 1691. Dutch Reformed minister Jacobus op den Akker would complete the unfinished translation of the Old Testament, finally published in two volumes in 1748 and 1753.

1754

North America: United States
Christianity

John Woolman publishes *Some Considerations on the Keeping of Negroes,* which launches two decades of antislavery activity among the Quakers.

Fellow Quaker Anthony Benezet, who has been teaching at the Friends' English School, establishes his own school, the first public girls' school in North America.

1754

North America: United States
Christianity

The assembly of the Dutch Reformed Church in the British American colonies (formed in 1747) declares itself independent of the classis (synod) of Amsterdam (Netherlands).

1754

South Asia: India
Islam

Mughal emperor Ahmad Shah Bahadur is deposed and blinded. He is replaced by Aziz-ud-din Alamgir II (r. 1754–1759), the son of former emperor Jahandar Shah.

1754

East and Southeast Asia: China
Buddhism

The Qianlong emperor orders a major renovation and reconstruction of Ciren Monastery in Beijing, which justifies its renaming as the Grand Baoguo Ciren Monastery.

1754

Europe: Spain
Christianity

Pope Benedict XIV erects the Diocese of Santander (Spain) and designates the former Collegiate Church of the Holy Bodies as the diocese's cathedral, now known as the Cathedral of the Assumption of the Virgin Mary of Santander.

1754

Southwest Asia and North Africa: Asia Minor
Islam

Ottoman sultan Mahmud I dies and is succeeded by his brother Osman III (r. 1754–1757). His brief reign was marked by a rise in intolerance of the Jews and Christians residing in the empire, especially in Asia Minor. Both communities are required to wear distinctive clothing so to distinguish them as they move among the Muslim majority.

1754–1755

Europe: Ukraine
Judaism

Jacob Frank settles in Podolia after years of travels in Asia Minor and southeastern Europe. He initiates a new messianic movement in the tradition of Sabbatai Zevi. As his following grows, a rabbinical court gathers at Brody and excommunicates him. Frank subsequently converts to Christianity and joins forces with Christian anti-Semites in attacking the rabbis.

ca. 1755

Europe: England
Unbelief

James Relly, an independent Methodist minister from Wales, settles in London and authors a series of books, most notably *Union; or a Treatise of the Consanguinity between Christ and His Church* (1759), expounding belief in universal salvation, a doctrine he had developed from John Wesley's idea of free grace and the universal atonement. He later teaches his ideas to John Murray, who would become one of the founders of the Universalist Church in the United States.

1755

North America: United States
Christianity

Shubal Stearns leads in the formation of the Sandy Creek Baptist Church in North Carolina.

1755

East and Southeast Asia: Taiwan
Chinese Religions

Immigrants from Fujien, mostly from Tongan County, who worship the local deity Baosheng Dadi, begin construction of the Dalongdong Baoan Temple in what will become Taipei. It will grow to become one of Taiwan's largest traditional temples. While originally devoted exclusively to the worship of Baosheng Dadi, over the years additional halls supporting veneration of a spectrum of traditional Chinese deities emerge.

1755

Europe: Holy Roman Empire
Christianity

Maria Theresa, the empress of the Holy Roman Empire, bears a daughter, Marie Antoinette (1755–1793), the future queen of France.

Drawing of the Lisbon earthquake of November 1, 1755. The earthquake was the greatest natural disaster to strike Europe in the 18th century, killing tens of thousands of people and leveling the city of Lisbon, Portugal. Many believed the disaster was God's retribution for the sinfulness of Lisbon's citizens. (Jupiterimages)

1755–1756

Southwest Asia and North Africa: Asia Minor
Christianity

Three years after the ecumenical patriarch Cyril V rules that both Armenian and Catholic converts to Orthodoxy should be rebaptized, the Holy Synod of the Ecumenical Patriarchate meets to consider Cyril's decision. They reject it as an innovation not in accord with the tradition. Cyril counters by exiling all the bishops who oppose him. He then issues an encyclical, *Anathema of those who accept papal sacraments,* which is followed by the *Oros (Tome) of the Holy Great Church of Christ,* a decree that requires rebaptism of any converts to Orthodoxy, especially those from Roman Catholicism. The *Oros* would be reissued a year later with the added signatures of the patriarchs Matthew of Alexandria and Parthenius of Jerusalem.

Though accepted only by the three Greek patriarchates, the *Oros* creates another significant theological barrier to the reestablishment of cordial relations between Roman Catholic and Eastern Orthodox churches. At issue is not the doctrine of baptism, but its mode, as the Orthodox churches generally baptize by triune immersion.

November 1 (All Saints' Day), 1755

Europe: Portugal
Christianity

A major earthquake, followed by a tsunami, strikes Lisbon, Portugal, largely destroying the city. Significant damage spreads through central Portugal and into adjacent areas of Spain. Among the major ecclesiastical buildings included in the destruction are the Lisbon Cathedral, the Misericórdia Church, the basilicas of São Paulo, Santa Catarina, and São

Vicente de For, and the Carmo Convent. The convent was left in its ruined state as a reminder of the event, and damage from the quake remains visible in the cathedral at Salamanca, Spain. That the quake hit on an important church holy day and destroyed almost all of the key churches in the city would become an issue discussed by theologians and church leaders for several centuries.

In Morocco, cities along the Atlantic coast, such as Rabat, suffer significant damage, but the effects also reach into the interior to Meknes, Fez, and Marrakesh. Mosques, synagogues, and churches, many centuries old, collapsed and had to be rebuilt.

For Christians, the damage of the earthquake occasions broad discussions of theodicy, the question of the presence of significant innocent suffering in a world reputedly created by a God of immense goodness and power.

1756

North America: United States
Christianity
With the support of both the Philadelphia and Charleston Baptist Associations, Rev. Isaac Eaton founds Hopewell Academy, the first Baptist seminary in the Americas, at Hopewell, New Jersey.

1756

North America: United States
Christianity
Fort Herkimer is built to protect colonial interests in New York's Mohawk Valley. Integral to the fort's defenses is the Reformed Church, a stone building with three-foot-thick walls. Over two centuries later, the church continues to house an active congregation.

1756–1757

South Asia: India
Islam
In what becomes his fourth invasion of India, Ahmad Shah sacks Delhi and moves on to plunder Agra, Mathura, and Vrindavan. His actions do not, however, destroy the Mughal Dynasty, which retains control over the Punjab, Sindh, and Kashmir, as Ahmad's vassal. Ahmad installs a puppet emperor, Alamgir II, on the Mughal throne.

1756–1758

East and Southeast Asia: Mongolia
Buddhism
Chingunjav, a Mongolian military leader, initiates a rebellion against the Qianlong emperor. The rebellion never takes hold and lasts only because of the great distances involved and the time the emperor needs to recruit and send an army to reoccupy the land.

The Jebtsundamba Khutugtu, the Mongolian Buddhist leader, did not join the rebellion and his silence was a major reason that more did not rally to Chingunjav's cause. He dies in 1758, and the emperor declares that the future incarnations of the Jebtsundamba Khutugtu, heretofore drawn from Mongolian nobility, will in the future be "found" in Tibet.

1757

North America: United States
Christianity
King Charles III expels the Jesuits from the American lands controlled by Spain and confiscates their property.

1757

North America: United States
Christianity
Franciscans create the Mission Santa Cruz de San Sabá located along the San Saba River to serve the Lipan Apache.

1757

South Asia: India
Islam, Sikhism
Forces of Afghani king Ahmed Shah Abdali attack and plunder Delhi, Agra, Mathura, and Vrindavan. On their return to Afghanistan they march on Amritsar, blow up the Sikh Golden Temple, and fill the sacred pool with the entrails of slaughtered cows. This latter act establishes deeply embittered feelings in Sikhs toward Afghanis.

1757

South Asia: India
Islam, Christianity
The Battle of Plassey. At a site on the Bhagirathi River (aka Hooghly River) upstream from Calcutta, British

forces attached to the British East India Company defeat the combined forces of the nawab of Bengal, the ruler of Bengal, Bihar, and Orissa, and the French. The battle establishes the British East India Company rule over Bengal and sets the stage for the expansion of British rule across the subcontinent. The coming of the British, in spite of the overall hostility of the company to religious missionaries, opened India to the influx of a spectrum of Protestant missionaries.

1757

Europe: Germany
Christianity

Church historian Johann Salomo Semler assumes the leadership of the faculty of theology at the University of Halle. During his lengthy career, he will emerge as a critical student of the ancient church documents, including the Bible, and become a pioneering champion of a spectrum of views that will become part of the modern approach to religious history. He will insist on the distinctions between religion and theology, and draw out the differences between the local and temporal as opposed to the eternal and permanent aspects of religion.

His work also leads him to reject a spectrum of largely assumed propositions relative to Christian origins, including the consideration of the Old and New Testaments as of equal value; the uniform authority of all parts of the Bible; the establishment of the canon of Scripture by divine authority, and the integrity and accuracy of the texts of the Old and New Testaments. He also refused to identify revelation with scripture. His work led the way in considering the Bible texts as historical documents and the proper objects of the techniques of historical research. His controversial views made him a popular figure with both his colleagues and the student body.

1757

Europe: Netherlands
Christianity

Peter Jan Meindaerts, who has succeeded to the leadership of the independent Archdiocese of Utrecht, revives the vacant Diocese of Deventer, which becomes a new suffragan diocese of Utrecht. The pope excommunicates all who act in support of the Archdiocese of Utrecht and its suffragan dioceses of Haarlam and Deventer.

1757

Europe: Spain
Christianity

Charles III, the king of Spain, expels the Jesuits from Spain and all the territories under Spanish control, which includes Sicily, Naples, and Parma, and confiscates all their property.

1757

Southwest Asia and North Africa: Asia Minor
Christianity

Ecumenical Patriarch Cyril V moves to suppress opposition to his rule by exiling the metropolitan of Proilavo (i.e., Brăila, Romania) Callinicus (r. 1757) to the Sinai Peninsula. He refuses to leave Istanbul and takes refuge in the French embassy. While there, he receives a large gift of money, which he passes to Sultan Osman III and which facilitates his being able to depose Cyril and succeed to the office. He is, however, unable to hold the office for long and is forced to move to the Sinai by the new patriarch Seraphim II (r. 1757–1761).

1757

Southwest Asia and North Africa: Asia Minor
Islam

Ottoman sultan Osman III dies and is succeeded by his nephew Mustafa III (r. 1757–1774). Shortly before his death, Osman issues a decree (a firman) that defines and makes provisions for preserving the present sites of the Christian, Muslim, and Jewish communities in Palestine.

November 11, 1757

South Asia: India

The Battle of Amritsar. Sikhs under the aging holy man Baba Deep Singh (1682–1757) attack Afghani forces who have destroyed and desecrated the Golden Temple. They lose the battle and Singh is decapitated. The sword he used in the battle has become a sacred Sikh relic.

1757–1758

Europe: England
Christianity

Thomas Herring, the archbishop of Canterbury, dies and is succeeded by Matthew Hutton (r. 1757–1758), who had also succeeded Herring as the archbishop of York. Hutton dies after only a year in his new role and is succeeded by Thomas Secker (r. 1758–1768), the former bishop of Oxford.

1758

North America: United States
Christianity

The Philadelphia Yearly Meeting of the Society of Friends declares slavery inconsistent with Christianity.

1758

South America: Brazil
Christianity

The Jesuits' missions along the Uruguay River are caught in a border dispute between Spain and Portugal. Anti-Jesuit sentiment in Portugal leads to the order being stripped of all its property and expelled from Portuguese territory (Brazil).

1758

Europe: England
Christianity

Ann Lee joins a small informal group of believers that had gathered around Jane and James Wardley. She eventually assumes leadership of the group, which comes to be known as the Shakers from the movements they made during their worship. Lee taught that the shaking and trembling were a sign of the Holy Spirit purifying the body by sin being purged away.

1758

Europe: Italy
Christianity

Pope Benedict XIV dies and is succeeded by Pope Clement XIII (r. 1758–1769).

1758–1759

Europe: Portugal
Christianity

A series of controversies involving the Jesuits, culminating in the accusation that they were behind the attempted assassination of the country's king, led to the order losing its mission property in Brazil, being banished from Portugal, and then formally suppressed throughout Portuguese territory.

1759

North America: Canada
Christianity

The British capture Quebec, where Roman Catholicism is the dominant form of religion. The new British leadership, who are primarily Anglicans, guarantees free exercise of religion to the residents. During the siege of the city, the original Cathedral of Notre Dame is destroyed by fire and must be rebuilt.

1759

South Asia: India
Islam

Mughal emperor Alamgir II, having heard that a holy man had come to meet him, journeys to greet the unknown person only to encounter assassins sent by one of his empire's officials who felt threatened by a possible loss of position. The relatively popular emperor is mourned by the Muslim populace who organize against the Hindu-led Maratha kingdom, which is defeated at the Third Battle of Panipat. Alamgir II is eventually succeeded by his son Shah Alam II (r. 1761–1806), who will hold the throne for the rest of the century.

1759

Europe: France
Unbelief

François-Marie Arouet, better known by his nom de plume Voltaire, publishes his satirical classic *Candide: or, The Optimist,* just a few years after the devastating earthquake that destroys Lisbon. It is a satirical attack upon the naïve optimism of the German philosopher Gottfried Wilhelm Leibniz. The story describes a youth indoctrinated with optimism, which is stripped away by his own experiences of disillusionment and hardships. True to Voltaire's skepticism, God is largely absent from Candide's existence, and he can no longer believe that he lives in the best of all possible worlds.

1759

Europe: Portugal
Christianity

The marquis of Pombal, prime minister of King José I, announces the banning of the Jesuits from Portugal. Their church and formation house in Coimbra are abandoned.

1759

Europe: Sweden
Western Esotericism
From 300 miles away, Swedish seer Emanuel Swedenborg has a vision of fire in Stockholm.

1760

North America: United States
Judaism
An English translation of *Evening Services for Rosh-Hashanah and Yom Kippur* appears in New York. The volume, attributed to a Jewish merchant, Isaac Peters, is the first English translation of a Jewish prayer book to be published. It will be followed by an additional volume, *Prayers for Sabbath, Rosh-Hashanah and Yom Kippur,* published in 1766.

1760

East and Southeast Asia: Japan
Buddhism
Shogun Tokugawa Ieshige formally retires just a year before his death and installs his son Tokugawa Ieharu (r. 1760–1786).

1760

Europe: England
Christianity
King George II dies and is succeeded by his grandson who reigns as George III (r. 1760–1820). His reign is the longest in British history prior to the 20th century.

1760

Europe: France
Christianity
Having purchased a new residence at the Château de Choisy, King Louis XV of France commissioned a new church building in which he might worship when in the area. Upon its completion, the king, his court, and the archbishop of Paris attended the ceremonies dedicating the building. For several decades in the 20th century, the church served as the cathedral for the newly created Diocese of Créteil (1966–1987).

1760

Europe: Germany
Christianity
Jesuits erect a large Baroque-style church at Mannheim and dedicate it to Ignatius Loyola and Francis Xavier. It is noteworthy for its large dome and interior decorations to which a number of artists contributed.

1760

Russia, Central Asia, and the Caucasus: Russia
Christianity
A wooden building, the Church of the Smolensk Icon of the Mother of God, is completed and consecrated at the Smolensk Cemetery on Vasilevsky Island in St. Petersburg.

1760–1769

South Asia: India
Sikhism
Sikhs, reacting to the desecration of their holy temple, stay in a state of hostility toward the Afghani Empire to their north. Afghani ruler Ahmad Shah feels compelled to invade the Punjab in 1761, 1762, 1764, and 1766, with the Sikhs showing themselves better able to withstand attack with each encounter. Those who died in the battles are hailed as martyrs of the faith.

1761

East and Southeast Asia: China
Buddhism
The two-year-old Jamphel Gyatso, the future eighth Dalai Lama, is taken to Tashilhunpo monastery in Shigatse, Tibet, after the stories of extraordinary occurrences associated with him become more generally known. The Panchen Lama performs the recognition ceremony and gives the boy his name.

1761

Europe: England
Christianity
Scottish Bible scholar Alexander Cruden presents the second edition of his concordance of the King James

Version of the Bible to British king George III, to whom it is also dedicated. The king awards Cruden £100 for his effort. This second edition enjoyed brisk sales and became a standard tool for anyone wishing to study the Bible in English, and it remains in print to the present day.

1761

Southwest Asia and North Africa: Asia Minor
Christianity
The pro-Russian sympathies of Ecumenical Patriarch Seraphim I bring him into conflict with the Ottoman authorities and lead to his deposition and exile to Mount Athos. The Ottomans replace him with Joannicios III (r. 1761–1763), the metropolitan of Chalcedon. Joannicios's brief tenure as patriarch would again introduce a generation in which instability ruled the office and little could be accomplished by the succession of patriarchs serving but brief terms in office.

January 1761

South Asia: India
Hinduism, Islam
Third Battle of Panipa. Afghani king Ahmed Shah Abdali declares a jihad (holy war) against the Hindu-led Maratha kingdom, which now controlled most of India. After several years of indecisive battle, the two armies met at Panipat, Haryana State, in north India where Ahmad Shad won a significant victory.

December 25, 1761

Russia, Central Asia, and the Caucasus: Russia
Christianity
Russian empress Elizabeth dies and is succeeded by her nephew and designated heir, Peter III. During his brief reign, he publishes a proclamation of religious freedom throughout the country. He was assassinated after only six months on the throne, his wife and successor, Catherine II, being high on any list of suspects.

1762

North America: United States
Judaism

Rhode Island refuses to grant Jews Aaron Lopez and Isaac Eliezer citizenship, stating "no person who is not of the Christian religion can be admitted free to this colony."

1762

South Asia: India
Sikhism
In a battle with Afghani forces in February, some 25,000 Sikhs, including many women and children, are killed. In the following October, with the memory of the heavy losses suffered earlier in the year, Sikh forces engage the Afghanis at Amritsar. In the midst of the battle, in which the losses are heavy by both sides, a total eclipse of the sun occurs. The Afghan leader Shah Durrani takes advantage of the darkness to disengage and withdraw from a battle he appears to have been losing.

1762

East and Southeast Asia: China
Buddhism
The future Dalai Lama, Jamphel Gyatso, now three years old, is taken to Lhasa and enthroned at the Potala Palace.

1762

East and Southeast Asia: China, Hong Kong
Chinese Religions
Residents of Pen Chau Island, located in the body of water between Hong Kong Island and Lantau Island, construct a temple dedicated to Gum Fa, a patron saint of pregnant women. Gum Fa is a special favorite in a culture that values children and constantly hopes for more births, such as in the world of fishermen, where a large family is an economic asset.

1762

Europe: Bulgaria
Christianity
The Bulgarian monk Paisius of Hilendar writes what is the first work written in modern Bulgarian. The brief book, *History of Slav-Bulgarians,* calls for a national awakening by getting rid of the domination of the Greek language and culture in Bulgaria.

1762

Europe: Netherlands
Judaism

Jewish philosopher Isaac de Pinto attempts to answer Voltaire's anti-Semitic remarks against the Jews. In his *Apology for the Jewish Nation,* he describes his own Sephardic community as highly cultured and enlightened, and suggests that Voltaire's remarks are more descriptive of the Ashkenazi Jews.

1762

Russia, Central Asia, and the Caucasus: Russia
Christianity

Elizabeth, the empress of Russia, dies. She is succeeded by Peter III (r. 1762), who would rule Russia a scant six months. His rivals for the throne arrest him, depose him, and then send him into exile, where he died a short time later. He is succeeded by his wife Catherine II (1762–1796), who would later be known as Catherine the Great. She would become the longest-ruling female monarch of Russia.

1762

Russia, Central Asia, and the Caucasus: Russia
Islam

Catherine the Great prohibits Muslims from owning any serfs of the Russian Orthodox faith.

1762

Russia, Central Asia, and the Caucasus: Russia
Christianity

As part of an attempt to heal the break in the Russian Orthodox community between the Orthodox Church and the Old Believers, Russian empress Catherine issues a decree permitting Old Believers to practice their faith openly without interference from the authorities.

1763

North America: United States
Judaism

The Sephardic community of Rhode Island erects the second synagogue in America. Jeshuat Israel (Salvation of Israel), later known as the Touro Synagogue,

For more than 30 years, Catherine II ruled Russia with such energy and flair that she stamped an entire epoch with her name. She is admired as Catherine the Great by most Russians because the country became strong enough under her rule to threaten the other great powers. (Dmitry Levitzky, *Portrait of Catherine II as Legislator in the Temple of the Goddess of Justice,* 1783, The Russian Museum, St. Petersburg, Russia)

is the oldest synagogue structure in the United States. It is designed by leading Rhode Island architect Peter Harrison.

1763

North America: United States
Christianity

Anglican minister James Maury sued for back salary, the dispute resulting from contrary rulings concerning the payment of clergy salaries. In 1758, Virginia had agreed to a payment in currency rather than tobacco, an action disavowed in England by the king's Privy Council. The case is remembered as an opportunity for a young lawyer, Patrick Henry (1736–1799), to voice his belief that the king had broken his trust with those whom he governed, and hence had forfeited his rights to their allegiance.

1763

Central America and the Caribbean: Antigua
Christianity

Following his conversion to Methodism while in England, Nathaniel Gilbert returns home to Antigua where he begins the Methodist Church by spreading his new faith among his own slaves.

1763

South America: Brazil
Christianity

Brazil moves its capital from Salvador to Rio de Janeiro.

1763

Europe: England
Christianity

Anglican minister and poet Augustus Toplady writes his most famous hymn, "Rock of Ages." Toplady had been originally converted by the Methodists, but later left them when he became convinced that Calvinism's predestinarian perspective was a more biblical position. He met Selena, the countess of Huntington, and associated with the connection of churches she sponsored.

1763

Europe: France
Christianity, Judaism, Traditional Religions

The Treaty of Paris ends the global Seven Years' War (sometimes referred to in North America as the French and Indian War) between predominantly Protestant England and predominantly Catholic France and Spain. As a result, in North America France cedes its Canadian territory (except the islands of St. Pierre and Miquelon) and all territory south of the St. Lawrence and east of the Mississippi River except the city of New Orleans. In the Caribbean, France secured Martinique and Guadeloupe, while England maintained title to St. Vincent, Dominica, and Tobago. Spain relinquished control of Florida to England, but regained control of Cuba. It also received New Orleans and French Louisiana west of the Mississippi River.

1763

Europe: Germany
Christianity

Under the pseudonym of Justinus Febronius, Johann Nikolaus von Hontheim, the coadjutor bishop of Treves (or Trier), publishes a book attacking the power of the papacy and raising in Germany the same issues that had entertained the powerful in Gallican France relative to the pope acting as a monarch. Febronius suggests that while respecting the pope as the first among equals, he is subordinate to the universal church. The church is based on its common episcopacy, power shared by all bishops; and the papal claims to infallibility are questionable. The Febronian movement would gain significant strength over the next century in Germany and would be reflected in numerous decisions by secular monarchs.

1763

Russia, Central Asia, and the Caucasus: Russia
Christianity

The saintly Tikhon, the bishop of Keksgolma and Ladoga of the Russian Orthodox Church, becomes the bishop of the emerging Diocese of Voronezh. During his four and a half years in office, he authors several books, completes the eradication of Paganism (especially the continuing worship of Yarila, a local Pagan fertility deity), and founds a seminary. Exhausting himself, he will have to retire to the Tolshevsk monastery, where he will live the rest of his life.

1763–1765

North America: United States
Christianity

Irish Methodist preacher Robert Strawbridge founds several Methodist classes (small groups that meet weekly for prayer and support in the spiritual life) in Maryland, the first Methodist organizations in the

British American colonies. Barbara Heck leads in the founding of a similar class in New York in 1766. Each class includes both black and white members.

1764

North America: United States
Christianity
The British assume control of New Amsterdam and rename it New York. There are 13 Reformed churches in the colony. They will continue to use the Dutch language for another century.

1764

North America: United States
Christianity
The Philadelphia Baptist Association commissions Rev. James Manning, a graduate of Hopewell Academy, to take the lead in the organization of the College of Rhode Island (now Brown University). Though the college was to have a Baptist president, it had a religiously diverse board of trustees and prohibited any religious tests for admitting students.

1764

Europe: Austria
Christianity
Joseph II (r. 1764–1790), the eldest son of Empress Maria Theresa, is crowned as co-emperor of the Holy Roman Empire. He will begin to assume duties beside his father, Emperor Francis I.

1764

Europe: England
Christianity
Anglican lay reader John Newton, who had been frustrated in his attempt to become a minister, is accepted by the bishop of Chester, who ordains him and assigns him to the parish of Olney in Buckinghamshire.

1764

Russia, Central Asia, and the Caucasus: Russia
Christianity
Her attempt to assimilate the Old Believers back into the Orthodox Church having failed, Russian empress Catherine deports some 20,000 Old Believers to Siberia. At about the same time, in order to limit the growing power of the Russian Orthodox clergy, Catherine confiscates church lands across Russia.

1764

Southwest Asia and North Africa: Palestine
Judaism
Rabbis Nahman of Horodenka and Menahem Mendakl of Peremyshlany introduce Hasidim to Palestine by leading a group of believers to settle in Tiberias.

1764–1765

South Asia: India
Islam, Christianity
Forces of the British East India Company defeat the army of the Mughal Empire at the Battle of Buxar. Soon afterward, Shah Alam II signs the Treaty of Allahabad in which he grants the right to collect taxes to the British in Bengal, Bihar, and Orissa, a percentage of which they then pay to the empire. The British victory also opens India to further incursions by Christian missionaries.

ca. 1765

East and Southeast Asia: China, Hong Kong
Chinese Religions
Residents of Mong Tseng Wai in what is now the New Territories construct a temple to Pak Tai, a sea god also known to protect people from contagious disease.

1765

Central America and the Caribbean: Honduras
Christianity
Construction begins on the San Miguel Cathedral in Tegucigalpa, the capital of Honduras. It will take some 20 years to complete.

1765

Europe: France
Unbelief, Judaism
In Volume Nine of his *Encyclopedia,* Denis Diderot both praises Jews as the oldest nation on earth and perpetuators of the natural religion of the patriarchal

era, but simultaneously denounces them as a defective nation due to superstition and ignorance.

1765

Europe: Holy Roman Empire
Christianity

Emperor Francis I of the Holy Roman Empire dies unexpectedly. His son, Joseph II, already crowned as his successor, assumes his duties, though the real power is maintained by his mother, Empress Maria Theresa. Maria Theresa is deeply affected by the loss of her husband and dresses in mourning for the remaining 15 years of her life, and gradually allows her son to assume more duties than he would have otherwise.

1765

Europe: Italy
Christianity

Pope Clement XIII backs the Jesuits and praises their work, which had come under heavy criticism throughout Europe, and dismisses criticisms against them as false slander. In Austria, Maria Theresa blocks the publication of Clement's statement.

1765

Europe: Italy, Poland
Christianity

At the request of the bishops of Poland, Pope Clement XIII gives approval for the celebration of the Feast of the Sacred Heart of Jesus and simultaneously, prompted by a request of the queen of France, the French bishops give the feast a quasi-official status in the country.

1765–1769

North America: United States
Christianity

Irish immigrant Robert Strawbridge organizes the first Methodist class in the British American colonies in rural Frederick County. Among the members is a black woman known as "Auntie Ann." Methodism spreads quickly through the middle colonies with the initial classes being organized in New York City, Brooklyn, Philadelphia, Leesburg (Virginia), and

Baltimore. From the beginning, African Americans join and become an integral part of the fellowship.

1766

North America: United States
Christianity

Reacting to the establishment of Princeton University by the Presbyterians, ministers of the Dutch Reformed Church, Rev. Theodorus Jacobus Frelinghuysen and Rev. Jacob Rutsen Hardenbergh (1736–1790), establish a college to train the church's ministers within the church. Their effort culminates in the chartering of Queen's College, which is named in honor of King George III's queen consort, Charlotte of Mecklenburg-Strelitz. It will evolve to become Rutgers University.

1766

North America: United States
Christianity

Presbyterian ministers George Duffield and Charles Clinton Beatty travel through western Pennsylvania, Maryland, and Virginia on a missionary tour designed to meet with families scattered throughout the region and preach to any Native peoples they encounter.

1766

South Asia: India
Christianity

Lutheran missionary Johann Phillip Fabricius oversees the printing of the complete New Testament of his translation in Tamil, followed by an edition of the Psalms. This translation would be the standard Tamil text into the 20th century.

1766

Europe: England
Christianity

Anglican minister and Methodist founder John Wesley publishes the first edition of *A Plain Account of Christian Perfection,* in which he offers Christians the possibility of becoming perfect in this life, by which he meant to be "sanctified throughout" and "to have a heart so all-flaming with the love of God, as continually to offer up every thought, word, and work, as a spiritual sacrifice, acceptable to God through Christ." In every thought of our hearts, in every word of our tongues, in every work of our hands, to "show forth his praise, who hath called us out of darkness into his marvelous light."

1766

Russia, Central Asia, and the Caucasus: Armenia
Islam

The Persian rulers of Yerevan, in a region of Armenia where Islam was the dominant religion, complete construction on the Blue Mosque, the largest mosque serving the Muslims of the city.

1766

Southwest Asia and North Africa: Asia Minor
Islam

A major earthquake hits Istanbul. The Fatih Mosque is completely destroyed and has to be largely rebuilt.

1767

South America: Brazil, Paraguay
Christianity

Jesuits are expelled from Spanish lands in the Americas, and work they had led is largely reassigned to Franciscans and Dominicans.

1767

South Asia: India
Hinduism

Ahilya Bai Holkar (r. 1767–1795), who has married into the family of the rulers of Malwa, a district of the Maratha Empire in western India, emerges as queen when the men around her die unexpectedly. With the sanction of the Maratha peshwa (prime minister), she emerges as a capable ruler and a great patron of Hinduism. She supplies resources to build new temples, especially replacement temples for those destroyed by the Muslims during the reign of Aurangzeb, and to repair and expand others not only in her kingdom, but across India from the Himalayas to the far south. She transforms her capital Maheshwar into a notable literary, musical, and artistic center.

The Holkar family are Saivites, that is, devotees of the Hindu deity Shiva. Her personal faith is evident in Ahilya Bai Holkar's particular attention to the most holy of the Saivite sites, the 12 Jyotirlingas, at which she made notable reconstructions and other improvements. She also built a number of new Shiva temples.

1767

East and Southeast Asia: Thailand
Buddhism

Burmese invaders destroy the Buddhist kingdom of Ayutthaya. The invaders systematically decapitate statues of the Buddha, including the Golden Buddha (officially known as Phra Phuttha Maha Suwan Patimakon), the world's largest solid gold statue. The gold statue went otherwise unnoticed as it had been coated with plaster prior to the invasion. It would later be recovered and carried to Bangkok.

1767

Europe: Spain, Italy
Christianity

King Charles III of Spain moves against the Jesuits. He has all their centers surrounded, the residents detained and shipped to the nearest Spanish port. Placed on ships, they were all sent to Civitavecchia, the port of Rome in central Italy. He gave them an allowance, but promised to withdraw it should any of them write in their defense or against his action.

1768

North America: Canada
Judaism

Sephardic Jews in Montreal establish Shearith Israel, the first Jewish congregation in Canada.

1768

North America: United States
Christianity

Scottish physician Andrew Turnbull organizes the largest attempt at British colonization in the New World with the founding of New Smyrna, Florida. He had married a woman from Smyrna, the Greek city on the west coast of Turkey, and named his colony in honor of her birthplace. He also invites Greek immigrants to settle there, thus creating an environment for

Franciscan friar Junipero Serra (1713–1784) led the establishment of 21 Spanish missions throughout the area of Alta California, which was then part of the Spanish Empire. (Bettmann/Corbis)

the primal emergence of the Greek Orthodox Church in North America.

1768

Central America and the Caribbean: Mexico
Christianity

Spanish king Carlos III orders all Jesuits forcibly expelled from New Spain. As a result, their work in Baja California is taken over by the Franciscans under the leadership of Father Junipero Serra.

1768

East and Southeast Asia: China
Chinese Religions

The Qianlong emperor orders the renovation of the Confucius Temple complex in Beijing. All of the buildings, except the Chongsheng Temple, which serves as the ancestral temple of the Confucius family, are cov-

ered with yellow tile (the color limited to the exclusive use of the imperial family).

1768

East and Southeast Asia: Myanmar
Buddhism

An earthquake hits Yangon and topples the steeple that caps the Shwedagon Pagoda, a Buddhist stupa containing sacred relics. King Hsinbyushin of the Konbaung Dynasty responds with repairs that raise the stupa to its current height of 325 feet.

1768

Europe: England
Christianity

Thomas Secker, the archbishop of Canterbury, dies and is succeeded by Frederick Cornwallis (r. 1768–1783), the former bishop of Lichfield.

1768

Europe: Germany
Unbelief

Deist philosopher Hermann Samuel Reimarus dies. He had denied the supernatural origin of Christianity and championed the perspective that knowledge of God and the basic principles of nature can be deduced from the rational observation of nature and there was no need of revelation. His major work, a study of the historical Jesus, would remain unpublished during his lifetime, but would upon publication lead to the 19th-century search for the historical Jesus.

1768

Europe: Netherlands
Christianity

Johannes van Stiphout, the bishop of Haarlem, consecrates Walter Michael van Nieuwenhuisen as the 11th archbishop of the independent Archdiocese of Utrecht. The archdiocese continues its search for vindication from a church council and resolves its differences with Rome. Following his consecration, van Nieuwenhuisen receives letters of support from other bishops across Europe who oppose the pope's claims to universal authority.

1769

North America: United States
Christianity
Franciscan priest Junipero Serra accompanies Mexican governor Gaspar de Portolà on an expedition to California. The expedition reaches what is now San Diego. Fr. Serra stays behind as it moves on and founds Mission San Diego de Alcalá, the first of 21 missions along the coast of California founded by him and those under his direction.

1769

North America: United States
Christianity
Methodist founder John Wesley sends Joseph Pilmore and Richard Boardman as lay preachers to travel among the members of the emerging Methodist movement in the colonies.

1769

North America: United States
Christianity
Congregationalist minister Eleazar Wheelock founds what becomes Dartmouth College with a primary goal of training Native Americans as missionaries. Wheelock had previously trained Samson Occom, a Mohegan who had been ordained and became a missionary among the Montauks of Long Island. Occom accompanied Wheelock on his initial tour to raise financial support for the school. The school would ultimately receive its primary support from a Methodist, William Legge, second earl of Dartmouth.

1769

Europe: England
Christianity
Anglican minister Augustus Toplady enters the ongoing polemics between the Arminians and Calvinists in the Church of England after six students with Calvinist leanings are dismissed from St. Edmund Hall at the University of Oxford. Toplady offered his support in a book, *The Church of England Vindicated from the Charge of Arminianism,* in which he argues that Calvinism, not Arminianism, is the primary historical position promulgated by the Church of England. About the same time, Toplady publishes his translation of Heidelburg professor Girolamo Zanchius's *Confession of the Christian Religion,* a book that originally helped convince Toplady of the truth of Calvinism a decade earlier.

Toplady's publication prompts Methodist leader John Wesley to enter the fray on the issue of the position of the Church of England. Wesley, a committed Arminian who champions the cause of free grace and the universal atonement offer in Christ, carries on a pamphlet war with Toplady through the 1770s, which finally exhausts both sides.

1769

Europe: Germany
Judaism
Moses Mendelssohn refuses the invitation of Lutheran theologian John Caspar Lavater to publicly make the case for Judaism's superiority over Christianity. Mendelssohn suggests that religious polemics are out of step with the spirit of religious tolerance he hopes to represent.

1769

Europe: Italy
Christianity
Pope Clement XIII dies and is succeeded by Pope Clement XIV (r. 1769–1774).

1769

Europe: Italy
Christianity
Roman Catholic archbishop Antonio Martini publishes the first volume of his translation of the Bible into Italian. The several volumes of the New Testament appear between 1769 and 1771 followed by the Old Testament between 1776 and 1781. This critical edition includes both the Latin Vulgate and the Italian translation in parallel columns and a set of lengthy footnotes. The pope gives it his official approval. It will be the most used Italian Bible for the next two centuries.

ca. 1770

Europe: England
Christianity

Members of the group that has gathered around the charismatic Ann Lee designate her as their "Mother in spiritual things" and she begins to refer to herself as "Ann, the Word." She has recently spent two weeks in jail in Manchester where she has experienced a revelation that salvation requires that a complete confession of sins be made before witnesses. She confirms the revelation by performing a number of miracles, most notably healing the sick.

The group around Lee slowly evolves into a new religious community, the United Society of Believers in Christ's Second Appearing. Members are called to give up all their worldly goods, live communally, and assume a celibate existence. Their worship includes singing, dancing, shaking, and shouting. Members often speak in unknown tongues and prophesy.

1770

North America: United States
Christianity

Quaker educator Anthony Benezet, who has worked for abolition of slavery for several decades, founds the Negro School at Philadelphia for the education of African American children. Benezet has joined fellow Quaker John Woolman in taking the lead in pressing the idea that the buying, selling, and owning of slaves is incompatible with Christian faith.

1770

North America: United States
Christianity

Mennonites who have settled in Germantown, Pennsylvania, construct the first Mennonite meetinghouse in North America.

1770

North America: United States
Christianity

Members of the Church of the Brethren, who had generally met in private homes, construct their first meetinghouse in America at Germantown, Pennsylvania.

1770

East and Southeast Asia: China, Hong Kong
Chinese Religions

Chang Po Chai, a pirate, takes control of Hong Kong Island and establishes his headquarters on the southern coast where the present town of Stanley is located. He is in possession of a bell that had been cast in 1767 and a drum, which he uses to communicate with his ships. When he dies, the bell and drum are given to the local temple dedicated to Tienhou, where they remain to the present.

1770

Europe: France
Unbelief, Judaism

Atheist philosopher Baron d'Holbach publishes his essay "The Spirit of Judaism," in which he characterizes Jews as full of self-interest and avarice.

1770

Europe: Sweden
Western Esotericism

A royal ordinance declares the writings of seer Emanuel Swedenborg are "clearly mistaken" and Lutheran clerics who have been attracted to Swedenborg's teachings are ordered to stop using them. The edict also directs customs officials to impound his books as a means to prevent any further circulation.

1771

Europe: England
Western Esotericism

The Grand Lodge of England is formed by the merger of four Masonic lodges.

1771

Europe: France
Christianity

The future emperor Napoleon Bonaparte is baptized at the Cathedral of Our Lady of the Assumption in Ajaccio, Corsica.

1771

Europe: France
Judaism, Unbelief

In his *Letter of Memmius to Cicero,* Voltaire captures his lifelong attitude toward the Jews, "They are, all of them, born with raging fanaticism in their hearts, just as the Bretons and the Germans are born with blond hair."

1771

Europe: Hungary
Christianity

At the request of Holy Roman empress Maria-Theresa, Pope Clement XIV erects the Ruthenian eparchy of Mukaèevo (Transcarpathian Ruthenia) and designates it a suffragan of the Primate of Hungary. The Catholics of this area follow an Eastern rite that continues a liturgy from the time when they were Eastern Orthodox believers. In 1778, a seminary for the training of Ruthenian Catholic priests will be established at Uzhorod.

1771

Europe: Netherlands
Western Esotericism

While on a trip to Amsterdam, Emanuel Swedenborg publishes his last work, *Vera Christiana Religio* (*The True Christian Religion*). It attempts to explain his teachings to Christians, especially Lutherans.

1771

Russia, Central Asia, and the Caucasus: Russia
Christianity

An epidemic sweeps through Vladimir. An icon of the Blessed Virgin Mary brought from the nearby Bogoliubskii Monastery is credited with ending the plague. To commemorate this deliverance, the citizens began to hold an annual procession with the miracle-working icon, which is carried from Bogolubov to Vladimir.

1771

Southwest Asia and North Africa: Egypt
Christianity

A new church dedicated to St. Michael is erected at the monastery of St. Paul (dedicated to St. Paul of Thebes) in the Egyptian desert. It is the fourth church at the large monastic complex, which had been abandoned and then reinhabited in 1701, and a sign of the reemergence of the community through the century.

1772

Europe: England
Christianity

A committee of clergy under the direction of Mark Hildesley, the Anglican bishop of Sodor and Man, completes and publishes their translation of the Bible into the Manxa dialect of the Gaelic language. The New Testament had previously been published in 1767.

1772

Europe: Lithuania
Judaism

The rabbis of Vilna (Vinius), the capital of Lithuania, denounce the growing Hasidic movement and place it under a ban. They accuse the Hasidim of disregarding tradition and creating a schism within the Jewish community. The ban does not stop the spread of the movement, but heralds similar actions that will soon be taken by other Jewish communities across eastern Europe.

1772

Europe: Poland
Judaism, Christianity

The first Partition of Poland (the former Polish Lithuanian Commonwealth) adds a significant number of Jews to the Russian population. In response, Jews were asked to pay taxes at a rate twice that of the members of the Russian Orthodox church. Should they convert to Christianity, the tax was taken away.

1772

Europe: Portugal
Christianity

The Roman Catholic bishop of Coimbra transfers his seat from the old Romanesque cathedral to the relatively new and spacious Jesuit church, which had sat vacant since the Jesuits had been banned in Portugal.

1772

Southwest Asia and North Africa: Persia
Islam

Yusuf Al Bahrani, the dean of scholarship in Karbala and a leading Shi'a Muslim theologian, dies. He has led one school of Shi'a theology, the Akhbari, into a dominant role in Shi'a thought. He has been opposed by Vahid Behbahani, who represented the Usuli school. The Usuli attempted to use reason to derive general principles of right behavior from the Qur'an and Hadith (using the Shi'a text of the Hadith). The Usuli approach also projected the necessity of jurists who had the ability to reason and the power to enforce their findings. Following Bahrani's death, Behbahani led a revival of Usuli thinking, going so far as to term those who disagreed with him heretics. His success promoted Islamic jurists into a position of significant authority in Persia, and he is considered a major architect of contemporary Iranian Shi'a theocracy. The Usuli school became and remains the dominant theological perspective in Shi'ite Islam.

1773

Central America and the Caribbean: Guatemala
Christianity

A massive earthquake strikes Antigua, Guatemala, the capital of Guatemala, and destroys most of the town. Severe damage is inflicted on the massive St. Joseph Cathedral. The event leads the country's officials to again move the capital to its present location in Guatemala City. As the Catholic Church develops in the country, the cathedral remains the seat of a bishop, though the country's archdiocese is reestablished in the new capital.

1773

South India: India
Islam

Afghan ruler Ahmad Shah Durrani dies and is buried in Kandahar, where a large mausoleum with a turquoise dome will be erected. The mausoleum also serves as a mosque and houses what is believed to be the sacred cloak of Prophet Mohammed, considered one of the holiest relics in the Islamic world. His successors prove to be incompetent in keeping the empire together and over the next generation it largely disintegrates.

1773

East and Southeast Asia: China
Islam

Yining's reputation as a major Muslim learning center is bolstered by the opening of the Beytulla Mosque, one of the mosques in China that gained royal financial support.

1773

East and Southeast Asia: China, Hong Kong
Chinese Religions

Seafaring people who reside in Apleichai, a small island off the southern coast of Hong Kong, build a temple to Hung Sing Heh, a god of the sea who is seen as a patron saint by boat people. It is believed that he was an official in the era of the Tang Dynasty who was later deified.

1773

Europe: Italy
Christianity

Yielding to pressure primarily from France, Pope Clement XIV issues *Dominus ac Redemptor* calling for the suppression of the Society of Jesus. The Jesuits included some 23,000 members who offered personal allegiance to the pope and to the service of the church. Jesuit property would be confiscated, libraries lost. France has the most hostile reaction, combining formal disbanding of the order with charges of the immorality of its members. Austria, where Maria Theresa had already turned on the order, follows a similar course, and confiscates all the order's property.

In contrast, Catherine, the empress of Russia, rejects the suppression and forbids the promulgation of the papal document. Some 200 Jesuits continue to function in Russia. American Jesuit John Carroll, who was studying in Europe, was forced to return to Maryland just as revolutionary fervor was on the rise.

1773

Russia, Central Asia, and the Caucasus: Russia
Islam

Russian empress Catherine issues an edict on "Toleration of All Faiths." It allows Muslims permission to build mosques and practice all of their traditions, including the making of the hajj and the pilgrimage to Mecca, which were formerly prohibited.

1773–1774

Europe: England
Unbelief

Anglican clergyman Theophilus Lindsey, who had been among the petitioners to Parliament in 1771 asking to be relieved of subscribing to the 39 Articles of Religion of the Church of England, resigns his parish. Parliament rejected the petition and Lindsey, who had developed anti-Trinitarian views, felt he had no place left in the Church of England. He went on to found the first avowedly Unitarian congregation in England, the Essex Street Chapel in London. At the time, the holding of Unitarian beliefs was against the law in England.

1774

North America: Canada
Christianity

The Quebec Act provides for a permanent civil government for Quebec and among its provisions, it grants a privileged position to the Roman Catholic Church.

1774

North America: United States
Christianity

The Continental Congress chooses Rev. Jacob Duche to open its sessions with prayer.

1774

North America: United States
Christianity

Mother Ann Lee accompanied by eight of her followers emigrate to America and settle in New York where they found the first of a number of Shaker communities. They adopt a communal celibate existence and practice equality of the sexes. They will become known for their many contributions to the emerging American culture from their unique furniture to their musical creativity. Shakers will also serve as the orphanage for the American frontier, and an element of their growth derives from their taking in children whose parents had died.

1774

North America: United States
Christianity

Jesuit priest John Carroll founds Saint John the Evangelist Catholic Church in Silver Spring, Maryland.

1774

North America: United States
Christianity

Reformed Presbyterian congregations in North America, aligned with the Reformed Presbytery of Scotland, popularly termed the Covenanter Church, organize the reformed Presbytery of America, a step along the way to the formation of the Reformed Presbyterian Church of North America.

1774

Europe: England
Christianity

Methodist founder John Wesley makes his definitive statement against slavery in his pamphlet "Thoughts on Slavery," in which he draws heavily from the writings of Philadelphia Quaker Anthony Benezet.

1774

Europe: Italy
Christianity

Pope Clement XIV dies and is succeeded by Pope Pius VI (r. 1775–1799).

1774

Southwest Asia and North Africa: Asia Minor
Islam

Ottoman sultan Mustafa III dies and is succeeded by his brother Abdülhamid I (r. 1774–1789). The new sultan is immediately confronted by a humiliating defeat by the Russians at the Battle of Kozluja, which is followed by the publicly embarrassing Treaty of Küçük Kaynarca, which ends the Russo-Turkish War of 1768–1774. Strategically, the Crimea was declared independent and, among other territorial accessions, Russia gained its long sought ice-free ports on the Black Sea and access to the Dardanelles. Among the religious provisions of the treaty, Russia was assigned the right to protect Christians throughout the Ottoman Empire; Eastern Orthodox Christians were granted the right to sail under the Russian flag; and the Russian Orthodox Church was given permission to build a new church in Istanbul (though it would never be constructed).

1774–1775

Europe: Germany
Christianity

German biblical scholar Johann Jacob Griesbach publishes his critical edition of the New Testament, which appeared in three successive volumes. The first volume contains the first three Gospels (Matthew, Mark, and Luke), which share a significant amount of text, arranged in parallel columns (synoptically). From his work, Griesbach would propose a theory of the literary dependence of the first three gospels on each other, though his theory of the priority of the gospel of Matthew has generally been discarded in favor of the priority of Mark.

1775

North America: United States
Christianity

In Philadelphia, Quaker educator Anthony Benezet takes the lead in forming the Society for the Relief of Free Negroes Unlawfully Held in Bondage, the first American society for the abolition of slavery. Most of the original members were fellow Quakers, but among the non-Quaker members is Thomas Paine.

1775

North America: United States
Christianity

Quakers take the lead in the formation of the Pennsylvania Society for the Abolition of Slavery.

1775

North America: United States
Christianity

In one of the most famous events in American history, church sexton Robert Newman, Captain John Pulling, and Thomas Bernard place lanterns in the tower of the Old North Church (the Anglican church in Boston) to pass information to revolutionaries across the Charles River about the movements of the British army prior to the Battle of Lexington, an early skirmish in the American Revolution.

1775

North America: United States
Judaism

Frances Salomon is elected to the South Carolina Provisional Congress, the first Jew to hold elected office in America.

1775

East and Southeast Asia: China
Chinese Religions

The Qing emperor Qianlong completes a renovation and enlargement of the Maha Gela Temple in Beijing, which emerges as the Pudu Temple.

1775

Europe: England
Unbelief

Anglican minister John Jebb, an instructor at Cambridge University, resigns all of his positions that involve income from the Church of England. He had developed a variety of minority views including a Unitarian perspective on the Trinity, soul sleep (that the soul is unconscious between death and resurrection), and female equality. His resignation was occasioned by the failure of a movement to drop the requirement of Anglican clergy to formally subscribe to the 39 Articles of Religion. He would spend the rest of his life as a social-change activist.

1775

Europe: Italy
Christianity, Judaism

Pope Pius VI issues his Edict on the Jews, which reiterates a set of anti-Jewish regulations accumulated over the centuries operative in papal territories.

1775–1854

North America: United States
Judaism

America merchant and philanthropist Judah Touro funded the first New Orleans synagogue.

1776

North America: Canada
Christianity
Henry Alline begins his preaching ministry in Nova Scotia.

1776

North America: United States
Christianity
Charles Carroll becomes the only Roman Catholic to sign the Declaration of Independence. With his Jesuit cousin John Carroll, Samuel Chase, and Benjamin Franklin, he travels to Quebec and attempts to persuade the French Canadians to join the revolution. The mission was unsuccessful, but cemented the relationship between the Carrolls and the government that emerged after the war.

1776

North America: United States
Christianity
As the American Revolution begins, Anglican establishments exist, at least formally, in New York, New Jersey, Delaware, Maryland, Virginia, North Carolina, South Carolina, and Georgia.

1776

North America: United States
Judaism
Following the British occupation of New York, Gershon Mendes Seixas, the leader of Congregation Shearith Israel, flees the city with the congregation's Torah scrolls and other items to safety in Connecticut.

1776

Europe: Italy, France
Christianity
Pope Pius VI orders his representatives in Avignon to stop any forced baptisms of Jewish children.

1776

Europe: Spain
Christianity

Reconstruction of the cathedral for Cadiz, Spain, begins. The cathedral had burned in 1596, and in 1635 another church had been constructed close to the site on the same Plaza de la Catedral.

1776

Europe: Ukraine
Judaism
Hasidic founder Ba'al Shem Tov dies and is succeeded by Dov Baer of Mezhirech who launches an effort to disseminate his mentor's teachings throughout Eastern Europe.

1776

Russia, Central Asia, and the Caucasus: Russia
Christianity
The wooden Church of the Smolensk Icon of the Mother of God at the Smolensk Cemetery on Vasilevsky Island in St. Petersburg is replaced with a stone church. This new building is identified with St. Ksenia, a local St. Petersburg resident, who was said to have aided the builders of the church by carrying bricks for their use secretly each evening after they finished their daily shift. The icon for which it is now named was a 19th-century gift from the monks of Mount Athos.

January 21, 1776

North America: United States
Christianity
Peter Muhlenberg, pastor of the Lutheran church in Woodstock, Virginia, preaches from Ecclesiastes, "To every thing there is a season." He declares that the congregation now lives in a time of war, removes his clerical robe revealing his military uniform, and opens enlistment in the Continental Army: 162 men sign up.

July 4, 1776

North America: United States
Christianity, Unbelief
The Declaration of Independence is approved by the Continental Congress convened in Philadelphia. Most of the signers were members of various Protestant churches (Anglican, Congregationalist, or

China's Qianlong emperor, ca. 1737, Qing Dynasty. The long reign of the Qianlong emperor was a watershed in the history of China, the most wealthy and populous nation in the world in the late 18th century. (RMN-Grand Palais/Art Resource, NY)

Presbyterian). John Witherspoon, the only clergyman to sign the declaration, was president of the Presbyterians' College of New Jersey (now Princeton University). Charles Carroll was a Roman Catholic. John Adams was a Unitarian. Thomas Jefferson was a Deist. Deism was a movement that grew up in the Anglican Church whose adherents, like the Unitarians, had lost faith in a variety of orthodox Christian propositions, including the Trinity. Though the Baptists were possibly the strongest supporters of the Revolution, none had been selected to sit in the Continental Congress (though Stephen Hopkins was the grandson of a Baptist minister). Methodists, like the Baptists a relatively small group at the time, were generally viewed as among the least sympathetic to the Revolution.

As the American Revolution begins, a number of clergymen offer themselves in various ways to the army. George Duffield, the chaplain to the Continental Congress, becomes an army chaplain, while Lutheran minister Peter Muhlenberg is authorized to raise and command a regiment of the Continental Army, and he is later joined by his minister brother Fredrick Augustus Muhlenberg.

1777

Sub-Saharan Africa: Gabon
Christianity
Portuguese authorities expel the Italian Capuchin missionaries who had worked in the country since the previous century.

1777

St. Kitts
Christianity
Missionaries from the Moravian Church begin work on the Caribbean island of St. Kitts.

1777

East and Southeast Asia: Thailand
Buddhism
King Rama I of Thailand, having obtained copies of the Tripitaka from Sri Lanka, calls a council to standardize the Thai version of the Tripitaka, and subsequently distributes copies to temples throughout the country.

1777

Russia, Central Asia, and the Caucasus: Russia
Islam
Russian empress Catherine II creates the Orenburg Muslim Spiritual Assembly to provide state oversight and administration for the Muslim community in Siberia, the Volga-Ural region, and most of central Asia. On September 22, Mukhammed-zhan Khusainov is appointed the first mufti of the Orenburg Muslim Spiritual Assembly, but given limited powers.

1777–1778

East and Southeast Asia: China
Chinese Religions
The Qing Empire conquers Xinjiang, an area whose Mongol and Uyghur population is largely Muslim. In 1777, the Qing emperor Qianlong began building the Emin Minaret, the largest in China, at a mosque located along the old Silk Road to commemorate a local military leader, Emin Khoja.

1778

North America: United States
Christianity
The Brethren (later the Church of the Brethren) hold the first "recorded" Annual Meeting.

1778

East and Southeast Asia: China
Buddhism
The Qianlong emperor invites Palden Yeshe, the Panchen Lama, to Beijing. Upon his arrival, the Panchen Lama is treated royally and extends his stay. Unfortunately, his visit concludes in 1780 with his contracting smallpox and dying.

1778

East and Southeast Asia: China
Islam
Muslims in Xingiang build Sugong Tower, a round minaret attached to a mosque near Turphan City. Made of yellow brick, it stands over 100 feet high, the tallest premodern minaret in China. The tower honors the local military hero, Emin Khoja, who worked for China's unification.

1778

Europe: Germany
Judaism
As part of a larger effort to integrate Judaism in German society, David Friedlaender founds a school in Berlin. It attempts to inculcate the values enunciated by Friedlaender's mentor Moses Mendelssohn of religious tolerance and brotherhood.

1778–1779

North America: United States
Christianity
Shortly before his death, Henry Sharp, a church deacon and slaveowner, frees his slave George Lisle, whom he has previously encouraged to preach to other slaves. Lisle moves to Savannah, Georgia, where he joins with both slaves and other free blacks in forming one of the first African American Baptist congregations in America.

1778–1780

Europe: England
Christianity
Parliament passes the Catholic Relief Act, which allows Roman Catholics in England to own property, inherit land, and join the army—significant steps on their way to full citizenship. Scottish politician Lord George Gordon assumes leadership of the Protestant Association (1779) through which he hopes to get the legislation repealed. His lack of success will lead to a set of violent riots that are named for him, the Gordon Riots of 1780. Rioters target buildings in London associated in any way with Catholicism.

1779

North America: United States
Christianity
John Murray organizes the first American Universalist congregation in Gloucester, Massachusetts.

1779

Europe: Albania
Christianity
Ottoman authorities arrest Greek Orthodox priest Cosmas of Aetolia, whom they accuse of being a Russian agent, and execute him. As no formal charges are filed and no evidence of his Russian connection produced, it is assumed that he has made too many enemies with the effectiveness of his work, including moving between Ottoman lands and adjacent territory ruled by Venice. Most recently, he had been able to change the holding of the weekly bazaar from Sunday, the Christian holy day, to Saturday, which cut significantly into Jews' participation. Cosmas is later canonized by the Greek Orthodox Church.

1779

Europe: England
Christianity
John Newton, the rector of the small church at Olney, Buckinghamshire, collaborates with the poet William Cowper in the production of a volume published as *Olney Hymns*. This work would contain a number of Newton's most influential hymns, including "Glorious Things of Thee Are Spoken," but most notably

"Amazing Grace," originally published under the title "Faith's Review and Expectation." The volume also includes possibly Cowper's most famous hymns, "There Is a Fountain Filled with Blood" and "Light Shining out of Darkness," which contains the oft-quoted lines, "God moves in a mysterious way, His wonders to perform." The *Olney Hymns* emerges as the most popular of the new songbooks among Presbyterians, Independents (Congregationalists), and the evangelical wing of Anglicanism.

The popularity of hymn singing among the Methodists and the various dissenting groups would create a groundswell for the adoption of hymns into the order of worship of the Church of England and during the next century lead to significant change in Anglican worship.

1779

Europe: France
Christianity

The new Diocese of Chambéry is set aside in southeastern France. A local church, originally built as a chapel for a Franciscan monastery, is designated as the diocese's cathedral and dedicated to Saint Francis de Sales.

1779

Europe: Germany
Judaism

German philosopher Gotthold Lessing authors a play, *Nathan the Wise,* whose title character is based on his friend Moses Mendelssohn, who articulates the values of tolerance and brotherhood. The drama is a great success and signals the rise of Judaism to a place of importance in German society. Lessing, unfortunately, dies before the play is initially performed in 1783.

1780

North America: United States
Christianity

Rev. Benjamin N. Randall founds the first Free-will Baptist church in the New England states at New Durham, New Hampshire.

1780

North America: United States
Judaism

Gershon Mendes Seixas, previously the leader of Congregation Shearith Israel in New York, assumes leadership of Congregation Mikvah Israel in Philadelphia.

1780

South America: Guyana
Western Esotericism

The first known lodge of freemasonry emerges in Guyana at Essequibo on Fort Island, which was then the capital of the colony. Its name, Three Friends, appears to be a reference to Three Rivers, a nickname of the colony, which consisted of three major rivers, the Essequibo, Demerara, and Berbice.

1780

South India: India
Hinduism

Ahilya Bai Holkar, the Hindu Maratha queen of the Malwa kingdom of India, rebuilds the Kashi Vishwanath Temple, a Vaishnava Hindu temple that commemorates the site of Lord Krishna's birth on earth. As the traditional site of the temple was occupied by a mosque built in 1669 by Mughal emperor Aurangzeb, she had the new temple constructed immediately adjacent to the mosque. A barricade separates them. There is also a well, the Gyanvapi, located between the temple and the mosque. Many believe that Aurangzeb hid the sacred lingam, the symbol of Shiva from the old temple, in the well, but to date it has not been located.

In 1835, the Sikh maharaja Ranjit Singh of Punjab donates 1,000 kg of gold, which is used to cover the spire and the dome of the temple.

1780

East and Southeast Asia: China
Buddhism

Qadain Yexe, the sixth Pachen Lama, the second highest official in Gelugpa Tibetan Buddhism, visits Beijing to celebrate the birthday of the Qianlong emperor, who is 70 years old. He stays at the West Yellow Temple, the Gelugpa temple north of the Forbidden City. While there, he passes away. The Qianlong emperor orders a pagoda erected on the temple grounds to preserve the lama's relics.

1780

Europe: England
Christianity

Philanthropist Robert Raikes opens a school for boys in the slums of Gloucester. It operates only on Sunday, as the boys work the other six days of the week. He recruited Christian laypeople as teachers and they initially taught the boys to read and then began instruction in the Christian faith using the catechism. The movement catches on, in spite of notable initial opposition, and soon becomes a continuing major structure in Christian lay education.

1780

Europe: Holy Roman Empire
Christianity

Holy Roman empress Maria Theresa dies and her son, Joseph II (r. 1764–1790), who had been crowned in 1764, becomes the sole ruler of the Holy Roman Empire. He would pursue a policy of religious toleration, the Protestants and Jews enjoying the benefits most. He also promoted the establishment of schools for Jews and various Protestant groups, part of a policy supportive of universal education.

Simultaneously, he advocated reform in the Roman Catholic Church aimed at modernizing its worship, weakening its power in his court, and lessening the control of the papacy over the Austrian dioceses. He manipulated the income of the Austrian bishops and forced them to take an oath to the crown. He confiscated land owned by monasteries and from the income was able to finance those bishops and dioceses perceived to be most loyal to him. The number of monks and nuns decreased sharply during his regime, especially the number in contemplative orders, which he considered useless burdens. He also secularized marriage.

Relative to Catholic worship, he moved to simplify the ritual of the mass and cut the number of holy days celebrated throughout the empire. He allowed anticlericalism, an attitude associated with the Enlightenment, to gain public support, and his opponents accused him of being both pro-Protestant and a proponent of Enlightenment rationalism.

While never initiated, Joseph proved an ally of Freemasonry, which he saw as compatible with many of his views. Freemasons also tended to be anticlerical in their approach to the established religion.

1780

Europe: Ukraine
Christianity

The new Uspensky Cathedral at Pochayiv Monastery is consecrated. It had been promoted and largely financed by Ukrainian nobleman Count Mykola Pototcki (from a family of distinguished nobles) who made a worthy contribution to the development of what was conceived as the largest Uniate Church (a Roman Catholic church that follows the Greek Catholic rite). In a concession to the terrain, the builders abandon the tradition demanding that cathedrals be oriented along an east-west axis. In 1831 when the monastery was returned to the control of the Ukrainian Orthodox Church, the interior of the cathedral was refurbished in Orthodox style, most notably by the addition of an iconostasis.

1780–1781

East and Southeast Asia: Japan
Shinto

Two of the four main shrines at Suwa Taisha, a Shinto site in Nagano, are built. Suwa Taisha is unique among the thousands of Shinto shrines in Japan, as it is one of three shrines that provides for the direct worship of the mountain before which the shrine was constructed. There is no *honden* to house the deities, only prayer halls for believers to gather for their worship. The mountain is designated as the shintaizan (the kami-body mountain). The two new buildings, which join two older similar buildings, are designated *haidens,* halls for worship.

1781

North America: United States
Christianity

With the British defeat in the Revolution, most Anglican priests return to England.

1781

North America: United States
Christianity

The original Lutheran Ministerium, founded in 1748, adopts a formal constitution and chooses a new name, the German Evangelical Lutheran Ministerium of

North America. Still under the influence of Pietism, it does not insist on a strict adherence to the Lutheran Confessions, though they form its teaching perspective.

1781

North America: United States
Unbelief

Adams Streeter, a Baptist minister who has independently arrived at a Universalist position that he has been spreading among the churches he serves, is excommunicated by the Baptists, immediately affiliates with the Universalists, and serves early Universalist congregations in New England, located at Oxford and Milford, Massachusetts.

1781

North America: United States
Judaism

Haym Solomon, a Polish Jew who arrived in New York in 1772, helps raise funds to finance the American cause in the Revolutionary War.

1781

East and Southeast Asia: China
Islam

Ma Ming Hsin, having recently returned from a pilgrimage to Mecca and being heavily influenced by the Naqshbandi Sufi order, founds a new Islamic movement that opposes traditional Chinese Muslim accommodation to Confucianist thought. Disagreement within the Muslim community would later lead to armed conflict beginning at Lauchou, a major Chinese Muslim center, and then evolve into open rebellion against Chinese rule.

1781

Europe: Holy Roman Empire
Judaism

Joseph II, the Holy Roman emperor, initiates a series of reforms relative to the Jewish community. He abolishes the requirement that Jews must wear a yellow badge and removes several special taxes. He introduces new educational opportunities and demands that those Jews in the business community stop the use of Hebrew or Yiddish in keeping their commer-cial records. These reforms are aligned with the policies of enlightened rule he pursued in other empire matters.

May 13, 1781

North America: United States
Christianity

Methodist preacher Harry Hosier preaches the first sermon known to have been delivered by an African American.

1782

Central America and the Caribbean: Guatemala
Christianity

Construction begins on the Cathedral of Guatemala City, aka the Catedral Primada Metropolitana de Santiago, the headquarters church of the Roman Catholic Archdiocese of Guatemala. Located in the center of Guatemala City, the site of the capital of Guatemala since 1777, it will take a generation to complete and survives in spite of several destructive earthquakes that have hit the region.

1782

Central America and the Caribbean: Jamaica
Christianity

African American George Lisle arrives in Jamaica and begins to preach among the slaves. He thus becomes the first Baptist missionary in Jamaica, though at the time he has no support or recognition from any Baptist church or association. He forms a congregation near Kingston and would eventually turn to the Baptists in London for support.

1782

Europe: Greece
Christianity

Two monks from Mt. Athos, Nikodemos of the Holy Mountain and Makarios of Corinth, complete their compilation of Orthodox spiritual writings, the *Philokalia*. It is published in Vienna and a translation into Church Slavonic followed in 1793. In the mid-nineteenth century, a translation would appear in Russian, with Romanian, Italian French, and English translations appearing in the 20th century.

Dionisiou Monastery on Mount Athos in Greece. Mount Athos is widely considered the most famous Orthodox monastic center in the world. (Nikos Pavlakis/Dreamstime.com)

The book would become the definitive volume of modern hesychasm, an inner spiritual tradition with deep roots in Eastern Orthodox spiritual practice as practiced at Mount Athos. The central practice is based in the repetition of the Jesus Prayer, "Lord Jesus Christ, Son of God, have mercy on me, the sinner."

The publication of the *Philokalia* became a key event in the emerging Kollyvades Movement, a renewal movement among the monastic communities on Mount Athos. The movement focused on restoring traditional practices and getting rid of unwarranted innovations. Key to the movement were the frequent reception of Holy Communion and the practice of unceasing prayer using the Jesus Prayer. Both Nikodemos and Makarios would later be recognized as saints.

1782

Europe: Holy Roman Empire
Christianity

Pope Pius VI visits Austria and the court of Holy Roman emperor Joseph II, who had made a variety of attempts to reform the Roman Catholic Church in his realm, and also gave haven to a rising tide of anticlericalism sweeping across Europe. Joseph politely hosted the pope and put his own Catholic faith in the forefront, but refused to back away from his efforts at reform.

1782

Europe: Holy Roman Empire
Judaism

Jewish educator Naptali Herz Wessely publishes *Words of Peace and Truth* in which he argues for educational reforms in light of the more tolerant policies toward Jews introduced by Joseph II, the Holy Roman emperor. He suggests a curriculum combining secular and religious education and instruction in German. More traditional rabbis oppose him as they fear it would lead to Jewish integration into Gentile society.

1783

North America: United States
Christianity

The Treaty of Paris (along with the three related treaties of Versailles) formally ends the American Revolution and revises Great Britain's relationship with France, Spain, and Holland. Most importantly, Great Britain recognizes the United States. Florida, which Britain had taken from Spain in 1763, is returned to Spanish control.

In the Caribbean, Britain receives permanent control of the island of St. Vincent over which the French and British had fought for a generation. At this time the Church of England, now an integral part of the Church of the Province of the West Indies, emerges as the strongest religious group. Spain returns the Bahama Islands to Britain.

1783

North America: United States
Christianity

Franciscan missionary Fr. Juan Bautista Velderrain initiates construction on the new church for the Mission San Xavier du Bac, a few miles south of what will become Tucson, Arizona. It will take 14 years to complete.

1783

Central America and the Caribbean: Jamaica
Christianity

Former slave George Lisle (1750–1829), the first American Baptist missionary, begins ministry work in Kingston, Jamaica.

1783

Central America and the Caribbean: Trinidad
Christianity

Missionaries of the Moravian Church begin work in Trinidad.

1783

South Asia: India
Hinduism

Several members of Hindu royalty merge their resources and rebuild the Somnath Temple, a prominent Shiva temple located on the western coast of Gujarat, one of the 12 Jyotirlinga shrines. It had been destroyed by Mughal emperor Aurangzeb (1701), who then proceeded to use the stone of the temple to erect a mosque on the site. The new Somnath Temple is rebuilt immediately adjacent to the mosque.

1783

East and Southeast Asia: China, Hong Kong
Chinese Religions

Fishermen on Cheung Chau, a small island close to Hong Kong Island, begin construction of a temple to Pak Tai, often referred to as the Barefoot Emperor from the North, a deity whose worship was popular in their native Fujien province on the Chinese mainland. When a epidemic had hit the residents of Cheung Chau in 1677, the fishermen had brought an image of Pak Tai to the island and launched an effort to raise the money to construct a proper temple. Construction will take five years to complete. The main image in the temple is a black three-foot-tall wooden statue of Pak Tai discovered floating in the water by fishermen.

1783

Europe: England
Christianity

Frederick Cornwallis, the archbishop of Canterbury, dies and is succeeded by John Moore (r. 1783–1805), the former bishop of Bangor.

1783

Europe: France
Christianity

The Treaty of Paris and associated Treaty of Versailles formally end the American Revolution and revise the relationships between England and other natural participants in the hostilities, France, Holland, and Spain. Most changes of territory relate to the New World, but Spain receives control of Minorca, an island in the Mediterranean that had been ceded to Britain by the 1763 Treaty of Paris.

1783

Europe: Germany
Christianity, Judaism

German Protestant theologian Johann Gottfried Herder uses his study of *The Spirit of Hebrew Poetry* to argue not only for the value of Jewish culture but also for the complete emancipation of German Jews from all the regulations inhibiting their participation in German society.

1783

Europe: Germany
Judaism

Jewish writer Isaac Abraham Euchel founds the Society for the Proponents of the Hebrew language, a representative organization of the Jewish Enlightenment (Haskalah) centered on the study of biblical Hebrew and of Hebraic writings on cultural, scientific, and literary subjects. Euchel is considered the founder of the Haskalah or Jewish Enlightenment movement.

1783

Russia, Central Asia, and the Caucasus: Russia
Christianity

A stone building replaces the original wooden Church of the Vladimir Icon of the Mother of God in St. Petersburg, Russia. The church features five onion-shaped cupolas and a four-tiered bell tower.

March 1, 1783

South Asia: India
Sikhism

Sikhs briefly enter the Red Fort in Delhi and occupy the Diwan-i-Am, its hall for public audiences.

1784

North America: United States
Christianity

The priests of the Church of England who remain in the United States formally organize the Protestant Episcopal Church in the United States. Having formally separated from their British brethren, they are no longer obliged to recognize the leadership of the king of England in either secular or ecclesiastical affairs. They set about the task of obtaining a bishop with Anglican orders and apostolic succession.

Samuel Seabury, chosen as bishop by the clergy in New England, contacts the bishops of the Episcopal Church of Scotland, who consecrate him in his office.

1784

North America: United States
Christianity

Following the death of founder Anthony Benezet, Benjamin Franklin and Benjamin Rush reorganize the Society for the Relief of Free Negroes Unlawfully Held in Bondage, America's original abolitionist society, as the Pennsylvania Society for Promoting the Abolition of Slavery and for the Relief of Free Negroes Unlawfully Held in Bondage. As president of the society in 1790, Franklin would petition the U.S. Congress to rid the country of slavery.

1784

North America: United States
Christianity

Thomas Coke, having been commissioned by John Wesley to set up the American Methodists as an independent church, arrives in Maryland and proceeds to Baltimore to meet with the gathered American preachers (all lay preachers) during Christmas week. They elect Coke and Francis Asbury to lead them, but choose the designation of bishop rather than superintendent. Coke ordains a number of the preachers as deacons and then elders, and then consecrates Asbury as the bishop. The gathering also organizes the Methodist Episcopal Church.

1784

North America: United States
Christianity

Lutheran minister Frederick A. Muhlenberg leads in the organization of the Ministerium of New York, the second Lutheran synod in North America.

1784

North America: United States
Unbelief

Ethan Allen completes *Reason the Only Oracle of Man*, the first atheist text published in America.

1784

North America: United States
Christianity

Mother Ann Lee, founder of the Shakers (The United Society of Believers in Christ's Second Appearing), dies at Watervliet, New York, and is succeeded by one of the group's elders, James Whittaker.

1784

North America: United States
Christianity

John Carroll is named the Superior of Missions in the United States of North America, the highest office held by an American Roman Catholic in the country at the time.

1784

South Asia: India
Islam

Asaf-ud-Daula, nawab of Lucknow, builds the Bara Imambara, an imambara complex in Lucknow. An imambara, also known as a Hussainia, is a hall at which Shi'a Muslims gather for commemorative ceremonies, most notably those associated with the Remembrance of Muharram, which marks the anniversary of the Battle of Karbala when Imam Hussein ibn Ali, the grandson of the Prophet Muhammad and a Shi'a Imam, died at the hands of the forces of the second Umayyad caliph Yazid I.

An imambara is not a mosque, where Friday prayers are offered, and is primarily used for Muharram gatherings. The Lucknow imambara complex also includes the large Asfi Mosque as part of the buildings erected by Asaf-ud-Daula.

1784

East and Southeast Asia: China, Korea
Christianity

While in China with his father on a diplomatic mission, Korean nobleman Yi Seung-hun converts to Roman Catholicism and is baptized, the first Korean person of noble birth to become a Catholic. Upon his return to Korea he gathers a group of believers that begins to meet regularly for prayer and worship.

1784

East and Southeast Asia: Japan
Buddhism

On the 950th anniversary of his death, Japan holds countrywide celebrations to honor Kūkai (aka Kōbō-Daishi), the founder of Shingon Buddhism.

1784

East and Southeast Asia: Thailand
Buddhism

Thai general Chao Phra Chakri seizes the reins of government from King Taksin, changes his name to Rama I, and founds Bangkok as his new capital. In Bangkok, he builds a new temple especially designed to display holy buildings, statues, and pagodas, and brings the Emerald Buddha, the country's most valuable treasure, to the new temple, Wat Phra Kaeo (aka Phra Sri Rattana Satsadaram, "the residence of the Holy Jewel Buddha"). Besides the main temple with the Emerald Buddha, Wat Phra Kaeo is home to some 100 additional buildings scattered over its 234 acres.

1784

Europe: England
Christianity

Baptist ministers John Sutcliff, Andrew Fuller, and John Ryland issue the "Prayer Call of 1784," which admonishes the Baptist churches to pray monthly for "the revival of real religion, and the extension of Christ's kingdom in the world." The Prayer Call is credited with initiating the movement that would lead to the formation of the Baptist Missionary Society in 1792.

1784

Europe: England
Christianity

In light of the changes wrought by the successful American Revolution, Methodist founder and Anglican minister John Wesley requests Robert Lowth, the bishop of London, to ordain some ministers for the New World. When he refuses, Wesley rethinks his position and decides that since he has been doing the work of a bishop, he has a bishop's authority. He therefore "sets aside" his close colleague and fellow Anglican minister Thomas Coke as a "superintendent" and sends him to America to reorganize and set in order the Methodist work there. As Coke is commissioned to ordain ministers once in America, he is often considered to have also become a bishop, though lacking the apostolic succession claimed by Roman Catholics and Anglicans for their bishops.

Wesley issues the Deed of Declaration by which he relinquishes control of the Methodist movement in England and turns it over to the preachers as a self-perpetuating group, the Conference, which continues to administer the British phase of the movement.

1784

Europe: France
Western Esotericism
The French Academy of Science denounces the magnetic theories of Franz Anton Mesmer.

1785

North America: United States
Unbelief
King's Chapel, Boston, the first Anglican congregation in New England, adopts a revised Book of Common Prayer, edited by their unordained minister James Freeman Clarke, to accommodate Unitarian perspectives. Refused ordination by the Episcopal Church, Clarke was ordained by the congregation, which later became a part of the American Unitarian Association.

1785

North America: United States
Christianity
Franciscan priest Fermin Lasuén founds Mission Santa Barbara as part of the effort to convert the Chumash people of California. It is the first of nine missions founded by Lasuén at the end of the century.

1785

Europe: England
Christianity
Baptist minister Andrew Fuller publishes *The Gospel Worthy of All Acceptance,* in which he argues against

what is termed hyper-Calvinism, which gave such allegiance to the idea of God's predestination that it saw no need for missionary work. Without giving up Calvinism, Fuller argued for a theology that understood the need of missionary endeavor. His work laid the theological foundations for the Baptist phase of the modern missionary movement.

1785

Europe: England
Hinduism
British scholar Charles Wilkins translates the Bhagavad Gita into English.

1785

Europe: England
Christianity
William Fox, a lay leader among the Particular Baptists of London, forms the Society for the Establishment and Support of Sunday Schools to facilitate the education of London's poor. He is able to secure the support both of Anglicans and members of various dissenting sects, and the society is able to found multiple Sunday schools within a few years.

1785

Russia, Central Asia, and the Caucasus: Russia
Judaism
Russian empress Catherine II officially declares Jews to be foreigners, thus reaffirming Judaism's separate identity from the main body of the Russian citizenry. The decree defined Jewish rights against those accorded status as either a native Orthodox Christian or a naturalized citizen of Russia.

1785

Russia, Central Asia, and the Caucasus: Russia
Islam
Russian empress Catherine II begins to establish new towns in Muslim areas of her regime, each town centered on a new mosque. Muslims, many of whom were heir to a nomadic lifestyle, were invited to settle these towns, which were seen by the Russians as a tool to regulate and control elements of the previously mobile peoples.

1785

Russia, Central Asia, and the Caucasus: Russia
Christianity

Russian empress Catherine II reevaluates her position relative to the Old Believers and allows them to participate in the government by holding elected positions in the cities. She also promises religious freedom to those she has deported who wish to resettle in Russia.

1785

Southwest Asia and North Africa: Arabia
Islam

Abdul Aziz ibn Muhammad ibn Saud (r. 1765–1803) succeeds his recently deceased father Muhammad ibn Saud as the ruler of the first Saudi state, the country that will evolve to become the modern Saudi Arabia.

1786

North America: United States
Christianity

The New York Ministerium, the second Lutheran jurisdiction in the Americas, is formed.

1786

North America: United States
Christianity

The Methodist Church in the Bahamas traces its beginning to the arrival in Abaco of former slave Joseph Paul, a Methodist who left the United States and settled in Abaco. After a few years he moved to Nassau where he gathered the first class, which became the core of the first Methodist congregation.

1786

North America: United States
Christianity

John Carroll convenes a meeting of the priests of the Roman Catholic Church at Sacred Heart Church in White Marsh, outside Annapolis, Maryland. This group decided to start a school to be located in Georgetown, which would be founded in stages and finally open in 1792 as Georgetown College (now Georgetown University). Land was secured in 1789, the date recognized by the school as its founding date.

1786

East and Southeast Asia: Japan
Buddhism

Shogun Tokugawa Ieharu dies. He is succeeded by Tokugawa Ienari (1786–1841), who will enjoy more than five decades on the throne. The early years of his lengthy reign are marred by the country suffering a set of disasters, most notably the great fire that hit Kyoto (1788) and a series of major volcanic eruptions and earthquakes in 1792–1793.

1786

East and Southeast Asia: Korea
Christianity

The initial group of Roman Catholics in Korea deals with the problem created by there being no priests in the country by having some of their lay leaders act as temporary priests. Several years later, upon hearing what is occuring, Mgr. Gouvea, the bishop in Beijing, forbids such practice as contrary to church teachings.

1786

East and Southeast Asia: Malaysia
Christianity, Islam

The sultan of Kedah, Abdullah Mukarram Shah, cedes the island of Penang to the British in return for Britain's assistance in protecting the small Malaysian sultanate from Siam and Burma. Captain Francis Light becomes the founder of modern Penang over which he assumes control. As Prince of Wales Island, it becomes the first British possession in Southeast Asia.

1786

Europe: England
Christianity

Methodist minister Thomas Coke lays the foundation for the British Methodist world missionary enterprise in his pamphlet "An Address to the Pious and Benevolent proposing an annual Subscription for the Support of Missionaries." He subsequently visits Antigua and out of his understanding of the needs there, develops a passion for missions that continues for the rest of his life.

1786

Europe: Italy
Christianity

Scipione de' Ricci, the Roman Catholic bishop of Pistoia, with the support and encouragement of Leopold, grand-duke of Tuscany, calls the Synod of Pistoia together to initiate a reform of the Catholic Church in Tuscany. While some elements of the rationale of the synod are quite positive—the education of the clergy, the editing of missals and breviaries removing questionable legendary material—the major agenda is the assertion of the authority of the secular authority relative to the church and the power of bishops within their own diocese relative to the universal authority of the pope. Leopold also hopes to find a means of curtailing the growing power exercised by monastic orders in his realm.

Within a year the synod meeting provokes a reaction among the other bishops of Tuscany and eventually Pope Pius VII denounces its work (1794).

1786

Russia, Central Asia, and the Caucasus: Russia
Christianity

Russian empress Catherine II excludes all religion and clerical studies programs, including those of the Russian Orthodox Church, from the public schools. This action continues a step by step program she has pursued to isolate the church and its clergy from the Russian government and to segregate the community by taking over its lands (and thus its means of financing itself) and making it financially dependent on the state. This process had the effect of distancing the Orthodox Church's clergy from the affairs of state and decreasing their influence.

1786

Russia, Central Asia, and the Caucasus: Russia
Islam

In a further attempt to control the Russian Islamic population, especially the wandering nomads, Empress Catherine II moves to assimilate the Islamic schools into the Russian public school system, and hence the regulations of the government.

January 16, 1786

North America: United States
Christianity

The General Assembly of the state of Virginia adopts its Statute on Religious Liberty, which prohibits public support of religious institutions and grants religious liberty for all citizens. Originally authored by Thomas Jefferson, the statute declares that no one can be compelled to support any given religion nor suffer discrimination for his or her religious beliefs.

1787

North America: Canada
Christianity

British king George III authorizes the formation of the Diocese of Nova Scotia of the Church of England and designates the loyalist priest Charles Inglis as its first bishop. He is consecrated in London in a ceremony presided over by the archbishop of Canterbury, who is assisted by the bishops of Rochester and Chester.

There is already an Anglican bishop in the United States—Samuel Seabury—but he has received his orders from the Episcopal Church of Scotland. Inglis is thus the first bishop directly consecrated by the Church of England and expected both to reside and exercise authority outside of England. His territory would include Nova Scotia, all of British Canada, and Bermuda.

1787

North America: United States
Christianity

The bishop of London consecrates William White and Samuel Provost as bishops for the new Protestant Episcopal Church of the United States of America.

1787

North America: United States
Christianity

The Northwest Ordinance, a plan to govern the territory north of the Ohio River, includes a provision for freedom of worship.

1787

North America: United States
Christianity

Methodist preacher Richard Allen joins with a group of African American leaders in organizing the Free

Richard Allen (1760–1831), founder and first bishop of the African Methodist Episcopal Church in Philadelphia, Pennsylvania. While he was still enslaved, Allen had been converted by a traveling Methodist preacher. (Daniel Alexander Payne, *History of the African Methodist Episcopal Church*, 1891)

African Society, a mutual aid society for Philadelphia's black residents.

1787

North America: United States
Christianity, Judaism

The new Constitution of the United States, which has been sent to the states for ratification, contains a clause prohibiting any religious test being required as a qualification to hold public office. This requirement is interpreted as applying to offices of the federal government, but all but two states have a similar clause in their constitutions. Maryland and North Carolina continue to restrict Jews and various religious dissenters from holding public office at the state level for the next generation.

1787

South India: India
Hinduism

Devi Ahilya Bai Holkar, the ruler of the Malwa kingdom, part of the Maratha Empire of eastern India, rebuilds an enlarged Vishnupada Mandir (a Vaishnava temple) at Gaya.

1787

Europe: England
Christianity

The growing acceptance of hymn singing as an integral part of Baptist church worship is signaled in the success accorded John Rippon's *A Selection of Hymns from the best authors, intended as an appendix to Dr. Watts's Psalms and Hymns.* Apart from reprints of Watts's hymn book, Rippon's songbook became the most popular one adopted by Baptist churches for several generations. Rippon's work also introduced the widely acclaimed "How Firm a Foundation, Ye Saints of the Lord."

1787

Europe: England
Western Esotericism

Disciples of the writings of Emanuel Swedenborg found a new church, an ecclesiastical organization that adheres to his teachings. The movement quickly acquires a number of centers of activity across the country.

1787

Europe: France
Unbelief, Christianity

The French promulgate the Declaration of the Rights of Man and of the Citizen, which guarantees freedom of religion and free exercise of worship, provided that it does not contradict public order.

1787–1788

North America: United States
Christianity

Elder James Whittaker dies and Joseph Meacham becomes the first elder of the United Society of Believers in Christ's Second Appearing, more popularly known as the Shakers. He begins to gather the somewhat scattered group together and organize them into communal clusters. He also introduces Lucy Wright as his co-leader and together they establish the group's administrative structure, ordered to promote the idea of equality of the sexes. They also found the first Shaker community at New Lebanon, New York.

1788

North America: United States
Christianity

Abraham Marshall, a white Baptist minister, and Jesse Peters, an African American minister, arrive in Savannah and officially recognize the Baptist group that had been founded by George Lisle. They baptize some 40 members and ordain Lisle's successor, Andrew Bryan, as the church's pastor.

1788

South India: India
Hinduism

Sardar Rangarao Odhekar of Nasik, Maharashtra, has a dream of a black statue of the Hindu deity Rama, an incarnation of Vishnu, lost in the river Godavari. A search uncovers the statue, which is retrieved. Odhekar subsequently funds the erection of the Kalaram Temple to house the statue. Nasik had once been the home to dozens of temples, most destroyed by Aurangzeb. The new Kalaram Temple emerges as the most prominent temple in Nasik.

1788

East and Southeast Asia: Japan
Buddhism

A fire swept through Kyoto. Burning for five days until put out by a heavy rain, it destroyed the imperial palace and most of the major religious structures. Reconstruction began with the palace, no other work being allowed to commence until it was ready for inhabitation.

1788

Europe: England
Christianity

John Newton, the parish minister at Olney, Buckinghamshire, who had once been a captain of a slave trading ship, breaks his silence on the subject of slavery with the publication of *Thoughts Upon the Slave Trade,* in which he vividly describes the horrific conditions of slavery and apologizes for his role in it. He subsequently becomes a friend and ally of William Wilberforce and joins his crusade to eliminate the slave trade.

1788

Russia, Central Asia, and the Caucasus: Russia
Islam

Russian empress Catherine II establishes the Orenburg Muslim Spiritual Assembly, which is given jurisdiction over aspects of Islamic activity in Siberia, the Volga-Ural region, and parts of central Asia, including the Kazakh steppe. It places the administration of the Islamic community in the hands of a mufti, the first being Mukhammed-zhan Khusainov (r. 1788–1824).

1788

Oceania and Antarctica: Australia
Christianity

A British fleet of eleven vessels arrives in Port Jackson on the east coast of Australia carrying among its thousand passengers 778 convicts who establish a settlement at Sydney Cove. Among their number is Richard Johnson, an Anglican chaplain who will erect the first Christian chapel in the new colony. Above and beyond his parish duties, he is made responsible for public morals by the governor and later assumes a spectrum of duties relative to education and health.

1789

North America: United States
Christianity

The first Congress chooses Rev. William Lynn, a Presbyterian from Philadelphia, as the official chaplain of the U.S. House of Representatives.

The newly organized Presbyterian General Assembly chooses Rev. George Duffield as its first stated clerk.

1789

North America: United States
Christianity

The Roman Catholic Diocese of Baltimore, the first diocese in the United States, is erected. It will be elevated as an archdiocese in 1808. On November 6, John Carroll, who has been elected by the American clergy as their new bishop, is confirmed by the pope as the first bishop of Baltimore.

1789

North America: United States
Judaism

Gershom Mendes Seixas, minister of New York's Jewish congregation, is invited to Washington's inaugural.

1789

North America: United States
Christianity

The U.S. Senate elects Episcopal bishop Samuel Provost as its first chaplain.

1789

North America: United States
Christianity

George Washington is inaugurated as president of the United States, the first of 12 Episcopalians to hold that office.

1789

Europe: England
Western Esotericism

Followers of the writings of Emanuel Swedenborg hold the first General Conference of the New Church in London.

1789

Europe: France
Unbelief

The French Revolution begins. On July 14 a mob storms the Paris prison known as the Bastille. On August 27, the National Constituent Assembly issues a Declaration of the Rights of Man and of the Citizen, one of the most historically important statements concerning human rights. Like the U.S. Constitution, it is based on the idea of natural rights. It defines humans as born free and equal, and all political associations are called into existence to preserve the natural human rights.

Like the preceding American documents, the Declaration did not enfranchise women nor dispense with slavery. Following its promulgation, a group of women offers the Assembly a petition to grant women equality. Its defeat would lead to Olympe de Gouges publishing the Declaration of the Rights of Woman and the Female Citizen in 1791. Slavery in the French colonies would be abolished in 1794.

Article 10 of the Declaration states, "No one shall be disquieted on account of his opinions, including his religious views, provided their manifestation does not disturb the public order established by law." Shortly after passing the Declaration, the revolutionary government moved to abolish the collecting of all taxes for use of the church and then nationalized all revenue-producing church property, that is, all property owned by the Roman Catholic Church whose revenue provided the financial support for the church.

1789

Europe: Germany
Judaism

Holy Roman emperor Joseph II issues a charter of religious toleration for the Jews of Galicia, a region of the empire with an especially large concentration of Jews in its population. Toleration had a price, as Jews lost some of their communal self-governing powers and were pushed toward secularization and integration into the larger German-speaking community.

1789

Europe: Holy Roman Empire
Judaism

As part of his continuing efforts to reform the Jewish community, Joseph II, the Holy Roman emperor, orders Jews to adopt a German-sounding name from a list his officials have prepared and decrees that Jews are eligible for service in the empire's army.

1789

Southwest Asia and North Africa: Asia Minor
Islam

Ottoman sultan Abdülhamid I dies and is succeeded by his nephew Selim III (r. 1789–1807). Finding an empire in decline, he would attempt to reform the state and the military, but would be constantly harassed by Russia, which is locked into an expansionist policy.

Selim III is a devotee of the Mevlevi Sufi order, the Sufis made famous for their twirling dance as the Whirling Dervishes. His participation in the order provided an outlet for his musical abilities, and he composed a variety of pieces of Sufi Islamic music, which the Mevlevi use in their worship.

1789–1791

Europe: France
Judaism
The French General Assembly debates the status of French Jews in light of the Revolution. Initially, a limited citizenship is extended to the Sephardic Jews who reside in Bordeaux and southern France, but in the end, all French Jews including the heretofore unofficial community in Paris and the Ashkenazi community in Alsace and Lorraine are granted full emancipation.

May 21, 1789

North America: United States
Christianity
The first General Assembly of the Presbyterian Church in the United States of America meets in Philadelphia.

September 9, 1789

North America: United States
Christianity
The U.S. House of Representatives approves the Bill of Rights, a set of amendments to the Constitution, and recommends them to the states for adoption. The First Amendment begins with the provision that "Congress shall make no law respecting an establishment of religion, or prohibiting the free exercise thereof."

ca. 1790

East and Southeast Asia: Japan
Buddhism
Through the 1780s and 1790s, master artisan Jingoro Eirei Ono and his apprentices carve a massive statue of Yakushi Nyorai (i.e., the Medicine Buddha) out of

the stone cliff near 8th-century Nihon-ji Temple in Chiba Prefecture. Reaching some 90 feet in height, it is the largest of Japan's premodern Buddha statues. The Nihon-ji Temple itself dates back to 725 CE.

Associated with the giant Buddha are contemporaneous carvings of some 500 arhats (or rakans) (known as the Gohyaku Rakan) and a large stone carving of Kannon (Guan Yin), a project of the chief priest of Nihon-ji.

ca. 1790

Europe: England
Christianity
A network of like-minded Church of England social reformers emerges in the Clapham district in south London around politician William Wilberforce. They share an evangelical faith, a zeal for social activism, and a set of moral and spiritual values. The group is given much of the credit for the eventual passage of the Slave Trade Act (1807) and the Slavery Abolition Act (1833). They also participated in the founding of such diverse organizations as the Society for Suppression of Vice, the Church Mission Society, and the Society for the Prevention of Cruelty to Animals. In the next century, historians will begin to refer to them as the Clapham Sect.

Henry Venn, an evangelical Anglican minister, is generally considered the founder of the group, which included among its outstanding members activist Granville Sharp, Anglican minister William Dealtry, evangelist/poet Katherine Hankey, and writer Hannah More.

1790

North America: United States
Judaism
Jews of Newport, Rhode Island welcome President George Washington. George Washington writes a letter to the Jewish community proclaiming religious liberty.

1790

North America: United States
Christianity
John Carroll is consecrated as the first Roman Catholic bishop for the United States.

1790

North America: United States
Judaism

President George Washington visits the Jewish synagogue at Newport, Rhode Island, and promises that the United States is a nation that "to bigotry gives no sanction, to persecution no assistance."

1790

North America: United States
Christianity

The nation's first Naturalization Law limited naturalization (citizenship) to aliens who were "free white persons."

1790

North America: United States
Christianity

Additional Shaker communities open in Hancock, Massachusetts, and Enfield, Connecticut. They are followed by ones in Canterbury, New Hampshire, and Tyringham, Massachusetts (1792); Alfred, Maine, Enfield, New Hampshire, and Harvard and Shirley, Massachusetts (1793); and New Gloucester (or Sabbathday Lake), Maine (1794).

1790

North America: United States
Unbelief

The ministers and churches adhering to the Universalist doctrine, primarily the affirmation of universal salvation, meet in Philadelphia and adopt a "Faith and Plan of Church Government," a pan-congregational association that will facilitate ordaining ministers, issuing preaching licenses, and chartering local congregations.

1790

Europe: England
Christianity

Thomas Coke is named head of the newly formed Methodist missionary committee, to which he would donate much of his family's wealth.

1790

Europe: England
Judaism

The Ashkenazi community in London inaugurates its new Great Synagogue, which has seating for some 500 males, plus a gallery for some 250 females.

1790

Europe: Holy Roman Empire
Christianity

Holy Roman emperor Joseph II dies. He had pursued policies considered enlightened by many, but has raised much opposition as he attempted to build numerous structures that concentrated power in his centralized administration in Vienna. He faced opposition, especially in the non-German-speaking parts of his empire in northern Italy, Hungary, and Belgium. He is succeeded by his brother, Leopold II (r. 1790–1792). He had for many years served as the duke of Tuscany, where he had with little success attempted to reform the Roman Catholic Church. During his brief rule as Holy Roman emperor, he would move aggressively to quiet the rebellions that were erupting throughout the empire due to the unpopular policies of his predecessor.

1791

North America: Canada
Christianity

Priests of the predominantly French Sulpician order settle in Baltimore, Maryland, and establish the first American seminary.

1791

North America: Canada
Christianity

African Canadian Thomas Peters travels to London, where with the assistance of social activist Granville Sharpe he is able to convince the royal government to resettle the former slaves now residing in Nova Scotia in a new colony, which would be named Freetown, Sierra Leone, on the west coast of Africa. Peters is well received in London and is able to meet some notable people who agree to assist him in the proposed resettlement.

1791

North America: United States
Christianity
Methodist circuit rider Ezekiel Cooper preaches at the chapel erected by "a number of religious black people" at Oxon Hill, Maryland. That congregation, now known as the St. Paul United Methodist Church, is the oldest known congregation of African American Methodists.

1791

South Asia: India
Hinduism
Armed forces of the Maratha Empire under Raghunath Rao Patwardhan raid the Sringeri Sharada Peetham, Karnataka, founded in the 8th century by Adi Shankara Shringeri. Many are killed by the soldiers who rob the temple and monastery of all their treasures and valuables. Though the ruler of Mysore made a generous donation to the temple, it took many years for the *matha* to recover from its losses.

1791

Europe: England
Christianity
The British parliament passes the Roman Catholic Relief Act, which continues the process of granting Roman Catholics the same rights as Protestants. In particular, it allows Roman Catholics to practice law, grants free exercise of the Catholic faith, and provides for the existence of Catholic parochial schools. At the same time, a variety of restrictions remain. For example, Catholic churches could not have locks on their doors, or either steeples or bells on the chapels. Priests could not wear clerical garb in public nor conduct worship in the open air.

1791

Europe: France
Unbelief
In the wake of the French Revolution, the French government seizes and annexes the papal territory in Provence, the Comtat Venaissin, and Avignon. The government also appropriates the famous Citeau Abbey, forces the monks to leave, and sells it.

As the French Revolution proceeds, the government passes the Civil Constitution of the Clergy, which disbands all monastic orders and their centers.

1791

Europe: France, Italy
Christianity
Pope Pius VI condemns the Civil Constitution of the Clergy passed by the revolutionary French government and suspends all priests who accept it.

1791

Russia, Central Asia, and the Caucasus: Russia
Judaism
Russian empress Catherine II creates the Pale of Settlement, a region comprising about 20 percent of eastern Russia in which Jews were allowed to establish a permanent residency and beyond which they were not allowed to reside on any permanent basis.

May 1791

Central America and the Caribbean: Haiti
Christianity
The French revolutionary government grants citizenship to wealthy free people of color in its colonies, but whites in Haiti refuse to recognize the action.

August 21, 1791

Central America and the Caribbean: Haiti
Christianity
The slaves of Saint Domingue (Haiti) rise in revolt. The signal to begin the revolt had been given by Dutty Boukman, a Voudou high priest among the Maroon slaves, who had led a ceremony at Bois Caïman a week earlier.

1792

Sub-Saharan Africa: South Africa
Christianity
Three Moravian missionaries enter South Africa and discover that the original Moravian missionary congregation at Genadendal, founded in the 1730s, is still active. The Moravian Church will now obtain a

FRANÇOIS MAKANDAL (D. 1758)

Historical sources say little about the origins of François Makandal, an Islamic prophet who led a resistance movement that was a precursor to the Haitian Revolution. François Makandal was probably born and socialized in West Africa during the first half of the 18th century and at some point enslaved (perhaps at age 12) and sold into bondage in the French colony of Saint-Domingue. Some scholars cite evidence, such as his name and the names of his closest conspirators, Mayombe and Teyselo, that Makandal hailed from central Africa rather than West Africa. These suggestions, along with others concerning reports of Makandal's orchestration of Voudou rituals derived from central Africa (the Petwo rite, for example) and his adept use of poisons, are tenuous because it is just as likely that he learned Petwo rites in Saint-Domingue and that his knowledge of poison came with him from West Africa.

Makandal's fluent Arabic and Islamic devotion are the strongest evidence of his West African origins (not unlike those of his contemporary, the African American poet Phillis Wheatley). It is possible that in Africa he had been a Qur'anic scholar and cleric.

By 1740, Makandal had escaped from the plantation on which he labored to become a leading figure in a Maroon (escaped slave) community in the island's northwestern mountains. Although organized armed uprisings involving small clusters from among the island's half-million slaves occurred as early as 1522, and several others erupted during the 25-year period between 1679 and 1704, such violent insurrections were relatively infrequent in Saint-Domingue.

The impressive longevity (18 years) and defiant success of Makandal's movement was due chiefly to its development as a Maroon community. Operating from a Maroon base, Makandal is said to have had the power to transform himself into a variety of animals to evade capture and bring messages to satellite Maroon communities to ferment resistance. Although finally captured and burned at the stake in 1758 (though some believe that he escaped execution by transforming himself into a fly), he set an important precedent as a charismatic leader of resistance to the slave regime and thus, as historian Carolyn Fick puts it, "his memory was sufficient to nourish the long and bitter struggle that would one day lead to emancipation." Beyond the Haitian Revolution, Makandal's name has been adopted in Haitian Creole to designate a particular class of poisons and other paraphernalia associated with sorcery. He is also one of the few human beings to have been deified as a spirit in Haitian Voudou.

TERRY REY

permanent place in the region and spread throughout the Cape colony.

1792

North America: United States
Christianity

With the multiplication of Lutheran synods in North America, the original Lutheran Ministerium based in Philadelphia changes its name to the Ministerium of Pennsylvania and Adjacent States.

1792

North America: United States
Christianity

Pope Pius VI erects the Roman Catholic Diocese of New Orleans.

1792

North America: United States
Western Esotericism

The first American Swedenborgian society is founded in Baltimore, Maryland.

1792

North America: United States
Christianity

The first African American Methodist congregation (now St. Paul United Methodist Church) is founded in Oxon Hill, Maryland. Richard Allen, Absalom Jones, and Lunar Brown lead African American members out of St. George's Church in Philadelphia. This group will later create three congregations—the Bethel and Zoar Methodist churches and St. Thomas Episcopal Church.

1792

North America: United States
Christianity

Dutch Reformed congregations organize what becomes the Reformed Church in America.

1792

East and Southeast Asia: China, Hong Kong
Chinese Religions

Residents of Pen Chau Island, located in the body of water between Hong Kong Island and Lantau Island, construct a temple dedicated to Tianhou, the empress of heaven, a deity much beloved by those who make their living in the ocean. Resting in front of Tianhou is a large eight-foot whale bone, which fishermen brought to the temple and left as a good-luck piece.

1792

East and Southeast Asia: China, Tibet
Buddhism

The Chinese government revises the process by which the leading lamas for Tibet and Inner Mongolia are chosen. They present a golden bottle to the Yonghe Lama Temple in Beijong and to Jokhang Monastery in Lhasa. When it is time to search for the next Dalai Lama, Panchen Lama, or Changkya Khutukhtu (for Inner Mongolia), the names of the candidates chosen for consideration shall be placed in one of the golden bottles and chosen by lot. With the subsequent approval of the central government, the chosen candidate may assume the title and undergo the enthronement ceremony. This method is initially a solution to the problem of drawing the Changkya Khutukhtu from a limited list of Mongolian nobles.

1792

East and Southeast Asia: Japan
Buddhism

Mount Unzen near Shimabara, Nagasaki, erupts. The resulting tsunami destroys most of the town. The 15,000 deaths constitute one of Japan's worst volcanic disasters.

1792

Europe: England
Christianity

Baptist minister William Carey publishes *An Enquiry into the Obligations of Christians to Use Means for the Conversion of the Heathens*, in which he makes the argument for the need of organized missionary endeavors to spread the gospel to his Particular Baptist colleagues, most of whom because of their Calvinist theology do not believe in evangelizing the non-Christian world. Carey draws inspiration from the history of Christian missions, which he surveys

Considered by some to be the father of modern Protestant missionary efforts, Baptist minister William Carey (1761–1834) left Great Britain at a young age for British India. (John Brown Myers, *William Carey: The Shoemaker Who Became the Founder of Modern Missions*, 1887)

from the time of the early church to the most recent activity of the Methodists.

Carey then takes the lead, along with Andrew Fuller, John Ryland, and John Sutcliff, in the formation of the Particular Baptist Society for the Propagation of the Gospel Amongst the Heathen, known more popularly as simply the Baptist Missionary Society (and since 2000 as BMS World Mission). It succeeds in involving the Baptists in the growing concern for the propagation of Christianity around the globe previously in the hands of the (Anglican) Society for the Propagation of the Gospel, the Moravians, and the Methodists.

1792

Europe: Denmark
Christianity

Denmark takes the lead and becomes the first nation to abolish the slave trade.

1792

Europe: Holy Roman Empire
Christianity

Holy Roman emperor Leopold II dies after only two years on the throne. He is succeeded by his son Francis II (r. 1792–1806), who would be the last Holy Roman emperor. His reign was marked by his relationship with France, which had been changed radically by the French Revolution and the subsequent rise of Napoleon Bonaparte to power.

1792–1793

Europe: France
Unbelief

The newly elected French National Convention establishes the French First Republic and officially strips King Louis XVI of all political powers. The former king is then tried for crimes of high treason (December) and eventually found guilty and executed (January). During the following unrest, the convention appoints a Committee of Public Safety, which suspends the guarantees of the Declaration of the Rights of Man and of the Citizen and introduces the infamous Reign of Terror. Along with executing a number of perceived enemies of the state, the committee introduces a new revolutionary calendar and closes a number of churches in Paris and its environs as a part of a movement of de-Christianizing the nation.

1792–1794

North America: United States
Christianity

African American preachers Richard Allen and Absalom Jones lead a walkout of African members of St. George's Methodist Church in Philadelphia. The minister in charge of St. George's threatens to excommunicate Allen and those who leave with him and form an independent African Union Church. The majority of the members decide to form St. Thomas Episcopal Church over which Absalom Jones is ordained as the priest. The remaining members form two churches, Bethel Methodist Church in Philadelphia and Zoar Methodist Church located in Kensington, just outside the city limits. St. Thomas is the first African American Episcopal congregation. Bethel will later become the founding congregation of the African Methodist Episcopal Church (1816). Zoar remains attached to the Methodist Episcopal Church and continues today as Zoar United Methodist Church.

March 1792

Central America and the Caribbean: Haiti
Christianity

The French revolutionary government grants full civil and political rights to all free people of color in its colonies.

1793

North America: Canada
Christianity

A new Anglican Diocese of Quebec is created by taking the majority of the territory previously in the Diocese of Nova Scotia.

1793

North America: United States
Unbelief

Thomas Paine's *The Age of Reason* advocates Deism while denouncing traditional Jewish and Christian beliefs. Paine suggests, for example, that Jews pose a danger to an enlightened society.

1793

North America: United States
Christianity

Bishop John Carroll ordains Stephen Badin, the first Roman Catholic priest ordained in the United States.

1793

Europe: England
Christianity

The newly formed Baptist Missionary Society commissions its first missionaries, William Carey and John Thomas, and sends them to Bengal, India.

1793

South Asia: India
Christianity

Baptist missionary William Carey arrives in Bengal and settles in Calcutta. He and his colleague John Thomas find work at a factory, and Carey begins to learn the local language and to translate the Bible into Bengali. He also establishes some basic ground rules that will allow them to survive with a minimum of support from home—economic communalism and financial self-sufficiency, and the education of local leaders as ministers.

1793

Europe: France
Unbelief

As a result of the French Revolution, Notre Dame Cathedral is initially rededicated to the Cult of Reason (and later to the Cult of the Supreme Being). Supporters of the revolution destroy or remove items considered offensive, and a statue of Lady Liberty replaces that of the Virgin Mary on the altar. Eventually, the cathedral came to be used as a warehouse for the storage of food.

1793

Europe: Germany
Judaism

German philosopher Lazarus Bendavid calls his fellow Jews to discard the Jewish ritual laws. In his *Notes regarding the Characteristics of Jews,* he suggests that reform is the only course to prevent massive defections of young Jews to Christianity.

September 24, 1793

Europe: France
Unbelief, Christianity

French revolutionists enter the cathedral at Chartres and take possession of the *Sancta Camisia* (or saint's shirt), a prized relic believed to have been originally worn by the Blessed Virgin Mary. The revolutionaries divide the garment and distribute pieces to those present. The largest piece is retained by a devout Catholic and returned to the possession of the cathedral, though much of the garment is permanently lost.

1794

North America: United States
Christianity

Shakers found a community at Sabbath Lake, Maine.

1794

North America: United States
Christianity

Metropolitan Gabriel of Novgorod and St. Petersburg assigns Hieromonk Nazarius of Sarov, the superior of Valaam Monastery, the task of recruiting a group of monks to evangelize the residents of the Aleutian Islands. He selects 10 men including a young monk named Herman, who in 1794 travel to the island of Kodiak in the Gulf of Alaska, the headquarters of the Russian colonies in North America. They found a school, construct a church dedicated to Christ's Resurrection near Kodiak Harbor, and create a monastery where the members of the mission reside. The mission is short-lived, as the Russian-American Trading Company opposed their interference in their exploitation of the Native population. Most of the monks return to Russia, and only Herman remains. Of saintly reputation, he will later be canonized by the Russian Orthodox Church for his effort.

1794

North America: United States
Unbelief

Minister and theologian Hosea Ballou, who had converted to Universalism in 1789, becomes the pastor of a Universalist congregation in Dana, Massachusetts. He will subsequently become the most notable advocate of Universalism in the United States.

1794

North America: United States
Judaism

The Charleston, South Carolina, Jewish community dedicates its new synagogue building, which will house Congregation Beth Elohim. It is the second oldest synagogue building in the United States.

1794

Europe: England
Christianity

Anglican clergyman and theologian William Paley publishes his apologetic classic, *View of the Evidences of Christianity,* a presentation of what is termed the teleological argument for the existence of God, which compares creation to a watch, the existence of both, he asserts, implying the work of a creator. The book would be widely read and quoted into the 20th century. Out of their appreciation of the book, both the bishop of London and the bishop of Lincoln offered Paley positions in their dioceses. He developed the argument in his 1802 book, *Natural Theology.*

1794

Europe: Lithuania
Judaism

Elijah Ben Solomon Zalman, the head of the Jewish community, reiterates its condemnation of Hasidism by advocating the public burning of *The Testament* of the Hasidic leader, Rabbi Israel Ba'al Shem Tov.

1794

Russia, Central Asia, and the Caucasus: Russia
Judaism

Russian empress Catherine II doubles the taxes on Jews and officially declares that Jews bore no relation to Russians.

1795

North America: United States
Christianity

Congregational minister Timothy Dwight accepted the presidency of Yale College and during his quarter of a century of leadership builds it into a first-rate scholarly institution, while also serving as its professor of divinity and regularly preaching in the college church.

1795

North America: United States
Judaism

Ashkenazi Jews in Philadelphia who had formerly worshipped at Mikvah Israel Synagogue leave to found Rodeph Shalom, the first synagogue in North America to follow the Ashkenazi form of service.

1795

East and Southeast Asia: China
Chinese Religions

The Chinese Qing emperor Qianlong resigns the throne and is succeeded by his son, the Jiaqing emperor (r. 1795–1820).

1795

East and Southeast Asia: Korea
Christianity
A Roman Catholic lay movement in Korea, concentrated in Seoul, had grown to include some 4,000 members and finally is rewarded with the arrival of the first priest in the country, Zhu Wenmiao, from China.

1795

Europe: England
Christianity
Baptist John Ryland, who had been instrumental in the founding of the Baptist Missionary Society, suggests that Evangelical Anglicans and other Protestants join together in a cooperative missionary effort. His suggestion is well received, especially among the Congregationalists, and results in the formation of the London Missionary Society, started as an inter-denominational organization. Most of the groups will drop away as the number of denominational missionary societies multiply, and it will emerge in the next century as primarily a Congregational mission.

The first missionaries recruited and commissioned by the society went to Tahiti. It would later initiate work in China under the leadership of Robert Morrison.

1795

Europe: France
Christianity
With the worst of the French Revolution seemingly behind them, the priests at the Basilique Saint-Denys in Argenteuil begin to assemble the pieces of what they believe to be a tunic worn by Jesus of Nazareth, the most prized relic owned by the church. It seems to have been given to the church by the emperor Charlemagne in the ninth century. It had been divided and hidden as the Revolution entered its most virulent antireligious phase.

1795

Europe: Poland
Christianity

The Third Partition of Poland sees the division of the country with Austria, Prussia, and Russia each taking their portion. As one result, hundreds of thousands of Jews residing in eastern Poland are incorporated into Russia, which has for several centuries prohibited Jews from residing within it. Ironically, Russia has now become home to more Jews than any other country.

1796

North America: United States
Christianity
The Treaty of Tripoli includes a statement that "the government of the United States of America is not in any sense founded on the Christian Religion."

1796

North America: United States
Christianity
Shaker leader Joseph Meacham dies. His co-leader Lucy Wright remains in her leadership role until her death (1821).

1796

South Asia: India
Judaism
Samuel Ezekiel Decker builds a synagogue to accommodate the Indian Jews (the Bene Israel) who have over the previous decades moved to Bombay (Mumbai).

1796

South Asia: India
Christianity
Baptist missionary William Carey, based in Calcutta, baptizes his first convert, a Portuguese man residing in India at the time.

1796

Europe: Belarus
Judaism
Shneur Zalman of Liadi, the first rebbe of Chabad, an innovative branch of Hasidism, a mystical form of Judaism, who resides in Belarus (then part of imperial Russia), publishes *Tanya,* his systematic presentation

of the Chabad perspective. While advocating a mystical Kabbalistic emphasis, he also supports rigorous intellectual endeavor.

1796

Europe: Scotland
Christianity

Inspired by the founding of the Baptist Missionary Society and the London Missionary Society, Scottish Protestants (members of both the Church of Scotland and several dissenting groups) form the Glasgow Missionary Society and the Edinburgh Missionary Society. They initiate work on the coast of West Africa.

1796

Russia, Central Asia, and the Caucasus: Russia
Christianity

Russian empress Catherine II dies. She is succeeded by her son Paul I (1796–1801).

1797

North America: United States
Judaism

Solomon Etting petitions the Maryland state legislature to end its prohibition on Jews holding public office. The legislature ignores his request, and a three-decade struggle ensues to admit Jews to full citizenship.

1797

Central America and the Caribbean: Trinidad
Christianity

Spain surrenders Trinidad to England.

1797

Europe: France
Christianity

Secularized in 1790, the Cathedral of Our Lady at Boulogue, France, was closed to worship and eventually sold. The new owner began to demolish it. The destruction culminated in 1797 with the burning of the celebrated miraculous statue of the Virgin called "Our Lady of the Sea." Only a small part of the statue's hand survived the fire, but later when the property was returned and the church rebuilt, the

surviving fragment would again be placed on display and remains a target of pilgrimages.

1797

Europe: Netherlands
Judaism

Jews in Amsterdam who have taken up the cause of reform open the first Reform congregation, Asa Jeshurun. A product of the Jewish Enlightenment, the Reform movement will attempt to find a way of practicing Judaism while accommodating current intellectual traditions and the findings of contemporary science and allowing assimilation of Jews into modern society.

1797

Oceania and Antarctica: Tahiti
Christianity

A group of missionaries commissioned by the London Missionary Society lands in Tahiti. One of their number, Henry Nott, will begin the work of translating the Bible into Tahitian.

1797–1798

Europe: Italy
Christianity, Judaism

The French forces of Napoleon invade the Papal States, move Pope Pius VI into exile in France, and declare the existence of a new republic headquartered in Rome. The pope is forced to sign the Treaty of Tolentino, which surrenders part of the Papal States to France.

French forces visit Loreto, and while there invade the basilica that covers the Holy House, a structure believed miraculously transported to Italy from Palestine in the 13th century. They steal the statue of the Virgin and Child, which eventually reappears in the Louvre Museum. While in Rome, French forces commit a number of sacrileges, including the theft of the crown that had been placed on the portrait of the Virgin Mary at the Basilica of Santa Maria in Aracoeli.

The new French authorities in Rome grant Jews equal rights and revoke all traditional restrictions upon them.

1798

Sub-Saharan Africa: South Africa
Christianity

Johannes Theodorus van der Kemp, a physician who had been ordained by the London Missionary Society, becomes the first missionary commissioned by the Netherlands Missionary Society, arrives in Cape Town, and will work among the Xhosa and Khoikhoi (aka the Hottentots) for the rest of his life.

1798

South Asia: India
Christianity

The complete Bible using the new translation into Tamil produced by German Lutheran missionary Johann Phillip Fabricius is finally published. It will become the standard Tamil edition of the Bible into the 20th century.

1798

Europe: Austria
Christianity

Composer Joseph Haydn completes his great sacred oratorio *The Creation*, which is initially performed to great acclaim in Vienna. In the remaining years of his life he will frequently appear in public to lead a performance of *The Creation* for various charity functions.

1798

Europe: France
Christianity, Islam

Napoleon plans a invasion of Egypt with the intent of creating a connection to Tipu Sultan, a Muslim enemy of the British in southern India.

1798

Europe: Malta
Christianity

Napoleon captures Malta on his way to Egypt. Following the fall of Valletta, the stronghold of the Knights Hospitaller, a military religious order that had ruled Malta since the 14th century, the knights are dispersed though Europe. The Russian czar Paul I gives sanctuary to the single largest number of knights, who settle in St. Petersburg. In return, the knights elect Paul as their next grand master. The arrival of the knights led to the emergence of some sanctioned space for Roman Catholics in the otherwise Russian

Orthodox realms, as Grand Master Paul I created a Roman Catholic grand priory into which the order's members were organized.

1798

Europe: Netherlands
Christianity

Reformed Protestants meet in Rotterdam where they form the Netherlands Missionary Society.

1798

Southwest Asia and North Africa: Egypt
Christianity

While in Egypt, Napoleon places St. Catherine's Monastery in the Sinai Desert under his protection and grants recognition of its traditional status and privileges.

1798

Southwest Asia and North Africa: Palestine
Christianity

As countries (especially Russia) where Eastern Orthodoxy is the predominant faith unite against the Ottoman Empire, Patriarch Anthimios of Jerusalem comes to the empire's defense, arguing that it has been part of God's dispensation to protect Eastern Orthodoxy from being tainted with Roman Catholic innovations as well as Western secularist and irreligious perspectives.

July 1, 1798

Southwest Asia and North Africa: Egypt
Christianity

Napoleon and his army land at Alexandria, Egypt. A month later, on August 1 at the Battle of the Nile, British naval forces under Horatio Nelson decisively defeat the French navy, capturing or destroying all but two French ships.

1799

North America: United States
Christianity

Archimandrite Joasaph Bolotov, one of the original Russian monks sent to Alaska in 1793, had left the Aleutian Islands and returned to Russia where he had reported on the opposition they encountered and the harsh treatment being received by the Native people. Little is done with his report, but he is later consecrated as the first bishop of Alaska. He journeys back to his new diocese in 1799, but dies before reaching the Aleutians as his ship is lost at sea.

1799

North America: United States
Christianity

The official memorial service for the recently deceased Geroge Washington is held at Zion Lutheran Church in Philadelphia, the same church where services had been held for Benjamin Franklin in 1790.

1799

North America: United States
Christianity

Methodist bishop Francis Asbury ordains Richard Allen as a deacon (the first of two steps in the ordained ministry in Methodism). He thus becomes the first African American to be ordained as a Methodist minister, though he is never offered elder's orders. It will be another generation before black ministers are fully ordained by the Methodists.

1799

North America: United States
Christianity

Leonard Neale, the president of Georgetown College, invites three sisters of the Roman Catholic Order of the Visitation of Holy Mary to open a convent at Georgetown, and in their facilities they launch a Saturday school for young women, which will evolve into the present-day Georgetown Visitation Preparatory School.

1799

Europe: England
Christianity

A group of Evangelical Anglicans, including members of the activist Clapham Sect, found the Society for Missions to Africa and the East (which soon changes its name to the Church Missionary Society, the name under which it became famous). William Wilberforce served as one of its original vice presidents. It initially cooperated with the Evangelical Lutheran Church in Württemberg, which supplied its early missionary personnel. As the Society for the Propagation of the Gospel tended to represent high-church Anglicans, the CMS tended to find its support under the more evangelical low-church wing of the Church of England.

1799

Europe: France
Christianity, Judaism

In August, Napoleon leaves Egypt and returns to France. Back home, the Roman Republic declared in 1798 is dissolved and the Papal States are restored under Pope Pius VII. The rights granted Jews by the French are abandoned, the Jews are forced to return to their ghettos, and the old anti-Jewish laws are reinstituted. In November, Napoleon participates in a coup in France, which results in his being named the First Consul.

1799

Europe: Germany
Christianity

Friedrich Schleiermacher, a German theologian and biblical scholar, launches his career as the leading exponent of the new liberal Protestant theology that will dominate Europe through the 19th century with the release of his *Speeches on Religion to Its Cultured Despisers,* attempts to defend traditional Lutheran and Reformed Protestantism in the face of intense criticism from spokespersons of the Enlightenment. He would become an early champion of the merger of Lutheran and Reformed churches that occurred in the German Evangelical Church.

1799

Europe: Italy
Christianity

Just short of a quarter of a century on the papal throne, Pope Pius VI dies and is succeeded by Pope Pius VII (r. 1800–1823).

1799

Southwest Asia and North Africa: Syria, Egypt
Christianity, Islam

Pius VII was pope from 1800 to 1823. He is credited with reestablishing the papacy after Napoleon I all but destroyed both the office and its land holdings. (William M. Sloane, *The Life of Napoleon Bonaparte*, 1909)

Napoleon moves his army against Syria, a province in the Ottoman Empire, and begins taking cities along the Mediterranean coast—Arish, Gaza, Jaffa, and Haifa. He is stopped at Avre, where his weakened troops fail to take the city.

1800–1849 CE

Introduction: 1800–1849

The emergence of a new independent country in the place of the British American colonies along the Atlantic coast of North America would prove the decisive new factor redirecting European trajectories for world history as the 19th century began. It would herald the pushing aside of the European powers from most of the Americas—their control primarily surviving in the Caribbean islands and a few spots on the coast of the mainland (British Honduras, Suriname, French Guinea). From its base in the cities along the Atlantic, the new United States would begin the push westward to the Mississippi River and then more than double its territory with the purchase of Louisiana. Few doubted its future role after it withstood the attempt of the British to reassert their hegemony in the War of 1812.

A largely unchurched nation, the United States started the new century with the emergence of a decentralized and largely uncoordinated but massive movement on the part of its different Christian denominations to bring the American public into its folds. That effort would see a steady growth of both the numbers and percentage of the public who attached themselves to the Methodists and Baptists or one of the several dozen alternatives that opened their doors to potential recruits, but only about a fourth of the adult population found their way to membership in one of the churches by midcentury.

The older churches—Anglican, Presbyterian, and Congregationalist—would grow significantly through the early decades, but would be far outstripped by the Methodists, who initially grew the fastest, but who were closely followed by the Baptists. When both split over the slavery issue in the mid-1840s, the Roman Catholics suddenly jumped to the fore and became the largest single denomination in the country, a fact often lost in the growth of the fiercely competitive Protestant groups, united in but a single fact—their mutual opposition to Catholicism.

Catholicism was, in fact, doing quite well throughout the Americas. It survived largely intact through the change of power (French to English) in Canada. It emerged as the dominant religious institution from Mexico to Chile and Argentina as each of the South and Central American countries became independent of Spain and Portugal. And it maintained strong centuries-old establishments in the Caribbean on the larger islands—Cuba, Haiti and the Dominican Republic, and Puerto Rico. Meanwhile, the real challenge to the church's power would emerge in Europe.

The European century began with the arrival of Napoleon Bonaparte. He began the century as First Consul but within a few years was crowned as Emperor of France. He had already moved to alter Europe's map but as emperor moved about the continent in seemingly unstoppable fashion. While reestablishing the Roman Catholic Church's position in France, a role temporarily lost due to the French Revolution, the Napoleonic church was a new, highly regulated institution. Only with the horrendous mistake of invading Russia and the destruction of his army was Napoleon finally slowed and then utterly defeated. Along the way he had finished off the Holy Roman Empire, long in decline, sped up the process of secularization across the continent, and largely abandoned France's role in the Americas.

In the wake of Napoleon, Europe's religious communities would enjoy a vital renaissance with a number of outstanding intellectuals, not the least being the father of German liberal theology, Friedrich Schleiermacher, who sought to recast Christian theology in a form that responded positively to the new currents of Enlightenment thought. His effort would dominate European Protestantism for the rest of the century.

While old modes of thought remained firmly entrenched among European elites, new visions of culture, religion, and political life had been unleashed in the previous century and as the disenfranchised masses yearned for a better life, would bear fruit as democratic imperatives gained in popularity. The new ideas would erupt in 1830 in France with the July Revolution that ended the Bourbon regime instituted after Napoleon's defeat and brought the House of Orleans in the person of King Louis Philippe. The 1830 revolution marked the beginning of the end of the idea of the divine right of kings in European thought and pointed to the arrival of a new idea in which political power was seen as being derived from the people, an idea to be embodied in future democratic systems in which the people could exercise their right to withdraw their consent to be governed from any monarch, or indeed, any government.

Further to the east, the Ottoman Empire still looked impressive as it stretched from Europe to the Arabian Peninsula and across North Africa, but internally the leadership knew that it was facing severe problems. The growing strength of its neighbors to the north, most notably Austria and Russia, which had begun to slowly acquire territory once under undisputed Ottoman control, accelerated the pressure on the Ottomans with their increasingly more powerful weaponry. Yet even as the sultans attempted to modernize, a conservative Muslim clergy became a major obstacle to any effort to reform the system, most notably by blocking much-needed improvements in communication and military acumen. Greece revolted and gained its independence in the 1820s and further unrest spread through the Balkans in the 1830s. By midcentury,

Ottoman partisans looked for a prescription that could save the "sick man" whose empire faced the possibility of complete collapse.

The Hindu Maratha kingdom opened the century in control of most of India, but faced a new challenge from forces under the control of the British East India Company, which had initially (and successfully) intervened in India affairs in the First Anglo-Maratha War (1775). As the 19th century progressed, the British now fought two wars with the Marathas for control of the subcontinent, and the victories of the Third Anglo-Maratha War (1817–1818) left the British East India Company in control of most of India. While the company was no friend of religion, their victory had the long-term effect of opening India to Christian missionaries, and representatives of the major churches of Europe responded by establishing outposts in every area of the land.

India had been one of two major targets of the developing missionary movement by Protestants in Europe and America. Missionary-minded Europeans had first looked at the Americas in the 18th century, and only toward the end of the century had Asia been targeted, though one early effort by German Lutheran Pietists had opened a singular mission in southern India early in the 1700s. Protestants now looked to China and the South Seas, the Dutch East Indies, Malaysia and the surrounding lands, Sri Lanka (then called Ceylon), and the Indian subcontinent. The early groups that initiated the Protestant missionary enterprise had formed missionary associations (the Anglicans) or turned their ecclesiastical structure into such an association (the Moravians and Methodists). However, beginning with the British Baptists, European Christians who adopted the missionary imperative began to found new missionary associations (each based in a single or a few closely related denominations) to recruit missionary personnel, raise money for their support, and strategize on winning the world for Christ. The Baptists sent their first missionaries to Burma (India being initially inhospitable), the Congregationalists to China and the South Seas, and the Dutch Reformed to Malaysia and Indonesia.

Interest in Africa would follow as British intervention in South Africa opened the door. Interestingly, it would be David Livingstone, a missionary who arrived in Africa initially in 1840, but who subsequently quit his job to become an explorer of the African interior, who would inspire later generations to focus on the conversion of Africa.

Possibly the most notable changes of the early 19th century would come in China and Japan, two countries that had self-consciously cut themselves off from the changing world around them. Europeans, especially the British, were knocking on China's door as they applied pressure to enlarge the very lucrative but very limited trade with the subjects of the Qing rulers. By the beginning of the 19th century, opium had become an essential part of that trade, even as the Qing government sought to eliminate the spread of opium and its harmful effects.

Conflicts over a number of issues, most focused on disagreements over opium, led to the first Opium War, which culminated in a British victory and the 1842 Treaty of Nanking that gave the British a land base on Hong Kong Island and Westerners an expansive new opening in China with the establishment of five treaty ports spread along China's coast. The treaty allowed China to be penetrated by Western trade and Western ideas. Relative to religion, the Nanking Treaty allowed missionaries to settle in the five ports and as a result China soon became the single largest mission field for Protestant churches.

The opening of China and the profits that flowed from it led other Westerners to cast their attention on Japan, which more than China had closed its borders to any relationship with European nations. Only the Dutch were allowed a trading post and any relationship with the shogunate, which had ruled Japan for centuries. However, with China now open, it was only a matter of time before the effort would be made to create a new Japanese market. Korea, which existed in a tense relationship with the Manchurian Qing government, also hesitated to develop any relationship with potential trading partners in the West, and certainly had little use for Western culture and religion. A new world, however, was just beyond the horizon.

ca. 1800

Europe: England
Western Esotericism
Francisco de Miranda, a Venezuelan and Freemason who fought for the independence of South America from Spain, founds "The Great American Reunion" lodge in London. It would become the meeting place for fellow revolutionaries, such as Simon Bolivar, when they visited England in the early 19th century. Soon after the lodge's founding, Miranda meets

Bernardo O'Higgins, future Chilean revolutionary leader, and O'Higgins begins his Masonic career in the London lodge. O'Higgins later aligns with another Mason, José de San Martin, in the effort to free Argentina and Chile from Spanish rule.

1800

North America: United States
Christianity
German Americans influenced by Methodism found the Church of the United Brethren (led by William Philip Otterbein and Martin Boehm) and the Evangelical Association (later the Evangelical Church), under the leadership of Jacob Albright.

1800

Central America and the Caribbean: Haiti
Traditional Religions
Inspired by the French revolution, the slave population of Haiti under the leadership of Toussaint-Louverture revolts and takes control of the country.

1800

South Asia: India
Christianity
William Carey, the first Baptist missionary in India, baptizes his first convert, Krishna Pal.

1800

Oceania and Antarctica: Australia
Christianity
The first Roman Catholic priests arrive in Australia as convicts. James Harold, James Dixon, and Peter O'Neill have been convicted on charges related to the Irish rebellion of 1798. Fr. Dixon is subsequently freed and permitted to celebrate mass for the small community of Roman Catholics, almost all of Irish heritage, who had previously been sent to the penal colony. Catholicism would have a slow start in Australia due to its lack of legal status in England.

1800–1899

Oceania and Antarctica: Micronesia
Traditional Religions, Christianity

The term "Micronesia" (meaning "small islands") describes three archipelagos: the Marshall Islands, the Mariana Islands, and the Caroline Islands. They were inhabited in prehistoric times by Micronesians of various groupings. The traditional religions of Micronesia followed a polytheism that recognized a variety of deities under a supreme being known as Ialulep. The first Europeans, Ferdinand Magellan (ca. 1480–1521) and his crew, visited the Marianas in 1521. They would be named for Queen Maria Ana of Austria (1667–1740) during her time as regent to the Spanish throne. The Spanish claimed hegemony over the islands and in 1885 were able to keep the Germans from trying to place a protectorate over them. The Spanish brought Catholicism with them and slowly transformed the indigenous religions of the islands into distinct forms of Catholicism.

1800–1899

Oceania and Antarctica: Marshall Islands
Traditional Religions, Christianity

Like the rest of Micronesia, the Marshall Islands are influenced primarily by Spanish Catholicism in the 19th century. Catholic missionaries slowly wiped out the indigenous religion, a form of polytheism that gave a central place to two deities: the Great Spirit and the Lord of the Nether Regions. That religion has all but disappeared.

March 14, 1800

Europe: Italy
Christianity

Pope Pius VII (r. 1800–1823) begins his reign as head of the Roman Catholic Church. He will be crowned while wearing a papier-mâché papal tiara, as Napoleon's French troops had carried the tiara away when they left Rome,

July 6, 1800

Southwest Asia and North Africa: Asia Minor
Traditional Religions

Lord Elgin, in Istanbul on a mission from the British government, convinces the Ottoman sultan to issue orders that will allow him to remove the sculptures from the Parthenon on the Acropolis in Athens, then under Ottoman rule. Elgin will subsequently have the sculptures taken from Athens to London, where they remain.

August 1800

North America: United States
Christianity

Gabriel Prosser, intending to create a free black state in Virginia, plots with other slaves in the spring of 1800 to seize the arsenal at Richmond and kill whites. Upon learning of the plan, Governor James Monroe dispatched the state militia. Prosser and some 35 of his comrades were captured and executed. Prosser had planned to kill all of the whites with the exception of Quakers, Methodists, and Frenchmen (whom he viewed as being antislavery). Subsequently, Virginia passes a law forbidding African Americans to assemble between sunset and sunrise for religious worship or instruction.

October 1, 1800

North America: United States
Christianity

By the Treaty of San Ildefonso, Spain quietly returned the Louisiana Territory west of the Mississippi River to France.

December 24, 1800

Europe: France
Christianity

Amid the turmoil and anti-Catholic feeling released by the French Revolution, Father Pierre Coudrin and Henriette Aymer de Chevalerie, both of whom had separately experienced visions of creating a new religious institute, officially establish the new Congregation of the Sacred Hearts of Jesus and Mary. Its focus will center on spreading a devotional life based on adoration of the hearts of Jesus and Mary and the Blessed Sacrament.

1801

North America: United States
Christianity

Congregationalists and Presbyterians approve a Plan of Union outlining the development of congregations west of the Allegheny Mountains.

1801

North America: United States
Unbelief

POPE PIUS VII (1742–1823)

Pius VII was pope from 1800 to 1823 during the age of Napoleon I. He is credited with reestablishing the papacy after Napoleon all but destroyed both the office and its land holdings. Open to modern ideas, Pius had declared in 1797 that there was no conflict between Christianity and democracy, a radical view for the time.

Pius reached an agreement with Napoleon on July 16, 1801. The concordat recognized that Catholicism was the religious choice of the majority of French citizens, in effect recognizing the rights of the church. In 1802, Napoleon unilaterally promulgated the Organic Articles, which strengthened French control over the church and restricted papal intervention. Pius traveled to Paris in 1804 to take part in Napoleon's coronation as emperor. At this event, instead of receiving the crown from the pope, Napoleon took the crown from Pius's hands and placed it on his own head; he then crowned Empress Josephine.

Relations with France deteriorated after the papacy refused to take sides against England. French troops occupied Rome in February 1808 and annexed what remained of the Papal States in May 1809. Pius then excommunicated Napoleon. The pope was arrested and interned at Savona, a town near Genoa, until mid-1812, when he was carted off to Fontainebleau. Pius remained in France until early 1814, when Napoleon, suffering military defeats, sent the pope back to Italy.

During his captivity, Pius's prestige was enhanced because he bore his chains with courage. The favorable political climate after Napoleon's downfall enabled the Vatican to sign concordats with Russia in 1818 and Prussia in 1821.

In other matters, Pius restored the Society of Jesus in 1814 after 40 years in hiatus. He condemned Protestant Bible societies in 1816 and Freemasons in 1821. He tried to steer a moderate course between the old ways and new ideas introduced by the French Revolution.

RICHARD SAUERS

Elihu Palmer launches his career as a Deist leader with his book *Principles of Nature.*

1801

North America: United States
Judaism
The first American Jewish orphan care society is established in Charleston, South Carolina.

1801

Central America and the Caribbean: Haiti
Traditional Religions

François-Dominique Toussaint-Louverture (1743–1803), a former slave who emerged as a brilliant military commander, proposes a new constitution for Haiti. It provides for local autonomy and names him governor for life. As the revolt proceeds, the African traditional religions followed by the slaves reassert themselves and emerge as an important faith in Haiti, where it will be known as Voudou.

1801

South Asia: India
Hinduism

An earthquake does extensive damage to the main temple at Badrinath, a site especially revered by Vaishnava Hindus, and the king of Jaipur takes the lead in the rebuilding effort. The temple is home to a 45-foot mega-statue of Vishnu as Lord Narayana.

1801

East and Southeast Asia: Korea
Christianity

King Sunjo begins his reign in Korea. He turns on the Christian community, which has already attained outlaw status, and kills many, mostly Roman Catholics. Among the martyrs is Yi Seung-hun, who had attempted to reintroduce Christianity into the country in 1785.

1801

Europe: United Kingdom
Western Esotericism

Francis Barrett's *The Magus* marks the beginning of the post-Enlightenment magical revival.

1801

Russia, Central Asia, and the Caucasus: Georgia
Christianity

Georgia, a largely Orthodox Christian nation with a substantial Muslim minority, already a Russian protectorate, is fully absorbed into the Russian Empire.

1801

Russia, Central Asia, and the Caucasus: Russia
Christianity

Czar Paul I, the emperor of Russia, is assassinated by a small group of former army officers. He is succeeded by his son, the 23-year-old Alexander I (r. 1801–1825). Though highly disliked by the nobility, Paul will be venerated as a saint by many of the members of the Russian Orthodox Church who benefited by his measures that improved their daily life substantively.

1801–1818

Southwest Asia and North Africa: Asia Minor
Christianity

Neophytus VII (r. 1798–1801), who had been installed as the ecumenical patriarch for the second time in 1798, is again deposed. He is sent into exile on Mount Athos. He will be followed by a series of patriarchs who will reign briefly, possess only a modest amount of power, and about whom little is known—Callinicus V (1801–1806, 1808–1809); Gregory V (1806–1808); Jeremias IV (1809–1813); and Cyril VI (1813–1818).

In 1818, Gregory V, who had already served two terms as the patriarch (1797–1798, 1806–1808), is brought to Istanbul for a third time and begins serving an additional three years, which will end in tragedy.

January 1, 1801

Europe: England, Ireland
Christianity

Great Britain merges with the Kingdom of Ireland and forms the United Kingdom of Great Britain and Ireland. As prime minister, William Pitt the Younger (r. 1783–1801) emerges as the major architect of the union. Pitt's plans to grant concessions to Roman Catholics, the majority of the population in Ireland, and abolish a spectrum of political restrictions that had been imposed on Catholics by the British since the Protestant Reformation were opposed by King George III. He saw any concessions to the Catholics as violating his oath to protect the Church of England. Unable to change the king's opinion, Pitt resigns on February 16. He is succeeded by Henry Addington.

As an integral element of the union between England and Ireland, the Church of England and Church of Ireland are united into a single Protestant Episcopal church, to be called the United Church of England and Ireland. Anglicans assume control of the property of the Roman Catholic Church, most notably the main churches and cathedrals. A struggle to maintain Catholic worship is initiated, and the majority of the people remain Catholic in faith and practice. The Roman Catholic Church becomes identified with the struggle for Irish independence over the next two centuries.

March 23, 1801

Europe: Russia
Christianity

Russian czar Paul I is murdered. He is succeeded by his son Alexander.

April 21, 1801

Southwest Asia and North Africa: Iraq, Arabia
Islam

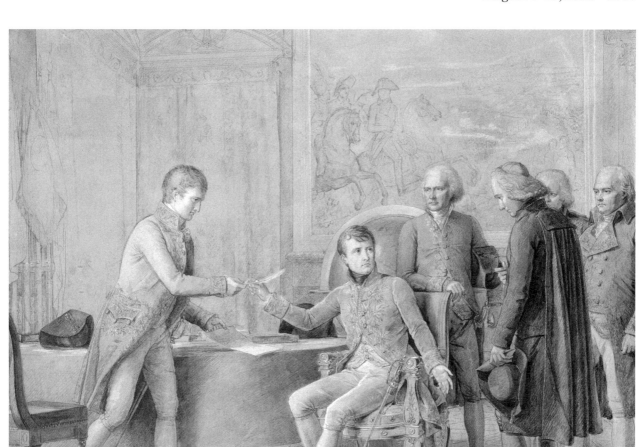

French leader and future emperor Napoleon Bonaparte signs the Concordat of 1801. In an attempt to ease the discord over the rightful control of the Catholic Church, Napoleon signed an agreement with Pope Pius VII to reestablish the Catholic Church in France. (Château de Versailles, France/Giraudon/The Bridgeman Art Library)

Sunni Muslim Saudi Arabs lead raids into Karbala, Iraq, a sacred site for Shi'a Muslims, and kill some 5,000 people. The city is commemorated as the place where Hussein ibn Ali died and his tomb is visited annually by millions of Shi'as.

July 15, 1801

Europe: France
Christianity

Napoleon reaches an agreement with Pope Pius VII, the Concordat of 1801, which aims at restoring much of what had been lost to the Roman Catholic Church during the French Revolution, recognizes its role as the majority faith of the country, and reasserts its civil status. It stops short of recognizing the Catholic

Church as the French state church and preserves rights for the country's Protestant minority.

Napoleon agrees to pay the salaries of the priests, but they are expected to swear an oath of allegiance to the state.

As a result of the Concordat, a number of the smaller and weaker French dioceses are consolidated with a neighboring diocese, thus substantially reducing the number of dioceses nationally.

August 6–13, 1801

North America: United States
Christianity

Thousands of people who have settled on the American frontier gather at Cane Ridge, Kentucky for a camp meeting. The meeting becomes the model of many to follow and ignites a movement to convert the settlers and organize them into congregations. This process of churching the West will come to be called the Second Great Awakening. It will be led by the new Church of Christ Restoration movement (which largely develops from Cane Ridge), the Methodists, Baptists, and Cumberland Presbyterians.

August 30, 1801

Southwest Asia and North Africa: Egypt
Islam, Christianity

The remainder of Napoleon's French army in Egypt surrenders to the British.

1802

North America: United States
Unbelief

In a letter to Baptists in Danbury, Connecticut, President Thomas Jefferson introduces the phrase "separation of church and state."

1802

North America: United States
Judaism

Ashkenazi (Central European) Jews in Philadelphia create a second synagogue, Rodeph Shalom.

1802

North America: United States
Christianity

New England Baptists organize the Massachusetts Baptist Missionary Society.

1802

South Asia: Sri Lanka
Buddhism

The Treaty of Amiens. While formally creating a temporary peace between France and the United Kingdom, the treaty cedes the Dutch half of the island of Sri Lanka to the British, who immediately transform it into a crown colony. The other part of the island continues to be locally ruled by the king of Kandy.

1802

Europe: France
Christianity

The Genius of Christianity, a work by François-René de Chateaubriand while in exile from the French Revolution, is published in France. It defends Roman Catholicism against the attacks of the Enlightenment ideas expressed by the revolution's leaders. He emphasizes the church's social, cultural, and spiritual benefits.

April 2, 1802

South Asia: India
Sikhism

Having united the various local divisions of the confederacy that had ruled the Sikhs, Ranjit Singh (1780–1839) was crowned the maharajah of the new Sikh Empire. He established his capital at Lahore. His rule would be known for its relative egalitarianism and pluralistic religious environment.

April 8, 1802

Europe: France
Christianity

Napoleon issues the Organic Articles, a law aimed at managing public worship in France. The majority of the law regulates the Roman Catholic Church. It provides for state supervision of church life and allows the state veto power on issues from the promulgation of papal encyclicals inside France to the building of new churches. It also provides for the state to pay the salaries of the clergy. A second set of regulations also regulate the French Reformed Church, which becomes both state-supported and controlled.

April 9, 1802

Europe: France
Christianity

Napoleon releases the Organic Articles, a set of regulations relative to public worship, 77 of which relate to Catholicism and 44 to Protestantism. The articles were designed to provide oversight of the churches in case any groups became subversive. The articles had as one goal the prevention of conflicts between the various churches.

April 18, 1802

Europe: France
Christianity

A provision of the Concordat of 1801 goes into effect with the reestablishment of the Sabbath as a "festival" on the French calendar. France still operated under the French Republican Calendar, which had been designed in part to remove all religious influences from the calendar. France would return to the Gregorian Calendar on January 1, 1806.

May 20, 1802

Europe: France
Christianity

Napoleon issues the Law of 20 May 1802, which reestablishes slavery in France's colonial possessions, most notably Haiti. It had been banned by the revolutionary French government.

May 20, 1802

Central America and the Caribbean: Haiti
Traditional Religions

Napoleon reinstitutes slavery in France's colonial possessions, reversing the ban imposed following the French Revolution. He sends an army to suppress the slave revolt on the island of Hispaniola.

August 2, 1802

Europe: France
Christianity

A national referendum confirms Napoleon as First Consul for life, a major step in his acquisition of dictatorial powers.

1803

Sub-Saharan Africa: South Africa
Christianity

Dutch missionary Johannes Theodorus van der Kemp, sponsored by the London Missionary Society, establishes Bethelsdorp near Port Elizabeth as a haven to protect a group of some 600 native Khoikhoi people from the harsh realities of the colonial system.

1803

North America: United States
Unbelief

American Universalists issue their statement of belief, the Winchester Profession.

1803

Central America and the Caribbean: Haiti

With the army largely destroyed in the unsuccessful attempt to reimpose French authority on Haiti, Napoleon withdraws the remaining troops from the island. Napoleon abandons his idea of reestablishing a North American empire.

1803

Central America and the Caribbean: Haiti
Traditional Religions

Battle of Vertieres. A Haitian army led by Jean-Jacques Dessalines defeats French forces sent to quell the uprising by former slaves.

1803

Central America and the Caribbean: Cuba
Christianity

Pope Pius VII elevates the Roman Catholic Diocese of Santiago de Cuba, originally erected in 1518, to become a new archdiocese.

1803

South America: Venezuela
Western Esotericism

Venezuelan Simon Bolivar is initiated in the Masonic lodge of Lautaro in Cadiz, Spain. It is believed that this lodge becomes the meeting place of Bolivar with other South American revolutionaries such as José de San Martín. Bolivar will become a master mason in 1806 at a lodge in Paris.

1803

South America: Venezuela
Christianity

Pope Pius VII designates the Roman Catholic Diocese of Caracas, originally erected in 1531, as a new archdiocese.

1803

South Asia: Sri Lanka
Buddhism

Unitarian Universalist Association

The Unitarian Universalist Association (UUA) is the primary carrier of the several strains of the liberal religious tradition that developed in 19th-century America in dissent from the orthodox Christian faith. The Universalist Church of America and the American Unitarian Association grew up side by side through the 19th and 20th centuries. Although they saw themselves as the more liberal wing of the Protestant churches, many felt that they were far more than just another Christian sect. They felt that in denying the Trinity and the doctrine of hell, both groups had placed themselves beyond the boundaries of the faith. Neither group was invited to participate in ecumenical organizations.

American Unitarianism was exported by missionaries to India and Japan in the 19th century. As a result of its work in India, the Unitarians became aware of the Brahmo Samaj and the similarity of their beliefs. Eventually the Unitarians withdrew from India and have continued their fraternal ties to the Brahmo Samaj. Through the 20th century, the association developed followings among expatriate communities in Europe. Universalists, meanwhile, developed a missionary program in Japan.

The Unitarian Association and the Universalist Church merged in 1961 to form the Unitarian Universalist Association. Although the UUA acknowledges its roots in Christianity, in the decades since the merger it has steadily moved away from those roots in the acceptance of a broad spectrum of religious perspectives within its membership. Not only are humanism and other nontheist perspectives acceptable but, in addition, Eastern religious systems have taken root among the members. Possibly the most interesting of recent developments has been the growth of neo-Pagan Witchcraft (or Wicca) in the UUA, which has been given structure through the Covenant of Unitarian Universalist Pagans (CUUPs). Christian Unitarians continue to exist as one caucus among many.

J. Gordon Melton

The British invade the kingdom of Kandy, but are unsuccessful.

1803

East and Southeast Asia: Myanmar
Buddhism
Some Sri Lankan monks with ordination from Amarapura (Burma) found the Amarapura Nikaya in Sri Lanka. The formerly established Siyam Nikaya admitted only high-caste brahmins to its membership.

1803

Europe: Denmark
Christianity

The Danish regent Prince Frederick issues a ban on his country's continued participation in the slave trade. Denmark becomes the first country to move against slavery.

1803

Europe: Gibraltar
Christianity
The Methodist bishop initiates five years of journeys on behalf of Methodist missions with a visit to Gibraltar, where he establishes Methodist work.

1803

Europe: Switzerland
Christianity

After having imposed a highly unpopular centralized government on Switzerland, Napoleon confers with Swiss leaders on ameliorating the situation. Their meeting results in the Act of Mediation, which largely restores Swiss autonomy and creates a confederation of 19 cantons.

1803

Southwest Asia and North Africa: Arabia
Islam

An assassin kills Abdul Aziz, the head of the Saud family, which is expanding its territory on the Arabian Peninsula. The assassin is believed to be a Shi'a Muslim who is seeking revenge over the sacking of the Shi'ite holy city of Karbala by the Saudis (who are Wahhabi Sunni Muslims) in 1802.

1803

Southwest Asia and North Africa: Arabia
Islam

Arabic forces led by Saud ibn Abdul Aziz, the son of Abdul Aziz, capture the holy city of Mecca.

1803

Southwest Asia and North Africa: Afghanistan
Islam

Mahmud Shah Durrani (r. 1803–1818), the formerly deposed ruler of the Durrani Empire based in Afghanistan, again ascends the throne. The empire extends from Iran to Turkmenistan and south into India, having reached its height in the mid-18th century.

1803

Oceania and Antarctica: Australia
Christianity

The first Irish priests arrive in Australia. They come to minister to Irish political prisoners, who formed the core settlers from which the Roman Catholic Church in Australia would grow.

1803

Oceania and Antarctica: French Polynesia
Christianity

Pōmare I, a ruler on Tahiti, dies and is succeeded by his son Vaira'atoa, who takes the name/title Pomare II. He closely associates with the recently arrived missionaries from the London Missionary Society, who taught him to read, an activity that allowed them to work toward his conversion. He becomes a Christian in 1812 and begins to work toward the unification of the island.

April 5, 1803

Europe: Austria
Christianity

Ludwig van Beethoven's *Christus am Ölberge* (*Christ on the Mount of Olives*), an oratorio inspired by an incident in the life of Jesus of Nazareth, his visit to the garden of Gethsemane prior to his crucifixion, is initially performed at the Theater an der Wien in Vienna. It was perceived as a more humanistic presentation of the passion of Christ than had been present in, for example, the earlier works of Johann Sebastian Bach.

November 30, 1803

North America: United States
Christianity

In a ceremony at New Orleans, Spain completes the process of ceding Louisiana to France, which in turn, with the war in Haiti going badly, sells it to the United States.

1804

Sub-Saharan Africa: South Africa
Islam

The Dutch, who had brought political prisoners from India to South Africa, most of them Muslim, grant Muslims the freedom to practice their religion. While Islam is tolerated, Muslims still experience discrimination and outright hostility.

1804

North America: United States
Christianity

The United States, having purchased the Louisiana Territory west of the Mississippi River from France, sends representatives to a formal ceremony in St. Louis at which France transfers ownership.

1804

North America: United States
Christianity

ABSALOM JONES (1746–1818)

Absalom Jones was an African American activist and abolitionist in Philadelphia who helped found the first African-led Episcopal Church. As part of the free black community in the north, Jones was imbued with the rhetoric of the American Revolution and sought to advocate for African Americans through the organization offered by the church.

Jones was born enslaved sometime in 1746 in Sussex County, Delaware, where at an early age he taught himself to read. At 16 years of age, he was taken to Philadelphia and put to work as a clerk and handyman in a retail store. By the 1780s, he had earned his freedom, married and bought his wife's freedom, and purchased property in Philadelphia.

As a lay minister and teacher at St. George's Methodist Church in Philadelphia, Jones met and joined forces with another lay minister there, Richard Allen. In their role at St. George's, they ministered to the African Americans attending the established church for the white community. Although the Free African Society and the African American members of St. George's Methodist Church flourished under Allen and Jones, increasing racial tensions and incidents led to concerns that the African American members of St. George's would separate from the church's main congregation. In 1792, an official split did occur when the white trustees of St. George's tried to prevent Jones from praying in what they perceived as the "white" section of the church. Grievously insulted, the African American congregants left the church as a whole.

With this break in the congregation of St. George's Methodist Church, Jones began to organize "the African Church." Although a number of the white members of St. George's fought the division—the established African American congregants had brought a solid economic base to the church—many white abolitionists supported Jones's efforts to establish an independent church. When Jones began construction on his new facility in 1793, donations from these same abolitionists aided the building fund. Another divide in the former St. George's congregation took place in 1794 when Jones and Allen disagreed on the denomination of the new church. In 1802, Jones was ordained an Episcopal priest, the first Episcopal priest of African American descent. Allen went on to establish Bethel African Methodist Episcopal Church in the Methodist tradition in Philadelphia and several decades later became the first African American Methodist Episcopal (AME) Church bishop.

JANE M. ALDRICH

Absalom Jones, the pastor of the African Episcopal Church of St. Thomas in Philadelphia, is ordained as a priest, the first African American priest and the first African American ordained by the Episcopal Church.

1804

East and Southeast Asia: China, Tibet
Buddhism
Jamphel Gyatso, the eighth Dalai Lama, dies.

1804

Europe: France
Christianity
The Brothers of the Christian Schools (aka the Christian Brothers or the De La Salle Brothers), a French religious order that had been dissolved by the French National Assembly in February 1790, is called back into existence by Napoleon I, formally recognized by the French government in 1808, and subsequently flourishes in France and internationally. By the end of the century, it is the largest Roman Catholic male order in the world.

1804

Europe: Scotland
Christianity
The Scottish Episcopal Church had been largely destroyed by a set of laws designed to inhibit it that passed in the 18th century. The laws allowed the confiscation of all the church's buildings, which were given to the Church of Scotland. An attempt to revive the church begins at the Synod of Laurencekirk at which those in attendance accept the Anglican Prayer Book, the 39 Articles of Religion, and the oath of allegiance to the king of England. In the wake of the synod, the church began to build new sanctuaries for worship and work for the full repeal of the penal laws that blocked its growth. It would experience slow but steady growth through the next century and reemerge as a viable Anglican community.

1804

Europe: United Kingdom
Christianity
Protestants in England found the British and Foreign Bible Society.

1804

Southwest Asia and North Africa: Arabia
Islam
Saudi Wahhabi Muslims capture Medina, the second most holy city for Sunni Muslims, and take control of the region from the Ottoman Empire. The Wahhabis differ from the Hanafi Sunni Muslims on several points of Muslim belief and practice, most notably in the strictness of practice that they advocate.

1804–1813

Southwest Asia and North Africa: Persia, Georgia
Islam
Pressured by the Shi'a Muslim clergy, Fat'h Ali Shah invades Georgia, then controlled by Russia. The war proves a disaster and the Persian army is ill-equipped to fight the modernized Russian forces. After a series of defeats, the Persians are forced to sign the Treaty of Gulistan with Russia.

January 1, 1804

Central America and the Caribbean: Haiti
Traditional Religions
Declaring Saint-Domingue (Haiti) an independent nation in 1804, Jean-Jacques Dessalines is chosen by a council of generals as the island nation's first governor-general. In September, he proclaims himself emperor.

Haiti emerges as the only contemporary nation born directly out of a slave revolt. A number of slave owners, many with their slaves, flee to Cuba and then on to Louisiana.

March 4, 1804

Europe: United Kingdom
Christianity
An interdenominational group of British Evangelicals, including William Wilberforce and Thomas Charles, found the British and Foreign Bible Society to publish Bibles and distribute them in the United Kingdom and throughout the British colonies. The immediate problem faced by the organization was a shortage of Bibles in the Welsh language.

May 10, 1804

Europe: United Kingdom
Christianity
William Pitt again becomes the British prime minister (r. 1804–1806).

May 18, 1804

Europe: France
The French Senate passes a bill that introduces the concept of a French Empire and names Napoleon as the first emperor.

August 28, 1804

North America: Canada
Christianity

Canadian Anglicans consecrate the Cathedral of the Holy Trinity in Quebec City, the first Anglican cathedral to be built outside the British Isles. The older St. Paul's Cathedral then in Halifax had originally been constructed as a parish church and then designated a cathedral in 1878. It remains the cathedral for the Diocese of Quebec. To mark Holy Trinity's completion, King George III, as head of the Church of England, donates a number of religious objects. It is one of many churches modeled after the Church of St. Martin-in-the-Fields, London.

December 2, 1804

Europe: France
Christianity

In a ceremony at Notre Dame Cathedral, the seat of the Roman Catholic archbishop of Paris, Napoleon crowns himself Emperor Napoleon I and then crowns his wife Josephine as Empress. Pope Pius VII is present and offers a prayer of consecration, but is not allowed to place the crown on him.

1805

Sub-Saharan Africa: Namibia
Christianity

The first missionaries of the London Missionary Society (now an integral part of the Council for World Missions) sent to Africa arrive on the west coast of southern Africa (what is now Namibia).

1805

North America: United States
Unbelief

Henry Ware, a Unitarian, is appointed as the Hollis Professorship of Divinity at Harvard College. Trinitarian conservatives leave Harvard to found Andover Theological Seminary.

LONDON MISSIONARY SOCIETY

The London Missionary Society was founded to spread the Christian gospel in areas newly controlled by the British. One result of the missionary activities was to unify the British Empire around the world.

One of the areas in which the London Missionary Society was first active was the South Pacific. The London Missionary Society also desired to spread the gospel to India, but quickly encountered the opposition of the British East India Company, which was attempting to establish economic control over the subcontinent.

The London Missionary Society was also active in South Africa. The earliest missionary was Dr. J. T. Vanderkemp, who landed at Cape Town in 1799. Both he and his assistant, John Philip, were outspoken advocates of the rights of black natives and criticized white rule. Other missionaries followed, expanding the society's area of operations into the center of the continent. As in other places, the Bible was translated into native languages, encouraging native peoples to join the church. Among the London Missionary Society's agents in Africa was noted explorer David Livingstone. Livingstone was forced by the Boers to travel across Africa looking for suitable places to establish missions. By 1875, the missions of South Africa were sufficiently established to become churches. In that year, they were united in the Congregational Union of South Africa.

TIM WATTS

1805

North America: United States
Christianity
A German Protestant under the leadership of George Rapp founds Harmony, Pennsylvania, a utopian community.

1805

Europe: Germany
Christianity
Prussia becomes the first Protestant country to send an envoy, in the person of Baron Wilhelm von Humboldt, to the court of the pope, as the sovereign of the Papal States, in Rome.

1805

Europe: Italy
Western Esotericism
Freemasons in Italy form the Grand Orient of Italy, a national organization for what will become the umbrella in the yet to be united Italian state. Future grand masters will include Giuseppe Garibaldi, one of the major military leaders of the unification effort and next generation, and Giuseppe Mazzini, a major advocate of the unification.

January 18, 1805

Europe: United Kingdom
Christianity
John Moore, the archbishop of Canterbury, dies. He is succeeded by Charles Manners-Sutton (r. 1805–1828), formerly the bishop of Norwich.

March 23, 1805

Europe: France
Christianity
The emperor Napoleon signs the decree reinstating the Paris Foreign Missions Society, a Roman Catholic missionary agency founded in the 17th century.

April 8, 1805

Europe: Hungary
Christianity

Three years after it had been burned to the ground (1802) during the great fire that destroyed most of Debrecen, construction begins on the Great Church, the main Protestant Reformed church in Hungary. Construction will take over a decade with the western tower completed in 1818 and the eastern tower in 1821.

April 28, 1805

Sub-Saharan Africa: South Africa
Christianity
The Huguenots, members of the French Calvinist Reformed Church, consecrated the Strooidakkerk (or thatched church) in Paarl, the third oldest European settlement in South Africa.

May 17, 1805

Southwest Asia and North Africa: Egypt
Islam
Muhammad Ali Pasha (aka Mehmet Ali Pasha), an Albanian who became a commander in the Ottoman army, is named Wāli (governor) of Egypt and later declares himself the Khedive (viceroy) of the Ottomans for Egypt and Sudan.

May 26, 1805

Europe: Italy
Christianity
Napoleon crowns himself King of Italy using the Iron Crown of Lombardy in a ceremony at Milan Cathedral.

December 2, 1805

Europe: Czech Republic
Christianity
The Battle of Austerlitz. On the first anniversary of his coronation, Napoleon Bonaparte defeats a combined Russian-Austrian army at a site in what is now the Czech Republic.

1806

Sub-Saharan Africa: South Africa
Christianity

Muhammad Ali Pasha (1769–1849) was a professional soldier of the Ottoman Empire who seized control of Egypt in 1805 and ruled the country for more than four decades. (Library of Congress)

The British troops land at Losperds Bay in the Cape Colony, defeat the Dutch at the Battle of Blaauwberg, and following the surrender, Sir David Baird becomes the new governor of the Cape.

1806

North America: United States
Christianity

Five students from Williams College in western Massachusetts take refuge from the rain under a haystack and while waiting out the storm engage in prayer. During this time, later memorialized as the Haystack Prayer Meeting, they arrive at a common conviction that they should look upon the world as the object of their ministry. They will later (1810) take the lead in the formation of the American Board of Commissioners for Foreign Missions, which will emerge as the missionary arm of America's Congregationalist Churches.

1806

Central America and the Caribbean: Haiti
Traditional Religions

Jean-Jacques Dessalines, the emperor of Haiti, is assassinated.

1806

South Asia: India
Christianity

Henry Martyn travels to India as an Anglican chaplain. During his stay, he translates the New Testament into Hindi and Persian, the Psalter into Persian, and the Prayer Book into Hindi, and revises an Arabic translation of the New Testament. He will move on from India to Persia but dies soon thereafter.

1806

East and Southeast Asia: Japan
Buddhism

Inzan Ien establishes a Rinzai Zen community at Zuiryo-Ji in Gifu and founds the Inzan school of Japanese Zen. He and his contemporary, Takuju Kosen, are credited with completing the process of systematizing the use of koans in the practice of Rinzai Zen, and Inzan's disciples form one of the two main branches of contemporary Rinzai Zen.

1806

Europe: Netherlands
Christianity

Napoleon establishes the new Kingdom of Holland and names his brother Louis Bonaparte as king.

January 23, 1806

Europe: United Kingdom
Christianity

British prime minister William Pitt dies. He is succeeded in office by William Wyndham Grenville, first Baron Grenville (r. 1806–1807).

April 1806

Europe: France
Judaism

ZEN BUDDHISM

Zen Buddhism is a branch of Mahayana Buddhism. According to legend, the Buddha established the foundations of Zen Buddhism during a discourse on Vulture Peak in which he held up a flower. Only Maha Kashyapa understood this message, becoming the first Indian patriarch in the Zen Buddhist lineage. Legend continues that an Indian monk named Bodhidharma transmitted this new form of Buddhism to China around 500 CE.

Bodhidharma's teachings mixed with Daoism to form a new school of Mahayana Buddhism called Chan. Chan is the Chinese pronunciation of the Sanskrit word *dhyana,* which means "meditation." In Japan, Chan became known as Zen, which is the Japanese pronunciation of Chan. The two main schools of Japanese Zen Buddhism, Rinzai and Soto, were introduced into Japan from China in the 12th and 13th centuries, respectively. Both schools adapted to Japanese culture, while still retaining elements of their Chinese roots.

The aim of Zen Buddhism is to achieve enlightenment. The essential nature of Zen is often summarized as follows: a special transmission outside the scriptures, not depending upon words and letters, directly pointing at the human heart; seeing into one's nature and the realization of Buddhahood.

Zen claims to differ from other Buddhist schools in its emphasis on seated meditation. In contrast with his contemporaries, Bodhidharma deemphasized the existing focus on priestly ritual and the endless chanting of the sutras or Buddhist scriptures. Although other Buddhist schools often balance meditation with other religious practices such as intellectual analysis of doctrines or devotional practices, Zen considers those practices useless in attaining enlightenment. The core of Zen practice is seated meditation, called *zazen.* Meditation practices differ in different schools: generally, Soto Zen teaches *shikantaza,* and Rinzai Zen teaches *koan* practice. Shikantaza (nothing but sitting) involves sitting in a state of alert attention that is free of thoughts. Koans are paradoxical questions, phrases, or stories posed to the Zen practitioner as tools to assist the attainment of enlightenment. These koans such as "What is the sound of one hand clapping?" cannot be solved or understood using intellectual reasoning.

The vast majority of Zen practitioners outside of Japan are converts. There are now indigenous Zen teachers from a variety of lineages leading Zen groups in countries as diverse as the United States, Canada, the United Kingdom, France, Germany, Poland, Spain, Sweden, Switzerland, Australia, New Zealand, Argentina, Brazil, India, and the Philippines. As Zen has developed it has been recontextualized to suit Western cultures. Major changes include an emphasis on lay practice, equality for women, the application of democratic principles, an emphasis on ethics, and secularization and the linkage to some sciences, particularly psychology and psychotherapy.

MICHELLE BARKER

Napoleon convenes an Assembly of Jewish Notables to consider and respond to 12 questions. As they supplied satisfactory answers to the questions, many of which concerned the Jewish community's relationship to the state, to Christians, and to various outsiders, Napoleon orders the notables to select 71 men (of whom two-thirds would be rabbis) to constitute a Grand Sanhedrin (Jewish Court), which would have the authority to convert the answers to the 12 questions into decisions that would become the foundation of the future Jewish community in the empire.

April 21, 1806

Southwest Asia and North Africa: Arabia
Islam
Saudi Arabs lead Sunni raids into Najaf, Iraq, a holy place for Shi'a Muslims, whom the Sunnis consider heretics, and kill some 5,000 people.

May 1806

North America: United States
Christianity
Methodist bishop Francis Asbury ordains three African Americans—James Varick, Abraham Thompson, and June Scott—as deacons, a step to full ordination as elders, in New York City. The action recognizes the growing number of African American members in the Methodist Episcopal Church in the northern states and their need of ministerial leadership. He will subsequently ordain Daniel Coker (1808) and Jacob Tapsico and James Champion (1809), but afterward refuses further requests from African Americans for ordination and never raises any to eldership.

July 12, 1806

Europe: Liechtenstein
Christianity
Napoleon grants sovereignty to the small kingdom of Liechtenstein. It is the sixth smallest country in the world, consisting of only 62 square miles.

August 6, 1806

Europe: Germany, Austria
Christianity

With the abdication of Emperor Francis I, the Holy Roman Empire goes out of existence. Following his defeat at the hands of Napoleon at the Battle of Austerlitz, Holy Roman emperor Francis I dissolves the empire. Two years earlier he had founded the Austrian Empire, which he would continue to rule. Napoleon subsequently organizes those German states over which he now exercises hegemony as the Confederation of the Rhine. Napoleon commissions the Arc de Triomphe in Paris to commemorate the victory at Austerlitz.

1807

Sub-Saharan Africa: South Africa
Christianity
The British ban the slave trade and stop the importation of slaves to the Cape.

1807

Sub-Saharan Africa: Sierra Leone
Christianity
After outlawing the slave trade, the British bring liberated slaves, the "Recaptives," to Sierra Leone. They do not mix well with either the settlers repatriated from North America nor the native tribes around Freetown, and they create a new tribe called the Kri and create a language called Krio.

1807

South America: Colombia
Construction begins on a new cathedral in Bogota, where a bishopric had been located since the 16th century. It will take some 16 years to complete and be dedicated in 1823. After completion, it would become known as the Archbishopric Cathedral of Bogota.

1807

North America: United States
Christianity
A German-speaking Methodist movement that had developed around the ministry of Jacob Albright organizes more formally and names him as their first bishop. The group would later take the name Evangelical Church.

1807

East and Southeast Asia: China, Tibet
Buddhism
Lungtok Gyatso is recognized by Gedun Choekyi Nyima, seventh Panchen Lama, as the next Dalai Lama. The Panchen Lama will the next year perform the tonsure ceremony and give the new three-year-old lama his new name, Lobzang Tenpai Wangchuk Lungtok Gyatso.

1807

East and Southeast Asia: China
Christianity
Robert Morrison, a Scotsman sent out by the London Missionary Society, arrives in Canton (Guangzhou), China. Soon after settling, he will begin work on compiling a Chinese dictionary and translating the Bible into Chinese.

1807

Europe: France
Judaism, Christianity
Napoleon includes Judaism, beside the Roman Catholic Church and the Lutheran and Calvinist Protestants, as an official religion of France.

1807

Southwest Asia and North Africa: Iraq
Islam
Saud al-Saud, the head of the Saudi Arabs, again invades Karbala, Iraq, a holy city for Shi'a Muslims, for the second time in less than a year. He does much damage, but is unable to occupy the city for very long.

1807

Southwest Asia and North Africa: Asia Minor
Islam
The reforms introduced by Selim III, the sultan of the Ottoman Empire, become increasingly unpopular and a fatwa is issued against him for introducing the manners of infidels among the community of believing Muslims. He is also attacked for attempting to suppress the Janissaries. In the wake of the fatwa, Selim attempted to save his life by swearing fealty to his cousin, who comes to the throne as Mustafa IV (r. 1807–1808).

1807

Southwest Asia and North Africa: Arabia, Iraq
Islam
Sunni Arab Muslims lead raids into the Iraqi Shi'a holy city of Karbala, which they had devastated in 1801.

January 18, 1807

Europe: Germany
Christianity
Prussian nobleman Baron Clemens August von Droste-Vischering is named bishop coadjutor of Münster, and later in the year, following the resignation of the bishop, becomes the bishop of Münster.

February 9, 1807

Europe: France
Judaism
Delays push the opening of the new Sanhedrin that will lead the Jewish community until four days after the adjournment of the Assembly of Notables. Its 71 members include the rabbis who had sat in the Assembly, an additional 29 other rabbis, and 25 laymen. Its presiding officers, appointed by the minister of the interior, include Joseph David Sinzheim, the rabbi of Strasbourg (serving as president); Joshua Benzion Segre, a rabbi and member of the municipal council of Vercelli (first vice president); and Abraham de Cologna, a rabbi at Mantua (second vice president).

February 23, 1807

Europe: United Kingdom
Christianity
Under the leadership of Anglican William Wilberforce, Parliament passes "An Act for the Abolition of the Slave Trade" (aka the Slave Trade Act), which abolishes the trade in slaves (though not slavery) in the United Kingdom and its colonies. Wilberforce had been assisted in the effort by a group of concerned Protestants and Quakers who had allied to expose the evils of slavery.

After receiving significant support, 283 to 16, the bill subsequently received the formal assent of the king on March 25, 1807. Over the next decade, the British would use their international clout to pressure other nations to end the slave trade.

May 1807

South America: Uruguay
As part of a largely unsuccessful attempt to take control of the Rio Plata, the river flowing out of central South America and forming the entrance to Argentina and Uruguay, the British occupy Montevideo. They will remain for five months.

May 12, 1807

Europe: France
Christianity
Roman Catholic bishop Imberties of Autun bestows religious habits upon Anne Marie Javouhey and eight other women, an act that officially founds the Society of St. Joseph of Cluny.

Autumn 1807

Europe: Portugal
Christianity
Napoleon's French army enters Portugal. The royal family and most of the Portuguese nobility relocate to Brazil, then Portuguese territory.

1808

North America: United States
Christianity
Congregationalists who hold to an orthodox Trinitarian theology found Andover Theological Seminary in Andover, Massachusetts, to counter the influence of Unitarianism that had become popular at Harvard.

1808

North America: United States
Judaism
Polonies Talmud Torah, the first Jewish school on record in the United States, is established in New York.

1808

Central America and the Caribbean: Dominican Republic
Christianity
After a decade of chaos in which the island is under shifting rule by France and by revolting former slaves, Spain is finally able to retake control of the eastern half of Hispaniola, then known as Santo Domingo, now the Dominican Republic.

1808

South America: Brazil
Christianity
When Napoleon invades Portugal, the Portuguese royal family, along with most of the Portuguese nobles, flee to Brazil and reestablish themselves in a new capital, Rio de Janeiro. Soon after settling in, Prince Regent John (later King John VI of Portugal) and his courtiers begin to use the nearby Carmelite Church of Our Lady of Mount Carmel of the Ancient See, attached to the Carmelite monastery, as the royal chapel. A short time later it is transformed to become the new Cathedral of Rio de Janeiro. The bishop of Rio de Janeiro becomes the chaplain to the king.

1808

South Asia: India
Sikhism
Sikh maharajah Ranjit Singh (1780–1839) begins work on Gobindghar Fort at Amritsar, the sign of a coming transition of the center of the Sikh community from Lahore to Amritsar.

1808

Europe: France
Christianity
Construction begins on the new L'Église de la Madeleine, now a prominent Roman Catholic church in Paris, but originally designed as a temple to the glory of Napoleon's army.

February 1808

Europe: Italy
Christianity
Napoleon occupies Rome, arrests many of the cardinals, and imprisons the pope within the Quirinal Palace in Rome. He will subsequently annex the Papal States to France. In the process, Pope Pius VII excommunicates the emperor, and the French army exiles the pope to Savona.

February 22, 1808

Europe: Ukraine
Christianity
Pope Pius VII raises the Eparchy of Lviv to become the Archeparchy of Lviv. In the aftermath of the Partition of the Ukraine in 1785, the western part of the land had come under the aegis of the Austro-Hungarian Empire. The Roman Catholic rulers favored the Ukrainian Greek Catholic Church, an Eastern rite church in communion with Rome, and it prospered.

March 2, 1808

North America: United States
Christianity
Congress passes legislation forbidding the further importation of slaves into the United States.

March 19, 1808

Europe: Spain
Christianity
Charles IV, the king of Spain, abdicates his office. In the wake of his father's forced abdication, Ferdinand VII (r. 1808) fills the vacuum.

April 8, 1808

North America: United States
Christianity
Pope Pius VII elevates the diocese of Baltimore as the United States' first Roman Catholic archdiocese, and at the same time erects four new dioceses based in Boston, New York, Philadelphia, and Bardstown (Kentucky).

May 5–6, 1808

Europe: Spain
Christianity
In a precarious and unstable position, King Ferdinand VII of Spain turns to Napoleon for support. Instead, Napoleon forces him off the throne. On May 5, former king Charles IV relinquishes *his* right to the Spanish throne in favor of Napoleon. The next day, Ferdinand is forced to abdicate. Napoleon takes Ferdinand into custody and appoints his brother Joseph Bonaparte (r. 1808–1813) as the new ruler of Spain. Joseph assumes his new position on June 6.

July 20, 1808

Europe: France
Judaism
Napoleon orders the Jews of France to adopt family names.

July 29, 1808

Southwest Asia and North Africa: Asia Minor
Islam
Selim III (r. 1789–1807), the former sultan of the Ottoman Empire, is assassinated on orders from the sultan Mustafa IV. The Janissaries, who had helped Mustafa on the throne, carry out the murder of Selim. They fail, however, to kill Selim's brother Mahmud, who is able to emerge and depose Mustafa. The effort to turn back the reforms introduced by Selim is thwarted.

Mahmud II (r. 1808–1839) assumes authority as the sultan of the Ottoman Empire and the caliph of the Sunni Islamic community.

1809

South America: French Guiana
Christianity
The Portuguese, now based in Brazil, invade and capture French Guiana.

1809

Europe: United Kingdom
Christianity, Judaism
A group of influential Protestant church leaders, including William Wilberforce, Charles Simeon, and missionary Joseph Frey, conclude that there is a need for focused attention on converting Jews to Christianity and form the London Society for Promoting Christianity Amongst the Jews (now known as the Church's Ministry Among Jewish People). Beginning with a mission in London's East End, it soon spreads globally through the Jewish diaspora.

1809

Oceania and Antarctica: Australia
Christianity
The first Protestant missionaries to Australia are the Presbyterians, who build their first church, the

Mahmud II (1789–1839)

Ruling the Ottoman Empire from 1808 until his death in 1839, Sultan Mahmud II was known as a reformer who was responsible for the many changes that occurred in the empire during his time. He sought to modernize and Westernize his empire in an attempt to make it once again competitive with the great powers of Europe.

Mahmud consolidated his power over the empire by building up the regular army and creating an officer corps that would be loyal to him. Development of the army was slowed by the empire's military problems. War with Russia had begun in 1806 and posed a serious threat to the Ottomans. Russia's conflict with France in the summer of 1812, however, saved Mahmud, as the Russians were forced to back down. Mahmud declared war on Persia in October 1820 over border disputes but suffered serious setbacks and was forced to make peace in 1823.

During the summer of 1826, thousands were massacred as the Janissaries were defeated and dissolved. During the same summer, Mahmud also destroyed such powerful religious dervish orders as the Bektashi. By the autumn of 1826, Mahmud had secured a powerful place for himself in the empire by eliminating rival groups committed to the status quo.

Once secure in his power, Mahmud enacted many reforms in the empire. His goal was to make the empire a more viable force in the Western world by reforming it along the lines of the European powers. After destroying the Janissaries, he began to create a more modern, Westernized army and also built a much larger and modernized navy. He transferred the imperial palace from Topkapi to Dolmabahçe, which he fashioned in a much more Westernized style. He began to dress in European clothes and in 1829 issued a decree making European dress mandatory for men. From then on, the use of turbans and robes became permitted only for religious figures. Mahmud's reforms could not reverse the declining state of his empire, however, a trend that continued throughout the 19th century.

CHRISTOPHER BORHANI

Ebenezer Church, in 1809. It is the oldest existing church in Australia, and as it doubled as a school, also the oldest school building. They are soon followed by the Baptists, Methodists, Anglicans, and other missionary societies like the Salvation Army, but their growth is very slow for the first few decades.

Following its being overrun by the armies of Czar Alexander I, Sweden loses its eastern territory, which emerges as the autonomous Grand Duchy of Finland within the Russian Empire. The change does not affect Sweden's or Finland's status as predominantly Lutheran Protestant lands.

March 29, 1809

Europe: Sweden, Finland
Christianity

May 5, 1809

Europe: Switzerland
Judaism

The Canton of Aargau denies citizenship to its resident Jews.

May 17, 1809

Europe: Italy
Christianity

France annexes the Papal States, which leads Pope Pius VII to excommunicate Napoleon. As the relations between Pope Pius VII and Napoleon reach a new low, Napoleon makes Pius a prisoner. He is exiled to Savona, an Italian city on the Mediterranean, and then (July 5) to France.

May 25, 1809

South America: Bolivia
Christianity

The struggle for independence from Spain in South America starts in the city of Chuquisaca (now known as Sucre) in what is now Bolivia. Early attempts to organize an independent government would be crushed by Spanish forces and Bolivia would change hands on several occasions as the various wars for independence were fought out in neighboring Argentina, Chile, and Peru.

July 5, 1809

Europe: Italy, France
Christianity

Napoleon makes Pope Pius VII a prisoner and as French troops withdraw from Italy, takes him to France where he will hold him until 1814.

December 16, 1809

Europe: France, Austria
Christianity

The French Senate acts to allow Napoleon Bonaparte's divorce from Empress Josephine. Count Clemens von Metternich has already convinced Francis I of Austria to offer his daughter Marie-Louise's hand to Napoleon. The divorce would lead to open conflict between Napoleon, Francis, and the pope.

1810

North America: United States
Christianity

New England Congregationalists found the American Board of Commissioners for Foreign Missions as a means of engaging in the emerging Protestant World Missions enterprise. It will serve as the missionary arm of the Congregationalist churches and later serve as a sending agency for several sister Calvinist denominations including the Presbyterians (1812–1870) and Dutch Reformed (1819–1857).

1810

North America: United States
Christianity

Roman Catholic bishop John Carroll is named the first archbishop in the United States.

1810

South America: Chile
Christianity

Chile becomes independent of Spain. The new government establishes the Roman Catholic Church as the state religion.

1810

South America: Peru
Christianity

While most of South America is being swept by revolutionary ideals, prompted by negative reactions to Napoleon's entrance into Spain, the Viceroyalty of Peru remains the center of conservative Spanish loyalists. The largest Spanish army in South America is also stationed in Peru, which becomes the ultimate force to be dealt with by those seeking to establish independent and locally led countries on the continent.

1810

Europe: Scotland
Christianity

The Scottish Episcopal Church founds Edinburgh Theological College as a school to train Anglican clergy.

January 10, 1810

Europe: France
Christianity

The bishops of the Roman Catholic Church in France give in and against their better judgment annul the marriage of Napoleon to Josephine, which will allow him to remarry in a way believed to strengthen his political position in Europe.

March 11, 1810

Europe: France, Austria
Christianity

Lacking an heir, Napoleon divorces the empress Josephine and marries Archduchess Marie-Louise of Austria. Since he was unable to attend his wedding, Archduke Charles stood in for him at the ceremonies held at the Augustinian Church in Vienna.

Thirteen cardinals who opposed the divorce and remarriage of Napoleon were imprisoned for nonattendance at the marriage and stripped of their red robes. They would become known as the "Black Cardinals."

May 25, 1810

South America: Argentina
Christianity

The May Revolution. The takeover of Spain by Napoleon has significant consequences in Argentina and the whole of the Viceroyalty of the Río de la Plata, which included what today is Argentina, Bolivia, Paraguay, and Uruguay. Rejection of any French influence in the viceroyalty leads to open revolt that culminates in the deposition of Viceroy Baltasar Hidalgo de Cisneros and the emergence of local rule by the Primera Junta, which claims authority by ruling in the name of deposed king Ferdinand VII.

July 31, 1810

North America: United States
Christianity

Elizabeth Ann Bayley Seton establishes the Sisters of Charity, a new religious order in Emmitsburg, Maryland, dedicated to the care of the children of the poor. It was the first new Roman Catholic religious order for women to be founded in the United States. As head of the order she became known as "Mother Seton" and would later (1973) be canonized by the church.

September 16, 1810

Central America and the Caribbean: Mexico
Christianity

From the small town of Dolores, Guanajuato, Roman Catholic priest Miguel Hidalgo y Costilla declares Mexico's independence from Spanish rule, and an insurgent force begins to assemble under Hidalgo's leadership. In reacting to the independence move, Spanish authorities capture Hidalgo and some confederates and execute them.

September 18, 1810

South America: Chile
Christianity

In the wake of the Napoleonic invasion of Spain, the Government Junta of Chile proclaims Chile's independence as an autonomous republic, which nevertheless asserts its continuing allegiance to the now deposed king of Spain. This initial declaration initiates a move toward total independence led by General José Miguel Carrera. A struggle between those seeking independence and royalists follows. Eventually Carrera will be pushed aside in favor of Bernardo O'Higgins, who challenges Carrera's leadership.

1811

Sub-Saharan Africa: South Africa
Christianity

The town of Caledon, South Africa, is established and the Dutch Reformed Church is constructed.

1811

Sub-Saharan Africa: Sierra Leone
Christianity

George Warren, a Wesleyan Methodist missionary from Great Britain, arrives in Sierra Leone and integrates the Methodist work founded in the 1790s into the larger British Methodist community.

1811

North America: United States
Traditional Religions

Shawnee chief Tecumseh, with the aid of his brother, the prophet and visionary Tenskwatawa (1775–1836),

A Shawnee mystic and brother of Tecumseh, Tenskwatawa (1775–1836) was known as The Prophet. Tenskwatawa created a prophetic movement that tied Native people together against the United States' encroachment onto their traditional homeland. (Thomas L. McKenney and James Hall, *The Indian Tribes of North America*, 1836–1844)

organizes a confederacy of Native people with headquarters on Tippecanoe Creek (Indiana). U.S. forces under the command of William H. Harrison defeated Tecumseh in the Battle of Tippecanoe. After the battle, Tenskwatawa lost his influence among the Native people and left for Canada.

1811

South America: Colombia
Christianity
A movement against Spanish rule led by Antonio Nariño found early success in establishing an independent Cartagena by the end of 1811. The following year, he was able to proclaim the new United Provinces of New Granada. The success was short-lived, however, and eventually (1816) Spain regained control.

1811

South Asia: India
Christianity
The first Bible Society in Asia is founded in Calcutta.

1811

East and Southeast Asia: China
Christianity
Qing officials modify the Great Qing (legal) Code with an addition to the statute on "Prohibitions Concerning Sorcerers and Sorceresses." They outlaw the spreading of Roman Catholicism among either Chinese or Manchus. Attempted proselytization is a capital offense. In addition, any who refuse to repent of their conversion to Christianity are condemned to be sent to Xinjiang and to be assigned to Muslims as slaves. This law would be strengthened in steps over the next generation.

1811

Europe: England
Unbelief
Romantic poet Percy Bysshe Shelley is expelled from Oxford University in 1811 for writing *The Necessity of Atheism*. This pamphlet, originally published anonymously, is now considered the first atheistic text originally published in the English language.

1811

Europe: United Kingdom
Christianity
Methodists who have introduced American-style evangelism and camp meetings in northern England found the Primitive Methodist Church.

1811–1814

Southwest Asia and North Africa: Arabia
Islam
The Ottoman sultan sends the Egyptian ruler Muhammad Ali to retake the holy cities of Mecca and Medina from the emerging Saudi leadership. While both the ottomans and the Saudis are Muslims, there is a religious dimension in the effort as the Ottomans advocate Hanafi Sunni Islam, and the Saudis follow

Wahhabi Sunni Islam. Ali succeeds in driving the Saudis from Mecca (1813) and the following year captures Hijaz and takes the son of Saud ibn Abdul Aziz as a prisoner. He is sent to Istanbul where the sultan orders his execution.

1811–1823

Europe: France
Christianity

The abandoned abbey at Cluny, which had been shut down by French Revolutionaries, has stood vacant for over a decade, and locals begin to quarry it for stone.

March 1, 1811

Southwest Asia and North Africa: Egypt
Islam

Muhammad Ali Pasha, the new governor of Egypt, kills the leaders of the Mamluks, who had previously ruled Egypt, his major rivals for control of the country. Ali invites the Mamluk leaders to a celebration to honor his son, Tusun, who has been appointed head of the forces commissioned to recover the holy cities of Mecca and Medina from the Saudi forces in Arabia. When the Mamluks arrive, they are killed.

May 15, 1811

South America: Paraguay
Unbelief

Paraguay overthrows the local Spanish administration and names José Gaspar Rodríguez de Francia as ruler for life with dictatorial powers. He is a disciple of Jean Jacques Rousseau's *Social Contract* and attempts to build a utopian society utilizing its insights.

Without suppressing it, he curtailed the powers of the Roman Catholic Church. He forbids Europeans from marrying other Europeans. They may only marry native Paraguayans, Africans, or mulattoes. His policies build hostilities, as they curtail many assumed personal freedoms among European residents, but he is able to suppress opposition and to maintain his rule. His policies isolate Paraguay from events in the rest of South America for a generation.

May 18, 1811

South America: Uruguay
Christianity

The Battle of Las Piedras. Forces led by José Gervasio Artigas defeat the Spanish and successfully set up an independent Uruguay (known as Banda Oriental), which is in league with Argentina as part of the continuing Viceroyalty of the Río de la Plata.

July 18, 1811

Russia, Central Asia, and the Caucasus: Georgia
Christianity

Russian authorities abolish the autocephalous status of the Georgian Orthodox Church, which is placed under the direct authority of the Russian Orthodox Church. Through most of the 19th century, the church would be headed by a Russian metropolitan bishop.

July 31, 1811

South America: Mexico
Christianity

Roman Catholic priest Miguel Hidalgo y Costilla is executed by a firing squad in Chihuahua. Leadership of the independence movement passes to another priest, José María Morelos, who is able to occupy several key cities in southern Mexico.

November 5, 1811

South America: El Salvador
Christianity

A Roman Catholic priest working in what is now El Salvador, José Matías Delgado, launches the first effort of the citizens to break free of Spanish control. He calls the people together by ringing the bells at his church, the Iglesia La Merced in San Salvador, and calls for insurrection. His effort gives birth to the 1811 Independence Movement, which is quickly suppressed and its leaders arrested.

1812

North America: United States
Christianity

Presbyterians found Princeton Theological Seminary and name theologian Archibald Alexander as the first instructor. The initial class has three students.

1812

South Asia: Sri Lanka
Christianity
James Chater moves to Sri Lanka from Burma to initiate Baptist missionary work on the island.

1812

Europe: Greece
Christianity
Construction begins on the new katholikon (major sanctuary for worship) at St. Panteleimon's Monastery, the primary monastic center on Mount Athos for Russian monks. It will take a decade to complete.

May 11, 1812

Europe: United Kingdom
Christianity
British prime minister Spencer Perceval is assassinated, the only British prime minister to so die. He is succeeded in office by Robert Banks Jenkinson, second earl of Liverpool (r. 1812–1827). He comes to office having voiced his opinion that the restrictions on Roman Catholics in England and Ireland should remain in place. The attempts to have those restrictions removed will remain an important issue throughout his term in office.

June 17, 1812

South Asia: India
Christianity
Adoniram Judson and his wife arrive in Calcutta as missionaries of the Congregational church, sent out by the American Board of Commissioners for Foreign Missions. On their trip, Adoniram had been presented with the claims of the Baptists relative to believer's baptism, which he has accepted.

August 12, 1812

Europe: Spain
Christianity
British commander the duke of Wellington occupies Madrid, Spain, which forces out Joseph Bonaparte and his small occupying French force.

August 17, 1812

Europe: Russia
Christianity
The Battle of Smolensk. Napoleon Bonaparte's army defeats the Russians during the Russian retreat to Moscow.

September 6, 1812

South Asia: India
Christianity
Adoniram Judson and his wife, having accepted the Baptist position on believer's baptism, formally convert to the Baptist church and are baptized by William Ward, an English Baptist and missionary associate of William Carey.

September 18, 1812

Russia, Central Asia, and the Caucasus: Russia
Christianity
As Napoleon's troops enter Moscow, a fire destroys the overwhelming majority of the buildings, which had been constructed close together of wood. An estimated 80 percent of the city burns, including almost all of its churches.

1813

North America: United States
Christianity
African Methodists in Wilmington, Delaware, separate from the Methodist Episcopal Church and form the African Union Church, the first independent African American denomination, which continues to the present as the African Union First Methodist Protestant Church and the Union American Methodist Episcopal Church (UAMEC).

1813

North America: United States
Christianity
Conflict within Presbyterianism over revivalism in the western states led those supportive of the revivals to form the Cumberland Synod (later the Cumberland Presbyterians Church).

1813

North America: United States
Judaism
President Madison appoints Mordechai Noah as consul to Tunis and then rescinds the appointment when the Tunisians object to dealing with a Jew.

1813

South America: Argentina, Uruguay
Christianity
Representatives of the Viceroyalty of the Rio de la Plata convene in Buenos Aires to plan their future, now free of Spanish control. Uruguayan José Gervasio Artigas advocates a federal system with loose central control of member states. He especially argues for an autonomous Banda Oriental (Uruguay). The majority ultimately vote for a more centralized state based in Argentina.

1813

South America: Colombia, Venezuela
Christianity
Simon Bolivar is given his initial command of an army under the direction of the Congress of United Provinces of New Granada, which was attempting to establish itself independently of Spain. Bolivar initiates what has been termed the Admirable Campaign. He successively conquers Mérida, Trujillo, and Caracas (Venezuela). Bolívar is declared "El Libertador."

1813

South Asia: India
Sikhism
Sikh maharajah Ranjit Singh obtains the famous "Ko-he-noor" diamond, then the largest diamond in the world, from the deposed ruler of Afghanistan seeking help to restore his throne. In a great military parade, Ranjit Singh marches it through the streets of Amritsar.

1813

East and Southeast Asia: China, Indonesia
Christianity
Dutch Reformed missionary Joseph Kam arrives in Java under the auspices of the London Missionary Society and begins two decades of pioneering work on the Moluccas. At about the same time William Milne joins Robert Morrison in Guangzhou but stays only a short time before relocating to Malacca, Malaysia (1815), where he manages a publishing concern and works among the Chinese-speaking people in what was then the Straits Settlement.

1813

East and Southeast Asia: China, Japan
Buddhism
Takuju Kosen, one of the two most important Rinzai Zen teachers at the beginning of the 19th century, becomes abbot at Myoshin-ji and receives the purple robe, symbolic of his accomplishments. He is recognized for having completed, along with his contemporary Inzan Ien, the process of systematization of the use of koans by Rinzai practitioners. Almost all Rinzai schools today are in the lineage of either Takuju Kosen or Inzan Ien.

1813

Europe: England
Christianity
Parliament defeats a new Roman Catholic Relief bill, which has the effect of pushing the issue of Catholic emancipation in England and Ireland aside for the rest of the decade.

1813

Europe: United Kingdom
Christianity
Particular (Calvinist) Baptists in England found the Baptist Union.

1813

Europe: United Kingdom
Christianity, Judaism
The London Society for Promoting Christianity Amongst the Jews founds a Christian congregation called Benei Abraham (Children of Abraham), the first modern assembly of Jewish believers in Jesus, now seen as the forerunner of the 20th-century Messianic Jewish movement.

1813

Russia, Central Asia, and the Caucasus: Russia
Islam

The Treaty of Gulistan. As a result of losing the Russo-Persian War (1804–1813), Persia transfers control of Georgia and Chechnya to Russia. Chechnya is a Shafi'ite Sunni Muslim land with a significant number of Sufis, most of whom follow either the Qadiri or Naqshbandi order.

January 25, 1813

Europe: France
Christianity

The exile of Pope Pius VII ends with his signing of the Concordat of Fontainebleau. He and the various cardinals who had also been exiled return to Rome. The pope has been forced to make a number of concessions to Napoleon on a range of issues, but these are not put into effect as Napoleon abdicates on April 11, 1814.

February 18, 1813

Europe: Poland
Christianity

In the wake of Napoleon's retreat from Moscow, Czar Alexander leads the Russian army into Warsaw and reasserts control over Poland.

June 1, 1813

North America: United States
Christianity

Peter Spencer, a member of the Ezion Methodist Episcopal Church in Wilmington, Delaware, an African American congregation, withdraws from the white-controlled Methodist Episcopal Church and founds the African Union Church, the first African American Christian denomination. It will later be known as the African Union Methodist Protestant Church.

July 13, 1813

South Asia: India, Burma
Christianity

Authorities with the British East India Company order Adoniram Judson and his wife out of India, and they move to Burma (Myanmar). They initially settle in Yangon, Burma. to begin what will become the Myanmar Baptist Convention. He begins work on a Burmese grammar and a translation of the Bible.

October 16–19, 1813

Europe: Germany
Christianity

The Battle at Leipzig (aka the Battle of the Nations). Napoleon faces off against the combined forces of Prussia, Austria, and Russia and suffers one of his worst defeats, a sign of things to come in the next year.

November 6, 1813

Central America and the Caribbean: Mexico
Christianity

The insurgents attempting to throw off Spanish rule convene the Congress of Chilpancingo where they sign the Solemn Act of the Declaration of Independence of Northern America.

December 11, 1813

Europe: Spain, France
Christianity

French emperor Napoleon signs the Treaty of Valençay in which he acknowledges Ferdinand VII (r. 1813–1833) as the rightful king of Spain and allows him to return to his homeland from years of confinement in France.

December 13, 1813

Europe: Spain
Christianity

King Joseph (Bonaparte) of Spain has been an unpopular foreign king of Spain. The French defeat by the British at the Battle of Vitoria provided the occasion of his abdicating the throne and returning to France.

1814

Sub-Saharan Africa: South Africa
Christianity

In the multiple agreements reached between the allies following their defeat of Napoleon, the Cape Colony is removed from Dutch hegemony and assigned to the United Kingdom.

1814

North America: United States
Christianity
The Rappite community in Pennsylvania purchases 30,000 acres of land in Indiana and founds New Harmony.

1814

Central America and the Caribbean: Nicaragua
Christianity
Construction of the Cathedral of León (aka the Real and Renowned Basilica Cathedral of the Assumption of the Blessed Virgin Mary) is completed. Begun in 1747, it is the largest cathedral in Central America. It is formally consecrated by Pope Pius IX in 1860.

1814

Oceania and Antarctica: New Zealand
Traditional Religions, Christianity
Two tradesmen-missionaries, Thomas Kendall (1778–1832) and William Hall, arrive in New Zealand, distribute religious literature to Maori people, and hold shipboard services. Their arrival marks the beginning of the erosion of traditional Maori religion. Maori religion revolves around the idea that the world of physical existence and the world of supernatural beings are two separate but interrelated spheres. Maori ritual is designed to produce benefits from gods (*atua*) and spirits (*wairua*). Ancestors (*tipuna*) and ghosts (*kehu*) also loom large in Maori religion. It is claimed that the first Christian service was held in New Zealand on Christmas Day, 1814, by Samuel Marsden (1764–1838). Marsden was an Anglican chaplain from Australia and a representative of the Church Missionary Society. His sermon, delivered in English, was translated into Maori.

January 14, 1814

Europe: Norway
Christianity
The Treaty of Kiel. Denmark, which had aligned with Napoleon, is forced to cede Norway to Sweden. Denmark retains control of Iceland, Greenland, and the Faroe Islands. Norway declares independence, adopts a constitution, but declares a personal union between Sweden and Norway under Charles XIII of Sweden; another group selects the crown prince Christian Frederick

A 19th-century wood carving of an ancestor of the Maori Tuwharetoa people depicted on the *tekoteko* (gable finial) of a chief's storehouse. (Werner Forman/Corbis)

as its king (May 17). The constitution recognizes the Lutheran Church of Norway as the established church and the king as its leading representative.

April 11, 1814

Europe: France
Christianity
Napoleon abdicates. When Paris fell in March, Napoleon had initially proposed marching on its occupiers, but his generals refused. This action leaves him with

MAORI RELIGION (NEW ZEALAND)

Maori stories of creation often begin with the embrace of the Sky-father, Ranginui (Rangi), and the Earth-mother, Papa-tuanuku (Papa). The offspring of their union and other early descendants include a number of figures common to many regions. Early sources usually refer to these as ancestors (*tupuna*) rather than gods (*atua*).

The more recent ancestral dead, especially dead chiefs, are frequently referred to as gods in early sources. These more recent ancestors were thought to continue their interest in tribal affairs even after death. Offerings, often of food, were made to *atua*. In the case of the more recently dead, the food was offered by suspending it near the sacred place where the body was kept. In the case of earlier ancestral figures, these offerings might be made to carved figures, stones, or other objects representing them. Every community had at least one shrine (*tuahu*) that was the main site where offerings were made to *atua* and where the priests (*tohunga*) performed rituals.

The Maori had a cyclic view of life and death. Spirits of the dead were said to go either to Te Po (the underworld) or to Hawaiki (a paradisiacal homeland). Hawaiki was not only the realm of the ancestors but also a source of life and fertility.

A near male relative of the chief often took the role of chief priest. A special role was also accorded one or more high-ranking women. These women performed protective rites at sacred activities such as warfare, house-building, and childbirth.

The distinction between tapu or taboo (sacred) and *noa* (ordinary) was particularly important in Maori religion and ritual. These concepts also reflected and shaped Maori social structure and the division of labor. The lives of *rangatira* (chiefs and their near relatives), who had the closest connection to the tribal gods, were the most ritualized. *Tutua* (ordinary people) pursued their own rituals and observed tapu restrictions to a lesser extent.

ADELE FLETCHER

little choice and he is forced to leave office. Napoleon formally renounces for himself and his heirs the rights to the thrones of both France and Italy. He is subsequently exiled to the island of Elba in the Mediterranean off the coast of Italy.

Louis XVIII (r. 1814–1824), the brother of former king Louis XVI, is called from exile to become the new ruler of France. He had become the heir to the Bourbon dynasty following the death of Louis XVI's son in 1795.

May 4, 1814

Europe: France
Christianity

With Napoleon's abdication, the monarchy reemerges, and Bourbon reign is restored to France. Royalists crown Louis XVIII as the successor to his guillotined brother. The possibility of turning back many of the changes wrought by the revolution appears on the horizon.

May 8, 1814

South Asia: India
Christianity
Thomas F. Middleton is consecrated as the first bishop of Calcutta and assumes leadership of the Church of England's work throughout the territory controlled

by the East India Company. Among his major accomplishments is the founding of Bishop's College in Calcutta.

May 16–17, 1814

Europe: Norway
Christianity

Norway signs and promulgates a new constitution. It is the second oldest national constitution in the world still in force as law, only the United States' Constitution being older. In absorbing ideas from both France and the United States, it is viewed as a radically liberal document by politicians in surrounding countries. Relative to religion, it acknowledges the Evangelical-Lutheran Church as the official religion of the state and demands that parents raise their children in the faith. It forbids monastic orders, especially Jesuits, who are mentioned by name. It also forbids the entry of Jews into the country.

May 18, 1814

North America: United States
Christianity

American Baptists meet in Philadelphia and organize the General Missionary Convention of the Baptist Denomination in the United States of America. Previously, British missionary William Carey and future American missionaries Adoniram Judson Jr. and his wife Ann Hasseltine Judson had convinced the majority of American Baptists to form a national organization to support the Judsons' planned mission trip to Burma. The convention, which would continue to meet every three years, became popularly known as the Triennial Convention. It would evolve to become the Northern Baptist Convention (1907) and later the American Baptist Churches in the United States.

May 20, 1814

Europe: Italy
Christianity

The first public showing of the Shroud of Turin since 1775 is occasioned by the return of the monarchy in the person of King Victor Emanuel. The shroud is removed from its resting place inside the Guarini Chapel.

May 30, 1814

Sub-Saharan Africa: South Africa
Christianity

The First Treaty of Paris, negotiated after Napoleon's abdication, grants the United Kingdom hegemony over the Cape of Good Hope. Later in the year (August 13), the British sign the Treaty of London-Netherlands in which they agree to pay the Dutch £6 million for the Cape of Good Hope.

May 30, 1814

Europe: Malta
Christianity

Under provisions of the Treaty of Paris, Malta, which had been a British Protectorate since 1800, is officially incorporated into the British Empire. Malta is a predominantly Roman Catholic country. British rule provides an opening for the emergence of Anglicanism on the island.

July 1, 1814

Europe: Spain
Christianity

Ferdinand VII, who had been pushed aside as the king of Spain by Napoleon, recovers his throne. Among his early actions, he reestablishes the Spanish Inquisition, which Napoleon had closed. The Inquisition will again be temporarily closed during the time of the liberal government that comes to power in 1820, but is reestablished when Ferdinand again reasserts his power in 1823.

July 19, 1814

Europe: Italy
Christianity

Pope Pius VII transforms the former Congregation *Super Negotiis Ecclesiasticis Regni Galliarum,* established by Pius VI to handle the special circumstances created by the French revolution, into the Congregation for the Extraordinary Ecclesiastical Affairs, which is assigned duties in dealing with the Vatican's relations with governments outside of Italy.

August 7, 1814

Europe: Italy
Christianity

Upon his return from exile in France, Pope Pius VII reinstates the Jesuits.

August 24–25, 1814

North America: United States
Christianity
British capture and burn Washington, D.C., and begin an attack on Baltimore. The free black community of Philadelphia, headed by James Forten (Epicopalian) and Richard Allen (Methodist), leads in the organization of the African Americans to build defenses for the city.

October 10, 1814

Europe: Norway, Sweden
Christianity
Sweden, which has invaded and conquered Norway, allows Norway to keep its recently adopted constitution. Following the negotiations, King Christian Frederick delegates his powers to the parliament and abdicates. The parliament elects the Swedish king Charles XIII king of Norway. This action perpetuated the concept that Charles was king of Norway by the will of the people rather than by divine right.

November 1, 1814–June 8, 1815

Europe: Austria
Christianity
The nations of Europe, most notably England, France, Prussia, Russia, and Austria, met as the Congress of Europe to settle numerous boundary disputes that arose with the fall of Napoleon's empire and the final dissolution of the Holy Roman Empire (1806), which has held the German states together. Among its major actions would be the creation of a German Confederation, a precursor to the modern states of Germany, and the partition of Poland, most of which was given to Russia.

The Congress of Vienna approves the restoration of the Papal States, annexed to France in 1808, and Pope Pius VII returns to his throne. He also uses this occasion to restore the Society of Jesus (the Jesuits), which had been suppressed in 1757–1759 in many of the Catholic countries of Europe, most notably Spain and Portugal.

The new German Confederation bound some 39 German states, the most powerful being Prussia, in a very loose association, primarily economic in na-

ture. It was seen as the successor to the former Holy Roman Empire

The congress reestablishes the Kingdom of Piedmont-Sardinia and returns the deposed Charles Emmanuel IV to the throne. It gives the former Republic of Genoa to Piedmont and thus initiates the kingdom's rise to prominence on the Italian Peninsula.

ca. 1815

North America: United States
Christianity
Mary T. Ogle, an adherent of the Stone-Campbell movement, founds a church in Pennsylvania that is one of the earliest to use the name Disciples of Christ. Women emerge quite early in the movement as missionaries and evangelists and assume functions generally reserved for ordained ministers, such as baptizing new converts.

1815

Sub-Saharan Africa: South Africa
Traditional Religions
Shaka becomes the king of the Zulus.

1815

North America: United States
Christianity
Two white Baptists, William and James Crane, found the Richmond African Missionary Society in Virginia. The society will later fund African American missionaries Lott Cary and Colin Teague.

1815

North America: United States
Christianity
Monk missionaries of the Orthodox Church build the first Russian Orthodox church in what is now the United States in Sitka, Alaska.

1815

Central America and the Caribbean: Guatemala
Christianity
Construction is completed on the Cathedral of Guatemala City (aka the Metropolitan Cathedral of Saint

James), which serves as the diocesan church of the archbishop of Guatemala. Work on the church began in 1782, and its towers were not completed until 1867.

1815

Central America and the Caribbean: Netherlands
   Antilles
Christianity
The Kingdom of the Netherlands creates a new colonial establishment in the Caribbean, which it names Curaçao and Dependencies.

1815

Central America and the Caribbean: Puerto Rico
Christianity
In an attempt to bolster the economy and undercut independence efforts, Spain publishes the Royal Decree of Graces of 1815, which allows non-Spanish Europeans the privilege of moving to Puerto Rico and grants a variety of inducements. A variety of immigrants arrive from both Roman Catholic and non-Catholic countries. Free land is offered, but only on the condition that the immigrant swears loyalty to the Spanish Crown and allegiance to the Roman Catholic Church.

1815

Central America and the Caribbean: St. Pierre and
   Miquelon
Christianity
Following Napoleon's final surrender, the islands of St. Pierre and Miquelon in the Atlantic off the Canadian coast are returned to French control, and the Catholic church on the islands revives under the guidance of several French religious orders.

1815

South America: Brazil
Christianity
Portuguese king Dom João VI (now serving as regent for his mother) elevates Brazil from the status of a mere colony to a sovereign kingdom united with Portugal.

1815

South America: Colombia
Christianity

Spain reenters the territory acquired by the independent United Provinces of New Granada and begins a reconquest of its lost territory. After early successes in 1813 and 1814, including the capturing of Caracas and Bogota, Simon Bolivar is forced to leave South America. He goes to Jamaica and Haiti seeking support for his return.

1815

South America: Uruguay
Christianity
Led by Uruguayan José Gervasio Artigas, Montevideo breaks with Buenos Aires, and Banda Oriental (Uruguay) establishes an autonomous government. Four of the six original provinces will later become part of Argentina.

1815

South Asia: Sri Lanka
Buddhism
The British again invade the Kingdom of Kandy and this time succeed in conquering all of Sri Lanka and incorporating it into the crown colony of Ceylon. In the document by which they assume control, the British promise to safeguard Buddhism and declare its rites and ceremonies sacred and inviolate. Over the next years, the British governor participates in the annual ceremonies conducted around the Sacred Tooth relic of the Buddha.

1815

Europe: Germany
Christianity
In Prussia, all of the religious communities (both Christian and Jewish) are placed under a single consistory in each Prussian province. Protestant believers are divided into Lutheran, Mennonite, Moravian, and Reformed (Calvinist) congregations.

1815

Europe: Portugal
Christianity
With the capital of Portugal now located in Rio de Janeiro, Brazil, King John VI changes the name of the Portuguese Empire to the United Kingdom of

Portugal, Brazil, and the Algarves. Though Napoleon is no longer a threat, the king decides to remain in Brazil rather than return to Portugal.

1815

Europe: Switzerland
Christianity
The Congress of Vienna reestablishes Swiss independence, and the European powers agree to recognize Swiss neutrality. Switzerland admits the cantons of Valais, Neuchâtel, and Geneva, thus establishing its national borders to the present. Switzerland has no official state religion, though all of the cantons except Geneva and Neuchâtel recognize official churches. Switzerland has a multiple set of cantons in which either French or German is the primary language, and one in which Italian is spoken. The Reformed Church is dominant in one set of cantons and second in the remaining cantons in which the Roman Catholic Church is dominant. Both churches, along with the Old Catholic Church and the Jewish congregations, receive a substantial portion of their financial resources from tax money.

1815

Russia, Central Asia, and the Caucasus: Azerbaijan
Islam
Following the two Russo-Persian Wars, Russia gains hegemony over the several Shi'a Muslim khanates that existed in what is now the country of Azerbaijan. The first Russian Orthodox church opens in Baku, the capital.

1815

Southwest Asia and North Africa: Arabia
Islam
Britain allies with Egypt and the sheikhdom of Muscat and Oman against the Saudi forces (Wahhabi Muslims) to suppress the pirate sheikhs in Arabia that were being protected by the Saudis.

February 26, 1815

Europe: France
Christianity
Napoleon escapes from his exile on the island of Elba and begins his attempt to regain the French throne.

March 1, 1815

Europe: Netherlands
Christianity
The Netherlands passes a new law that regulates Sunday observance.

March 6, 1815

East and Southeast Asia: China, Tibet
Buddhism
The Dalai Lama, only nine years old, dies from a cold he caught at the annual Monlam Prayer Festival. During the next years while waiting for the next Dalai Lama to appear and then come of age, Palden Tenpai Nyima, who serves as the seventh Panchen Lama, emerges as the most powerful figure in Tibet.

March 16, 1815

Europe: Netherlands
Christianity
With the defeat of Napoleon, William I of the Netherlands returns home and is named King of the Netherlands. He will later assume authority over Luxembourg and what today is known as Belgium.

April 1815

East and Southeast Asia: China: Indonesia
Islam
The eruption of Mount Tambora in Indonesia throws an estimated 400 million tons of sulfuric gases into the atmosphere and leads to global climatic distortions including the year without a summer in the United States and Europe.

June 9, 1815

Europe: Austria
Christianity
Representatives of the major powers of Europe meeting at what has been termed the Congress of Vienna conclude nine months of deliberations by signing the Final Act, an agreement that embodies a number of separate treaties anticipating the final defeat of Napoleon and which redraws the map of Europe. Russia, Austria, Prussia, and England emerge as clear winners. A new United Netherlands is created. A German

Confederation emerges from the old Holy Roman Empire. The Papal States were given their pre-Napoleon borders, and the pope was restored as the ruler. A post-Napoleonic France survives and its boundaries are confirmed.

June 18, 1815

Europe: France
Christianity

The Battle of Waterloo. British forces under Wellington, assisted by a Prussian force, defeat Napoleon's French army. Following the defeat, Napoleon surrenders himself and accepts exile to the island of St. Helena.

June 29, 1815

Europe: Italy
Christianity

With the proliferation of Protestant Bible societies and the circulation of Protestant translations of the Bible in many of the various European languages, and countries in which Roman Catholicism has long had control, Pope Pius VII reacts to the new competition and condemns the work of the societies.

August 15, 1815

Europe: Italy
Christianity

Pope Pius VII returns from exile to find a declining spiritual environment in Rome. In response, he invites Gaspar del Bufalo to found the Missionaries of the Precious Blood with a mandate to establish missions throughout the Papal States. The new religious order is composed of secular priests and lay brothers who live in community without vows but share a dedication to evangelize in those places deemed most needy. The work would later spread from the Papal States across Europe and to the United States. The founder would also later be canonized and the order has subsequently become a worldwide organization.

September 16, 1815

Europe: Switzerland
Christianity

Pietist Lutherans and Reformed Church leaders found the Basel Missionary Society, which will emerge as one of the main Protestant sending agencies through the next century.

November 12, 1815

Oceania and Antarctica: French Polynesia
Christianity

Pōmare II wins a decisive battle against the most powerful rival clan and becomes the monarch of Tahiti. As the missionaries had encouraged his rise to power, he privileged Protestantism and it quickly spread throughout the island. The next year, John Williams, a missionary sponsored by the London Missionary Society, arrives and begins work on a Tahitian translation of the Gospels. As the Native population accepts Christianity, the practice of human sacrifice is abandoned, the last reported incident being in 1816.

December 22, 1815

Central America and the Caribbean: Mexico
Christianity

The Roman Catholic priest José María Morelos, who has been leading the effort to throw off Spanish rule in Mexico, is captured and executed. In the following years, the insurgency almost completely collapses.

1816

North America: United States
Christianity

A number of prominent Americans including Henry Clay, John Randolph, Richard Bland Lee, and Presbyterian minister Robert Finley found the American Colonization Society (aka the Society for the Colonization of Free People of Color of America) to return free blacks to Africa. It will recruit African American ministers and laypeople as colonists, and they will in turn found some of the first congregations in Sierra Leone and Liberia. Black leaders such as Richard Allen in Philadelphia will emerge as major critics of the colonization program. The program of the society had been partially inspired by the work of Paul Cuffee, an African American Quaker and ship owner, who had taken 38 American blacks to Freetown, Sierra Leone.

The Christian evangelization of Africa is a lesser, but no less real theme in the deliberations of the society and accounts for much of its support.

1816

North America: United States
Christianity
American Protestant leaders form the American Bible Society to publish and distribute the Christian scriptures. It selects Elias Boudinot, former president of the Continental Congress, as its first president.

1816

North America: United States
Christianity
The archbishop of Canterbury launches an Anglican mission in the Hawaiian Islands.

1816

North America: United States
Christianity
Richard Allen leads in the formation of the African Methodist Episcopal Church (AME) centered on the Bethel congregation in Philadelphia. He is selected as the church's first bishop.

1816

South America: Colombia, Venezuela
Christianity
Spain scores some success in its reconquest of Colombia and destroys the independent United Provinces of New Granada. However, having been able to recruit an army primarily of Haitian soldiers and having promised to abolish slavery if successful, Simon Bolívar lands in Venezuela and initiates a war of liberation of Venezuela and Colombia from Spanish control.

March 6, 1816

Europe: Germany
Judaism
The Free City of Lübeck expels all of its Jewish residents.

March 8, 1816

Europe: Macedonia
Christianity
Matthaes Crasnich is named archbishop of Skopje, and subsequently becomes the first Roman Catholic bishop to take up residence in Macedonia since the beginning of the Ottoman Muslim occupation of the country some 500 years earlier.

April 9, 1816

North America: United States
Christianity
Richard Allen, who has led the Bethel church, the African Methodist Episcopal congregation in Philadelphia, for the last quarter of a century, leaves the white-controlled Methodist Episcopal Church and founds a new denomination, the African Methodist Episcopal Church. At the founding meeting, he is joined by Daniel Coker, Jacob Tapsico, and James Champion, who select him as their bishop. Episcopal priest and former Methodist Absalom Jones joins them to participate in the consecration of Allen to the bishop's office.

June 3, 1816

Southwest Asia and North Africa: Syria
Christianity
Pope Pius VII condemns the writings of the late Bishop Germanos Adam of the Melkite Catholic Church, an Eastern rite church in communion with Rome. He had advocated conciliarism, championing the authority of ecumenical councils over that of the papacy.

July 9, 1816

South America: Argentina
Christianity
The Congress of Tucumán. The defeat of Napoleon in Europe led to consideration of the reestablishment of Spanish rule in Argentina and the nearby territories that together constituted the Viceroyalty of the Río de la Plata, which had been locally ruled for the last five years. A congress to deal with the range of issues gathers at San Miguel de Tucumán on March 24, 1816. The first major action would be on July 9, the declaration of independence of the United Provinces of South America (modern Argentina), a name chosen in hopes of incorporating the entire region in the new country.

The declaration moved Argentina into the events that would over the next decade remake the southern half of South America. General José de San Martin emerges with a plan to defeat the Spanish forces centered on the Viceroyalty of Peru that desired to turn back the clock and reestablish the Spanish rule of the pre-Napoleonic era.

Argentina assumed that the Malvina Islands (aka the Falkland Islands) are included in the territory assigned to it by the Congress of Tucumán. That is not an assumption shared by others.

July 23, 1816

Europe: France
Christianity
French priest William Joseph Chaminade founds the Society of Mary (aka the Marianists), a new Roman Catholic religious order whose members have taken the Blessed Virgin Mary as their model for the development of their faith and spirituality. Chaminade had survived the anticlericalism that had been so prevalent through the previous two decades and wanted to help revive the church in postrevolutionary France.

November 4, 1816

Europe: Italy
Christianity
An Italian priest, Gaspar Bertoni, founds the Congregation of the Sacred Stigmata (aka Stigmatines), a new Roman Catholic religious order, in Verona, Italy. The first members had an immediate calling to assist the victims of the ongoing war then causing so much destruction in Bertoni's hometown, and later attempted to reform the clergy then known to be deeply infected with contemporary worldliness.

1817

Sub-Saharan Africa: Ghana
Christianity
The British-chartered African Company of Merchants signs a treaty of friendship that recognizes the Asante Empire's claims to sovereignty over large areas of the Gold Coast of western Africa, now known as Ghana.

1817

North America: United States
Christianity

Episcopalians in New York found General Theological Seminary, their first school for the training of ministers.

1817

North America: United States
Western Esotericism
The General Convention of the New Jerusalem in the United States of America is organized at Baltimore, Maryland.

1817

South America: French Guiana
Christianity
Portugal (whose government is based in Brazil) is forced to return control of French Guiana (which it had captured in 1809) to France.

1817

South America: Uruguay
Christianity
Portugal invades the briefly independent Uruguay (since 1811) and incorporates it into Brazil.

1817

Southwest Asia and North Africa: Persia
Islam
A Shi'a Muslim cleric, Mulla Husayn Yazdi, an influential Muslim cleric among the main body of Shi'a Muslims, incites a mob to attack the house of Shāh Khalīlullāh, the head of the Nizari Shi'a Ismaili Muslims, in Kahak, Qom. Shāh Khalīlullāh is killed and later buried in the holy city of Najaf, Iraq, in a family mausoleum. He is succeeded by his eldest son Shāh Hassan 'Alī (r. 1817–1881), 46th imam of the Nizari Ismailis and the first to use the title Aga Khan.

1817

Europe: Belgium
Christianity
Constant Guillaume van Crombrugghe, a Roman Catholic priest, founds the Institute of the Josephites of Belgium, a new Roman Catholic order focused on work among the younger generation, and opens its first mother house at Geraardsbergen, near Ghent.

1817

Oceania and Antarctica: Australia
Judaism

The first Jewish burial society is formed in Australia, marking the new influence of Judaism on the continent. It was common for a cemetery to be the first visible structure of a new Jewish community.

January 1817

Sub-Saharan Africa: Réunion
Christianity

The Sisters of St. Joseph of Cluny, a Roman Catholic religious order founded in France in 1807, begin their global expansion by sending a group of the sisters to the island of Bourbon (now known as Réunion) in the Indian Ocean west of Madagascar. Two years later, a second group initiates work in Saint-Louis, Senegal.

January 1817

Sub-Saharan Africa: South Africa
Christianity

Robert Moffat, a Scottish Congregationalist minister and missionary to Africa, arrives in South Africa along with three colleagues, all under the sponsorship of the Church Missionary Society.

February 1817

South America: Argentina, Chile
Christianity

José de San Martin leads a combined army of Argentineans and Chileans across the Andes Mountains, They score their initial victory at the Battle of Chacabuco on February 12, 1817, which initiates the Chilean War for Independence (1817–1818). When San Martin refuses, Bernardo O'Higgins, a Chilean who has accompanied the army across the Andes, accepts the leadership of the now anticipated independent Chile. He is subsequently granted dictatorial powers as the Supreme Director on February 16, 1817

July 4, 1817

North America: Canada
Christianity

Scottish Congregationalist missionary Robert Moffat (1795–1883), with a depiction of his missionary work in Africa. (Michael Nicholson/Corbis)

Pope Pius VII erects the Vicariate Apostolic of Nova Scotia, the first Roman Catholic jurisdiction designated to serve primarily English-speaking Catholics.

September 1817

East and Southeast Asia: Japan
Buddhism

Tokugawa Ienari, the shogun of Japan, orders the expulsion of Titia Bergsma, the first European woman known to have visited the islands.

October 31, 1817

Europe: Germany
Christianity

A series of decrees by Prussian king Frederick William III unites the Lutheran Church and the Reformed

(Calvinist) Church into the Prussian Union of churches, popularly known as the Evangelical Church. Frederick William uses the 300th anniversary of the Protestant Reformation (the day Martin Luther posted his 95 Theses) as the occasion for the formal merger. Two congregations in Potsdam would showcase the merger and other congregations were encouraged to follow their example. This united Protestant church was for much of the 19th century the largest Protestant body in Europe but was opposed on each side by conservative Lutherans and Reformed believers who found the two churches incompatible theologically.

The theological faculty at the Rhenish Frederick William's University in Bonn adheres to the union. Beginning in 1820, to increase support for the united church, all candidates for ministry are required to state that they would be willing to join the union, and a new ordination vow is created that states the pastor's allegiance to the Evangelical Church.

December 6, 1817

North America: Canada
Christianity

Two ships collide in Halifax, Nova Scotia, one of which is loaded with war munitions. The resulting explosion, the largest human-generated explosion prior to the atomic era, destroys much of the city and causes hundreds of deaths.

1818

Sub-Saharan Africa: Madagascar
Christianity

Missionary work begins in Madagascar with the reluctant approval of the king.

1818

North America: United States
Christianity

In 1818 Mother Philippine-Rose Duchesne arrives in New Orleans from France with four sisters of the Society of the Sacred Heart to begin work in America. She settles in St. Charles, Missouri. She would later open work in Florissant and St. Louis, Missouri, and in St. Michael, Grand Côteau, and New Orleans, Louisiana. She will later be canonized.

1818

Europe: Italy
Christianity

While in Salerno attending a retreat at a center of the Redemptorist order, Gaetano Errico, a priest from Naples, experiences an apparition of St. Alphonsus Liguori who instructs him to found a new religious order and also to build a church in Secondigliano in honor of the Blessed Virgin Mary as Our Lady of Sorrows. The church would be finally completed and consecrated in 1930.

1818

Southwest Asia and North Africa: Asia Minor
Christianity

Gregory V (r. 1818–1821), who had already served twice as ecumenical patriarch (1797–1798, 1806–1808) with two depositions, is called to assume the patriarch's role a third time. He will devote his time to the much-needed restoration of the Patriarchal Cathedral of St. George, which still showed the damage from the fire of 1738.

1818

Southwest Asia and North Africa: Egypt
Christianity

The Church Missionary Society (of the Church of England) initiates work in Egypt.

1818

Oceania and Antarctica: French Polynesia
Christianity

Rev. William Pascoe Crook, a missionary of the London Missionary Society, founds the city of Papeete, which will later become the capital of Tahiti.

February 12, 1818

South America: Chile
Christianity

After a year of struggle, Chile proclaims itself an independent republic.

February 23, 1818

Central America and the Caribbean:
   Trinidad and Tobago
Christianity

Pope Pius VII erects the Vicariate Apostolic of Trinidad, which will become the Prefecture Apostolic of the West Indies in 1850 and is eventually elevated as the Archdiocese of Port of Spain in 1956.

April 5, 1818

South America: Chile
Christianity

The Battle of Maipú. Chilean forces led by General José de San Martin defeat and largely destroy the Spanish army sent against it. A decisive battle, it largely ensures the establishment of the modern state of Chile. After the battle, San Martin turned his attention to Peru, the center of royalist support.

June 2, 1818

South Asia: India
Christianity, Hinduism

The British army's defeat of the Maratha alliance at Bombay signals the rising control of the subcontinent by Britain. The United Kingdom, through the British East India Company, has been gradually taking control first of the economy and then of the political administration of India.

October 20, 1818

North America: Canada, United States
Christianity

The United States and the United Kingdom established the 49th Parallel as the boundary between Canada and the United States, west of the Great Lakes.

December 25, 1818

Europe: Austria
Christianity

Franz Gruber's "Silent Night," destined to become one of the most beloved of Christmas carols, is initially heard by the public at the Church of St. Nikolaus in Oberndorff, Austria.

1819

North America: United States
Unbelief

William Ellery Channing, the pastor of the Federal Street Congregational Church in Boston, preaches the ordination sermon for Jared Sparks, who will subsequently become the pastor of First Independent Church (Unitarian) in Baltimore. In his address, entitled "Unitarian Christianity," Channing outlines the distinctive opinions held by the Unitarian movement, at the time a dissenting group within the larger Congregationalist church. He rejects the Trinity, but also speaks about his faith in human goodness and the subjection of theological affirmations to the critique of reason. Following the sermon, he will be recognized as the leading spokesperson for Unitarianism in the United States.

1819

North America: United States
Judaism

Rebecca Gratz establishes the first independent Jewish women's charitable society in Philadelphia.

1819

South America: Colombia
Christianity

Colombia becomes independent from Spain under the name New Granada.

1819

Southwest Asia and North Africa: Egypt
Traditional Religions

Egypt presents the United Kingdom with the obelisk of Alexandria, originally set up in Heliopolis in 1461 BCE. It had been moved to Alexandria in 14 BCE, but had been toppled in an earthquake around 1300.

1819

Southwest Asia and North Africa: Ottoman Empire
Christianity

Ecumenical Patriarch Gregory V, writing in opposition to the monks on Mount Athos, who were in the midst of a revival movement (the Kollyvades movement) that advocated the frequent and regular partaking of Holy Communion (the Eucharist), tells the monks that the Eucharist should not be received at set times, but reserved for those times when the individual feels ready to receive it, and only after confession and other necessary preparations. Council at Constantinople responds to the patriarch by endorsing the position of the Kollyvades fathers that Holy Communion should be partaken of regularly and frequently by both clergy and laity.

1819

Oceania and Antarctica: French Polynesia
Christianity

Pōmare II, encouraged by the Protestant missionaries on Tahiti, introduces the first Tahitian legal code. Greatly influenced by the missionaries, it bans nudity, dancing and chanting, and costumes made largely of flowers. In the future, the women will be encouraged to wear a dress that covers their entire body.

1819–1840

Oceania and Antarctica: New Zealand
Christianity

Missionary activity increases in New Zealand. The first Anglican priest arrives in 1819, along with the first Wesleyan missionary. The first Roman Catholic, Baptiste Pompallier, comes in 1838, and the first Presbyterian, John McFarlane, preaches at Petone in 1840.

January 12, 1819

North America: Canada
Christianity

Pope Pius VII elevates the Diocese of Quebec to become the Archdiocese of Quebec, the first archdiocese in Canada.

February 22, 1819

North America: United States
Christianity

The Adams-Onis Treaty. Spain cedes East Florida to the United States and renounces any claim to West Florida. It also cedes land in Louisiana east of the Sabine River, which establishes part of the boundary with Texas. The United States recognizes Spain's hegemony over Texas and sets the boundary between it and Texas. Spain subsequently opens Texas to immigrants from the United States, but stipulates that Catholicism is the state religion and that all immigrants must embrace it, and other religions (including varieties of Christianity) are prohibited. Included in the stipulations is an understanding that only marriages performed by a priest would be recognized by the state.

May 16, 1819

Oceania and Antarctica: Polynesia
Traditional Religions, Christianity

Pomare II, the second king of Tahiti who ruled between 1782 and 1821, converts to Christianity. Pomare believed that he had lost favor with the local god, 'Oro, and with the help of Henry Nott, a British Protestant missionary with the London Missionary Society, he begins to turn toward Christianity. Three other representatives of the London Missionary Society preach at Pomare's baptism, Henry Bicknell, William Henry, and Charles Wilson. Pomare would soon oversee the construction of the island's first church, and at his urging, most of his people convert to Christianity.

1820

North America: United States
Christianity

Spain opens Texas to immigrants from the United States, but stipulates that Catholicism is the state religion and that all immigrants must embrace it, and other religions (including varieties of Christianity) are prohibited. Included in the stipulations is an understanding that only marriages performed by a priest would be recognized by the state.

1820

North America: United States
Christianity

The first general, national Lutheran body, the General Synod, is organized in Hagerstown, Maryland.

1820

North America: United States
Christianity

Joseph Smith claims to have received a visit from God the Father and Jesus Christ who tells him all churches are wrong.

Joseph Smith (1805–1844) founded the Church of Jesus Christ of Latter-day Saints (the Mormon Church), an indigenous church in the United States that today is one of the fastest-growing denominations, with a world membership of seven million. (Library of Congress)

1820

East and Southeast Asia: China, Tibet
Buddhism

Five years after the death of the previous Dalai Lama, his successor Tsultrim Gyatso is recognized as the 10th Dalai Lama. He is enthroned at the Potala Palace in 1822.

1820

Europe: France
Christianity

The Sisters of the Immaculate Conception emerge initially as an ordered branch of the more inclusive Institute of the Holy Family, which Abbé Pierre Bonaventure Noailles founds while a student at the Seminary of the Society of Saint-Sulpice, in Paris. The first members settle in Bordeaux as the Ladies of Loreto

and evolve into the Sisters of the Immaculate Conception as they develop a special vocation for educational work. They will expand their work internationally to Spain, England, Ireland, South Africa, and Canada.

1820–1821

Europe: Germany
Christianity

Theologian Friedrich Schleiermacher publishes his monumental theological treatise *The Christian Faith,* in which he attempts to deal with the criticisms of Christianity leveled by the Enlightenment thinkers against the affirmations of traditional Protestant orthodoxy. Continuing his earlier explorations of religious sensibilities, he famously describes religion as the "feeling of absolute dependence."

1820–1850

Oceania and Antarctica: Australia
Judaism

A small Jewish community expands across Australia. A congregation was founded in Sydney in 1828 and an initial synagogue opened in 1844. Meanwhile worshipping communities emerged in Melbourne, Ballarat, Geelong, and Adelaide. By the beginning of the 20th century, Jews had spread across the continent, and many had risen to positions of prominence in business and government.

January 29, 1820

Europe: England
Christianity

British king George III dies. He is succeeded by his son, who reigns as George IV (r. 1820–1830).

February 6, 1820

Sub-Saharan Africa: Sierra Leone
Christianity

The first group of free blacks from the United States sponsored by the American Colonization Society heads for Sierra Leone.

March 5, 1820

Europe: Netherlands
Judaism

JOSEPH SMITH (1805–1844)

Joseph Smith founded the Church of Jesus Christ of Latter-day Saints (the Mormon Church), an indigenous American church which today is one of the fastest-growing denominations, with a world membership of more than 12 million.

Born in Sharon, Vermont on December 23, 1805, Smith moved with his family to Palmyra in western New York in 1816. At the time, this part of the state was known as "the burned-over district" because it had undergone successive waves of religious enthusiasm and was filled with many competing religious sects. Smith was deeply troubled by the existence of so many sects, each claiming to be the true faith. In 1820 and again in 1823, Smith experienced visions in which an angelic figure appeared to him and told him not to join any of the sects because none of them represented God's will. According to Smith, the angel said that the true church had been withdrawn from the world and that it was Smith's mission to bring it back. The angel also instructed him where to find a book written on gold plates that contained the history of this true church.

According to Smith, in 1827, he uncovered the plates from a stone box under a large rock at a hill called Cumorah near Manchester, New York. He then set to work translating them from the language (known as reformed Egyptian) in which they were written with the help of two magic stones called Urim and Thummim. Smith published this work as *The Book of Mormon* in 1830. The book, together with Smith's later revelations contained in the *Doctrine and Covenants* (1835) and *The Pearl of Great Price* (1851), form the scriptures of the Mormon faith.

The Book of Mormon tells how the Hebrews came from Israel to the Americas in ancient times. Although their communities were destroyed by warfare long ago and few survived, their descendants lived on as the American Indians. On April 6, 1830, at Fayette, New York, Smith formally founded the Church of Jesus Christ of Latter-day Saints. Smith convinced his followers that God had chosen him to save a doomed world.

In 1831, Smith moved his community to Kirtland, Ohio and then, after his involvement in a bank fraud made him a fugitive from the law, to Jackson County, Missouri in 1838. Friction between the Mormons and their neighbors forced another move a year later, this time to Illinois to a community that Smith renamed Nauvoo. The Mormons thrived and their numbers grew, increased by many converts from Europe as well as the United States who were drawn by Mormonism's offer of certainty in troubled times. Allowed a free rein by the Illinois government, Smith served as mayor of Nauvoo and exercised virtual one-man rule. Smith's dreams of glory were cut short by his death on June 27, 1844. Most of Smith's followers moved with Brigham Young, who emerged as Smith's successor, to Utah a few years later.

JED WOODWORTH

The Dutch city of Leeuwarden forbids Jews to attend the synagogues on Sundays.

March 30, 1820

North America: United States
Christianity

Congregationalist missionaries sent out by the American Board of Commissioners for Foreign Missions begin work in the Hawaiian Islands.

July 11, 1820

North America: United States
Christianity

Pope Pius VII designates the new dioceses of Richmond and Charleston for the rapidly growing church in the United States.

August 20, 1820

South America: Chile
Christianity

General José de San Martin initiates his campaign against the Spanish in Peru. He sails from Santiago with his Army of the Andes, consisting of Chilean and Argentinean troops.

September 2, 1820

East and Southeast Asia: China
Buddhism

The Jiaqing emperor dies at a summer palace outside Beijing. He is succeeded by his son, the Daoguang emperor (r. 1820–1850).

1821

Sub-Saharan Africa: Liberia
Christianity

Liberia is formed by former slaves from America, among whom are a number of Christian ministers and laypeople.

1821

Sub-Saharan Africa: Sierra Leone
Christianity

African American Lott Carey, a Baptist missionary, sails with 28 colleagues from Norfolk, Virginia, heading to Sierra Leone.

1821

North America: United States
Christianity

African Methodists in New York organize what will become the African Methodist Episcopal Zion Church (AMEZ) and select William Varick as their first bishop.

1821

Central America and the Caribbean: Mexico
Christianity

Mexico wins its independence from Spain and soon afterwards permits Stephen F. Austin to start Texas colonization and bring Americans, many of whom are Protestants, into the land.

1821

South America: Uruguay
Christianity

Brazil, which had taken control of Banda Oriental (Uruguay), formally annexes the territory as a province that it names Cisplatina.

1821

Europe: Germany
Christianity

The united Protestant church being created in Prussia takes the name Evangelical Church in Prussia. Lutheran opposition becomes most visible as reference to the real presence of Christ in the Eucharist liturgy is missing. Equally, as coercion to conform to the union of Lutheran and Reformed theology increases, church leaders voice a concern about the threat to Protestant freedom, with some likening the pressure on them to Roman Catholic pressure in the 16th century.

1821

Europe: Portugal
Christianity

LIBERIA

The African nation of Liberia is located on the continent's Atlantic coast between Sierra Leone and Cote d'Ivoire. The country also shares a northern border with Guinea. It is home to 3.3 million people, overwhelmingly members of the several groups that settled the land prior to the 19th century. About 2.5 percent are descendants of the African Americans who migrated there beginning in the 1820s.

At the end of the 18th century, Liberia was part of Sierra Leone, the area set aside by the British for the relocation of people liberated by their antislavery activity. However, in 1821 the American Colonization Society, an organization devoted to relocating African Americans to Africa, purchased what became Liberia and founded the port city of Monrovia. Some 20,000 African Americans, descendants from various peoples of western Africa, moved to Liberia. Several American scholars coauthored a new constitution for what in 1847 became the independent country of Liberia. The descendants of the repatriated African Americans formed a ruling elite in the country, a development that has affected its politics to the present.

In spite of strong Christian missionary activity, less than half of the Liberian people have become Christian. The largest segment, some 40 percent, retain their traditional religions. Traditional religions have as major themes the veneration of ancestors, the working of magic, and the prominence of religious functionaries, popularly known as medicine men, who establish their authority by the demonstration of a spectrum of mystical competence—healing, divining, prognosticating, and so on.

J. GORDON MELTON

A wave of anticlericalism sweeping through Portugal leads to the abolition of the Inquisition, the banning of religious orders, and the confiscation of much property previously owned by the Roman Catholic Church.

1821

Oceania and Antarctica: Australia
Christianity
Major-General Lachlan Macquarie (r. 1810–1821) the governor of New South Wales, Australia, lays the cornerstone of St. Mary's Church (later to be designated St. Mary's Cathedral), the first Roman Catholic church in Sydney.

1821

Oceania and Antarctica: Cook Island
Christianity

Tahitian converts take the lead in introducing Christianity to the Cook Islands. They accompany John Williams, a missionary sponsored by the London Missionary Society.

1821–1832

Southwest Asia and North Africa: Asia Minor
Christianity
Along with Ecumenical Patriarch Gregory V, Sultan Mahmud II arrests Eugenius II (r. 1821–1822), the archbishop of Anchialos (Bulgaria), when the Greek War of Independence erupts in 1821. After Gregory is executed, he appoints Eugenius to succeed to Gregory's office. Eugenius lasts only a year and is followed by a set of successors who, in part because of the continuing and ultimately successful Greek War of Independence, would have little authority and be able to accomplish little beyond maintaining the

office—Anthimus III (r. 1822–1824), Chrysanthus I (r. 1824–1826), Agathangelus I (r. 1826–1830), Constantius I (r. 1830–1834), and Constantius II (r. 1834–1835).

January 4, 1821

Europe: Germany
Christianity

Moravians at Niesky, Germany, hang an illuminated star with 110 points at their school as a part of their commemoration of Epiphany, the Christian remembrance of the Three Wise Men who saw a new star in the sky and followed it to the infant Jesus of Nazareth. It is the origin of the now widespread use of the star as an integral part of the celebration of the Christmas season.

March 25, 1821

Europe: Greece
Christianity, Islam

The southern half of Greece proclaims independence from Turkey. The action will set off a lengthy war for domination of the Greek peninsula.

April 10 (Easter Sunday), 1821

Southwest Asia and North Africa: Asia Minor
Islam, Christianity

Ottoman authorities accuse Gregory V, the ecumenical patriarch residing in Istanbul, of ineffectiveness in the effort to prevent the Greek War of Independence that had recently arisen as one element in Russia's ongoing campaign to reclaim lands long dominated by the Ottoman Empire in Europe. Under orders directly from the sultan, at the close of the Easter service at the Patriarchal Cathedral of St. George, authorities grabbed Gregory and executed him by hanging at the main gate of the patriarchal compound. They left his body still in its ritual vestments for three days and then had a small group recruited from the city's Jewish community drag the body through the streets of Istanbul and throw it into the Bosporus Straits. Greek sailors would eventually recover the body and take it to Athens, where it was laid to rest amid full ceremonies in the Metropolitan Cathedral.

The execution of Gregory backfires on the sultan as he is seen as a modern martyr saint and his death commemorated as an important event in emerging Greek nationalism. In Istanbul, Saint Peter Gate, where his body was hung, would be quietly closed and welded shut. It has never been opened in the years since Gregory's death, which would be referenced in the "Hymn to Liberty," the modern Greek national anthem.

June 19, 1821

North America: United States
Christianity

Pope Pius VII erects the new Diocese of Cincinnati (Ohio), a community that has grown quickly by the influx of German-speaking immigrants, many bringing their Catholic faith with them.

July 28, 1821

South America: Peru
Christianity

After a year of fighting that included many small victories but no decisive battles, the Spanish desert Lima. Though the struggle is not yet over, General José de San Martín declares the independence of Peru and the end of the Viceroyalty of Peru. He also steps into the vacuum of leadership and becomes the leader of the revolutionary government.

San Martin takes a series of steps to ensure the support of Peru's Native population. He abolishes the forms of servitude that had been imposed on the Native people and grants them full citizenship. He takes the first step to abolish slavery. He declares the slaves of those Spanish who had abandoned Peru free, and declares all as yet unborn children of the remaining slaves to be free. He discontinues the Inquisition, ends corporal punishment, and proclaims freedom of speech.

August 24, 1821

Central America and the Caribbean: Mexico
Christianity

Spanish general Agustín de Iturbide joins his forces with the troops of insurgency general Vicente Guerrero. Together they force the representatives of the Spanish Crown in Mexico to sign the Treaty of Córdoba and the accompanying Declaration of Independence of the Mexican Empire, which recognizes

José de San Martin proclaiming independence of Peru, July 28, 1821. San Martin (1778–1850) led the rebellion against Spain that liberated Argentina, Chile, and Peru. (DeAgostini/Getty Images)

the independence of Mexico. Immediately afterward Agustín de Iturbide proclaims himself the emperor of the First Mexican Empire.

Soon after independence is declared, Mexico permits Stephen F. Austin to start colonization in what will become the state of Texas.

September 7, 1821

South America: Colombia, Venezuela
Christianity

Following a lengthy war and with key victories behind him, Simon Bolivar is finally able to create the Gran Colombia (a country that included what is now Colombia, Venezuela, Panama, Ecuador, and parts of Peru and Brazil). It names Bolivar as its first president.

September 15, 1821

Central America and the Caribbean: Guatemala
Christianity

Spanish authorities issue the Deed of Independence that releases the Captaincy of Guatemala (which included what is now Guatemala, El Salvador, Honduras, Nicaragua, Costa Rica, and the Mexican state of Chiapas) from Spanish rule. The captaincy is superseded by the Federal Republic of Central America (aka the United Provinces of Central America).

1822

Sub-Saharan Africa: South Africa
Christianity

Missionary John Philip is appointed superintendent of the London Missionary Society in South Africa at the height of the debates concerning the abolition of slavery in England. Philip contributes by documenting the harsh activity of the South African settlers and the colonial government toward the local Native population.

1822

Southwest Asia and North Africa: Egypt
Traditional Religions

Jean-François Champollion (a French classical scholar and philologist) publishes the translation of the text of the Rosetta Stone hieroglyphs, in which he demonstrates that the Egyptian writing system was a combination of phonetic and ideographic signs. His work opens a new era of modern archeological research on ancient Egypt and makes the deciphering of its many religious texts possible.

1822

Central America and the Caribbean:
  Haiti, Dominican Republic
Christianity

Haitian president Jean-Pierre Boyer (r. 1818–1843) takes control of Santo Domingo and brings the entirety of Hispaniola under one government. Haiti and Santo Domingo continue forward as separate nations.

1822

Central America and the Caribbean: Mexico
Christianity

The Central American countries of the newly formed Federal Republic of Central America meet in Guatemala City and vote to join the newly constituted First Mexican Empire founded by Agustín de Iturbide. All of the countries share a common attachment to the Roman Catholic Church.

1822

South America: Ecuador
Christianity
Ecuador gains independence from Spain.

1822

Europe: France
Christianity

A group of 10 priests who had been operating a clandestine Roman Catholic school in postrevolutionary France found the Congregation of Saint Basil, a new religious order to ensure the continuation of the school, then located in Annonay. In the ups and downs of the next decades, the school would eventually be closed, but by that time the Congregation of St. Basil had grown and developed new centers of operation in North America.

1822

Europe: Germany
Christianity

Evangelical Church authorities direct Protestant congregations to use the new order of worship, reflecting the attempt to unite Lutheran and Reformed approaches to congregational life. Approximately one-third of the congregations refuse the new approach.

1822–1831

Oceania and Antarctica: Tonga
Christianity

Australian Methodist Walter Lowrey arrives in Tonga in 1822. Just some 20 years earlier, Natives had killed three representatives of the London Missionary Society. Lowrey has better luck, and in 1831, King George Tupou I, King of Tonga and admirer of all things British, converts to Methodism. Following his conversion nearly all of Tonga converts to Christianity. Thanks to King George, however, the Methodist church splits into two rival branches.

January 1, 1822

Europe: Greece
Christianity

In the wake of the successful Greek revolution, the Provisional Regime of Greece adopts the provisional Greek constitution of 1822, now considered to be the first constitution of the modern state of Greece, which had since the 15th century been under the control of the Ottoman Empire. The document establishes Christianity in its Eastern Orthodox manifestation as the prevailing religion of the new country and understands the Greek Orthodox Church to be a definitive element of Greek ethnic identity.

February 4, 1822

Sub-Saharan Africa: Liberia
Christianity

The first group of African Americans, including the founders of the Methodist and Baptist churches of Liberia, arrives at Cape Mesurado and founds Monrovia, which they name in honor of President James Monroe, who has offered his support for the efforts of the American Colonization Society. They are the first of some 20,000 free blacks who will migrate to Liberia over the next 80 years.

February 5, 1822

Europe: Albania
Christianity, Islam

Agents of the Ottoman Empire kill Albanian leader Ali Pasha of Tepelena who had emerged as a power governor within the empire and operated as an independent leader of his assigned territory. The Ottoman sultan decides that he can no longer tolerate the competition he represented. The Ottoman action puts Albania in play even as the empire is attempting to quell a revolt against Ottoman rule in Greece. Simultaneously, Russia is pressuring the empire from the northeast as it attempts to gain an ice-free port on the Black Sea.

May 24, 1822

South America: Ecuador
Christianity

Following Antonio José de Sucre's defeat of the Spanish forces at the Battle of Pichincha (near Quito), Ecuador gains its independence. It then moves quickly to align with the Republic of Gran Colombia, which Simon Bolivar had created.

July 26–27, 1822

South America: Peru
Christianity

Simon Bolívar confers with Argentinian general José de San Martín at the Guayaquil conference. San Martín, who had liberated part of Peru from Spanish control, agreed to Bolívar completing the task of fully liberating Peru.

September 7, 1822

South America: Brazil
Christianity

When Portuguese king João VI returns to Europe (April 1821), he leaves his elder son Prince Pedro de Alcântara to control Brazil as regent. When the government in Portugal attempts to turn Brazil back into a colony, the Brazilians refuse to accept the idea and Prince Pedro steps forward to declare the country's independence from Portugal.

October 12, 1822

South America: Brazil
Christianity

Brazilian regent Prince Pedro de Alcântara is declared the first emperor of Brazil and begins his rule as Dom Pedro I.

November 22, 1822

Sub-Saharan Africa: Morocco
Islam

Mulay Suleiman, the sultan of Morocco, whose Alaoute Dynasty had ruled the land since the 17th century, dies. He is succeeded by his nephew Moulay al-Rahman (r. 1822–1859).

1823

Sub-Saharan Africa: South Africa
Christianity

Scottish minister Robert Moffat, a missionary sponsored by the Church Missionary Society, settles in Kuruman in Bechuanaland, where he will spend the next 50 years.

1823

North America: United States
Judaism

The first American Jewish periodical, *The Jew,* is published in New York.

1823

Central America and the Caribbean: Jamaica
Christianity

The Moravian missionaries in Jamaica sell their property at New Carmel, which they had used to support themselves from the labor of some 40 slaves. Their becoming slave owners had greatly weakened their credibility and become a major obstacle to their ministry among African Jamaicans. After they rid themselves of their slaves, their work prospers and grows dramatically during the 1830s.

Sir George Henry Rose, a member of the British Parliament, writes an open letter in which he argues that slave unrest in the West Indies could only be quelled by converting them to Christianity. He attributes the slaves' condition to their lack of proper instruction in Christianity, which would lead them to be obedient, orderly, industrious, and moral.

1823

Europe: Germany
Christianity

Prussian king Frederick William III appoints Saxon Lutheran theologian Daniel Amadeus Gottlieb Neander as the provost of St. Petri Church in Berlin, thus making him the highest ranking ecclesiastical official in Prussia. As a confidant of the king and his major policy makers, Neander emerges as the most powerful German church leader.

1823–1824

North America: United States
Christianity

Representatives of a number of local unions from various American cities promoting Sunday schools, at a time when they are about teaching youth to read and write using the Bible and religious literature, gather in December 1823 in Philadelphia and hold initial discussions aimed at the formation of a national organization to promote the Sunday school cause. Out of these discussions, the American Sunday-School Union is formed early in 1824, its initial leadership coming from laypeople of the major Protestant denominations. The union will become a major publisher of printed material for children and youth for the rest of the century, and survive through the transition that saw Sunday schools transform from their original purpose of teaching literacy to become an instrument in training and educating people in Christian faith and life.

1823–1824

Central America and the Caribbean: Mexico
Christianity

A revolution overthrows Agustín de Iturbide and establishes the United Mexican States. The new Republican Constitution (1824) designates Catholicism as the official and unique religion of the Mexican people. Guadalupe Victoria is named as the first president.

1823–1825

South America: Chile, Peru
Christianity

Pope Pius VII sends the apostolic nuncio, Monsignore Giovanni Muzi, Monsignore Bradley Kane, and Fr. Giovanni Maria Mastai-Ferretti (later Pope Pius IX) to Chile and Peru on a mission to assess postrevolutionary South America and map out a plan for the development of the Roman Catholic Church in the emerging South American republics. When elected, Mastai-Ferretti thus becomes the first pope ever to have been in the Americas.

January 3, 1823

North America: United States
Christianity

The Mexican government issues a grant to Stephen F. Austin who initiates colonization in the Brazos River valley. Given the legal status of the Roman Catholic Church, Austin petitions Mexican authorities to send English-speaking priests to the Texas colonies. The Mexican authorities are unable (and/or unwilling) to comply.

Joseph L. Bays, a Baptist preacher traveling with a group of settlers heading from Missouri to Louisiana, preaches in San Felipe de Austin and is arrested by order of the Mexican governor. He later escapes his confinement. The incident leads Stephen Austin to warn Methodist preacher William Stevenson to not violate the law on non-Catholic religious activity.

January 28, 1823

South America: Chile
Christianity

Bernardo O'Higgins, the first ruler of an independent Chile, is deposed and replaced with a new dictator, Ramón Freire. O'Higgins had lost support over a spectrum of liberal reforms he attempted to introduce. He had in the process offended the Roman Catholic bishop of Santiago, Jose Rodriguez Zorrilla, and lost the support of the church.

May 1823

Oceania and Antarctica: French Polynesia
Christianity

By this time, almost all of the native residents of Tahiti have converted to Christianity.

May 3, 1823

Europe: France
Christianity

Pope Pius XI shows his support of the Society for the Propagation of the Faith, designed to support missionary work around the world by the Roman Catholic Church by declaring it a "pontifical" organization. It will become the largest society advocating for and sponsoring Catholic missionaries. The society had been founded the year before by the devout laywoman Pauline-Marie Jaricot of Lyon, who would four years later found the Association of the Living Rosary.

July 15–16, 1823

Europe: Italy
Christianity

A fire in Rome destroys the basilica that had been built by the emperor Theodosius over what was believed to be the burial site of Paul the Apostle just outside the walls of Rome. A new Basilica of St. Paul Outside the Walls is constructed over the site.

August 23, 1823

Europe: Italy
Christianity

Pope Pius VII dies. He is succeeded by Pope Leo XII (r. 1823–1829) who begins his reign over the Roman Catholic Church on September 28. Leo will be among the more unpopular popes as he attempts to impose a very conservative and detailed behavioral code on the citizens of the Papal States.

1824

Sub-Saharan Africa: Lesotho
Christianity

The Basotho chieftain Moshoeshoe founds what will become Lesotho, a relatively small land completely surrounded by South Africa, as a settlement on a natural rock fortress called the Mountain of the Night.

1824

North America: United States
Judaism

The Society of Reformed Israelites, the first American experiment with reforming Judaism, emerges in Charleston, South Carolina

1824

North America: United States
Christianity

The governor of California, appointed by Mexico, offers all the property of the missions established by the Franciscans a century earlier for sale under a program of secularization.

1824

Central America and the Caribbean: Jamaica
Christianity

British Baptist missionary William Knibb arrives in Jamaica and launches his work among Jamaica's slaves at Falmouth, where he builds a chapel. Knibb supported the slaves in their bid for emancipation, and the small church would come to act as the headquarters of Jamaica's antislavery movement.

1824

Central America and the Caribbean: Jamaica
Christianity

The Church of England erects the Diocese of Jamaica. This multi-island diocese reaches across the Caribbean to other British colonies such as the Bahamas and the Turks and Caicos Islands. The first bishop is Christopher Lipscombe.

1824

South America: Brazil
Christianity

German immigrants arrive in Brazil and begin to build German-speaking communities (the first at San Leopoldo) in the country. Many are Lutheran and found the first German-speaking Lutheran churches. The original Synod of Rio Grande do Sol (1886) evolved to become the present Evangelical Church of the Lutheran Confession in Brazil.

1824

South America: Chile
Christianity

Mission San Diego de Alcalá, founded by Father Junipero Serra in 1769, was the first of the California missions. (National Oceanic and Atmospheric Administration)

The government of Chile moves against the Roman Catholic Church and confiscates the church's property. It subsequently abolishes church tithes, establishes a salary for the clergy, and closes most of the religious houses (monasteries).

1824

East and Southeast Asia: China
Christianity

Robert Morrison ordains Liang Fa, one of his early converts, who becomes the first Chinese Protestant evangelist.

1824

Europe: Scotland
Christianity

Calls for the Church of Scotland (Presbyterian) to found its own missionary society leads the Assembly of the church to appoint a committee to inaugurate a foreign mission program. The committee's work comes to fruition five years later when the church commissions Alexander Duff as its first missionary and sends him to Calcutta, where he becomes the headmaster of an educational institution, the beginning of a significant missionary career. His work in Calcutta will lead to the adoption of English in all of the government-sponsored schools of India and contribute to its broad use throughout the land.

1824

Southwest Asia and North Africa: Arabia
Islam

The Saud family, who are expanding their control of the Arabian Peninsula, establish a new capital at Riyadh.

CALIFORNIA MISSIONS

Spain's excursions into what is now California was a foray into what would be the absolute outskirts of an already overextended empire. An abject inability to deal with much resistance among Native peoples of the interior part of the state gave Spain the impetus to allow the church to establish missions as a means of "converting" various Native communities, with the hope of turning these missions into pueblos, or towns, that the Spanish Crown could then control. Hence the colonization process for Alta California differed greatly from Spain's earlier and much more violent colonization of Mexico and Central and South America. This new method, however, was no less insidious and devastating to the Native populations of the region.

The missions of Alta California were organized and overseen by a Franciscan with Inquisition experience and a severe personality, Padre Junipero Serra. A man who had had designs on martyrdom among the "savages" since childhood, this astute and driven administrator founded, or planned and directed, the establishment of 21 missions in California along the coast or at a short distance inland, reaching from San Diego in the south to Sonoma, beyond San Francisco Bay, in the north.

In spite of somewhat romantic visions of kindly padres ushering docile Natives into the modern world, California missions were essentially religious plantations designed to benefit Spain and its ruling elite. In terms of the religious effects of the mission system, California, in precontact times, supported a vast number of relatively independent, village-oriented tribal groups. California Native religious philosophies were extremely different from Western, Judeo-Christian sacred narratives, and many California tribal traditions employed a host of other-than-human participants, from plant, animal, and environmental spirits to heroes, deities, and sacred beings of human origin.

For many California Mission Indians, the stories of the "before time" were brought to them by their ancestors despite the seemingly total disruption by the colonial process of missionization. Today, many Native Californians see no sharp distinction between their Native traditional ways and their Catholic upbringing. While many modern California Indian people do reject, often totally, anything having to do with the church because of its bloody and oppressive history, it is nevertheless true that one is as likely to find the elders of these former mission Native communities at mass on Sunday as not.

DENNIS F. KELLEY

February 2, 1824

Europe: France
Christianity

The Congregation of the Holy Spirit under the protection of the Immaculate Heart of Mary (aka the Spiritians) was almost destroyed by the French Revolution. Its one remaining member in France, Fr. James Bertout, reorganizes it and Pope Leo XII gives his formal approval of the revived work. Once reestablished, the Holy Ghost Fathers would develop extensive missions and ultimately send more missionaries to Africa than any other religious order in the Roman Catholic Church.

February 10, 1824

South America: Peru
Christianity

After he completes the liberation of Peru, the country's Congress names Simon Bolivar the dictator of Peru. He begins the task of reorganizing the government and through the end of the year completes the defeat of the last remnants of the Spanish forces.

February 29, 1824

Europe: Germany
Christianity

A group of Lutheran laymen in Berlin founds the Society for the Advancement of Evangelistic Missions amongst the Heathen (better known as simply the Berlin Missionary Society). The society continues the individual work of Pastor Jänicke who had for a number of years trained missionaries to go out from the Bohemian-Lutheran congregation he pastored in Berlin.

April 1824

Europe: England
Western Esotericism

While visiting London, South American liberator Simon Bolivar, a Freemason for many years, visits the Great American Reunion Lodge, where he receives the 33rd degree of Inspector General Honorary.

May 17, 1824

Europe: Italy
Christianity

Pope Leo XII returns the Pontifical Gregorian University in Rome to the refounded Society of Jesus, which had been disbanded in the previous century.

July 29, 1824

North America: United States
Christianity

A Russian–United States treaty blocks Russian claims to North American territory below latitude 54°50'. Father John Veniaminov (later known as Bishop Innocent of Alaska) arrives on Unalaska Island in the Aleutians to begin work as a Russian Orthodox Church missionary.

August 15, 1824

Sub-Saharan Africa: Liberia
Christianity

The African American residents at Monrovia formally organize the new country of Liberia.

September 16, 1824

Europe: France
Christianity

French king Louis XVIII dies and is interred at the Basilica of St. Denis outside Paris. He is succeeded by his younger brother Charles X (r. 1824–1830).

December 9, 1824

South America: Peru
Christianity

The Battle of Ayacucho (aka the Battle of La Quinua). South American revolutionary forces defeat the Spanish army. The battle culminates the lengthy war for independence in South America led by Simon Bolivar. Following the battle, the Spanish viceroy signs a capitulation agreement that includes a provision for Spain to abandon Peru completely.

1825

North America: United States
Christianity

The Rappists abandon the New Harmony, Indiana, colony, return to Pennsylvania, and found Economy, 20 miles from Pittsburgh.

1825

North America: United States
Judaism

Mordechai Emmanual Lassalle leads a movement, which ultimately failed, to colonize New York's Grand Island with Jewish refugees.

1825

North America: United States
Christianity

Baptists in Massachusetts found Newton Theological Institution near Boston.

BATTLE OF AYACUCHO (1824)

The Battle of Ayacucho on December 9, 1824, was the final major battle of the wars for the independence of Spanish America. Bolivian general Antonio de Sucre led the outnumbered patriot forces against the royalists and managed a decisive victory at Ayacucho in the Peruvian highlands. The battle was the last in the military effort to achieve independence from the Spanish Empire that had begun in Venezuela and Argentina in 1810. The patriot armies, liberating as they went, had gradually converged on Peru, the center of Spain's empire in South America and home to a wide variety of staunchly loyalist groups.

In May 1823, the independent Peruvian Congress called on Simón Bolívar for help against the Spanish Army. Bolívar took a year to consolidate patriot forces and produce a degree of political stability. His army finally engaged Spanish forces near the lake of Junín high in the Andes Mountains on August 6, 1824. Bolívar returned to Lima for reinforcements, leaving Sucre in charge in the field.

On December 9, 1824, Sucre engaged the Spanish army. It was a daring move since he was outnumbered more than two to one by an army that had superior firepower and occupied the strategically advantageous heights overlooking the plains. Sucre managed a stunning defeat of the Spanish forces with a desperate cavalry charge, capturing the Spanish commander, General José de la Serna. The royalists lost 1,400 men in the battle, and 700 more were wounded. In contrast, the patriots suffered a total of 900 casualties. The royalists surrendered in the mountains and in Lima. This last battle of the wars of independence marked the end of Spanish rule in South America.

ABC-CLIO

1825

Central America and the Caribbean: Honduras
Christianity

Pope Pius XI declares the Virgin Mary, under the form of Our Lady of Suyapa (aka Nuestra Señora de Suyapa, a statue that resides at the basilica that serves as her shrine in Suyapa, a suburb of the city of Tegucigalpa), as Patroness of Honduras. He selects February 3 as her feast day.

1825

Central America and the Caribbean:
   Netherlands Antilles
Christianity

By decree of King William I of the Netherlands, the Netherlands Reformed Church and the Lutheran Church unite to form the United Protestant Church.

1825

South Asia: India
Christianity

Bishop Heber of Calcutta ordains Abdul Masih, a former Muslim and just the second Indian national to be ordained to the Anglican ministry. He will subsequently become one of the most influential indigenous Christians in the shaping of 19th-century Christian missions in India.

1825

East and Southeast Asia: Japan
Buddhism

Japan issues an edict that strengthens its antiforeign stance. It suggests, "Should any foreigners land anywhere, they must be arrested or killed."

1825

Russia, Central Asia, and the Caucasus: Russia
Christianity

Czar Alexander I, the emperor of Russia, dies of typhus and is interred at the Cathedral of Sts. Peter and Paul in Saint Petersburg. A rumor later spreads through Russia that he had faked his death and spent the remainder of his life as a hermit. Some suggested that he was actually the Russian Orthodox saint Feodor Kuzmich, who would later be visited by Czar Alexander II. The Romanovs did little to squelch such speculation. Alexander I is succeeded by his son Nicolas I (r. 1825–1855).

1825

Oceania and Antarctica: French Polynesia (Tahiti)
Christianity

The Propaganda Fide, the department of the Vatican charged with the spread of the Catholic faith, assigns the Society of the Sacred Hearts of Jesus and Mary the task of evangelizing the South Pacific.

March 21, 1825

Europe: Italy, Netherlands
Christianity

Pope Leo XII names Bartolomeo Alberto Cappellaria (the future pope Benedict XVI) a cardinal, and shortly afterward sends him to the Netherlands to negotiate a concordat guaranteeing the rights of Catholics in the Low Countries. He carries out his task with a high degree of success.

May 26, 1825

North America: United States
Christianity

Unitarians in the United States and Canada, heretofore existing as a minority within the Congregationalist Church, form the American Unitarian Association. They are most distinguished from their Congregationalist peers by their disavowal of the doctrine of the Trinity. Coincidentally, on the same day, Unitarians in England found the British and Foreign Unitarian Association.

August 6, 1825

South America: Bolivia
Christianity

Though early to call for revolution, Bolivia is rather late in attaining it, but finally forces led by Antonio José de Sucre win the fight against royalist forces supportive of Spain. After 16 years of revolution, with the Spanish finally driven from the continent, the Congress of Upper Peru creates the Republic of Bolivia, which they name after Simon Bolivar, whom they see as the continent's liberator.

August 29, 1825

South America: Brazil
Christianity

After an unsuccessful military operation, Portugal relents and recognizes the independence of Brazil.

December 5, 1825

North America: United States
Christianity

Elizabeth Ka'ahumanu, the queen regent of the Kingdom of Hawai'i and widow of King Kamehameha I, having earlier acknowledged her conversion to Protestant Christianity and having encouraged her subjects to be baptized, accepts baptism from the hands of the Congregational Church missionaries who had been working in the islands. A short time later she promulgates Hawaii's first codified body of laws, drawing on the ethical principles she had learned from the missionaries, most notably the Ten Commandments.

1826

North America: United States
Christianity

Samuel S. Schmucker takes the lead in the founding of the Lutheran Theological Seminary at Gettysburg, Pennsylvania.

1826

Oceania and Antarctica: Australia
Christianity

The Anglican Church initiates its first mission among the Aborigines of Australia. Its progress was slow, as the church's attempts to build settled Christian congregations and communities clashed with the Aboriginal nomadic life.

1826

Oceania and Antarctica: French Polynesia
New Religions

As Christianity comes to dominate religion in Tahiti, the Mamaia movement emerges combining Christian and elements of traditional Tahitian religion. The founding local prophets, many being women, predicted the imminent return of Jesus Christ while rejecting many of the restrictive rules governing women's behavior that had been imposed on the Christian community.

1826–1828

Europe: United Kingdom
Christianity

Henry Drummond, a former member of the British House of Commons, hosts the Albury Park prophetic conferences in Surrey.

January 25, 1826

Europe: France
Christianity

Eugene de Mazenod, a French priest, founds the Missionary Oblates of Mary Immaculate, a new religious order dedicated to reviving the church in postrevolutionary France. Less than a month later (February 17) Pope Leo XII recognizes it. It later develops a major focus on missions and would become especially important in the development of the Roman Catholic Church in Canada and in Texas.

1827

North America: United States
Unbelief

The Freethought Press Association is founded in New York City.

1827

North America: United States
Christianity

The angel Moroni gives Joseph Smith some gold plates that had been buried in Cumorah Hill (near Palmyra, New York). Smith claims that they were written in "Reformed Egyptian."

1827

North America: United States
Christianity

Two years after Pope Leo XII creates the Prefecture Apostolic of the Sandwich Islands, a group of French religious associated with the Congregation of the Sacred Hearts of Jesus and Mary establish a mission in Hawaii. A priest of the congregation, Father Alexis Bachelot, becomes the first prefect. Their work will meet with an immediate response and lead to the founding of what will become the Roman Catholic Diocese of Honolulu and the building of the Cathedral of Our Lady of Peace, which later emerges as the oldest continuously used Roman Catholic cathedral in the United States. It would contribute the first six bishops to the Hawaiian diocese.

1827

Europe: Finland
Christianity

The Great Fire of Turku severely damages the cathedral church, the headquarters church for the Evangelical Lutheran Church of Finland. It is largely rebuilt, and the new spire on the tower is elevated to 101 meters (331 feet).

1827

Europe: United Kingdom
Christianity

Anglican minister John Keble completes and publishes *The Christian Year,* a book of poems for each Sunday and the major feasts of the liturgical year of the Church of England. The book heralds Keble's move to a high church position within the Anglican community, that stance which is closest to traditional Roman Catholicism.

April 1827

North America: United States
Christianity

The preaching of Elias Hicks emphasizing the "Inner Light" leads to a major schism among American Quakers beginning with the Philadelphia Yearly Meeting. Hicksite Quakers later form the Friends General Conference.

Hicks would teach that attention to the Inner Light was more important than yielding to the authority of the Bible, and denies a number of what many believe to be Christian essentials—the virgin birth of Christ, the divinity of Christ, and the atonement. His views would be compared favorably with Deism.

July 7, 1827

The first Catholic missionaries to the Kingdom of Hawaii are allowed to disembark at Honolulu. The Catholic priests are members of a religious order, the Congregation of the Sacred Hearts of Jesus and Mary, aka the Picpus Fathers. The small group is led by Alexis Bachelot, whom Pope Leo XII has named Prefect Apostolic of the Sandwich Islands (as Hawaii was then known).

October 20, 1827

Europe: Greece
Christianity

The Battle of Navarino. One of the decisive battles of the Greek War of Independence, during which a combined force of British, French, and Russian naval vessels destroys the Ottoman Empire's Mediterranean naval fleet. The battle occurs in Navarino Bay (modern-day Pylos) off the Greek coast in the Ionian Sea. The victory came at a time in which the Greek cause appeared to be on the verge of collapse. The battle is one in a series that has pitted Christian European forces against the Muslim Ottomans in the Mediterranean waters since the 15th century.

Shortly after the battle, Count Ioannis Antonios Kapodistrias, who had been selected as the first head of state of the postrevolutionary country, arrives in

View showing Quakers walking past the first Philadelphia Hicksite meeting house. In 1827, the Society of Friends split into the Orthodox and Hicksite Quakers as a result of a theological division over the role of scripture within the faith. (Library Company of Philadelphia, PA, USA/The Bridgeman Art Library)

SOCIETY OF FRIENDS (QUAKERS)

The Friends movement, commonly known as the Quakers, emerged in 17th-century England as the most radical expression of the Puritan movement, which attempted to complete the work of the Reformation in the Church of England by purifying it of nonbiblical elements that had accumulated over the centuries. George Fox, the movement's founder, was a mystic and social activist who began to preach in 1647 during the English Civil War.

The beginnings of a movement became visible in 1667 when Fox's followers organized a set of Monthly (congregations), Quarterly (district), and Yearly (national) Meetings. The Society of Friends was built around Fox's idea that the Bible was not the end of revelation, but that each believer had access to the Inner Light that provided immediate contact with the Living Spirit. Gatherings were centered upon quietly waiting for the Spirit to speak. Bodily movements that appeared in these meetings gave members the popular appellation Quakers. The messages received and the guidance they offered would then be tested by the teachings and example of Jesus.

Fox taught that Friends should lead simple lives, avoiding the vanities of the world. Members did not wear colorful clothing, wigs, or jewelry. Their language was characterized by their refusal to use the formal "you" when addressing social superiors, as was customary; they addressed everyone with the familiar "thee" and "thou," which further set them apart. They became known for their participation in various social causes, including abolition of slavery, prison reform, and, most notably, pacifism. Heightened tension over their pacifism regularly arose in times of war.

Persecuted in England, Quakers found a haven in the American colonies when William Penn founded Pennsylvania and invited his fellow believers to settle there. They first arrived in 1655.

The Friends remained a small minority group in both England and the United States, and their support for the antislavery cause further limited their growth in the American South. However, through the 19th and early 20th centuries, they spread across North America. As early as 1681 the first General Meeting of Friends was held in New Jersey. It evolved into the General Yearly Meeting of Friends in Philadelphia, East Jersey, and Adjacent Provinces, and as the Philadelphia Yearly Meeting continues as the oldest Quaker association in North America.

J. GORDON MELTON

Greece, unites the divided revolutionary forces, and oversees the final stages of the movement toward liberation.

After a decade of work, construction is completed on St. George's Cathedral, built by the Anglican Church Missionary Society in Freetown.

1828

Sub-Saharan Africa: Sierra Leone
Christianity

1828

Sub-Saharan Africa: South Africa
Traditional Religions

Shaka, the Zulu chief who had unified the Nguni peoples and created an impressive fighting force, is assassinated, though Zulu power continues on an upward trajectory.

1828

Sub-Saharan Africa: Ghana
Christianity

The Basel Mission sends its first missionaries to the Gold Coast where they become involved in the development of cocoa farming.

1828

North America: United States
Christianity

Joseph Smith begins translating what will later be published as *The Book of Mormon.*

1828

North America: United States
Christianity

Methodists who reject its episcopal leadership leave the Methodist Episcopal Church, form the Methodist Protestant Church (MPC), and adopt a congregational polity.

1828

Central America and the Caribbean: Mexico
Christianity

General Manuel Mier y Teran, the military commander of Mexico's northeastern provinces, conducts a tour of the Texas border and reports that Anglos are importing slaves illegally and violating Mexican laws regarding the courts and religion. Relative to the state of religion, he concludes that freedom of religion would be preferable to no religion at all.

1828

Central America and the Caribbean: Mexico
Western Esotericism

Stephen F. Austin calls together an initial meeting of Freemasons at San Felipe de Austin, Texas. The group subsequently petitions the York Grand Lodge of Mexico for a charter to form a lodge. The petition is never acted upon, as the Mexican government reacts to what it fears is a liberal political philosophy influencing English-speaking Freemasons and outlaws Freemasonry in Texas.

1828

South America: Uruguay
Christianity

Uruguay becomes independent of Brazil.

1828

South Asia: India
Hinduism

Ram Mohun Roy founds the Brahmo Samaj to emphasize Hindu Vedantic philosophy. He argued against idol worship as contrary to the purity of the original Hindu faith.

1828

East and Southeast Asia: Thailand
Buddhism

Prince Mongkut (later to reign as King Rama IV of Thailand) founds a movement to reform and modernize the country's Buddhist monkhood that later evolved into the Dhammayut sect.

1828

East and Southeast Asia: Thailand
Christianity

Karl Friedrich August Gützlaff, a German missionary originally sent to Java by the Netherlands Missionary Society, breaks with the society and joins Jacob Tomlin, under the sponsorship of the London Missionary Society, in opening Protestant work in Siam/Thailand. The pair worked together in producing the first Bible translation in Thai and later on a dictionary of Cambodian and Lao.

1828

Europe: Ireland
Christianity

John Nelson Darby, a priest, separates from the Church of Ireland (Anglican) and begins to break bread with a group of independent believers.

FREEMASONRY

Although there is much debate over the ties of modern Freemasonry to medieval guilds of stone masons, there is little doubt that what is today called Freemasonry emerged at the end of the 17th century with the formation of the lodges of speculative Freemasons in Great Britain culminating in the formation of the first Grand Lodge in 1717 by the merger of four previously existing lodges in England. These initial lodges had emerged as older Masonic organizations accepted non-Masons into their community. Devoid of any interest in erecting buildings, these non-Masons used their gatherings to speculate about metaphysical issues quite apart from the theological perspectives of either the Church of England or the other dissenting churches operating in the country at the time, choosing instead to follow the Western Esoteric teachings previously spread under the label of Rosicrucianism.

The first papal statements against Freemasonry were issued in 1738 and 1751. The Grand Lodge of Massachusetts was founded in 1733, and others followed beginning with South Carolina in 1737. The Masonic lodges would become hotbeds not only of metaphysical speculation but of new democratic political ideals. These Masonic ideals would flow through the salons of Paris in the decades prior to the French Revolution and would become part of the consensus shared by many of the American revolutionaries. The Marquis de Lafayette was a Mason as were Benjamin Franklin (who largely financed the American Revolution) and future American presidents George Washington, James Madison, and James Monroe.

English Masons led in the founding of speculative lodges in France early in the 18th century. The French work became important in the 19th century as Freethought became important to French intellectual and political culture. In 1849, the Grand Lodge declared that the existence of God and the immortality of the soul were foundational principles of Freemasonry. However, in 1877, the French declared that absolute liberty of conscience and the solidarity of humanity were the basic principles. Thus, all references to God were removed from the rituals. These actions led to the British or American lodges severing relations with the French.

There are a variety of rites used in the different Masonic lodges. A Grand Lodge unites lodges that use the same rite. A Grand Orient unites lodges that may use a variety of rites. The Eastern Star was founded in 1876 as a Masonic auxiliary for women, Masonry being basically a male endeavor. Through the 20th century several forms of Masonry termed Co-Masonry, which accepted female members, have been founded. Today, the Supreme Council 33 Degrees of Ancient and Accepted Scottish Rite of Freemasonry of the Southern Jurisdiction of the United States of America is the leading American organization.

J. GORDON MELTON

1828

Europe: Italy
Christianity

Two Roman Catholic priests, Antonio Rosmini-Serbati and Abbé Jean-Baptiste Löwenstein, found the Institute of Charity as a new religious order dedicated to evangelizing the more isolated regions of northern Italy. They establish a motherhouse in Domodossola, Piedmont. As their work progressed, they encountered women who wished to enter the religious life and thus in 1832, they established a new order for them, which they named the Sisters of Providence of the Institute of Charity, aka the Rosiminian Sisters of Providence.

1828

Oceania and Antarctica: Samoa
Christianity

The Methodist church establishes a mission in the Samoan islands. They are soon followed by the London Missionary Society in 1830 and the Roman Catholic Church in 1845. The arrival of missionaries heralds a sweeping change for Samoan religious life.

July 21, 1828

Europe: United Kingdom
Christianity

Charles Manners-Sutton, who had served as archbishop of Canterbury for more than two decades, dies. He is succeeded by William Howley (r. 1828–1848), formerly the bishop of London. He would represent the bishops in their opposition to parliaments passing legislation that expanded the rights of Roman Catholics (the Emancipation of the Catholics) in 1829 and the Great Reform Act of 1832, which reformed the voting rights of the citizenry.

December 1828

Central America and the Caribbean: Mexico
Christianity

General Santa Anna and Vicente Guerrero lead a coup against Mexican president Guadalupe Victoria. The recent election results are set aside, and Guerrero assumes power as the president.

1829

North America: United States
Christianity

Mother Mary Elizabeth Lange, a young woman of Haitian background, and Fr. James Nicholas Joubert, a French-born priest of the Society of Saint-Sulpice, found the Oblate Sisters of Providence, the first Roman Catholic religious order designed from its conception for Catholic women of African descent. It begins operation in Baltimore, Maryland, with a mission to provide education to young girls of African descent. Along with its spread in the United States, it will develop centers throughout the Caribbean.

1829

Europe: Ireland
Christianity

Upon election to Parliament, Irish Catholic Daniel O'Connell immediately begins to work for the repeal of the union between Britain and Ireland, even as British Catholics are working to reestablish the Roman Catholic Church in the land. From this time, Roman Catholicism begins to be identified with Irish nationalist interests.

1829

Southwest Asia and North Africa: Egypt
Traditional Religions

Egypt presents France with the Obelisk of Luxor, which is erected in the Place de la Concorde in Paris.

February 10, 1829

Europe: Italy
Christianity

Pope Leo XIII dies. He is succeeded by Pope Pius VIII (r. 1829–1830) who begins his reign on March 31.

May 24, 1829

Europe: Italy
Christianity

Soon after taking the throne, Pope Leo XII issues his first encyclical, *Traditi humilitati,* in which he condemns religious pluralism and its implications that Catholicism exists on a par with other religions. He also condemns new Bible translations (and the Bible societies promoting them) as they provide occasions for non-Catholic interpretations of scripture.

June 1829

Europe: Germany
Christianity

Prussian king Frederick William orders all Protestant congregations and clergy in his realm to discard the names *Lutheran* or *Reformed* and use the name *Evangelical*. Though this change carries with it no demand to make any substantive theological or worship changes, the name alteration has a significant impact on the believers' self-image.

September 15, 1829

Central America and the Caribbean: Mexico
Christianity

Mexican president Vicente Guerrero frees all slaves, but Texans obtain a one-year exemption from the national slave emancipation decree.

October 4, 1829

North America: United States
Christianity

The American bishops of the Roman Catholic Church gather in Baltimore for the first Provincial Council.

November 8, 1829

South Asia: India
Hinduism

Though it is not a common practice among Hindus, William Bentinck, the governor-general of the East India Company, calls for the abolition of sati, the practice of a widow burning herself to death at the time of her husband's cremation. A month later, British colonial authorities outlaw the practice.

1830

Sub-Saharan Africa: Ethiopia
Christianity

Samuel Gobat, a Swiss Lutheran who later became the Protestant bishop of Jerusalem, accompanies Christian Kugler to Abyssinia under the sponsorship of the Church Missionary Society. The pair introduces Protestantism to Ethiopia.

1830

North America: United States
Christianity

A group of abolitionists, most with either Quaker or Methodist backgrounds, gather in Philadelphia to found the America Anti-Slavery Society. Lucretia Mott, the wife of one of the founders, is the only woman who is allowed to speak at the organizational meeting. A few days after the founding of the American Anti-Slavery society, Mott joins with other women in the city to found the Philadelphia Female Anti-Slavery Society.

1830

Central America and the Caribbean: Mexico
Christianity

Mexico passes a law forbidding slavery in Texas as well as any further settlement there by U.S. citizens.

1830

Southwest Asia and North Africa: Algeria
Christianity

The French begin their conquest of Algeria by occupying Algiers.

1830

Europe: Germany
Christianity

In recognition for his work in strengthening the Evangelical Church in Prussia, Prussian king Frederick William III bestowed the honorary title of bishop on Daniel Amadeus Gottlieb Neander, who has emerged as the major architect of the new church. Neander had been instrumental in the publication of a new revised edition of the order of worship that incorporated a greater level of acknowledgment of the uniquely Lutheran liturgical tradition and at least temporarily satisfied Lutheran theological concerns with the Prussian church union.

1830

Oceania and Antarctica: Fiji
Christianity

Hatai, Arue, and Tahaara, three native Christian missionaries from Tahiti, arrive at Lakeba as representatives of the London Missionary Society. They are the first Christian missionaries to come to the Fijian Islands. However, by agreement among the Protestant missionaries working in the South Seas, the Methodists received hegemony over Fiji, and in 1835 the LMS missionaries withdrew and two British Methodists, William Cross and David Cargill, assumed their post.

1830

Oceania and Antarctica: Samoa
Christianity
John Williams leads a group of missionaries from the London Missionary Society in introducing Christianity to the Samoan islands.

1830

Oceania and Antarctica: Samoa
Traditional Religions, Christianity
As Christianity made significant inroads in Samoa, a new religion combining elements of Christianity with the traditional religion of the island arose. Named for its founder, Siovili, it claimed a large following with its message of the imminent arrival of God's son, Sisu, who would bring judgment on the people. It offered direct access to God through the words of female mediums.

1830–1865

Oceania and Antarctica: New Zealand
Traditional Religions, Christianity, New Religions
From 1830 to 1850, at least 10 religious movements arise out of a combination of millenarian sentiment and charismatic leadership. Another nine flourish briefly in the 1850s, mainly based on healing. Disputes between Maori and the new colonials regarding sovereignty, land ownership, and land confiscation led to the onset of the Land Wars from 1860 to 1865, a further catalyst for Maori to develop religious movements that suited their circumstances. At least 16 major prophetic movements arose, including the Pai-Marire, more commonly known as Hauhau. Hauhau transposed Old Testament prophecies about the Promised Land into the contemporary Maori situation.

March 23, 1830

Europe: Italy
Western Esotericism
Pope Pius VIII issues *Litteris altero,* in which he condemns Freemasonry and the associated secret societies and also attacks the new vernacular translations of the Bible.

April 6, 1830

North America: United States
Christianity
Joseph Smith Jr. leads in the formation of what becomes the Church of Jesus Christ of Latter-day Saints. The church emerges in reaction to his visionary experiences and his reception of the text of the Book of Mormon, which joins the Bible as scripture for the new movement.

April 6, 1830

Central America and the Caribbean: Mexico
Christianity
Mexico forbids further emigration of settlers from the United States, which results in a further decline of relations between the Texans (Anglos who previously migrated to Texas) and the Mexican government. The Texans also disagree with a provision of the law forbidding the further importation of slaves.

June 26, 1830

Europe: England
Christianity
King George IV dies. He is succeeded by William IV (r. 1830–1837).

July 5, 1830

Southwest Asia and North Africa: Algeria
Islam
French troops invade Algiers, ostensibly to suppress the Mediterranean pirates operating from the Algerian coast.

July 18, 1830

Europe: France
Christianity

Catherine Labouré, a nun in Paris with the Daughters of Charity of Saint Vincent de Paul, has an initial vision of the Blessed Virgin Mary in which she is given a mission tied to the negative situation of the church in postrevolutionary France.

July 18, 1830

America: Uruguay
Christianity

Two years after becoming independent, Uruguay promulgates a constitution drawing inspiration from the French and American models, but naming the Roman Catholic Church the religion of the state and subsidizing missions to the Native peoples. The president includes in his oath of office a promise to protect the church. About that same time, Pope Pius VIII erects the Vicariate Apostolic of Montevideo. It later becomes the Diocese of Montevideo (1878) and the Archdiocese of Montevideo (1897).

July 25, 1830

Europe: France
Christianity

With his government in crisis, King Charles issues four ordinances that seek to suppress the press, dissolve the recently elected Chamber of Deputies, alter the electoral system, and call for new elections. The ordinances occasion open revolt in Paris. On August 2, Charles abdicates and on August 16 leaves France for exile in England.

August 9, 1830

Europe: France
Christianity

The French Chamber of Deputies selects Louis Philippe (r. 1830–1848), a distant relative of the former king Charles X, as the new ruler of France with the title King of the French.

October 1830

North America: United States
Christianity

After Baptist minister Sidney Rigdon in Kirtland, Ohio, joins the Latter-day Saints and brings his congregation with him, Joseph Smith Jr. responds to a vision and moves the Mormon community to Kirtland, where the first Mormon temple will be constructed.

November 27, 1830

Europe: France
Christianity

The Blessed Virgin Mary again appears to Catherine Labouré, a nun in Paris. The Virgin appears inside an oval frame, standing upon a globe, wearing many rings of different colors. Around her are the words "O Mary, conceived without sin, pray for us who have recourse to thee." Catherine was instructed to take the images she had seen to her father confessor and convey to him Mary's request that they be placed on a medallion, which when it is distributed becomes known as the Miraculous Medal. Stamped on the medal are the words, "All who wear them will receive great graces."

The vision to Catherine initiates a new wave of popular veneration of the Virgin, which grows decade by decade through the century.

November 30, 1830

Europe: Italy
Christianity

Pope Pius VIII dies after only a year in office. He is succeeded by Pope Gregory XVI (r. 1831–1846) whose reign begins on February 2, 1831. Pope Gregory, though a cardinal, is not yet a bishop at the time he was named the new pope. He is the last nonbishop so chosen.

December 9, 1830

Europe: Italy
Christianity

A new church dedicated to the Blessed Virgin Mary as Our Lady of Sorrows is consecrated in Secondigliano (near Naples). Its opening occasions the beginning of a process of realizing the goals laid out in a vision experienced by the Roman Catholic priest Gaetano Errico. He has a statue of Our Lady of Sorrows commissioned, which arrives in Secondigliano in May 1835, turning the church into a pilgrimage site. He also begins to assemble the first brothers who will become the original member of his new order, the Missionaries of the Sacred Hearts of Jesus and Mary.

He gains initial approval for the new order in 1836 and papal approbation two years later. Errico would be canonized in 2008.

December 17, 1830

South America: Colombia
Christianity

Liberator turned dictator Simón Bolívar dies. He is buried in the cathedral at Santa Marta on the Caribbean coast of Colombia.

Gran Colombia, which had largely been held together by his presence, has already begun to disintegrate. Ecuador separates from Gran Colombia. It initially claims lands to the west and south of its present borders, but these claims are not accepted by its more powerful neighbors. Venezuela also gains full independence from Gran Colombia. Some attempt is made to separate Panama, but it will remain a department of Colombia through the 19th century.

December 20, 1830

Europe: Belgium, Netherlands
Christianity

An international conference meeting in London declares the dissolution of the old Kingdom of the Netherlands and, with Belgians in the streets opposing rule from the north, recognizes the independence of Belgium.

1831

North America: United States
Christianity

As a group, the Latter-day Saints move to Kirtland, Ohio.

1831

Central America and the Caribbean: Jamaica
Judaism

Although Jews had been living in Jamaica since 1655, they are finally given the right to vote.

1831

South America: Argentina
Christianity

Anglicans complete the construction of the Cathedral of St. John the Baptist, which survives today as the oldest non-Catholic church building in South America. The occasion for the building is a treaty signed between the United Kingdom and Argentina in 1825 that granted religious tolerance for British subjects who reside in the country.

1831

East and Southeast Asia: China, Tibet
Buddhism

The 19-year-old Dalai Lama takes his vows as a Buddhist priest and initiates his first major project, the reconstruction of the Potala Palace.

1831

Europe: Croatia
Christianity

A Bible translation closely following the text of the Roman Catholic Vulgate is published in the Croatian language.

1831

Europe: Ireland
Christianity

With a large inheritance from her family, Catherine McAuley founds the Sisters of Mercy, a religious order dedicated to serving the poor, the ill, and the educationally disadvantaged. Beginning in Dublin, the order will grow to become one of the largest religious orders in Ireland, and indeed in the whole Roman Catholic world.

1831

Oceania and Antarctica: Samoa
Christianity

Taufa'ahau, a chief on Tonga, is baptized and given the Christian name George. He later emerges as King George Tupou I.

1831–1833

Europe: Ireland
Christianity

View of the Potala Palace, traditional home of the Dalai Lama, in Tibet's capital, Lhasa. The palace is a revered location that was spared in the destruction that followed China's invasion of Tibet in 1950. (Kim Pin Tan/Dreamstime.com)

Lady Theodosia Powerscourt hosts conferences on biblical prophecy near Dublin, Ireland.

May 1831

Europe: United Kingdom
Christianity
Eighty-two Congregational ministers gather and form the Congregational Union of England and Wales. Scottish Congregationalists had organized a decade earlier.

May 11, 1831

South Asia: India
Christianity
Frs. Palackal Thoma Malpan, Porukara Thoma Kathanar, and Kuriakose Elias Chavara, Roman Catholic priests, found a new monastery and religious order known as the Congregation of the Servants of Mary Immaculate of Mount Carmel. The order will become part of the push to define the doctrine of the Immaculate Conception of the Blessed Virgin Mary as dogma (which finally occurs in 1854).

July 21, 1831

Europe: Belgium
Christianity
With the separation of the southern and predominantly Roman Catholic provinces of the Netherlands, a new nation, Belgium, is formed and Leopold I is crowned as the country's first king. He operates over a constitutional monarchy. The constitution includes a French laicist concept that blocks religious involvement in government affairs and the like absence of government involvement in religious affairs.

August 7, 1831

North America: United States
Christianity
At Dresden, New York, William Miller delivers his first lecture in which he makes public the conclusions he had reached concerning the Second Coming of Christ, namely that it would occur on or before 1843. From this point forward, he would write, speak, and gather followers who believed in his understanding of the imminent culmination of human history.

POTALA PALACE

Potala Palace, the imposing former palace of the Dalai Lama, spiritual head of Tibetan Buddhism and exiled ruler of Tibet, towers 13 stories (330 feet) above the city of Lhasa on a tall hill.

The Potala's earliest sections can be traced to the seventh century CE, but the great building periods occurred in the late 17th century and the early 20th. With more than 1,000 rooms, the Potala stretches more than 1,300 feet east to west and more than 1,100 feet north to south. At its base, the stone walls are 16 feet thick, yet the upper stories are so finely fitted together that no nails were used in the construction. As the home of the Dalai Lama and the center of his government, the palace was until the Chinese occupation the religious and political focus of Tibet.

The Potala is divided between the White Palace and the Red Palace, which are joined by a smaller structure used to store the sacred banners hung on the face of the palace on the first and 30th days of the second lunar month. The White Palace contained the apartments of the Dalai Lama and other high officials, the seminary for training court and national officials, the printery for printing Buddhist scriptures, and government offices.

The Red Palace is primarily religious and houses the lavish tombs of the Dalai Lamas. The Buddhist scriptures are preserved here in special libraries; they are hand-printed from carved wooden blocks and total 335 volumes. Many chapels and shrines contain the full panoply of Tibet's pantheon of Buddhas, bodhisattvas, saints, and demons.

The Red Palace highlights the life and works of the fifth Dalai Lama (1617–1682). It was he who unified Tibet, made the Yellow Hat sect of monasticism the state religion, and built the Potala. He is the most important figure in Tibetan history. His life is presented in murals, and in one chapel he is shown seated on a throne parallel to a seated Buddha, equal in dignity. The tomb of the fifth Dalai Lama is rivaled only by the tomb of the last Dalai Lama, who died in 1933 after making Tibet an independent country for the first time.

NORBERT C. BROCKMAN

September 9, 1831

East and Southeast Asia: Korea
Christianity

Pope Gregory XVI erects the Apostolic Vicariate of Korea and appoints missionary bishop Barthélemy Bruguière as the first bishop. It will later be known as the Apostolic Vicariate of Seoul.

November 3, 1831

Europe: France
Christianity

Fr. Louis Querbes, a Roman Catholic priest, founds the Clerics of Saint Viator (aka the Viatorians), a new Roman Catholic religious order in Lyon. An order dedicated to education and teaching, it takes its inspiration from Saint Viator, a fourth-century catechist who had lived in Lyon. It currently operates schools in North America, the Caribbean, and Japan.

December 1831

Central America and the Caribbean: Jamaica
Christianity

The Baptist War. During the Christmas holidays of 1831, Jamaican slaves, responding to a peaceful strike led by Baptist minister Samuel Sharpe, revolt. The militia, organized by the Jamaican plantation owners, suppresses the rebellion with great loss of life and property. It will destroy the chapel built by Thomas Kribb at Falmouth along with others that had been built by Baptists, Methodists, and Moravians, who were suspected of inciting the slaves. Afterward the missionaries were loved by the slaves and widely distrusted by the plantation owners. The British Parliament will conduct two inquiries, which contribute to raising the issue of the horrors of slavery and lead directly to the Slavery Abolition Act of 1833.

1832

North America: United States
Judaism
Canada grants Jews political rights.

1832

North America: United States
Christianity
Baptist preacher William Miller voices his views, based on the 2,300-day prophecy of Daniel 8:14, about the second coming of Christ in a set of articles in *Vermont Telegraph,* a Baptist periodical.

1832

North America: United States
Christianity
The American Baptist Home Mission Society is organized to initiate work in the American West.

1832

Europe: France
Christianity
Michael Garicoïts, a French Roman Catholic priest, founds the Priests of the Sacred Heart of Jesus of Betharram. Garicoïts saw the members as leading a spiritual life rooted in a union with Christ, who would give themselves to meeting the needs of humanity out of love symbolized by the Sacred Heart. Members eventually spread to four continents.

1832

Europe: Greece
Christianity
In the wake of the 1831 assassination of independent Greece's first head of state, Count Ioannis Kapodistrias, the European powers decided to establish a monarchy in the country as the best option to end the chaos of the previous few years. They select Otto (r. 1832–1862), a Bavarian prince, to become the first of a new lineage of modern kings of Greece. He is a Roman Catholic ruling what is essentially a Greek Orthodox nation, with many Greeks viewing him as a heretic.

1832

Europe: Italy
Christianity
Pope Gregory XVI issues his first encyclical, *Mirari Vos.* It deals with a spectrum of issues that have arisen with the social and intellectual changes of the early 19th century and begins with a condemnation of religious pluralism. It also condemns Freemasonry and offers arguments supportive of the ecclesiastical supremacy of the papacy.

1832

Europe: United Kingdom
Christianity
A initial gathering of the Brethren formed at Plymouth, England.

1833

North America: United States
Christianity
American Baptists issue the New Hampshire Confession based on the London Confession of Faith.

1833

North America: United States
Christianity
Presbyterian minister John J. Shipherd and missionary Philo P. Stewart found Oberlin College in Ohio to train teachers and other Christian leaders for service in the American West. The college will over the next generation emerge as one of the most liberal

institutions of learning in the United States, admitting both African American and female students.

1833

North America: United States
Christianity
Joseph Smith Jr., the founder of the Church of Jesus Christ of Latter-day Saints, publishes a volume of early revelations from God received by himself and another church member, Oliver Cowdery, under the title *The Book of Commandments*. It contains some 65 revelations, most offering guidance on immediate decisions.

1833

Central America and the Caribbean: Mexico
Christianity
A cholera epidemic strikes Iztapalapa, Mexico. Following a procession to an image of Christ called the "Señor de la Cuevita" (Lord of the Little Cave), the epidemic subsided. In gratitude, the people began to hold the annual Fiesta de Solteras de Septiembre, a mass in honor of this image and an annual presentation of a Passion Play. The play is held each Holy Week with reenactments of the events in the life and death of Jesus from Palm Sunday through Easter Sunday. The Passion Play has continued to the present and become a large event attracting visitors from across Mexico and beyond.

1833

South Asia: India
Christianity
In a major shift of power, the British government in India takes away the British East India Company's monopoly of trade with China and bans it from trading in India entirely.

1833

East and Southeast Asia: Thailand
Christianity
Baptist missionaries enter Thailand and found the Maitrichit Chinese Baptist Church in Bangkok, the first Protestant church in Thailand.

1833

Europe: Belgium
Christianity
Canon Jean-Baptiste-Victor Kinet, a Belgian priest, founds the Sisters of Providence of the Immaculate Conception at Jodoigne. The new religious order is dedicated to the education of children, the care of orphans, and service to the sick. From its motherhouse at Champion, it will eventually establish work in England, Italy, and the United States.

1833

Europe: England
Christianity
Anglican minister John Keble preaches his famous Assize Sermon duirng which he attacks the recently passed Irish Church Temporalities Bill, which, among other changes it forces on the church in Ireland, alters the rules on the leasing of church lands, opening the possibility of the government ultimately seizing those lands. Keble labels the bill an act of "national apostasy." The sermon energizes other high-church Anglicans, most notably John Henry Newman and Edward Pusey, to form what becomes known as the Oxford movement. They will begin to articulate what became known as the branch theory of ecclesiology, which views Eastern Orthodoxy, Anglicanism, and Roman Catholicism as three "branches" of the one "Catholic Church."

Spokespersons of the movement begin to issue a set of short writings, the *Tracts for the Times*, published between 1833 and 1841, and it is often termed the Tractarian movement.

1833

Europe: Germany
Unbelief
David Friedrich Strauss, a professor at Tübingen, resigns his post to devote himself full time to the writing of a book on Jesus of Nazareth, which is published in two volumes in 1835/1836 as *The Life of Jesus, Critically Examined*. The book sells well, but creates a storm of controversy as Strauss treats the miraculous elements in the gospels as being "mythical" in character.

January 3, 1833

South America: Argentina
Christianity

Britain removes a small group of Argentine settlers from the Malvina Islands (Falkland Islands) and takes control of the South Atlantic territory, which becomes a valuable stopping point for ships sailing through the region.

April 1, 1833

Central America and the Caribbean: Mexico
Unbelief

The Congress of Mexico elects General Santa Anna as president. The new president then appoints Valentín Gómez Farías as vice president, and almost immediately Farías begins to implement a set of reforms relative to the Catholic Church, the country's state religion, including abolishing obligatory tithing. He also seizes a number of properties formerly owned by the church. The unpopular reforms lead to his dismissal and exile. Santa Ana assumes greater and greater power and eventually emerges with dictatorial control.

Summer 1833

North America: United States
Traditional Religions

In Texas, the Osage attack the Kiowas, many of whom are killed. They also steal three Kiowa *taimes,* stone statues used in the annual Sun Dance ceremony. The stones will be returned two years later after a peace treaty is negotiated between the two tribes.

July 23, 1833

Europe: Greece
Christianity

In the wake of the successful Greek revolution, the Orthodox Church of Greece declared itself autocephalous, that is, independent and self-governing, relative to the Ecumenical Patriarchate.

September 29, 1833

Europe: Spain
Christianity

King Ferdinand VII of Spain dies. He is succeeded by his three-year-old daughter Isabella II (r. 1833–1868).

Her rule was challenged by a group of conservatives, the Carlists, who oppose the idea of the country being ruled by a female. They kept the country in some degree of turmoil through most of Isabella's rule.

October 1833

Europe: United States
Christianity

Pope Pius IX donates a stone to be placed on the Mall near the Washington Monument in Washington, D.C. A year after it is given a place, it is stolen by an unknown group of men, most likely members of the nativist Known-Nothing Party, who were staunchly anti-Catholic. The stone disappeared and was never seen again. A replica was donated by the Vatican in 1982.

December 22, 1833

South America: Chile
Christianity

Pope Gregory XVI erects the Vicariate Apostolic of Oriental Oceania, a missionary jurisdiction with responsibility for the South Pacific. He oversees the consecration of Étienne Jérôme Rouchouze as a bishop and names him the first vicar apostolic. Rouchouze will reside in Valparaiso, Chile, and direct the efforts of the Congregation of the Sacred Hearts of Jesus and Mary (aka the Picpus Fathers) who have been assigned responsibility for the evangelization of the Hawaiian Islands and the eastern Pacific.

1834

Sub-Saharan Africa: Zimbabwe
Traditional Religions

The Ndebele people arrive in Zimbabwe after fleeing from the Zulu leader Shaka and create their new homeland, which they term Matabeleland.

1834

Sub-Saharan Africa: South Africa
Christianity

The first missionaries sent out by the Berlin Missionary Society (Lutheran) arrive in South Africa.

1834

North America: United States
Christianity

Baptist preacher William Miller of New York summarizes his views on the imminent second coming of Christ in a booklet, *Evidence from Scripture and History of the Second Coming of Christ, about the Year 1843: Exhibited in a Course of Lectures.*

1834

North America: United States
Christianity

Padre José Antonio Díaz de León, the one remaining Franciscan friar in East Texas, is killed in Polk County, bringing to an end the several centuries of Spanish Catholic activity in Texas.

1834

Europe: Belgium
Christianity

The Roman Catholic bishops of Belgium found a new church-sponsored university, Mechelen, which a year later moves to Leuven, emerges as the Catholic University of Leuven, and later becomes one of the leading universities of Europe.

1834

Europe: Portugal
Unbelief, Christianity

Portugal abolishes all Roman Catholic religious orders.

1834

Russia, Central Asia, and the Caucasus: Russia
Islam

A Muslim leader, Imam Shamil, organizes a Muslim theocratic state in Russia's Chechnya province. It will take Russia some 27 years to reintegrate the predominantly Islamic region back into the empire.

1834

Southwest Asia and North Africa: Afghanistan
Islam

Kohendil Khan (r. 1829–1834), who had briefly ruled in Kandahar at the time of a divided Afghanistan, is defeated by Persians who take control of the city. Kohendil Khan has recently built the Mosque of the Hair of the Prophet, a new mosque that comes to

hold a relic of the Prophet Muhammad that had been brought to Afghanistan in 1768.

1834–1842

Oceania and Antarctica: Polynesia
Traditional Religions, Christianity

The French begin to colonize Polynesia. Catholic missionaries arrive in Tahiti in 1834. At first they encounter major resistance, forcing them to leave the island in 1836. In response, France sends a gunboat in 1838, and in 1842 France declares Tahiti and Tahuata a French protectorate. Prior to the coming of Christianity, the residents of the islands worshipped a pantheon of deities headed by a supreme god called Taaroa. The other deities were ascribed hegemony over vital areas of island life, such as the sea or the weather.

January 1, 1834

Central America and the Caribbean: Jamaica, Trinidad
Christianity, Hinduism

Catholic missionary with two Tahitian converts, ca. 1845. (Henry Guttmann/Getty Images)

British legislation abolishing slavery throughout the empire takes effect. It has its primary effect among the British colonies throughout the Caribbean.

To meet the demands for plantation labor, the British authorize the importing of indentured servants from India to the Caribbean colonies, which has the effect of introducing Hinduism and, to a lesser extent, Islam to the region. The largest percentage of Hindus would develop in Trinidad and Guyana.

January 1, 1834

Europe: United Kingdom
Christianity

The recently passed Slavery Abolition Act of 1833, to which the king assented on August 28, 1833, abolishes slavery throughout the British Empire (with a few exceptions, namely the "territories controlled by the East India Company," the "Island of Ceylon," and "the Island of Saint Helena"). The exceptions were eliminated a decade later. The act had its greatest effect in Jamaica and Canada, the latter becoming a target of escaped American slaves.

The act formally emancipates the slaves, which meant no new persons are to be admitted to the slave state, but actual freedom will come in stages. Slaves are indentured to their former owners in an apprenticeship system. The first set of apprenticeships end on August 1, 1838, with the last ending August 1, 1840.

Among those receiving compensation for slaves who are freed is the bishop of Exeter, who receives payment for releasing 665 slaves.

April 22–23, 1834

Europe: Germany
Christianity

English Baptist Barnas Sears visits Germany and baptizes J. G. Oncken, his wife, and five others and the next day, in Hamburg, constitutes the seven as the first Baptist church in Germany, indeed in continental Europe.

June 12, 1834

Central America and the Caribbean: Mexico
Christianity

Mexican president Santa Anna dissolves Congress and announces his decision to implement the Plan of Cuernavaca, which had appeared the previous year. It calls for repeal of the liberal and anti-Catholic reforms pushed by Santa Anna's vice president. Santa Anna puts together a new Catholic centralist coalition and announces the abandonment of the 1824 constitution.

July 15, 1834

Europe: Spain
Christianity

Spanish regent Maria Christina of the Two Sicilies, the widow of Ferdinand VII, issues a royal decree officially abolishing the Spanish Inquisition. She has the approval of the president of her cabinet, Francisco Martínez de la Rosa. The Inquisition had been largely inactive over the last 20 years.

August 1, 1834

North America: Canada
Christianity

The British Parliament having ordered the abolition of slavery throughout its colonial empire, the law takes effect in Canada.

August 1, 1834

Central America and the Caribbean: Trinidad
Christianity

The governor of Trinidad is shouted down during a speech on slavery at Port of Spain. Peaceful protests follow and the local government passes a resolution abolishing the forced apprenticeships that in fact continued slavery after the slaves' formal emancipation on January 1. Full emancipation is scheduled for August 1, 1838, two years ahead of the schedule suggested in the British antislavery law of 1833. Trinidad becomes the first British territory to abolish slavery completely.

August 11–12, 1834

North America: United States
Christianity

During a wave of anti-Catholicism that swept through the United States, a Protestant mob riots and burns the convent of the Ursuline sisters in Charlestown, Massachusetts. The riots had been occasioned by the circulation of a rumor that a member of the Ursulines had been abused.

October 23, 1834

Southwest Asia and North Africa: Persia
Islam

Fat'h Ali Shah Qajar, who has ruled as the shah of Persia for a half century, dies. He is succeeded by his grandson Mohammad Shah Qajar (r. 1834–1848).

December 14, 1834

Europe: Netherlands
Christianity

Rev. Hendrik de Cock, pastor of the Reformed Church in Ulrum, is forbidden to preach and ordered to refrain from condemning the teachings of his ministerial colleagues. In response, the majority of the congregation in Ulrum sign the Act of Secession and Return, leave the State Church, and form the independent Christelijke Gereformeerde Kerken (Christian Reformed Church).

1835

Sub-Saharan Africa: Madagascar
Traditional Religions, Christianity

Queen Ranavalona I (r. 1828–1861), who will rule Madagascar for over three decades, rejects Western influences invading her land by issuing a royal edict that prohibits the practice of Christianity and banishes most foreigners from the island monarchy.

1835

North America: United States
Christianity

Evangelist Charles Grandison Finney (1792–1875) accepts a position as professor of theology at Oberlin Collegiate Institute (later Oberlin College). While continuing his evangelistic activity, he becomes deeply involved with the abolitionist movement and frequently denounces slavery from the pulpit. He leads Oberlin College to commit itself to admit both African Americans and women to the student body.

1835

North America: United States
Christianity

Joseph Smith Jr. publishes a new edition of his collected revelations, originally published two years earlier as the *Book of Commandments*. The new edition, released under the title *Doctrines and Covenants,* contains 138 separate revelations, the earlier edition having only 65. *Doctrines and Covenants* will be added to the recognized scriptures of the Latter-day Saints, and more recent additions will have additional revelations received by Smith and various church presidents over the years.

1835

Central America and the Caribbean: Mexico
Christianity

As the Mexican president's conservative measures spread through the country, several states openly rebel against the central government and create the Republic of the Rio Grande, the Republic of Yucatan, and the Republic of Texas. Santa Anna is able to suppress the rebels in the Rio Grande and Yucatan, but Texas proves a different situation.

1835

Europe: Germany
Judaism, Christianity

Composer Felix Mendelssohn, at the height of his musical career, accepts the position of conductor of the Leipzig Gewandhaus Orchestra. Though born into a prominent Jewish family and raised without religion, he accepts baptism and joins the Lutheran Church. He becomes a representative figure of the movement of Jews to leave the ghetto and the Jewish community and integrate into the dominant Christian society, though he does so as one grateful for and acknowledging his Jewish heritage.

1835

Southwest Asia and North Africa: Asia Minor
Christianity

Following a period of extreme instability in the office of the Ecumenical Patriarchate introduced by the 1821 execution of Gregory V, Gregory VI (r. 1835–1840) takes the throne and is able to survive for five years.

1835–1836

East and Southeast Asia: China
Christianity

In the face of China's law against spreading Roman Catholicism in the country, Protestant missionaries in Canton, hopeful that they will be seen as distinct

CHARLES GRANDISON FINNEY (1792–1875)

Charles Grandison Finney was the leading Protestant evangelist of the great religious revival that swept 19th-century America and helped to spark the many social reform movements of the mid-century.

Finney received little religious training as a child, and although he regularly attended church as a young man, he was unmoved by traditional preaching and worshipping. His legal studies introduced him to the Bible, prompting him to embark on a self-led spiritual exploration. He underwent a religious epiphany and decided to renounce his legal practice and become an evangelist.

Finney was ordained a Presbyterian minister in 1824. In his sermons, he stressed the dire consequences of disobedience to God's will, emphasizing repentance and urging converts to accept salvation. People responded strongly to his charismatic preaching. Congregants frequently expressed their religious fervor through emotional outbursts and trances, which became a standard feature of Finney-led revivals.

In 1832, a group of merchants invited Finney to come to New York City as pastor of the Second Free Presbyterian Church. In New York, Finney again made many converts. Within a few years, several other churches had been established, including the Broadway Tabernacle. Increasingly dissatisfied with conservative Presbyterian theology and discipline, Finney withdrew from the Presbyterian Church and embraced Congregationalism while preaching at the tabernacle.

Finney took a stand against intemperance and slavery, two of the major social movements of the time. His followers, eager for causes to which they could dedicate their energies, quickly took up his call for action on these issues. Finney's supporters became the basis for both movements. He publicly and actively supported Theodore Weld when Weld left the Lane Theological Seminary in Cincinnati, Ohio because discussion of slavery was forbidden, urging religious leaders to exert themselves on behalf of the antislavery cause. In 1835, he became the chairman of Oberlin College's department of theology. Two years later, he left his post at the Broadway Tabernacle and moved permanently to Oberlin.

At Oberlin, Finney served as pastor of the First Congregational Church from 1835 to 1872 and as president of the college from 1851 to 1866. Under his guidance, the school became a center of antislavery agitation and a station on the Underground Railroad. Finney also made evangelistic tours of the United States and Great Britain. By the time of his death in 1875, the evangelical movement that he had done so much to shape and direct was firmly established within American Protestantism.

ABC-CLIO

from Catholics, pass along Christian books to some Chinese. The Daoguang emperor calls them "traitorous natives" and has the missionaries arrested. They were subsequently either strangled or expelled from the country. In 1839, the law against Christianity would be expanded to include non-Catholic Christians.

April 4, 1835

Europe: Italy
Christianity
Fr. Vincent Pallotti, a priest in Rome, founds the Society of the Catholic Apostolate (aka the Pallottines), a religious order designed to lead in the revitalization of the Catholic faithful through the promotion of a revived faith and rekindled love. Among the society's more interesting contemporary duties is the administration of one of the claimants to being the largest church in the world, the Basilica of Our Lady of Peace of Yamoussoukro in Côte d'Ivoire.

October 2, 1835

Central America and the Caribbean: Mexico
Christianity
The Battle of Gonzales. The revolution against Mexican rule in Texas begins with Texans repulsing a detachment of Mexican cavalry. Texas is but one of several states of Mexico that reject Santa Anna's authority, but Texas will be the only one successful in its efforts at independence.

October 28, 1835

Oceania and Antarctica: New Zealand
Traditional Religions
Before 1835, New Zealand was technically considered part of the British colony of New South Wales, a colony comprising many island territories in the South Pacific. New Zealand was rather peripheral to the interests of the New South Wales colony, however, so in 1835 the British sent James Busby to act as British Resident in New Zealand. Busby convenes a meeting of the United Tribes of New Zealand, and tribal representatives sign a Declaration of Independence. By 1839, 52 chiefs will have signed. The declaration attempted to protect the sovereignty of tribal chiefs, but it was not well received in Britain. The meaning of the Declaration is still debated.

December 1, 1835

Europe: Germany
Christianity
The cathedral chapter of Cologne elects Clemens August, the bishop of Münster, as the new archbishop of Cologne. He subsequently receives papal confirmation (February 1, 1836) and is enthroned (May 29, 1836).

December 15, 1835

Central America and the Caribbean: Mexico
Christianity
President Antonio López de Santa Anna leads in passing a set of constitutional amendments that at a fundamental level change the governmental structures of the first Mexican republic. The Siete Leyes (Seven Laws) have the effect of centralizing and strengthening the federal government.

1836

Sub-Saharan Africa: Ghana
Christianity
Dutch soldiers enter the territory of the kingdom of the Ashanti people as a first step in setting up a colony in which they plan to continue the slave trade and mine for gold. The British maintain control of most of the coast, the land of the Fante people.

1836

Sub-Saharan Africa: South Africa
Christianity
The Boers, French and Dutch settlers in South Africa, most of the Reformed Protestant faith, begin the great trek, a mass migration from those areas of the country controlled by the British into the interior. Once arrived, they will form two new republics, Transvaal and the Orange Free State.

1836

North America: United States
Christianity
Albert Barnes, pastor of First Presbyterian Church of Philadelphia, is tried for heresy over views he expressed on atonement in his book *Notes on Romans*. Though he was not convicted, his trial energized the growing division between the conservative Old School and more liberal New School factions in the Presbyterian Church.

1836

North America: United States
Western Esotericism
Ralph Waldo Emerson's essay "Nature" marks the beginning of Transcendentalism as a popular intellectual movement.

1836

North America: United States
Christianity
Marcus Whitman, a Presbyterian missionary, and his wife Narcissa establish a settlement called Waiilatpu (meaning "place of the rye grass"), which becomes the headquarters of a mission to the Cayuse and the Nez Perce peoples. It is located just west of what today is the city of Walla Walla, Washington. Whitman preached, farmed, and provided medical care. Narcissa established a school for the Native American youth.

1836

North America: United States
Christianity
Presbyterians in New York City found Union Theological Seminary, an independent school with a Presbyterian orientation. The school would become a conduit for the new directions in liberal Protestant thought being developed in Germany.

1836

North America: United States
Unbelief
Abner Kneeland is convicted of blasphemy in Massachusetts (the last such case in American history).

1836

North America: United States
Christianity
The Church of Christ's name evolves into the Church of Jesus Christ of Latter-day Saints. Joseph Smith moves to Far West, Missouri.

1836

North America: United States
Western Esotericism
Phineas Parkhurst Quimby takes up the practice of mesmerism (mesmeric sleep or hypnotism) after attending a lecture in Belfast, Maine by a traveling French physician/mesmerist, Dr. Robert Collyer.

1836

Central America and the Caribbean:
 Trinidad and Tobago
Christianity
Missionaries of the Society for the Propagation of the Gospel (Church of England) arrive in Trinidad and Tobago.

1836

South America: Argentina
Christianity
Following up on early suggestions to open missionary work in South America, the Methodist Episcopal Church launches a mission in Buenos Aires, which soon expands to other Argentine cities and then into other nearby countries. The work will evolve into the Evangelical Methodist Church of Argentina.

1836

East and Southeast Asia: Korea
Christianity
Roman Catholic missionaries from the Paris Foreign Missions Society begin to enter Korea on a clandestine basis where they discover an already existing lay-led practicing Christian community that had been started by Koreans who had discovered Roman Catholicism in China.

1836

Oceania and Antarctica
Christianity
The task of evangelizing the islands of the South Pacific proving too large for the Society of the Sacred Hearts of Jesus and Mary, Pope Gregory XVI sets Western Oceania apart and designates it the Vicariate Apostolic of Western Oceania. Jean-Baptiste François Pompallier, a member of the society, is consecrated as a bishop and named the vicar apostolic for the new missionary district.

1836

Europe: France
Christianity

Fire destroys the medieval timber roof of the Chartres cathedral. Architect J. B. Lassus leads the effort to replace it with an innovative iron roof.

1836

Europe: France
Christianity
Fr. Basil Anthony-Marie Moreau, a Roman Catholic priest of the diocese of Le Mons, founds the Congregation of Holy Cross, a new religious order. It is designed to respond to the secularization of education in France, which leaves many Catholics without a place to be educated or even to learn the catechism. Initially designed to serve the needs of the diocese, it will soon grow to become an international organization.

1836

Southwest Asia and North Africa: Palestine
Christianity, Judaism
The London Society for Promoting Christianity Amongst the Jews sends two missionaries to Jerusalem, one a physician, Albert Gerstmann, and the other a pharmacist, Melville Bergheim, who open a clinic providing free medical services. The British missionary effort among Palestinian Jews will lead to the placing of an Anglican bishop in Jerusalem.

February 17, 1836

Europe: France
Christianity
Beginning in 1831, a number of Poles immigrate to France. Three of these immigrants, Bogdan Jański, Peter Semenenko, and Hieronim Kajsiewicz, found a new Roman Catholic religious order, the Congregation of the Resurrection of Our Lord Jesus Christ (aka the Resurrectionists). The first group of seven members would take their vow in Rome on Easter Day, 1842. The name assumed by the group recalls that second beginning commemorating Christ's resurrection.

March 2, 1836

Central America and the Caribbean: Mexico
Christianity
In the midst of hostilities with Mexico, Texans declare the establishment of the independent Republic of Texas.

March 6, 1836

Central America and the Caribbean: Mexico
Western Esotericism
The Siege of the Alamo. A Mexican army under General Santa Anna overruns an abandoned Roman Catholic mission held by Texans under Col. William B. Travis. Among those who die are Freemasons Travis, James Bowie, and Davy Crockett.

April 21, 1836

Central America and the Caribbean: Mexico, Christianity
The Battle of San Jacinto. Texans under Sam Houston rout the Mexican forces of Santa Anna and finally win independence.

April 22, 1836

Central America and the Caribbean: Mexico
Christianity
Texan forces under the command of James Sylvester capture Mexican president Santa Anna. He is hiding in a marsh, dressed in the uniform of a dragoon private.

Meanwhile, Texas politicians move to separate church and state when writing the Constitution of the Republic, which includes as a provision, "Ministers of the gospel being, by their profession, dedicated to God and the care of souls, ought not to be diverted from the great duties of their functions, therefore, no minister of the gospel or priest of any denomination whatever shall be eligible to the office of the Executive of the Republic, nor to a seat of either branch of the Congress." The prohibition was carried over into the state constitutions of 1845 and 1866 after Texas joined the Union.

The constitution declares, "No preference shall be given by law to any religious denomination or mode of worship over another, but every person shall be permitted to worship God according to the dictates of his own conscience."

June 5, 1836

Oceania and Antarctica: Australia
Christianity
William Grant Broughton is enthroned as the Anglican bishop of Australia in ceremonies at St James's Church in Sydney. He is the first and only bishop to have jurisdiction over all of Australia as the diocese will soon be divided.

1837

Sub-Saharan Africa: Ethiopia
Christianity
Lutheran missionary Johann Ludwig Krapf arrives in Ethiopia under the auspices of the Anglican Church Missionary Society. He has prepared himself by learning both Ge'ez and Amharic, two Ethiopian languages, and works on translating the Bible into them.

1837

North America: United States
Judaism
The first Passover Haggadah is printed in America.

1837

North America: United States
Christianity
A spectrum of issues divides Presbyterians into more conservative Old School and more liberal New School factions. Auburn Seminary will become a center of the New School Presbyterians. They issue a statement, the Auburn Declaration, supporting the doctrinal openness of the New School position.

1837

East and Southeast Asia: China, Tibet
Buddhism
The 10th Dalai Lama, who had been in poor health all his life, dies.

1837

East and Southeast Asia: Japan
Buddhism
A four-year famine calls into question the leadership of Shogun Tokugawa Ienari. He steps aside in favor of his son Tokugawa Ieyoshi (r. 1837–1853).

1837

East and Southeast Asia: China, Japan
Christianity
Karl Gutzlaff, a missionary with the London Missionary Society residing in Macau, translates the Gospel of John into Japanese. Over the next two decades, other books of the New Testament will be translated, but as many Japanese could read Chinese and access to Japan was limited, the need for further translation was not primary.

1837

Russia, Central Asia, and the Caucasus: Russia
Christianity
Construction begins on the Epiphany Cathedral at Yelokhovo in Moscow. It will be completed in 1845. In 1938, it became the cathedral of the patriarch of Moscow following the closing of the Dorogomilovo Cathedral, and as the largest open church in Moscow, remained as such through the rest of the Soviet era.

1837

Southwest Asia and North Africa: Arabia
Islam

Epiphany Cathedral at Yelokhovo, Moscow, is the vicarial church of the Holy Patriarch of Moscow and all Rus. The present building was designed and built during 1837–1845. (Валерия Попова/iStockphoto.com)

An Algerian-born Berber tribesman, Muhammad ibn Ali al-Sanusi, who claimed a lineage from Muhammad through his daughter Fatima, founds the Sanusi Sufi order in Mecca. It subsequently became popular among the Berber and Bedouin people of North Africa.

1837–1838

Sub-Saharan Africa: Zimbabwe
Traditional Religions

The Rozwi Empire of Zimbabwe (along with other Shona states) is pushed aside by the entering Ndebele people, who have entered the region from south of the Limpopo River. They force the Rozwi to pay tribute and concentrate themselves in northern Zimbabwe.

January 10, 1837

Central America and the Caribbean: Jamaica
Christianity

The formation of the Vicariate Apostolic of Giamaica o Jamaica signals the revival of the Roman Catholic Church in Jamaica, which had been suppressed after the British takeover of the island in 1855. The vicariate would be superseded by the Diocese of Kingston (1956) and the Archdiocese of Kingston (1967). Later in the year, Pope Gregory XVI will also erect a new Vicariate Apostolic of British Guiana (Guyana).

March 24, 1837

North America: Canada
Christianity

Canada grants the recently freed slaves and all of its African Canadian citizens the right to vote.

June 20, 1837

Europe: England
Christianity

William IV dies without any legitimate heirs. He is succeeded by his niece Victoria (r. 1837–1901) who will remain on the throne for the rest of the century. She comes to the throne in the wake of the Reform Act of 1832, which had placed legislative authority in the House of Lords and executive authority in a cabinet composed of members of the House of Commons. Though kept informed of what was happening in the government, she had no direct input on matters of policy. She worked with Lord Melbourne, who served as the prime minister during the early years of her reign.

November 20, 1837

Europe: Germany
Christianity

The archbishop of Cologne comes into conflict with the ruler of Prussia, Frederick William III, over the issue of regulations concerning mixed marriages, when Roman Catholics marry Protestants. The conflict leads to the archbishop's arrest and confinement in the fortress of Minden. His arrest led to a major controversy between the government of Prussia and the Roman Catholic Church, with other German bishops coming to the archbishop's support.

1838

Sub-Saharan Africa: Nigeria
Christianity

Nigerians transported to Brazil by the Portuguese, who had absorbed Roman Catholicism during their sojourn, return to Lagos and gather each Sunday in the Popo Maro district for worship in the house of Senhor Isidore Ezechiel de Souza, a devout layman whom they know as "Padre Anthonio," who led Catholic worship until the arrival of the first priest in 1863.

1838

North America: United States
Western Esotericism

At a meeting in Houston, Freemasons in Texas form the Grand Lodge of the Republic of Texas, A.F. & A.M. Representatives of the three Texas lodges (Houston, Nacogdoches, and St. Augustine) had previously met in 1837 and projected plans for a grand lodge. Sam Houston is among the Houston delegates, who select Anson Jones as the first grand master of Masons for Texas.

1838

North America: United States
Judaism

Rebecca Gratz creates the first Hebrew Sunday school in Philadelphia.

1838

Southwest Asia and North Africa: Palestine
Judaism, Christianity

Edward Robinson, the professor of biblical literature at Union Theological Seminary, a Presbyterian school in New York City, travels to Palestine accompanied by the Protestant missionary Eli Smith in search of the location and modern name of the many places mentioned in the Bible. The result of the trip is a book, *Biblical Researches in Palestine and Adjacent Countries,* in which Robinson and Smith report on their identifications of the ancient sites. Their work opens a new era in biblical archeology and the grounding of much of the Jewish Bible and the Christian New Testament in the geography of Palestine and the adjacent countries.

1838

Oceania and Antarctica: Australia
Christianity

Clamor Schurmann, appointed by the recently formed Dresden Missionary Society, arrives in Australia and begins work at Adelaide among the local Aboriginal people. She will produce an Aboriginal dictionary, establish a school for Native children, and attempt interventions against the periodic indiscriminate killings of Aboriginal people.

May 5, 1838

South America: Guyana
Hinduism, Islam

The first indentured servants from India arrive in Guyana primarily from the states of Uttar Pradesh and Bihar and bring their Hinduism and, to a lesser extent, Islam with them. Hindus will eventually constitute more than a third of the Guyanese population. The immigrants will introduce both Hinduism and Islam to South America.

August 16, 1838

East and Southeast Asia: China
Christianity

As work expands in China, Pope Gregory XVI erects the Vicariate Apostolic of Manchuria, one of four new vicariates erected in the Chinese empire this year.

October 24, 1838

Europe: France
Christianity

Fr. Pierre Mermier, a French priest, founds the Missionaries of St. Francis de Sales (aka the Fransalians) in Annecy, France. The new religious order is inspired by the life and work of St. Francis de Sales, most noted for his writings on the spiritual life, especially his *Introduction to the Devout Life.* Mermier saw France as being in the midst of a deep spiritual crisis brought on by the antireligious attitudes fostered by the French Revolution, and hoped to lead a revival throughout the land.

November 5, 1838

Central America and the Caribbean: Guatemala
Christianity

The beginning of the end of the Captaincy of Guatemala, which united the Central American states, begins with the withdrawal of Nicaragua. As civil war erupts, Costa Rica and Nicaragua also withdraw. The union officially ends when El Salvador proclaims its independent republic in February 1841.

1839

Sub-Saharan Africa: Ethiopia
Christianity

Roman Catholic priest Justin De Jacobis, a Vincentian brother, reintroduces Roman Catholicism into Ethiopia. He works primarily in northern Ethiopia and initiates what is now the Ethiopian Catholic community.

1839

North America: United States
Christianity

Methodist Episcopal Church (MEC) minister Timothy Merritt, in Boston, begins a periodical, *A Guide to Christian Perfection,* to revive interest in Wesley's understanding of the doctrine of sanctification.

1839

North America: United States
Christianity

Evangelist Charles G. Finney reads Wesley's *Plain Account,* experiences sanctification, and goes on to become a social reformer and the most prominent evangelist in America.

1839

North America: United States
Christianity
The Book of Mormon is published and the Church of Christ (later known as the Church of Jesus Christ of Latter-day Saints) founded. Latter-day Saints begin to settle what becomes Nauvoo, Illinois.

1839

North America: United States
Christianity
Hiram Bingham and colleagues with the Congregational Church in Hawaii publish the second volume of the Bible in Hawaiian, the New Testament. They had completed the translation of the Old Testament seven years previously.

1839

East and Southeast Asia: Malaysia
Islam
After aiding the sultan of Brunei to subdue a rebel force on the island of Borneo, Sir James Brooke, an Englishman, is named raja of Sarawak (now part of East Malaysia). His descendants will continue to rule until 1946.

1839

Europe: Belgium
Christianity
Motivated by a recent stint in North America, Theodore James Ryken, a lay catechist, founds the Xaverian Brothers (aka the Congregation of St. Francis Xavier), a new Roman Catholic religious order based in Bruges. This lay order was designed to provide workers who would operate beside missionary priests, assisting and supplementing their work. It was originally founded with Native Americans in mind, but Ryken finally decides that the children of European immigrants in the United States are most in need of

help. The congregation now supports work in Belgium, England, and the United States.

1839

Europe: Belgium
Christianity
Trappist monks at St. Sixtus in Belgium began brewing Westvleteren beer to finance construction of a new monastery.

1839

Europe: United Kingdom
Christianity
Growing and largely superseding the older Agency Committee of the Society for the Mitigation and Gradual Abolition of Slavery Throughout the British Dominions, which had been an important factor in the passing of the 1833 antislavery law in the United Kingdom, the British and Foreign Anti-Slavery Society is founded by abolitionists to work against the practice of slavery beyond the British Empire. Now known as Anti-Slavery International, it is the oldest still active international human rights organization.

1839

Russia, Central Asia, and the Caucasus: Russia
Christianity
The cornerstone is laid for the Russian Orthodox Church's Cathedral of Christ the Savior in Moscow, located on the banks of the Moskva River, not far from the Kremlin. It will rise to 344 feet and becomes the tallest Orthodox church in the world.

1839

Southwest Asia and North Africa: Persia
Islam, Judaism
A pogrom targeting Jews in Mashad, Iran, leads to their forcible conversion to Shi'a Islam.

1839

Oceania and Antarctica: Vanuatu
Traditional Religions, Christianity
Several Samoan Christian teachers, supported by the London Missionary Society, arrive in Vanuatu.

They make slow headway, partly because several outbreaks of disease are blamed on the missionaries, and the indigenous religion survives well into the 20th century. The local religion is called Custom and is especially strong on the islands of Tanan and Aniwa, with a significant presence also on Santo and Vao. Almost 20 languages are spoken in the islands, and there is a similar number of variations on the indigenous religion.

March 1839

East and Southeast Asia: China
Chinese Religions
The Daoguang emperor appointed a new strict Confucian commissioner, Lin Zexu, to control the opium trade at the port of Canton.

March 20, 1839

Europe: Malta
Christianity
Dowager queen Adelaide of England lays the foundation stone for the new St. Paul's Pro-Cathedral, an Anglican church in Valletta. She had commissioned the building of the church after discovering that there was no place for Anglican worship on the island, which was British territory.

April 1839

North America: United States
Christianity
Joseph Smith Jr. leaves Missouri and relocates to Illinois, where he purchases land along the Mississippi River for a new community that will be named Nauvoo. Here a new Mormon temple will be erected.

April 19, 1839

Europe: Belgium, Luxembourg
Christianity
The Treaty of London. The nations of Europe recognize and guarantee the independence of the recently formed Belgium and establish the independent Province of Luxembourg. Both countries are heavily Roman Catholic and are thus freed from the predominantly Protestant Netherlands.

April 22, 1839

Europe: Germany
Christianity
After a year and a half of confinement, Prussian ruler Frederick William III attempts to reverse his mistake relative to relations with the Roman Catholic Church and has the archbishop of Cologne released from his confinement.

June 17, 1839

North America: United States
Christianity
Under pressure from France, Kamehameha III issues an Edict of Toleration, which allows Roman Catholics freedom to spread their faith through the Hawaiian Islands. His action had been opposed by the Protestant ministers who had previously enjoyed an exclusive opportunity to evangelize the Native Hawaiians. As a result of the edict, Bishop Etienne Rouchouze, the vicar apostolic of Oriental Oceania, moves from Chile to Honolulu and creates a permanent Catholic presence in the islands.

July 1, 1839

Southwest Asia and North Africa: Asia Minor
Islam
Mahmud II, the sultan of the Ottoman Empire, dies of tuberculosis. He is succeeded by his son Abdülmecid (r. 1839–1861).

August 23, 1839

East and Southeast Asia: China
Christianity
The British take control of Hong Kong.

September 21, 1839

East and Southeast Asia: Korea
Christianity
At Saenamteo, Korean authorities execute by beheading Laurent-Joseph-Marius Imbert, the Roman Catholic vicar apostolic of Korea, and two priests, Frs. Pierre-Philibert Maubant and Jacques-Honoré Chastan, who proved unwilling under torture to reveal the locations of the small communities of Catholic converts whom they had been quietly leading.

November 1839

Oceania and Antarctica: Vanuatu
Christianity
John Williams, a Congregationalist missionary who had pioneered Protestant Christianity in the South Seas for more than two decades, ventures along with fellow missionary James Harris to the island of Erromango in the New Hebrides (now Vanuatu) where they are killed and eaten by cannibals.

November 3, 1839

East and Southeast Asia: China
Chinese Religions
Lin Zexu, a Qing official, initiates the first Opium War by ordering the dumping of 3 million pounds of Western-owned opium into the sea. Forces of Britain engage those of the Qing regime in the Guangzhou region of southern China over the next three years.

November 9, 1839

Oceania and Antarctica: Australia
Christianity
Anglicans lay the cornerstone for what becomes St. James Old Cathedral, the oldest church building in Melbourne. In 1848, St. James becomes the cathedral church for the first Anglican bishop of Melbourne.

December 3, 1839

Europe: Italy
Christianity
Following a broad consultation with the church's cardinals, Pope Gregory XVI issues *In Supremo Apostolatus,* a papal bull in which he denounces the slave trade and the continuance of the institution of slavery. The bull is largely ignored by Roman Catholics in Maryland and the American South. They accepted his opposition to the slave trade (already outlawed by Congress), but could not accept his condemnation of slavery itself as many owned slaves and saw it as necessary for their economic survival.

1840

Sub-Saharan Africa: Malawi
Christianity
David Livingstone settles in what today is Malawi as a missionary with the London Missionary Society.

1840

North America: United States
Christianity
Saxon Germans in the Mississippi Valley organize the German Evangelical Church Society of the West, later the Evangelical Synod.

1840

North America: United States
Christianity
Boston minister Joshua V. Himes established a periodical, *Signs of the Times,* in which to discuss and publicize Baptist preacher William Miller's views that the return of Jesus Christ was imminent.

1840

North America: United States
Judaism
The first ordained rabbi, Abraham Rice, comes to the United States.

1840

North America: United States
Judaism
The first organized movement by American Jewry to protest false accusations of blood libel takes place in Damascus, Syria.

1840

North America: United States
Christianity
The Texas Congress passes a law that prohibits the immigration of free people of color into the republic and requires all free blacks either to remove themselves from Texas or face being sold into slavery. Any exceptions must be specifically exempted by an act of Congress.

1840

North America: United States
Christianity
Following his tour of Texas by horseback, Fr. John Timon is named Prefect Apostolic of Texas with power to administer confirmation. Roman Catholicism is officially reinaugurated in Texas.

DAVID LIVINGSTONE (1813–1873)

David Livingstone, a Scottish missionary and explorer, is known for his travels deep into the interior of the African continent. He was the first European to see Victoria Falls and searched for many years for the source of the Nile.

Reading about missionaries in China inspired the young Livingstone to travel to Asia as a medical missionary. After earning his medical degree in 1840, he planned to head east, but his departure was delayed by the Opium War. Livingstone attended a lecture by Dr. Robert Moffat, who headed a missionary station in Africa. Moffat's description of the vast expanses of the African continent as yet unpenetrated by any European piqued Livingstone's interest, and he approached the missionary to offer his services. By July 1841, Livingstone found himself at Moffat's headquarters about 500 miles north of Cape Town in present-day South Africa.

Livingstone sequestered himself in a village to learn the languages and customs of the Africans. He then turned his attention to territories further north, looking for locations to set up new missions. He journeyed deep into the African interior, preaching and providing medical care as he went.

Livingstone soon came into contact with the African slave trade for the first time. Though the 1833 Act of Abolition in Britain had banned such commerce in West Africa, it persisted farther east on the continent. Livingstone decided that the slave trade was the result of paltry economic opportunities and that it could be halted by opening up trading routes. He turned his attention to learning more about Africa's rivers.

At the behest of the Royal Geographical Society, Livingstone set out to explore the great African watersheds looking for the source of the Nile River. Livingstone was hampered by the suspicions of the Africans he encountered who believed that he was a slave trader. Disease was also a constant problem. His long absence spurred rumors of his possible demise. Such fears prompted the *New York Herald* to send a journalist, Henry Morton Stanley, in search of Livingstone. In a now famous incident, Stanley, on finding Livingstone alive but ailing at his base camp in Ujiji, quipped, "Dr. Livingstone, I presume?"

Heading out again with his African companions, Livingstone's strength soon failed him, and the other members of the expedition were soon forced to carry him in a litter. The expedition stopped in the village of a friendly chief, where a hut was built for him. On May 1, 1873, Livingstone was found dead in his hut, kneeling by his bedside, apparently in prayer. His longtime African comrades buried his heart under a tree and then carried his body to the coast for the return trip to England. Livingstone was buried at Westminster Abbey on a day of national mourning.

ABC-CLIO

1840

East and Southeast Asia: China, Tibet
Buddhism

Khedrup Gyatso is recognized as the 11th Dalai Lama. He is enthroned at the Potala Palace in Lhasa two years later. Meanwhile, the seventh Panchen Lama, Palden Tenpai Nyima, continues as the most powerful person in Tibet.

1840

Europe: France
Christianity

The rather limited work of the Congregation of the Holy Cross, operating in the Diocese of Le Mans, is radically altered by a request from Algeria to send representatives of the congregation to North Africa with the goal of establishing schools, including a seminary for the training of priests. Founder Fr. Basil Anthony-Marie Moreau reorganizes the congregation, and the first members take formal vows of the religious life. He also organizes a group of women who had become associated with the work to form the Marianites of Holy Cross.

1840

Europe: United Kingdom
Christianity

John Nelton Darby and Benjamin Wills Newton, the principal persons among the Brethren and Plymouth, part company over doctrinal differences. Those who follow Darby become the several sects of the Exclusive Brethren and those who follow Newton become the Open or Christian brethren.

1840

Oceania and Antarctica: New Zealand
Traditional Religions, Christianity

Governor William Hobson (1793–1842) signed the Treaty of Waitangi with Maori chiefs, annexing New Zealand as a British colony and sparking new efforts at religious colonization. Maori responded to the Christian influence by developing indigenous Christian sects that helped maintain their Maori identity. The basic theology of the Maori-Christian syncretism identifies the Hebrew Jehovah with Io, a figure in Polynesian myth. It is debatable whether Io's traditional role is that of a supreme being and thus comparable to the Christian God, but that is clearly the case in syncretistic Maori religious movements. This correlation then allows the genealogies of both traditions to be aligned, providing Maori with an ethnic identity that can be placed within Jewish, Christian, Mormon, and even Rastafarian belief systems. Although Maori have undoubtedly participated in this construction, the origin of these concepts can also be attributed to Samuel Marsden. An emphasis on charismatic prophets and imminent millenarianism is also a common feature of these movements.

1840–1855

Oceania and Antarctica: New Caledonia
Traditional Religions, Christianity

Two Samoan missionaries, supported by the London Missionary Society, arrive in New Caledonia (now the country of Kanaky) in 1841. They are joined by European missionaries in 1853, about the same time that the French took possession of the area. During this time period the local inhabitants are raided by slavers who capture slaves to work in plantations in Fiji and Queensland.

February 6, 1840

Oceania and Antarctica: New Zealand
Traditional Religions, Christianity

After a decade of negotiations and disagreements about the rights of European settlers and New Zealand natives, a coalition of Maori chiefs and British signatories sign the Treaty of Waitangi. The history of the document and the intentions of all signatories are somewhat unclear, and the affiliations of different parties to the transaction are surprising. Catholic leaders, both Maori and European, objected to the treaty, while Protestant leaders were more likely to support it. The effect of the document was to trade Maori sovereignty for protection by the British crown. The treaty has been understood to supersede the Declaration of Independence of 1835, and it is now treated as the founding document of the nation of New Zealand. Over the next two decades, the New Zealand parliament struggle, to implement a constitution.

Maori chiefs recognize British sovereignty by signing the Treaty of Waitangi on May 21, 1840. With the signing of the treaty, New Zealand was annexed as a British colony. (Mary Evans Picture Library/The Image Works)

March 17, 1840

Europe: Ireland
Christianity

The foundation-stone is laid for the new Roman Catholic cathedral in Armagh. It replaces the medieval cathedral that had been taken over by the Church of Ireland. St. Patrick's will take some six decades to complete.

April 22, 1840

North America: United States
Christianity

The Roman Catholic work in California, long administered from Mexico City, is separated and placed in a new Diocese of the Two Californias, which Pope Pius XI erects. This diocese will later become the diocese of Monterey, which is the capital of the Two Californias.

May 21, 1840

South America: Chile
Christianity

Pope Gregory XVI elevates the diocese of Santiago de Chile as the new Archdiocese of Santiago de Chile. He then designates the new dioceses of La Serena and of San Carlos de Ancud, which become suffragan dioceses.

June 7, 1840

Europe: Germany
Christianity

Frederick William III dies. He is succeeded by his eldest son, Frederick William IV (r. 1840–1861).

June 8, 1840

Europe: United Kingdom
Christianity

Pope Gregory XVI consecrates Nicolas Wiseman, a British Roman Catholic priest, as bishop, several weeks after naming him the vicar apostolic to England.

July 9, 1840

North America: United States
Christianity

Roman Catholic missionaries in Hawaii break ground for the first permanent church on what is the feast day of Mary as Our Lady of Peace, the patron saint of the Congregation of the Sacred Hearts of Jesus and Mary, of which the missionaries are members. During the service, some 280 Native Hawaiian converts are baptized and confirmed.

August 28, 1840

East and Southeast Asia: Mongolia
Christianity

Pope Gregory XVI erects the Vicariate Apostolic of Mongolia.

November 1840

Europe: United Kingdom
Christianity

David Livingstone completes his studies, is licensed as a physician, and moves from Glasgow to London where he is ordained as a missionary by the London Missionary Society. The next month he sails for South Africa.

1841

Sub-Saharan Africa: South Africa
Christianity

The Glasgow Missionary Society, a Scottish Presbyterian sending agency, founds Lovedale High School in the Cape Colony, South Africa, and places missionary William Govan in charge. Govan builds the school as a integrated institution offering the best education to potential college students who did manual labor to assist in supporting the school. He hoped to produce a Christian academic elite (both black and white) to lead the nation.

1841

North America: United States
Unbelief

Having left the Unitarian Church, former minister George Ripley forms a communal experiment based on Charles Fourier's Utopian ideals. Among the founding members is writer Nathaniel Hawthorne.

1841

North America: United States
Hinduism

Yale University establishes a chair in Sanskrit and Indology.

1841

North America: United States
Judaism

David Levy Yulee of Florida is elected to the United States Senate, the first Jew in Congress.

1841

North America: United States
Christianity

Pope Gregory XVI elevates the Prefecture Apostolic of Texas into a Vicariate Apostolic. Rt. Rev. Jean-Marie Odin, previously vice prefect apostolic, was consecrated Bishop of Claudiopolis and made Vicar Apostolic.

1841

Central America and the Caribbean: Jamaica
Christianity

Jamaican Methodists erect a large new church in Kingston, now known as Coke Memorial Church, in honor of Thomas Coke who originally organized the movement on the island in the previous century.

1841

Central America and the Caribbean: Bahama Islands
Christianity

Construction on a new Christ Church, the main Anglican church in Nassau, is completed. The church houses the first congregation gathered in the Bahamas, and this new building is the fifth the congregation has inhabited. It is also the cathedral church for the Anglican Diocese of the Bahamas and the Turks and Caicos Islands.

1841

South America: Paraguay
Unbelief

After a brief transition following the death of his uncle José Gaspar Rodríguez de Francia, who had ruled Paraguay for more than three decades, Carlos Antonio López (r. 1841–1862) steps into the leadership of Paraguay. He will build on the utopian society envisioned by his uncle but modernize the country, open it to relationships with neighboring states, and introduce its first constitution.

1841

East and Southeast Asia: Malaysia, Brunei
Islam

In return for the help he gave the sultan of Brunei in putting down several challenges to his rule, James Brooke, a British adventurer, receives the governorship of Sarawak. He emerges as the raja of the territory.

1841

Europe: France
Christianity

Francis Mary Paul Libermann, a Jewish convert to Roman Catholicism, founds the Congregation of the Sacred Heart for the purpose of initiating missionary activity among the recently freed slaves in Réunion, Haiti, and Mauritius. It will later merge into the Congregation of the Holy Ghost.

1841

Europe: Germany
Unbelief

German philosopher and anthropologist Ludwig Feuerbach publishes his magnum opus *The Essence of Christianity* in which he argues that God is in essence the outward projection of a human's inward nature. He concludes that the false essence of religion is the idea that God has a separate existence apart from the believer.

January 20, 1841

East and Southeast Asia: China
Christianity

By the Convention of Chuenpi, the Chinese cede the island of Hong Kong, already in British hands, to the United Kingdom as the Opium War comes to a conclusion. With the arrival of the British, Anglican worship is introduced to the island from Macau, and initial hegemony is assigned to the new Diocese of Victoria, the original name of the colony on Hong Kong Island.

March 1841

Southwest Asia and North Africa: Persia, Afghanistan
Islam

Hasan Ali Shah, the governor of Kerman Province in Persia and the 46th imam of the Nizari Ismaili Muslim community, is driven out of Kerman and flees to Kandahar, Afghanistan. He aligns with the British but is unable to reclaim his position within Persia.

October 17, 1841

Oceania and Antarctica: New Zealand
Christianity

Anglican priest George Augustus Selwyn is appointed the first Anglican bishop of New Zealand, and before leaving for his post, he is consecrated in ceremonies at Lambeth Palace. He sails for New Zealand on December 26.

1842

Central America and the Caribbean: El Salvador
Christianity

The Roman Catholic Diocese of San Salvador is erected. It becomes an archdiocese in 1913.

1842

East and Southeast Asia: Japan
Shinto

Amid a general consensus that Japan faced an array of problems, the shogun Tokugawa Ieyoshi introduces a set of reforms that are carried out by his chief councilor Mizuno Tadakuni. The Tenpo Reforms had as their major theme a return to frugality, simplicity, and discipline and begin with a ban on most forms of entertainment and displays of wealth. The reforms include the introduction of a new annual calendar under which families are required to register themselves at their nearby Shinto shrine twice annually on the 16th day of the first and seventh months. A Shinto festival, meeting, or pilgrimage was also scheduled once each month on the new calendar.

1842

Europe: Germany
Christianity

The discovery of the original plans for the façade of Cologne Cathedral provides an opportunity for Prussian ruler Frederick William IV, a Protestant, to improve his strained relations with his Roman Catholic subjects, relations strongly marred by his arrest of the archbishop of Cologne. He orders the completion of the cathedral and makes a substantial contribution out of state funds to that end. Two years later he visits the cathedral and becomes the first king of Prussia to enter a Roman Catholic building.

1842

Oceania and Antarctica: French Polynesia
Christianity

The French take control of Tahiti. The English-speaking Protestant missionaries leave and are replaced with Roman Catholics and French-speaking Protestants.

1842–1844

Europe: France
Christianity

The group of women that has grown around Jeanne Jugun moves into a former convent that had been vacated during the French Revolution. The women slowly assume the structure of an ordered religious community and call themselves the Servants of the Poor. They select Jugun as their superior, and she leads them to take initial vows of obedience. In 1844 the group changes their name to Sisters of the Poor, by which they have been known ever since, and adopt a program aimed at assisting the poor and elderly.

January 1842

Sub-Saharan Africa: Sierra Leone
Christianity

Thirty-five African survivors of the *Amistad* incident arrive in Sierra Leone. They are accompanied by representatives of the American Missionary Association. The Congregationalist missionaries establish an outpost from which they spread Protestant Christianity and minister to the needs, educational and otherwise, of the local people. The *Amistad,* a Spanish slave ship, had been captured by the U.S. Navy and its cargo of Africans was taken to Connecticut where they became involved in a two-year ordeal before the courts. Eventually their case reached the Supreme Court where they were finally freed. During this time, they were introduced to Christianity, to which some converted.

January 1842

North America: United States
Christianity

Bishop Etienne Rouchouze, the Roman Catholic vicar apostolic of Oriental Oceania, sails from Honolulu on a trip to Paris to recruit more missionaries for the Sandwich Islands (Hawaii). His ship is lost at sea and he is never seen again.

July 12, 1842

North America: United States
Christianity

Joseph Smith Jr., the founder of the Church of Jesus Christ of Latter-day Saints, announces two new revelations he has received to the church's leadership. The first concerns the practice of baptizing the dead and the second initiates the practice of polygamy. The latter doctrine is not shared with the general membership, but divides the leadership and, as Smith begins to act on the revelation, leads to rumors and accusations of immoral behavior on Smith's part. It will ultimately lead to Smith's assassination.

August 29, 1842

East and Southeast Asia: China
Christianity

China is forced to sign the Treaty of Nanking as the Opium War ends. The treaty opens five ports—Canton, Amoy, Foochowfoo (aka Fuzhou), Ningpo, and Shanghai–through which Western business, culture, and religion begin to flow into the country. The treaty confirms Britain's hegemony over Hong Kong in perpetuity, and the following year it becomes a crown colony. The treaty proves the beginning of a new era in Protestant missions.

1843

Sub-Saharan Africa: Ethiopia
Christianity

Johann Ludwig Krapf, a Lutheran missionary under the sponsorship of the Anglican Church Missionary Society, is expelled with all the Western missionaries from Ethiopia. With his fellow missionary Carl Wilhelm Isenberg, he authors a memoir of his work and then moves on to Kenya.

1843

North America: United States
Christianity
The Wesleyan Methodist Church is founded by advocates of abolitionism who were forced out of the MEC.

1843

North America: United States
Christianity
Joseph Smith Jr. receives secret revelations relating to polygamy.

1843

Central America and the Caribbean: Dominican Republic
Christianity
Forces opposed to the Haitian control of the eastern half of Hispaniola revolt, overthrow Jean-Pierre Boyer, and reestablish an independent Santo Domingo.

1843

East and Southeast Asia: China
Christianity
Anglican minister William Jones Boone moves to Amoy and shortly thereafter is appointed the missionary bishop of Shanghai.

1843

Europe: France
Christianity
Roman Catholic bishop Forbin-Janson of Nancy, a friend of the wealthy Catholic lay leader Pauline Jaricot, who had founded the Society for the Propagation of the Faith and had recently returned from two years in North America, develops a vision of the role of the children of Christian countries joining in the effort to assist the children in the lands where the church was directing its missional focus. His idea leads to the founding of the Holy Childhood Association, through which Bishop Forbin-Janson appeals to the children of France to help the children in the mission field, especially in America and China. The association would grow to become one of the four large pontifical missionary societies serving the Roman Catholic Church globally.

1843

Europe: France
Unbelief
Karl Marx publishes *On the Jewish Question* in which he argues that Judaism and Christianity represent stages in human development that must be surpassed if humanity is to gain political emancipation.

1843–1847

Europe: France
Christianity
Sister Mary of St. Peter, a Carmelite nun residing in Tours, experiences revelations from Jesus of Nazareth on the development of a new devotion to his Holy Face, which appears on a piece of cloth kept in the Vatican, believed by many to be Veronica's Veil, a miraculous picture that appears when she wipes the sweat from Jesus's face as he carries the cross to Golgotha. The devotion is to offset the effects of the many modern blasphemies and profanities.

April 5, 1843

East and Southeast Asia: China
Christianity
Queen Victoria proclaims Hong Kong to be a British crown colony.

May 23, 1843

Europe: Scotland
Christianity
Presbyterian minister Thomas Chambers leads a major schism in the Church of Scotland that sees more than 400 clergy withdraw and form the Free Church of Scotland. They select Chambers as their first moderator.

August 15, 1843

North America: United States
Christianity
Roman Catholics in Hawaii complete construction and dedicate the Cathedral of Our Lady of Peace to serve what was then the Vicariate Apostolic of the Hawaiian Islands. Now serving the Diocese of Honolulu, it is the oldest cathedral in continuous use in the United States.

September 3, 1843

Europe: Greece
Christianity
The Greek army, with significant public support, challenges the autocratic rule of the Roman Catholic king Otto. They demand a constitution and the removal of the many Bavarians (also Roman Catholics) that had come into the government. The revolution succeeds, and a constitution is quickly written and proclaimed as law the next year. Among its provisions are that Otto's successors on the throne must be of the Orthodox faith.

November 28, 1843

North America: United States
Christianity
Pope Benedict XVI erects four new American dioceses—Chicago, Milwaukee, Hartford, and Little Rock.

ca. 1844

Europe: Germany
Christianity
The career of Lutheran pastor Johann Christoph Blumhardt is upset by his becoming known as a healer. He resigns from the Lutheran Church, joins the Reformed Church, and moves to Bad Boll, where he purchases an abandoned resort hotel. He transforms the hotel into a healing retreat center where people come for rest, meditation, study, and pastoral counseling. He would continue to operate his healing center for the rest of his life.

1844

North America: United States
Christianity

The first issue of *The Nauvoo Expositor* claims polygamy is being practiced in Nauvoo and claims that Joseph Smith is teaching that there is more than one God. Latter-day Saint leaders order *The Nauvoo Expositor* press destroyed, and subsequently deny that polygamy is being practiced.

1844

North America: United States
Christianity
Asa Mahan, a colleague of evangelist/professor Charles G. Finney at Oberlin, publishes his holiness study, *Scriptural Doctrine of Christian Perfection.*

1844

North America: United States
Christianity
When March 21 passed without Christ appearing, Adventist leaders offer several alternate dates.

1844

North America: United States
Christianity
Adventists in Washington, New Hampshire, begin keeping the Sabbath (Saturday) as their main day of worship.

1844

North America: United States
Christianity
Samuel S. Snow suggests that Christ will return on October 22, 1844. The failure of Christ to return on that date becomes known as the Great Disappointment.

1844

North America: United States
Judaism
Lewis Charles Levin becomes the first Jew elected to the U.S. House of Representatives.

1844

Central America and the Caribbean: Dominican Republic
Christianity
The Dominican Republic attains independence from Spain.

1844

East and Southeast Asia: Japan
Christianity

French Roman Catholics attempt to introduce Christianity back into Japan through the Ryūkyū Kingdom (i.e., Okinawa), at the time a vassal of Japan. Fr. Théodore-Augustin Forcade of the Paris Foreign Missions Society takes up residence in Tomari, though he is confined to the Buddhist Temple of Amiku. He is able to make use of his time by learning Japanese from the temple monks. Pope Gregory XVI will later name Forcade Bishop of Samos and Vicar Apostolic of Japan.

1844

East and Southeast Asia: Vietnam
Christianity

Bishop Dominique Lefevre, a Catholic missionary and French citizen, engaged in a plot with other priests to overthrow Thieu Tri, the emperor of Cochin China (now known as Vietnam). Lefevre is imprisoned and condemned to death.

1844

Europe: France
Unbelief

Karl Marx, in his *Economic and Philosophic Manuscripts* of 1844, argues that religion should be abolished in order to liberate humanity, which would no longer accept the consolation of the "opiate of the people."

1844

Oceania and Antarctica: Micronesia
Christianity

Pope Gregory XVI takes territory previously assigned to the Vicariate Apostolic of Western Oceania and creates two new vicariates apostolic, one for Micronesia and one for Melanesia.

1844

Oceania and Antarctica: Polynesia
Traditional Religions, Christianity

Both the Church of Jesus Christ of Latter-day Saints (the Mormons) and the Reorganized Church of Jesus

Karl Marx (1818–1883) was an important figure in 19th-century Europe, but his status as the founder of modern communism has placed him among the most influential people in the history of the modern world. (Library of Congress)

Christ of Latter-day Saints (now known as the Christian Community) establish missions in the islands. The former arrive first in 1844 and begin a long history of work in the area, as they believe that the Polynesians play a special role in their scheme of salvation. The work begun by Elder Addison Pratt is considered the first Mormon mission to a non-English-speaking area of the world.

1844–1845

North America: United States
Christianity

Now the largest church in America, the Methodist Episcopal Church splits into two jurisdictions over the slavery issue: the Methodist Episcopal Church and the Methodist Episcopal Church, South (MEC,S). As a result, the Roman Catholic Church becomes the largest church in America.

KARL MARX (1818–1883)

Born in Prussia in 1818, Karl Marx was a social philosopher credited with founding international communism. Marx was educated at universities in Bonn, Berlin, and Jena. In the early 1840s, he edited the radical newspaper *Rheinische Zeitung,* contributing controversial articles that criticized current social conditions. When the paper was censored, Marx moved to Paris (where he encountered and began collaborating with Friedrich Engels), and then Brussels. Eventually banished from Belgium because of the intensification of revolutionary thinking and his alliance with unpopular political movements and growing social struggles, Marx finally settled permanently in London in 1849.

Marx believed that the material base of economics lay in the nature of objects and the value of objects. He described objects as having value because human labor was used to create or manufacture them. Therefore, via this "labor theory of value," workers became more important than the capitalists who exploited their labor. He objected to capitalism's exploitation of workers and the ways in which mass production prevents them from taking pride and satisfaction in their work. He imagined instead a working society in which everyone contributes according to their talents and means and receives according to their needs.

Marx was also convinced that philosophy was not simply abstract thought and idealism, but should be viewed from an economic perspective and practiced to make changes in society. One of his favorite sayings was "Everything should be doubted." While not especially influential during his lifetime, Marx is now recognized as one of the most important thinkers ever. His views are now known as Marxism or scientific socialism. Marxist ideas are often reflected in contemporary criticism of consumer culture. Marx died in London, England on March 14, 1883.

PATRICIA H. HINCHEY

March 13, 1844

South America: Paraguay
Christianity
With the approval of President Carlos Antonio Lopez, Paraguay approve its first constitution. It provides sanctions for Lopez's dictatorial powers and offers no mention of human rights, civil rights, or liberties. However, soon after the constitution is set in place, Lopez releases all of the country's political prisoners and formally abolishes slavery and torture.

June 6, 1844

United Kingdom
George Williams, a young executive involved in the drapery trade, concerned about the lack of moral and uplifting activities for single young men involved in business in Britain, founds the first Young Men's Christian Association. It will quickly grow into a national and international enterprise and spawn a like organization for women.

June 27, 1844

North America: United States
Christianity
A mob enters the Carthage jail where four Latter-day Saints leaders are being held and kill Joseph Smith and his brother Hyrum. Also confined with him, Willard Richards escapes unscathed, while future church president John Taylor receives several bullets but survives.

Following Smith's death, three claimants arise for the office of the presidency of the Church of Jesus Christ of Latter-day Saints—Sidney Rigdon, Brigham Young, and James Strang. Each receives some support, though most flows to Brigham Young. Rigdon and Strang form small splinter groups.

Prior to his death, Joseph Smith considers a plan to move to Texas, which is at the time outside the borders of the United States. To that end he corresponds with Sam Houston, seeking the southern and western portions of Texas as a future Latter-day Saint nation. Lucien Woodworth in Austin, as Smith's representative to pursue the idea with Houston, drops negotiations following Smith's death.

October 22, 1844

North America: United States
Christianity
A wave of expectation of the end of the world that has swept across America over the last decade initially climaxed during the period between March 21, 1843, and March 21, 1844, during which time Baptist preacher William Miller predicted Christ would return. Shortly after the failure of the prediction, a new date, October 22, 1944, is proposed. The failure of the second date, known as the Great Disappointment among Adventists, would ultimately lead to the division of the movement into three major segments that would become known as the Advent Christian Church, the Church of God (Seventh-day), and the Seventh Day Adventists.

1845

North America: United States
Christianity
Adventists meet in New York. Those attending the Albany Conference form the loosely associated Evangelical Adventists.

1845

North America: United States
Christianity
Hiram Edson publishes the view that the event highlighted by the prophecy of Daniel 8, the cleansing of the sanctuary, did not refer to Christ's return but to a heavenly event presaging his return.

1845

North America: United States
Judaism
Isaac Leeser publishes his translation of the Pentateuch from Hebrew into English.

1845

North America: United States
Hinduism
Ralph Waldo Emerson reads the Bhagavad Gita and Henry Colebrooke's *Essays on the Vedas.*

1845

Central America and the Caribbean: Bahamas
Christianity
The first Roman Catholic priest to visit the Bahamas, a Father Duquesney, stays in Nassau six weeks and leads worship in private homes.

1845

Central America and the Caribbean:
    Trinidad and Tobago
Hinduism
The first indentured servants from India arrive in Trinidad and Tobago primarily from the states of Uttar Pradesh and Bihar and bring their Hinduism with them. A generation later, Hindus will constitute more than 20 percent of the Trinidadi population.

1845

South Asia: India
Christianity
The Vatican accepts the offer of the Missionaries of St. Francis de Sales to supply missionaries for India. Their work will lead to the formation of the Roman Catholic dioceses of Nagpur and Visakhapatnam, to which the society continues to offer leadership to the present.

1845

Europe: Italy
Christianity
Don John Bosco, an Italian Roman Catholic priest, founds a night school for boys in Valdocco, just outside Turin. He will subsequently open additional schools.

The workers in these schools will eventually come together as a new religious order, the Society of St. Francis de Sales, popularly known as the Salesians.

The society's formal recognition by Pope Pius IX in 1873 would become the catalyst for its international expansion, initially to France and Argentina, quickly followed by Austria, Britain, Spain, and additional countries in South America. Today it has over 2,000 centers from which it conducts its work.

1845

Oceania and Antarctica: New Zealand
Christianity

Jean Baptiste Pompallier, the first Roman Catholic bishop in New Zealand, commissions the building of the Cathedral of St. Patrick and St. Joseph in Auckland. Its construction will follow in stages through the rest of the century.

1845–1852

Europe: Ireland
Christianity

The Great Famine (aka the Irish Potato Famine), a period of mass starvation, disease, and emigration, becomes a watershed event in Irish history. Caused by a disease that attacked the potato crop upon which the majority of the population were dependent, the famine led to a million deaths while another million migrated primarily to the United States. Long term, the event soured relations between primarily Roman Catholic Ireland and predominantly Anglican England, and changed the makeup of the Catholic Church in the United States, just in the process of becoming the largest religious body in the new nation, where the Irish came to dominate the hierarchy.

In Ireland, the famine motivated the desire for home rule and independence from England. Through the last half of the 19th century, Irish nationalism gained strength and remained the dominating factor in Irish-British relations through the 20th century. Integral to the issue is the struggle between Protestants and Roman Catholics for control of Ireland's religious life.

March 1, 1845

North America: United States
Christianity

The Republic of Texas is annexed by the United States.

April 17, 1845

East and Southeast Asia: Korea
Christianity

Kim Taegon (aka Angrew Taegon) becomes the first native Korean to be ordained as a Roman Catholic priest. He is martyred a year later, and is subsequently canonized.

May 8–12, 1845

North America: United States
Christianity

For a decade, differences between northern and southern Baptists, especially over the issue of slavery, had prompted heated debates at the gatherings of the Triennial Convention, the major national gathering of Baptists. They had argued that a disproportionate share of mission funds was being spent in the South and disagreed over the Triennial conventions' policy of not supporting missionaries who happened to be slave owners. Southern Baptists respond to a call from Virginia Baptists for Baptists from across the South to meet at Augusta, Georgia, in early May 1845 for the purpose of consulting "on the best means of promoting the Foreign Mission cause, and other interests of the Baptist denomination in the South." Delegates gather at First Baptist Church, Augusta, Georgia, and form the Southern Baptist Convention.

July 15–28, 1845

Europe: Germany
Judaism

A conference of Reform Jewish rabbis held at Frankfurt am Main rejects the idea of a "return to Zion" by the Jewish people. They subsequently delete all prayers for a return to Zion and a restoration of a Jewish state from the Sabbath ritual.

July 25, 1845

Central America and the Caribbean: Antigua
Christianity

The Cathedral of St. John the Divine, the cathedral church of the Anglican Diocese of North Eastern Caribbean and Aruba, is completed and dedicated. Located on a hill overlooking St. John's, Antigua, and Barbuda, the immediate occasion dictating its construction is the 1842 erection of the former Diocese of Antigua.

October 9, 1845

Europe: United Kingdom
Christianity

Anglican priest John Henry Newman, a leading advocate of the Oxford movement, finds inadequacies with the branch theory of the church, the idea that the one church of Jesus Christ exists in three branches, of which Anglicanism is one. His change of opinion leads him to convert to Roman Catholicism, and he is formally received into the Catholic Church. Before the year is out, he is reordained as a Catholic priest. Some critics of the Oxford movement view his conversion as proof that the Oxford movement is seeking to "Romanize" the Church of England.

November 10, 1845

North America: United States
Christianity

In Monroe, Michigan, Theresa Maxis Duchemin, a founding member of the Oblates of Providence, the first congregation of women religious of color in the world, and Fr. Louis Florent Gillet, a Roman Catholic priest of the Redemptorist Order, found the Congregation of the Sisters, Servants of the Immaculate Heart of Mary. The sisters are assigned the immediate task of bringing the Catholic faith to French Canadian immigrants who had come to reside on the shores of the Raisin River in Michigan.

December 25, 1845

Europe: France
Christianity

Fr. Emmanuel d'Alzon, a Roman Catholic priest, founds the Augustinians of the Assumption (aka the Assumptionists), a new religious order based at Nîmes in southern France. The Assumptionists will become the center of a group of closely related orders including the Oblates of the Assumption, which Fr. d'Alzon and Marie Correnson found in May 1865. Correnson, later known as Mother Emmanuel-Marie de la Compassion, will become the Oblates' first superior general. The energetic founders developed a broad range of programs from foreign missions to educational endeavors that led to the diversification and global spread of the new order.

1846

North America: United States
Hinduism

Henry David Thoreau's *A Week on the Concord and Merrimack Rivers* is heavily influenced by his having read Emerson's copy of the Bhagavad Gita.

1846

East and Southeast Asia: Brunei
Islam

The British attack Brunei and force Sultan Saifuddin II to sign a treaty that opens trade and later cedes territory to neighboring Sarawak.

1846

Europe: Belgium
Christianity

In Brussels, the Sisters of Charity, a Roman Catholic religious order, open the tavern La Fleur en Papier, which in the 1920s will become a meeting place for painters.

1846

Europe: United Kingdom
Christianity

At a conference held in London, some 800 people from 52 Protestant churches in eight countries launch the modern ecumenical movement by forming the Evangelical Alliance.

1846

Europe: United Kingdom
Unbelief

The prominent British literary figure Mary Anne Evans (better known by her pen name George Eliot) begins her literary career by translating into English David Strauss's *Life of Jesus,* which had treated the biblical miracle stories as mythological. While continuing to maintain a façade of Christianity, regularly attending church over the years, she further manifested her liberal beliefs by translating Ludwig Feuerbach's *The Essence of Christianity* (1854). As the opportunity presented itself, she met and conversed with such liberal thinkers as Robert Owen, Herbert Spencer, Harriet Martineau, and Ralph Waldo Emerson.

George Eliot was the *nom de plume* of Mary Ann (or Marian) Evans, one of the leading British novelists of the 19th century. Eliot's method of analyzing her characters' inner and outer lives gives her work its particularly modern quality. (Library of Congress)

1846

Oceania and Antarctica: New Zealand
Traditional Religions, Christianity

The New Zealand Parliament passes the New Zealand Constitution Act, but the act is never fully implemented. To this day the constitution is still not codified, and instead a collection of documents outline the government and the rights and duties of citizens. The government generally respects freedom of religion, but New Zealand does not have a specific document guaranteeing religious freedom until the Bill of Rights Act in 1990.

1846–1848

North America: United States
Christianity

The Mexican-American War. The American annexation of Texas leads to armed conflict with and the subsequent invasion of Mexico. Major fighting ends after a year and a half when an American army occupies Mexico City.

The war officially ends with the signing of the Treaty of Guadalupe Hidalgo in which Mexico agrees to transfer control of California, Arizona, New Mexico, Nevada, and Utah to the United States. Mexico also relinquishes its claim to Texas in exchange for $20 million, and the Rio Grande is set as the Mexican-American boundary. American armed forces arrive in El Paso. El Paso begins to grow in 1849 as people initially headed for the California gold fields stop in the area and go no further.

However, the war proves one of the most divisive in U.S. history with antislavery exponents forming part of the intense opposition. Northern Baptists generally support the war effort, but oppose any annexation of Mexican territory.

February 1846

South Asia: India
Islam

After fleeing Persia, Hasan Ali Shah, the 46th imam of the Nizari Ismaili Muslim community, settles in Bombay (Mumbai). The Persian government demands his extradition, but the British refuse. They do, however, force his temporary relocation to Calcutta.

February 10, 1846

South Asia: India
Sikhism

The Battle of Sobraon. British forces under General Sir Hugh Gough decisively defeat the Punjabi Sikh forces under Tej Singh.

March 6, 1846

South Asia: India
Sikhism

The Treaty of Lahore marks the end of the First Anglo-Sikh War. The British subsequently take possession of the Punjab. One item in the treaty demands that the Sikh ruler surrender the "Ko-he-noor" diamond to the British. It would then be placed in the crown for the coronation of Queen Victoria.

June 1, 1846

Europe: Italy
Christianity, Judaism

ANGLO-SIKH WARS

Two wars were fought between 1845 and 1849 by the British and the Sikhs in India. The British victories in both wars ended any serious threat to British hegemony in India. With no serious rival on the subcontinent, the British were able to consolidate India under their total control.

The Sikhs were one of the most martial groups in the country. During the first part of the 19th century, they conquered most of northwestern India. The founder of the empire was Raja Ranjit Singh. Singh witnessed the power of the disciplined British regiments and was greatly impressed. He organized his army on the lines of the European example and armed them with European weapons. The Sikh society was organized along military lines, and all energies were devoted to expansion and conquest. Singh's successes in war led to great devotion by his army to him. By the time of his death in 1839, the Sikhs were the only power left that could rival the British in India. They had an army of 100,000 well-armed and well-equipped men. They were known as the Khalsa, literally "the pure" or "soldier-saints." For six years after Singh's death, the army made and unmade Sikh rulers. To give an external venue to the army's energies, the Sikh leaders began to consider a war with the British.

The British watched the growing power of the Sikhs with concern. They signed a treaty with Singh making the Sutlej River the boundary between their spheres of influence. On December 11, 1845, a Sikh army crossed the Sutlej border near Ferozepur. The British under Gen. Hugh Gough were allowed to concentrate and march on the Sikhs. Gough arrived at Mudki on December 18, 1845.

On December 21, the two armies fought the Battle of Ferozeshah. The British were outnumbered almost two to one, and their artillery was inferior. Nonetheless, Gough again attacked and forced his way into the Sikh camp. Darkness forced a halt in the battle. When the British attacked the next morning, the Sikhs offered little resistance because of dissension among their leaders. The Sikhs retreated to the Sutlej River and established a position near Aliwal. On January 28, Gough defeated them again in the Battle of Aliwal and caused great losses in men and materiel because the Sikhs had trouble trying to retreat across the river. Several British victories in 62 days forced the Sikhs to come to terms. They signed the Treaty of Lahore on March 9, 1846.

The Second Sikh War resulted from the nationalistic feelings of the Sikh people. They were humiliated by their defeat and by the British occupation of Lahore. The people and the army rose up in the summer of 1848 and killed several British officers.

Gough was forced to gather troops for a long campaign. On February 21, Gough fought a large Sikh army at Gujrat. The British artillery inflicted heavy casualties on the Sikhs, while British losses were light. The Sikhs were forced to retreat. Gough followed them and forced the Sikh army to surrender unconditionally on March 14, 1849, at Rawalpindi. The surrender brought the Second Sikh War to an end.

TIM WATTS

Pope Gregory XVI dies. He is succeeded by Pope Pius IX (r. 1846–1878) who begins his 32-year reign, the longest in papal history, on June 16.

Shortly after taking office, Pope Pius opens the Jewish ghetto in Rome in an effort to integrate the segregated Jewish community into the larger Roman social and economic world.

July 24, 1846

North America: United States
Christianity

Pope Pius IX erects two new dioceses, the first on the American Pacific coast at Oregon City and Walla Walla. The Roman Catholic Church is now the largest single denomination in the United States, a position it will retain to the present.

September 19, 1846

Europe: France
Christianity

Two children, Maximin Giraud and Melanie Calvat, report that they have had an apparition of the Blessed Virgin Mary. It occurs at La Salette on Mount Sous-Les Baisses near their home. According to their account, she spoke to them in French, then added words in their local dialect. She wept throughout the time she was visible to them.

Along with the items of her distinctive dress, the Virgin at La Salette wore a unique crucifix that had an attached hammer and pincers. The hammer symbolizes the instrument that was used to nail Jesus of Nazareth to the cross, and the pincers the instrument that removed those same nails.

On the day after the apparition, the two children gave a full account of what had occurred and it was written down and signed by them and others present at the time. The story quickly spread beyond the village and reached the ears of the bishop of Grenoble, who soon launched an investigation of the apparition. He gave it his initial approval in 1851.

1847

North America: United States
Christianity

The Lutheran Church–Missouri Synod is founded by immigrants from Saxony who have rejected the merger of the Lutheran and Reformed churches in their homeland.

1847

North America: United States
Christianity

John Oberholtzer leads in the formation of the General Conference Mennonite Church.

1847

Central America and the Caribbean: Nicaragua
Christianity

Moravian Church missionaries begin work along the Caribbean coast among both African Caribbean residents and the Native Nicaraguans. The work evolves into the Moravian church of Nicaragua.

1847

South Asia: India
Christianity

Anglicans in Bengal complete construction and consecrate St. Paul's Cathedral in Kolkata (Calcutta), West Bengal. It currently serves as a cathedral for the Church of North India.

1847

South Asia: Sri Lanka
Buddhism

The British governor withdraws from Buddhist affairs and thus distances the Buddhist leadership from the ruling British authorities. He requires the Buddhist monks to select their own chiefs, a task formally in the hands of the ruler of Kandy.

This action follows 30 years of favoritism by British authorities toward Christian missionary endeavors on the island.

1847

East and Southeast Asia: Hong Kong
Christianity

The cornerstone is laid for the first Anglican church in Hong Kong, later (1849) to be consecrated as the cathedral of St. John the Evangelist.

POPE PIUS IX (1792–1878)

Pope Pius IX was one of the most important figures in the Catholic Church during the 19th century. During his reign from the Vatican in Italy, the longest in history, he steered the church in a conservative direction. He is most famous for defining the doctrine of papal infallibility.

Pius appointed a liberal as secretary of state for the Papal States, declared an amnesty for political prisoners, and introduced several democratic reforms into the administration of the Papal States and the city of Rome. However, the revolutions of 1848 cooled his enthusiasm for reform considerably. Pius was forced to disband the papal guard and grant a radical democratic government to his possessions. In effect, he was a prisoner of the revolutionaries, and he fled Rome for Naples.

On April 12, 1850, Pius returned with the help of French troops granted to him by President Louis-Napoleon Bonaparte (soon to be Emperor Napoleon III). Throughout the 1850s, he refused to negotiate with democratic forces, and after Italian unification, he refused to recognize the new kingdom. In 1869, Napoleon withdrew the French troops that had supported papal authority in Rome. In a plebiscite held to determine the political future of Rome and the Papal States, Italians voted overwhelmingly to join the Kingdom of Italy under King Victor Emmanuel II. Thus, the pope had lost control over all territory in Italy except for the huge Vatican palace in Rome, and Pius now considered himself a "prisoner."

Pius showed himself to be conservative in doctrinal matters as well. On December 8, 1854, he proclaimed the dogma of the Immaculate Conception of Mary (according to which God miraculously cleansed Mary of original sin at the moment of her conception), fostering a movement of devotion to the Virgin Mother. In 1864, he published the encyclical *Quanta cura,* which contained his famous "Syllabus of Errors," defending the temporal power of the pope and the church, among other things.

Pius continued his struggle against the forces of the modern world and strengthened papal authority within the church by calling the Vatican Council in 1869. The high point of the proceedings came when the council voted to declare the doctrine of papal infallibility to be the accepted belief within the Catholic Church. Pius succeeded in obtaining a decisive statement that the pope cannot err when speaking in the capacity of his office (*ex cathedra*) on an issue of doctrine and faith. Infallibility is considered to be a special charism that adheres to the reigning pope in virtue of his office when, as the teacher of all belivers, he proclaims in a definitive manner a particular doctrine of faith or morals.

RICHARD FOGARTY

1847

East and Southeast Asia: Japan
Buddhism

Tokuryo, a Buddhist apologist, becomes head of Hongan-ji, the academy of the Higashi Honganji, one of the two large Jodo Shinshu sects in Japan. He has become a popular voice of Buddhism in opposition to the spread of Western teachings in the country, especially alternative secular ethical systems.

1847

Europe: Belgium
Unbelief

Karl Marx and Friedrich Engels found the Communist League in Brussels.

1847

Europe: Russia
Christianity

Pope Pius IX begins a brief period of cordial relations with the Russian government. He negotiates an "Accomodamento," an agreement that allows him to name bishops to head vacant diocesans serving the Latin rite Catholics in both Russia (primarily in the Baltic countries) and the Polish provinces then in Russia. As those appointments are made, opposition quickly emerges in the Russian Orthodox Church and gradually the era of good feelings comes to an end.

1847–1860

North America: United States
Unbelief

Some 1,000 German Freethinkers migrate to the Texas hill country. The first group, led by Dr. Ferdinand von Herff, found the Bertina colony at a juncture of Elm Creek and the Llano River. Later arrivals found the original communities of Castell, Cypress Hill, Tusculum (later Boerne), Sisterdale, and Luckenbach. Of these several communities, Sisterdale proved the most successful. Among these settlers, a knowledge of Latin was highly valued and considered an essential element of the cultured intellectual life, and the societies became known as the "Latin Colonies."

February 7, 1847

North America: United States
Christianity

Responding to the request of the American Roman Catholic bishops, Pope Pius IX names the Virgin Mary to be the patroness of the United States.

April 26, 1847

North America: United States
Christianity

Representatives from 15 German Lutheran congregations found the German Lutheran Church Synod of Missouri, Ohio, and other States (now known as the Lutheran Church—Missouri Synod).

May 4, 1847

North America: United States
Christianity

Recognizing the addition of the former Republic of Texas to the United States as a new state, Pope Pius IX designates the former Vicariate Apostolic of Texas as the new Diocese of Galveston. It includes all of the State of Texas, with the exception of El Paso County. Bishop Jean-Marie Odin is named as the first bishop. All 15 priests of the diocese are from the Vincentian order.

July 11, 1847

North America: United States
Christianity

Pope Pius IX erects the Vicariate Apostolic of the Sandwich Islands and appoints Louis Desiré Maigret as its first vicar apostolic. He succeeds the late bishop Etienne Rouchouze, the vicar apostolic of Oriental Oceania.

July 20, 1847

North America: United States
Christianity

Pope Pius XI raises another center of German immigration to the United States, St. Louis, from diocese to archdiocese.

July 24, 1847

North America: United States
Christianity

Brigham Young, who has led the Latter-day Saints (aka the Mormons) west from their settlement at Nauvoo, Illinois, arrives in the Salt Lake Valley, Utah, and begins the process of building a new settlement for the members of the Church of Jesus Christ of Latter-day Saints who have followed him.

November 29, 1847

North America: United States
Traditional Religions

During an epidemic of measles, the surviving members of the Cayuse people blame missionaries Marcus Whitman and his wife Narcissa Whitman for the extremely high death rate among their children and kill both of them.

December 21, 1847

North America: United States
Christianity

Though he had led the church for three years since the death of founder Joseph Smith Jr., Brigham Young is finally and formally declared president of the Church of Jesus Christ of Latter-day Saints.

1848

Sub-Saharan Africa: Botswana
Christianity

At Kolobeng, David Livingstone makes his first important Christian convert in what is now Botswana in the person of Kgosi Sechele I, the chief of the Bakwena people. He agrees to abandon any ceremonies of his Native religion, like rain-making, and to leave all his wives but one. Livingstone is subsequently blamed for the drought later in the year and the problems encountered by the chief's now unattached former wives.

1848

North America: United States
Christianity

Saint Innocent of Alaska is consecrated as North America's first Orthodox bishop.

1848

North America: United States
Christianity

Church president Brigham Young places a ban on African American members of the Church of Jesus Christ of Latter-day Saints. They are prohibited from holding the priesthood, which means that they cannot participate in the primary temple rituals conferring the endowment or sealing their marriage. These restrictions remain effective until 1978.

1848

North America: United States
Christianity

John Humphrey Noyes founds the Oneida community in Vermont, a communal society that becomes known for its belief in perfectionism, the possibility that one could be free of sin in this lifetime, and the unique system of sexual sharing that evolved from it.

1848

North America: United States
Christianity

Dr. John Thomas, who had associated with the Restoration movement founded by Barton Stone and Alexander Campbell, breaks with the movement and develops his own following that will come to be known as the Christadelphians.

1848

North America: United States
Western Esotericism

Reports of spirit rappings in the home of the Fox sisters gives birth to modern Spiritualism in North America.

1848

North America: United States
Christianity

Brigham Young, the second president of the Latter-day Saints church, leads the former Nauvoo residents to the Salt Lake Valley.

1848

Central America and the Caribbean: Belize
Christianity

An Indian revolt in Mexico leads some 7,000 Roman Catholics to migrate to what is now the nation of

Belize and found what has become the majority faith of the country.

1848

Europe: France
Christianity

Members of two religious orders, Congregation of the Sacred Heart, founded in 1842 by Francis Mary Paul Liberman, and Congregation of the Holy Spirit under the protection of the Immaculate Heart of Mary (aka the Holy Ghost Fathers), develop close relations and in 1848 merge. Liberman becomes the leader of the merged order and is often considered its second founder.

1848

Europe: Italy
Christianity

Pope Pius IX appoints Antonio Rosmini, the founder of a new but quickly emerging religious order, the Institute of Charity, as the prime minister of the Papal States. A patriot philosopher, he has a vision of a confederation of Italian states free of foreign (especially Austrian) control and under the leadership of the pope. His rise to power angered the leadership of the Society of Jesus, who opposed his liberal spirit. They challenge his ideas and have his writings placed on the Index of Prohibited Books. He was forced to retire (1849), though he lives to see his work declared without error and removed from the Index.

1848

Europe: United Kingdom
Christianity

William Howley, the archbishop of Canterbury, dies. He is succeeded by John Bird Sumner (r. 1848–1862), formerly the bishop of Chester.

1848

Oceania and Antarctica: Vanuatu
Traditional Religions, Christianity

The work of the LMS is absorbed into the Presbyterian mission when Nova Scotian John Geddie arrives. The Reformed Presbyterian Church of Scotland becomes the major force in Vanuatu with the arrival of John G. Paton, one of the more famous of the missionaries in the South Sea Islands. Among other things, the Presbyterians translate the Bible into indigenous languages. By 1870, the scriptures would be translated into the four main languages. By 1901, the Bible would be published in 21 languages. Today, the independent Presbyterian Church of Vanuatu includes approximately one-third of Vanuatu's population.

January 5, 1848

Europe: Italy
Christianity

A set of revolutionary impulses in the various states on the Italian Peninsula begins with a civil disobedience movement in Lombardy. The Italian citizenry stop smoking and abandon the national lottery, which has the effect of denying the tax revenue to the ruling Austrian government.

January 13, 1848

South America: Ecuador
Christianity

Pope Pius IX elevates the Diocese of Quito to the Archdiocese of Quito.

January 24, 1848

North America: United States
Buddhism, Chinese Religions

Gold discovered at Sutter's Mill on the American River in California prompts a three-year period of intensive migration to the state. Included in the migration are many Chinese, among whom are the first Buddhists and Taoists to settle in the United States.

February 1848

Sub-Saharan Africa: South Africa
Christianity

The recently consecrated Robert Gray (1809–1872), the first Anglican bishop of Cape Town, arrives in South Africa.

February 2, 1848

Central America and the Caribbean: Mexico
Christianity

Chinese gold miners stand next to a sluice box, Aubine Ravine, California, about 1852. (Fotosearch/Getty Images)

In the Treaty of Guadelupe Hildalgo, Mexico relinquishes claims to Texas, cedes New Mexico and California to the United States, and sets the U.S.-Mexican border at the Rio Grande River.

February 2, 1848

North America: United States
Chinese Religions, Buddhism
The first ship of Chinese immigrants arrives in San Francisco.

February 21, 1848

Europe: Italy
Christianity
Surprising many, Pope Pius IX grants a constitution to the Papal States, an unexpected move in light of the history of the monarchial rights historically claimed by the popes through the centuries.

February 24, 1848

Europe: France
Christianity, Unbelief
With the country in the midst of the February 1848 revolution, King Louis Philippe abdicates in favor of his nine-year-old grandson, Philippe, Comte de Paris. He leaves Paris and flees into exile in England. Two days later, the French National Assembly proclaims the establishment of the Second Republic.

The changes in France provide the context in which Karl Marx and Friedrich Engels will issue the *Communist Manifesto.*

July 1, 1848

Europe: Spain
Christianity

Fr. Joachim Masmitjá, a Roman Catholic priest, founds the Daughters of the Most Holy and Immaculate Heart of the Blessed Virgin Mary (later known as the Sisters of the Immaculate Heart of Mary), a new religious order for women. He saw the order as an instrument in the revitalization of society through educating the next generation of young women.

July 19–20, 1848

North America: United States
Christianity, Unbelief

A group of women of various backgrounds—Quakers, Methodists, Freethinkers, and so on—meet at the Wesleyan Methodist Chapel at Seneca Falls, New York, and adopt a series of resolutions outlining their demands for women's rights, including the right to vote. Among the few men in attendance, abolitionist Frederick Douglass makes a significant speech urging the attendees to pass a resolution demanding that women be given the vote.

November 15, 1848

Europe: Italy
Christianity

Recently appointed the minister of justice for the Papal States by Pope Pius IX, Pellegrino Rossi is assassinated on the opening day of the Parliament. Fearful for his own life, Pope Pius flees Rome and begins to question the liberal reforms going on around him in Europe.

December 10, 1848

Europe: France
Christianity

Prince Louis Napoléon Bonaparte is elected president of the French Republic.

1849

Sub-Saharan Africa: South Africa
Christianity

Anglican bishop Robert Gray founds Diocesan College, Rondebosch, Cape Town.

1849

Sub-Saharan Africa: Ethiopia
Christianity

Guglielmo Massaja, who leads the Capuchin mission in Ethiopia (founded in 1846), consecrates Justin de Jacobis as the bishop of Nilopolis and vicar apostolic of Ethiopia. Against strong local resistance, they build the Roman Catholic community in the country.

1849

North America: United States
Christianity

James White obeys a vision of his wife, Ellen G. White, and begins publishing *The Present Truth,* an Adventist periodical supporting the Sabbath.

1849

North America: United States
Christianity

Adventist minister John T. Walsh proposes 1854 as the date for Christ's return.

1849

North America: United States
Unbelief

A group of German colonists settle in the hill country of central Texas and found the town of Börne, named after Ludwig Börne, a Socialist writer who encouraged them to come to Texas and freedom. For the first few years, it was called Tusculum, after Cicero's home in ancient Rome.

1849

Central America and the Caribbean: Jamaica
Christianity

With the support of the British Baptist Missionary Society, Baptists form the Jamaica Baptist Union.

1849

Europe: Italy
Christianity

Pope Pius IX orders public prayers for the Papal States, which are being negatively affected by the move to unite Italy into one political entity. As these prayer proceed, he allows a three-day showing of Veronica's Veil, a relic believed by many to be a piece of cloth used by a woman to wipe the sweat from Jesus of

Nazareth's face during his walk to his crucifixion. A picture of his face appears on the cloth. During the showing, many report the face on the veil glowing with a soft light. The priests at St. Peter's Basilica, where the veil is kept, ring the church bells to celebrate the happening.

As the account of the miraculous glow spreads, people bring representations of the veil to it and touch the relic. These representations were subsequently sent across Italy and abroad and became the origin of a practice of bringing copies of the veil to Rome to be touched to the original. Also, locally, copies verified to have been touched to the veil become available for pilgrims.

February 2, 1849

Europe: Italy
Christianity

A young Roman Catholic priest, the Abbé Arduini, speaks at a large political rally in the Apollo Theater in Rome. He declares papal temporal power to be a "historical lie, a political imposture, and a religious immorality."

February 2, 1849

Europe: Italy
Christianity

From his exile, Pope Pius IX addresses an encyclical, *Ubi Primum,* to the bishops of the Roman Catholic Church in which he inquires about their stance relative to his defining the doctrine of the Immaculate Conception of the Blessed Virgin Mary. This document is doubly important as it prepares the way for the definition of the new dogma five years later and for its naming Mary as the mediatrix of salvation. By this time, Pius had already appointed a theological study commission to review the implications of the Immaculate Conception becoming dogma.

February 9, 1849

Europe: Italy
Christianity, Western Esotericism

With the pope out of the picture for the moment, Carlo Armellini, Giuseppe Mazzini, and Aurelio Saffi declare the formation of a new Roman republic modeled on ancient Rome. They hope to propagate a constitution that allows all religions to be practiced freely with a provision that the pope be guaranteed governance of the Catholic Church. At this time, the Papal States allowed only Catholicism and Judaism to be practiced within its boundaries. The constitution also abolished capital punishment.

At this point, Giuseppe Garibaldi, a military leader and an active Freemason, emerges on the scene in Italy and moves to Rome to support the republic. He will eventually be elected Grand Master of the Grand Orient of Italy.

April 14, 1849

Europe: Hungary
Christianity

Hungary proclaims its independence after 150 years of Habsburg rule at a gathering in the Great Church in Debrecen. The new government accepts Lajos Kossuth as governor (and virtual dictator) of the new Hungarian Republic.

June 5, 1849

Europe: Denmark
Christianity

Denmark becomes a constitutional monarchy and establishes a two-chamber parliament. According to its constitution, the Lutheran Church of Denmark is the established religion and the royal family must be members of it. The remainder of the population may be of any religion, though the great majority remain adherents of the Danish Church.

June 11–12, 1949

Europe: France
Christianity

A bill of impeachment of President Louis Bonaparte of France is introduced but defeated by the French Parliament. The occasion of the bill is Louis's intervention in Rome on behalf of reestablishing Pope Pius IX in power. Louis is pursuing a plan to create a unified Italy free of Austrian control (Austria is then in control of Lombardy). In the process of intervening in the Italian crisis that had been created by the assassination of the Papal States' minister for finance and the proclamation of the new Roman republic, France becomes aligned to the pope and emerges as the pope's protector.

June 29, 1849

Europe: Italy.
Christianity

French forces under Charles Oudinot enter Rome after a two-month siege. The Roman republic declared at the beginning of the year comes to an end, Pope Pius IX is restored to his throne, and revolutionary leaders Giuseppe Garibaldi and Giuseppe Mazzini flee into exile.

July 2, 1849

Europe: Italy
Western Esotericism

As the leaders of the Republic of Rome surrender their rule to the invading French and Austrian forces, revolutionary and Freemason Giuseppe Garibaldi and some 4,700 men leave Rome and prepare to launch a guerrilla war against Austria.

July 16, 1849

Europe: Spain
Christianity

Antonio Mariá Claret y Clará, a Spanish priest, organizes five young priests at the seminary at Vic (near Barcelona) in the process of founding the Congregation of Missionary Sons of the Immaculate Heart of Mary (aka the Claretians), an evangelistic religious order with a special devotion to the Blessed Virgin Mary. A mere 20 days after the founding event, Pope Pius IX names Claret as the new archbishop of Cuba. He departs for the Caribbean island and leaves the new order in the hands of his colleague Esteban Sala. In spite of its early loss, the Claretians thrive.

Index

Barkyaruq (sultan), 715
Barlaam (abbot), 911
Barleus, Caspar, 1199
Barnabas, 285, 286, 287
Barnabites, 1079
Barot, Clement, 1094
Barreira, Balthazar, 1159
Barrett, Francis, 1374
Barth, Karl, 1698, 1700
Bartoldus of Calabria, 759
Basel Missionary Society, 1404
Basilades, 314, 316
Basil I (emperor), 608, 615, 616, 627, 757
Basil I (patriarch), 646, 647
Basilica Cathedral of the Assumption of the Blessed Virgin
    Mary, 1315
Basilica of Our Lady of Peace of Yamoussoukro, Ivory Coast,
    1935, 1936
Basilica of Saint Lawrence, 482
Basilica of Saint Mary, 570
Basilica of Saint Mary of the Flower, 871
Basilica of San Giovanni Evangilista, 797
Basilica of San Isidoro, 694
Basilica of Santa Maria, 842
Basilica of Santa Maria Maggiore, 391
Basilica of Sant'Apollinare, 474
Basilica of St. Anne de Beaupre, 1225
Basilica of St. Denis, 745, 747
Basilica of St. John Lateran, 749, 880
Basilica of St. Mark, 693, 714, 735
Basilica of St. Nicholas, 710, 760
Basilica of St. Paul, 292, 1420
Basilica of St Paul Outside the Walls, 599, 601
Basilica of St. Peter, 292, 735
Basilica of St. Sernin, 705
Basilicus (emperor), 757
Basil II (emperor), 648, 656, 670, 675
Basil III (patriarch), 1674, 1689
Basil II Kamateros, 779, 782
Basil of Caesarea, 569
Basil of Cappadocia, 399, 402
Basil the Physician, 734
Basimon, Jacob, 1220
Basnage, Jacques Christian, 1282
Basques, 576
Bassandyne, Thomas, 1134
Bast (goddess), 194
Bath Cathedral, 1090–1091
Bathyra, Judah ben, 291
Batista, Fulgencio, 1714, 1766, 1786
Batu Khan, 832
Bavaria, Christianity, 1221
Ibn al-Bawwab, 664
Baxter, Richard, 1223, 1230
Bayazid II (sultan), 955, 1006, 1017–1018
Bayezid I (sultan), 941
Bayle, Pierre, 1254
Al-Bayyasi, Abdallah, 821, 820
Beaton, David, 1098

Beatty, Charles Clinton, 1332
Beaty, John, 1763
Beaufort, Henry, 970
Beaufort, Margaret, 1020
Becker, Peter, 1288, 1289
Becket, Thomas, 765, 766, 771, 772, 773, 777, 778, 816
Becket, Thomas (saint), 765, 765, 766, 925
Bede, 528, 547
Bedell, William, 1166, 1248
Beeldenstorm, 1123
Beethoven, Ludwig van, 1379
Begin, Menachem, 1844
Behbahani, Vahid, 1337–1338
Behistun Inscription, 147
Beirut, 251
Beissel, Conrad, 1299
Beissel, Johann Conrad, 1302
Beis Yaakov Synagogue, 1515
Bekkos, John, 867
Belarus, 1899
    Christianity, 1048, 1713, 1719, 1881
    constitution, 1910
    independence, 1887
    Judaism, 1120, 1365–1366, 1726, 1729
Belgic Confession of Faith, 1118, 1119, 1123
Belgium, 973, 1511, 1612
    Christianity, 683, 918, 1060, 1073, 1083–1084, 1088, 1184,
        1406, 1435, 1436, 1439, 1441, 1451, 1452, 1466, 1697,
        1731, 1847
    constitution, 1898
    freedom of religion, 2012
    homosexuality, 1955, 1981
    Judaism, 917, 1065, 1102
    Reformed Church, 1125
    traditional religions, 1869
    unbelief in, 1471
Belgrade, 198
Belize, 1510
    Christianity, 1472–1473, 1571, 1761
    constitution, 1854
    Holy Redeemer Cathedral, 1501
Bellamy, Edward, 1571
Bellarmine, Roberto Cardinal, 1176
Bellona (goddess), 195, 256, 257
Belshazaar (king), 137
Ben Ashak, Ali (aka Ali Ibn Ghaniya), 777
Ben Asher, Jacob, 904
Bendavid, Lazarus, 1363
Benedict, Saint, 471, 572, 612, 626, 632, 633
Benedict II, 527
Benedict III (bishop), 603
Benedictine Order, 559, 622, 626, 612, 673, 699, 717, 807
Benedict IX (pope), 678, 679, 683, 684
Benedict of Nursia, 453, 472
Benedict V (pope), 644
Benedict VI (pope), 647
Benedict VIII (pope), 669, 671, 673, 673
Benedict X (pope), 689
Benedict XI (pope), 876, 878, 879

Islam, 794, 1241, 1770, 1771, 1771, 1804, 1836, 1851, 1865,
1871, 1872, 1914, 1920, 1921, 1926, 1932–1933, 1933,
1939, 1945, 1945–1946, 1946, 1947, 1957, 1965, 1979,
1989, 1991, 2008
Judaism, 1447
Shariah law, 1957
Western estotercisim, 285
Pak Tai (god), 1331, 1348
Pal, Krishna, 1371
Palace of Eternal Harmony Lama Temple, 1313
Palace of Knossis, 45, 46
Palácios, Pedro, 1111
Palatine Chapel, 573, 583
Palatine Hill, 215
Palau, 1631, 1747, 1848, 1899
Paleario, Aonio, 1126
Palermo, 162–163
Palermo, Battle of, 699
Palestine, 39, 53, 55, 1646
Academy of the Hebrew Language, 1557
Baha'i faith, 1800
Battle of Hatin, 782
birth of Jesus, 243
British mandate, 1656
Christianity, 271, 275, 279–280, 280, 284, 287–288, 291,
314–315, 320, 326, 344, 349, 371, 375, 380, 383–384, 384,
386, 388, 390, 397, 399, 406, 419, 421, 426, 437, 444, 505,
555, 662, 669, 670, 674, 682, 699, 705, 716, 717, 719, 723,
725, 734, 739, 742, 748, 749, 751, 754, 759, 764, 772, 773,
781, 782, 785, 813, 823, 825, 868, 855, 911, 1005, 1160,
1447, 1450, 1704, 1968, 1971
Islam, 501, 511, 530, 540, 555, 647, 669, 670, 672, 699, 716,
719, 739, 782, 785, 825, 838, 868, 873, 1708
Judaism, 71–72, 76, 83, 83–84, 84–85, 87, 87–88, 90–91,
91–93, 94, 98, 98–99, 100, 103–107, 105, 106–107, 108,
112, 116, 117, 118, 121, 128, 128–129, 129–130, 130,
130–131, 137–138, 140, 144, 147, 162, 163, 179, 181, 182,
187, 189, 199, 210, 217, 219, 223, 226, 226–227, 227, 228,
229, 230, 231, 234, 236, 237, 240, 241, 246, 247, 248, 249,
250, 251, 252, 253, 254, 257, 260, 261, 262, 263, 264, 265,
267, 268, 269, 271, 272, 277, 278, 279, 280, 281, 282, 283,
284, 289, 291, 292, 293, 293–294, 296–297, 297–298, 303,
304, 309, 310, 313–314, 314, 315, 318, 319, 338, 392, 395,
428, 430, 431, 499, 500, 505, 555, 632, 653, 672, 804,
1001, 1100, 1309, 1320, 1331, 1450, 1688, 1967–1968
post-WWI, 1656
traditional religions, 56, 58, 68, 69, 71, 72, 73, 74–75, 76, 78,
79–80, 84, 88, 103, 117, 122, 126–127, 127, 128–129, 179,
181–182, 183–184, 187, 194, 211, 226, 247, 252, 260, 268,
269, 271, 275, 279, 281, 295, 308, 311, 314–315, 319, 321,
326, 329, 356, 850
Palestine Liberation Organization (PLO), 1786, 1802, 1803,
1817, 1824, 1834, 1858, 1871
Paley, William, 1364
Pali Canon of Theravada Buddhism, 229
Pali Tripitaka, 242, 256
Palladius, 430
Pallava Dynasty, 486
Pallava kingdom, 476, 505, 533

Pallavamalla. *See* Nandivarman II
Pallottines, 1445
Pallu, François (bishop), 1226, 1247
Palmer, Elihu, 1373
Palmcr, Paul, 1295
Palmer, Phoebe, 1500, 1502, 1514
Palymra, 278
Pami (pharaoh), 99
Pan (god), 154
Panama, 1612, 1676, 1743, 1826, 1877
Panama Canal, 1638
Panamara, 261
Panangkaran (king), 566
Pancharata Vaishnavite sect, 191
Panchen Lama, 1204, 1289, 1294, 1296, 1802, 1842,
1842–1843, 1865, 1874, 1902, 1912
Panday, Basdeo, 1981
Pandukabhaya (king), 164
Pandyan, Maravarman Sundara, 833
Pandyan Dynasty, 486, 626
Pandyas, 799, 814, 843, 861
Panebtawy (god), 226
Panias, Battle of, 217
Panipat, Battle of, 1027
Panium, Battle of, 219
Panth, 1277
Pantheon, 264, 301, 313
Pap (king), 401, 402
Papacy, 434–435, 660–662
See also specific popes
Avignon papacy, 879, 890, 904
Papal infallibility, 1483, 1529, 1532, 1535
Papal States, 560, 561, 567, 570, 649, 940, 1401, 1474, 1475,
1476, 1504, 1531
Papias of Hierapolis (bishop), 311
Papua Act, 1616
Papua New Guinea, 1548, 1609, 1619, 1814, 1836, 1837,
1838–1839, 1948
Paracelsus, 1088
Paradesi Synagogue, 1125
Paraguay
Christianity, 1089, 1318, 1463, 1869, 1893, 2002
constitution, 1893
Jesuits in, 1168, 1333
Roman Catholic Church, 1533, 2009
unbelief in, 1394, 1458
Unification Church, 1931, 1970, 1992
wars against Triple Alliance, 1515
Parakramabahu I (king), 756, 760, 767
Parakramabahu III (king), 861
Paramesvaravarman I (king), 523
Paramesvaravarman II (king), 523, 548–549
Parantaka Chola I (emperor), 624
Parantaka Chola II (emperor), 638
Parapsychology, 1697
Pardes Rimonim (Orchard of Pomegranates), 1100
Paris Evangelical Missionary Society, 1509
Parker, Matthew, 1113, 1125, 1133
Parks, Rosa, 1777